Kenneth

The SAGE Handbook of
Housing Studies

SAGE has been part of the global academic community since 1965, supporting high quality research and learning that transforms society and our understanding of individuals, groups, and cultures. SAGE is the independent, innovative, natural home for authors, editors and societies who share our commitment and passion for the social sciences.

Find out more at: **www.sagepublications.com**

The SAGE Handbook of
Housing Studies

Edited by
David F. Clapham,
William A. V. Clark
and Kenneth Gibb

Los Angeles | London | New Delhi
Singapore | Washington DC

Introductions © David F. Clapham, William A. V. Clark and Kenneth Gibb 2012
Chapter 1 © Duncan Maclennan 2012
Chapter 2 © Michael Ball 2012
Chapter 3 © Maarten van Ham 2012
Chapter 4 © William A.V. Clark 2012
Chapter 5 © George Galster 2012
Chapter 6 © Christine M.E. Whitehead 2012
Chapter 7 © Kenneth Gibb 2012
Chapter 8 © Tim Butler and Chris Hamnett 2012
Chapters 9 and 10 © David Clapham 2012
Chapter 11 © Julie Lawson 2012
Chapter 12 © Bo Bengtsson 2012
Chapter 13 © Roderick Lawrence 2012
Chapter 14 © Geoffrey Meen 2012
Chapter 15 © Walter Matznetter and Alexis Mundt 2012
Chapter 16 © Christopher Bitter and David A. Plane 2012
Chapter 17 © Ray Forrest 2012
Chapter 18 © Phil Jones 2012
Chapter 19 © Suzanne Fitzpatrick 2012
Chapter 20 © Chris Leishman and Steven Rowley 2012
Chapter 21 © Judith Yates 2012
Chapter 22 © Sako Musterd 2012
Chapter 23 © Ronald van Kempen and Gideon Bolt 2012
Chapter 24 © Hugo Priemus 2012

First published 2012

Apart from any fair dealing for the purposes of research or private study, or criticism or review, as permitted under the Copyright, Designs and Patents Act, 1988, this publication may be reproduced, stored or transmitted in any form, or by any means, only with the prior permission in writing of the publishers, or in the case of reprographic reproduction, in accordance with the terms of licences issued by the Copyright Licensing Agency. Enquiries concerning reproduction outside those terms should be sent to the publishers.

SAGE Publications Ltd
1 Oliver's Yard
55 City Road
London EC1Y 1SP

SAGE Publications Inc.
2455 Teller Road
Thousand Oaks, California 91320

SAGE Publications India Pvt Ltd
B 1/I 1 Mohan Cooperative Industrial Area
Mathura Road, Post Bag 7
New Delhi 110 044

SAGE Publications Asia-Pacific Pte Ltd
3, Church Street
10-04 Samsung Hub
Singapore 049483

Library of Congress Control Number 2011938474

British Library Cataloguing in Publication data

A catalogue record for this book is available from the British Library

ISBN 978-1-84787-430-6

Typeset by Cenveo Publisher Services
Printed in India by Replika Press Pvt. Ltd
Printed on paper from sustainable resources

Contents

	List of Contributors	ix
	Preface	xv
SECTION 1	**HOUSING MARKETS**	**1**
	Edited by Kenneth Gibb	
1	Understanding Housing Markets: Real Progress or Stalled Agendas? *Duncan Maclennan*	5
2	Housebuilding and Housing Supply *Michael Ball*	27
3	Housing Behaviour *Maarten van Ham*	47
4	Residential Mobility and the Housing Market *William A.V. Clark*	66
5	Neighborhoods and Their Role in Creating and Changing Housing *George Galster*	84
SECTION 2	**APPROACHES**	**107**
	Edited by David Clapham	
6	The Neo-Liberal Legacy to Housing Research *Christine M.E. Whitehead*	113
7	Institutional Economics *Kenneth Gibb*	131
8	Social Geographic Interpretations of Housing Spaces *Tim Butler and Chris Hamnett*	147
9	Social Policy Approaches to Housing Research *David Clapham*	163

10	Social Constructionism and Beyond in Housing Research *David Clapham*	174
11	A Review of Structurally Inspired Approaches in Housing Studies – Concepts, Contributions and Future Perspectives *Julie Lawson*	188
12	Housing Politics and Political Science *Bo Bengtsson*	206
13	People–Environment Studies *Roderick Lawrence*	230

SECTION 3   CONTEXT — **245**
Edited by William A.V. Clark

14	Housing and the Economy *Geoffrey Meen*	251
15	Housing and Welfare Regimes *Walter Matznetter and Alexis Mundt*	274
16	Housing Markets, the Life Course, and Migration Up and Down the Urban Hierarchy *Christopher Bitter and David A. Plane*	295
17	Housing and Social Life *Ray Forrest*	313
18	Housing: From Low Energy to Zero Carbon *Phillip Jones*	327

SECTION 4   POLICY ISSUES — **355**
Edited by Kenneth Gibb

19	Homelessness *Suzanne Fitzpatrick*	359
20	Affordable Housing *Chris Leishman and Steven Rowley*	379
21	Housing Subsidies *Judith Yates*	397
22	Ethnic Residential Segregation – Reflections on Concepts, Levels and Effects *Sako Musterd*	419

23	Social Consequences of Residential Segregation and Mixed Neighborhoods *Ronald van Kempen and Gideon Bolt*	439
24	Managing Social Housing *Hugo Priemus*	461
	Conclusion *David Clapham*	484
	Index	488

List of Contributors

Michael Ball is Professor of Urban and Property Economics in the School of Real Estate and Planning, Henley Business School, University of Reading. His books include *Markets and Institutions in Real Estate and Construction* (Blackwell Publishing, 2006) and the co-authored textbook, *The Economics of Commercial Property Markets* (Routledge, 1998). He jointly chairs the housing economics group of the European Network for Housing Research; led the expert advisory panel on housing markets and planning for the UK government's Communities and Local Government department from 2007 to 2010. He has produced a series of reports for the UK government which have focused on the economics of the housebuilding industry; the impact of regulation and land-use planning on housing supply; and the consequences of the economic downturn on housing supply. His recent research has focused on issues related to inter-relations between markets and institutional frameworks, specifically concerning housing supply, the private rented sector, and specialist housing for the elderly.

Bo Bengtsson is a Professor of Political Science at Uppsala University, Sweden, where he divides his time between the Department of Government and the Institute for Housing and Urban Research. He has published extensively in the field of housing policy and politics, and in recent years also on integration politics and ethnic organization. He has analysed housing policy and politics on the macro level in perspectives of citizenship, rights, and universal vs selective housing regimes. On a micro level he has explored the role of housing organisations, and the conditions of tenant participation and collective action in housing. He has been keynote speaker at a number of international conferences and is a member of the editorial board of *Housing, Theory and Society*.

Christopher Bitter is an Assistant Professor of Urban Design and Planning at the University of Washington in Seattle and is affiliated with the Runstad Center for Real Estate Studies. He earned his doctorate in Geography at the University of Arizona, and, prior to pursuing an academic career, he worked for many years as a real estate and urban economist in the private sector. His current research focuses on clarifying the implications of demographic change for cities and housing markets and the market context for more compact and sustainable forms of urban development.

Gideon Bolt is an Assistant Professor of Urban Geography at the Faculty of Geosciences of Utrecht University, the Netherlands. His research focuses on urban policy, residential segregation and neighbourhood choice. He was (co-) guest editor of three recent special issues on this theme: Combating residential segregation of ethnic minorities (*Journal of Housing and the Built Environment*, 2009) Housing policy and (de)segregation: An international perspective (*Housing Studies*, 2010), and Linking integration and residential segregation (*Journal of Ethnic* *and Migration Studies*, 2010). Dr Bolt is an editor of *Journal of Housing and the Built Environment* and *Tijdschrift voor de Volkshuisvesting (Housing Sector Journal)*.

Tim Butler is Professor of Geography at King's College London and the Vincent Wright Professor in the Centre for European Studies at Sciences Po. He is the author of several books on the gentrification of London and most recently (with Chris Hamnett) of *Ethnicity, Class and Aspiration: Understanding London's New East End* (Policy Press, 2011). He has also edited two books on the regeneration of East London and one (with Michael Savage) on *Social Change and the Middle Classes (*UCL Press, 1995*)*. He is the author (with Paul Watt) of *Understanding Social Inequality* (Sage, 2007). He has edited a book on social mixing and urban regeneration (with Gary Bridge and Loretta Lees) *Mixed Communities: Gentrification by Stealth?* (Policy Press, 2011 and University of Chicago Press, 2012). He has authored several articles on gentrification and more recently on the geography of education and specifically on school choice. He is currently involved in a joint ESRC–ANR research project (with Gary Bridge and Marie Hélène Bacqué) on the Middle Class, Social Mixing and the City (MiCCY), comparing the relations between the middle classes and the city in London and Paris. He is a trustee and treasurer of the Foundation of Urban and Regional Studies (FURS) and a Board Member of the Research Committee (RC21) on urban and regional research of the International Sociological Association and a member of the Editorial Board of the *London Journal.*

David Clapham is Professor of Housing in the School of City and Regional Planning at Cardiff University in the UK. Recent books include *The Meaning of Housing* (Policy Press, 2005). He is also editor of the journal *Housing, Theory and Society* published by Routledge. His current research interests include homelessness, the application of social theory to housing, housing for disadvantaged people, and the inter-disciplinary analysis of the housing market.

William A.V. Clark is Professor of Geography at the University of California Los Angeles with a joint appointment in Statistics. His research focuses on demographic change, models of residential mobility and the sorting processes that bring about residential segregation in the urban mosaic. He has been a visiting scholar at the Universities of Amsterdam, Utrecht, Victoria University Wellington and St Andrews, Scotland. He is an honorary member of the Royal Society of New Zealand and a member of the National Academy of Sciences of the USA. He has published extensively on both internal and international migration, including most recently *Immigrants and the American Dream: Remaking the Middle Class* (2003).

Suzanne Fitzpatrick completed her PhD on youth homelessness at the University of Glasgow in 1998 and subsequently held a number of posts in the Department of Urban Studies at the University of Glasgow. From 2003 to 2010, Suzanne was Joseph Rowntree Professor of Housing Policy and Director of the Centre for Housing Policy at the University of York, and took up her current post as Professor of Housing and Social Policy at Heriot-Watt University in July 2010. Suzanne specialises in research on homelessness and housing exclusion, and much of her work has an international comparative dimension. Suzanne is Editor of the *International Journal of Housing Policy.*

Ray Forrest is Professor of Urban Studies in the School for Policy Studies, University of Bristol, UK and Chair Professor in Housing and Urban Studies, City University of Hong Kong. He has been Head of the School for Policy Studies at Bristol (2001–2004), co-Director of the ESRC Centre for Neighbourhood Research (2001–2005), and Acting Head of the Centre for East Asian Studies (2007–2008). He is a founding member of the Asia-Pacific Network of

Housing Researchers. His research interests focus on social change and social division in the contemporary city. His most recent book (co-edited with Yip, Ngai-ming) is *Housing Markets and the Global Financial Crisis – The Uneven Impact on Households*.

George Galster is the Clarence Hilberry Professor of Urban Affairs at the Department of Geography and Urban Planning, Wayne State University, Michigan. He earned his PhD in Economics from MIT. He has published over 150 scholarly articles, primarily on the topics of metropolitan housing markets, racial discrimination and segregation, neighborhood dynamics, and urban poverty. His authored and edited books include *Homeowners and Neighborhood Reinvestment, The Maze of Urban Housing Markets, The Metropolis in Black and White, Reality and Research, Why NOT in My Back Yard?, Life in Poverty Neighborhoods,* and *Quantifying Neighborhood Effects*.

Kenneth Gibb is a Professor in Housing Economics at the University of Glasgow. Current research interests include the economics of social housing, behavioural economics and urban housing market analysis. He has published widely in journals such as *Housing Studies, Housing, Theory and Society, Environment and Planning A and C, Journal of Housing Economics, Real Estate Economics, International Journal of Housing Markets and Analysis* and the *Journal of Property Research*. He is co-editor of Sage's forthcoming *Reader in Housing Economics* (with Alex Marsh). He is also the editor-in-chief of *Urban Studies*.

Chris Hamnett is Professor of Geography at King's College London. He is the author of several books, including *Unequal City, London in the Global Arena* (Routledge, 2003) and *Winners and Losers: Home Ownership in Britain* (Taylor & Francis, 1999). He is co-author (with Tim Butler) of *Ethnicity, Class and Aspiration* (Policy Press, 2011) and co-author of number of other books on the housing market. He has held a variety of visiting positions, including Sciences Po, Paris; the Netherlands Institute for Advanced Studies; Nuffield College Oxford, and George Washington University. In addition to his previous work on gentrification, social polarisation and housing in London, he has recently published several articles with Tim Butler on education in London and is currently working on ethnic change in secondary schools in England and the impact of government policies on housing benefit in Britain.

Phillip Jones is Chair of Architectural Science and Head of School at the Welsh School of Architecture, Cardiff University. He also chairs the Wales Low Carbon Research Institute (LCRI), which is a consortium of six universities in Wales representing energy research across a broad range of subjects. His teaching and research activities are in the field of energy use, environmental design and sustainability in the built environment. He is a visiting professor at Chongqing University and Tianjin University. He chaired the EU COST Action C23 'Low Carbon Urban Built Environment', which produced the *European Carbon Atlas* (2009).

Roderick Lawrence is a Professor of the Faculty of Social and Economic Sciences at the University of Geneva and heads the Human Ecology Group at the Institute of Environmental Sciences. He has been an Associate Member of the New York Academy of Sciences since 1997. His recent research and publications focus on interdisciplinary and transdisciplinary contributions to tackle housing and urban planning while promoting health and quality of life. He has been a Scientific Advisor to the World Health Organization on housing and health and also to the WHO Healthy Cities project.

Julie Lawson is a Senior Research Associate for the Australian Housing and Urban Research Institute. Her interests include international comparative research, urban development, land and housing policy and social housing finance. She has worked for institutes and universities (OTB TU Delft, RMIT University, University of NSW, University of Sydney, University of Amsterdam and Institute of Housing and Urban Studies, Erasmus), the United Nations (Habitat, Nairobi), the Dutch and Australian government as well as city governments and community organisations. Julie has published numerous investigations on housing finance and urban planning including *International Measures to Channel Investment Towards Affordable Housing* (AHURI, 2010) and *International Trends in Housing and Policy Responses* (AHURI, 2007). She is on the editorial advisory board of *Housing Theory and Society* and is author of *Critical Realism and Housing Research* (Routledge, 2006) as well as numerous articles in the field of path dependence, comparative historical analysis such as *Path dependency and emergent relations* (Routledge, 2010), *Comparative housing research in the new millennium* (UNSW, 2010) and *Comparing the causal mechanisms underlying housing networks over time and space* (Springer, 2001). She is currently based in Geneva, Switzerland and is writing about federal state structures and designing a bond financing instrument to channel investment towards limited-profit housing.

Chris Leishman is Professor of Housing and Urban Economics at the University of Glasgow. His work centres on modelling housing markets, including determination of house prices, rents, development activity, tenure choice and affordability. He specialises in working with large scale micro and macro datasets, econometric modelling and simulation models. A particularly imporant aspect of his work involves bridging academic research and sophisticated modelling approaches with the needs of policy makers and advisors. As such, a great deal of his career has been spent working on public sector policy-related research projects. Chris is currently Editor-in-Chief of the leading housing journal *Housing Studies*.

Duncan Maclennan is an applied economist with interests in cities, neighbourhoods and housing. He is currently the Director of the Centre for Housing Research and Professor of Economic Geography at the University of St Andrews and Adjunct Professor at RMIT, Melbourne. He was previously at the University of Glasgow and Directed the ESRC Centre for Housing Research there from 1984–99. He has also held major posts in public policy as adviser to the First Minister of Scotland and as Chief Economist (DSE) in the Government of Victoria (Australia) and at Infrastructure Canada: (Federal Government of Canada).

Walter Matznetter is Assistant Professor at the Department of Geography of the University of Vienna, Austria. In 2004, he was a Fulbright Visiting Professor at the University of Minnesota, USA. His research is in comparative urban and housing research, mainly within Europe. He is (co-) author and/or (co-) editor of eight books and 54 articles, mainly in German, and some in English, such as *European Integration and Housing* (1998, Routledge, with Mark Kleinman and Mark Stephens). He is currently co-editing a special issue of *BELGEO*, on international student migration (in English), and a book on European metropolises (in German, 2011, Mandelbaum).

Geoffrey Meen is currently Professor of Applied Economics and Head of the School of Politics, Economics and International Relations at the University of Reading. He also holds an Adjunct Professorship at RMIT University, Melbourne. Prior to joining the University of Reading, he worked in the private sector and in the Government Economic Service. Professor

Meen specialises in quantitative housing market analysis at different spatial scales. He has published in most of the major academic journals in housing, and in numerous policy publications, as well as being author of *Modelling Spatial Housing Markets: Theory, Analysis and Policy* (Kluwer Academic Publishers, 2001).

Alexis Mundt is research associate at the Vienna-based IIBW – Institute for Real Estate, Construction and Housing Ltd. He received universal training in economics and history at the University of Vienna and the Vienna University of Economics and Business. His areas of research include the history of the welfare state, social policy evaluation, international housing policy and social housing. He has worked on a number of projects that have investigated and evaluated housing policy in Austria and Europe.

Sako Musterd is Professor of Urban Geography and Director of the Centre for Urban Studies at the University of Amsterdam, the Netherlands. His main research interests are in the fields of spatial segregation, integration and neighbourhood effects. He has written and (co-)edited a dozen books in this field, including *Urban Segregation and the Welfare State* (Routledge, 1998); *Neighbourhoods of Poverty* (Palgrave MacMillan 2006); *Mass Housing in Europe* (Palgrave Macmillan, 2009), and wrote extensively in international scientific journals as well (http://dare.uva.nl/author/musterd,s). He is a member of the editorial/management/advisory boards of the journals *Urban Geography*; *Urban Studies*; *International Journal of Urban and Regional Research*; and *Housing Studies*.

David A. Plane is Professor of Geography and Regional Development at the University of Arizona, Tucson. His research focuses on migration systems, population distribution in the United States, and the modelling of spatial interaction. A Fellow of the Western Regional Science Association and of the Regional Science Association International, he has served as President of the Association of Pacific Coast Geographers, the Population Specialty Group of the Association of American Geographers, the Pacific Regional Science Conference Organization, and the North American Regional Science Council. He co-authored, with Peter Rogerson, the highly acclaimed text: *The Geographical Analysis of Population: With Applications to Planning and Business*.

Hugo Priemus is Professor Emeritus in Housing at OTB Research Institute for the Built Environment, Delft University of Technology. He was educated in architecture (Delft) and general economics (Erasmus University, Rotterdam). He was Dean of the Faculty of Architecture and Dean of the Faculty of Technology, Policy and Management of TU Delft. He has written many books and journal articles on housing, spatial planning, urban development and infrastructure, and planning. He has conducted advisory work for the United Nations, the World Bank, the European Commission, the Dutch Parliament, Dutch Ministries and local governments.

Steven Rowley is Associate Professor and Head of the Department of Property Studies, Curtin Business School, Curtin University, Perth. Steven is also Director of the Australian Housing and Urban Research Institute's Western Australian Research Centre. Steven holds a PhD in property valuation and has published numerous reports for the UK Government, as well as book chapters and papers in journals such as *Urban Studies* and *Town Planning Review*. He is currently working on research aimed at increasing the supply of affordable housing in metropolitan and regional Australia.

Maarten van Ham is Professor of Urban Renewal at the OTB Research Institute for the Built Environment, Delft University of Technology, the Netherlands. His research interest can be broadly defined as the causes and consequences of family migration: Why do people move residence and what are the consequences of moving for the housing, household and labour career? Maarten is an expert on neighbourhood effects, residential mobility, housing and tenure choice, urban and neighbourhood change, segregation, population and household change, and the geography of labour markets. He has published widely in these areas, and currently has projects in the UK, Sweden, Germany, Estonia and the Netherlands.

Ronald van Kempen is Professor of Urban Geography at the Faculty of Geosciences of Utrecht University, the Netherlands. His research focuses on urban spatial segregation, divided cities, the effects of housing and urban policy on neighbourhoods and residents, urban enclaves, high-rise housing estates, social cohesion and residential mobility, especially of low-income and minority-ethnic groups. He has co-edited a number of special issues of international journals on this theme (*Urban Studies, Housing Studies, Urban Geography, Housing, Theory and Society, Journal of Economic and Social Geography*). He also co-edited *Restructuring Large Housing Estates in Europe* (Policy Press), *Mass Housing in Europe* (Palgrave Macmillan) and *Globalizing Cities* (Blackwell).

Christine M.E. Whitehead is an internationally respected housing economist. She is currently Professor in Housing in the Department of Economics, London School of Economics. Until the end of 2010 she was also Director of the Cambridge Centre of Housing and Planning Research, which celebrated its 20th anniversary last September. Her latest book with Sarah Monk, *Making Housing More Affordable*, published by Wiley Blackwell, was launched at the celebratory conference. She has been working in the fields of housing economics, finance and policy for many years, covering both UK and international issues. She was awarded an OBE for services to housing in 1991.

Judith Yates is currently an Honorary Associate in Economics at the University of Sydney, following a career of more than 30 years in academia. Her research has been in the fields of housing economics, finance and policy and, in the past few years, has focused on housing affordability, the supply of low-rent housing and housing taxation. She has served on numerous government advisory committees and on a number of boards and is currently a member of the government's National Housing Supply Council and on the board of the not-for-profit National Housing Company.

Preface

Housing studies as a field of study in the social sciences has a relatively recent pedigree. There have been studies of housing dating back to the Industrial Revolution, but before the 1970s they tended to be few and situated within particular social science disciplines. From the 1970s onwards, housing became a subject in its own right, largely because of government interest in research for the policy process in a number of European countries. In Britain, this coincided with a growth in professional education in the housing field, supported by government concerned with a perceived lack of skilled professionals to cope with housing problems. There developed a specific field that one can call housing studies. Although many academics reached into the field from their own disciplinary base, others saw themselves as 'housing specialists' who often drew from a range of disciplines to analyse housing phenomena. In the field of economics, the growth of the sub-specialty urban economics included specific studies of housing and housing markets. Within urban economics a number of people specialised in housing and there developed a subdiscipline – somewhat peripheral to mainstream economics – but drawing inspiration from it and from links with housing researchers from other disciplines.

Although there are no university departments devoted entirely to housing studies, a number of research centres were established with housing as their primary focus and in this way the development of a housing field of research became institutionalised. In Britain, the Housing Studies Association was formed to organise dialogue between housing academics and policy-makers. The European Network for Housing Research soon followed, with the Asia Pacific Network for Housing Research close behind.

This Handbook is designed to review the 'state of the art' of this field of housing studies. It is a diverse field, with research being undertaken from a number of disciplines as well as some multi-disciplinary work. The focus of research varies from ethnographic studies of homeless people to econometric studies of the relationship between the housing market and the wider economy. Therefore, any review cannot hope to be comprehensive, and we are aware that there are many gaps not covered in this volume. Nevertheless, we have attempted to capture as many as possible of the different dimensions of the field. Furthermore, we have attempted to highlight ways in which there is potential for the field to develop in the future. Contributors have been asked to review where we have got to and to chart future directions, which may be research topics or the development of particular concepts or approaches or policy directions. It is the belief of the editors that much can be gained through multi-disciplinary research and so contributors have been specifically asked to highlight areas where there is potential for this.

We have divided the Handbook into four sections. The first section examines the basic structures of a housing market. First, the concept of a market is reviewed and our existing ways of thinking about it are re-examined. How do we think about a market and how does it operate? There follow chapters on different elements of the market. One reviews knowledge of the supply of housing. Another examines household decision making and the factors that influence that. A third looks at the processes of housing mobility that are the essence of the sale and purchase of the housing product. The final chapter in this section examines the concept of neighbourhood that is at the heart of the functioning of housing markets.

With the basics established, Section 2 reviews different approaches to the study of housing. We argued earlier that housing has been a multi-disciplinary field and the major elements are reviewed in this section. It starts with a review of the neo-liberal economics approach to housing markets that can perhaps be seen as the dominant approach to the analysis of housing markets. But this is followed by a chapter that examines alternative economic approaches such as behavioural and new institutional economics. Other disciplinary approaches are also reviewed, such as the geographical focus on space and the psychological emphasis on people–environment studies. Political science is included by means of a chapter that takes a politics perspective and reviews research on housing that focuses on political institutions (state and non-state) and processes of interaction between political elite actors as well as between elite actors and citizens in general. Sociology is represented by two chapters: one evaluates the contribution of the social constructionist perspective to housing studies ; the other reviews structuralist sociological paradigms and their application to the field of housing. A theme running through many of these contributions is the need for a more multi- or inter-disciplinary approach to the housing field and some ways forward in identifying possible starting points are charted.

Section 3 focuses on the different elements of the context within which housing markets operate. Housing is related to many other fields in reciprocal relationships of influence and five such areas are highlighted here. Perhaps the most important is the relationship between housing and the wider economy covered in the first chapter. But a growing influence is the concern about the natural environment and its finite resources. One element of this, which is receiving increased attention from governments, is the need to reduce carbon emissions in the construction and use of houses and this is the focus in the another chapter in this section. Other chapters examine the link between housing and urban form; the concept of neighbourhood and the link between housing and social life. Housing is also linked to other elements of state welfare spending, and the final chapter of this section reviews the research on these links through the concept of welfare regimes in different countries in which there are different scales and types of housing intervention, linked to differences in state provision in other fields.

The final section focuses on government policy towards housing. The first chapter examines research on the nature of homelessness and government responses to it. Another reviews the provision of affordable housing in its many forms. Two chapters look at residential segregation, examining the processes involved and on government attempts to counteract it. One focuses on the concentration of ethnic minorities in particular neighbourhoods and the other on poverty or social exclusion. Another chapter examines the rationale and impact of different types of government subsidies to the producers and consumers of housing. The final chapter looks at research on the management of public housing stock.

In the conclusion, the editors tie together some of the themes emerging from the contributions on the future direction of housing studies. It offers some thoughts on future research priorities and trends. What are the hot topics for the future and where is there most potential for developing the inter-disciplinary approaches that are so badly needed?

Finally, at the outset Bengt Turner was one of the three editors. Unfortunately, Bengt passed away before the project could be completed. Therefore, we would like to dedicate this volume to him. He contributed as much as anyone to the field of housing studies, both through his writing and in his capacity as Chair of the European Network of Housing Research for many years. He was a personal inspiration to many scholars in the field and will be missed.

David Clapham
Bill Clark
Ken Gibb

SECTION 1

Housing Markets

Kenneth Gibb

INTRODUCTION TO SECTION 1

Section 1 of the handbook consists of five chapters concerned with fundamental aspects of housing markets. This section is largely about households, their choices and behaviour in terms of housing decisions and the delivery of new housing supply; the scale is primarily local – indeed, one chapter focuses on the neighbourhood scale. However, as Maclennan emphasises in Chapter 1, developing a more coherent and realistic account of micro market processes and behaviour is essential if housing research is to provide a useful contribution to better understand housing's relationship with the monetary and the real macroeconomy, an issue catapulted to the forefront of policymakers' minds the world over in recent years. In other words, the micro foundations of the housing market remain an essential (contested) cornerstone of housing analysis at all spatial scales.

Section 1 examines the basic structures of a housing market. In Chapter 1 the concept of a market in general is reviewed and our existing ways of thinking about it are re-examined. Market mechanisms dominate housing provision in Western economies and this is not simply a matter of tenure distribution. Maclennan discusses the importance of markets and market relationships within local housing systems. It is of course correct that urban housing in many countries often has disproportionately large non-market housing sectors but, even so, we should not neglect the impact of market processes and choices on non-market housing in terms of demand, neighbourhood effects and the widened choice set presented to households (and vice versa – social housing can influence the competitiveness of private housing).

Maclennan's opening chapter asks fundamental questions about markets and the multidimensional complexity of housing. If researchers are to take these dimensions of durability, spatial fixity, heterogeneity and the like seriously, this has consequences for future housing research programmes. Maclennan argues that developing models and future analysis should be based on relevant, realistic assumptions, taking proper account of complexity and combining insights from other areas of applied economics (e.g. labour economics), behavioural economics and specific market contexts and institutional settings. Not only does this project speak to the housing–macroeconomy nexus but also it is directly relevant to policymaking.

Chapter 2 is also from the economics discipline. Michael Ball's review of the housebuilding process adopts the methods and techniques of industrial organisation. Whereas much recent research has been devoted to questions of land availability, far less has sought to understand the underlying behaviour of housebuilding firms in different institutional and international contexts – their scale, structure, behaviour, plans and performance. In the previous chapter Maclennan calls for more empirical work on supply elasticities and Ball in his chapter takes the argument one stage further back to explore the market mechanisms that actually deliver new housing.

In Chapter 3, Van Ham focuses on household choice and behaviour, examining how needs and preferences, conditioned by resources and what is available (the choice set), leads to decisions about house type and size, location, tenure and, indeed, whether or not to move. Van Ham argues that these decisions – critically informed by economic status, education, household composition and the cultural basis of preferences – are best understood through the lens of dynamic life course, though stressing this to be a framework for a range of analyses rather than a full working theory.

In a related vein, Chapter 4 on residential mobility also draws on life-course theory, though it also reviews a long and established body of work on search, mobility and choice in the housing market. In this case, however, space is devoted to examining the implications of empirical strategies involving discrete choice modelling including nested and other multilevel statistical modelling. For Clark, mobility is the engine of the housing market, allowing households to exercise choice (within constraints) and create vacancy chains that allow further moves to occur. Clark also stresses the strong overlap with labour market decisions by household members (and the increased complexity created by multiple working within households) in relation to short distance mobility and longer migration decisions.

In Chapter 5, the final chapter in the opening section Galster considers neighbourhoods. Again, the focus is on individual agents and their decisions, but also on neighbourhood processes and how we might measure and separate out causes and effects conceptually and empirically. This very clear account identifies the problems defining and bounding neighbourhoods, before coming up with proposed solutions for both difficulties. The chapter also sets out to explain processes of neighbourhood change, employing filtering and housing market concepts to do so.

Neighbourhoods are shown by Galster to be both a useful unit of observation for understanding urban dynamics and also a multidimensional bundle of attributes that can help us make more sense of outcomes (housing quality, job opportunities, discrimination, poverty, etc.) for individuals, households and communities. Galster stresses the analytical value of non-linear effects such as cumulative causation and threshold effects operating at neighbourhood levels. He also unpacks and helps explain the diverse and contradictory evidence about neighbourhood effects on disadvantaged individuals and groups.

Although these five chapters are quite diverse in coverage, focus and analytical antecedents, they share a number of key ideas and common themes which are worth further emphasis. It would not be unreasonable to argue that all of the chapters share the concern expressed by Maclennan to make models and analysis more relevant and realistic, but there are – beyond that general level – several themes that repeatedly emerge.

The first of these common themes is risk. The high transactions costs and uncertainty associated with household housing search decisions (for what is an experiential good) creates risks that have to be quantified and handled. Households (and other local actors) also have to understand, evaluate and manage neighbourhood-level risks. Galster argues that neighbourhood change is typically set in motion by external shocks or drivers, adding another layer of considerations for residential decision-makers. Ball clearly sets out the risks facing housebuilders and how they attempt to cope with development and various market risks that they confront that also lead to decisions about contracting or providing elements of the development, building and selling process in-house.

A second recurring idea concerns the multidimensional nature of housing. Part of the reason that housing markets characteristically exhibit risk is because of the fundamental heterogeneity of housing and its commodity complexity, which expands to encompass neighbourhoods too. Housing economists are of course well-versed in hedonic estimation techniques with which to uncover the implicit values of many of these multiple attributes but, as Galster points out, it is not at all clear that the willingness to pay for a neighbourhood can be recovered in such a way (essentially because of its experiential nature). Multidimensionality is a well-known problem for the analyst trying to isolate specific causal relationships but is equally important as a barrier to good policy-making; the root problem is the same in both cases – uncertainty over the precise transmission mechanisms and indirect and sometimes confounding effects of third factors which are often found in housing markets (for instance the spatial externalities linked to the joint nature of the housing commodity).

A third common theme is the importance of real time (as opposed to theoretical time) in housing decisions. Clark and Van Ham both recognise the utility of setting household decision-making in some form of dynamic life-course framework. This sense of the importance of events and external shocks affecting housing preferences and needs at different life stages is suggestive of the importance of the flow of family history and of real time elapsing. Housing lasts a long time; housing search takes place over a real-time trajectory and Maclennan goes as far as to argue that markets are really constituted by flows of information. Moreover, here and elsewhere, he stresses the Austrian economics notions of market information discovery (and its corollary, information ignorance), historical market contexts, path dependency and the cumulative redundancy of relevant market information held by non-mobile households (Maclennan, 1982). Galster's exposition of neighbourhoods repeatedly also emphasizes the importance of these real-time processes on decision-making at that scale of analysis.

A fourth issue is the shared concern with future research agendas. Apart from reviewing recent and otherwise important research in their respective areas of analysis, each of the five chapters makes a case for a lively and important programme of further research. This is for several reasons: the need for reliable empirical magnitudes at local and other spatial scales; evident gaps in our existing conceptual and empirical knowledge; an inability of the present body of work to tackle and inform current real-world problems (e.g. the global financial crisis or the inability to tackle poverty neighbourhoods); and also scope to augment existing housing research frameworks with emerging or new research tools (e.g. behavioural economics).

Finally, the five chapters draw on a range of research, predominantly from North America, continental Europe, the UK and one or two other countries such as Australia. On the one hand, this is where the great preponderance of housing research has been done and been published. However, we should recognise that the contexts for housing market operation, household housing behaviour, housing supply and neighbourhoods analysis will be quite different once we step out of the Western housing market environment. While it is not clear that researchers studying other types of housing systems are eschewing the traditional methods of housing market analysis (indeed this may be a weakness, for instance in research on contemporary Chinese housing, in so far as it is often premised on norms operating in North America), it is certainly the case that institutional and contextual differences are being analysed and attempts are made to isolate them in comparative work. The five chapters in Section 1 make repeated use of international comparisons, and do so effectively, indicating that national institutional contextual factors such as social security systems, foreclosure laws and transactions costs do matter and need to be adequately factored-in to any analysis of housing markets and household housing behaviour.

REFERENCE

Maclennan, D (1982) *Housing Economics.* Longmans, Harlow, Essex.

Understanding Housing Markets: Real Progress or Stalled Agendas?

Duncan Maclennan

HOUSING MARKETS: WIDE INTERESTS, NARROW THEORIES?

Discussions about housing markets appear daily in the media and press of most countries and they underpin, along with individuals' experiences, frequent conversations around dinner tables, on aeroplanes, elevators and staff common rooms. Everybody, now, has a model of the housing market. Different, more technical and more evidence-rich debates about housing market outcomes are commonplace in municipalities, planning departments and the law courts. Diverse analytical perspectives, with equally varied empirical content and approaches, on housing markets are recurrently unfolded in the academic journals of core disciplines and, more commonly, specialist housing and urban journals.

The currency of 'housing markets' as an area of interest is hardly surprising given both the causes and consequences of the recent Great Financial Crash (GFC); see Smith and Searle (2010). However, public debate and published literature contains not one understanding of the notion of housing market but many. Again, that variety is unsurprising as there are commonly simplifications between the academy and the polity. But in the context of housing market analysis and debate there is a reasonable concern that while there are different conceptions of housing market that are valid and useful, they lack any intellectual coherence. The burden on analysts and commentators is to be clear on what conception of housing market they are using and why. In reality, even within academia there is a lack of clarity about the meanings of 'housing markets', why they are important and why they need to be researched and rethought (see Chapters 6 and 7).

Some writing within academia aims to push forward theoretical understandings and to develop new conceptual models. Although theoretically informed, the vast bulk of published research on housing and cities is potentially valuable because it provides 'applied' evidence on patterns and processes. But applied to what, and for whom? This chapter argues that there remain unsettling gaps between how academia conceptualises and analyses housing markets and how serious commercial sector interests such as banks, major builders, real estate investment companies and governments, both local and national, grapple with the most basic questions of market structure and functioning let alone more nuanced estimates of housing demand and supply. It is argued below that economists and others have fashioned more elaborate models and developed better datasets for housing market analysis over the last two decades. However, there remains a valid question whether economics research on housing has accepted too readily the restrictions and reductionisms of conventional theoretical frameworks and paid too little attention to the insights of cognate disciplines and indeed new evolving ideas at the edge of core economics.

More worryingly, a concern remains that conventional economic reductionisms in housing market analysis throw out key babies along with the bathwater. Our assumptions can define away important research questions and issues and there can often be prolonged debate about the efficacy of econometric techniques rather than whether we have garnered the most important data in the first place. Housing economics research may be interesting, but is it ever useful? The beginnings of wisdom, according to Burns and Mitchell (1946), lie in asking the right questions. This chapter tries to identify key questions asked and omitted in housing market identification and analysis.

The purpose of this chapter is to consider how what has been 'learned' about housing markets over recent decades can be used to provide an economically based notion of housing market. That notion has to be: first, conceptually well based; secondly, provide hooks to connect model assumptions and processes to emerging insights in related disciplines: and, thirdly, credibly connect to and inform real housing policy and planning decisions. Clearly, the reductionisms tolerated in developing a framework with such aims will be rather different from an intendedly, high-level and abstract view of housing markets that nests neatly within core equilibrium economic models. The perspective here is still economic in nature but emphasises real systems, policy connections and interdisciplinary connections. It is an outward-looking and policy-relevant synthesis that is sought.

The chapter proceeds, in the next (second) section, to consider how to link housing markets to core economic theories and why such linkage is often likely to be too reductionist to achieve the three goals espoused above. The economic significance of the nature of housing as a commodity is explored in some detail to emphasise how what we often regard as important about housing and housing markets is assumed away in high-level theorising. It aims to set out key questions as to what a housing market is and the different ways in which the likely features of markets can be conceptualised. The subsequent sections then briefly review the main, different ways in which housing markets are subjected to empirical analysis and how these approaches might be improved. The third section considers how housing market to economy connections may be thought of at the aggregative national or multi-regional scale (How does the 'housing market' matter in the national economy?) and the fourth section moves to the local or metropolitan scale of analysis and policy. The fifth section is a brief conclusion.

FROM CORE THEORY TO SORRY REALITIES: MARKETS AS REAL PROCESSES

Core meanings of market

The vast majority of economists, in academia or government, carry with them an intellectual framework that is firmly rooted in the neoclassical synthesis. Somewhat greater varieties of approach prevail in relation to macroeconomic issues. When confronted with a question about changing drivers for housing demand, such as rising incomes or growing household numbers, or the shifting costs of housing supply, such as rising borrowing rates for the construction sector or rising land costs, there is a stripped down, *ex ante* model that can be applied to suggest likely housing market outcomes. Such unqualified discussion is somewhat rarer now than 20 years ago within academia but is still prevalent in government and financial sectors.

In essence this high-level approach applies neoclassical choice, and equilibrium-oriented models to an 'in principle' market called housing. The systematic peculiarities of the commodity involved and the particularities of the markets that are inevitable consequences of these characteristics are not allowed to destroy the logic of the story. That is, a very high-level and *ex ante* position on the connection between economic change and housing market outcomes can be drawn. Although it may be logically sound and usually directionally correct it will often be generally devoid of any practical use and can, in some settings, lead to the wrong measures for policy being adopted.

In 2007 as the long housing boom was manifesting worrying symptoms of excess household debt, housing equity withdrawal and accelerated consumption, the Federal Reserve convened, at Jacksons' Hole, a major colloquium on housing macroeconomics, to assess how policies needed to be reset to shape more effective market outcomes. The seminar had a stellar cast of analysts and officials. The papers for the seminar were about housing and the economy but in only a few of them − for instance, Muellbauer's contribution (Muellbauer, 2005) − was there any real attempt to incorporate key, basic features of housing markets: most did not, and in consequence the emerging policy debate was not at all about how to reshape housing markets or housing market policies but rather about the more familiar terrain of monetary policy and macro policy. For instance, it has had no impact on the reshaping of national housing policies in the advanced economies post the GFC. Similarly, the IMF's World Economy Report for 2008 raised housing economy issues to an unprecedented status in global policy discussion, but did so without any firm foundation in informed housing market analysis (IMF, 2008). Good real estate analysis needs a basis in good real estate economics.

In high theory the notion of market employed is, in many ways, a relatively unimportant part of the economic story and it operates not as a real or stylised system but simply as a logical construct. The market in standard Walrasian theory, for instance, is a frictionless device that smoothly and predictably transmits logical cause into precise maximising effect. This emphasis is, of course, rather different from the 'market' focus of Adam Smith where the great significance of the 'invisible hand' was that it served as a signalling mechanism and there is much of real markets in the Wealth of Nations. Lachmann (1986) stresses the contrast of neoclassical and Austrian perspectives on markets. The economics of Hayek, Von Mises and others emphasised the subjectivity of decisions, the complexity of processes and the multitude of networks or connections within a (single) market. That more micro, even messy, view of markets forms a useful contrasting intellectual standpoint to the Walrasian synthesis. Modern economic psychology and political economy would not necessarily finish with the same subjectivist assumptions and free-market conclusions as the Austrians (Anderson, 1996). But their emphasis on real market processes remain valid. After the Walrasians it was only the relatively disregarded Austrians who stressed the nature of markets as real discovery processes (Langlois, 1986).

But what is it that makes a market? In the most general terms, a market is the term used to connote a system, or institutional device, for exchange. It is a set of mechanisms or arrangements that facilitates flows of information between buyers and sellers. In consequence, it allows trades to be agreed and goods or services to flow from sellers to buyers and payments to move in the reverse direction. Traditionally, there was an assumption that a market was a venue, a well-defined place. It was the market of the medieval town, the cheese or fish or meat market of the Victorian city, or the stock or futures exchanges of Wall Street and Chicago. The term implied presence in place of buyers and sellers, as well as their goods and their means of payment. In due course, for instance the development of ideas about central place theory, it was recognised that markets could spread or connect over extensive areas, but usually with consumers moving to sales points (Maclennan, 1982).

Early neoclassical synthesis did little to reformalise or expand this notion of market. For instance, in Walras the forms of information gathering and bidding (the *cries au hasard*) presumed sellers and buyers in proximity. Recent developments on the internet provide a sharp contrast, where transactions do not require sellers and buyers to be in spatial proximity to exchange information, but rather to connect via cyberspace (although there may be proximity effects in the physical delivery of goods exchanged). There is an extensive literature emerging on transactions in cyberspace but it has had little application in real estate markets to date.

Where goods are costly, or even impossible, to move to a single market point then two obvious options arise. If the immobile good is relatively simple and can be described by a few key verifiable features, then centralised information will still allow centralised exchanges (the price of oil reserves, for instance). However, if the locationally fixed good is complex and has key attributes that are difficult to measure or describe, then trade is likely to require dispersed exchange involving search behaviour at the different points of single exchange across the market.

Thus, markets are not necessarily single points or places but rather connected information networks. Even where networks are well established, information flow is not always full or costless so that for trade to take place the market may require specialised information intermediaries who not only spread key messages but also verify the content and quality of proposed exchanges. These information services are important because these networks and places are not necessarily populated by fully informed consumers with firmly fixed preferences. Where individuals trade infrequently or do not enter a market with a well-defined list of what they might buy the market becomes, in Hayek's terms, not just an exchange process but a discovery process. And discovery can apply to sellers too, who may find new ways to position, present and sell their goods (Lachmann, 1986).

Within the market there are not only institutions that shape information flows and structures that separate potentially interactive trades but also there are rules and conventions that influence the ways in which offers are made. Multiple sites may coexist, offering identical products at advertised prices, such as the typical 'supermarket'. Within these systems, bargaining around advertised prices may or may not be culturally accepted (shopping in Scotland and Canada is a very different experience – in the former, a price tends to be a price; in the latter, it is often a starting suggestion for a negotiation). Or there may be auctions, and auctions have a multiplicity of rules, such as the English versus the Dutch auction. And for major assets, such as homes, there are likely to be even greater varieties, such as sealed bidding systems. The implications of these differences for price formation in housing markets are considered, for example, in Gibb (1992) and Antonides (1990).

When we move beyond the notion of market as a logical construct, then it has to be recognised that markets have different spatial and non-place forms and dimensions, and that participants learn in the market process. Furthermore, information flows and bidding systems can create a system that not only has frictional exchange costs but also may, as a result of them, fashion quite separate exchange sub-sets within apparently the same system. There may be market institutions and devices that encourage such separations and, in consequence, no longer act as a single market fashioning an equilibrium price, but as a partly partitioned system with some price diversity.

It would be unfair to leap from the abstract microeconomics of Walras, for instance, to a conclusion that core economic theory misses the point of housing markets. Developments in microeconomic theory, for instance game theory, have added some notes of reality to the core mechanisms of general equilibrium theory. However, it is clear then that any real housing economics has to be based not in a notion of market that is merely a logical construct, but rather one that recognises fundamental features of housing as a commodity, and that trader effort will unfold in a potentially complex device in which information agents and institutions have significant roles. In moving beyond a 'black box' approach to the housing market it is important to consider how the economic nature of housing as a commodity is likely to shape particular kinds of market process and structure that lead us some way from the frictionless *deus ex machina* of high theory.

Such de-reductionism in applied sub-specialisms in economics is by no means rare. Much progress in understanding labour markets, capital markets and financial systems has been made. And insights and approaches developed within these specialisms have fed back into new core modelling, or more commonly respecified macroeconomic models. However, feedback from the insights of applied housing economics are less apparent in economic discussion of the housing system. The encouraging development for housing analysis is that there has been a growing volume of informed housing economics in the last two decades.

The worry for the interest area is that there is little sign of core respecifications to reflect the lessons of intersectoral research. For instance, it was noted above that in the World Economy Report for 2008 (IMF, 2008), housing issues were a top policy concern but the analytical models used in the report, for instance those developed to report on the over- and undervaluation of national housing stocks, reflected more or less none of the research learnings from housing economics in prior decades and, in consequence, the estimates were probably misspecified and inaccurate. As housing looms so large in the budgets and wealth portfolios of households and touches significant components of employment, production and the financial sector, there is really now no excuse for national governments and international agencies to have a modelling approach for housing that is not rooted in realistic reductions in abstraction. We can learn much from high-level theoretical thinking on housing but applying such ideas to real markets, without qualification, is analytically misplaced concreteness. Market analysis, for housing or anything else, deserves more than a logical construct as the centre-piece but rather a well-constructed model of the key transmission mechanism that is the housing market. How can we define and identify housing markets? What is there systematic about the nature of housing? What stylised facts are there than can be used to construct definitions and models of housing markets that are operable? Are such models and definitions more or less likely to leave us comfortable with an equilibrium perspective on the markets we model?

Housing and housing markets

At first sight it may seem somewhat pedantic to take time to define and give meaning to the terms 'housing' and 'house'. The *Oxford Dictionary* defines the word simply as 'building for human habitation'. 'Housing' is both a noun and a verb. The term is applied both to dwellings (my house, town house, council house, etc.) and the set of actions which (*inter alia*) plans, produces, finances, allocates and maintains dwellings. Both of these notions, 'housing' as noun and verb, need to be explored if housing economics is to provide some useful insights about the notion of housing market. This arises because the nature of housing as a commodity has direct, unavoidable, implications for the ways in which effective market exchange arrangements may operate. Making these systems work involves process.

How we define housing will have implications for how we define and identify housing markets. Sociologists, anthropologists and economists have all explored the meaning of the words 'home', 'dwelling' and 'house' (Saunders 1989; Mallett, 2004). Within more economically oriented literature there has been long emphasis on the product variety, spatial fixity, neighbourhood and asset aspects of housing: for instance, see Maclennan (1982), Quigley (2002), Galster (1987) and Smith and Searle (2008), respectively. It is useful, from time to time, to look at the variety of these approaches across disciplines, as it is a reminder of how reductionist we are within each discipline. If we wish to connect housing market analyses to broader concerns about well-being, psychological and material, or to consider how housing is embedded in complex social relationships, then a regular revisit to where we start as disciplinary reductionists is useful. The focus below is more narrowly on economic notions of the market.

From an economic perspective, a house (or 'housing') consists of a designed physical structure of connected and sheltered spaces and systems, constructed of materials and components (pipes, wires, etc.) through the use of capital (e.g. developers' ingenuity and equipment), labour (from designers to bricklayers) and land or existing property. That is, houses are complex, durable, locationally fixed structures with multiple attributes that are invariably purchased and consumed jointly with the neighbourhood characteristics that surround them. This concept, broadly speaking, has been at the heart of housing economics for four decades or more and they are important features that make housing different from simple goods, such as the apples and widgets beloved of mainstream economic models.

Complexity

Economics research has been good at establishing the existence of the complexity of housing as a good. For almost four decades hedonic house price studies have been used to identify the economic significance of different, distinctive attributes of housing (Rosen, 1974; Brown and Rosen, 1982; Malpezzi, 2002). These studies, that almost invariably have high levels of explanatory power, confirm that housing prices are influenced by attributes or characteristics such as:

- Size, style, layout and internal amenity (variety).
- The location of the dwelling: households pay not just for size, type, quality but for the characteristics of the location; these (place and space) influences include:
  ○ the costs of accessibility to the wider spread of locations used by household such as employment, shopping and leisure locations
  ○ the quality and availability of neighbourhood amenity, including neighbours
  ○ access to local retail and service facilities (both public and private)
- The asset importance of their home and possibilities for (relative) gain and loss as well as quality and maintenance obligations (fixity and durability)

The range of attributes involved can be grouped under the three broad headings of *product variety*, *place and space*, and *fixity and durability*. The pros and cons of hedonic studies are considered further in the fourth section, below, but it can be argued that they have been widely, and often productively, used in research but without housing economics paying much regard to the consequences of that complexity for market processes and choices: or indeed, how that complexity may complicate the implementation of hedonic studies in the first instance.

How do product variety, place and space and fixity and durability (the real features of housing) impact the structure and process of the market? With these fundamental features of housing, how can the exchange system work to ensure that efficient and well-informed prices emerge (and that revealed hedonic prices are based on such processes)?

Product variety

The real and diverse characteristics of housing have a number of implications for market structures and processes. The first characteristic is that the range of significant elements of household well-being, or utility, influenced by housing characteristics, is such that the costs associated with the house will always be a significant element of households' budgets, so that mistakes matter. The second characteristic is that the costs of search and exchange (where dwellings are bought and sold rather than rented), allied to their budget significance, means that residential moves, and therefore well-informed trading by individual consumers, are relatively infrequent. With so many complex characteristics, this means that households, to avoid difficulties of adverse selection and moral hazard, are likely to deploy market experts to inform price bids (Quigley, 2002). This is likely to mean that not only do mistakes matters but also that with positive transaction costs they may be expensive to reverse.

Sellers will have an interest to conceal information in some instances and there may be significant information asymmetries about issues such as true dwelling condition (the central heating defects that you only know when you live in a house) and the nature of some externalities (the atmosphere of a neighbourhood, the propensity to form or avoid informal contacts, etc.). In some jurisdictions there are regulations requiring sellers to disclose relevant property information but even where they do exist there are potential neighbourhood effects that will be customer- as well as property-dependent.

Attribute complexity, in the case of housing, invariably leads to the need for agents and institutions. Their views can matter in shaping the choice sets that households can make effective. The question then arises as to whether the information and agent structure operating within the market is competitive or influences choices made and prices set in particular times and places.

Consumer assessment of the quality and implicit price of a diverse set of housing attributes is clearly a demanding information-processing exercise if strict neoclassical behaviours are assumed. This remains the case even where consumers have assessment procedures that are hierarchical or that eliminate by aspects (for more detailed consideration, see Chapter 3). More recent interest in new behavioural economics implies that different approaches to understanding the information processing involved in housing choices may be required, and this is considered in the final section (see Hogarth and Reder, 1987; Egidi and Marris, 1992; Rabin, 2001; Camerer et al., 2003).

The nature of housing attributes, given the complexity of design and attribute interactions, is such that they often have to be physically seen by buyers to be truly valued. There are important exceptions to this. For example, in some larger nations such as the USA, Canada and Australia, where interregional distances are on a grand scale, some households are prepared to rent and buy homes without visits but on the basis of an expert assessment associated with an electronic virtual tour. And in the UK there have been significant instances in the last decade of London-based buy-to-let investors purchasing properties in northern British cities without visiting them. In the first of these instances, the significant housing search costs involved explain unseen choice, and in the second case the detailed arrangement of the attributes were unimportant as the purchase had no consumption dimensions for the purchaser. More complex households, with multiple consumption uses of the dwelling, will usually be anxious to search homes and neighbourhoods prior to purchase. Search costs are likely to be significant, especially in 'hotter' housing markets, and they are also likely to be significant because of the spatial nature of housing markets (Novy-Marx, 2009; Piazzesi and Schneider, 2009).

Place and space, fixity and durability

Space effects interact with variety and durability in shaping the functioning of housing markets. First, space and place (geography) matters because households are choosing places, neighbourhoods and locations when they choose their home. Home and neighbourhood is an ineluctably conjoined choice. This jointness not only adds to the variety of attributes that have to be considered but also adds other distinctive aspects to housing choice that are considered below.

Secondly, unless we are living in a world of tents and mobile homes, space matters in market functioning because properties cannot be brought feasibly to some central market place. Purchasers have to search the spatially dispersed sales sites and know which sites to search (Clark, 1982). Aside from the search costs involved, there is a further, important market functioning consequence. Searchers, agents and institutions will not in reality be selecting or selling across a fully connected or centralised set of possibilities. Rather, searchers for immobile sales offers will have to choose within a (probably) localised set of a limited number of options. Preferences and information flows, and expert advice, will mean that the housing market in, say, a city at some point in time is not a single market but rather a collection of relatively localised exchanges. To assume that searchers, sellers or agents can equilibrate the price/quality relationships for the whole set of properties traded at any immediate time is an onerous demand to place on the market mechanism.

A metropolitan housing system may have multiple localised simultaneous trades but this does not necessarily mean that the market will be singular in its price outcomes and perfectly competitive in its structures.

Spatial search and informed choice, and the potential roles of market experts and institutions, are likely to be given even greater salience by the interaction of locational and fixity characteristics of dwellings. A further crucial consideration is that a house, when built, also has an absolutely fixed location. Although houses are spatially fixed, the geographies of employment, social composition, crime, etc., around about them might change (homes are absolutely fixed but their relative location might change over time).

This absolute fixity of a dwelling, combined with its durability in a potential matrix of changing locational attributes, means that owners face risks of price depreciation (appreciation) and asset losses (gains) that lie beyond their own control. Purchasers require information about options and risks, and this reinforces the roles that 'expert views' (surveyors, estate agents, lawyers and lenders) may have in choices. Geography and time interact to make consumer and expert expectations about prices and areas an important feature of how housing systems operate.

A further problem for smooth equilibrating tendencies in housing markets is that an important attribute of housing choices, often associated with neighbourhood attributes, is that they are often a 'social situational good'. Choice of housing makes statements about chosen lifestyles, relative status and social standing (see Chapter 3). There is clear evidence that for many, though not all, households that individuals choose houses where they wish to live amongst people like themselves. That is, neighbours are an important determinant of neighbourhood quality so that households are extensively interdependent in their decisions. This observation, allied to the conclusion of the previous paragraph that expectational effects are also important, means that the prices, vacancy rates and resident composition of neighbourhoods can change sharply and quickly (see Chapters 4 and 5).

In brief, the key features of housing are likely to mean that in some neighbourhoods, and particularly those regarded as problematic for policy, change patterns may be complex/chaotic rather than smoothly adjusting. Fast, non-linear demand responses may play out in a context of rather slow supply-side responses and where non-price adjustments have key roles in shaping final equilibria.

This last point brings us to issues of change rather than choice (given some fixed set of housing opportunities) and moves into the medium and long term.

It is important to ask why supply-side responses are typically sluggish, not least because in the absence of that reflection too many polemicists and more than a few economists lay supply inelasticity at the door of planning system constraints.

There are surprisingly few contemporary estimates of the price elasticity of housing supply for given markets over different periods. We have been happier to pontificate about supply elasticity than to measure it. Some neoclassical-based analyses of planning and supply issues, for instance Glaeser et al. (2008), have used well-defined models and good data to test plausible hypotheses about supply-side limits and there has been equally diligent work in other contexts: for instance, Grimes and Aitken (2010).

Analyses of the construction sector, and the labour, money and materials markets it relies upon, also suggest a range of characteristics of housing production systems and land markets that are likely to lead to sticky supply. Michael Ball has long argued that the real economics of the housing construction sector is oversimplified in competitive economic theorising about the housing market (Ball, 1996) (see Chapter 2). In some ways confirming this, policymakers from Lyndon Johnston in the 1960s (who lamented that the USA could send people to the moon but could not build enough homes fast enough, to house a growing population) through the UK Barker Reviews (Barker, 2004) to the current Donald Reviews (National Housing Supply Council, 2009) in Australia all express concern and some surprise at the sluggishness of housing supply.

It is more than unbalanced analysis to assume that slow supply-side responses always and everywhere stem from the planning system stilling the responsive hand of an otherwise competitive, informed housing provision system. However, when emphasis shifts from cross-section, consumers and space to supply, the emphasis is on adjustment over time and on production. Firms face real uncertainties, on cost and demands. Firms face incomplete information about preferences, as well as uncertainties about where and how the market will develop, planning systems and market instabilities. The construction industry is fragmented, often, productivity gains are slow and much of the return to construction (in some countries) is made from landholding. There may be localised monopolies of land hoarding. Lagged information and incomplete adjustments prevail. The market may be far from perfection, but still in some ways competitive. And in that context the challenge for applied analysis is to identify the balance of 'market' failures versus planning restrictions.

Housing fundamentals: so what?

So how will the invisible hand work in markets that have characteristics of the kind discussed above: namely, the potential for short-term submarkets and the near certainty of supply inelasticity? In the short and long term it requires information flows to emerge from market action and to be available to traders across the system as a whole. In essence, if searchers searched intensively over quite short periods of time until they make a successful bid, then this requires price and bid information to be available more or less immediately to potential buyers (and sellers), or at least their market agents.

Fast revelation of exchange price and bid information is not a characteristic of most housing markets in the advanced economies. In the UK, open auction prices only tend to be available in periods of sharp market downturn and home repossession when financial institutions auction off repossessed stock. Price statistics emerge to inform decision taking either through indices developed in a variety of ways by large lenders or market agents, or they are official statistics that emerge with a lag (and influence planners but less so the public). Sold dwelling prices in the UK are public information, but there is usually a minimum lag of a month in identifying sales prices.

In Victoria, Australia, half of homes are still sold in street auctions. Consumers, potential sellers (and aghast housing researchers) can stand in the street and watch prices being formed in the raw. And the results of these sales are listed, street by street, in the general press the following week. In Ontario, Canada, it is almost impossible for consumers to independently establish market-relevant housing prices. Realtors have a near monopoly on local market information and few make standardised information available to consumers at the scales at which they might search. Banks do publish lagged, usually quarterly prices but official price series are poor.

Price information in many systems of urban housing markets is only available on a lagged, incomplete basis and through market agents. Research makes too little allowance for the paucity of adequate price signals for consumers, especially in cross-country studies but also in modelling particular markets. The 'invisible hand' will fumble in such circumstances. More to the point, this incomplete information system is likely to localise searches into particular market locations or niches, so that locally noisy price signals may be prolonged and non-price signals given relevance. It is not being asserted that the market becomes a permanently disconnected catallaxy but that inter-area price adjustments and short-term market equilibration may take some time. The market as a self-organising system may involve more than fast adjustments driven by clear price signals (see Tabuchi, 2009).

Of course, supply-side fixity may mean that longer-term price equilibrium may also be, at best, a prolonged process. But clearly these features of supply (allied to consumer choice realities) can further complicate the mechanisms of the market in the longer term. Do we see the system of land and real estate as a random walk, efficiently valued and priced by the capital market? The efficacy of efficient market models is, post GFC, open to renewed debate. Do we see the market as a more chaotic mechanism? Arguably, we can, especially over short periods. Small, local and complex systems are quite likely to be open to complex and chaotic change with endogenous reinforcing mechanisms. There may also be periods of such change in wider housing markets, when at the peak or bottom of the cycle behaviours have interactive crowd features, when uncertainties are at their greatest and have their greatest impacts. Perhaps a system of punctuated equilibria may prevail, where periods of well-functioning, steady market behaviour become disrupted by chaotic bursts of change before a new period of order emerges?

These different forms of market behaviour may all have some relevance for housing markets in some places at some times. But there is also enough evidence to suggest that many markets have some equilibrating propensities. They may not be in equilibrium, but moving in that direction. This then poses a difficult choice for market analysts. Not only do they now have to identify the spatial extent of the market and its product features but also which conceptual notion of market meshes with the problem they are addressing. Faced with a real housing market question, analysts cannot, *ex ante*, resort to pervasive in-equilibrium assumptions. The skill in applied economics is to identify what the problem is and to choose the most useful framework for the issues on hand: *ex cathedra* and *ex ante* don't count. If the analytical interest is in the economic processes of housing markets, it is dangerous to throw out any real consideration of how adjustment mechanisms in the market are influenced by the inherent nature of the commodity.

If any or all of the above reservations about the functioning of housing markets have salience, then there are significant implications for core work in housing economics. Market structures and processes used in analysis need to be justified rather than simply assumed. Hedonic studies will need to be carefully constructed. If consumers are localised into a set of areas and products, and this may be because there is not a complete range of housing type-area substitutes as well as because of search cost and agent effects, then the set of choices may have some distinctiveness for consumers. In these circumstances it would be technically imprecise to consider that market as perfectly competitive (and that implicit assumption underpins most studies of housing choices and markets). Rather, each set of products, the area-type combinations, has some degree of lasting distinctiveness. Market structures will be more akin to monopolistic competition and this may mean that there is incomplete attribute price equalisation over the market as whole in the short and medium period.

In summary, then, the key real features of housing mean that it is:

- a multiple-attribute or composite commodity and its value reflects internal/structure attributes as well as neighbourhood and locational characteristics – standardisation of price and quality data is imperative, therefore, even for the most basic description of the market
- the set of attributes in dwellings varies from type to type and place to place within a market so that consumers are confronted with product variety, and of course consumers differ also in age, income, preferences, etc; the key issue is what product group choices are best for different household groups
- the fixity and durability of housing means that choices made are inherently risky
- social and neighbourhood interconnections between households, allied to economic expectations behaviour, are likely to mean that market trends in small area are likely to be non-linear when change ensues
- infrequent search behaviour and the risks and returns involved mean that households, especially, in buying homes are likely to use agents and experts in the housing choice process
- the fundamental features of housing and the range of markets that home construction has to interface with means that the housing supply process is likely to be sticky and encounter market failures and imperfections despite a deconcentrated structure of ownership.

Rejecting these considerations denies the real nature of commodity complexity. If economists are going to stick with their recognition of commodity complexity in housing, and that would be wise, they need to get to grips with how that complexity actually influences market outcomes and processes. How is this reflected in market analyses at national and local scales? In the sections that follow the argument is presented by moving from the micro and the metropolitan (next section) to the macro (fourth section) scales.

METROPOLITAN MARKETS AND LOCAL MARKET ANALYSIS

Access-space: old foundations

Whereas macro models of 'the market', as discussed in the next section, have been concerned with cycles and medium-term change, local housing market analysis, including both markets specified at metropolitan scales and more localised segments or submarkets within them, has primarily focussed on cross-section or short-term analysis. For the last half century, the dominant paradigm for urban economic analysis of the housing market has been the access-space model rooted in the work of Alonso (1964), Muth (1969) and Evans (1973). It is a framework that implies highly ordered spatial (ring and gradient) patterns and it is based on competitive equilibrium assumptions processes. However, the model has very limited usefulness for most of the important contemporary questions about the aggregative structure and functioning or metropolitan housing markets. Over the last 25 years a number of contributors, for example Maclennan (1982) and Rothenberg et al. (1992), have argued for a shift to understanding real market processes and real structures as a better basis for applied economic analysis of housing markets. Decentralisation of homes and jobs, growing incomes, diversification of preferences and lifestyles have all contributed to the emergence of the metropolitan market as a complex choice mosaic of housing and neighbourhood 'products' for 'consumer' groups. The core employment location and ring structures of the old model now mask so many important aspects of cities that they need to be pushed to the background of research and teaching. Access is required to a multiplicity of non-CBD (central business district) household activity points and households of the same incomes make quite different choices of what to do and where to do it.

That emergent diversity of structure and preferences, paradoxically, make it more important for researchers and planners to know the actual structures of housing market and behaviours within them. It is not that access and space tradeoffs are unimportant; indeed we are moving to a time when rising fuel costs and carbon charging will put a new premium on accessibility. But we need to establish clearly, as a matter of fact, what and where our metropolitan housing markets are?

Housing market analysis clearly needs to be less reductionist if it is to answer the real questions of participants, planners and policymakers dealing with these systems. Housing market analysis for markets with real dimensions is required. Should we proceed with an equilibrium neoclassical analysis, with simply more localised labour markets and household activity points? This approach has produced useful results from Straszheim (1987) onwards and is now the most common approach used in North America. But does such a starting point implicitly restrict our techniques and our range of conclusions? The answer depends on at least two considerations. First, either nationally or locally, is there reason to believe that the local housing system is in a period of particularly rapid change (unduly hot or cold; see Novy-Marx, 2009), or does it appear to be closer to some more balanced or equilibrium position. If rapid change is driving the interest, then a short-term equilibrium framework may not address key issues of concern. Secondly, the approach selected will have to reflect the questions asked: for instance, a model of perfectly informed households with competitive mortgage and housing markets may not be too helpful in getting to evident problems of limited consumer information and non-price rationing of housing finance. Without abandoning a long-term equilibrium framework as a pointer for the direction of change it may be important to look for non-equilibrium signs to indicate how markets are operating and with what consequences. In the UK, at least, it is often safer to assume that local housing systems are not in equilibrium and to proceed accordingly. Arguably, given the rather different intensities and forms of government intervention, US researchers might make the different call – that the equilibrium framework will do for most important questions.

Regardless of the choice made, how can local housing market analysis proceed? In what follows we examine how markets are defined and internal structures identified, how observed *ex post* choices and prices can be interpreted and the revelation and role of underlying behaviours and adjustments for the longer term. In all these areas of analysis there has been significant progress over the last two decades, but yet there remain significant new approaches and areas to address.

The market: boundaries and structures

Analysis invariably proceeds with the assumption that housing markets will have a strong spatial element. For much of the last century housing market analysts had to work with poor-quality house price information that was rarely available in geo-coded form at disaggregated levels. Markets, more often than not, were defined by administrative, often municipal, boundaries. The advent of geographic information systems (GIS) has, in most countries, revolutionised the quality of housing market information and access to it.

Detailed geographies of housing market outcomes can be used to define market limits band structures. For instance, in Scotland the Land Registry lists, *inter alia*, sales prices and the locational origins of purchasers. Broad housing market boundaries can then be constructed by identifying flows of moves between neighbourhoods and suburbs. If moves take place within some defined set of areas, then the degree of 'closure' of that local system can be proxied by the proportion of intra-group moves. A bounded housing market area can then be defined when some degree of local closure is accepted for analysis purposes (often 70–80% of moves).

An alternative approach to identifying market boundaries, as well as submarket structures within some wider bounded area, is to examine price structures. In essence this approach revolves around the notion that in a single, well-connected market there will be a single equilibrium price for identical commodities. In housing market analysis the term 'submarket' is often used rather casually to mean just some disaggregated part of the overall system. But it has a precise technical meaning: namely, an area where there are statistically significant and enduring price differences for some commodity or housing characteristic in relation to the overall market or other similarly defined areas within it (Maclennan and Tu, 1996). In housing markets this means either identifying, via hedonic price analysis, persistence in attribute price differences within the overall bounded area or, less precisely, identifying the relative price change of small areas over time. A recent review and development of the basic ideas involved can be found in Pryce (2009).

There is a significant literature on housing submarkets that confirms that they can exist and persist: see, for example, Schnare and Struyk (1976), Goodman and Thibodeau (1998), Watkins (2001), Bourassa et al (2003, 2007), Jones et al. (2003) and Tu et al (2007). This means that aggregative cross-section estimates of consumer choice parameters that ignore them may be biased (see further below).

A considerable intellectual effort has been made to understand and identify housing submarkets and, arguably, it has qualified rather than radically changed the broad insights of equilibrium analysis. Much less effort has been paid in structuring market analysis to identify consumer groups (with choice analysis usually entering data on incomes, household sizes, etc.) or to combine spatial opportunity data with other characteristics of dwellings to identify what might be called product groups (i.e. groups of properties defined by key bundles of characteristics): that is, in housing market analysis, issues are often being addressed that lie at a scale somewhere between the individual and the metropolitan area as a whole. The 'meso' level needs to be understood as submarket outcomes driven by the interaction of 'consumer groups' and 'product groups' but market analysis tends to stick resolutely to the overall market of the individual chooser and property.

This 'group' notion needs more thought in housing market analysis. The analysis above has already discussed housing submarkets and product groups. The case for having some notion of consumer groups becomes clearer when present approaches to explaining market choice outcomes are considered (see also Chapter 3).

Choices, choice outcomes and hedonics

In analysing household choices within housing markets analysts have tended to either develop specific tenure, size or location choice models (see Chapter 3) or to consider conventional economic parameterisation of household choices – that is, income and price elasticities of demand. Over a long period of time and in different contexts academic research has estimated that the income elasticity of demand for housing lies above 0.5 and below 1; households spend more on housing as incomes increase but they do so at a rate less than their growth in income. There are remarkably few estimates of price elasticities of demand.

Although the income elasticity of demand estimates comes close to a stylised fact, the question arises as to whether it is a useful parameter for many local housing planning and policy purposes. The latter usually require some sense of which housing attributes – such as size, quality or locational accessibility – will be sought as incomes rise. There are relatively few studies of how the demand for different attributes of housing respond to income change, and this is a surprising omission given the interests both of developers and planners. Those that have been completed – and Cheshire and Sheppard (1998) provide an excellent recent example – suggest that the demand for both structure quality and neighbourhood quality is more income elastic than the demand for size of units.

Economists, in making attribute specific estimates, deal with the fundamental complexity of housing by using hedonic methods for house price analysis. Hedonic analysis, well reviewed by Malpezzi (2005), has to be careful and not cavalier in its construction and interpretation. There are few market studies in which some list of characteristics fails to explain 60–70% of price variation. But which specification should be deployed and how should the interaction between different attributes be interpreted, always assuming that the estimates can be assumed to have been generated within an equilibrium system?

Hedonic price approaches are at the core of consumer research in housing economics and their apparent robust appearance can be misleading. Even assuming that the market is in equilibrium, caution is still needed. How can households logically value some of the attributes that can only be known by *ex post* experience? How do households process implicit values when up to 30 characteristics in hedonic regressions show significant effects? What is the information-processing skill that allows households to make these weightings? Or do they? Is there some other information and price formation process at work, ranging from the complex economics of the subconscious to the convergent influence of market experts?

Recent work on the general use of hedonic indices demonstrates how housing sector applications of the technique can be more refined than has been commonplace in the past. However, housing economics have invested significantly more effort in improving the econometric specification of models and housing price/quality databases than in probing the preferences and beliefs that underpin choices. The variety of attributes in dwellings raises important possibilities for households to display non-standard preferences and to confront information-processing issues in making housing choices, and indeed for households within a given area to exhibit strongly different *ex ante* preference sets. Until recently, in the development of new behavioural economics, the identification of preferences was not regarded as an important part of housing market analysis. Rather, only revealed preferences, i.e. well-behaved and group-wide rankings, mattered: in essence, they are derived by econometric interpretation rather than asking or observing individuals.

In reality, multiplicity of attributes and household services involved means that households – even of a similar age and with similar incomes – may have quite different preferences about lifestyles and, consequently, desired housing attributes and locations. Somewhat surprisingly, as economics sees itself as at least partly about the exploration of preferences in choices, conventional economic analysis of housing markets has been very limited in its methodology for preference assessments.

The changing balance of income and demographic drivers in housing markets has challenged forecasting approaches. However, within the economics-choice framework there is also growing concern about the relevance of aggregate market measures such as elasticities. The growth in household incomes and the growing diversity of household types has meant that housing choices are now more diverse. Quite different housing choices are now associated with different households on similar incomes or even similar-aged households with similar incomes: that is, aggregate measures are becoming increasingly imprecise and no longer convey the nuanced market information required by individuals, agents and policymakers.

Matching processes and behaviours

With this conception of unfolding and disaggregated markets, separate but connected, how does the price formation process unfold and market adjustment occur? In the short term, markets produce search and quantity signals as well as price signals so that market adjustment processes within as well as between markets may be important. Housing economics has historically emphasised the *ex post* analysis of actual housing choices and relatively little emphasis on the processes by which choices are made. For instance, the volume of research on housing market search pales into insignificance with respect to labour market search (and this has been true for three decades; see Clark and Moore, 1982). But a convincing housing economics has to understand market processes and not merely outcomes.

It is important to think of markets as complex processes that generate system signals. The way in which signals are generated, as searchers from different housing consumer groups strive to mesh with vacancies spread across product groups, is complex. And the signals generated are not just out-turn prices but failed bids, search activity and migration behaviour. These interrelated signals are what appear to shape housing market adjustment. Over the last 20 years a number of academic research studies – see for instance Wheaton (see DiPasquale and Wheaton, 1996) – have demonstrated the feasibility and relevance of housing search analysis and they have been, fruitfully, used by a number of housing and planning authorities.

Research reveals that, in most instances, the early stages of a search process involve a degree of orientation, usually by non-intensive search methods such as reading newspaper adverts or drive-through visits, which eliminate broad locations that are either beyond the resources of the household or are less preferred. After area/sector orientation, households become involved in the more detailed assessment of particular vacancies. Assessing some of these attributes requires expert opinions, for which potential customers must pay. Yet more attributes may require subjective assessment (the view from the room) or may only be capable of assessment after taking up residence (for instance, the friendliness of neighbours). Unless potential purchasers are risk lovers, intensive assessment of uncertain characteristics will be required prior to purchase. Even with the development of videos of houses for sale, and their extension into virtual reality techniques of information spread, potential purchasers will generally want to see and assess units.

This need to search and see specific units has at least two important implications for the way the market operates. First, the search area or areas in which more detailed assessments are made constitute the market area in which the individual is operating. They are also likely to be well-defined product groups. The extent to which there is a local market will then depend on (1) how other households – say for similar or the same consumer group – have a similar set of search areas and on (2) the extent to which such areas are geographically localised. Secondly, spatially (or sectorally) structured search behaviour will separate, at any point in time, the population of buyers and sellers into a number of dispersed trades and auctions. There is, as noted above, no single market clearing auction shaping the price of houses in a metropolitan area. Different prices for similar or standardised housing units could potentially prevail, though price differences between places may divert search behaviour, over time, from higher- to lower-priced areas and, in the longer term, supply additions may occur.

The pricing and search procedures for new housing developments usually differ from the second-hand market. Quality may be more readily ascertained and the sales transaction does not usually involve a bidding process. In the short term, developer prices are likely to be fixed and advertised with properties restricted on a queue or 'first come first served' basis. Developers may then adjust prices for subsequent tranches of homes, or stock unsold from previous periods, in relation to past observed levels of search. Specific dwelling searches in the new sector are generally likely to be more rapid and less costly than in the second-hand market.

The brief review of the information problems of housing markets hints at the importance of signals in the consumer search process. A two- or even three-stage 'matching' process is likely to emerge. First, as noted above, consumers may undertake an 'orientation' search in which the locational/ house-type characteristics desired may lead to a low-cost first scan of suitable product groups. Secondly, once broad product groups have been selected, more intensive search of specific vacancies takes place prior to bidding. Thirdly, after purchase bids are made, some, indeed the majority in all but the slackest housing markets, fail. Consumers, either learning new preferences or confronting real constraints, may then adjust the product groups in which they regard, on the basis of past bidding, purchase as feasible. The alternative is to remain in the same product groups and raise price bids. The expected costs of failed future searches are likely to influence the extent to which price bids are revised upwards.

The way in which households adapt product group search and price bids – i.e. the search adjustment process – contains important information for developers and planners. If consumers only adjust price bids for the same product groups, and do not adjust locations, etc,, the planner/developer implication is to increase output in such localities or in as close substitutes as possible. In short, sustained relative price appreciation signals shortages in specific places or product groups. On the other hand, if households switch search patterns, this shift sequentially reveals what consumers regard as close substitutes.

Analysis of household search processes can reveal key pressures and linkages within local markets and suggest where latent demands really exist. More work needs to be done in this area, not least in identifying the search patterns of different consumer groups and the extent to which consumers use hierarchical search processes: that is, establishing whether households focus on area, or type or some other attribute in selecting possible dwellings and then refocus on a second attribute and so on. Evidence already suggests that households have different and hierarchic search processes. For instance, whereas many Scottish households first select housing tenure, there is evidence that some younger households have strong area/ house-type preferences that dominate the tenure attribute. Some households may place house type and size ahead of area.

If, for a particular group, we are seeking to define the limits of a housing market, then the areas/types actually searched, the search field, may constitute a suitable interaction basis for defining the extent and structure of the market. Yet this approach has had more or less no significant purchase in applied housing research in the last three decades. But search costs, information asymmetries and market agents are inevitable in housing markets, given the nature of the commodity, even if they disappear in typical pricing and exchange models. Search is likely to matter not just because commodities are complex, but because they are spatially based and fixed.

Housing economics has become a diverse and interesting field of research over the last three decades. But despite the interest in economists in individual preferences, and mechanisms by which they might be most effectively expressed, the field remains paradoxically weak on research revelations about household preferences. Most empirical studies explore how variation in constraints shifts choices, and not in how preferences differ, change and form. Housing research, in the main, has been unwilling to get to grips with market processes of search and matching. Three decades of the application of information economics has moved much applied economics well beyond simple supply and demand analysis; yet it would be hard to argue that housing economics has kept pace over that period. In the majority of applied economics research on housing it seems that there remains an unwillingness to get to grips with market matching mechanisms and the behaviours of agents. Housing economists have either chosen or been forced by research funders to seek new datasets on outcomes and to presume the processes and the psychologies that shape housing choices. This has limited the range of change situations economists can understand and model. In many ways housing economics still has to confront the revolution in paradigms that occurred in labour economics over the last 30 years. At the same time, as noted above, housing economics research has to connect quickly to the new behavioural economics. In overviews of the latter, mainstream economists often cite home purchase as the kind of process that new economic psychology can help explain (Viale, 1992) Rabin, 2002; Friedman and Cassar, 2004; Guala, 2005; Della Vigna, 2009). Yet the housing research literature using new behavioural economics remains sparse.

Supply in the long term: an apologetic note

The sections above have emphasised the consumer, demand and choice aspects of housing markets. Housing investment and supply behaviour deserves at least similar attention but space constrains other than a few general remarks here.

It was noted in the second section that supply-side analyses in reality seldom produces robust estimates of housing supply elasticities. Planning and policy bodies should remedy that omission because the future pattern of metropolitan growth may face expansion constraints, and supply elasticities that differ from the present. However, they also need to give attention to broader conceptions of the supply side of the housing market for the long term. Some market systems, whether chaotic or homeostatic, may also have what are called 'emergent' properties: that is to say that change at more local levels, even if it is chaotic, can induce coherent and obvious patterns at larger levels of aggregation. For example, in the housing sector, there may be rapid and chaotic change processes, which take a neighbourhood from a stable middle-income standing to one of rapidly deteriorating quality and low- income occupation. Although the change process of that neighbourhood may be individually disorderly, it may help shape a more obvious aggregative pattern of income separation across different neighbourhoods. As future fuel costs change, it is important to ask what the likely 'emergent' properties of metropolitan housing markets might be.

Finally, it is important to recognise that some systems are evolutionary Connectivity and feedback: for example, do not simply lead to new equilibrium flows but may alter the nature of individuals and their behaviour, so that the qualities of the nodes change. Housing markets may display some or even all of these features and it is important that implicit assumptions as well as major change patterns are identified. There should be no a priori value judgement that self-balancing or emergent or evolutionary systems are per se superior to others in shaping housing and human well-being. But we need to understand better how housing markets will evolve in the longer term. In the UK, at least, there are currently no serious funded academic efforts to address that issue. Across the advanced economies more generally there does not seem to be an up-welling of applied microeconomic analysis to help us understand the individual and local market behaviours that have both underpinned and reflected the great housing boom and bust of the last 15 years. The opportunity to push paradigm exploration or change that might put in place a real micro basis for housing macroeconomics is in acute danger of being lost as housing research drops further down the priorities of national research councils. What have we learned about 'markets' in the macro context?

FROM REGIONAL TO NATIONAL NOTIONS OF HOUSING MARKETS

Over the last decade there has been a renewed interest in the role of 'the housing market' in the national economy. The long boom, from the early 1990s to 2007 and the subsequent GFC, have all featured housing prices, wealth and equity withdrawal as key elements of instability (see Smith and Searle, 2010). In consequence, for the vast majority of economists the phrase 'housing market' connotes not an interest per se in the real functioning of housing markets but how the incorporation of macro housing outcomes, such as price changes and aggregate shifts in housing debts and equity, changes the forecasts of macro models.

Macroeconomic models or assessments involving housing have typically been concerned, as in recent fiscal stimulus programmes, with the multiplier effects of housing investment or with the role of housing markets in economic cycles. There has been a resolute disregard of how housing market outcomes influence national productivity, growth and competitiveness. Glaeser (2009) has recently argued that 'the wealth of cities' is influenced by labour migration and that to understand metropolitan growth there has to be a focus beyond wage rates to a wider 'net advantages' perspective. In that broader view, Glaeser emphasises how housing costs and varieties can influence labour market outcomes, human capital and city growth. But there is a broad range of housing outcomes, affecting existing as well as mobile households, that could conceivably impact human capital, and business investment decisions too (see Maclennan, 2008). Housing research and housing policy has much work to do in confirming that often locally argued benefits of good housing outcomes can have productivity and growth effects. Strong policy efforts – for instance neighbourhood renewal programmes in the UK – often stand upon a rather empirically empty black box connecting housing to the economy.

Setting housing in the context of a macro-modelling framework has some important virtues. The drivers of demand and supply, such as incomes, taxes and interest rates, can be linked to national housing outcomes. If anything, such analysis also draws attention to the major markets of functions connected to the business of constructing, financing and selling housing: what was labelled above as 'housing the verb'. These housing activities then have strong connections to labour, capital, land and materials markets.

However, and again emphasised by recent events, the strong reductionism of mainstream economic analysis removes from the core framework inherently important features of the housing market. This is valid insofar as macroeconomists confront different concerns from those concerned with local housing market functioning and policies. For instance, many housing researchers, used to analysis of household data and local housing systems, show some signs of agitation with macroeconomists, such as Buiter (2009), who suggest that house price gains have little net impact on household consumption, largely because one person's gain is another's loss (either now or in the future). Microanalysts need to recognise that aggregate analyses have validity.

But it is also reasonable for housing market analysts to seek to challenge the relevance of reductionist macro assumptions and whether better stylised facts about housing can be incorporated in macro thinking. This micro-to-macro learning was the great success of labour economics in the second half of the last century; micro results shifted macro thinking, but this process has operated very weakly and slowly in housing sector analyses. For instance, since 2008 the key question in most countries has been whether housing price slowdowns (and reductions in some settings) have bottomed out and reversed or whether a double-dip will ensue into 2011. In reality, there are no predictive answers to such questions, unless there is an understanding of the psychology of housing market choices and household behaviours as regards housing wealth. This is an area governments will not pay to research adequately.

Recent experience also draws attention to the spatial aggregations involved, so that market imbalance and instability is neither adequately measured nor understood by aggregating the performance of quite different regions or metropolitan areas. The innovative work of Muellbauer (2005), Meen (2001) and others has helped abate the reductionism of macro models so that at least some aspects of the broad spatial structure of national and regional housing markets, that fundamental dimension of space, is allowed to have influence in analysis (see Chapter 14). Building on his earlier work on the different spatial dimensions or levels of housing market economics, Meen has developed a series of housing market models that move from nation, to regional then sub-regional scales. These models, as used by Meen, have important roles in systematically simulating the consequences of different demographic and economic futures for relatively small spaces. In a similar and related vein, Bramley (2002) and others have pushed this towards more formal modelling of future housing needs and demands within regional housing planning areas. These models have strengths and weaknesses (they rely on relatively simple house price to income ratios to split households into those capable of making affordable and unaffordable choices) but their major limitation is how they are used in the planning system In many planning authorities, planners – generally unfamiliar with housing economics – fixate upon a singular estimate of future affordable housing needs and demands. They use tentative forecasts as a target rather than as a consideration in a rather complex decision that needs to meld other sources of information as well as constant market monitoring.

So top-down interest in housing markets is important and there are developing strands of research. Aside from the downward shift of Meen-type modelling, there have been sustained studies of housing wealth behaviour, housing finance and economic outcomes that shift from national to local scales. In a series of papers, Case, Quigley and Shiller (Case and Siller, 2003; Case et al, 2005a, 2005b) have unravelled the consumption effects and economic consequences of housing price change at local, metropolitan, regional and national levels. These have been separate pieces of work and not conducted in a single local to national modelling framework, but each scale of work has been convincingly informed by the levels of analysis that lie above and below it. This persistent, consistent approach to housing market analysis that uses the strengths of conventional frameworks without being constrained by them is an exemplar of the kinds of housing market analysis required to make housing economics credible.

However, the macro models and debates of the present would be much better informed if we had better understandings of local housing market behaviours, turning points, etc. Recent developments in national to regional modelling of markets have been helpful, but as they still remain reductionist in the mechanisms or market processes involved they might be described as the same intellectual engine, just a smaller version. The concern in the third section was that there needs to be a different emphasis in the 'engineering' of how we think about local housing markets, not just adopting smaller spatial scales.

If a better-informed housing microeconomics is to emerge, the question remains as to whether we can capture something less reductionist in modelling at the macro scale. We have to set new micro research on local drivers and transmission mechanism in a macro context because the recent, spectacular and damaging outcomes in many metropolitan housing systems have involved the local absorption and transformation of national and global drivers in local systems. We have to improve, and link, our understandings of housing market analysis at both local and national levels.

INTEREST IN POLICY: ENDNOTE?

Some economists rapidly move from the status of market analysts to what the late George Stigler referred to as 'preachers': that is, there is a propensity to make the moral judgement that a well-functioning market system is to be preferred and should be largely left to its own devices to allocate resources, reward efforts, etc. For many economists, the market is a preferred, ethically imbued system. Individuals are assumed to be the best judge of their own well-being and the system is assumed to be relatively well informed, and generally free from market failures and monopolies.

The discussion in this chapter would not support the view that unfettered housing markets would always work well as systems, even if the underlying distribution of income and wealth were widely acceptable. There are too many possible flaws in the market, too many potential fumbles for the invisible hand, to assume *ex ante* that local markets should be policy-free. And the experience of the GFC suggests that if macro policy applies too reductionist a view of how housing markets operate (for instance in assuming that sectoral asset price booms should not be the concern of monetary policy) then there may be damaging economy-wide effects. The British economy, at least, now faces a minimum of five hard years as a result of a policy judgement that deregulated markets needed little scrutiny and would work well (and they have had significant benefits too) and the capital market would be efficient in shaping instruments and assessing risks. The mistake was that the markets did not operate in the expected *ex ante* fashion. And that is why in the enduringly important housing sector there is a need to improve real understandings of housing systems.

As researchers, we still need to make a modest assessment of what we actually know about the operation of housing markets over space and time. Our research agendas have stalled, precisely when we need to make real progress. Policymakers need to listen to these notes of caution as they confront a challenging decade ahead for housing market adjustment across the advanced economies.

REFERENCES

Alonso, W. (1964) *Location and Land Use.* Harvard University Press, Cambridge, MA.

Anderson, E.S. (1996) *Evolutionary Economics: Post-Schumpterian Contributions.* Pinter, London.

Antonides, G. (1990) 'A model of negotiations for the sale of a house', in S.E.G. Lea, P. Webley and B.M. Young, (eds), *New Directions in Economic Psychology: Theory, Experiment and Application.* Edward Elgar, Sussex.

Ball, Michael (1996) *Housing and Construction: A Troubled Relationship.* Joseph Rowntree Foundation, York.

Barker, K. (2004) *Review of Housing Supply.* London: The Treasury, Her Majesty's Stationery Office.

Bourassa, S., Hoesli, M. and Peng, V.S. (2003) 'Do housing submarkets really matter?', *Journal of Housing Economics*, Vol. 17, No.1, pp. 12–18.

Bourassa, S., Cantoni, E. and Hoesli, M. (2007) 'Spatial dependence, house submarkets and house price prediction', *Journal of Real Estate Finance and Economics*, Vol. 35, No. 2, pp. 143–160.

Bramley, G. (2003) 'Planning Regulation and Housing Supply in a Market System', In T. O'Sullivan and K. Gibb. *Housing Economics and Public Policy: Essays in honor of Duncan Maclennan*. Blackwell Science. Oxford, pp. 193–216.

Brown, J. and Rosen, H. (1982) 'On the estimation of structural hedonic price models', *Econometrica*, Vol. 50, pp. 765–768.

Buiter, W.H. (2009) 'Housing Wealth Isn't Wealth', *Economics*, Discussion Paper No 209–56.

Burns, Arthur F. and Mitchell, Wesley C. (1946) *Measuring Business Cycles NBER*. Harvard University Press, Cambridge, MA.

Camerer, Colin F., Loewenstein, George and Rabin, Matthew (2003) *Advances in Behavioural Economics*. Princeton University Books, Princeton, NJ.

Case, K.E. and Shiller, R.J. (2003) 'Is there a bubble in the housing market?', *Brookings Papers on Economic Activity*, Vol. 2, pp. 299–342.

Case, Karl E., Quigley, John M. and Shiller, Robert J. (2005a) 'Comparing wealth effects: The stock market versus the housing market', *Advances in Macroeconomics*, Vol. 5, Issue 1.

Case, Karl, Quigley, John M. and Shiller, Robert J. (2005b) 'Home-buyers, hHousing and the macroeconomy'. Paper presented to the Reserve Bank of Australia Conference on Asset Prices and Monetary Policy.

Cheshire, P. and Sheppard, S. (1998) 'Estimating thd-Demand for housing land, and neighbourhood characteristics', *Oxford Bulletin of Economics and Statistics*, Vol. 60, No. 3, pp. 357–382.

Clark, W.A.V. (1982) *Modelling Housing Market Search*. Croom Helm, London.

Della Vigna, S. (2009) 'Psychology and economics: Evidence from the field', *Journal of Economic Literature*, Vol. 67, No. 2, pp. 315–372.

DiPasquale, D. and Wheaton, W.C. (1996) *Urban Economics and Real Estate Markets*. Prentice Hall, Englewood Cliffs, NJ.

Egidi, M. and Marris, R. (1992) *Economics, Bounded Rationality and the Cognitive Revolution*. Edward Elgar, Cheltenham.

Evans, A. (1973) *The Economics of Residential Location*. Macmillan & Co, London.

Friedman, D. and Cassar, A. (2004) *Economics Lab: An Intensive Course in Experimental Economics*. Routledge, London.

Galster, G. (1987) *Homeowners and Neighbourhood Reinvestment*. Duke University Press.

Gibb, K.D. (1992) 'Bidding auctions and house purchase', *Environment and Planning A*, Vol. 24, No. 6, pp. 853–869.

Glaeser, E.L. (2009) 'The wealth of cities: Agglomeration economies and spatial equilibrium in the US', *Journal of Economic Literature*, Vol. 47, No. 7, pp. 983–1028.

Glaeser, E.L., Gyourko, J., Saiz, A. (2008) 'Housing supply and housing bubbles', *Journal of Urban Economics*, Vol. 64, No. 2, pp. 198–217.

Grimes, Arthur and Aitken, Andrew (2010) 'Housing supply, land costs and price adjustment', *Real Estate Economics*, Vol. 38, No. 2, pp. 325–353.

Guala, F. (2005) *The Methodology of Experimental Economics*. Cambridge University Press, Cambridge.

Goodman, A.C. and Thibodeau, T.G. (1998) 'Housing market segmentation', *Journal of Housing Economics*, Vol. 7, No. 2, pp. 121–143.

Hogarth, R.M. and Reder, M.W. (eds) (1987) *Rational Choice: The Contrast between Economics and Psychology*. University of Chicago Press, Chicago, IL, pp. 67, 117.

IMF (2008) *World Economic Outlook: Housing and the Business Cycle*. IMF, Washington D.C.

Jones, C., Leishman, C. and Watkins, C. (2003) 'Structural change in a local urban housing market', *Environment and Planning A*, Vol. 34, pp. 1315–1326.

Lachmann, L.M. (1986) *The Market as an Economic Process*. Basil Blackwell, Oxford.

Langlois, R.N. (ed.) (1986) *Economics as a Process: Essays in the New Institutional Economics*. Cambridge University Press, Cambridge.

Maclennan, D. (1982) *Housing Economics*. Longman, Harlow, Essex.

Maclennan, D. and Tu, Y. (1996) 'Economic perspectives on the structure of local housing markets', *Housing Studies*. Vol. 11, No. 3, pp. 387–486.

Maclennan, D. (2008) *Housing for the Toronto Economy*. Cities Centre Discussion Paper 216. University of Toronto.

Mallett, S. (2004) 'Understanding home: a critical review of the literature', *Sociological Review*, pp. 62–89.

Malpezzi, S. (2003) 'Hedonic Pricing Models: A selective and applied review'. In T. O'Sullivan and K. Gibb. *Housing Economics and Public Policy: Essays in Honor of Duncan Maclennan*. Blackwell Science. Oxford, pp. 67–85.

Meen, G. (2001) *Modelling Spatial Housing Markets: Theory, Analysis and Policy*. Kluwer Academic Publishers, Boston, MA.

Muellbauer, J. (2005) 'Property taxation and the economy after the Barker Review', *Economic Journal*, Vol. 115, pp. 99–117.

Muth, R. (1969) *Cities and Housing*. University of Chicago Press, Chicago, IL.

National Housing Supply Council (2009) State of Supply Report. Australian Government, Canberra.

Novy-Marx, R. (2009) 'Hot and cold markets', *Real Estate Economics*, Vol. 37, pp.1–22.

O'Sullivan, T. and Gibb, K. (2003) *Housing Economics and Public Policy*. Blackwell, Oxford, pp. 22, 38, 56, 67, 173.

Piazzesi, M. and Schneider, M. (2009) 'Momentum traders in the housing market: Survey evidence and a search model', *American Economic Review*, Papers and Proceedings, Vol. 99, pp. 466–477.

Pryce, Gwilym (2009) 'Dwelling substitutability and the delineation of submarkets', *Centre for Public Policy for the Regions*, Discussion Paper 21. University of Glasgow.

Quigley, John. M. (2003) 'Transaction costs and housing markets', in A.J. O'Sullivan and K.D. Gibb (eds), *Housing Economics and Public Policy*. Blackwell Publishing, Oxford, pp. 56–64.

Rabin, Matthew (2002) 'A perspective on psychology and economics', *European Economic Review* Vol. 46, Nos. 4–5, pp. 637–685.

Rosen, S. (1974) 'Hedonic prices and implicit markets: Product differentiation in pure competition', *Journal of Political Economy*, Vol. 82, pp. 34–55.

Rothenberg, J., Galster, G., Butler, R. and Pitkin, J. (1992) *The Maze of Urban Housing Markets*. University of Chicago Press, Chicago, IL.

Saunders, P. (1989) 'The meaning of the "home" in contemporary English culture', *Housing Studies*, Vol. 4, pp. 155–166.

Schnare, A. and Struyk, R. (1976) 'Segmentation in urban housing markets', *Journal of Urban Economics*, Vol. 3, pp. 146–166.

Smith, Susan J. and Searle, Beverley A. (2008) 'Dematerialising money? Observations on the flow of wealth from housing to other things', *Housing Studies*, Vol. 20, No. 2. pp. 21–43.

Smith, Susan J. and Searle, Beverley A. (2010) *The Blackwell Companion to the Economics of Housing: Housing and the Wealth of Nations*. Wiley-Blackwell, West Sussex.

Straszheim, M. (1987) 'The theory of residential structure', in: E.S. Mills (ed.), *Handbook of Regional and Urban Economics*, Vol. 11, North-Holland, Amsterdam.

Tabuchi, T. (2009) 'Self-organising markets', *Journal of Urban Economics*, Vol. 66, pp. 179–185.

Thomsen, E.F. (1992) *Prices and Knowledge – A Market-Process Perspective*. Routledge, London.

Tu, Y., Sun.H. and Yu, S.M. (2007) 'Spatial autocorrelations and urban housing market segmentation', *Journal of Real Estate Finance and Economics*, Vol. 34, No. 3, pp. 285–406.

Viale, R. (1992) 'Cognitive constraints of economic rationality', in H. Simon, M. Egidi, R. Marris and Viale, R. (eds), *Economics, Bounded Rationality and the Cognitive Revolution*. Edward Elgar, Cheltenham.

Watkins, C.A. (2001) 'The definition and identification of housing submarkets', *Environment and Planning A*, Vol. 33, No. 12, pp. 2235–2253.

Housebuilding and Housing Supply

Michael Ball

INTRODUCTION

The purpose of this chapter is to address and explain the broad dimensions of housebuilding. Housebuilding is only part of the supply side of new housing; the inputs the industry uses are the other. Land is the key supply resource needed to build housing and its supply is constrained by physical geography, planning rules and infrastructure provision. In recent years, a growing amount of research has been undertaken on residential land availability, which has highlighted problems of varying degrees of severity.[1] In contrast, little research is undertaken on housebuilding itself. Yet, the ways in which that operates has key implications for supply responsiveness to house price signals. The supply side has important influences on the housing market cycle – Why, for example, did some countries have homebuilders with massive unsold stocks and others with few in the extensive housing market crashes associated with the recent world financial crisis? Housebuilding economics has impacts on attempts to improve the energy efficiency of new building. Long-run productivity changes shape housing costs, product innovations and quality. Housing has changed much over the years but not in comparison to many manufactured products and has become more expensive relative to many other consumer goods (see Chapter 15).

Housebuilders come in many different forms: from large-scale specialists producing thousands of homes a year to small firms, self-builders constructing a home for themselves, and non-specialists constructing housing as a sideline to some other activity. Generally, there is substantial competition, encouraged by ease of entry and exit, though in some countries specialist areas may be dominated by few major producers, as with apartment building in Sweden (Barlow and King, 1992). Although regulatory constraints may hinder the adoption of some processes and components, they are broad barriers rather than firm-specific. They may affect different types of producer more than others and so distort competition, but typically much competition remains.

There is little international trade in housebuilding in contrast to that of the manufactured products used in the building and fitting out of dwellings. This is partly explained by the locational fixity of dwellings and also by the public good nature of building technology and design (Ball, 2006a). Building technologies are rarely proprietary. Instead, firms are able to select from the best techniques around when choosing their production strategies. But, this means that innovative firms can rarely temporarily corner a technical or product innovation in ways common with other consumer goods. This characteristic would suggest that housebuilding industries should be quite similar across market economies in the world, whereas in practice they often have divergent features. The prime reasons for that are regulatory factors and other institutional features, which vary widely between countries.

The limited ability in housebuilding to utilise product differentiation as a business strategy, either through design or innovation, highlights a similarity of housebuilding with many service activities. It also reflects skill divisions within the construction industry and the separation of professional specialists as repositories of building knowledge (Ball, 2006a). In commercial building, it is common to use leading architects as a means of product differentiation. The smaller scale of housing and the ease with which designs can be copied, as observed throughout history, means that this route is far more limited, being found in only the luxury, bespoke sector.

Overall, there is no reason to think that any countries' housebuilding industry is any worse, or any better, than elsewhere as long as it is allowed to be competitive. The problem is that many regulations hold back market initiative, with insufficient offsetting public benefits. Even so, there are no easy profits to be made on efficiency grounds by foreign entrants, because on entry they are subject to the same regulatory constraints as incumbents. The exception is in markets that have previously been closed to international competition and ideas for many years in the past or that are going through rapid phases of economic development for which domestic resources are insufficient. International housebuilding activity bears out this observation, as, for example, in the Middle East (*Building Magazine*, 2010).

There is an important distinction to be made between the competences of individual firms and those of the industry as a whole. Individual firm competences are influenced by competition and the feasibility of takeover. If a firm is underperforming, it may fold or be acquired. By contrast, the competence of the industry as a whole is affected by what it can or is allowed to do. Influences on that will include the optimisation of production methods given feasible technologies, input costs and market conditions; the availability of land and the terms under which it can be developed; finance and its impact on firm sizes and operations; regulations and their costs; the quality, relative costs and availability of inputs; innovations in inputs, processes and products; and what is acceptable to consumers and their funders. An analysis of housebuilding is best focused on industry-wide issues, therefore, and it will contain much country-specific contextualisation.

The central hypothesis here is that the prime causes of differences in countries' housebuilding industries lie in regulatory differences and in country-specific features, such as the nature of the financial system. However, there remains considerable variety in actual types of producers and in firm sizes even within countries. For example, in all countries smaller firms prosper next to their larger brethren rather than there being a standardised type of organisation. This variety of firm types arises through long process of competitive evolution within the institutional framework surrounding housing supply in any country.

Housebuilding invariably operates via a network of enterprises. These may take the managerial form of principals, such as developers or building firms, using agents in the form of subcontractors and professional specialists in parts of their operations or, alternatively, be associated with market-oriented chains of independent firms undertaking particular parts of the construction process. Common market-oriented subdivisions are those between land developers and homebuilders in greenfield building. In apartment building, in contrast, the managerial approach is overwhelmingly adopted with developer-sellers subcontracting construction work out to building contractors that actually build the structures. Why do these divisions take place? What benefits do they have? How do they affect the firm size hierarchy? How do they compare across countries and why do specific institutional forms exist?

Supply chain linkages play a key part in understanding the nature of housing supply. These extend through to materials producers that may simply sell their products to builders or supply-and-fix; to the land acquisition process; and to various forms of labour organisation and procurement in an industry where many are employed for only short periods of time before moving onto other projects. There are also close links to the rest of the construction industry. In the UK, for example, roughly, a third of all dwellings are estimated to be produced by general building contractors, usually working under instruction from residential developers (Ball, 2010b).

In general, empirical evidence related to housebuilding is limited, beyond knowledge of how many dwellings have been built in a particular year and some broad descriptions of the industry's features in specific countries. Away from them, details are often hard to pin down (Ball, 2003). The lack of good empirical material has helped to contribute to a lack of research on the industry (DiPasquale, 1999). The available literature is also scant, as is reflected in the references here, and it is hard to find the repeat testing of hypotheses from different angles common elsewhere in the housing literature. However, there is a reasonable enough body of material in economic and management theory which can be applied to housebuilding so that some reasonably robust conclusions can be derived (Roberts, 2007). But much remains unanswered.

It will be argued here that housebuilding industries are influenced by *three core features*:

1. The longevity and cost of residential development
Housebuilding from raw land to finished product takes a long time and imposes substantial costs on producers. This leads to:

- Substantial capital requirements and typically highly leveraged enterprises.
- High levels of risk over long periods of time. So, development is driven by expectations that may well not be met, given the existence of pronounced housing market cycles and other uncertainties.

2. The nature of the production process and product
The housing production process involves four separate stages: land acquisition; project conception, feasibility and planning; regulatory compliance and approval; and site works and building. These stages are often recursive in nature, because external circumstances alter or issues arise within the development itself during the lengthy development period. Production is also site-specific, meaning that it is unlike factory production because activity moves from site to site and products remain where they were made.

There is potential for separation of each building function through divisions of labour and networks of enterprises. Importantly, production operates within a framework of imperfect information. Imperfect information arises for a variety of reasons. For example, in relation to future market conditions and because of the divisions of labour that exist and resultant asymmetrical information that arises between principal and agent about tasks undertaken, with what effort, and how well they are done. Consequently, monitoring and the appropriate use of incentives are significant activities that influence agent relations and firm structures.

3. High degree of regulation
Housebuilding is associated with a high degree of regulation. Many of these regulations are associated with land-use planning.

Yet, there are also many other building regulations and controls concerned with structural and production process matters, such as structural integrity, fire risk and safety, or related to energy use, labour markets and other areas. Such regulations vary widely across countries, but mark housing production out as a highly regulated industry.

Recognition of these three features has influenced the argument that follows. Next, a more detailed breakdown of the housebuilding process is investigated; then, features of housebuilding as a continuous production process are considered; attention then switches to firm types and business models and their influence on the organisation of the industry. Firm size hierarchies are then considered; and the nature of risk and where it is highest in housebuilding are then examined to help understand how organisational differences arise. Some comments are then made on the links between housebuilding and the rest of the construction industry; followed by a discussion of subcontracting.

THE HOUSEBUILDING PROCESS

Housebuilding involves a wide range of activities when bringing forward land to create finished dwellings. For firms, these activities are part of a continuous process. As some sites are completed, others will be being started or planned. In the case of large firms, building will also be spread across regions in order to serve distinct markets. For example, towards the end of 2009, TaylorWimpey, the largest UK firm, was active on 223 sites throughout the country and the US' largest firms' activities are spread across an even larger number of widely spread sites (Taylor Wimpey, 2009).

Figure 2.1 describes the principal activities undertaken in private housebuilding. They are listed in the typical order in which they occur, though in practice several tasks might take place at different times (e.g. pre-sales before construction). The sequence is drawn as a circle to highlight the fact that firms will be undertaking these activities

A: Project Conception and Evaluation
- Identification of site
- Formulating and designing scheme
- Planning control feasibility
- Evaluation of viability
- Time line estimation
- Setting up finance

B: Land Preparation
- Site preparation
- Planning permission
- Charges and levies (CIL/s106)
- Site works
- Connecting and servicing

C: Building Construction
- Assembling build team, components and materials
- Foundations and services installation
- Superstructure
- Internal subdivison and fitting out

D: Marketing and Sales
- Branding
- Marketing
- Selling
- Bespoke fittings, etc
- After sales e.g. snagging
- Client relations

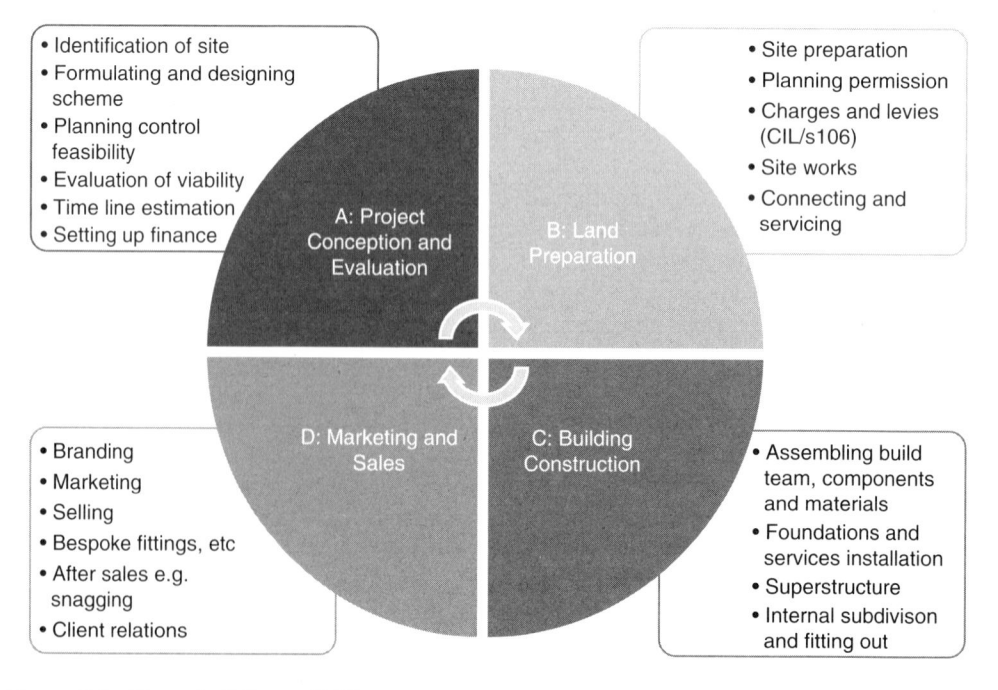

Figure 2.1 Housebuilding activities

repeatedly on different sites, with the arrows illustrating the continuous flow of production across those sites. For one-off housebuilders, the flow nature of development and production will obviously be limited to one site only but they will still be concerned to dovetail activities in order to minimise costs.

The four broad ranges of tasks involved in relation to any specific site are listed below.

A. Project conception and evaluation

Housing projects have to be formulated, evaluated and financed and be related to land sites identified as ripe for development:

- identifying a site, which may be bought on the open market or drawn from a 'land bank' of sites already owned outright or on option
- devising and designing a scheme – including layout, roads and other infrastructure
- arrangement and mix of dwelling types; and external and internal building design
- assessing the probability of a scheme winning planning consent and conformity with other regulations
- estimating the time line when the development will be in production, based on build and market demand factors
- weighing up financing requirements and costs
- viability analysis of likely streams of revenues and costs (including overheads and public charges) to ensure profitability, including consideration of potential risks and uncertainties.

B. Land preparation

Land has to be made ready for building, both in terms of site preparation and works and, also, in regulatory terms, particularly by gaining planning/building control approval and paying the assigned charges:

- application for and negotiation of permission to build, which varies considerably across countries depending on their planning and building control systems
- site preparation, including any demolitions and remedial works
- payment of charges and levies, such as those associated with impact fees (s106 in England)
- implementation of site works
- making connections to utility networks and provision of other site services and facilities.

C. Building construction

Building superstructures have to be erected and internally fitted out. This requires the detailed logistics of bringing work teams, materials and components in the appropriate sequence to site over an extended period of time, plus actual construction and the management and monitoring of it:

- initiating supply chains, including construction teams, manufactured components and other materials and having them on site at the appropriate times
- foundation works and installation of services to the building
- erection of the building superstructure
- internal subdivision and fitting out of the building.

D. Marketing and sales

Homes have to be sold and transferred to their new owners. This is achieved through site-related activity and through the general promulgation of the housebuilders' brand. Some sales will occur before building commences:

- branding – promoting brands to assist company-wide sales
- marketing – use of a range of marketing tools to create consumer awareness of developments
- selling – agreeing dwelling reservations and purchase, conveyancing, etc.
- bespoke fittings, etc. – carrying out additional purchaser requirements
- after sales, e.g. snagging – fixing faults, site and road maintenance until handover
- client relations – ensuring customer satisfaction.

FUNCTIONAL CONTINUITY

The activities described above occur in a variety of ways in all types of housebuilding enterprise, large and small. For most firms, production is continuous in nature. Furthermore, activities are undertaken simultaneously at separate locations (such as on-site, in the office, and in dialogue with third parties elsewhere).

Housebuilding as an industry relies on seven interrelated production principles:

1. *Continuous production*, dwellings are built sequentially on a site and when sites are completed activity moves rapidly onto others using –
2. *A complex division of labour*, based on –
3. *Simplification of component tasks*, which is made possible through –
4. *Standardisation*, which facilitates –
5. *Repetition*, so that actions can be practised, quick and effective with minimum unproductive time
6. *Effective monitoring and control*, so that problems can be resolved, costs controlled and innovations made
7. *Innovation and product enhancement*, generated by technical change and organisational improvement, in relation to consumer demand, or because of changing regulatory requirements.

These principles are generally recognised as the foundations of modern, efficient industries in manufacturing but also in others, such as retailing. The use of examples outside of manufacturing is important, because housebuilding is often mistakenly seen as akin to a pure manufacturing process and, then, criticised for not being a 'modern' highly capital intensive one. A better analogy is that housebuilding is a hybrid mixture of input assembly, production and distribution.

Land and project designs, property rights and regulatory approval, people and materials all have to be present and correct and the built products sold to willing clients. Moreover, all these factors take place at changing locations because dwellings are made where they are going to be used. The logistics and principles of manufacturing are different from this so, unsurprisingly, housebuilding as a process differs from it and also, to a lesser extent, from other types of construction because of the distinctive integration of land development and construction in the housebuilding sector (Winch, 2002; Ball, 2006a). Such process differences contribute to the distinctive networks of enterprises in housebuilding.

FIRM TYPES AND BUSINESS MODELS

Development and building

Many prior construction works, related to preparation, roads and parking, utilities, etc., have to be undertaken on sites before dwellings can be erected and fitted out. They can be expensive and may involve a substantial amount of work, potentially absorbing a half or more of total project build costs. An additional large amount of work is done off-site by firms prior to building and also as it continues, due to land purchase, design, evaluation, project planning and procurement and other activities. There is substantial regulatory engagement, such as obtaining planning/building permission and acquiring a series of other consents and undertaking subsequent actions. The aim of profit-maximising enterprises is to ensure that the optimal process flow principles pertain in these areas as well as in the actual process of building itself in order to achieve cost minimisation.

The stages prior to housebuilding are often termed *development*, in contrast to the actual *building* stages of *erecting* and *fitting out* structures, either as standalone or linked (terraced, semi-detached) dwellings or as blocks of flats. New housing may also be found in large mixed-use built structures, such as in currently the world's tallest building: the 162-floor Burj Khalifa in Dubai.

Specific development functions are often contracted out to, say, planning specialists or architects. Within the building stage itself, activities are associated with complex supply chains. Firms may have core staff to plan and manage these activities, but often contract out building work or parts of it. When directly involved in the building stage, they will typically use specialist and general subcontractors to undertake on-site building tasks under the control of the firm's own site managers and senior management teams. Within all but the smallest firms, management teams themselves are associated with substantial divisions of labour into specialist activities, whereas in the smallest firms the proprietor may do most management tasks directly.

Organisation of housebuilding industry

The distinction between development and building stages is an important one in terms of understanding the organisation of housebuilding and how and why it varies across the world. Development and building functions are often separated between different types of enterprise, with the sales of the finally completed dwellings undertaken by either the developer or the builder, depending on the precise institutional framework.

There are three main types but the variations can be substantial.

1. *Land developers and housebuilders.* In many countries, including Australia, Canada and the USA, suburban single-family housebuilding frequently begins with large developers buying up agricultural or other land at the urban fringe, obtaining the necessary permits, plugging the site into the local infrastructure networks and subdividing the area into plots in order to sell them onto smaller builders that erect and sell the actual dwellings.
2. *Residential developers and contractors.* Many private housing developers – and, in Europe, social housing providers – buy residential land and then contract out all of the design and building work (either as turnkey projects or with separate contracts in relation to groundwork, superstructure and fitting out, or various combinations and subsets of them). However, housing developers still own the dwellings rather than simply sell on serviced land like the previous category of developers. They either hold onto them on completion as rental investments or sell them onto owner occupiers or investors, partly off-plan and partly on completion.

Retaining the completed product as a long-term rental investment is common in areas like student housing and other types of specialist rental property: e.g. REIT (real estate investment trust) residential holdings. Even so, selling the completed homes is the most common outcome throughout the world. This reflects a typical separation between the ownership and production of dwellings.

Such housing developers can be found across the range of firm sizes. Many specialise in urban apartment blocks, often in only one or a handful of cities and regions, while others are cross-national and part of global conglomerates.

3. *Combined developer-builders.* With such firms, the development and building aspects are combined into single enterprises that undertake the whole of the housebuilding process. These firms typically manage construction themselves, and directly purchase most of the materials, but subcontract most actual building work out to specialist sub-contractors and labour-only gangs. Specialist tasks in other parts of their businesses will often be done by independent agencies as well, working to contract: for example, in areas of specialist advice, law, planning and design. Standard house designs are generally built, although configurations will vary substantially from site to site. Most new houses in Ireland and the UK are built in this way and firms of all sizes adopt this business model. With respect to blocks of flats and more complex structures, there is a greater likelihood that the building work will be let out in full on the housing developer-contractor model.

It is tempting to argue that such a wide variety of potential housebuilding business models are simply a result of 'tradition': i.e. historic institutional differences between specific countries. However, there are many economic reasons for these differences and they help to illustrate the economic principles of housebuilding in market economies, the problems that may arise in housebuilding and how market processes evolve in attempts to overcome them. Country differences, of course, still matter but many of them relate to variations in the form and scale of regulation than to tradition in its purest sense (Table 2.1).

Table 2.1 Types of housebuilding enterprise

1. Fully integrated private housebuilder

Integrated operation, selling on general market
- Subcontract out building on task basis, retaining site management

2. Residential developer

Common in standalone brownfield schemes of apartment blocks
- Undertakes land development and dwelling sales, but neither building nor design
- Let out build or design and build (D&B) contract to contractor (+ architect, etc.)

3. Land developer and housebuilder

Separated land development and housebuilding. Is common form for suburban building in Australia and USA; occurs in land swaps between housebuilders on large sites or mixed-use schemes in UK.
- Land developer buys land; ensures broad planning approval; adds infrastructure; sells subdivisions and housebuilder builds and sells

4. Variants:

  (i) Land developer/residential developer

As type 3 (above), but subdivided land bought by a developer that lets out a build or D&B contract as before

  (ii) Investor developer

Buys land, conceives a project, lets out D&B contracts, holds completed development as investment, e.g. student housing, some private renting, most social housing
- Most investors prefer to buy completed properties rather than to be involved in development risks

5. Self-builder

Typically build as owner-occupier, using land purchased 'raw' or from a land developer, and full- or part-letting out of design & build.

Self-building

Self-build housing, in which the future owner/user institutes and organises the building process, is a distinctive type of housing supply, providing particular benefits to particular types of housing consumer. Working out its real scale is not easy because of data difficulties, but its scale varies widely across countries. Again, this reflects institutional differences. Self-building is particularly large in the Third World, where it is associated with informal housing and there is a huge literature associated with the topic (Keivani and Werna, 2001). Many would argue that the extent of self-build in many parts of the Third World is a consequence of regulatory failure, which holds back 'formal' housing markets (World Bank, 1993; Ball, 2006a).

In contrast, self-build in the advanced economies is more associated with affluence in the sense of people trying to get an individualised home, one in a specific location or, alternatively, with the avoidance of restrictive rules. For example, it is used in a number of European countries, such as France, Germany and Italy, to avoid labour market legislation, taxation or building and planning controls (Ball, 2003).

The actual amount of self-building undertaken varies as architects and other professionals may be used and builders may be hired to undertake part or all of the works. But, in all cases, the self-builder takes on key development tasks. These tasks include raising the finance, acquiring the land, applying for (or avoiding) planning or building control permission, deciding on designs, opting for building methods and standards, and choosing the final dwelling fit-out. Self-builders are often involved in project management as well (Barlow et al., 2001).

Self-building is a potential option for those wanting a distinctive home, and who are willing and able to make the time and financial commitments. In such contexts, the benefits of self-build relate primarily to the ability of people to exercise detailed choice in the location and nature of their property, mainly for its characteristics but also, for the minority, because of the ability it brings to fulfil an interest in creating a dwelling or an ability to live under higher than normal environmental standards. Properties may also be cheaper relative to equivalents from a homebuilder and of higher quality, though there is no reliable evidence to support this claim.

It is possible to hire an agent to undertake all the procurement, which typically is done for the bespoke homes of the very wealthy. But self-building is more generally typified as a self-managed alternative to the standardised products of building firms. The costs of self-building are associated with all the responsibilities of development the self-builder takes on, and, in addition, some or all of those associated with the construction process itself. Many self-builders may relish the prospect but the exercise all the same is time consuming and carries with it many of the standard costs and risks of development. Once the value of the self-builders' own time plus the development costs and risks they face are brought into the calculation, many of the apparent financial benefits of self-build may vanish. Regulatory avoidance apart, this cost dimension puts a cap on the expansion of self-build. Many people would not think the benefits of self-build outweighed the time commitment required, and would not wish to bear the costs associated with self-build or be capable of absorbing the downside of the potential risks.

Partnerships

One way in which housebuilding often takes place is through partnerships, a common form being the 'joint venture'. Partnerships may involve housebuilders working together or acting in conjunction with other private agencies, such as investment funds, landowners and commercial developers. In addition, the public sector at local or national level may be a development partner. Public–private partnerships are prevalent throughout the world but are most common in countries where states have specific agendas within the land development process in general, as in the Netherlands (Needham, 1997); or in social housing, as in several European countries; or with respect to urban regeneration where the offer of land or funding is dependent on local government or regeneration agency involvement in development (Ball et al., 2003).

Partnership benefits are varied: they spread risk; allow the potential for subsidy when the public sector is involved or when regeneration grants can be accessed in consequence; smooth planning negotiations; make development funding more attractive for lenders; and possibly enable knowledge transfer and innovation derived from working in new ways with partners.

For developers, however, partnerships involving a wide variety of participants are not unequivocal benefits, because they involve the trading-off of some of the value added of their skills as developers for some potential improvements in items, such as liquidity and reduction in project risk. There are also costs in terms of partnership transaction costs, potential conflict and less flexibility because binding commitments have to be entered into with partners over project content, timing and the division of costs and rewards (Ball, 2004; Ball and Maginn, 2005). In good times, the trade-offs mean that large regeneration schemes will be the focus of such development models, because of their exceptional scale, the conditions related to public subsidies, their mixed-use character, the need to bring landowners on board, knowledge transfer and in order to raise finance. But, in bad times, the conditions of the trade-off alter and they may become more attractive across a wider range of development contexts.

For the public sector, partnerships offer benefits in terms of enhancing the range of feasible policy aims over other potential policy models, such as subsidy with no managerial involvement: e.g. steering regeneration of a locality; improving value-for-money from subsidies; involving local communities; and generally strengthened negotiation positions (Carley et al., 2000).

When the aims of the public and private sectors coalesce public–private partnerships can work well. But they can create problems if handled badly: such as a lack of clear aims, decision-making processes and responsibility; excessive delay and cost over-runs; and confrontational rather than cooperative working practices. There is also a danger that partnerships dampen competitive pressures, because, once appointed, private sector partners are relatively protected from market forces through the existence of public sector partners with deep pockets. They may adopt rent-seeking practices in consequence.

FIRM SIZES

Housebuilding firms come in all shapes and sizes. Some commentators have highlighted how small-scale and ephemeral local housebuilding firms can be (Buzelli and Harris, 2003), while others across the years have pointed to the existence of significant numbers of large enterprises (Grebler, 1973; Sommerville, 1999; Ball, 2006a). Many of the world's largest construction firms have housebuilding divisions and, at the same time, producers may be tiny enterprises building only a few homes a year or be active only intermittently.

Differences in firm size have some physical causes. For example, some house types are built on a small-scale basis and some firms undertake only part of overall homebuilding, say, through buying ready-serviced plots from residential land developers.

There are no rigorous studies of housebuilders' cost functions, so it is not possible to devise accurate understandings of scale economies within the industry. However, there are reasons to surmise that scale economies do exist in a number of key respects, such as through having continuous production, being able to reap the benefits of specialisation in a variety of ways through working across a variety of sites, risk pooling, having better access to finance, improved marketing possibilities and other aspects of housebuilding activities where size makes the difference. However, housebuilding is not a type of activity which uses extensive dedicated assets in the form of fixed capital, unlike say a car plant. This puts limits on the nature of increasing cost economies with size.

The heterogeneity of new housing encourages substantial variations in production technologies and practices. Moreover, markets and demand functions within them differ. This means that distinct production methods can coexist simultaneously in practice. Bespoke custom housing may, for example, be more expensive to build than standardised units but generate price premiums. In other words, scale economies are not everything. Moreover, different firms can specialise within production process and be of substantially different sizes. Some may be large with simultaneous multi-site operations and others may be small and active at only one place, yet still both may be involved in a particular project. Networks of producers can optimise across a range of potential scale economies and diseconomies because fragmentation of the building process enables distinct firms to reap economies where they exist, while others avoid potential diseconomies by remaining small.

An important difference in terms of scale relates to land development versus homebuilding itself. Land purchase, regulatory approval and site preparation, as noted earlier, require large inputs of capital. It is also often advantageous to develop a number of sites at the same time in order to limit the impact of individual site risks. In consequence, scale benefits that often exist at the land development stage are not necessarily found to the same degree at the building stage. This may help to explain the distinction in several countries between well-funded land developers and relatively small homebuilders. Of course, not all developers will necessarily be large in scale. Some may be original landowners looking to develop their land for residential use, either independently or in partnership. Alternatively, an investor may have purchased only a single site and be progressing it through the development pipeline. Such one-off schemes, however, do not afford the benefits of risk pooling and financial muscle that larger-scale developers have. (The differentiation of risks between the development and housebuilding stages is explored in greater depth in the next section.)

However, there are many reasons for differences in firm sizes and the relative market success of particular firm types and only limited research on this question. Some studies have argued that access to finance is a significant influence on size and competitive advantage (Ambrose and Peek, 2009). Development finance has also been highlighted as an important influence on the cyclical behaviour of firms' outputs (Mayer and Sommerville, 1996). Others have suggested regulatory constraints as another factor (Ball, 2006a). Cultural and local institutional frameworks have further been highlighted as potentially significant influences (Guy and Henneberry, 2002, 2004). The expectation of being able to explain all firm types may be low, but analysis is more convincing in terms of being able to demonstrate the feasibility of a wide variety of firm practices and influences on them.

A recent study by the author showed that the UK large housebuilders have a much higher market share than in Australia and the USA (Ball, 2008). In many other countries, housing markets are more fragmented between large conglomerate developers, land developers, small housebuilding enterprises, and various types of self-building, including utilisation of off-site-produced building systems.

In many countries, the shares of different sizes of housebuilder in total output does not change in a consistent manner over time. Yet one feature of the UK industry has been a growing market share for the largest producers. Between the early 1990s and the mid-2000s, the market share of the top 11 firms doubled to around 45% of all dwelling sales. The top 25's market share grew from 38% in 1990 to 57% in 2009, according to National House Building Council data. Takeovers amongst them further heightened the market shares of the top few firms towards the end of the boom. Nonetheless, over 50% of all output is produced by a variety of other providers: small and medium builders and developers; firms where housebuilding is a sideline; social housing providers building for the market; and self-builders. A note of caution may be worthwhile in pointing out the meaning of the term 'small'. In the UK, as elsewhere, a single block of flats by itself can be worth millions. For example, building 15 flats selling for an average price of £150,000 each would generate revenue of £2.25 million, so even small developers can be quite substantial businesses in terms of their turnover. They are classified as small here relative to other larger producers and in relation to the business models and limited specialist in-house staff they are likely to have.

A recent survey of residential development sites in the UK gives some indication of the variety of firm sizes and the nature of residential development schemes. Data were derived from 45 English local authority areas, encompassing most large cites and also smaller suburban and rural areas, and it excludes the smallest of firms and self-builders as only investigated 'major' schemes with more than 10 dwellings are recorded. Almost two-thirds of projects surveyed in that study involved the construction of 25 dwellings or less, highlighting the dispersed brownfield nature of much modern

Table 2.2 Developer-type shares of sites and dwellings. Survey of 45 English local authorities 2005/6

Developer type	Per cent of schemes	Per cent of dwellings
Large developer	19	38
Medium developer	9	12
Small developer	40	31
Non-developer	20	12
Social housing	12	8

Source: Ball (2010c).

English housebuilding. The market shares of the various types of producer are shown in Table 2.2. Large builders only built on around one-fifth of sites but constructed almost two-fifths of the dwellings, because they specialise more in larger developments.

One-fifth of sites were associated with non-traditional developers. They are firms or other landowners with a predominant activity in a non-property sphere but have some land suitable for residential development and hire contractors to undertake the work. These enterprises include supermarket chains building mixed-use schemes, schools and existing businesses in many spheres that have land available for housing. Some were individuals interested in developing land adjacent to their own dwelling, such as a large garden. Some of the housing built may not be for the general market but rather for the enterprise's employees, but the vast majority is put up for sale. Whatever their motivation, non-developers are clearly a significant factor in the development for housing and add to the diversity of providers. They also can start and stop whenever they like and, so, are often not particularly adversely affected by downturns; instead, they stop housebuilding until better times come again.

THE IMPORTANCE OF VIABILITY AND RISK

Housebuilders are profit-making entities, so projects have to achieve target rates of return to be viable. Those target rates of return will factor in risk and, as risks are high in housebuilding, expected rates of return will have to be high to compensate for them. Expected profitability will be determined by a combination of factors related to site, construction and finance costs, and marketability of the completed development. These factors are shown in Figure 2.2: each of them contains substantial risks, which are broadly identified under the 'contingencies' categorization in the figure.

The significance of risks in housebuilding operations cannot be overemphasised. The recent sudden and unexpected collapse of housing demand in the wake of the world financial crisis has brought the riskiness of housebuilding to the fore, but that has only highlighted several aspects of risk – those related to overall market conditions and finance. Many others also exist in the four areas identified in Figure 2.2.

Dealing with risk helps to explain why the housebuilding industry is organised in the way in which it is and how much it builds. Moreover, at any point in time, the risks of development are going to make some sites unprofitable and the number will be greater in downswings and periods of recovery when margins are squeezed.

Furthermore, builders have to decide on design issues with respect to both site layout and detailed dwelling types. Dwelling types are often of a standard design but can be mixed on individual projects. Getting the dwelling mix right can have significant implications for consumer satisfaction,

The multi-dimensional housing development decision-making process

Marketable?
Location, configuration, price, design, quality

Land site?
'Oven-ready': Planning permission, infrastructure and services

Viable?
Meets risk-adjusted hurdle rate of return
= Revenues
less land, overhead, build and finance costs
less levies (e.g. s106) and taxes

Finance?
Purchasers able to borrow; development finance in place

Buildable?
Technique, cost, regulation compatible

Contingencies
Forecastable and unexpected changes over life of project

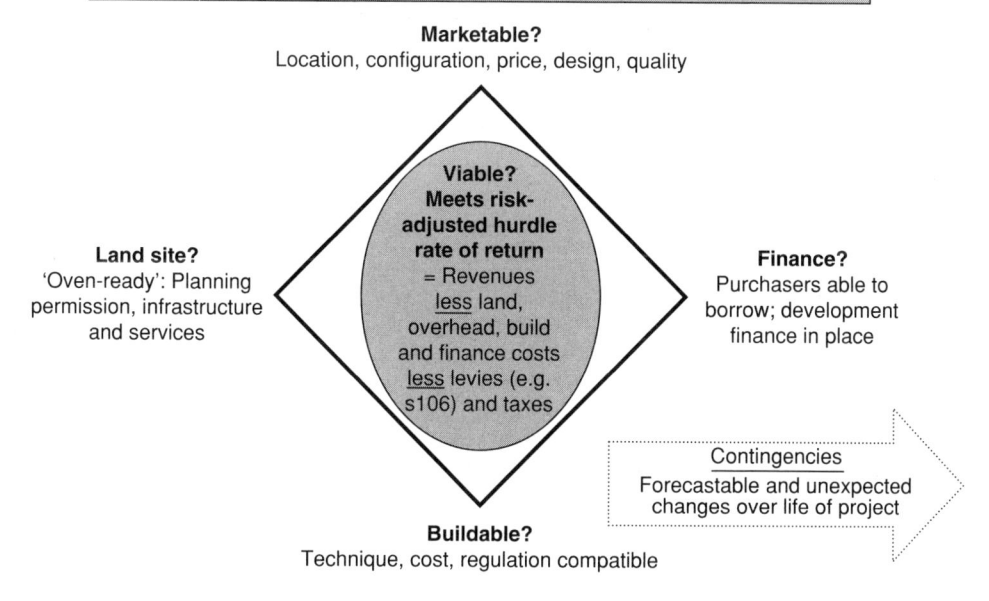

Figure 2.2 Assessing project viability

profitability and project viability (Leishman and Warren, 2005, 2006).

Site build-out times are an additional factor (Adams et al., 2009). To an extent, these are determined by the nature of the structures being built. For example, apartment blocks have to be constructed as a unity, so the timing of their commencement is often only triggered when a target number of off-plan pre-sales are achieved. Whether projects are at greenfield or brownfield locations may also influence project trajectories (Adams, 2004). Large sites may be divided into phases to limit capital requirements, to give more flexibility in relation to demand, and to avoid a flood of similar dwellings coming onto the market at the same time. With regard to single-family dwellings, on all but the smallest of sites there is the option of building them at a rate similar to sales levels. In this way, working capital is minimised and there is a much reduced risk of supply overhang if the market turned sour. In consequence, large sites may take many years to build out.

Where do the risks lie in housebuilding?

Land development is generally the most risky part of the housebuilding process. So many things can go wrong in it. An indication of the greater riskiness of land development can be seen in the generally higher volatility of 'oven ready' residential land prices compared to house prices themselves.

Risks are affected by several key factors associated with the site, the building process, finance and market conditions:

- individual project success – whether a scheme will sell quickly at the predicted prices
- general housing market conditions

- the degree of leverage, as lenders may call in loans unexpectedly or when agreed ratios (e.g. loan-to-asset value ratios) are unexpectedly exceeded
- interest rates, as much capital has to be invested a long time before returns from dwelling sales can be made
- regulatory hurdles, particularly in respect to building regulations and land-use planning controls
- the price paid for the land
- the size of impact fees/planning obligations required by local government before permitting development
- the costs and uncertainties of preparing sites for housing construction
- the time taken, which may stretch out way beyond what was anticipated, delaying revenue streams and raising costs and debt.

By contrast, the housebuilding process itself has a lower (though non-zero) profile of risks, because

- the technologies used in housebuilding are generally well-known and repeatedly used in thousands of other instances
- the tasks can be well specified and monitored as work goes along
- the time to build is relatively short, particularly for single-family homes, lowering though not eradicating market sales risk in contrast to development
- less capital is generally required for less time than in development, especially with regard to single-family homes.

Evidence of the lower risk in building can be seen in the experience of letting housebuilding work out as fixed-price contracts. Detailed designs, work plans and bills of quantities (or their equivalent) are usually provided initially, narrowing risk profiles considerably, against which bidders can work out closely what has to be done and price accordingly. Therefore, contractors know what they are committing themselves to and can operate on typically low contracting margins.

Risk is further limited by the practice of paying contractors for work on a regular basis as it is done, so that contractors have to extend relatively little of their own capital or debt. In contrast, developers put at risk substantial and growing amounts of capital from the start of schemes.

The generally greater capital requirements of developers tend to result in them being larger enterprises – though smaller ones may prosper. Two clear benefits exist at greater scale. The first benefit is risk pooling across individual sites as individual project success may vary. If developers operate across a variety of sites simultaneously, they are able to pool that type of risk. The second benefit is that larger enterprises can more easily raise finance than smaller ones, because of the pooling effects just described and through their improved ability to signal financial and business competence to investors, either through private arrangements or through issuing equity.

By contrast, small builders that buy land plots from land developers operate in a context of easy entry and exit on limited capital bases and typically find it hard to raise finance, unless they have a good reputation with a local bank or investor. Surveys show that small firm production capital is often financed out of retained profits and short-term credit loans (Hildebrandt, 1971; Ambrose and Peek, 2008). They tend to come and go in consequence or, if they survive, remain relatively small in scale (Buzzelli and Harris, 2006). So, even though their risk profile may be less than that of developers, their resource profile is equally limited. All types of enterprise are subject to overall housing market volatility. However, housing markets generally have many more years of upswing than of downswing, so that firms may prosper for a long time and may only fold in a downturn if they become overambitious and take on excessive debt in relation to risk. Unfortunately, housebuilders are often as prone to euphoria about housing markets, as are house buyers. This feature, in combination with early general risk factors, gives a profile of generally high firm turnover, especially amongst the smaller enterprises, with peaks of entry during market booms and troughs of exit during downturns.

There is also risk associated with ensuring that agents undertake specific tasks adequately. Asymmetrical information arises because it is costly to monitor individual building tasks, and in consequence, agents have incentives to shirk, build cheaper below specified quality and to hide problems that may arise. These factors have an important bearing on incentive structures, subcontracting and how the building process is organised, and will be discussed later.

The consequences of risk

Several observations in relation to organisational divisions and risk are important here:

1. Residential development functions require high gross margins in order to compensate for the risks associated with them. These are necessary to create the incentives to build. The high risks make some developers wealthy when they are lucky, but doom others to losses and possible failure. The risks tend to be cyclical in nature and they are often masked in boom periods, when risks appear less, but become more apparent in times of crisis (Leishman et al., 2000). Unfortunately, by their nature, it is not possible to predict with any degree of accuracy the lower-risk phases of the housing market cycle from the higher-risk ones. However, these risk profiles are not often recognised. Common notions of 'property speculators' having one-way bets on land value uplift ignore such risks. Proponents of land values taxation equally gloss over the volatility of land values.
2. The standard 'residual' models of land values, which subtract the build costs of a typical housing development from expected sales revenues to leave a return to land, as described in the *Callcutt Review* (2007), can give a misleading impression of the dynamics of housebuilding, if they do not incorporate sufficient weighting for risk. There is a danger that they lead to a perception that development is a passive and low-risk operation by assuming a standard, relatively modest development profit margin, in contrast to the high risk and high return profile of development assumed above.

   What is of the greatest importance is that development is where much of the entrepreneurship takes place that is so essential to housing supply. Searching out profit opportunities pushes developers to take consumer preferences on board; to hunt out sites that others may not have thought worthwhile; to innovate in design, quality, process, methods and product; to attempt to limit costs; to bring together and mould teams focused on project success; to confront and try to beat the competition; to find better and cheaper sources of finance; to bring complex projects in on time or better; and, generally, to confront and overcome barriers. It is the rationale for a market-driven economy and the essence of a private housebuilding industry rather than a residual associated with it.
3. Housebuilding business models in both the development and building aspects are designed in order to incorporate flexibility so as to minimise the impact when the downsides of risk predominate. The ways housebuilders organise the whole of their operations aims to incorporate approaches that facilitate speedy responses to changing circumstances. Limiting that flexibility can consequently be highly detrimental to an effective and efficient industry (Figure 2.3).

THE INTEGRATION OF HOUSEBUILDING WITH THE REST OF THE CONSTRUCTION INDUSTRY AND SUPPLY CHAINS

The description of the housebuilding industry given so far suggests that it is an independent standalone industry, which in a number of respects it obviously is. Yet this should not detract from the supply chains that stretch back from the housebuilding site. They flow back through to the producers of materials and components; to the workforce, which is often organised into independent firms and quasi-firms, as professional practices or labour-gangs; and into the rest of the construction industry.

Materials and component producers tend to be the almost exact opposite of housebuilding in the technical sense because they

Appreciating the risks of housebuilding and the profit opportunities they bring are keys to understanding the nature of the industry. The information available to developers and builders at any point in time is limited, but they have to invest large sums of capital for long periods of time before they earn a return.

- One way of managing risks is to apportion tasks between different enterprises and to use subcontractors. Incentives can also be structured through this route to ensure task efficiency and quality.
- Flexible production techniques are more able to cope with risk and volatility than fixed capital intensive ones. This affects the nature of housebuilding innovations.
- Most risk is associated with land development and the pricing and timing of dwelling sales.
- Most actual building works can be set up as relatively low-risk, low-margin activities to be undertaken by building contractors – development cannot.
- Entrepreneurs need to be rewarded for their risk-taking. Development uplift calculations need to take that fact on board.
- Land scarcity raises rewards but may also heighten risks by requiring more capital to be invested upfront.
- Public sector bodies are poorly structured to deal with development risk and, so, would be advised to avoid undertaking development directly or getting into partnerships where they carry most of the risk burden.
- Residential development is not as easy as it seems, because loss-making projects by their nature receive little publicity.
- If housebuilding business models do not take account of risk, they fail or require substantial public subsidy.
- If housebuilding was a low-risk industry, it would look very different from the way it does now.

Figure 2.3 Coping with profiting from risk in housebuilding

rely on capital-intensive production processes that work best when dealing with steady, high volumes. They tend to be an important route through which innovations occur in housebuilding in new components and factory-based ways of doing things previously done on site.

The supply chain links to the rest of the construction industry exist through specialist and main/subcontractors and in substitutable workforces, materials and components. In the UK, given the prevalence of high-density apartment building in recent years, main contractors have probably been building around a third of all new dwellings, under the instruction of developers that then sell the completed product on the open market. Furthermore, much social housing will be completed in this way as well. This model is common throughout the world, so that housebuilding's organisational links with the rest of the construction industry are inevitably deep.

Financial aspects may also intensify the linkages between housebuilding and other types of construction activity, because contracting typically generates substantial cash flows that can be utilised in residential development (Ball, 2006). So, more extensive integration is observed when development credit is constrained, or where financial systems are based on 'relational banking' (Frankel and Montgomery, 1991; Yafeh and Yosha, 2001). The likelihood is increased that major housebuilders and developers will be divisions of larger construction conglomerates, or of firms with even wider industrial spreads, under relational banking systems because that organisational form confers a financial competitive advantage over independent, smaller housebuilding concerns. In contrast, the more market-based financial systems prevalent in countries like the UK and the USA encourage large homebuilders to specialise in the sector in order that their activities are more open to arms-length evaluation by lenders and investors. Smaller firms in the more arms-length financial systems have particular problems in signalling financial probity, putting them at a competitive disadvantage, which may help to explain why smaller builders in them have been under increasing pressure over time.

The integration of housebuilding with the rest of the construction industry helps to justify the absence of clearly separate statistics on much of the housebuilding industry, which in most countries gets grouped together with the rest of the construction industry as a whole. Current statistical practices are especially problematic with regard to housebuilding in two ways:

1 There is no clear understanding of input costs, because at present private housebuilding cost indices are based on standardised mixes of inputs and, occasionally, some arbitrary assumption about productivity adjustments.
2 A lack of information about the size of the housebuilding labour force (and other inputs) means that accurate productivity measures and benchmarks cannot be produced. Product heterogeneity in housing is a further bugbear for such exercises but equally found and at least partly surmounted in other industrial sectors.

In consequence, many cross-country comparisons of relative productivity and efficiency in housebuilding are of limited value (Crawford and Vogl, 2006).

SUBCONTRACTING AND HOUSEBUILDING ORGANISATION

Subcontracting has a number of important advantages for housebuilders and, so, influences the way in which they operate and the structure of the housebuilding industry itself. Amongst the benefits are that it lowers general overhead costs; enables activity specialisation, because specialists can be more fully employed working for several clients; facilitates responses to fluctuations in workloads; simplifies administration and some regulatory factors, such as taxation and employment legislation (and may facilitate tax advantages for subcontractors); encourages high work speeds; and lowers supervision costs as managers only have to check that work has been done properly and on time and, then, pay out the agreed sum, rather than have to monitor work effort continuously (Costantino and Pietroforte, 2002; Ball, 2003). The relative importance of each aspect is a matter for some speculation in the literature, but measurement difficulties mean that an accurate ranking of them is never likely to be achieved.

Housebuilders can impose financial penalties on non-performing subcontractors and build up long-term relationships with core ones to ensure that they are generally available, have access to the appropriate pools of skilled labour (which may including a training element), can cope with any innovations that may occur and can self-police their own quality and prices. Often, subcontractors are single individuals, providing tools and labour and Eccles (1981) has termed such 'quasi-firm' to indicate the relationships.

The average ratio of subcontracting to directly employed labour in the UK was 70% in a 2004 study of volume housebuilders that collectively produced a third of national output. With the exception of some tidying up and snagging, typically all manual work was subcontracted to individuals, gangs of trades people or to sub-assembly specialists. Some professional tasks were also outsourced, particularly those associated with design, law and land-use planning. Relationships with subcontractors were often long-term ones and close. Firms would purchase most general materials used by subcontractors to ensure their quality, delivery and fitness for purpose and to gain purchasing economies (Ball, 2006b). In the USA, the Bureau of Census returns suggested that around 65% of housebuilder's costs were subcontracting payments in 1997 and that this had hardly changed in the 20 years (Costantino, ibid). Although many subcontractors are very small enterprises, some are very large.

Above the smallest sizes, subcontractors themselves often hire part of their workforces on time-, price- and task-specific bases – while, at the same time, employing a core of competent skilled workers and supervisors. So, a hierarchical tree of work patterns – embodying market and non-market relationships – can frequently be observed in housing production.

Another common employment option for housebuilders is to hire workers on a temporary hourly or daily basis. In this situation, the problem of directly monitoring work effort arises. This encourages the use of standardisation and simple techniques of production with easily observed results, so that relatively unskilled workers can be hired.

Subcontracting and day working considerably aid the flexibility of the housebuilding industry in coping with uncertain demand. When housebuilders' output falls, they do not have to lay off workers, but instead merely issue fewer contracts or hire less workers; a similar situation exists with plant when it is hired.

In contrast to the 'flexible' labour practices just described, a number of European countries, including France and Germany, outlaw most labour-only subcontracting. As a result, firms face higher costs, have less control over work effort and may consequently be reluctant to employ workers because of future workload uncertainties or because of the cost. The result is a labour market regulation separation of housebuilding in which much single-family housebuilding is undertaken in informal or 'self-build' ways in order to circumvent the regulations and lower build costs.

Other influences on employment practices are features of local physical geography. In countries and regions where the climate makes it impossible to build in the deepest winter months, for example, the large-scale switching of resources between housebuilding and other activities is obviously imperative at different seasons of the year. Traditional migrations are made between, say, summer housebuilding and winter forestry. Similarly, in countries with large agricultural sectors that have heavy demands for labour only at peak times, such as harvests, another pattern of seasonal job shifts in and out of housebuilding tends to occur.

CONCLUSIONS

This chapter has laid out the dimensions of the housebuilding industry and its international variations. It has highlighted that the industry is diverse, both in what it does and who does it. However, it is an industry in which there is usually substantial competition driven by easy entry and exit. Building technologies are rarely proprietary, so that firms are able to choose from the best techniques when choosing their production strategies. Although regulatory constraints may hinder the adoption of some processes and components, they are universal barriers rather than firm-specific.

There is, consequently, an important distinction to be made between the competences of individual firms and those of the industry as a whole. Individual firm competences are influenced by competition and the possibility of takeover. If a firm is underperforming, it will more likely than not fold or be acquired. In contrast, the competence of the industry as a whole is affected by what it is allowed to do. Influences will include the juxtaposition of feasible technologies and market conditions; the availability of land and the terms under which it can be developed; regulations and their costs; the quality and costs of inputs and competition for them; feasible innovations; and what is acceptable to consumers and to those that provide mortgages and development loans. An analysis of potential barriers to housing supply is, therefore, best focused on industry-wide issues at the geographic level at which they become binding. Cross-county institutional differences explain much, though it is extremely difficult to put estimates on relative costs and benefits of them because of the difficulty of measuring building, land and others costs and productivity internationally.

A variety of business models are feasible within housebuilding. There is also a considerable degree of persistence in cross-country differences. Firms may come and go but they are broadly replaced by similar types. Obviously, dynamic changes do occur, as with the increasing concentration in the UK industry. Even so, there is little indication of international convergence, which highlights the importance of country-specific regulatory and other institutional frameworks.

The significance of risks in housebuilding operations cannot be overemphasised. Dealing with and profiting from risk helps to explain why the housebuilding industry is organised in the way in which it is.

NOTE

1 Malpezzi, 1999; Mayer and Somerville, 2000; Mayo and Sheppard, 2001; Bramley, 2002; Barker, 2004; Glaeser and Gyouko, 2005; Ihlanfeldt, 2007; Glaeser et al., 2008; Goodman and Thibodeau, 2008; Saks, 2008; Ball, 2010a; Saiz, 2010.

REFERENCES

Adams, D. (2004) 'The changing regulatory environment for speculative housebuilding and the construction of core competencies for brownfield development', *Environment and Planning A*, 36: 601–624.

Adams, D., Leishman, C. and Moore, C. (2009) 'Why not build faster? Explaining the speed at which British housebuilders develop new homes for owner occupation', *Town Planning Review*, 80(3): 291–314.

Ambrose, B.W. and Peek, J. (2008) 'Credit availability and the structure of the homebuilding industry', *Real Estate Economics*, 36(4): 659–692.

Ball, M. (2002) 'The organisation of property development professions', in J. Henneberry and S. Guy (eds), *Development and Developers: Perspectives on Property*, Blackwell, Oxford, 2002.

Ball, M. (2003) 'Markets and structure of the housebuilding industry: an international perspective', *Urban Studies*, 40: 5–6, 897–916.

Ball, M. (2004) 'Co-operation with the community in property-led urban regeneration', *Journal of Property Research*, 21(3): 119–142.

Ball, M. (2006a) *Markets and Institutions in Real Estate and Construction*, Blackwell, Oxford.

Ball, M. (2006b) *The Labour Needs of Extra Housing Output: Can The Housebuilding Industry Cope?* Homebuilders Federation/CITB-Constructionskills, London.

Ball, M. (2008) *Firm Size and Competition: A Comparison of the Housebuilding Industries in Australia, the United Kingdom and the USA*, RICS Research Report, 2008.

Ball, M. (2010a) 'Planning delay and the responsiveness of English housing supply', *Urban Studies*, forthcoming.

Ball, M. (2010b) *The Housebuilding Industry. Promoting Recovery in Housing Supply*, Dept. Communities and Local Government, London.

Ball, M. (2010c) *Housing Supply and Planning Controls*, NHPAU, DCLG, London.

Ball, M. and Maginn, P. (2005) 'Urban change and conflict: evaluating the role of partnerships in urban regeneration in the UK', *Housing Studies*, 20(1): 9–28.

Ball, M., Le Ny, L. and Maginn, P. (2003) 'Synergy in urban regeneration partnerships: property agents' perspectives', *Urban Studies*, 40(11): 2239–2254.

Barker, K. (2004), *Review of Housing Supply: Final Report – Recommendations*, HMSO, London.

Barlow, J. and King, A. (1992) 'The state, the market, and competitive strategy: the housebuilding industry in the United Kingdom, France, and Sweden', *Environment and Planning A*, 24(3): 381–400.

Barlow, J., Jackson, R. and Meikle, J. (2001) *Homes to DIY for. The UK's Self-Build Market in the Twenty-First Century*, Joseph Rowntree Foundation.

Bramley, G. (2002) 'Planning regulation and housing supply in a market system', in A. O'Sullivan and K. Gibb (eds), *Housing Economics and Public Policy*. Basil Blackwell, Oxford.

Building Magazine (2010) 'Is it time to leave the Middle East?', *Building*, 30(7): 10.

Buzzelli, M. and Harris, R. (2003) 'Small is transient: housebuilding firms in Ontario, Canada 1978–1998', *Housing Studies* 18.3, 369–386.

Buzzelli, M. and Harris, R. (2006) 'Cities as the industrial districts of housebuilding', *International Journal of Urban and Regional Research*, 30(4): 894–917.

Callcutt Review (2007) *Callcutt Review of Housebuilding Delivery*, DCLG, London. http://www.callcuttreview.co.uk/default.jsp

Carley, M., Chapman, M., Hastings, A., Kirk, K. and Young, R. (2000) *Urban Regeneration through Partnership: A Critical Appraisal*, Joseph Rowntree Foundation, York.

Costantino, N. and Pietroforte, T. (2002) 'Subcontracting practices in USA homebuilding – an empirical verification of Eccles's findings 20 years later', *European Journal of Purchasing & Supply Management*, 8(2): 15–23.

Crawford, P. and Vogl, B. (2006) 'Measuring productivity in the construction industry', *Building Research & Information*, 34(3): 208–219.

DiPasquale, D. (1999) 'Why don't we know more about housing supply?', *Journal of Real Estate Finance and Economics*, 18(1): 9–23.

Eccles, R.G. (1981) 'Bureaucratic versus craft administration: the relationship of market structure to the construction firm', *Administrative Science Quarterly*, 26(3): 449–469.

Frankel, A. and Montgomery, J. (1991) 'Financial structure: an international perspective', *Brookings Papers on Economic Activity*, 1: 257–310.

Glaeser, G.L., Gyourko, J. and Saiz, A. (2008) 'Housing supply and housing bubbles', *Journal of Urban Economics*, 64: 198–217.

Goodman, A.C. and Thibodeau, T.G. (2008) 'Where are the speculative bubbles in US housing markets?', *Journal of Housing Economics*, 17: 117–137.

Grebler, L. (1973) *The Large Builder. Growth of a New Phenomenon*, Praeger, New York.

Guy, S. and Henneberry, J. (eds) (2002) *Development and Developers: Perspectives on Property*, Blackwell Publishing/RICS Foundation, Oxford.

Guy, S. and Henneberry, J. (2004) 'Economic structures, urban responses: framing and negotiating urban property development', in M. Boddy, and M. Parkinson (eds), *City Matters: Competitiveness, Cohesion and Urban Governance*, Policy Press, Bristol, pp. 217–234.

Hillebrandt, P.M. (1971) *Small Firms in the Construction Industry*, Committee of Inquiry on Small Firms; Research Report No.10, HMSO, London.

Ihlanfeldt, K.R. (2007) 'The effect of land use regulation on housing and land prices', *Journal of Urban Economics*, 61: 420–435.

Keivani, R. and Werna, E. (2001) 'Modes of housing provision in developing countries', *Progress in Planning*, 55(2): 65–118.

Leishman, C. and Warren, F.J. (2005) 'Planning for consumers' new-build housing choices', in D. Adams, C. Watkins, and M. White (2005) (eds), *Planning, Public Policy and Property Markets*: Blackwell, Oxford.

Leishman, C. and Warren, F.J. (2006) 'Private housing design customisation through house type substitution', *Construction Management and Economics*, 24(2): 149–158.

Leishman, C., Jones, C. and Fraser, W. (2000) 'The influence of uncertainty on house builder behaviour and residential land values', *Journal of Property Research*, 17(2): 147–168.

Mayer, C.J. and Somerville, C.T. (1996) 'Housing supply and credit constraints', *New England Economic Review*, 39–51.

Mayer, C.J. and Somerville, C.T. (2000) 'Land use regulation and new construction', *Regional Science and Urban Economics*, 30: 639–662.

Mayo, S. and Sheppard, S. (2001) 'Housing supply and the effects of stochastic development control', *Journal of Housing Economics*, 10: 109–128.

Needham, B. (1997) 'Land policy in the Netherlands', *Tijdschrift voor Economische en Sociale Geografie*, 88(3): 291–296.

Roberts, J. (2007) *The Modern Firm. Organisational Design for Performance and Growth*, Oxford University Press, Oxford.

Saiz, A. (2010) 'The geographic determinants of housing supply', *Quarterly Journal of Economics*, forthcoming. (http://real.wharton.upenn.edu/~saiz/GEOGRAPHIC%20DETERMINANTS.pdf).

Sommerville, C.T. (1999) 'The industrial organization of housing supply: market activity, land supply and the size of homebuilder firms', *Real Estate Economics*, 37: 65–78.

Taylor Wimpey (November 2009) *Analyst and Investor Presentation*, London.

Winch, G. (2002) *Managing Construction Projects: An Information Processing Approach*. Blackwell, Oxford.

World Bank (1993) *Housing: Enabling Markets to Work*, World Bank, Washington, DC.

Yafeh, Y. and Yosha, O. (2001) 'Industrial organization of financial systems and strategic use of relationshipbanking', *European Finance Review*, 5: 63–78.

Housing Behaviour

Maarten van Ham

INTRODUCTION

Housing behaviour research is about understanding the choices households make with regard to the tenure, type, size and location of their dwelling (Clark & Dieleman, 1996). The concept of housing 'choice' – which has positive connotations – is often used in academic and policy-related housing literature. However, the idea of households *choosing* how and where they live can be somewhat misleading, as for most households the choice set of available and suitable housing is very limited (Van Ham & Manley, 2009). Clearly, nobody chooses to live in a substandard dwelling in a deprived neighbourhood because they prefer to live there, but under certain circumstances, and in certain phases of the life course, this might be the best dwelling available. Having *real choice* means being able to select a preferred option from distinctive alternatives (see Elster, 1999; Brown & King, 2005). In social housing – a safety net for those with limited options – distinctive alternatives are often not available and therefore social housing applicants often have no real choice (Brown & King, 2005). Although home owners have more choice in the housing market, even in the owner-occupied market real choice is limited for most households.

The choice of a particular dwelling depends on the needs and preferences of households within a choice set determined by household resources and restrictions and housing market opportunities and constraints (Mulder & Hooimeijer, 1999). The most basic need fulfilled by a dwelling is the need for shelter. This is a basic and universal human need, and most dwellings can fulfil this need. After basic needs are satisfied, higher-order needs and preferences start to influence housing behaviour, such as the needs for a house big enough for all children to have their own bedroom. Some households are better able to realize their preferences with regard to housing than others. On the one hand, resources, such as income, and opportunities, such as the availability of suitable dwellings in an area, widen the choice set for households. On the other hand, restrictions, such as having to live close to a job, and constraints, such as the lack of finance (a mortgage) and affordable homes, narrow the choice set for households. A small number of very wealthy households have virtually no restrictions in where and how they live, but on the other end of the spectrum there are far more households in social housing, or households at the bottom end of the owner-occupied sector, with very little choice. Even in wealthy countries, considerable numbers of households are homeless, not even able to satisfy the basic need for shelter. Most households find themselves between these two extremes and the dwelling they occupy is the result of some degree of choice within a limited choice set.

Understanding why people choose certain types of housing is complicated by the fact that housing is a composite good (Clark & Dieleman, 1996). A dwelling can be described by its various characteristics such as tenure, size, style, quality and (relative) location. One cannot buy a single aspect of a dwelling separately as dwellings are bundles of characteristics, including neighbourhood and access to jobs and public and private facilities. Because dwellings are composite goods, most households trade off various dwelling characteristics and choose a dwelling meeting their most important needs and preferences within their budget and the choice set offered by the housing market. This can lead to a large error term in models of housing behaviour as the models often aim to explain one particular characteristic, such as tenure, without taking trade-off mechanisms into account.

The literature on housing behaviour is diverse and can be categorized in many different ways. For example, by life events linked to housing behaviour such as leaving the parental home (Goldscheider & Goldscheider, 1993; Goldscheider et al., 1993; Clark & Mulder, 2000), household formation (Murphy & Sullivan, 1985; Mulder et al., 2006) and child birth (Felson & Solaun, 1975; Murphy, 1984; Feijten & Mulder, 2002; Kulu & Vikat, 2008), or by events linked to other life careers such as the labour career (Clark & Davies Withers, 1999; Robst et al., 1999; Böheim & Taylor, 2002). The housing behaviour literature can also be categorized by its focus on different sociodemographic groups such as singles (Hendershott et al., 1980), elderly (Clark & Deurloo, 2006), divorced (Dieleman & Schouw, 1989; Feijten, 2005b; Dewilde, 2008) and ethnic minorities (Coulson, 1999; Painter et al., 2001; Bolt et al., 2002; Murdie, 2002; Özüekren & Van Kempen, 2002). Another way to categorize literature is to focus on tenure choice (Henderson & Ioannides, 1983; Deurloo et al., 1987, 1997; Ermisch & Di Salvo, 1997; Haurin et al., 1997), long-term tenancy (Wulff & Maher, 1998), or first-time home ownership (Henretta, 1987; Courgeau & Lelièvre, 1992; Clark et al., 1994, 1997; Mulder & Smits, 1999; Mulder & Wagner, 2001; Feijten et al., 2003; Smits & Mulder, 2008). A large literature also focuses on moves up and down the 'housing ladder' in terms of size and type of dwellings (Feijten & Mulder, 2005) or moves between cities, suburbs and the countryside (Brun & Fagnani, 1994; South & Crowder, 1998) (see Chapter 16).

Cutting across the above categorizations is a division between studies investigating either stated or revealed preferences in housing (Timmermans et al., 1994). The bulk of the housing behaviour literature investigates revealed preferences, focusing on the outcomes of the choice process (see Rosen, 1974 on hedonic price theory; and McFadden, 1978 on random utility theory). These studies simply examine the distribution of household types over housing categories and implicitly assume that the current dwelling is the optimum available to a household under the present circumstances (see Pickles & Davies, 1985). However, the high costs of housing adjustment means that household might stay for a considerable time in dwellings which are suboptimal; only recent movers might live in a dwelling which represents their preferences (Onaka & Clark, 1983). Then there is a large body of literature investigating stated preferences or moving desires, wishes and intentions (Morris et al., 1976; Varady, 1989; Lu, 1999; Kearns and Parks, 2003; Van Ham & Feijten, 2008; Feijten & Van Ham, 2010). It is very difficult to measure housing preferences as households might adjust their preferences to what is possible within their realistic choice set (a form of cognitive dissonance reduction). A much smaller body of literature takes a dynamic approach advocated by Davies and Pickles (1985) and links stated and revealed preferences and studies the whole path from preferences to actual behaviour using longitudinal data (see also Myers, 1999).

The variety of studies of housing behaviour and the complexity of the mechanisms behind housing behaviour are reflected in the absence of a single theoretical framework capable of explaining housing behaviour (see Chapter 1). Several attempts have been made to develop such a theoretical framework – some of which will be explored in this chapter – but the nature of housing and the variety of factors influencing housing behaviour make it nearly impossible, and maybe not even desirable to develop a single theory (Allen, 2009). Kemeny (1992) has argued that housing cannot be a discipline of itself with its own theory, but instead should be studied using theories and concepts from various disciplines such as sociology, politics and economics. Recently, some have argued for the need to theorize from housing itself, creating unique housing theory (Clapham, 2009; King, 2009) (see Chapters 9 and 10). The study of housing behaviour is intrinsically multi-disciplinary (Bengtsson, 2009; Gibb, 2009) and the outcomes of housing behaviour vary strongly between different national and even regional contexts and over historical time and individual life courses.

This chapter will use the dynamic *life-course approach* (Elder, 1985) as a tool to organize the very broad literature on housing behaviour (see Clark & Dieleman, 1996; Mulder & Hooimeijer, 1999; Feijten, 2005a). The life-course approach, as illustrated in Figure 3.1, is a powerful tool in understanding housing behaviour as it is capable of bringing a variety of factors influencing housing behaviour together, including historical and individual time. The life-course approach starts at the micro level, the level of individuals and households. Live events originating from life-course trajectories of individuals lead to preferences and needs with respect to housing. The resources and restrictions of a household influence to what extent it can realize its preferences. At the macro level, economic, socio-cultural, political and housing market circumstances determine the opportunities and constraints that influence the choice set of individuals (Feijten, 2005a). As such, the life-course approach is capable of bringing together the various ways in which the literature on housing behaviour can be categorized as discussed above (see Chapter 4).

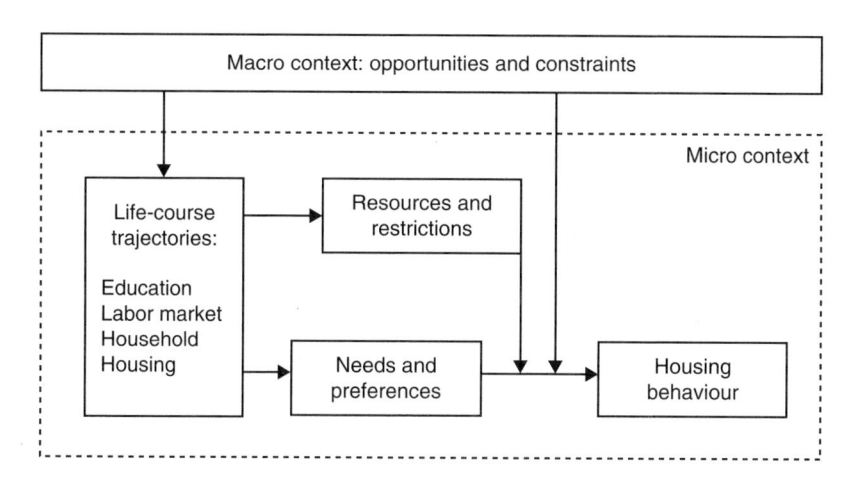

Figure 3.1 The life-course approach to housing behaviour

Source: based on Mulder & Hooimeijer, 1999

The remainder of this chapter is organized around five sections. The second section discusses household needs and preferences which arise from household composition, economic status, life-course phase and cultural preferences. These are the ingredients needed to understand why households choose a certain dwelling. The third section discusses household resources and restrictions, and the fourth section discusses the role of the housing market and society in shaping housing behaviour. The fifth section focuses on the specific question which households choose to rent, which to own and in what sectors of the housing market – private, social or some in-between status. The chapter ends with a section on the future of housing behaviour research and will look forward to future conceptual developments and information needs.

HOUSING NEEDS AND PREFERENCES

The choice of a certain type of dwelling is influenced by individual and household needs and preferences. The most basic need housing satisfies is shelter. This basic need is so important that it is part of the Universal Declaration of Human Rights:

> Everyone has the right to a standard of living adequate for the health and well-being of himself and of his family, including food, clothing, housing and medical care and necessary social services, and the right to security in the event of unemployment, sickness, disability, widowhood, old age or other lack of livelihood in circumstances beyond his control (United Nations, 1948).

For most people in Western societies housing behaviour is linked to more than just fulfilling the basic need of shelter, and some element of housing consumption comes into the equation (Pickles & Davies, 1985; Clark & Dieleman, 1996).

Housing consumption refers to housing behaviour driven by housing needs and preferences over and above the basic need for shelter. It is difficult to assess where basic needs end and consumption starts without making value judgements. It can be argued that all housing choices made after the basic need for shelter is satisfied can be seen as housing consumption. However, what is seen as a basic need varies over time and space and is influenced by societal norms. If it is the norm that all children in a household have their own bedroom, this will be seen as a basic housing need by many households.

However, most people would agree that owning very large houses and ownership of more than one home for a household's own use are examples of extreme forms of housing consumption well beyond basic needs. Increasingly too, households are seeing housing as a form of investment, and decisions on the tenure, type, size and location of the dwelling they live in are partly driven by the desire to make a profit from buying and selling their primary home. Housing behaviour can also be driven by a long-term income smoothing strategy where households see their investment in a dwelling as a form of old-age pension (Fahey, 2003).

Several attempts have been made to categorize, and order, the various needs related to housing. Maslow's (1943) theory of the hierarchy of needs has been used as the foundation for such attempts (see also Michelson, 1977). Maslow identified a hierarchy of human needs ranging from low-order physiological needs and safety needs to higher-order needs such as belonging, esteem and self-actualization. Higher-level needs become important when lower needs are satisfied. It is debatable whether there is a real hierarchy in needs, but it is clear that housing behaviour is linked to a complex range of needs. The needs of Maslow are related to the seven goals De Jong and Fawcett (1981) identified as underlying a decision to move: wealth, status, comfort, stimulation, autonomy, affiliation and morality. Each of these goals or values can lead to different outcomes in terms of housing choice. Specific goals (or preferences) may vary between individuals and change over an individual's life course (Mulder, 1996).

Status needs are an important driver of housing choice. Social scientists have for long argued that people use housing as an instrument in 'keeping up with the Joneses' (Michelson, 1977). Not only having resources drives people to become homeowners and buy certain houses in certain neighborhoods but also their desire to live in high-status neighborhoods with high-status neighbors (Duncan & Duncan, 1955; Tilly & Brown, 1967). Bell (1958, 1968) argued that people move to certain dwellings to be close to people who are like themselves or who they aim to be similar to. He argued that people do not move from cities to suburbs to increase their status, but to escape people dissimilar to themselves. Housing behaviour can be instrumental to other life careers, but housing can also be an aim in itself, leading to satisfaction and happiness. Saunders (1990) emphasized that homeownership not only represents status, but also has emotional value for many people. Many people derive a sense of security, comfort, accomplishment, freedom, independence and even identity from homeownership (Saunders, 1990). The choice for a particular dwelling or tenure type is also influenced by individual taste, lifestyles and identity (Michelson, 1977).

Cultural aspects also play role in housing choice, especially the choice of becoming a homeowner. The USA has often been described as a nation of homeowners where homeownership is part of the American Dream (Green & White, 1997), and this appears to be true within the UK as well (Merret & Gray, 1982; Saunders, 1990). In many Western countries homeownership has become the norm and public opinion is enforced by the media and governments. This is illustrated by quotations collected by Stegman and colleagues (1991) and Green and White (1997, pp. 441–442):

> Herbert Hoover: 'A family that owns its own home takes pride in it and has a more wholesome, healthful, and happy atmosphere in which to bring up children'; Franklin D. Roosevelt: 'A nation of homeowners is unconquerable'; and Lyndon B. Johnson: 'Owning a home can increase responsibility and stake out a man's place in his community' ... Jack Kemp: 'Democracy can't work without the component that goes to the heart of what freedom is all about – the chance to own a piece of property'; and the Clinton/Gore campaign: 'Homeownership and decent housing are an essential part of the American Dream'.

One of the most influential explanations of housing behaviour links housing needs and preferences to the family life cycle where stages in the life cycle of a family lead to the need for more or less space (Rossi, 1955; see also Doling, 1976). This approach emphasizes the importance of demographic need as an explanatory factor of housing behaviour. The life-cycle concept suggests a linear progression through a series of stages in the life cycle defined by the size of the family unit, the age of the head of the household and the presence of children (Lansing & Morgan, 1955; Glick, 1957). In a standard life cycle a young person leaves the parental home, starts his or her own family, gets children, and then once these children leave the parental home, retires. In each subsequent stage of the family life cycle, families expand or contract in size and these changes in the size and composition of the family lead to a need for more or less space. The life-cycle concept applied to housing is well illustrated by Clark and Dieleman (1996, p. 29): people usually start their housing career renting a small apartment, and over time move into a succession of increasingly bigger dwellings in line with the changing residential space needs of their growing household. Often these changes in the need for space coincide with moves from rented accommodation to homeownership.

Although a change in space needs is a major component of understanding housing behaviour, the life-cycle approach to housing has been heavily criticized (Clark & Dieleman, 1996). The life-cycle approach is both normative (it has set stages for all) and deterministic (the set stages are directly linked to housing behaviour). Although many people have similar household and housing careers, there is no such thing as a 'natural' progression in these careers. Also, the life-cycle approach strongly emphasizes upward moves, from smaller dwellings to larger dwellings and from renting to owning, while, in reality, many people follow alternative routes through their life careers. Since the life-cycle concept was developed in the 1950s, society has changed considerably and a range of alternative life paths has become mainstream. Stapleton (1980) acknowledged that households do not develop in a standard linear way and suggested an expanded life cycle with many alternative paths and outcomes allowing for remaining single, childless couples, divorce, remarriage, etc.

In the course of the 1990s the life-cycle approach has been gradually replaced by the life-course approach, which is a much more flexible and comprehensive and therefore a more powerful organizing approach for examining housing behaviour (Clark & Dieleman, 1996; Mulder & Hooimeijer, 1999; Feijten, 2005a). The life-course approach was developed in the early 1980s (Hareven, 1977; Elder, 1985; Willekens, 1991). The central idea of the life-course approach is that individual life histories consist of a succession of individual life events set within a specific historical and social time (Feijten, 2005a). Life events belonging to the same domain of life are grouped into a career (housing career, household career, educational career and labour market career). The use of the term 'career' does not necessarily refer to an upward progression, but to a succession of events. The various careers of an individual are interdependent and develop over time in parallel (Willekens, 1999).

The life course approach offers a framework for studying the interaction of parallel and interrelated careers of individuals and their household members in a changing social, political, institutional and spatial context. The life course approach has been successfully applied to housing behaviour (see Kendig, 1990). The framework used in this chapter (see Introduction) originates from Mulder and Hooimeijer (1999), who developed their approach on earlier work by Sandefur and Scott (1981), Courgeau (1985), Willekens (1987) and Wagner (1989). The life-course approach to housing stresses that life events alter needs and preferences with respect to housing and that each next step in a housing career cannot be understood without taking past life events and interdependencies between various parallel careers into account. It is important to stress that the life-course approach to housing behaviour is not a theory, but merely an interdisciplinary approach to study housing behaviour, drawing on various theories from other disciplines.

HOUSEHOLD RESOURCES AND RESTRICTIONS

The type of dwelling people live in is quite directly linked to their resources (income, accumulated wealth). The probability of being a homeowner and the probability of living in a large dwelling in a nice neighbourhood increase with the amount of resources available (including wealth accumulated in the dwelling itself). However, there is no simple one-to-one relationship between resources and housing choice. As discussed in the Introduction, housing is a composite good and preference for a particular characteristic of a dwelling (e.g. location) might lead to unexpected outcomes for another characteristic (such as tenure). For example, if there is a preference for inner-city living, even a relatively affluent household might end up renting in the private market simply because of a shortage of owner-occupied dwellings in inner cities. Lifestyle choices and subsequent trade-off mechanisms with regard to housing preferences might influence the link between resources and housing behaviour.

Household resources and restrictions are directly linked to the various life-course trajectories (housing, household, education and work) of household members. For most households, the resources available are a direct result of being in employment. Having a job, or having two jobs in the case of dual-earner households, generates the income needed to satisfy housing needs and preferences, but employment also leads to restrictions in housing choice, especially in location. Workers need to live within reasonable commuting time from their jobs, and dual earners, in particular, are restricted in their locational choices as they have to combine two job locations with one residential location (Van Ommeren et al., 1998, 1999; Van Ham, 2002, 2003). Especially for those individuals at the start of their labour career, it is important to live in places with good access to jobs as they often need to change jobs several times before they find a job matching their skills and aspirations (Van Ham, 2003; Mulder & Van Ham, 2005). These locational restrictions are likely to affect housing behaviour. Living close to concentrations of jobs means living in or close to cities where house prices are often high due to high housing demand (see also next section on macro-level constraints).

Resources influencing housing behaviour may also originate from outside the household. The tenure choice of individuals is inextricably linked to the tenure of their parents. Housing tenures of different generations in the same family often correlate (Henretta, 1984, 1987; Mulder & Smits, 1999; Helderman & Mulder, 2007). Intergenerational transmission of homeownership can take place through gifts and inheritance of (housing) wealth. Parental gifts have been found to influence tenure choice, the timing of homeownership, the quality of the dwelling and the size and period of a mortgage (Engelhardt & Mayer, 1998; Guiso & Jappelli, 1999). Boehm and Schlottmann (1999) found that the housing tenure of parents plays a primary role in determining whether or not children become homeowners in the USA (see also Helderman & Mulder, 2007 for the Netherlands).

Intergenerational transmission of homeownership is an important mechanism through which inequality is reproduced over generations (Jenkins & Maynard, 1983; Henretta, 1984; Thomas & Dorling, 2004). According to Thomas and Dorling (2004), between 1971 and 2002 the value of homes in the UK rose 50-fold and the share of wealth concentrated in housing has doubled from 22% to 42% over this period. Not all socio-economic groups have benefitted equally from these increases in wealth. Housing wealth has increased four-fold in the best-off areas and only doubled in the poorest areas over the 1990s. Children of homeowners are known to be better off during their childhood and early adult life than children from renters (they do better in school and in the labour market, Green & White, 1997; Boehm & Schlottmann, 1999), but also when their parents die and they inherit wealth. The fact that many homeowners help their children to buy their first home and climb the housing ladder increases inequality and disadvantages the children of (social) renters. This happens especially when parents downsize and free up a portion of their housing wealth which they can then transfer to their children (Thomas & Dorling, 2004). As house prices rise, the wealth gap will increase. According to Thomas and Dorling (2004, p. 6), 'By 2043 the richest tenth of children by area by family wealth would have recourse to 51 per cent of all housing wealth and the poorest tenth to 0.5 per cent, one hundred times less housing wealth per child'. Children of parents living in the most expensive areas will benefit most. Although house prices have dropped considerably in many areas during the 2008–2009 housing market crisis, the wealth gap between those who own their house and those who rent can be expected to remain very large.

HOUSING BEHAVIOUR AND THE HOUSING MARKET: OPPORTUNITIES AND CONSTRAINTS

The choices households make with regard to the tenure, type, size and location of their dwelling largely depends on what is available. The choice set of housing available to households is not only determined by household preferences, resources and restrictions but also by what is available on the housing market (Clark & Dieleman, 1996). For households with identical preferences, resources and restrictions, the choice set can vary considerably over time and space. There are large local, regional and national differences in the quantity, tenure, price, type and quality of housing available. The set of housing opportunities available to households is only a fraction of the total stock: only those dwellings vacant (for sale or available for renting) at a given point in time and within the desired local housing market form the potential choice set of households (Desbarats, 1983; Mulder, 1996). The fact that the choice set for most households is very limited means that not all households are able to live in a dwelling meeting their desired characteristics. Many households with the desire to move are not able to move because of a lack of suitable and affordable options and households that do move often have to trade-off desired housing characteristics. This section will give a short overview of housing market factors which influence the housing behaviour of households. (For a more detailed discussion of these macro factors see Chapters 14 and 18.)

Dwellings become vacant when households move out (moves to other dwellings, other housing markets or deaths) and when new stock is added to the existing stock (newly built housing and sales of former rented dwellings). The sale of a new or existing dwelling generally sets off a vacancy chain, freeing up several dwellings in the process (often including both owner-occupied and rented dwellings). There are large regional variations in the level of mobility of households, affecting the choice set of those searching for a dwelling. There are also large regional variations in the availability and affordability of housing by type and tenure. In inner-city areas rented apartments are often over-represented, whereas in suburbs owner-occupied detached family homes are over-represented. In places where housing demand is high relative to the supply of housing, prices are high. High prices directly affect the choice set of households, often leading to households trading off desired housing characteristics. The availability of housing can partly be explained by market forces, but government policies and behaviour of institutions also play an important role. The level of construction of new dwellings responds to the demand for housing (although often lagged), but is also regulated by governments through the allocation of building sites (planning permission). Tax rules, such as the level of stamp duty and whether or not mortgage interest rates are deductable from income tax, also influence the affordability of housing, and therefore the housing behaviour of households. In the social housing sector institutional constraints directly determine the size, type and location of social housing (Kintrea & Clapham, 1986).

The housing choice set available to households is partly determined by the stock available, and partly by institutions which regulate access to housing (Clapham & Kintrea, 1984). For those in social housing the level of housing choice is very limited. Brown and King (2005) state that choice in social housing is a gift from the bureaucracy which controls it. Even under choice-based letting, social landlords set the rules of the game as applicants may only bid on property deemed suitable for their needs. Because applicants are deprived of control, households in the social housing sector have little or no power (Brown & King, 2005). Having choice means being able to select a preferred option from distinctive alternatives. In social housing – a safety net for those without options – distinctive alternatives are often not available and choice is very limited. The housing behaviour of those who move into or within the social housing sector depends fully on the rules and regulations set by social landlords and eligibility for housing benefits.

In the UK the Right-to-Buy is an example of a housing policy with very significant consequences for the choice set of households. The Right-to-Buy legislation was introduced in the 1980 Housing Act by Thatcher's Conservative Government elected in 1979. Since it was introduced, over 2.7 million public sector dwellings have been sold to sitting tenants at prices well below market value (Jones & Murie, 2006). The large volume of houses sold under the Right-to-Buy since 1980 has dramatically altered the UK housing market and the distribution of dwellings by tenure changed radically: in 1981, 57.6% of all dwellings were owner-occupied and by 2003 this had risen to 72.3%; the share of local authority rented dwellings decreased from 29.2% to 13.0%; and the share of housing association dwellings increased from 2.2% to 7.4% (Jones & Murie, 2006). As a result of the Right-to-Buy programme, choice in the owner-occupied market has increased, but at the same time the availability of social housing has dramatically decreased. Because the most desirable public sector dwellings have been sold, the remaining stock is of relatively poor quality.

Also in the owner-occupied market institutions play an important role in the housing choice set available to households. In housing markets with very high demand the sale of newly constructed dwellings is sometimes regulated with waiting lists very similar to allocation mechanisms in the social housing sector. The most important institutional barrier to homeownership is the availability of credit. Mortgage lenders determine the conditions under which credit is available to households (stable income(s), loan-to-value ratio, age, etc.). The deposit needed to secure a dwelling is an important tool to reduce risks to lenders. The higher the deposit needed, the more difficult it is for potential first-time buyers to start climbing the property ladder. First-time buyers are highly dependent on credit, as they are less likely to have large amounts of savings and have no existing housing wealth. Interest rates are another way in which mortgage lenders influence the choice set of households. The higher the interest rates charged to households, the lower the amount a household can borrow, and the more limited the housing choice set. Interest rates fluctuate over time and are currently at an all time low. The March 2009 Bank of England interest rate was 0.5%, but interest rates have been as high as 16% (July 1980) and were close to 14% in the early 1990s. There is also some evidence that mortgage lenders limit the availability of credit to households looking to purchase dwellings in certain neighbourhoods. This is a(n) (illegal) practice known as redlining (Aalbers, 2006). Some argue that the evidence for redlining is rather weak, as it is difficult to empirically separate discrimination based on ethnic background and discrimination based on neighbourhood of residence (Tootell, 1996). Whatever the mechanism, the literature suggests that not all households have equal access to credit.

FROM RENTING TO OWNING AND FROM OWNING TO RENTING: TENURE CHOICE IN A LIFE-COURSE PERSPECTIVE

The literature on housing behaviour is dominated by studies on tenure choice, including topics such as first-time homeownership, transitions from renting to owning and falling out of homeownership. Much of the literature on tenure choice (still) uses (implicitly or explicitly) the life-cycle approach, which assumes a more or less linear progression from renting to owning and from smaller to larger dwellings. An underlying assumption seems to be that private homeownership is superior to (social) renting (which in most people's perception and in most societies is probably the case). Within the life-cycle approach to housing behaviour, transitions from homeownership to renting might take place at the end of housing careers when some households downsize.

However, transitions from owning to renting are not exclusively made at the end of a housing career. The life-course approach is much more suitable than the life-cycle approach to deal with these non-linear housing careers. This section does not aim to give a full overview of the literature on tenure choice, but will highlight some of the main factors influencing the tenure choice of nest leavers, first-time homeownership and factors behind transitions from owning to renting.

As mentioned earlier in this chapter, many households prefer to own rather than rent because homeownership is seen as an investment, gives more freedom in where and how to live, gives security, has more status than renting, has emotional value for many people and is often the norm. In addition, owner-occupied dwellings are often larger than rented dwellings, have gardens and garages, are detached and are located in suburban and rural areas (McCarthy et al., 2001). Renting, especially renting in the public sector, is often associated with failure in life, although there are large variations between countries and even within countries in the image of social renting.

There are large differences in rates of homeownership between countries. In the USA, rates of homeownership went up from 44% to 62% between 1940 and 1960 and then up to 78% in 2008. In the UK, the percentage of homeownership went up from 42% to 69% between 1960 and 2002. There are large differences in homeownership within Europe. Sweden (42%), Germany (42%), Denmark (51%) and the Netherlands (53%) were among the countries with the lowest levels of homeownership in 2002. Italy (80%), Slovenia (82%), Greece (83%), Lithuania (84%), Spain (85%) and Hungary (92%) are the countries with the highest levels of home ownership in 2002 (Doling, 2006; Hoover.org, 2009). It is interesting that some of the wealthiest countries in the world, such as Germany, have a relatively low rate of homeownership. This reflects the fact that homeownership is more than just an expression of wealth and that the political organization of societies (Lundqvist, 1992), the political and economic history of societies (Power, 1993), social structure (Kemeny, 1992) and financial institutions (Börsch-Supan, 1993) all play a role in explaining variations in tenure structure between countries (Clark et al., 1997).

For most young people who leave their parental home, becoming a homeowner sits high on the agenda and most want to start 'climbing the housing ladder' as soon as possible. Many associate renting with losing money and are worried that the longer they wait to buy, the less they will profit from a rise in house prices and the more they will have to pay for a house later (Ioannides & Rosenthal, 1994). Homeownership is seen as very desirable, despite the many risks attached to owning a home such as a drop in value, the risk of not being able to pay the mortgage and the transaction costs associated with buying and selling a home which limit household mobility. In the USA, where the vast majority of households are homeowners, a remarkable low percentage of those who leave the parental home become homeowners immediately (Clark & Mulder, 2000). Many nest leavers start their housing careers sharing a dwelling with others and in mobile homes (Leppel, 1987; Haurin et al., 1993). For the Netherlands it was found that there are important differences in tenure choice between those who leave their parental home to live alone and those who leave the parental home to live with a partner (Mulder & Hooimeijer, 1999). Singles are the least likely to become homeowners. The majority of those who leave the parental home to cohabit start in rented accommodation and those leaving the parental home to marry are as likely to become homeowners as they are to become renters in the Netherlands (Mulder & Manting, 1994).

As can be expected, income (resources) plays a very important role in the tenure choice of those who leave the parental home (Clark & Dieleman, 1996). Those who become homeowners immediately, or after a period of renting a dwelling, are typically those who have achieved financial stability (Clark et al., 1994). As discussed before (in the section on resources) financial contributions from parents can play an important role in first-time homeownership (Helderman & Mulder, 2007). However, financial stability alone is not enough to explain homeownership; it has been demonstrated repeatedly that households also need to be stable before becoming a homeowner (Rossi, 1955; Doling, 1976; Michelson, 1977; Henretta, 1987; Morrow-Jones, 1988; Clark et al., 1994; Clark & Dieleman, 1996; Davies Withers, 1998). Feijten and colleagues (2003, see also Feijten, 2005a) have theorized the role of stability in homeownership by using the term 'commitments'. With increasing commitments (which increase from cohabiting to getting married and having a child), it becomes more likely that a household becomes a homeowner. Stability does not only come from household commitments, but can also arise from ageing. As singles get older, their single status becomes more permanent and the stability that arises out of this stable household situation might lead to the decision to buy a home (Feijten et al., 2003).

The literature shows that the timing of first-time homeownership is strongly connected with the timing of marriage and childbirth (Deurloo et al., 1994; Mulder & Wagner, 1998). There is some evidence of reversed causality where the high cost of homeownership has been found to slow down the process of nest leaving and partner formation (Börsch-Supan, 1986; Hooimeijer & Mulder, 1998; Ermisch, 1999). Generally speaking, singles are the least likely to become homeowners and married couples are the most likely to become homeowners (Clark et al., 1994 for the USA; Mulder & Manting, 1994 for the Netherlands; Lauster & Fransson, 2006 for Sweden). Not just having children, but also the expectation to get children in the near future was found to play a role in the decision to become homeowner (Feijten & Mulder, 2002; Lauster & Fransson, 2006).

Most of the literature on tenure choice focuses on transitions from renting to owning. The opposite process of falling out of ownership has received much less attention (Dieleman et al., 1995; Feijten, 2005b). Dieleman and colleagues (1995) and Helderman (2007) identified several categories of households and their motives for moves from owner-occupied dwellings to rented accommodation. The first motive is related to the affordability of ownership in case of a drop in income or a rise in the cost of ownership. A drop in income could be the result of, for example, the loss of employment or separation or divorce (see Feijten, 2005b). Especially singles and single-parent families who have gone through a separation or divorce run the risk of falling out of homeownership. The cost of ownership can rise because of a rise in mortgage interest rates or because of a steep drop in housing prices.

For many decades housing was seen as a wealth escalator in which prices continued to rise. In the early 1990s, there was a growing awareness that house prices can also drop and that the housing market has a cyclical nature (Dieleman et al., 1995). In the 2008–2009 housing market crisis, there is renewed attention on the affordability of ownership: the decline in house prices puts pressure on those who bought their houses at the height of the property boom and not all households – especially those who bought on a 100% mortgage – can pay the cost of staying in the owners market.

The second set of motives is related to a change in the need for living space because of a decrease in household size (separation, divorce, death of partner, or children leaving the parental home). Rented dwellings are often smaller than owner-occupied dwellings and therefore more suitable for smaller households. A third set of motives is related to the urgency of moves. In the case of an urgent move, it is often easier to rent than to buy. The fourth motive is unfamiliarity with a housing market after a long-distance (job-related) move.

Familiarization with a housing market takes time and households might decide to rent temporarily before deciding what and where to buy. The fifth motive is a desire to avoid responsibility for an owner-occupied home. This motive is often related to ageing or losing a partner. Rented homes bring fewer responsibilities for the occupant than owner-occupied homes. The sixth motive is a desire to withdraw equity, and free up wealth locked in their dwelling. This motive is also often related to old age. Using data for the Netherlands, Helderman (2007) found separation and divorce, followed by motives related to ageing and health to be the most important reasons for moves from owner-occupied to rented dwellings.

There is a substantial body of literature on the effects of separation and divorce on housing careers (Sullivan, 1986; Schouw & Dieleman, 1987; Jackson, 1990; Murphy, 1990; Symon, 1990; Wasoff & Dobash, 1990; Watchman, 1990; McCarthy & Simpson, 1991; Van Noortwijk et al., 1992; Böheim & Taylor, 2000; Flowerdew & Al Hamad, 2004; Feijten & Van Ham, 2007). Divorce rates in many Western European countries have increased significantly over the last decades, especially between the 1960s and early 1980s. Since then, the divorce rate has remained fairly constant in most countries, although the incidence of 'splitting up' has increased strongly as a result of the rise in cohabitation (Feijten & Van Ham, 2010). The above-mentioned studies show that separation and divorce have a disruptive effect on the housing careers of those involved, often leading to downward moves on the housing ladder: moves from large to smaller and lower-quality dwellings, moves from owner-occupation into rented housing and from single-family dwellings into multi-family dwellings (Feijten, 2005b). Dewilde (2008), using panel data for 12 European countries, showed that the effect of divorce on moving out of ownership is fairly similar across European welfare states.

Cross-national differences in tenure changes for homeowners were only partly influenced by social housing policies, the extent of family support and institutional arrangements mitigating the economic consequences of divorce. Separation and divorce often have negative effects on housing careers because moves triggered by union dissolution are often urgent, financially restricted and spatially restricted (Feijten & Van Ham, 2007). The effects of separation and divorce on housing careers are found to be the most severe for women (Sullivan, 1986; Murphy, 1990; Symon, 1990; Feijten, 2005b). Several studies have shown that it takes a series of moves before divorced people have regained the housing quality they had before the divorce (Jackson, 1990; Watchman, 1990; McCarthy & Simpson, 1991), although for some households the damage is long-lasting.

FUTURE RESEARCH ON HOUSING BEHAVIOUR

The life-course approach offers a powerful tool in understanding housing behaviour as it is capable of bringing a variety of factors influencing housing behaviour together. It offers an integrated way of studying housing behaviour at the level of individual households within a macro context of the housing market and wider society. The last section of this chapter will identify three inter-linked areas for future research on housing behaviour within a life-course context.

The first area of research is the choice set households have in the housing market. This chapter started by questioning the concept of *choice* and it was stated that the use of the concept can be misleading, as for most households the choice set of available and suitable housing is actually very limited. It was identified that having *real choice* means being able to select a preferred option from distinctive alternatives, but for many people there may not be any alternatives. Housing behaviour is often modelled using a simple dichotomous variable: people move or do not move; people change tenure or not. Such models offer us very valuable information on the characteristics of those who exhibit certain behaviour, and reveal causal relationships between certain life events and certain housing behaviour. The implicit assumptions behind these models is that all cases (individuals or households) included in the data are actually at risk of exhibiting certain behaviour. In reality many households may not be at risk of housing behaviour due to the lack of real choice. Some households may indicate that they would like to move, and they may indicate preferences concerning the type of dwelling and location, but for many the reality is that these preferences are unlikely to lead to actual behaviour.

Our knowledge of the choice set of housing actually available to housing consumers is very limited. This choice set is influenced by individual resources and restrictions, but also by macro-level opportunities and constraints. There are many studies looking at housing preferences and many studies looking at actual behaviour, but few studies link the two literatures. The missing link between what people want and what they get is the choice set available to them. Individuals can influence their choice set by changing preferences, but they have limited influence on resources (income and wealth) and restrictions (for example, being tied to a regional labour market, and therefore a regional housing market). Individuals have no direct influence on the macro context of housing policy and the housing market. More research is needed, both theoretically and empirically, on the real housing choice set of households and how the choice set influences behaviour. Such research should be set within a multi-level context, taking into account the households, the regional housing market it operates in and the national housing policy context.

The second area for future research is the role of both macro-level time and individual time in housing careers (see Feijten, 2005a on which this section is based). A major notion in the life-course approach is that the situation at a certain moment in the life course can only be understood if past life events and their interdependencies are taken into account. Macro-level time refers to calendar time or historical time. All people in the same birth cohort experience the same macro time. People from different birth cohorts will have had different opportunities and experienced different constraints and this is likely to have a significant effect on housing careers. The opportunities and constraints people experience in their housing careers, especially those experienced early in their careers, may have long-lasting effects. For example, experiencing a housing crisis, being in negative equity or having to pay a very high mortgage interest rate for a prolonged period of time may severely disrupt a housing career. The way individual housing careers develop can only be understood within their specific historical and social context and housing careers are only comparable for those who have experienced the same macro circumstances. Consequently, the choice set does not only have a spatial but also a temporal dimension.

Individual time (micro-level time) can be expressed by age and the age at which life events are experienced. Experiencing life events (e.g. getting married) at an early age may mean that a housing event (e.g. becoming a homeowner) may also take place at an early age. Experiencing certain events early in life may give people an (accumulative) advantage or disadvantage later in life. Not just the timing of events, but also the order of events and the duration of the resulting states, are important in understanding housing careers. Individual variation in housing careers depends to a large extent on time-related differences in events and resulting states and time aspects such as timing, order, postponement and disruption are central (Feijten, 2005a). For example, a divorce is a serious disruption of the household career, with often far-reaching consequences for subsequent housing behaviour. If a divorced person forms a new couple, the individual life histories of both partners will influence their joint housing career.

Stronger commitments, such as getting married and/or having children, severely restrict people's potential pathways in life (their choice set shrinks). The fact that one has been married at some point in life cannot be undone. Commitments can also lead to stability, which can have positive effects on housing careers. Stability in various careers (household career, labour career) is important for the transition to first-time homeownership. Stability might bring the resources required to buy a house, and stability also takes away the necessity of the housing career to be flexible and people might settle down and make long-term housing decisions. The effects of life events on the housing career might be immediate, lagged, temporary or lasting. The timing of cause and effect may vary in order, as people might anticipate on certain events in the future. A good example is moving to an owner-occupied dwelling in a suburb because of a wish to have children. Theoretical debates on the life-course approach to housing behaviour have identified the value of looking at time aspects of live events and applying a long-term view, but empirical application remains limited.

A third and final area for future research is driven by information needs on several categories of people deserving more attention in housing market research. One such category is people with complex life histories. There are an increasing number of people whose life history includes multiple households. Some households are formed out of two previously married individuals, both with children from previous marriages and sometimes with joint children. Such complex household formations are beyond the standard categorizations of households in singles, couples and couples with children often used in housing research. In understanding housing behaviour, the complex life histories of individuals in households has to be taken into account. Another category deserving more attention is the elderly. An increasing number and proportion of people are over 65 years old and most of these people are not restricted in their housing career by job locations. Future birth cohorts reaching the age of 65 may have very different preferences with regard to housing than current and past birth cohorts reaching age 65, and housing careers at later age for various cohorts may develop in different ways. The very broad and growing category of singles deserves more attention in housing research. This category consists of young (temporary) singles, long-term (permanent) singles and those who became single through separation, divorce or widowhood. The timing of becoming single, the order of events and the duration of the single state can all be expected to have significant effects on the housing career.

The above three areas of future research combine information needs on particular categories of people and conceptual development of housing behaviour in a life-course framework. Successful implementation of the life-course framework requires large longitudinal and geo-coded data containing information on whole housing careers of individuals in their household context, including information on parallel careers. Longitudinal data allow for a more full understanding of housing behaviour by taking into account lagged effects, anticipative behaviour and long-term effects of events which took place early in life. Such an understanding not only will contribute to our conceptual understanding of housing behaviour but also will help to develop policies which take a long-term approach to solving inequality in housing.

ACKNOWLEDGEMENTS

I would like to thank Peteke Feijten and Bill Clark for their support in writing this chapter and their very helpful comments, suggestionsand corrections. Many thanks to David Manley for suggestions and proofreading the chapter.

REFERENCES

Aalbers, M. B. (2006). 'When the banks withdraw, slum landlords take over: The structuration of neighborhood decline through redlining, drug dealing, speculation and immigrant exploitation', *Urban Studies*, 43(7), 1061–1086.

Allen, C. (2009). 'The fallacy of "housing studies": Philosophical problems of knowledge and understanding in housing research', *Housing, Theory and Society*, 26(1), 53–79.

Bank of England (2009). http://www.bankofengland.co.uk. Accessed on 01.05.2009.

Bell, W. (1958). 'Social choice, life styles, and suburban residence', in W. M. Dobriner (ed.), *The Suburban Community* (pp. 225–247). New York: Putnam.

Bell, W. (1968). 'The city, suburb, and a theory of social choice', in S. Greer (ed.), *The New Urbanization* (pp. 132–168). New York: St. Martin's.

Bengtsson, B. (2009). 'Political science as the missing link in housing studies', *Housing, Theory and Society*, 26(1), 10–25.

Boehm, T. P. & Schlottmann, A. M. (1999). 'Does home ownership by parents have an economic impact on their children?', *Journal of Housing Economics*, 8(3), 217–232.

Böheim, R. & Taylor, M. P. (2000). 'My home was my castle: Evictions and repossessions in Britain', *Journal of Housing Economics*, 9, 287–319.

Böheim, R. & Taylor, M. P. (2002). 'The search for success: Do the unemployed find stable employment?', *Labour Economics*, 9(6), 717–735.

Bolt, G., Hooimeijer, P. & Van Kempen, R. (2002). 'Ethnic segregation in the Netherlands: New patterns, new policies?', *Tijdschrift voor Economische en Sociale Geografie*, 93(2), 214–220.

Börsch-Supan, A. (1986). 'Household formation, housing prices, and public policy impacts', *Journal of Public Economics*, 25, 145–164.

Börsch-Supan, A. (1993). 'Housing market regulations and housing market performance in the United States, Germany, and Japan', in R. Blank (ed.), *Social Protection Versus Economic Flexibility* (pp. 119–156). Chicago: University of Chicago Press.

Brown, T. & King, P. (2005). 'The power to choose: Effective choice and housing policy', *European Journal of Housing Policy*, 5(1), 59–97.

Brun, J. & Fagnani, J. (1994). 'Lifestyles and locational choices – trade-offs and compromises: A case-study of middle-class couples living in the Ille-de-France region', *Urban Studies*, 31(6), 921–934.

Clapham, D. (2009). Introduction to the special issue – a theory of housing: Problems and potential. *Housing, Theory and Society*, 26(1), 1–9.

Clapham, D. & Kintrea, K. (1984). 'Allocation systems and housing choice', *Urban Studies*, 21(3), 261–269.

Clark, W. A. V. & Davies Withers, S. (1999). 'Changing jobs and changing houses: Mobility outcomes of employment transitions', *Journal of Regional Science*, 39(4), 653–673.

Clark, W. A. V. & Deurloo, M. C. (2006). 'Aging in place and housing over-consumption', *Journal of Housing and the Built Environment*, 21(3), 257–270.

Clark, W. A. V. & Dieleman, F. M. (1996). *Households and Housing: Choice and Outcomes in the Housing Market*. Centre for Urban Policy Research. Rutgers – The State University of New Jersey.

Clark, W. A. V. & Mulder, C. H. (2000). 'Leaving home and entering the housing market', *Environment and Planning A*, 32(9), 1657–1672.

Clark, W. A. V., Deurloo, M. C. & Dieleman, F. M. (1994). 'Tenure changes in the context of micro-level family and macro-level economic shifts', *Urban Studies*, 31(1), 137–154.

Clark, W. A. V., Deurloo, M. C. & Dieleman, F. M. (1997). 'Entry to home-ownership in Germany: Some comparisons with the United States', *Urban Studies*, 34(1), 7–19.

Coulson, N. E. (1999). 'Why are Hispanic- and Asian-American homeownership rates so low? Immigration and other factors', *Journal of Urban Economics*, 45(2), 209–227.

Courgeau, D. (1985). 'Interaction between spatial mobility, family and career life-cycle: A French survey', *European Sociological Review*, 1(2), 139–162.

Courgeau, D. & Lelièvre, E. (1992). 'Interrelations between first home-ownership, constitution of the family, and professional occupation in France', in J. Trussell, R. Hankinson & J. Tilton (eds), *Demographic Applications of Event History Analysis* (pp. 120–139). Oxford: Clarendon Press.

Davies, R. B. & Pickles, A. R. (1985). 'Longitudinal versus cross-sectional methods for behavioural research: A first-round knockout', *Environment and Planning A*, 17, 1315–1329.

Davies Withers, S. (1998). 'Linking household transitions and housing transitions: A longitudinal analysis of renters', *Environment and Planning A*, 30(4), 615–630.

De Jong, G. F. & Fawcett, J. T. (1981). 'Motivations for migration: An assessment and a value-expectancy research model', in G. F. De Jong & R. W. Gardner (eds), *Migration Decision Making: Multidisciplinary Approaches to Microlevel Studies in Developed and Developing Countries* (pp. 13–58). New York: Pergamon Press.

Desbarats, J. (1983). 'Spatial choice and constraints on behavior', *Annals of the Association of American Geographers*, 73(3), 340–357.

Deurloo, R. C., Dieleman, F. M. & Clark, W. A. V. (1987). 'Tenure choice in the Dutch housing market', *Environment and Planning A*, 19, 763–781.

Deurloo, R. C., Clark, W. A. V. & Dieleman, F. M. (1994). 'The move to housing ownership in temporal and regional contexts', *Environment and Planning A*, 26, 1659–1670.

Deurloo, R. C., Dieleman, F. M. & Clark, W. A. V. (1997). 'Tenure choice in the German housing market: A competing risks model'. *Tijdschrift voor Economische en Sociale Geografie*, 88(4), 321–331.

Dewilde, C. (2008). 'Divorce and the housing movements of owner-occupiers: A European comparison', *Housing Studies*, 23(6), 809–832.

Dieleman, F. M. & Schouw, R. J. (1989). 'Divorce, mobility and housing demand', *European Journal of Population*, 5, 235–252.

Dieleman, F. M., Clark, W. A. V. & Deurloo, R. C. (1995). 'Falling out of the home owner market', *Housing Studies*, 10(1), 3–15.

Doling, J. (1976). 'The family life cycle and housing choice', *Urban Studies*, 13, 55–58.

Doling, J. (2006). Home ownership in Europe: Limits to growth. Paper presented at the CECODHAS Colloquium 'Current Developments in Housing Policies and Housing Markets in Europe: Implications for the Social Housing Sector', Brussels, 13 September 2006.

Duncan, O. D. & Duncan, B. (1955). 'Occupational stratification and residential distribution', *American Journal of Sociology*, 50, 493–503.

Elder, G. H. (1985). Perspectives on the life course. In G. H. Elder (ed.), *Life Course Dynamics: Trajectories and Transitions, 1968–1980* (pp. 23–49). Ithaca: Cornell University Press.

Elster, J. (1999). *Strong feelings: Emotion, addiction, and human behavior*. Cambridge, MA: MIT Press.

Engelhardt, G. V. & Mayer, C. J. (1998). 'Intergenerational transfers, borrowing constraints, and saving behavior: Evidence from the housing market', *Journal of Urban Economics*, 44(1), 135–157.

Ermisch, J. (1999). 'Prices, parents, and young people's household formation', *Journal of Urban Economics*, 45(1), 47–71.

Ermisch, J. & Di Salvo, P. (1997). 'The economic determinants of young people's household formation', *Economica*, 64, 627–644.

Fahey, T. (2003). 'Is there a trade-off between pensions and home ownership? An exploration of the Irish case', *Journal of European Social Policy*, 13(2), 159–173.

Feijten, P. (2005a). *Life Events and the Housing Career: A Retrospective Analysis of Timed Effects*: Delft: Eburon.

Feijten, P. (2005b). 'Union dissolution, unemployment and moving out of homeownership', *European Sociological Review*, 21(1), 59–71.

Feijten, P. & Mulder, C. H. (2002). 'The timing of household events and housing events in the Netherlands: A longitudinal perspective', *Housing Studies*, 17(5), 773–792.

Feijten, P. & Mulder, C. H. (2005). 'Life-course experience and housing quality', *Housing Studies*, 20(4), 571–587.

Feijten, P. & van Ham, M. (2008). 'Residential mobility and migration of the divorced and separated', *Demographic Research*, 17, 623–653.

Feijten P.M. and van Ham M. (2010). 'The impact of splitting up and divorce on housing careers in the UK', *Housing Studies*, 25, 483–507.

Feijten, P., Mulder, C. H. & Baizán, P. (2003). 'Age differentiation in the effect of household situation on first-time homeownership', *Journal of Housing and the Built Environment*, 18(3), 233–255.

Felson, M. & Solaun, M. (1975). 'The fertility-inhibiting effect of crowded apartment living in a tight housing market', *American Journal of Sociology*, 80(6), 1410.

Flowerdew, R. & Al-Hamad, A. (2004). 'The relationship between marriage, divorce and migration in a British dataset', *Journal of Ethnic and Migration Studies*, 30, 339–351.

Gibb, K. (2009). 'Housing studies and the role of economic theory: An (applied) disciplinary perspective' *Housing, Theory and Society*, 26(1), 26–40.

Glick, P. (1957). *American Families*. New York: John Wiley.

Goldscheider, F. & Goldscheider, C. (1993). 'Whose nest? A two-generational view of leaving home during the 1980s', *Journal of Marriage and the Family*, 55, 851–862.

Goldscheider, F., Thornton, A. & Young-DeMarco, L. (1993). 'A portrait of the nest-leaving process in early adulthood', *Demography*, 30(4), 683–699.

Green, R. K. & White, M .J. (1997). 'Measuring the benefits of homeowning: Effects on children', *Journal of Urban Economics*, 41, 441–461.

Guiso, L. & Jappelli, T. (2002). 'Private transfers, borrowing constraints and the timing of homeownership', *Journal of Money, Credit and Banking*, 34(2), 315–339.

Hareven, T. K. (1977). 'Family time and historical time', *Daedalus*, 106(2), 57–70.

Haurin, D. R., Hendershott, P. H. & Kim, D. (1993). 'The impact of real rents and wages on household formation', *The Review of Economics and Statistics*, 75, 284–293.

Haurin, R. J., Haurin, D. R., Hendershott, P. H. & Bourassa, S. C. (1997). 'Home or alone: The costs of independent living for youth', *Social Science Research*, 26(2), 135–152.

Helderman, A. & Mulder, C. (2007). 'Intergenerational transmission of homeownership: The roles of gifts and continuities in housing market characteristics', *Urban Studies*, 44(2), 231–247.

Helderman, A. C. (2007). 'Once a homeowner, always a homeowner? An analysis of moves out of owner-occupation', *Journal of Housing and the Built Environment*, 22(3), 239–261.

Hendershott, P. H., Bosworth, B. P. & Jaffee, D. M. (1980). 'Real user costs and the demand for single-family housing'. *Brookings Papers on Economic Activity*, 2, 401–452.

Henderson, J. V. & Ioannides, Y. M. (1983). 'A model of housing tenure choice', *The American Economic Review*, 73(1), 98–113.

Henretta, J. C. (1984). 'Parental status and child's home ownership', *American Sociological Review*, 49(1), 131–140.

Henretta, J. C. (1987). 'Family transitions, housing market context, and first home purchase by young married households', *Social Forces*, 66, 520.

Hooimeijer, P. & Mulder, C. H. (1998). 'Changing ways of leaving the parental home: With a partner or alone', in A. Kuijsten, H.De Gans, & H. De Feijter, H. (eds), *The Joy of Demography and Other Disciplines* (pp. 137–151). Amsterdam: Thela Thesis.

Hoover.org (2009). http://www.hoover.org/. Accessed on 01.05.2009.

Ioannides, Y. M. & Rosenthal, S. S. (1994). 'Estimating the consumption and investment demands for housing and their effect on housing tenure status', *The Review of Economics and Statistics*, 76(1), 127–141.

Jackson, A. A. (1990). 'Relationship breakdown: The individual and local authority response', in P.Symon (ed.), *Housing and Divorce* (pp. 77–91). Glasgow: Centre for Housing Research.

Jenkins, S. P. & Maynard, A. K. (1983). 'Intergenerational continuities in housing', *Urban Studies*, 20(4), 431–438.

Jones, C. & Murie, A. (2006). *The Right to Buy: Analysis and Evaluation of a Housing Policy*. Oxford: Blackwell.

Kearns, A., & Parkes, A. (2003). 'Living in and leaving poor neighborhood conditions in England', *Housing Studies*, 18(6), 827–851.

Kemeny, J. (1992). *Housing and Social Theory*. London: Routledge.

Kendig, H. (1990). 'A life course perspective on housing attainment', in D. Meyers (ed.), *Housing Demography: Linking Demographic Structure and Housing Markets* (pp. 133–156). Wisconsin: University of Wisconsin Press.

King, P. (2009). 'Using theory or making theory: Can there be theories of housing?', *Housing, Theory and Society*, 26(1), 41–52.

Kintrea, K. & Clapham, D. (1986). 'Housing choice and search strategies within an administered housing system', *Environment and Planning A*, 18, 1281–1296.

Kulu, H. & Vikat, A. (2008). 'Fertility differences by housing type: An effect of housing conditions or of selective moves?', *Demographic Research*, 17, 775–801.

Lansing, J. B. & Morgan, J. M. (1955). 'Consumer finances over the life cycle', *Consumer Behavior*, 2(4), 36–50.

Lauster, N. T. & Fransson, U. (2006). 'Of marriages and mortgages: The second demographic transition and the relationship between marriage and homeownership in Sweden', *Housing Studies*, 21(6), 909–927.

Leppel, K. (1987). 'Household formation and unrelated housemates', *American Economist*, 31, 38–47.

Lu, M. (1999). 'Do people move when they say they will? Inconsistencies in individual migration behaviour', *Population and Environment: A Journal of Interdisciplinary Studies*, 20, 467–488.

Lundqvist, L. (1992). *Dislodging the Welfare State? Housing and Privatization in Four European Nations*: Delft: Delft University Press.

McCarthy, P. & Simpson, B. (1991). *Issues in Post-Divorce Housing: Family Policy or Housing Policy?* Aldershot: Avebury.

McCarthy, G., Van Zandt, S. & Rohe, W. M. (2001). *The Economic Benefits and Costs of Homeownership: A Critical Assessment of the Research*, Research Institute for Housing America. Working Paper No. 01–02. Research Institute for Housing America: Arlington, VA.

McFadden, D. (1978). 'Modelling the choice of residential location', in: A. Karlqvist et al. (eds), *Spatial Interaction Theory and Planning Models*. Amsterdam: North-Holland.

Maslow, A. H. (1943). 'A theory of motivation', *Psychological Review*, 50(4), 370–396.
Merrett, S. & Gray, F. (1982). *Owner-Occupation in Britain*: London: Routledge & Kegan Paul Books.
Michelson, W. (1977). *Environmental Choice, Human Behavior, and Residential Satisfaction*. New York: Oxford University Press.
Morris, E. W., Crull S. R. & Winter, W. (1976). 'Housing norms, housing satisfaction and the propensity to move', *Journal of Marriage and the Family*, 38, 309–320.
Morrow-Jones, H. A. (1988). 'The housing life-cycle and the transition from renting to owning a home in the United States: A multistate analysis', *Environment and Planning A*, 20, 1165–1184.
Mulder, C. H. (1996). 'Housing choice: Assumptions and approaches', *Netherlands Journal of Housing and the Built Environment*, 11(3), 209–232.
Mulder, C. H. & Hooimeijer, P. (1999). Residential relocations in the life course', in L. J. G. Van Wissen & P. A. Dykstra (eds), *Population Issues: An Interdisciplinary Focus* (pp. 159–186). Den Haag: NIDI.
Mulder, C. H. & Manting, D. (1994). 'Strategies of nest-leavers: 'Settling down' versus flexibility', *European Sociological Review*, 10(2), 155–172.
Mulder, C. H. & Smits, J. (1999). 'First-time homeownership of couples: The effect of intergenerational transmission', *European Sociological Review*, 15(3), 323–337.
Mulder, C. H. & van Ham, M. (2005). 'Migration histories and occupational achievement', *Population, Space and Place*, 11(3), 173–186.
Mulder, C. H. & Wagner, M. (1998). 'First-time homeownership in the family life course: A West German–Dutch comparison', *Urban Studies*, 35(4), 687–713.
Mulder, C. H. & Wagner, M. (2001). 'The connections between family formation and first-time home ownership in the context of West Germany and the Netherlands', *European Journal of Population*, 17(2), 137–164.
Mulder, C. H., Clark, W. A. V. & Wagner, M. (2006). 'Resources, living arrangements and first union formation in the United States, the Netherlands and West Germany', *European Journal of Population*, 22(1), 3–35.
Murdie, R. A. (2002). 'The housing careers of Polish and Somali newcomers in Toronto's rental market', *Housing Studies*, 17(3), 423–443.
Murphy, M. J. (1984). 'The influence of fertility, early housing-career, and socioeconomic factors on tenure determination in contemporary Britain', *Environment and Planning A*, 16(10), 1303–1318.

Murphy, M. J. (1990). 'Housing consequences of marital breakdown and remarriage', in P.Symon (ed.), *Housing and Divorce*. Glasgow: Centre for Housing Research, University of Glasgow.
Murphy, M. J. & Sullivan, O. (1985). 'Housing tenure and family formation in contemporary Britain', *European Sociological Review*, 1(3), 230–243.
Myers, D. (1999). 'Cohort longitudinal estimation of housing careers', *Housing Studies*, 14(4), 473–490.
Onaka, J. & Clark, W. A. V. (1983). 'A disaggregate model of residential mobility and housing choice', *Geographical Analysis*, 15(4), 287–304.
Özüekren, A. S. & van Kempen, R. (2002). 'Housing careers of minority ethnic groups: Experiences, explanations and prospects', *Housing Studies*, 17(3), 365–379.
Painter, G., Gabriel, S. & Myers, D. (2001). 'Race, immigrant status, and housing tenure choice', *Journal of Urban Economics*, 49(1), 150–167.
Pickles, A. & Davies, R. (1985). 'The longitudinal analysis of housing careers', *Journal of Regional Science*, 25(1), 85–101.
Power, A. (1993). *Hovels to High Rise: State Housing in Europe since 1850*. New York: Routledge.
Robst, J., Deitz, R. & McGoldrick, K. M. (1999). 'Income variability, uncertainty and housing tenure choice', *Regional Science and Urban Economics*, 29(2), 219–229.
Rosen, S. (1974). 'Hedonic prices and implicit markets: Product differentiation in pure competition', *Journal of Political Economy*, 82(1), 34–55.
Rossi, P. H. (1955). *Why Families Move: A Study in the Social Psychology of Urban Residential Mobility*. Glencoe, IL: Free Press.
Sandefur, G. D. & Scott, W. J. (1981). 'A dynamic analysis of migration: An assessment of the effects of age, family and career variables', *Demography*, 18(3), 355–368.
Saunders, P. (1990). *A Nation of Home Owners*. London: Unwin Hyman.
Schouw, R. J. & Dieleman, F. M. (1987). *Echtscheiding en woningmarkt: een voorstudie naar de complexe relatie tussen echtscheiding en de woningmarkt*. Utrecht: KNAG.
Smits, A. & Mulder, C. H. (2008). 'Family dynamics and first-time homeownership', *Housing Studies*, 23(6), 917–933.
South, S. J. & Crowder, K. D. (1998). 'Avenues and barriers to residential mobility among single mothers', *Journal of Marriage and the Family*, 60, 866–877.
Stapleton, C. M. (1980). 'Reformulation of the family life-cycle concept: Implications for residential mobility', *Environment and Planning A*, 12, 1103–1118.

Stegman, M. A., Quercia, R., McCarthy, G. W. & Rohe, W. (1991). 'Using the P.S.I.D. to evaluate the affordability characteristics of alternative mortgage instruments and homeownership assistance programs', *Journal of Housing Research*, 2, 161–211.

Sullivan, O. (1986). 'Housing movements of the divorced and separated', *Housing Studies*, 1, 35–48.

Symon, P. (1990). 'Marital breakdown, gender and home ownership: The Owner-occupied Home in Separation and Divorce', in P. Symon (ed.), *Housing and Divorce* (pp. 110–138). Glasgow: Centre for Housing Research.

Thomas, B. & Dorling, D. (2004). *Know your place: Housing, Wealth and Inequality in Great Britain, 1980–2003 and Beyond.* London: Shelter.

Tilly, C. & Brown, C. H. (1967). 'On uprooting, kinship, and the auspices of migration', *International Journal of Comparative Sociology*, 8(2), 139–164.

Timmermans, H., Molin, E. & van Noortwijk, L. (1994). 'Housing choice processes: Stated versus revealed modelling approaches', *Journal of Housing and the Built Environment*, 9(3), 215–227.

Tootell, G. M. B. (1996). 'Redlining in Boston: Do mortgage lenders discriminate against neighborhoods?', *The Quarterly Journal of Economics*, 111(4), 1049–1079.

United Nations General Assembly (1948). Universal Declaration of Human Rights. Resolution 217 UN Doc. A/64.

Van Ham, M. (2002). *Job Access, Workplace Mobility, and Occupational Achievement.* Delft: Eburon.

Van Ham, M. (2003). 'Job access at labour market entry and occupational achievement in the life course', *International Journal of Population Geography*, 9(5), 387–398.

Van Ham, M. & Feijten, P. (2008). 'Who wants to leave the neighbourhood? The effect of being different from the neighborhood population on wishes to move', *Environment and Planning A*, 40(5), 1151.

Van Ham M. and Manley D. (2009). 'Social Housing Allocation, Choice and Neighbourhood Ethnic Mix in England', *Journal of Housing and the Built Environment* 24, 407–422.

Van Noortwijk, L., Hooimeijer, P. & Dieleman, F. M. (1992). 'Divorce and the disruption of the housing career', in P. Korcelli & J. Van Weesep (eds), *Housing and Urban Policy in Transition* (pp. 87–101). Warsaw: PAN IGiPZ.

Van Ommeren, J., Rietveld, P. and Nijkamp, P. (1998). 'Spatial moving behaviour of two-earner households', *Journal of Regional Science*, 38(1), 23–41.

Van Ommeren, J., Rietveld, P. and Nijkamp, P. (1999). 'Job moving, residential moving, and commuting: A search perspective', *Journal of Urban Economics*, 46, 230–253.

Varady, D. P. (1989). 'The impact of city/suburban location on moving plans: A Cincinnati study', *Growth and Change*, 20(2), 35–49.

Wagner, M. (1989). *Raümliche mobilität im lebenslauf. Eine empirische untersuchung sozialer bedingungen der migration.* Stuttgart: Enke.

Wasoff, F. & Dobash, R. (1990). 'Moving the family: Changing housing circumstances after divorce', in P. Symon (ed.), *Housing and Divorce* (pp. 139–165). Glasgow: Centre for Housing Research.

Watchman, P. Q. (1990). 'Relationship breakdown, homelessness and the law', in P. Symon (ed.), *Housing and Divorce* (pp. 92–108). Glasgow: Centre for Housing Research.

Willekens, F. J. (1987). 'Migration and development: a micro-perspective', *Journal of Institute of Economic Research*, 22, 51–68.

Willekens, F. J. (1991). 'Understanding the interdependence between parallel careers: A rational choice approach', in J. J. Siegers, J. De Jong Gierveld & E. van Imhoff (eds), *Female Labour Market Behaviour and Fertility* (pp. 11–31). Heidelberg: Springer Verlag.

Willekens, F. J. (1999). 'The life course: models and analysis', in P. A. Dykstra & L. J. G. van Wissen (eds) *Population Issues: An Interdisciplinary Focus* (pp. 23–52). New York: Kluwer Academic.

Wulff, M. N. N. & Maher, C. (1998). 'Long-term renters in the Australian housing market', *Housing Studies*, 13(1), 83–98.

Residential Mobility and the Housing Market

William A.V. Clark

INTRODUCTION

Residential mobility is the process by which households match their housing needs to the houses available to them and is central to understanding how the housing market operates. As households change their space needs, with changes in the life course, they make decisions about what housing to choose and where to move within the city. The choices are a function of their housing needs, external events and the housing stock available to them. This chapter will conceptualize mobility within the context of the life course and it emphasizes the way in which mobility is generated by the process of the evolving life course. It will examine the correlates of mobility – age, education, income and marital status – and examine the models that have been used to describe and understand residential change. The chapter will review what we have learned recently and examine attempts to apply our knowledge of mobility to intervention in the housing market.

Mobility is the core process which keeps the housing market working: it may even be said that mobility is the engine of the housing market. Of course, the financial engine of mortgage lending and construction financing is equally important, but the mobility engine is clearly one of the important mechanisms through which the housing market changes. Without the demand for new and/or different houses the market cannot operate as a clearing house for the supply and demand of housing units. However imperfectly it operates, it is mobility which brings about the matching between households and houses.

Mobility has always reflected new housing construction as it is the creation of vacancies which fuels change in urban areas and it is this change which is at the heart of understanding how mobility interacts with the wider processes of urban structural change. In fact a great deal of residential change is related to the transition from rental housing to ownership, and recent research has shown just how closely mobility and ownership changes are interconnected (Helderman et al., 2004, 2006). Ownership is a critical step in the housing career and almost always involves a residential change. Purchasing an existing house or a newly constructed house involves both selecting a house and selecting a location. That latter process is taken up more specifically in chapters on neighborhoods in other sections of the Handbook but neighborhood selection is an integral part of the mobility process, as the nested logit models show later in the chapter. Neighborhoods and their impacts on residential mobility are becoming more important as households evaluate their housing and community satisfaction (Van Ham and Clark, 2008; Van Ham and Feijten, 2008). Research is showing that it is not only objective characteristics of neighborhoods that are important but also that neighborhood reputations can play a role in creating and stimulating residential mobility (Permentier et al., 2007, 2009). (For a detailed discussion of household choices see Chapter 3.)

At the individual level, it is the intersection of household size and composition and the size of the dwelling which leads to housing changes. When households need more space, when they 'fall out' of equilibrium in their current housing, and when they make adjustments by moving from one house or apartment to another, especially when they move from apartments to houses and from smaller to larger houses, we call this process the housing career (Clark and Dieleman, 1996). The housing career is a central paradigm of how households adjust to both their individual household changes and changes in the housing availability. This conceptualization emphasizes the availability of living space and how much a household needs to meet the needs of the individual household. Thus, the difference between how much it needs and how much is available can be identified as the mismatch which is the trigger or driver that creates mobility and housing selection. Of course it is an imperfect mechanism and there is often considerable lag in the process of matching households to housing space, and budget constraints play a role too. Income limits and social and cultural values often keep households in particular houses or apartments far beyond the time when it would be useful for that household to move. At the other extreme, older households often stay on in houses which are much too large for their actual needs. Still, linking space needs to household size and composition is a central dimension to understanding the behavioural operation of the housing market.

THEORY AND THE LIFE COURSE

Over the past two decades research on residential mobility and the housing market has moved away from cross-sectional analyses of stage in the life cycle and associated likelihoods of moving to a more fluid conceptualization of mobility. The life course suggests that mobility from one dwelling to another is embedded in a sequence of changing family compositions, including marriages or cohabitation and fertility events. These events occur with relatively regular periodicity as individuals age, marry or cohabit, have children and divorce. The importance of the life course is that it emphasizes events, events which have specific outcomes in terms of relocations within the housing stock (Clark and Dieleman, 1996). The choices that we observe as outcomes of residential mobility are created by their links back to the changes in the life patterns of households, to the demographic underpinnings of the housing market (Myers, 1990).

It was a substantial breakthrough in the research and understanding of residential mobility when we moved from examining stages in a family *life cycle* to the notions of the family *life course* (Mulder, 1993; Clark and Dieleman, 1996). While the approach to family life stages emphasized cross-sectional approaches, the life-course approach emphasizes the dynamic nature of the process of residential mobility and its connection with the housing stock. Whereas the stage in the life-cycle approach was largely defined by age cohorts and the size of families, the life-course approach focuses less on age and more on the processes of adding children, changing marital status and the intersection of other social changes in the household's composition. Of course, age is an important dimension for much of the residential mobility behaviour, but the life-course approach recognizes that in fact couples of quite varying stages in their careers can have their first or additional children at quite different ages, which in turn creates the need for residential mobility and housing change.

Of course, we do know that young single adults are likely to live in apartments. Young couples may live in apartments, but families with children, especially in the United States, Canada, Australia, the United Kingdom and New Zealand, make their first moves to housing ownership followed by moves to larger housing as their families expand. We often identify marriage or first union formation as a central part of the process; we do not need to privilege marriage per se, and we recognize that this process occurs with cohabitation. But the focus on the life course is more than a focus on union formation and children. The focus on the life course is a rich conceptualization of change in family household structure and allows for other changes to be incorporated within the notion of the life-course trajectory. Not only do families change in their composition but men and also women enter and exit the labour market, often with associated occupational changes, and the timing of these events also influences their demand for, and ability to afford, various kinds of housing. We can think of the life course as a series of trajectories: trajectories of leaving home and forming unions, entering the labour market, having children and changing occupational careers. These changes, in turn, are linked to family responsibilities (increasingly including the care of elders), and they all influence the residential mobility process.

The life course is also an important advance in the sense that it provides a way to incorporate flexibility in the changing structure and nature of the family. In the last 30 years there has been a major shift from the traditional married couple and child/children family to a greater variety of family compositions, including more single-headed households and many more couples without children. With such changing compositions, delayed marriage and decreasing fertility, it is easier to examine changes as events than to try and classify families into particular family types. In addition, the life-course paradigm is designed to allow for the analysis of more than one process at a time so the changes in family composition, in housing, and in jobs can be linked in an interactive manner (Figure 4.1).

The process is far from linear, but the events of completing education, entering the workforce and forming a union (getting married) link the household career with the job career and mobility. Of course there are lags, and moves do not neatly coincide with changes in household's composition or changes in jobs. But it is these changes which are paralleled by shifting choices in the housing market which makes studying residential mobility a core element of understanding the housing market.

Thus, even though there have been substantial changes in family composition in the past several decades, the life course specifically recognizes that moving from one dwelling to another is embedded in the sequence of marital and fertility events and the associated changes in incomes and opportunities that go along with changes in occupational structures. Other chapters in this Handbook will examine issues of the composition of the stock and the way in which housing prices play an important role in the choices and outcomes in the housing market. Other chapters will also examine the nature of constraints on the mobility process, as will this chapter to some extent (for more about life-choice approach, see Chapter 3).

Residential mobility is not just of theoretical interest: it has an intense practical dimension. Moving companies, the media and increasingly professional corporations are focused on providing the services that allow households to move, and they evaluate their

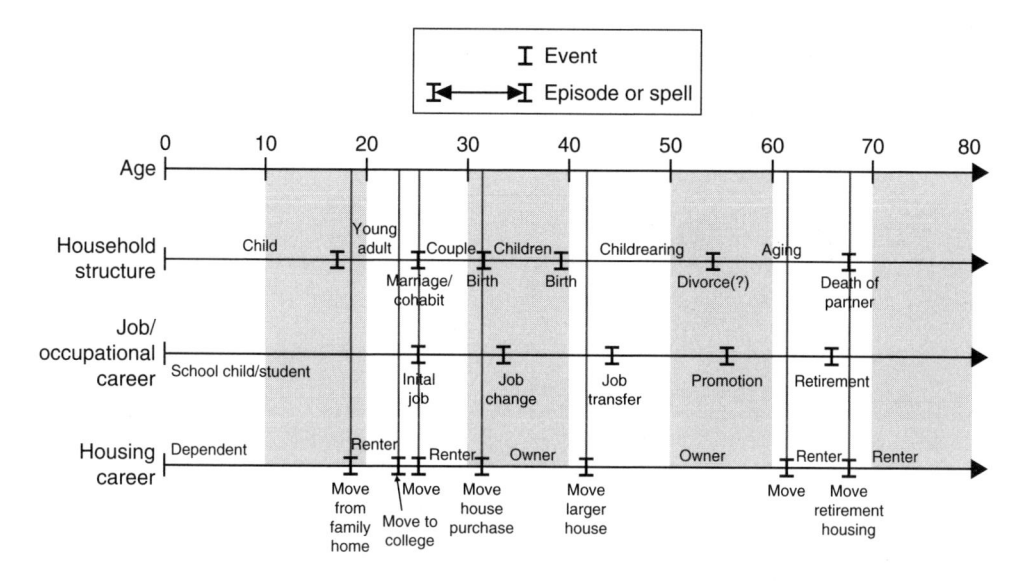

Figure 4.1 The life course and household/housing trajectories

satisfaction with particular neighborhoods and communities. Places change as people enter and leave them and if the composition of the population in a particular location is different from those arriving, there are a variety of implications for that community or neighborhood. When families with children move into a community there will be demands for schools and facilities that serve young families. When older households move into a community, there are very different demands placed on resources in those places (Clark and Davies Withers, 2007).

In the end it is these thousands of mobility decisions made every year in cities and towns in North America, Europe, Australia, New Zealand and the rest of the OECD (Organization for Economic Cooperation and Development) which fundamentally change neighborhoods, communities and housing markets themselves. Understanding the process of residential mobility helps housing specialists understand the broader changes in the housing market and, by implication, the changes in our society as individuals interact with communities and neighborhoods.

THE CORRELATES OF RESIDENTIAL MOBILITY

What do we know about residential mobility? What can we say about the relationships that describe this process in US, Canadian and Western European metropolitan areas generally? It is useful to utilize a now well-established schematic which distinguishes between residential mobility and longer-distance migration (Figure 4.2).

In this schematic we distinguish between partial and total displacement in which the new home either substantially disrupts the links with the workplace and previous locations or the move requires only modification of commuting and other local contacts. These partial displacement or adjustment moves are those within a housing market, while total displacement moves are moves between housing markets and involve a longer distance move. Of course it is difficult to provide a precise measure of the distance involved in partial and total displacement moves, although we commonly recognize moves of more than 50 km as likely to involve breaks with the web of contacts

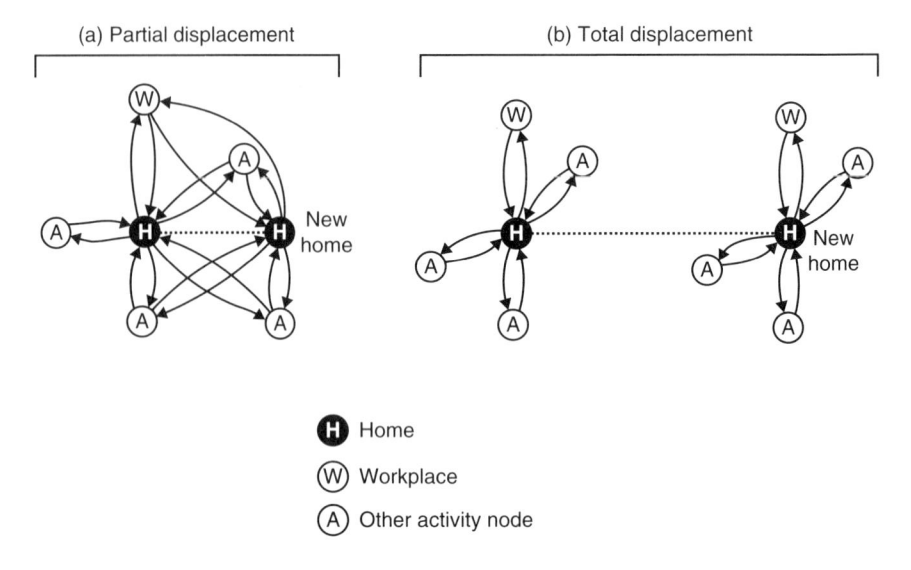

Figure 4.2 A schematic of partial and total displacement moves
Source: Adapted from Roseman 1971.

around the home. Some households drive even longer distances routinely but the proportion of households that regulate commute more than 50 km or more than an hour is relatively small proportion of all daily commuters. About 8% of all commuters in the United States had a travel time to work of more than an hour (Richardson et al., 2004). Average commute lengths are about 12 miles (19 km) and took approximately 24 minutes for all modes in the mid 2000s in the United States. Transit trips were longer but of course only a very small proportion of all work trips in the United States are by public transit – less than 10% overall.

Both long-distance and short-distance moves are related to age, tenure and space and socioeconomic status but while long-distance moves may involve job change as a primary stimulus for the move, short-distance moves are closely linked to the adjustment process of housing equilibrium and disequilibrium. Age is a primary correlate of the likelihood of residential mobility and longer-distance migration in young adults between the ages of 20 and 35. The distribution of the probability of moving by age across metropolitan areas shows that mobility peaks in the 20–24 age cohort in the United States, just the time when unions are occurring and young workers are finishing education and moving into the housing market. More than 35% of all individuals 20–24 years of age in the United States moved in the one-year period —2000–2001. That mobility rate declines slightly to 32% for the —25–29 cohort and further to 22% for the —30–34 age group (Schachter, 2001). Mobility varies across countries, with very high rates in the United States and much lower rates in Japan and European countries, but the classic young age cohort peak is consistent across countries. We can refer back to our discussion about the life course to understand and explain the periodicity and mobility in the young ages – household formation and expansion and growing incomes all fuel the demand for and the possibility of mobility. In some graphs we see a slight increase in mobility at older ages, which is related to retirement and will be an increasing indicator of changing mobility processes in aging societies.

Tenure – whether a household owns or rents – is intertwined with age and is an important dimension of the likelihood of moving. Renters are much more likely to move than owners. In the United States, 72% of renters moved in the past five years and about 31% of owners (US Census, 2000). Again, the results are tied to the life course. Households who rent are more likely to be in the initial stages of entering the housing market, setting up families and without the assets to buy into the housing market. More established households are already in the owner market, have put down roots and are making a long-term locational and emotional commitment to their neighborhoods and communities. The sunk costs of ownership are a serious deterrent to more frequent mobility. Recently the mobility rates have declined even further for both groups, a function of both an aging society and turmoil in the housing market. In the United States at least, mobility has declined from an average of about 20% per year in the 1960s to around 15% in the early 2000s.

A third dimension and correlate of the likelihood of mobility is the nature and amount of housing space and the level of 'room consumption'. Space consumption has increased over time, and households now live in considerably more spacious dwellings than they did only three decades ago. In the United States the average-sized single family house has increased from about 1000 square feet in 1950 to 2300 square feet 50 years later (National Association of Home Builders, 2006). Still, it is the same underlying process at work: the need or desire for adequate space for families.

In the introduction to the theory of residential mobility, I emphasized that the central component of the mobility process is the link between the needs for particular housing consumption, for the space for raising a family, which drives much of the housing search and relocation. I emphasized that it is the mismatch of housing and households which sets up residential mobility in cities and suburbs. Even a simple measure, like the number of rooms, is related to the likelihood that a family will change residences. As the number of rooms increases, the probability of moving decreases and once larger houses are occupied the length of residence increases in those houses. Of course this is in turn keyed into ownership, as larger dwellings with more rooms are often single-family homes, while smaller dwelling units, often apartments, have one or two rooms and are occupied by younger renters. Any plot between rooms stress (the difference between the number of rooms desired and the number of rooms available) shows quite clearly how the odds of moving in the future are related to the measure of available space (see Clark and Ledwith, 2006 for an example). At the same time there is considerable variability in the likelihood of moving with increased room stress. As we might expect, in the distribution of move probabilities, other intervening variables, income and budget constraints, play a role.

While age, tenure and room space are probably the most important correlates of mobility, income and socioeconomic status, family composition and a family's residence history also play a role in the likelihood of mobility. Income is clearly one of the important constraining and enabling variables as it is income which allows the households to translate needs into actualities. The higher the level of education of an individual or a household the greater the chance of moving at all ages. A college graduate is almost three times as likely to move as a person with elementary education. Two-earner households are considerably more likely to move than those households with only one worker, but at the same time once children become a part of a household mobility declines.

There is some debate about the role of previous mobility and its impact on the likelihood of moving again. There was earlier research which suggested that the longer a family stayed in a residence the longer they would continue to stay. This notion of cumulative inertia has been considerably deconstructed since its initial simplistic formulation and the emphasis is now on understanding when mobility occurred and what are the correlates, rather than classifying people as movers or stayers. Most would now argue that duration is only one of a plethora of factors that can influence mobility (Clark and Dieleman, 1996). Mobility likelihoods can decrease, increase or remain constant as a function of increasing lengths of stay; rather, it is the impact of a mixture of events which generates the mobility decision and the focus is more usefully directed to the events than to the durations between them.

In reviewing our discussion of the correlates of mobility, of age, marital status, the presence of children, income, tenure and the consumption of space, we can see how local moves are closely associated with the change from single to family status, a change which is in turn associated with age, and which is in turn influenced by income and previous tenure status. Each of these variables will be evaluated further in the models of mobility and their explanatory power.

CLASSIC AND CONTEMPORARY MODELS OF THE MOBILITY PROCESS

Simple and yet powerful models of the likelihood of moving in the housing market that incorporate the variables which are the central covariates of mobility have been developed in a variety of disciplines. These modeling strategies vary from the simple housing disequilibrium models first suggested by Hanuschek and Quigley (1978), which focus specifically on the difference between actual housing consumption and desired housing consumption, to nested logistic models, which focus on the behavior of households in the context not just of housing disequilibrium but of changes in household composition, number of workers in the family, as well as measures of age, marital status and socioeconomic status. Just as the initial models of migration suggested that the differences in net economic advantages, chiefly wages, caused (long-distance) migration, so differences in net housing differences cause residential mobility. Later, the chapter will show that the differences between long- and short-distance migration are less distinctive than older thinking about mobility and migration behavior.

All the modeling approaches have their genesis in some form of disequilibrium approach, whether it focuses on the stresses generated by the adequacy of house size, or changes in the neighborhood at large, or whether it is more specific economic and work-related opportunities: the models are essentially asking how does a household adjust to changing needs. Different modeling strategies and small variations in the variables used in the models still yield quite similar results and the predictive power is substantial across the alternative modeling strategies.

Three basic forms of the housing expenditure disequilibrium model have dominated the research and analysis literature. These forms revolve around forms of logit and nested logit models in which the decision to move is a function of some formulation that incorporates the housing market by focusing on the difference between actual and optimal amounts of housing consumed and controlled for age, income marital status and the presence and number of children. We conceptualize the difference between actual and desired housing characteristics as:

$$\frac{H^d_{t+1} - H_t}{H^d_t} \quad (1)$$

where H_t = the actual housing consumption at time t
H^d_t = the equilibrium housing consumption at time t and
H^d_{t+1} = the equilibrium housing consumption at time t+1.

Then we can conceptualize mobility – the probability P of moving between time t, and t+1 as

$$P_{t,t+1} = F \frac{H^d_{t+1} - H_t}{H^d_t} \quad (2)$$

Mobility in this formulation is seen as a response to the change in demands for housing and the associated services that the house provides such as access to schools, retail services and the myriad other activities that occur in the residential fabric.

Extensions of the same logit formulation, move or no move as a function of a series of independent variables often include both cross-sectional and time-dependent measures. In these formulations the probability of moving is related to age (and age squared to capture non-linear affects) and room stress as a measure of disequilibrium, but also to changes in household composition, number of workers in the family and changes in family income. These models are designed to uncover the nature of the links between households and the housing they consume. At the same time they purposefully include measures of what have been called household 'triggers' (the events that trigger a move from one house to another). Clearly, marriage (or divorce) can trigger a move of at least one of the partners and births are also a potential stimulus to move (Clark and Davies Withers, 2007).

Discrete choice modeling strategies for residential choices utilize the modeling strategies initially outlined in the work of McFadden (1974). The random utility model, the basis of a wide range of models in the choice literature assumes, as neoclassical economic theory, that the decision-maker has a perfect discrimination capability. But, the decision-maker has incomplete information and, as Manski (1993) has pointed out, uncertainty must be taken into account. Thus, the utility is modeled as a random variable in order to reflect uncertainty. More specifically, the utility that individual i is associating with alternative a is given by

$$U^i_a = V^i_a + E^i_a$$

where V^i_a is the deterministic part of the utility, and E^i_a is the stochastic part, capturing the uncertainty. Similarly to the neoclassical economic theory, the alternative with the highest utility is supposed to be chosen. Therefore, the probability that alternative a is chosen by decision-maker i within choice set C is:

$$P^i_c(a) = P(U^i_a = \max_{b \in c} U^i_b)$$

Random utility models are described in detail in several readily available sources and are not further covered in this chapter (see Ben-Akiva and Lerman, 1985 and Clark and van Lierop, 1986).

The results from discrete choice models have yielded useful and replicable results; more significantly, they have provided confirmation of the important role of the correlates that were discussed in the earlier section. The logit models of the likelihood of moving confirm the direction and size of the effects of age, room stress (room space) and tenure as explanations for distinguishing between families that moved and families that did not. What is most important for our understanding of mobility is that these models document that for families, in general, room stress has the expected negative effect: i.e., if the household has less than it needs, it is likely to move. As theory suggests, mobility can occur with either high negative values or high positive values of room stress, though (as it turns out) less space is more of a motivator than an excess of space (Clark and Deurloo, 2006). Naturally, both age and tenure are important variables in any model which predicts the likelihood of moving.

The results from the logit formulations have been confirmed by investigations of mobility within a multiple classification approach. This modeling strategy selects from a set of independent variables, and those variables (in order) that are most powerful classification indicators are selected. Using this approach for owners and renters separately, to control for the fundamental difference that we know exists with respect to mobility and tenure, we find that age, space and income are critical variables related to mobility for owners, and age, size of household (in essence a measure of space needs) and rent are powerful explanatory variables for renters (Clark and Dieleman, 1996).

Several different logit formulations have incorporated specific triggering events as additional elements for understanding the event of mobility. In these models, birth, divorce and other life-changing events are entered into the model and the coefficients reflect the impact of these 'triggering' events. Alternatively, we can plot the conditional probabilities of analogous families with and without the addition of a child. The analyses show that there is clearly a higher conditional probability of moving with the birth of a child in a sample of households from the Netherlands (Clark and Dieleman, 1996).

Now, the traditional modeling strategies for residential mobility are being extended with (1) more elaborate nested logit models, (2) simulation models that incorporate the mobility process as part of the wider decision-making process about residential location, transportation and land-use outcomes and (3) agent-based/automata models of residential mobility. Each of these approaches considerably enriches the simple first-level logit models of the decision to move, which were discussed above, and they make the important step of integrating the choice behavior of individuals into the wider decision-making that occurs in the housing market every day.

As Lee and Waddell (2010) point out, residential mobility and relocation choice are central parts of any attempt to construct integrated transportation and land-use models. Thus, these models move beyond simply looking at the mobility decision to how the mobility decision interacts with other decisions in the housing market. Clark and Onaka (1985) suggested a nested hierarchical model of the choice of moving and the choice of location, and the research by Lee and Waddell (2010) has expanded those ideas. They emphasize what of course is well known: that residential moves and location choices are interrelated decisions that together make up the housing process. Their research, which uses a two-tiered nested logit structure and simple random sampling, produces results that are similar to those found in earlier empirical studies, but what is important is the way in which the model introduces the housing market context. They show that housing price, building type, neighborhood composition and accessibility are important in the mobility locational choice outcomes. It is this multi-dimensional modeling which advances our thinking of mobility and the housing market and which has enabled more complex simulation modeling of the urban structure in general (Waddell, 2002: Waddell et al., 2008).

Residential mobility is only one part of the process of change in urban areas. The general models discussed above, which provide integrated approaches to land-use planning, transportation and environmental quality, are beyond the general review of residential mobility in this chapter but they are important strategies that incorporate residential decision-making as one of the important components of understanding urban growth and urban form (Waddell et al., 2008). A second, or perhaps third generation of these models – UrbanSim – is a disaggregate modeling approach that estimates the demand for real estate at each specified location and includes the decision making of actors (and their choice processes) that influence the patterns of urban development. (See www.urbansim.org for papers which discuss this approach to urban form and housing markets.) The UrbanSim strategies are designed not just to simulate urban growth patterns but to evaluate urban sprawl, housing affordability and the jobs housing balance in urban areas.

Specific models of residential mobility now include agent-based and automata approaches to explaining residential change (Torrens, 2007). These approaches are often hypothetical but provide rich understanding of the mobility process (Berenson, 1998). Agent-based modeling is good at handling human decisions within a structured (conceptual) framework although, as Torrens (2007) points out, the choice rules often do not deal very well with space. What Torrens in his research was able to do was create a special automata model in which individual households interacted with the real estate infrastructure to create 'synthetic communities and artificial property markets' (Torrens, 2007). The model uses a two-stage structure in which agents decide to search and then invoke preferences for different locations. In this sense it reflects the two-stage nested logit models that were discussed in the previous paragraphs. It is these modeling strategies which promise both experimental outcomes of alternative decision-making strategies and the opportunity to experiment with alternative simulation scenarios. Certainly the availability of more sophisticated computational strategies and high-speed computers is changing the way in which we are going about modeling the complex processes of choice in the housing market.

WHAT HAVE WE LEARNED FROM RECENT RESEARCH ON RESIDENTIAL MOBILITY?

We have now an excellent understanding of why people move and about the processes of choice that they engage in during the mobility process. We are fairly confident about our understanding of mobility in the context of age, tenure, the need for housing space and the triggers that lead to residential change. The research has also provided considerable detail on the spatial outcomes of those residential choices – outcomes which vary from the substantial suburbanization that occurred with the expansion of housebuilding and mobility in the two decades after the Second World War, to the spatial changes in inner-city neighborhoods as new ethnic groups moved into the large metropolitan areas of the United States and Europe. We also know a good deal about neighborhood selection and choice, and earlier in the chapter I noted the gains from embedding analyses of mobility within the wider land use and transportation modeling efforts. However, even within the specific analyses of mobility per se, there have been real advances in our understanding of the mobility process. These advances have been particularly important in linking mobility and the housing market. These recent findings have (1) questioned the simplicity of the old distinction between short- and long-distance moves, (2) raised the issue of housing costs in the mobility process, (3) examined the notion of unexpected mobility in the housing market and (4) introduced research on the impacts of two-worker households on residential change. Each of these research literatures is providing new ideas about the links between mobility and housing.

Migration versus mobility

In the past, the tendency for most geographers and spatial demographers was to draw a fairly marked distinction between local moves, which occurred in the same housing market, and longer-distance moves between cities and their labor market areas. Those long-distance moves were usually thought to involve job change and sometimes occupational change. However, recent research, both in the United Kingdom and the United States, suggests that there is a blurring in the distinction between reasons for long-distance and short-distance moves and that both short- and long-distance moves can be followed by either of these types of moves in a fairly short space of time. The suggestion that Goodman (1982) drew three decades ago between the frequent mover and the adjustment hypothesis is now being re-evaluated and, indeed, we would expect that these hypotheses might no longer be as relevant, simply because there has been a substantial change in family structures over the past four decades. The decline in married couple family households has been paralleled with a significant increase in married households without children and single-headed households, especially by women but also by men.

Once the focus was on an individual earner, and thus the decisions about residential movement seemed more straightforward. Movement occurred when the household head changed jobs and when households upgraded the housing required for a growing family. Now it seems that much of what we may be seeing within the framework of employment or housing-related choices and behavior is much more complex. Residential moves are being created by and involve complicated interactions of family change, employment change and housing selection. Sometimes, housing adjustment is the driving force in local moves and sometimes it is important in long-distance moves as well. Similarly, long-distance moves are often housing related and the movers do not report that they moved for jobs. Additionally, moves often reflect connections to family members who need care or who provide care for aging parents. It is true that housing-related moves are more important in local changes, but they only account in the aggregate for half of the reasons for these relocations. For long-distance moves it is much more complex than the previous notions of solely employment-driven moves. It appears that the housing market is playing an important role at both movement scales – locally, and for moves over longer distances between labor markets (Clark and Huang, 2004; Clark and Davies Withers, 2007).

Much of the complexity is created by the enhanced role of women in the long-distance migration process; their exits and entrances to the labor force are an integral part of understanding mobility behavior. Similarly, short-distance moves are not simply generated by changes in a family's interaction with the housing market. The reiteration that there is much less change in tenure with mobility and migration emphasizes that an economic concern with tenure change and ownership is a much less powerful explanation for relocation than is often asserted.

At a primary level, long-distance moves are somewhat explained by employment opportunities and the way in which couples interpret these opportunities. Similarly, short-distance moves are related to the housing market and the way in which households try and bring their housing aspirations into adjustment with the opportunities in the market. But the role of interruptions to the life course and complex family responses to changing opportunities and constraints clearly complicates this overly simplistic interpretation of sequential mobility. Many moves, and even those which are ostensibly for employment or housing reasons, are mixed and at odds with our dichotomous explanations. What does this mean for our analyses of family-related migration and mobility? At the simplest level it means that we must be aware of the greater complexity in human behavior than many of our current models allow and we need to search for sequential models that will allow us to capture the continuous time process of household change and residential relocation. This certainly emphasizes the importance of life-course approaches to migration and mobility.

Housing costs, migration and mobility

Not only do households report that they moved long distances for housing-related reasons but also housing affordability itself has become a central dimension in the residential mobility process. Where past analyses largely viewed the residential choices as occurring within a budget constraint, it now appears that long-distance migration is often specifically affected by the costs of housing in specific labor markets. The models of long-distance migration which assume that the households moved from areas with relatively low wages and/or full employment opportunities to areas with higher wages and more employment opportunities are incomplete at best. The labor theory of interregional migration has only partially recognized that costs of living more generally are central in the migration process. Housing costs can be viewed as a proxy for general costs of living impacts, in the migration process. There is now evidence that housing cost differentials, and the quality of life differences that they reflect, are important motivations for leaving large urban areas, particularly in the current context of hyper-appreciation in housing value (Withers et al., 2008). The challenges of family–work–life balance faced by so many households in the contemporary era of dual-earner families makes the change in housing costs associated with place-to-place migration arguably more important now than previously (Withers and Clark, 2006). Migration is associated with housing affordability adjustments and there are distinct demographic and regional differences in how families make housing cost adjustments with migration. It also appears that the movement down the urban hierarchy may be related to housing cost adjustments (Plane et al., 2005).

Mobility and workforce attachment

Mobility research has also provided important details on the way in which two-worker households have changed the dynamic of residential choice. There is now a very large body of work on the increasingly complex gender relationships in two-worker households and especially in dual-professional households (Green, et al 1999, 2004; Jarvis, 1999; Smits, 1999). Simply, the shift from a one-worker household to two- worker household complicates the mobility decision. It is no longer just a decision about tenure and space and neighborhood location but also about the journey to work for two individuals who may have very different spatial commuting patterns. The growth in the research on family and household mobility and migration reflects two important changes that have occurred in US labor markets in the last quarter of a century. In the 1970s, nearly all couple households (90%) relied on the husband for most of the family income. Twenty-five years later, the 2000 census reported almost the reverse. Only 25% of couple households had a sole-provider husband (Raley et al., 2006). The dramatic increase in wives labor-force participation has changed the migration dynamic. Now families are juggling two jobs when they make migration decisions, and it is no longer simply the husband's job that determines whether or not a move will be made and to where the household will move.

In the context of dual-worker and dual-career households, gendered theories of family migration provide an understanding beyond economic motivations for the rationales and adjustments made by couples in the migration process, particularly the way in which these decisions are embedded within other life-course issues (Boyle et al., 2001). Specifically, the decisions families make about the employment of wives within the context of inter-regional migration may not be explained by adjustments to long-term economic benefits of the husband alone. Thus, within the field of family migration there has been a significant shift in focus from economic outcomes for women towards the interconnection between family and work and, in particular, the non-economic elements of family life. These studies argue that migration outcomes for women need to be considered within the broader context of family structures, including parenting and the linked lives of dual-earner families (Cooke, 2001, 2003; Bailey et al., 2004). Boyle et al. (2001) suggest that migration is much more than a mechanism of economic adjustment, stressing family migrations and their outcomes, and are best understood as resulting from gendered family decision-making processes. This literature, which has been widely reviewed (Clark and Davies Withers, 2002; Cooke, 2003) demonstrates that the outcomes for women are not always positive and are frequently associated with lost earnings, interrupted labor-force participation and unemployment or underemployment, with consequent affects on housing market behavior (Clark and Huang, 2006).

Finally, we are beginning to recognize that the processes of entry and exit to the labor market are much more volatile and dynamic than at any time in the past. The labor market has changed and so has the nature of participation. Clark and Davies Withers (2002) and Clark and Huang (2006) established that, even though migrant wives are not necessarily disadvantaged by family migration, there was considerable job fluidity for migrants, local movers and even those who were residentially stable. While we often conceptualize employment as long spells with one employer and in one occupation, the shift to a service economy has destabilized employment spells. While long spells in employment are clearly relevant for professional workers, in fact, much of the mobility in and out of the labor force is not in the professional occupations and is frequent and unstable. A more detailed understanding of the dynamism of labor-force participation and the impacts and interactions of families will provide us with better ways to conceptualize the interdependencies of employment and mobility and housing market behavior.

Exogenous impacts on mobility

Mobility research until relatively recently tended to downplay unexpected or unanticipated residential relocation. Traditional research tended to emphasize the links of mobility and migration either to housing or to jobs, but recent studies of reasons for moves suggest that unintended moves are an increasing proportion of all relocations. Studies with the Panel Study of Income Dynamics (PSID) show that nearly a quarter of all moves are certainly reported as being unrelated to housing or jobs (Clark and Davies Withers, 2007). It is these moves, unrelated to what theory suggests, which emphasize the need for rethinking the impact of exogenous forces on mobility and migration decisions. The rising number of these moves reiterates studies in the England and Europe, more generally, on the role of deprivation and mobility outcomes (see Chapter 23). Moves can occur from a variety of outside events, such as being evicted, or changes in health status, or from family change including divorce and death, or from job loss. If a quarter of all moves are in fact unintended, it forces us to re-evaluate the tension between choice and constraint approaches to the mobility process. We might think of a continuum of moving intentions, from the unintended to the predetermined and planned, but all representing a complex link between family lives and residential needs. The research suggests that what we have been setting within the framework of purposive employment or housing-related choice and the following housing selection is much more complex and that serendipitous forces play an important role in the mobility process.

Numerous studies cite residential dissatisfaction as a common reason for local moves, but beyond this we have only limited substantive research on people's intentions to move and whether they act upon these intentions (Lu, 1999). There is still not very much research which actively investigates either unintended mobility or failed mobility – those who have moved and returned to their previous location. Two recent papers have made a call for greater consideration of the intentionality of migration and mobility. Smith (2004) builds on Halfacre's (1995) thesis of the intentional/unintentional agency of family migrants, and both authors call for fuller understanding of non-economic reasons and outcomes in the family migration process. Interestingly, while academia has been reticent, the law has not. The Internal Revenue Service has codified what constitutes the 'unforeseen circumstances' of moving in the context of liability for capital gains tax on income derived from the selling of a home. The allowable events include disasters, death of a spouse, becoming unemployed, financial burden due to employment changes, divorce or legal separation and multiple births from the same pregnancy (Silow, 2006). All of these are triggers for relocation, including the last one which depicts unexpected space stress. The common thread amongst these is the unintended nature of the event. To reiterate, that a quarter of all of US moves recorded in the PSID report that something other than jobs or housing adjustment was the most important fact in their mobility behavior emphasizes that our models are still far from complete in terms of explaining and predicting residential mobility in metropolitan areas.

What we have learned recently does not negate the findings from previous research but it does emphasize the need to situate the mobility research both within the changing family dynamic and in the changing economic contexts of our metropolitan areas.

POLICY AND MOBILITY – PUTTING OUR KNOWLEDGE TO WORK

Within the context of concerns over the potential for a growing urban underclass and the associated concerns with enlarging poverty *concentrations* (although the percent in poverty actually declined in the 1990s in the US), there has been increased interest in whether inner-city minority households can escape poverty neighborhoods and whether government assistance can increase those probabilities (Sampson et al., 2002; Varady and Walker, 2003; Briggs, 2005; Varady, 2005; Clark, 2008). To examine whether it is possible to change poverty concentrations, policymakers looked to residential mobility as a way to provide relocation opportunities for low-income families generally and families in poverty in particular. In the 1990s, a tentative consensus emerged that enabling low-income families to move from high- to low-poverty neighborhoods had the potential to reduce the levels of income segregation and, as a corollary, the degree of racial separation (for a discussion of ethnic residential segregation see Chapter 22).

Housing voucher programs were introduced to allow poor inner-city households to increase their access to neighborhoods beyond those often decaying inner-city blocks in large American cites. In turn, these moves might enhance their employment and educational opportunities and diminish their exposure to crime, violence and drugs. Certainly, some commentators suggested that these programs would both benefit individual families and have the potential to de-concentrate poverty. Although the program of housing vouchers was not specifically designed to integrate minority populations, the implication of moving to lower-poverty neighborhoods would have gains in living in more mixed neighborhoods as well.

Housing vouchers in the United States, also known as the Section 8 vouchers, are designed to provide a voucher to allow a household meeting certain program requirements to seek rental housing within specific urban communities. In some cases the vouchers were ' more portable' than in others: i.e. they could be used to rent housing outside of specific municipalities and so increase the housing opportunities for low-income families. The shift to housing vouchers was a move away from previous HUD (Housing and Urban Development) programs which authorize projects of fixed low-income housing largely in inner-city communities.

Because of the interest in an expanded voucher program and its potential for greater mobility on the part of low-income families, a 'Moving to Opportunity' (MTO) program was initiated in 1992 with a mandate from Congress to the Department of Housing and Urban Development. The program was designed to test the usefulness of housing vouchers for generating moves away from low-poverty areas and into integrated residential settings. Five cities – Baltimore, Boston, Chicago, Los Angeles and New York – were selected to participate in the experimental program. It examined the behavior of those who were given special help in moving (counseling and mobility assistance) in contrast with a group of regular Section 8 movers and a baseline control group who were not given either vouchers or special help. Of course, the baseline control group could move without assistance and many did. The Section 8 group received a voucher and regular housing assistance counseling; the experimental group, the special movers, received a voucher and special mobility counseling but they were required to move to a low-poverty neighborhood (less than 10% poverty according to the 1990 census).

Several reports and independent analyses of the MTO program have now been published and there is considerable debate about the gains from the special counseling section of the experiment. While the Orr (Orr et al., 2004) and Rosenbaum reports (1995) suggest that there are real gains from the special program and some suggest it could be the basis for a nationwide mobility program (Goering, 2005), others suggest the gains are more limited and may not be significantly greater than those achieved with the regular Section 8 program.

It is not straightforward to test whether or not there are gains from the additional counseling of the mobility program (MTO) over the simple provision of Section 8 vouchers. Should all cities be aggregated as the Orr report does, or should the tests be for individual cities? Should the tests be against the baseline group or should the MTO recipients be tested against the regular Section 8 voucher holders? Finally, should those who were participants in the study, but who were not able to find a house or apartment under the MTO rules, be 'added back in' to the sample before the tests. In other words, should the tests be only of movers or of all respondents (the 'intent to treat' group in the language of experimental medical testing, for example).

Tests of movers only, show that for all cities the original MTO movers are significantly more likely to be in low-poverty neighborhoods. But, over time, the MTO movers have not been able to maintain their low-poverty locations. Sometimes they have moved again; in other cases the neighborhood has changed to become poorer. On an individual city basis, in three cases the current MTO and the current Section 8 locations are different from each other, but for Los Angeles and Boston they are not. Geography matters, and the different contexts generate different outcomes. That for three cities there are greater gains in being in a lower-poverty neighborhood for experimental movers than for Section 8 movers is a finding which is evidence in support of the gains of the special MTO program. However, when movers and non-movers are aggregated, the story is less compelling. It is hard to make strong claims for the 'experiment' on the basis of the distributions of outcomes when there are few differences between the MTO outcomes and the outcomes for Section 8 vouchers.

An analysis of the mobility rates across the five cities provides additional data on the problems of controlled choice programs. While the Section 8 recipients had relatively high mobility rates, across all cities, only in Los Angeles was there a rate which provides confidence in the ability of a controlled program to generate successful mobility. For the other cities mobility rates hovered around 50%, with dramatically lower results in Chicago. These findings emphasize the difficulty of dispersing poverty with experimental programs. The fact that there are significant gains for households who receive no help speaks to the important role of residential mobility in general. It is certainly plausible that individually motivated choice is likely to make major changes in the patterns of poverty as much as program intervention itself.

The results from comparing aided and ordinary mobility reiterate the great difficulty of intervening in the dynamic of household relocation. Consistent with our knowledge of mobility in general, subsequent moves by the MTO group were often to neighborhoods like the ones they came from, and in some cases back to their old neighborhoods. Once again, we can identify the powerful role of housing choices and preferences, which favor known neighborhoods where there are friends, family and support relationships. Households vote with their feet, as Tiebout (1956) observed, and decisions by governments are always embedded in the dynamic demography of the city. Income and assets are important and integral parts of the choice process, as are preferences, and these forces play an ongoing role in the way in which households choose places to live.

The fact that many unaided households still managed to improve their housing situations further emphasizes that mobility is a powerful and fundamental force in the housing market. The fact that the unaided households also made changes is not unexpected though, as all households who participated in the sample – those who were selected to receive a voucher and those in the control group who did not – were all motivated to move. The fact that a significant number of the sample respondents without aid have made gains in moving to low-poverty neighborhoods is sufficient to raise questions about how we can best intervene in communities and neighborhoods.

Overall, it seems that while there are initial gains from moving, those gains decline over time as individuals make additional locational choices. It is a recurrent theme of work on mobility and housing that it is difficult to intervene in a dynamic system of residential choices and people do not 'stay put'; they move, often frequently, to bring their housing needs into adjustment with their housing space. Perhaps it is obvious now, but the notion that 'one-shot' intervention with a voucher and counseling would change spatial patterns was certainly overly optimistic and is an important policy lesson more generally.

SUMMARY OBSERVATIONS

An understanding of residential mobility and relocation in cities is a core part of understanding the operation of the housing market. It is the changes in household location which, in the end, create the change in the urban mosaic. While the unrelated individual moves operate without connection, their aggregate outcomes generate the changes in communities and neighborhoods which later become the visible signs of urban change from ethnic composition to changes in housing occupancy composition. As households move to newly built housing and leave older housing, they create the vacancy chains that allow movement in the housing market. While rates of mobility change over time, and while some households are more able to move than others, mobility remains the engine of behavioral change which is at the heart of our dynamic urban systems.

REFERENCES

Ben-Akiva, M. and Lerman, S. R. (1985) *Discrete Choice Analysis: Theory and Application to Travel Demand.* Cambridge, MA: MIT Press.

Berenson, I. (1998) Multi-agent simulation of residential dynamics in the city. *Computers, Environment and Urban Systems* 22: 25–42.

Boyle, P., Cooke, T. J., Halfacre, K. and Smith, D. (2001) A cross-national comparison of the impact of family migration on women's employment status. *Demography* 38: 201–213.

Briggs, X. (2005) *The Geography of Opportunity.* Washington, DC: Brookings Institution.

Clark, W. A. V. (2008) Re-examining the moving to opportunity study and its contribution to changing the distribution of poverty and ethnic concentration. *Demography* 45: 515–535.

Clark W. A. V. and Davies Withers, S. (2002) Disentangling the interaction of migration, mobility and labor force participation. *Environment and Planning A* 34: 923–945.

Clark, W. A.V. and Davies Withers, S. (2007) Family migration and mobility sequences in the United States: Spatial mobility in the context of the life course. *Demographic Research* (Max Planck Institute for Demographic Research) 17(20): 591–622.

Clark, W. A. V. and Deurloo, M. (2006) Aging in place and housing over-consumption. *Journal of the Built Environment* 21: 257–270.

Clark, W. A. V. and Dieleman, F. (1996) *Households and Housing: Choice and Outcomes in the*

Housing Market. Rutgers State University, Center for Urban Policy Research.

Clark, W. A. V. and Huang, Y. (2003) The life course and residential mobility in British Housing markets. *Environment and Planning A* 35: 323–339.

Clark, W. A. V. and Huang, Y. (2004) Linking migration and mobility: Individual and contextual effects in housing markets in the UK. *Regional Studies* 38: 617–628.

Clark W. A. V. and Huang, Y. (2006) Balancing move and work: Women's labour market exits and entries after family migration. *Population, Space and Place* 12: 31–44.

Clark W. A. V. and Ledwith, V. (2006) Mobility, housing stress and neighborhood contexts: Evidence from Los Angeles. *Environment and Planning A* 38: 1077–1093.

Clark, W. A. V. and Onaka, J. L. (1985) An empirical test of a joint model of residential mobility and housing choice, *Environment and Planning A* 17: 915–930.

Clark, W. A. V. and van Lierop, W. (1986) Residential mobility and household location modeling. In P. Nijkamp (ed.), *Handbook of Regional and Urban Economics*, Volume 1. Amsterdam: Elsevier.

Cooke, T. J. (2001) Trailing 'wife' or 'trailing mother? The effect of parental status on the relationship between family migration and the labor-market participation of married women. *Environment and Planning A* 33: 419–430.

Cooke, T. J. (2003) Family migration and the relative earnings of husbands and wives. *Annals, Association of American Geographers* 93: 338–349.

Cooke, T. J. (2008) Migration in a family way. *Population, Space and Place* 14: 255–265.

Goering, J. (2005) Expanding housing choice and integrating neighborhoods: The MTO experiment. In X. Briggs (ed.), *The Geography of Opportunity: Race and Housing Choice in Metropolitan America*. Washington, DC: Brookings Institution, pp.128–149.

Goodman, J. (1982) Linking local mobility rates to migration rates: Repeat movers and place effects. In Modeling Housing Market Search. Clark, W.A.V. (ed) London, Croom Helm, pp. 209–223.

Green, A. E., Hogarth, T. and Shackleton, R. E. (1999) Longer distance commuting as a substitute for migration in Britain: A review of trends, issues, and implications. *International Journal of Population Geography* 5: 49–67.

Green, A. (2004) Is relocation redundant? Observations on the changing nature and impacts of employment related geographical mobility in the UK. *Regional Studies* 38: 629–641.

Halfacre, K. (1995) Household migration and the structure of patriarchy: Evidence from the USA. *Progress in Human Geography* 19: 159–182.

Hanuschek, E. and Quigley, J. (1978). An explicit model of intra-metropolitan mobility. *Land Economics* 54: 411–429.

Helderman, A., Mulder, C. and van Ham, M. (2004) The changing effects of homeownership on residential mobility in the Netherlands, 1980–1998. *Housing Studies* 19: 601–616.

Helderman, A. van Ham, M. and Mulder, C. (2006) Migration and homeownership. *Tijdscrift voor Economische en Sociale Geografie* 97: 111–125.

Jarvis, H. (1999) Identifying the relative mobility prospects of a variety of household employment structures, 1981–1991. *Environment and Planning A* 31: 1031–1046.

Lee, B. H. and Waddell, P. (2010) Residential mobility and location choice: A nested logit model with sampling of alternatives. *Transportation* 37: 587–601.

Lu, M. (1999) Do people move when they say they will? Inconsistencies in individual migration behavior. *Population and Environment* 20: 467–488.

McFadden, D. (1974) Conditional logit model analysis of qualitative choice behavior, In P. Zarembka (ed.), *Frontiers in Econometrics*. New York: Academic Press.

Manski, S. (1993) Identification problem in the social sciences. In P. Marsden (ed.), *Sociological Methodology*. Cambridge: Blackwell.

Mulder, C. H. (1993). *Migration Dynamics: A Life Course Approach*. Amsterdam: Thesis Publishers – PDOD Publications.

Myers, D. (1990) *Housing Demography: Linking Demographic Structure and Housing Markets*. Madison, WI: University of Wisconsin Press.

National Association of Home Builders (2006) *Housing Facts, Figures and Trends for March 2006*.

Orr, L., Feins, J., Jacob, R. and Beecroft, E. (2003) *Moving to Opportunity: Interim Impacts Evaluation: Final Report*. Washington, DC: Department of Housing and Urban Development, Office of Policy Development and Research.

Permentier, M., van Ham, M. and Bolt, G. (2007). Behavioral responses to neighborhood reputations. *Journal of Housing and the Built Environment* 22: 199–213.

Permentier, M. van Ham, M. and Bolt, G. (2009) Neighborhood reputation and the intention to leave the neighborhood *Environment and Planning A* 41: 2162–2180.

Plane, D. A., Henrie, C. J. and Perry, M. J. (2005) Spatial demography special feature: Migration up and down the urban hierarchy and across the life course. *Proceedings of the National Academy of Sciences* 102: 15313–15318.

Raley, S., Mattingley, M. and Bianchi, S. (2006) How dual are dual income couples? Documenting change from 1970–2001. *Journal of Marriage and the Family* 68: 11–28.

Richardson, H., Gordon, P. and Lee, B. (2004) *Commuting Trends in US Cities in the 1990s*. Los Angeles, CA: USC Lusk Center for Real Estate.

Rosenbaum, J. (1995) Changing the geography of opportunity by expanding residential choice: Lessons from the Gautreaux program. *Housing Policy Debate* 6: 231–269.

Sampson, R. J., Morenoff, J. and Gannon-Rowley, T. (2002) Assessing neighborhood effects: Social processes and new directions in research. *Annual Review of Sociology* 28: 443–478.

Schachter, J. (2001) *Why People Move: Exploring the March 2000 Current Population Survey*. Washington, DC: US Census Bureau, Current Population Reports, P23–204.

Silow, M. (2006) Selling a home due to 'unforeseen circumstances'. *New Jersey Law Journal* 01/30/2006.

Smith, D. (2004) An untied research agenda for family migration: loosening the shackles of the past. *Journal of Ethnic and Migration Studies* 30: 263–282.

Smits, J. (1999) Family migration and the labor force participation of married women in the Netherlands 1977–1966. *International Journal of Population Geography* 5: 133–150.

Tiebout, C. (1956) A pure theory of local expenditures. *Journal of Political Economy* 64: 418–424.

Torrens, P. (2007) A geographic automata model of residential mobility. *Environment and Planning B: Planning and Design* 34: 200–222.

Van Ham, M. and Clark, W. A. V. (2009) Neighborhood mobility in context: household moves and changing neighborhoods in the Netherlands. *Environment and Planning A* 41: 1442–1459.

Van Ham, M and Feijten, P. (2008) Who wants to leave the neighborhood? The effect of being different from the neighborhood population on wishes to move. *Environment and Planning A* 40: 1151–1170.

Varady, D. (2005) *Desegregating the City: Ghettos, Enclaves and Inequality*. Albany, NY: State University of New York Press.

Varady, D. and Walker, C. (2003) Using housing vouchers to move to the suburbs: How do families fare? *Housing Policy Debate* 14: 347–382.

Waddell, P. (2002) UrbanSim: Modeling urban development for land use, transportation and environmental planning. *Journal of the American Planning Association* 68: 297–314.

Waddell, P., Wang, L. and Liu, X. (2008) UrbanSim: An evolving panning support system for evolving communities. In R. Brail (ed.), *Planning Support Systems for Cities and Regions*. Cambridge, MA: Lincoln Institute for Land Policy, pp. 103–138.

Withers, S. and Clark, W. A. V. (2006) Expectations and outcomes: The geography of family migration. *Population Space and Place* 12: 273–289.

Withers, Suzanne Davies, Clark, W. A. V. and Ruiz, T. 2008. Demographic variation in housing cost adjustments with US family migration. *Population Space and Place* 14: 305–325.

Neighborhoods and Their Role in Creating and Changing Housing

George Galster

In a fundamental sense, housing and neighborhood are inseparable. By its very nature, a dwelling unit is attached to a geographic place, typically for its entire lifetime. The demographic, socio-economic, architectural, political, topographical and environmental characteristics of these places vary dramatically, of course, both across places and, often, across time for a single place. But what is more important for the study of housing is that these variations matter greatly to all the key housing sector actors: households, dwelling owners, business owners, public officials, mortgage lenders, and home insurers. Households believe that the neighborhood affects their quality of life and the future opportunities of their children, property owners and business people believe that the neighborhood affects their risk-adjusted rates of financial return, and public officials believe that the neighborhood affects the quality of public services that will be demanded and the efficiency at which they can be supplied. All of these dimensions are summarized by the well-known adage about what is crucial in real estate: 'location, location, location.'

Given its central importance to so many key constituents, it is no wonder that the neighborhood has been the focus of scholarly investigations by economists, sociologists, political scientists, geographers, historians, and planners, among others.[1] In this chapter I will synthesize the main strands of this scholarship and offer suggestions of the central questions requiring further investigations. The chapter is structured around the following questions: What does neighborhood mean? Does a neighborhood have boundaries? What are the idiosyncrasies of neighborhoods? How do neighborhoods come to be? What causes neighborhoods to change? What is the nature of neighborhood change? Are neighborhood change processes socially efficient and equitable? Do neighborhoods independently shape the opportunities for adults and children residing in them?

WHAT DOES NEIGHBORHOOD MEAN?

Urban social scientists have provided disparate answers. Many scholars have employed a purely ecological perspective. For example, Keller (1968: 89) defines neighborhood as a 'place with physical and symbolic boundaries.' Morris and Hess (1975: 6) label it 'place and people, with the common sense limit as the area one can easily walk over. ' Golab (1982: 72) uses the phrase 'a physical or geographical entity with specific (subjective) boundaries.'

Others have attempted to integrate social and ecological perspectives, as in Hallman's (1984: 13) definition: 'a limited territory within a larger urban area, where people inhabit dwellings and interact socially.' Warren (1981: 62) defines neighborhood as 'a social organization of a population residing in a geographically proximate locale.' 'Geographic units within which certain social relationships exist,' is the term suggested by Downs (1981: 15). Schoenberg (1979: 69) specifies the neighborhood's defining characteristics as: 'common named boundaries, more than one institution identified with the area, and more than one tie of shared public space or social network.'

All these definitions suffer from common shortcomings. They presume either a certain (if unspecified) degree of spatial extent and/or social interrelationships within that space, and they underplay numerous other features of the local residential environment that clearly affect its quality from the perspective of residents, property owners, public officials, and investors.

I believe that our understanding can be advanced by defining neighborhood as follows:

> Neighborhood is the bundle of spatially based attributes associated with clusters of residences, sometimes in conjunction with other land uses.

This definition owes it intellectual genesis to the work of Lancaster (1966), who originally formulated the notion of complex commodities as a multi-dimensional bundle comprised of simpler (albeit sometimes abstract) goods. In this application, the spatially based attributes comprising the complex commodity called 'neighborhood' consist of:

- structural characteristics of the residential and non-residential buildings – type, scale, materials, design, state of repair, density, landscaping, etc.
- infrastructural characteristics – roads, sidewalks, streetscaping, utility services, etc.
- demographic characteristics of the resident population – age distribution, family composition, racial, ethnic, and religious group mix, etc.
- class status characteristics of the resident population – income, occupation, and education composition
- tax/public service package characteristics – the quality of safety forces, public schools, public administration, parks and recreation, etc., in relation to the local taxes assessed
- environmental characteristics – degree of land, air, water, and noise pollution, topographical features, views, etc.
- proximity characteristics – access to major destinations of employment, entertainment, shopping, etc., as influenced by both distance and transportation infrastructure
- political characteristics – the degree to which local political networks are mobilized, residents exert influence in local affairs through spatially rooted channels or elected representatives[2]
- social-interactive characteristics – intra- and extra-neighborhood networks, degree of inter-household familiarity, type and quality of interpersonal associations, residents' perceived commonality, participation in locally based voluntary associations, strength of socialization, and social control forces, etc.[3] sentimental characteristics – residents' sense of identification with place, historical significance of buildings or district, etc.

The unifying feature of these attributes constituting the bundle called neighborhood is that they are *spatially based*. The characteristics of any attribute can be observed and measured only after a particular *location* has been specified. This is not to say that neighborhoods are homogeneous on any attribute, merely that a distribution or profile can be ascertained once a space has been arbitrarily demarcated. Moreover, to say that attributes are spatially based does not mean that they are intrinsically coupled with the geography: some are (infrastructure, topography, buildings), whereas others are associated with individuals who lend their collective attribute to the space purely through aggregation (race, income, life-cycle stage).

I emphasize that, while most of the attributes above usually are present to some extent in all neighborhoods, the quantity and composition of constituent attributes typically vary dramatically across neighborhoods within a single metropolitan area, let alone internationally. This implies that, depending on the attribute package they embody, neighborhoods can be distinctly categorized by type and/or by quality. This is, of course, a tenet of social area analysis (Greer, 1962; Hunter, 1974). However, unlike that school of thought, I extend the dimensions over which neighborhoods can be classified beyond the demographic- and status-related. The extension is necessary if one is to understand neighborhood change, for key decision makers evaluate more than merely the demographic and status attributes of a space before investing in it or moving into it.

Moreover, in instances where a certain dimension (social-interactive or sentimental, for example) of the neighborhood bundle is virtually absent at a certain location, 'neighborhood' in this dimension can be thought of as being absent there. Thus, implicit in my definition is the notion that the *type and even existence* of neighborhoods can and often does vary across urban space. This could be termed 'the degree of presence of neighborhood'.[4]

Commodities are consumed, of course, and in this sense neighborhood is no exception. Four distinct types of users potentially reap benefits from the consumption of neighborhood: households, businesses, property owners, and local government.[5] Households consume neighborhood through the act of occupying a residential unit and using the surrounding private and public spaces, thereby gaining some degree of satisfaction or quality of residential life. Businesses consume neighborhood through the act of occupying a non-residential structure (store, office, factory), thereby gaining a certain flow of net revenues or profits associated with that venue. Property owners consume neighborhood by extracting rents and/or capital gains from the land and buildings owned in that location. Local governments consume neighborhood by extracting tax revenues, typically from owners based on the assessed values of residential and non-residential properties.

DOES A NEIGHBORHOOD HAVE BOUNDARIES?

The fact that, once a space has been arbitrarily specified, spatially based attributes can be measured does not imply, unfortunately, that *neighborhood* takes on an unambiguous spatial character. If all attributes were to vary across the same spatial scales *and* these scales could be demarcated by congruent boundaries, where one neighborhood stopped and another began (i.e., each attribute in the attribute bundle changed) could be designated in unambiguous geographic terms. However, the geographic scale across which an attribute varies often is wildly dissimilar among attributes. For example, structural characteristics may vary dramatically over a few meters, whereas public educational quality may only differ among enrollment zones for elementary schools, and air quality may be virtually constant across vast swaths of a metropolitan area. More scholarship is needed in this realm. It could profitably employ advances in geographic information system (GIS) technology to measure the scales over which these attributes vary.

Thus, my definition does not lead to the Holy Grail sought by much neighborhood analysis of the 20th century: a means of unambiguously, meaningfully bounding urban neighborhoods. On the contrary, it suggests that any particular space is *nested*, with a different level of the spatial hierarchy associated with different components of its attribute bundle. It follows that households, investors, and scholars should select a different parsing of urban space, depending on the particular neighborhood attributes (or, equivalently, the neighborhood typology) of interest.[6]

This implication is consonant with Suttles' (1972) conceptualization suggesting a multi-level spatial view of neighborhood. He argued that urban households could identify four scales of 'neighborhood.' At the smallest scale was the block face, the area over which children could be permitted to play without supervision. The second level was labeled the 'defended neighborhood,' the smallest area possessing a corporate identity as defined by mutual opposition or contrast to another area. The third level, the 'community of limited liability,' typically consisted of some local governmental body's district in which individuals' social participation was selective and voluntary. The highest geographic scale of neighborhood, the 'expanded community of limited liability,' was viewed as an entire sector of the city. Subsequent surveys (Birch et al., 1979, Ch. 3; Pebley and Vaiana, 2002) have revealed that residents do, indeed, conceive of distinct spatial levels of neighborhood, which correspond closely to Suttles' theory. In the context of my definition, I interpret the foregoing as suggesting that residents perceive clusters of neighborhood attributes that vary at the same scale across roughly congruent spaces.

Moreover, it is precisely these *perceptions* of boundaries that are most critical in constructing theories or predictive models of neighborhood change. As I will explicate further below, the stock of attributes constituting neighborhood at any point are produced by flows of resources, and these flows will be governed by perceptions of key actors. The extent to which they will modify their resource flows will depend on whether they perceive that attributes of relevance within *their* perceptual bounding of neighborhood have changed.

In earlier work (Galster, 1986), I attempted to formulate this in terms of 'neighborhood externality space.' I defined a person's externality space as the area over which changes in one or more spatially based attributes initiated by others are perceived as altering the well-being (use value, psychological, and/or financial benefits) the individual derives from the particular location.[7] I formulated three (quantifiable) features of these externality spaces:

- 'congruence' – the degree to which an individual's externality spaces correspond to particular, predetermined geographic boundaries
- 'generality' – the degree to which an individual's externality spaces for different spatially based attributes correspond
- 'accordance' – the degree to which externality spaces for different individuals located in close proximity correspond.

The specification of neighborhood as a bundle of spatially based attributes, coupled with the notion of externality space and its aforementioned three dimensions, allows for the potential empirical identification of behaviorally meaningful boundaries of 'neighborhood.' For a predetermined spatial set of individuals, should there be an area over which accordance and generality (for a certain subset of attributes) were high, it would imply that boundaries could be reasonably specified for that scale of neighborhood. If accordance and generality were low for all attributes, one would conclude that no meaningful spatial bounding existed for that group and their perceptual neighborhood.

The aforementioned works suggest in this context that, for a certain subset of attributes among which there is high generality, there are, indeed, high degrees of accordance and congruence at the block-face scale. Analogously, for a different subset of attributes, there are high degrees of accordance and congruence at the 'defended community' scale. The boundaries of this scale often seem to correspond to major streets

(Suttles, 1972; Appleyard and Lintell, 1986; Grannis, 1998). However, we know little about the degree to which these conclusions may be generalized across ethnic or income groups, or across national contexts. Future scholarship might well employ advances in portable microcomputing and GIS technology to uncover how residents and investors specify and modify their 'mental maps' of neighborhoods, and the degree to which specifications produce consistently bounded spaces at distinct, nested spatial scales.

WHAT ARE THE IDIOSYNCRASIES OF NEIGHBORHOODS?

Above, I explained how attributes comprising neighborhood are spatially based yet inconsistent in their geographic variability, which yielded some challenging implications for the potential bounding of neighborhood. Here I discuss four additional aspects of spatially based attributes and the idiosyncrasies that result for neighborhoods. These aspects are cross-attribute variation in durability, cross-attribute variation in ability to be priced, relativistic evaluations of attributes by consumers, and consumption impacts on attributes.

The spatially based attributes comprising neighborhood vary in their durability. Some, like certain topographical features, are permanent, save major cataclysms. Sewer infrastructure and buildings typically last generations. Others, such as tax/public service packages and demographic and status profiles of an area, can change over a year. The area's social interrelationships can be altered even more rapidly. The implication of this observation is as follows. Although some of the key features that define a desirable neighborhood from the perspective of its many consumers can be counted on to remain constant (and therefore predictable) for extended periods, others cannot. This means that consumers' *predictions* about future changes in these less-durable features will play a major role in determining decisions about mobility, financial investments, and psychological investments in neighborhoods over the long term.

The spatially based attributes comprising neighborhood vary in their ability to be priced by market mechanisms. In order for potential consumers to make bid offers for a commodity they must have some modicum of information about the quantity and quality of that commodity and what likely benefit they would receive from its consumption. Real estate markets have been shown to meet this criterion for a vast number of spatially based attributes: indeed, such is the foundation of over three decades of empirical work estimating 'hedonic indexes'.[8] These studies have shown that attributes like structural size and quality, accessibility, tax/public service packages, demographic and status composition of residents, and pollution can be priced and accurately reflect bidders' willingness to pay. However, most social interactive dimensions of neighborhood cannot be priced well because they are hard *ex ante* for prospective bidders to assess. The idiosyncratic and personalized nature of neighborhood social interactions means that prospective in-movers will only be able to ascertain how they will 'fit in' after an extended period of residence. One implication is that long-term residents may have considerably different market evaluations ('reservation prices') for their neighborhood than prospective residents or investors because the former have capitalized (positively or negatively) their assessments of the social interactive dimension. Thus, the former may be highly resistant to external market forces when they assess a positive social environment, and may be more easily outbid and eventually supplanted by new owners and residents when they assess a negative one. Another implication is that neighborhoods are particularly prone to forms of insider dealing, with privileged information communicated to preferred buyers and in-movers by current residents, owners, and their market intermediaries. The degree to which this selection occurs and affects the course of neighborhoods is a fertile area for future scholarship (for a discussion of socio-spatial interpretations of housing spaces see Chapter 8).

Even if the market can price attributes comprising neighborhood, however, their price will typically be based on a comparison of attributes in competing neighborhoods, not on the intrinsic characteristics of the attribute set.[9] Perhaps the most obvious example is the status dimension. The absolute income levels of households in a particular neighborhood may rise, but if they are rising at least as quickly in all other neighborhoods in the metropolitan area there likely will be no change in consumers' evaluations of that neighborhood's status attribute. Analogous arguments can be made regarding other attributes, such as proximity, school quality, and public safety. The upshot is that, when new neighborhoods are created through large-scale construction or rehabilitation projects, they can change the relative attractiveness of existing neighborhoods. And because *relative* evaluations will alter flows of resources across space, *absolute* changes in the existing neighborhoods will follow (Galster, 1987: Ch. 2; Grigsby et al., 1987). There need to be more empirical investigations aimed at uncovering how households and investors develop their evaluations of neighborhoods, what sources of information they use, and the extent to which they apply relativistic or absolutist criteria.

The final idiosyncrasy is that the spatially based attributes comprising neighborhood can change by the very act of consuming them. This can occur directly and indirectly. Directly, as households consume neighborhood by occupying residences in it, they may simultaneously alter the demographic and/or socioeconomic status profile of the neighborhood if the in-moving households differ systematically from longer-term residents. Analogously, a different type of ownership of homes or stores may emerge if the consumption changes to absentee-owned instead of owner-occupier, for example. Indirectly, changes in the occupancy and/or ownership profiles of a neighborhood not only change tautologically their current attributes but also may trigger longer-term changes in a wider variety of attributes. This can occur if the occupancy or ownership changes yield different decisions by current or prospective consumers of the neighborhood that affect the flows of resources into that space, a topic I discuss in more depth in the following section. Suffice it to note here the corollary of this point: attributes of neighborhood are mutually causal over time. Changes in one attribute may change decisions by one or more type of consumer, which lead, in turn, to changes in other attributes, and so on (Galster, 1987: Ch. 2; Grigsby et al., 1987; Temkin and Rohe, 1996).

HOW DO NEIGHBORHOODS COME TO BE?

Although it is tempting to conceive of neighborhood as a commodity with fixed, clearly defined characteristics, it is more appropriately viewed in a more dynamic perspective. The attributes comprising neighborhood at any moment are, in fact, the result of past and (typically) current flows of households and resources – financial, social-psychological, and time – into and out of the space in question (Galster, 1987: Ch.2). Certainly, when a subdivision of homes is newly constructed one might say that a neighborhood has come into being, though without household occupants it is not yet a fully formed neighborhood. From that moment of construction on, what attributes that place will possess – what that neighborhood will *be* – will be shaped by the decisions of current and prospective 'consumers.'

Thus, in a fundamental way, the *consumers* of neighborhood can be considered the *producers* of neighborhood as well. Households consume a neighborhood by choosing to occupy it, thereby producing an attribute to that location related to that household's demographic characteristics, status, civil behaviors, participation in local voluntary associations and social networks, and so forth. Property owners consume a neighborhood by buying land and/or buildings in it; they subsequently produce the neighborhood's attributes through their decisions regarding property construction, upkeep, rehabilitation, or abandonment. Business people consume a neighborhood by operating firms there, thereby producing attributes related to structure types, land use, pollution, and accessibility. Governments consume neighborhood by extracting tax revenue and, in turn, produce attributes associated with public services and infrastructure; in some contexts they also produce social housing in the neighborhood.

The list of producers of importance to any neighborhood is expansive and diverse. It includes not only the aforementioned consumers: households, property owners, business people, and local governments. It also includes, in a secondary but nevertheless important way, those in the real estate brokerage, insurance, and mortgage finance sectors. It includes those who currently reside, own property, and/or earn income or tax revenues there, and those who do not but *may* under certain future circumstances. It includes those who perceive a vested financial or social-psychological interest in the area and those who do not. It includes those who make decisions using the cold calculus of profit maximization, those who consider sentiment and personal satisfaction, and still others who are motivated by political pressures.

The mobility, purchasing, and resource allocation decisions related to neighborhoods (what I will refer to hereafter as generic 'investing') are inherently fraught with an unusual amount of uncertainty. First, although the neighborhood as a whole affects the well-being (variously measured) of each consumer/producer, what happens to that neighborhood is a function of changes in numerous constituent attributes, each of which has an indeterminate future to varying degrees. Secondly, there is the aforementioned large number of consumers/producers of different types and motivations. The aggregate behavior of this panoply of actors is difficult to gauge, yet the decisions by one will affect directly and indirectly the investment outcomes of all. Finally, the flows of resources (money, people, power) across all neighborhoods in a metropolitan area will be influenced by uncertain metro-wide factors related to the regional economy, technological innovation, population and immigration, national government policy, and vagaries of nature (Temkin and Rohe, 1996).

This high uncertainty translates into substantial long-term risk because, once made, investments of resources in neighborhoods are not easily reversible. Many sorts of potential investments, such as choosing to occupy or own a dwelling, have substantial out-of-pocket and psychological transactions costs, costs which consumers/producers are loathe to incur on a frequent basis. Other sorts of potential investments, especially structures and infrastructures, have long projected life spans and are spatially fixed. The high uncertainty and high-risk nature of neighborhood investments holds important implications for the characteristics associated with neighborhood change, the topic to which I turn next. Despite its importance, we know remarkably little at the micro level about how households, property owners, and residential developers go about assessing risks and making choices. Additional ethnographic and social survey work in this realm should prove fruitful.

WHAT CAUSES NEIGHBORHOODS TO CHANGE?

Above I argued that neighborhoods would change (i.e., their attributes would be altered) based on the risk-laden decisions by consumers/producers that influence the ongoing flow of resources to a neighborhood. These decisions are based heavily on relativistic, inter-neighborhood comparisons and futuristic expectations embedded within a highly interactive, multi-actor context. In the next three sections, I will more deeply probe the nature of the decision-making process related to neighborhood dynamics. Specifically, I will argue that changes in a neighborhood are (1) fundamentally driven by forces originating externally to the neighborhood that reverberate through the metropolitan housing market, (2) characterized by non-linear adjustment processes, and (3) socially inefficient.

For the first claim, I draw upon the model of the metropolitan housing market developed by Rothenberg, Galster, Butler, and Pitkin (1991) as a framework. Admittedly, this model is most applicable to a housing system dominated by decentralized, market-based actions, not centralized, state-based actions. This model begins by classifying the housing stock into 'quality submarkets,' sets of dwellings units that households perceive as closely substitutable, considering all the myriad attributes of the housing bundle (including spatially based attributes). Each submarket can be modeled as having its own supply and demand functions. Supply into one submarket (through new construction and net conversion of dwellings) will be influenced, among other things, by the relative rate of return that owners/developers can reap in this submarket compared to others. Demand by households in one submarket will be influenced, among other things, by the market valuations (sales prices or equivalent capitalized rents) in close-substitute submarkets. Shocks to equilibrium in any one submarket are transmitted sequentially throughout the submarket array by housing owners/developers altering their supply decisions in response to a new submarket pattern of rates of return, and by households altering their occupancy decisions in response to new relative market valuations across substitute submarkets.

This model of housing dynamics can be usefully applied to neighborhood dynamics (Rothenberg et al., 1991: Ch. 9). The connection between the metropolitan housing submarket and neighborhood is straightforward. Most neighborhoods in the market-based systems consist primarily of residences classified (by households, owners, and developers as close substitutes) in the same quality submarket, for three reasons (Vandell, 1995). First, economies of scale in construction lead private developers to build homes in subdivisions that typically have similar physical characteristics. Secondly, many households' willingness to pay premia for neighbors of higher socioeconomic status, often backed up with various land-use regulations that enhance the fiscal status of the jurisdiction, limits diversity of housing types developed within small geographic areas. Thirdly, because spatially based attributes contribute to a dwelling's quality and, hence, submarket designation, dwellings in close proximity will share many common attributes and thus tend to be classified in the same quality submarket tautologically.

The foregoing suggests first that any forces affecting a particular housing submarket will also affect the neighborhoods where such a type of dwelling is located; the greater the concentration of the given submarket type in a neighborhood, the greater the spatial impact there. Secondly, it suggests that forces originally impacting anywhere (either in terms of quality submarket or geographic location) in the metropolitan area will eventually have some impact everywhere, as the shock is transmitted (in progressively damped severity) across submarkets of increasingly dissimilar substitutability.

An illustration is the classic process of 'filtering' (Galster and Rothenberg, 1991). Developers may speculate and build a number of high-quality submarket homes on ex-urban, undeveloped tracts. Should this increase in supply exceed the increase in demand for the high-quality submarket (say, due to growth of high-income households), there will be a net decline in the market valuations and rate of return associated with such dwellings. Some households who previously chose not to occupy the high-quality submarket now do so, as affordability has risen. Concomitantly, some owners of pre-existing dwellings in the high-quality submarket may choose to downgrade the quality of their units to take advantage of comparatively superior rates of return in the somewhat lesser-quality submarket(s). They typically accomplish this by passive under-maintenance: investing insufficient upkeep to maintain the dwelling in its original submarket. These adjustments jointly restore equilibrium in the high-quality submarket but upset it in the lower-quality one(s): there, demand has fallen (from some erstwhile occupants choosing instead a superior-quality submarket) and supply has risen (from some owners downgrading from higher-quality submarkets), thereby driving down market valuations. An adjustment process on both supply and demand sides of the market ensues, analogous to the above, but disequilibrating forces are transmitted still farther down the submarket quality array.

By the time system-wide equilibrium is restored, the model predicts a series of changes in demographic and physical attributes of neighborhoods constituting submarkets. In every submarket, the least competitive neighborhoods have witnessed: (1) an in-migration of households of somewhat lower means than the typical residents who left, and (2) a decline in the physical quality of the dwellings – in the extreme: dilapidation and even abandonment. In each case, the new construction of high-quality dwellings in excess of household demand for such rendered the array of lower-quality neighborhoods relatively less attractive, and less expensive. This generated altered flows of resources (occupancy patterns by households, financial resources by owners) that ultimately changed absolutely the attributes of these neighborhoods.

What I wish to stress about this process is that the alterations of existing neighborhoods in this scenario were triggered by forces originating outside the confines of these neighbourhood.[10] These forces external to the neighborhood in question led those controlling resources flowing into it to change their decisions, based on the connections described by the quality submarket array of the metropolitan housing market. This leads me to suggest that the most fundamental sorts of neighborhood changes are *externally induced*.

Unfortunately, this proposition has largely remained untested in the empirical literature. To my knowledge, there have been no recent studies of metropolitan housing markets that have investigated longitudinally how metro-wide shocks have been transmitted through the array of housing quality submarkets and spawned adjustments by households and dwelling owner/developers. Advances in micro-simulation software technology also might be usefully applied to this endeavor.

In a related vein, there has been insufficient research on the spatial dimensions of housing submarkets. Though some have *defined* submarkets *a priori* in spatial terms (e.g., Tu, 2003), we have only seen exploratory work on how quality categories of dwellings may take on spatial patterns (Leishman, 2007; Pryce, 2008). Advancing such work is crucial for understanding the spatial dimensions of neighborhood change, such as modifications in neighborhood borders and spatial autocorrelation processes. Moreover, the microeconomic underpinnings of these aggregate processes need to be better understood. Both individual- and neighborhood-level dynamics could be probed using data gathered through a people-place panel survey. In overview, it would involve:

- *Wave 1 person-in-place* – in-depth, comprehensive questionnaire administered to spatially clustered samples of households (and/or owners); assesses baseline objective and subjective characteristics of individuals and (via aggregation of these individuals' responses) of neighborhoods sampled.
- *Wave 2 person* – comprehensive questionnaire administered to the households originally living at (and/owners of) addresses, as in wave 1 but now have moved (or sold); assesses characteristics of original individuals sampled who moved (sold) since wave 1.

- *Wave 2 place* – comprehensive questionnaire administered to the households (and/or owners) now living at same addresses as in wave 1; assesses later-period characteristics of sampled neighborhoods and individuals who did not move.

WHAT IS THE NATURE OF NEIGHBORHOOD CHANGE?

Once begun, the process of change from one collection of attributes to another is likely non-linear, even discontinuous: what I call a threshold effect. There are four distinct, not mutually exclusive, mechanisms suggested by extant theory through which thresholds may be produced: collective socialization, contagion, gaming, and preference models.[11] The first two rely upon collective actions and social intercourse to create thresholds; the other two involve more atomistic attitudes and behaviors. One can analyze: behavior of households to move out through collective socialization, gaming, and preference models; behavior of households to move in through gaming models; and behavior of households, dwelling owners, and business people who remain in the neighborhood through collective socialization, gaming, and contagion models.

Collective socialization theories focus on the role that social groups exert on shaping an individual's attitudes, values, and behaviors (e.g., Simmel, 1971; Weber, 1978). Such an effect can occur to the degree that (1) the individual comes in social contact with the group, and (2) the group can exert more powerful threats or inducement to conform to its positions than competing groups. These two preconditions may involve the existence of a threshold. Given the importance of interpersonal contact in enforcing conformity, if the individuals constituting the group in question were scattered innocuously over urban space, they would be less likely to be able either to convey their positions effectively to others with whom they might come in contact or to exert much pressure to conform. It is only when a group reaches some critical mass of density or power over a predefined area that it is likely to become effective in shaping the behaviors of others. Past this threshold, as more members are recruited, the group's power to sanction non-conformists probably grows non-linearly. This is especially likely when the position of the group becomes so dominant as to become normative in the area.[12]

The basic tenet of contagion models is that if decision makers live in a community where some of their neighbors exhibit non-normative behaviors, they will be more likely to adopt these behaviors themselves. In this way, social problems are believed to be contagious, spread through peer influence. Crane (1991) proposes a formal contagion model to explain the incidence and spread of social problems. He contends that the key implication of the contagion model is that there may be critical levels of incidence of social problems in neighborhoods. He states that

> If the incidence of problems stays below a critical point, the frequency or prevalence of the problem tends to gravitate toward some relatively low-level equilibrium. But if the incidence surpasses a critical point, the process will spread explosively. In other words, an epidemic may occur, raising the incidence to an equilibrium at a much higher level (Crane, 1991: 1227).

From our perspective, we would observe attributes such as crime and social incivilities rise disproportionately in the neighborhood.

Gaming models assume that, in many decisional situations involving neighborhoods, the costs and benefits of alternative courses of action are uncertain, depending on how many other actors choose various alternatives. The individual's expected payoff of an alternative varies, however, depending on the number or proportion of others who make a decision before the given actor does. Thus, the concept of a threshold amount of observed prior action is central in this type of model. The well-known prisoners' dilemma is the simplest form of gaming model (Schelling, 1978), but more sophisticated variants have been developed and applied to neighborhood change processes (Granovetter, 1978; Granovetter and Soong, 1986). As illustration, consider the situation of a dilapidated neighborhood for which the market is signaling potential gains in property values were its owners to improve their properties as a group. But, individual owners may believe that they will not earn back the value of their marginal investment if they were to upgrade but no others followed suit. A conservative gaming strategy of behaving to minimize maximum prospective loss, regardless of what others may do, will lead many owners to refrain from upgrading first. Only if a threshold proportion of owners were to upgrade would these skeptics be convinced to upgrade (Taub, Taylor, and Dunham, 1984), whereupon the neighborhood suddenly becomes radically transformed.

Preference models claim that actors in a residential environment will respond if the aggregate behavior of others (or, an exogenous event) raises an undesirable neighborhood attribute above the level they find tolerable. An endogenous process can be triggered once the attribute reaches the critical threshold. The trigger occurs because actors in a neighborhood are assumed to have different tolerance levels, with the least tolerant responding first. If additional change in the neighborhood attribute results from the course of action taken in response to the initial event by those with the lowest tolerance level, the new level of the neighborhood attribute may now be above the tolerance level of some of the less tolerant remaining actors. The process may continue with new rounds of attribute change and actor adjustment until the process is completed. At the extreme, the process may end when all the original actors in a neighborhood have responded. The theoretical development of preference models has focused on changes in a neighborhood's racial composition, though extensions to preferences for other sorts of neighborhood attributes are straightforward. For example, if some 'undesirable' household type were to move into a neighborhood, the original residents least tolerant of the new in-movers may leave. If their vacant dwellings were filled disproportionately by more members of the undesirable group, still more of the original residents may find the now-higher proportion of undesirables intolerable, and move out, and so on. Seminal theoretical work in this vein has been produced by Schelling (1971, 1978), Schnare and MacRae (1975), and Taub, Taylor, and Dunham (1984) (for a fuller discussion of residential segregation see Chapters 22 and 23).

The empirical study of non-linear dynamics of neighborhood change has thus far focused on changes in racial composition (e.g., Galster, 1990), but recent work has also identified thresholds of public investment required to engage private investors in efforts to revitalize distressed neighborhoods (Galster et al., 2005; Galster, Tatian, and Accordino, 2006). There are now emerging a number of data sets in the United States that provide for certain cities a long panel of annual observations of neighborhood indicators. Prototype analyses of such data sets have thus far not uncovered archetypical tipping points for many indicators (Galster, Cutsinger, and Lim, 2007; Lim and Galster, 2009), but more definitive work is to be done. As suggested earlier, surveys of individual households and owner/developers might probe the degree to which they indeed engage in behaviors like gaming.

Another new approach to non-linear transformation processes is through the use of cellular automata computer simulations. Seminal work in this realm (e.g., Fossett and Waren, 2005; Fossett, 2006) has indeed suggested that 'tipping' from one equilibrium spatial arrangement of actors to another can occur with relatively minor, random perturbations. The exciting empirical challenge is to link evidence on the racial preferences and tolerances of households to the simulation parameters in the cellular automata behavioral algorithm.

ARE NEIGHBORHOOD CHANGE PROCESSES SOCIALLY INEFFICIENT AND INEQUITABLE?

The foregoing discussion implies that changes in the flows of resources into neighborhoods are not likely to produce socially efficient outcomes. At least four reasons come to bear: externalities, gaming, expectations, and flawed pricing of attributes.

Because the act of consuming neighborhood can change its attributes directly and indirectly, and such changes affect the decision-making calculus of other consumers/producers, the act can be thought of as generating externalities. For example, the choice of a minority to move into an all-white occupied neighborhood imposes externalities on the bigots there. The choice of a property owner to repair the façade provides external benefits to neighbors. The choice of many higher-income households to move into a neighborhood currently occupied by low-income households may impose both external costs and benefits upon the latter. Because in all such cases external costs and benefits do not accrue to the decision-maker, a suboptimal amount of the activity is chosen in aggregate: the classic economic inefficiency.

The aforementioned discussion of gaming also serves as reference here. Individual neighborhood consumers/producers lack certainty about the decisions of a myriad other consumers/producers located in the neighborhood or considering investing in the neighborhood. Yet, the payoffs from their alternative choices depend upon such decisions of others. Thus, autonomous decision makers are likely to adopt strategies that do not produce the greatest good for the collective. The unwillingness to renovate dilapidated buildings in an area until other investors do so first is a classic example.

Expectations are, of course, imperfect and prone to major errors. But this in itself does not imply a systematic bias toward inefficient choices. Rather, expectations about the future may prove to be so 'certain' in the view of the decision maker that the resulting choice encourages the expectation to transpire. This is the famous 'self-fulfilling prophecy' phenomenon. An illustration is panic selling of homes. Because of some anticipated neighborhood change, several homeowners become convinced that property values will fall rapidly. They therefore try to sell their homes quickly, offering a discount. But the rash of 'For Sale' signs and the rumors that these homes are selling cheaply convinces other owners in the neighborhood that, indeed, values are on the way down. As they join in the attempt to unload their properties, panic ensues and prices do, as some prophesied, drop precipitously. The sorts of prices produced by these self-fulfilling prophecy dynamics are unlikely to allocate resources efficiently. Instead of accurately capitalizing the underlying quality (and replacement cost of the dwellings) in the neighborhood, these artificially deflated prices encourage the purchase by owners with less personal financial means. These owners are likely to invest less in home maintenance and repair activities than their higher-income forebears (Galster, 1987), thereby shortening the useful lifetimes of these valuable assets.

Finally, I explained above how certain attributes of the neighborhood, especially those associated with the sentimental and social-interactive dimensions, could not be evaluated well by potential consumers/producers not yet located in a given neighborhood, compared to those located there for some time. This divergence in information creates an agency problem in which inefficient transactions likely occur. Owners attempting to sell or rent their properties will have a bias toward disguising any undesirable attributes — and not discounting the price appropriately — of the neighborhood that may not be known to prospective buyers or renters. Conversely, the valuable social intercourse that owner-occupants may enjoy in their neighborhood will be difficult for the market to capitalize, dependent as it is on the idiosyncrasies of personal interrelationships. This means that the latter group will make inefficient choices: they would have chosen a different neighborhood had they but been fully informed.

Analogous to the efficiency analysis is one focusing on equity. I believe it reasonable to hypothesize that neighborhood change processes disproportionately impose personal and financial costs on lower-income households and property owners in lower-quality neighborhoods. Theory suggests, for example, that the filtering process in declining metro areas ultimately produces residential abandonment, the financial and quality of life externalities associated with which undoubtedly primarily affect the aforementioned groups. The well-documented problems associated with concentrated poverty neighborhoods (Wilson, 1987; Friedrichs, Galster, and Musterd, 2005) are similarly suggestive that the distress produced when neighborhoods surpass multiple physical, financial, and sociological thresholds are borne by disadvantaged households. Unfortunately, there have been few studies that have rigorously quantified the gains and losses incurred by different parties from market-driven neighborhood change dynamics, although work on gentrification-induced displacement is qualitatively indicative.

Several recent studies have found that home appreciation rates vary by low-income and high-income market segments as well as by race, but the findings have been inconsistent. Using US Panel Study of Income Dynamics (PSID) data for the 1984–1993 period, Boehm and Schlottmann (2004) found median annual rates of appreciation ranged from 4.2 percent for low-income whites and 4.3 percent for low-income minorities to 4.6 for high-income whites and 4.8 percent for high-income minorities. By contrast, in an evaluation of loans to low-income borrowers originated between 1998 and 2002, Stegman, Quercia, and Davis (2007) reported that blacks experienced 10 percent lower annual equity appreciation than whites. Santiago, Galster, and Kaiser (2008) observed even larger black–white gaps in home appreciation rates for low-income buyers graduating from a Denver public housing-run asset-building/counseling program; Hispanics evinced even lower appreciation rates than blacks. Flippen (2004) found dramatic geographic differences in home appreciation rates across neighborhoods delineated by racial–ethnic composition. For 1970–1990, US census data showed that homes in neighborhoods with less than 2 percent black residents appreciated over 22 percent, whereas those in neighborhoods with 2–30 percent black residents appreciated 10 percent, and those with more than 30 percent appreciated less than 8 percent, on average. Over the same period, the patterns were less clear for Hispanic composition, however. Homes in neighborhoods with less than 2 percent Hispanic residents appreciated over 14 percent, those with 2–5 percent appreciated 27 percent, those with 5–10 percent appreciated 23 percent, and those with over 10 percent appreciated 15 percent. Given this lack of consensus, more research into this and other equity dimensions of neighborhood change processes would be especially helpful.

DO NEIGHBORHOODS INDEPENDENTLY SHAPE THE OPPORTUNITIES FOR ADULTS AND CHILDREN RESIDING IN THEM?

The oft-heard aphorism states, 'We shape our environments, and then our environments shape us.' Indeed, a belief in this aphorism has led to numerous public policy initiatives on both sides of the Atlantic that are designed to equalize attributes across neighborhoods, especially with regard to public services and education, and the ethnic, income, and tenure mix of households. Regardless of the particular programmatic forms that this policy thrust has assumed internationally, all are founded on the belief that neighborhoods have a strong and independent effect upon the well-being and life chances of individuals. The posited mechanisms of effect include socialization, epidemics, norms, networks, stigmatization, and private and public resource restrictions[13] (for other discussion, see Chapters 22 and 23).

The adequacy of the evidence base to support this position has been the subject of spirited debate.[14] Indeed, though large in volume, most of the literature attempting to quantify neighborhood effects can be convincingly challenged on methodological grounds.[15] The central challenge in providing an unbiased estimate of the magnitude of neighborhood effects is selection bias. The most basic selection issue is that certain types of individuals who have certain (unmeasured) characteristics will move from/to certain types of neighborhoods. Any observed relationship between neighborhood conditions and outcomes for such individuals or their children may therefore be biased because of this systematic spatial selection process, *even if all the observable characteristics are controlled* (Manski, 1995, 2000; Duncan, Connell, and Klebanov, 1997). As Gennetian, Ludwig, and Sanbonmatsu (2008) show, these biases can be substantial enough to seriously distort conclusions about the magnitude and direction of neighborhood effects.

There have been three general approaches adopted in response to the challenge of selection bias. The most common approach consists of a variety of econometric techniques applied to non-experimentally generated data. The other two use natural or experimental designs to generate quasi-random or random assignments of households to neighborhoods.

Econometric models based on non-experimental data

Most studies of neighborhood effects have used cross-sectional or longitudinal data collected from surveys of individual households residing in a variety of neighborhoods as a result of mundane factors associated with normal market transactions. They employ multiple regression or other multivariate analysis techniques to control for observed individual characteristics to ascertain the relationship between neighborhood characteristics and a variety of outcomes for these individuals. The more sophisticated studies employ either (1) instrumental variables (Galster, Marcotte, et al., 2007; Cutler, Glaeser, and Vigdor, 2008), (2) differencing (Galster et al., 2008), (3) fixed effects (Weinberg, Reagan, and Yankow, 2004), or (4) comparisons of siblings (Aaronson, 1997; Plotnick and Hoffman, 1999) to correct for the selection problem. These studies almost without exception identify strong effects from neighborhoods on a variety of labor market and educational outcomes. Moreover, the relationships observed are often highly non-linear or associated with threshold points (Galster, 2002), as discussed above. Nevertheless, all of these approaches have their own shortcomings, which are beyond the scope of this chapter, so conclusions should be couched in some caveats.

Quasi-random assignment natural experiments

It is sometimes possible to observe non-market interventions into households' residential locations that mimic random assignment. In this way they may be viewed as second-best options for removing selection effects. The Gautreaux (Chicago) and Yonkers (NY) court-ordered, public housing racial–ethnic desegregation programs (Rosenbaum, 1995; Briggs, 1997; Rubinowitz and Rosenbaum, 2000; Fauth, Leventhal, and Brooks-Gunn, 2003; DeLuca et al., 2010) are illustrative. Evaluations of these programs revealed generally strong effects of neighborhoods in several dimensions. Recent evaluations of long-term impacts on Gautreaux (black) mothers found, for example, that residence in neighborhoods with the highest percentages of black and low-income residents were associated with significantly greater welfare usage, lower employment rates, and lower earnings. Sons of Gautreaux participants who moved far from their original, high-crime neighborhoods were less likely to run afoul of the criminal justice system, especially in matters related to drug offenses (DeLuca, et al., 2010).

However, although these natural experiments may indeed provide some exogenous variation in neighborhood locations, the selection problems are unlikely to be avoided completely. There is typically selection involved in who chooses to participate in these programs and who succeeds in locating rental vacancies in qualifying locations. In some cases (e.g., Gautreaux), participants have some non-trivial latitude in which locations they choose, both initially and subsequent to original placement. In other cases (e.g., Yonkers), there are limitations in the range of neighborhoods to which participants move because of where subsidized housing is located.

Random assignment experiments

Many researchers advocate a random assignment experimental approach for best avoiding biases from selection. Data on outcomes that can be produced by an experimental design whereby individuals or households are randomly assigned to different neighborhoods is, indeed, in theory, the preferred method. In this regard, the Moving to Opportunity (MTO) demonstration has been touted conventionally as *the* study from which to draw conclusions about the magnitude of neighborhood effects (e.g., Gennetian, Ludwig, and Sanbonmatsu, 2008). The MTO research design randomly assigns public housing residents who volunteer to participate to one of three experimental groups: (1) controls that get no voucher but can stay in public housing in disadvantaged neighborhoods; (2) recipients of rental vouchers; and (3) recipients of rental vouchers and relocation assistance who had to move to neighborhoods with less than 10 percent poverty rates and remain for at least a year. Most investigations of MTO data revealed no substantial neighborhood effects on educational and labor market outcomes (e.g., Ludwig, Duncan, and Pinkston, 2000; Katz, Kling, and Liebman, 2001; Ludwig, Duncan, and Hirschfield, 2001; Ludwig, Ladd, and Duncan, 2001; Goering and Feins, 2003; Orr et al., 2003; Kling, Liebman, and Katz, 2007). Based on this, it has been claimed that 'MTO is the gold standard ... [and] its results ... have proven discouraging ... neighborhood quality ... [has] little effect on desirable and measurable outcomes ...' (Smolensky, 2007: 1016).

Such a sweeping conclusion is unsupportable for four main reasons. First, although MTO *starts* with random assignment, thereafter it does not control the assignment of neighborhood characteristics to *any* of the experimental groups, and thus does not purge the relationship between neighborhood characteristics and unmeasured individual characteristics (Sampson, Morenoff, and Gannon-Rowley, 2002; Clampet-Lundquist and Massey, forthcoming). The 'control' group is not constrained to live perpetually in disadvantaged neighborhoods; indeed, many MTO controls moved to better neighborhoods on their own. The group that receives only a rental subsidy with no mobility counseling and no geographic restrictions can (and did) freely select from a wide range of neighborhoods. The treatment group receiving intensive mobility counseling and assistance, though constrained to move initially to a neighborhood with less than 10 percent poverty rates, has the ability nevertheless to choose neighborhoods varying on their school quality, homeownership rates, racial composition, local institutional resources, etc. That is, they can select many aspects of neighborhood opportunity structure within the poverty rate constraint. As Gennetian, Ludwig, and Sanbonmatsu (2008) explain, this selection within MTO can be addressed through instrumental variables techniques. But the adjustment remains imprecise, because the neighborhood poverty instrument is measured either at a single point in the observed family's trajectory of moves or represents the average across this trajectory.

Secondly, MTO fails to ensure adequate exposure to neighborhood conditions at any location. As amplified below, some neighborhood effects are likely to yield outcomes only after long-term exposure to the neighborhood context (Clampet-Lundquist and Massey, 2008). Unfortunately, all three experimental groups in MTO evinced significant residential mobility (typical of low-income households), thus minimizing the chance to observe neighborhood effects that require substantial duration of exposure. Clampet-Lundquist and Massey (2008) analyze MTO data from the perspective of only those who resided for substantial spells in low-poverty neighborhoods, and find (non-experimental) evidence that they experienced a variety of improved labor market outcomes.

Thirdly, the MTO design may not have been powerful enough to detect statistically the magnitude of spatial effects that may be present in certain outcome domains. Quigley and Raphael (2008) developed a statistical model of how much spatial mismatch might affect the employment rate of black workers and concluded that the experimental treatment involved in MTO *ex post* (after subsequent moves by the treatment group) could not be expected to yield detectable differences.

Fourthly, subsequent to their initial, low-poverty location they are free after one year to move to different, higher-poverty neighborhoods should they choose: indeed, 85 percent have done so (Kingsley and Pettit, 2007). This means that few effects from low-poverty neighborhoods will be observed if the mechanisms for such require some non-trivial degree of exposure duration.

Despite these methodological weaknesses, one should not lose sight of the fact that many important neighborhood effects nevertheless *can* be observed from MTO data, as Goering and Feins (2003) and Gennetian, Ludwig, and Sanbonmatsu (2008) summarize. Analysts have observed substantial improvements on mental health of mothers and daughters, rates of risky behaviors, perceptions of safety, and overall life satisfaction in lower-poverty neighborhoods. The picture for boys appears more complex, however, as they evinced reductions in violent crime but increases in property crime offending in lower-poverty neighborhoods.

Thus, despite its theoretical promise, MTO has not provided definitive evidence about the potential benefits to the poor from residence in non-poor neighborhoods. It fails to (1) overcome the selection bias challenge and must resort to imprecise instrumental variable estimates, (2) produce substantial exposure to a given neighborhood environment, (3) provide adequate statistical power for assessing impacts on key outcomes, and (4) provide adequate duration of exposure to a low-poverty neighborhood's environment. Unless a social experiment is designed wherein the precise neighborhood conditions are randomly assigned to a large number of participants, and then these conditions fixed for a substantial period (which is likely to be impractical), data gathered will still need to be analyzed using one of the econometric methods described above, and the power of the 'pure' random assignment experiment will thus be diluted.

A provisional conclusion about neighborhood effects and future directions

A substantial number of studies (employing sophisticated econometric methods with non-experimental data, natural quasi-experimental designs, and experimental designs for overcoming selection bias) have identified non-trivial, independent correlations between various aspects of the neighborhood and several dimensions of the well-being of disadvantaged children and adults. Many of these effects appear non-linear, such that certain neighborhood characteristics only appear to affect outcomes after a threshold has been exceeded. Nevertheless, one should not pretend that the issue of the magnitude or the mechanisms of neighborhood effects is settled.

I believe that there is untapped potential for exploiting 'natural quasi-experiments'. Either classic anthropological case study, control vs experimental group, or pre-post longitudinal designs (including retrospective comparisons) could be contemplated. There are ample opportunities emerging in the US public policy arena, including HOPE VI mixed-income redevelopments of distressed public housing complexes, court-ordered public housing authority desegregation consent decrees, and innovative local housing authority initiatives. My colleague, Anna Santiago, and I are currently gathering retrospective data from one such natural experiment involving scattered-site public housing in Denver, CO. In the Western European context, several nations have adopted policies for increasing the income and/or tenure diversity of large private and social housing estates, which may offer additional opportunities for testing neighborhood impacts in a quasi-experimental context.

SUMMARY AND CONCLUSION

In this chapter, I have proposed that the urban neighborhood could be usefully defined as the bundle of spatially based attributes associated with clusters of residences, sometimes in conjunction with other land uses. This bundle of attributes is multi-dimensional, consisting of everything from structures and topography to demography, public services, and social interactions. Implicit in my definition is the notion that, depending on the attributes present, the type and even existence of neighborhoods can and often does vary across urban space.

Bounding the neighborhood has been a long-standing concern. The specification of neighborhood as a bundle of spatially based attributes, coupled with the notion of 'externality space' that I introduced, allows for the potential empirical identification of behaviorally meaningful, multi-scaled boundaries of 'neighborhood.' This framework comports nicely with existing work indicating distinct spatial scales of the boundaries of different aspects of neighborhood.

The stock of attributes comprising neighborhood at any moment is the result of past and current flows of households and resources – financial, social-psychological, and time – into and out of the space in question. Four key users make decisions affecting these flows: households, businesses, property owners, and local government; they thus can be viewed as producers of neighborhood. However, these same actors play dual roles because they potentially reap benefits from the consumption of this complex commodity called neighborhood. To understand the factors and processes that influence these production and consumption decisions is to uncover the roots of neighborhood change.

Multi-dimensional commodities are common, but the neighborhood offers a variety of significant idiosyncrasies that suggest insights into these decisions:

- Different neighborhood attributes vary in their durability. Investors must take a long-term strategy with durable features, with concomitant reliance upon imperfect and socially influenced expectations. Self-fulfilling prophecies and gaming strategies that result yield inefficient outcomes.
- Social-interactive and sentimental attributes of neighborhood are not well-priced because of information asymmetries. The resultant agency problem leads to inefficient outcomes.
- Consumers evaluate neighborhood attributes relatively. This provides the vehicle by which changes elsewhere in the metropolitan area can lead to changes in the given neighborhood, as decision-makers alter flows of resources based on new, relativistic evaluations of attributes. This implies that the prime origins of a particular neighborhood changing are located outside that neighborhood.
- The act of households or property owners consuming neighborhood attributes typically changes the attributes. The direct effect occurs tautologically, based on a change in resident population or ownership profiles. The indirect effect occurs because changing attributes changes the

evaluations of neighborhoods made not only by consumers and potential consumers, but also by intermediaries such as lenders, insurers, and housing agents, thereby changing resource flows. This means that attributes of neighborhood are mutually causal over time. Changes in one attribute may change decisions by one or more types of consumer/producer, which lead, in turn, to changes in other attributes, and so on. Because this process generates externalities imposed on other consumers/producers operating in the neighborhood, socially inefficient outcomes are manifested.

- The attributes of a neighborhood, including the composition of its households, likely influences the behavior and opportunities of adults and children residing there. This means that uncoordinated actions by households, property owners, governments, and other institutions that alter the package of neighborhood attributes will create externalities. These externalities will be especially severe if processes exceed threshold points. This provides yet another rationale for deducing socially inefficient outcomes.

The foregoing suggests an unmistakable case of market failure. For a variety of reasons inherently associated with the concept of neighborhood, changes in flows of households and resources across space will produce socially inefficient outcomes. I have also suggested (though the evidence is sparse) that these outcomes are inequitable as well; they likely produce the largest penalties for the most vulnerable households. There is thus a prima facie case on efficiency and equity grounds for some sort of collective intervention, whether it come from informal social processes, non-profit, community-based organizations, or the governmental sector.

Informal social processes might take the form of sanctions and rewards meted out by neighbors that are designed to enforce compliance with collective norms regarding civil behavior and building upkeep. Community-based organizations might politically organize, establish neighborhood bonds of mutual solidarity, or foment a positive public image of the neighborhood. Governments might offer financial incentives, regulations, and investments of infrastructure and public services, and target them to neighborhoods at crucial threshold points. In concert, these actions can help alter perceptions of key neighborhood investors, provide compensatory resource flows, minimize destructive gaming behaviors, internalize externalities, and moderate expectations, thereby defusing self-fulfilling prophecies.

In closing, I wish to emphasize that much of this essay has been conjectural and based on deductive logic, although consistent with extant empirical evidence. I hope that my claims are viewed as hypotheses worthy of empirical testing. In this fashion we can enhance our understanding of neighborhood change, its consequences, the behavioral decisions that underpin it, and the policy options for effectively altering it, to improve the efficiency and equity of outcomes.

NOTES

1 For comprehensive reviews of the social scientific literature on neighborhood, see Hunter (1979), Schwirian (1983), Hallman (1984), Grigsby et al. (1987), and Temkin and Rohe (1996).

2 For more on this dimension, see Hunter (1979) and Temkin and Rohe (1996).

3 For more on this dimension, see Warren, (1975), Warren and Warren (1977), Fischer (1982), Sampson (1997), Sampson, Raudenbush and Earls (1997), and Sampson, Morenoff, and Earls (1999).

4 I am indebted to Ade Kearns for this expression.

5 Visitors may also consume neighborhoods in which they do not reside by the act of working, shopping, or seeking entertainment there. For simplicity I omit them as key consumers when analyzing the main determinants of neighborhood change.

6 For more on neighborhood typologies, see Warren (1975). My view is consonant with that expressed recently by Gephart (1997: 10): 'Insofar as neighborhood has a geographic referent, its meaning depends on context and function. The relevant units vary by behavior and domain, and they depend on the outcome or process of interest.'

7 Changes initiated by others, not the individual in question, are implicit in the notion of externality.

8 For a review of theory and evidence on hedonic indexes, see Rothenberg et al. (1991: Ch. 3) and Malpezzi (2003).

9 An amendment to this claim is that some attributes may have associated with them an absolute minimum threshold value below which no price will ever be bid, such as the case of air quality.

10 A similar position was articulated in Grigsby et al. (1987) and Temkin and Rohe (1996).

11 For a review, see Quercia and Galster (2000); for evidence, see Galster, Quercia, and Cortes (2000), Galster, Cutsinger, and Lim (2007), and Lim and Galster (forthcoming).

12 More modern sociological treatises closely related to collective socialization also suggest thresholds, such as Wilson's (1987) contention that as a critical mass of middle-class families leave the inner city, low-income blacks left behind become isolated from the positive role models that the erstwhile dominant class offered. Economists, also, have developed several mathematical treatises involving collective socialization effects in which thresholds often emerge as solutions to complex decision problems under certain assumptions (Akerlof, 1980; Galster, 1987: Ch. 3; Brock and Durlauf, 2000).

13 For reviews, see Jencks and Mayer (1990), Gephart (1997), Friedrichs (1998), Sampson, Morenoff, and Gannon-Rowley (2002), and Ioannides and Loury (2004).

14 See Galster and Zobel (1998), Atkinson and Kintrea (2001), Ostendorf, Musterd, and de Vos (2001), Friedrichs (2002), Kearns (2002), Musterd (2003), Kleinhans (2004), Delorenzi (2006), Joseph (2006), Joseph, Chaskin and Webber (2006), and Galster (2007).

15 For reviews, see Gephart (1997), van Kempen (1997), Friedrichs (1998), Leventhal and Brooks-Gunn (2000); Sampson, Morenoff, and Gannon-Rowley (2002), Friedrichs, Galster, and Musterd (2003), Ellen and Turner (2003), and Galster (2003).

REFERENCES

Aaronson, D. (1997) Sibling estimates of neighborhood effects, in: J. Brooks-Gunn, G. Duncan & J. Aber (eds), *Neighborhood Poverty: Vol. II, Policy Implications in Studying Neighborhoods*, pp. 80–93. New York: Russell Sage Foundation.

Akerlof, G. (1980) A theory of social custom, of which unemployment may be one consequence, *Quarterly Journal of Economics* 94, pp. 749–775.

Appleyard, D. & Lintell, M. (1986) The environmental quality of city streets: The residents' viewpoints,' in: E. de Boer (ed.), *Transport Sociology: Social Aspects of Transport Planning*, pp. 93–120. Oxford: Pergamon Press.

Atkinson, R. & Kintrea, K. (2001) Area effects: What do they mean for British housing and regeneration policy? *European Journal of Housing Policy* 2(2), pp. 147–166.

Birch, D., Brown, E., Coleman, R., Da Lomba, D., Parsons, W., Sharpe, L. and Weber, S. (1979) *The Behavioural Foundations of Neighborhood Change*. Washington, DC: USGPO/HUD.

Boehm, T. & Schlottman, A. (2004) The dynamics of race, income, and homeownership, *Journal of Urban Economics* 55: p. 113–30.

Briggs, X. (1997) Moving up versus moving out: researching and interpreting neighborhood effects in housing mobility programs, *Housing Policy Debate* 8, pp. 195–234.

Brock, W. & Durlauf, S. (2000) Interactions-based models, in J. Heckman and E. Learner (eds), *Handbook of Econometrics*, Vol. 5. Amsterdam: North-Holland.

Clampet-Lundquist, S., & Massey, D. (2008). Neighborhood effects on the economic self-sufficiency: A reconsideration of the Moving to Opportunity experiment, *American Journal of Sociology*, 114(1), 107–143.

Crane, J. (1991) The epidemic theory of ghettos and neighborhood effects on dropping out and teenage childbearing, *American Journal of Sociology* 96, pp. 1226–1259.

Cutler, D., Glaeser, E. & Vigdor, J. (2008) When are ghettos bad? Lessons from immigrant segregation in the United States, *Journal of Urban Economics* 63, 759–774.

Delorenzi, S. (2006) Introduction, in: S. Delorenzi (ed.), *Going Places: Neighbourhood, Ethnicity and Social Mobility*, pp. 1–11. London: Institute for Public Policy Research.

DeLuca, S., Duncan, G., Mendenhall, R. & Keels, M. (2010) *Gautreaux* mothers and their children: An update, *Housing Policy Debate* 20(1), pp. 7–25.

Downs, A. (1981) *Neighborhoods and Urban Development*. Washington, DC: Brookings Institution.

Duncan, G., Connell, J. & Klebanov, P. (1997) Conceptual and methodological issues in estimating causal effects of neighborhoods and family conditions on individual development, in: J. Brooks-Gunn, G. Duncan & J. Aber (eds), *Neighborhood Poverty: Vol. 1, Context and Consequences for Children*, pp. 219–250. New York: Russell Sage Foundation.

Ellen, I. & Turner, M. (2003) Do neighborhoods Matter and why? in: J. Goering & J. Feins (eds), *Choosing a Better Life? Evaluating the Moving To Opportunity*

Experiment, pp. 313–338. Washington, DC: Urban Institute Press.

Fauth, R., Leventhal, T. & Brooks-Gunn, J. (2003) Short-term effects of moving from public housing in poor to affluent neighborhoods on low-income, minority adults' outcomes. Unpublished paper, National Center for Children and Families, Columbia University.

Fischer, C. (1982) *To Dwell Among Friends*. Chicago, IL: University of Chicago Press.

Flippen, C. (2004) Unequal returns to housing investment? A study of real housing appreciation among black, white and Hispanic households, *Social Forces* 82: pp. 1523–1551.

Fossett, M. (2006) Ethnic preferences, social distance dynamics, and residential segregation: Theoretical explorations using simulation analysis, *Journal of Mathematical Sociology* 30: pp. 185–274.

Fossett, M. & Waren, W. (2005) Overlooked implications of ethnic preferences for residential segregation in agent-based models, *Urban Studies* 42(11), pp. 1893–1917.

Friedrichs, J. (1998) Do poor neighborhoods make their residents poorer? Context effects of poverty neighborhoods on their residents, in: H. Andress (ed.), *Empirical Poverty Research in a Comparative Perspective*, pp. 77–99. Aldershot: Ashgate.

Friedrichs, J. (2002) Response: contrasting U.S. and European findings on poverty neighborhoods, *Housing Studies* 17(1), pp. 101–106.

Friedrichs, J., Galster, G. & Musterd, S. (2003) Neighborhood effects on social opportunities: The European and American research and policy context, *Housing Studies* 18(6), pp. 797–806.

Friedrichs, J., Galster, G. & Musterd, S., eds. (2005) *Life in Poverty Neighbourhoods*. London & New York: Routledge.

Galster, G. (1986) What is neighborhood? An externality-space approach, *International Journal of Urban and Regional Research* 10(2), pp. 243–261.

Galster, G. (1987) *Homeowners and Neighborhood Reinvestment*. Durham, NC: Duke University Press.

Galster, G. (1990) White flight from integrated neighborhoods, *Urban Studies* 27(3): pp. 385–399.

Galster, G. (2002) An economic efficiency analysis of deconcentrating poverty populations, *Journal of Housing Economics* 11, pp. 303–329.

Galster, G. (2003) Investigating behavioural impacts of poor neighborhoods: Towards new data and analytic strategies, *Housing Studies* 18(3), pp. 893–914.

Galster, G. (2007) Neighbourhood social mix as a goal of housing policy: A theoretical analysis, *European Journal of Housing Policy* 7(1), pp. 19–43.

Galster, G. & Rothenberg, J. (1991) Filtering in urban housing: A graphical analysis of a quality-segmented market, *Journal of Planning Education and Research* 11, pp. 37–50.

Galster, G., Andersson, S., Musterd, S. & Kauppinen, T. (2008) Does neighborhood income mix affect earnings of adults?. *Journal of Urban Economics* 63, pp. 858–870.

Galster, G., Cutsinger, J. & Lim, U. (2007) 'Are neighborhoods self-stabilizing? Exploring endogenous dynamics,' *Urban Studies* 44(1): pp. 1–19.

Galster, G., Marcotte, D., Mandell, M., Wolman, H., & Augustine, N. (2007) The impacts of parental homeownership on children's outcomes during early adulthood, *Housing Policy Debate* 18(4): 785–827.

Galster, G., Quercia, R. & Cortes, A. (2000) Identifying neighborhood thresholds: An empirical exploration, *Housing Policy Debate* 11(3), pp. 701–732.

Galster, G. Tatian, P. & Accordino, J. (2006) Targeting investments for neighborhood revitalization, *Journal of the American Planning Association* 72(4): pp. 457–474.

Galster, G., Walker, C., Hayes, C., Johnson, J. & Boxall, P. (2005) Measuring the impact of community development block grant spending on urban neighborhoods, *Housing Policy Debate* 15(4): 903–934.

Galster, G. & Zobel, A. (1998) Will dispersed housing programs reduce social costs in the U.S.?, *Housing Studies* 13(5), pp. 605–622.

Gennetian, L., Ludwig, J. & Sanbonmatsu, L. (2008) Understanding neighborhood effects on low-income families. Paper presented at the How Does Place Matter Conference, Federal Reserve Bank of Philadelphia, Philadelphia, March 27.

Gephart, M. (1997) Neighborhoods and communities as contexts for development, in J. Brooks-Gunn, G. Duncan & J. Aber (eds), *Neighborhood Poverty, Vol. 1: Context and Consequences for Children*. New York: Russell Sage Foundation.

Golab, C. (1982) The geography of the neighborhood, in: R. Bayer (ed.), *Neighborhoods in Urban America*. Port Washington: Kennikat.

Goering, J. & Feins, J., eds (2003) *Choosing a Better Life? Evaluating the Moving To Opportunity Experiment*. Washington, DC: Urban Institute Press.

Grannis, R. (1998) The importance of trivial streets: Residential streets and residential segregation,

American Journal of Sociology 103(6): pp. 1530–1564.
Granovetter, M. (1978) Threshold models of collective behaviour, *American Journal of Sociology* 83, pp. 1420–1443.
Granovetter, M. & Soong, R. (1986) Threshold models of diversity: Chinese restaurants, residential segregation, and the spiral of silence, *Journal of Sociology* 18, pp. 69–104.
Greer, S. (1962) *The Emerging City: Myth and Reality*. New York: Free Press.
Grigsby, W., Baratz, G., Galster, G. & Maclennan, D. (1987) *The Dynamics of Neighborhood Change and Decline*. Progress in Planning Series # 28. London: Pergamon.
Hallman, H. (1984) *Neighborhoods: Their Place in Urban Life*. Beverly Hills, CA: SAGE Publications.
Hunter, A. (1974) *Symbolic Communities*. Chicago, IL: University of Chicago Press.
Hunter, A. (1979) The urban neighborhood: Its analytical and social contexts, *Urban Affairs Quarterly* 14(3), pp. 267–288.
Ioannides, Y. & Loury, L. (2004) Job information networks, neighborhood effects, and inequality. *Journal of Economic Literature* 42, pp. 1056–1093.
Jencks, C. & Mayer, S. (1990) The social consequences of growing up in a poor neighborhood, in: National Research Council (ed.), *Inner-City Poverty in the United States*. Washington, DC: National Academy Press.
Joseph, M. (2006) Is mixed-income development an antidote to urban poverty? *Housing Policy Debate* 17(2), pp. 209–234.
Joseph, M., Chaskin, R. & Webber, H. (2006) The theoretical basis for addressing poverty through mixed-income development, *Urban Affairs Review* 42(3), pp. 369–409.
Katz, L., Kling, J. & Liebman, J. (2001) A Moving to Opportunity in Boston: Early results of a randomized mobility experiment, *Quarterly Journal of Economics* 116, pp. 607–654.
Kearns, A. (2002) Response: From residential disadvantage to opportunity? Reflections on British and European policy and research. *Housing Studies* 17(1), pp. 145–150.
Keller, S. (1968) *The Urban Neighborhood*. New York: Random House.
Kingsley, T. & Pettit, K. (2007) Destination neighborhoods of multi-move families in the Moving to Opportunity demonstration. Paper presented at the Urban Affairs Association annual meeting, Seattle, April.
Kleinhans, R. (2004) Social implications of housing diversification in urban renewal: A review of recent literature, *Journal of Housing and the Built Environment* 19, pp. 367–390.
Kling, J., Liebman, J. & Katz, L. (2007) Experimental analysis of neighborhood effects, *Econometrica* 75(1): pp. 83–119.
Lancaster, K. (1966) A new approach to consumer theory, *Journal of Political Economy* 74, pp. 132–157.
Leishman, C. (2007) Hedonic methods and the housing market as a multi-level spatial system. Paper presented at EURA Conference, University of Glasgow.
Leventhal, T. & Brooks-Gunn, J. (2000) The neighborhoods they live in, *Psychological Bulletin* 126(2), pp. 309–337.
Lim, U. & Galster, G. (2009) The dynamics of neighborhood property crime rates, *Annals of Regional Science* 43 (4), pp. 925–945.
Ludwig, J., Duncan, G. & Pinkston, J. (2000) Neighborhood effects on economic self-sufficiency: Evidence from a randomized housing-mobility experiment. JCPR Working Paper159. [http://www.jcpr.org/wp/Wpprofile.cfm?ID=165]
Ludwig, J., Duncan, G. & Hirschfield, P. (2001) Urban poverty and juvenile crime: Evidence from a randomized housing-mobility experiment, *Quarterly Journal of Economics* 116(2), pp. 655–679.
Ludwig, J., Ladd, H. & Duncan, G. (2001) The effects of urban poverty on educational outcomes: Evidence from a randomized experiment, in: W. Gale & J. R. Pack (eds), *Brookings-Wharton Papers on Urban Affairs*, pp. 147–201. Washington, DC: Brookings Institution.
Malpezzi, S. (2003) Hedonic pricing models, in: T. O'Sullivan & K. Gibb (eds), *Housing Economics and Public Policy*, pp. 67–89. Oxford: Blackwell Publishing.
Manski, C. (1995) *Identification Problems in the Social Sciences*. Cambridge, MA: Harvard University Press.
Manski, C. (2000) Economic analysis of social interactions, *Journal of Economic Perspectives* 14, pp. 115–136.
Morris, D. & Hess, K. (1975) *Neighborhood Power*. Boston, MA: Beacon Press.
Musterd, S. (2003) Segregation and integration: A contested relationship, *Journal of Ethnic and Migration Studies* 29(4), pp. 623–641.
Orr, L., Feins, J., Jacob, R. & Beecroft, E. (2003) *Moving to Opportunity: Interim Impacts Evaluation, Final*

Report. Washington, DC: US Department of Housing and Urban Development.

Ostendorf, W., Musterd, S. & De Vos, S. (2001) Social mix and the neighborhood effect: Policy ambition and empirical support, *Housing Studies* 16(3), pp. 371–380.

Pebley, A. & Vaiana, M. (2002) *In Our Backyard.* Santa Monica, CA: RAND Corp.

Plotnick, R. & Hoffman, S. (1999) The effect of neighborhood characteristics on young adult outcomes: Alternative estimates, *Social Science Quarterly* 80(1), pp. 1–18.

Pryce, G. (2008) The nature of housing submarkets. Unpublished paper, Department of Urban Studies, University of Glasgow.

Quercia, R. & Galster, G. (2000) Threshold effects and neighborhood change, *Journal of Planning Education and Research* 20, pp. 146–163.

Quigley, J. & Raphael, S. (2008) Neighborhoods, economic self-sufficiency, and the MTO. Unpublished paper, Department of Economics, University of California-Berkeley.

Rosenbaum, J. (1995) Changing the geography of opportunity by expanding residential choice: Lessons from the Gautreaux program, *Housing Policy Debate* 6(1), pp. 231–269.

Rothenberg, J., Galster, G., Butler, R. & Pitkin, J. (1991) *The Maze of Urban Housing Markets: Theory, Practice and Evidence.* Chicago IL: University of Chicago Press.

Rubinowitz, L. & Rosenbaum, J. (2000) *Crossing the Class and Color Lines: From Public Housing to White Suburbia.* Chicago, IL: University of Chicago Press.

Sampson, R. (1997) Collective regulation of adolescent misbehaviour: Validation results for eighty Chicago neighborhoods, *Journal of Adolescent Research* 12(2), pp. 227–244.

Sampson, R., Morenoff, J. & Earls, F. (1999) Beyond social capital: Spatial dynamics of collective efficacy for children, *American Sociological Review* 64, pp. 633–660.

Sampson, R., Morenoff, J. & Gannon-Rowley, T. (2002) Assessing 'neighborhood effects': Social processes and new directions in research, *Annual Review of Sociology* 28, pp. 443–478.

Sampson, R., Raudenbush, S. & Earls, F. (1997) Neighborhoods and violent crime: A multilevel study of collective efficacy, *Science* 277, pp. 918–924.

Santiago, A., Galster, G. & Kaiser, A. (2008) The financial consequences of low-income homeownership. Unpublished paper, School of Social Work, Wayne State University, August.

Schelling, T. (1971) Dynamic models of segregation, *Journal of Mathematical Sociology* 1, pp. 143–186.

Schelling, T. (1978) *Micromotives and Macrobehaviour.* New York: Norton.

Schnare, A. & Macrae, C. (1975) *A Model of Neighborhood Change.* Contract Report No. 225–4. Washington, DC: The Urban Institute.

Schoenberg, S. (1979) Criteria for the evaluation of neighborhood viability in working class and low income areas in core cities, *Social Problems* 27, pp. 69–85.

Schwirian, K. (1983) Models of neighborhood change, *Annual Review of Sociology* 9, pp. 83–102.

Simmel, G. (1971) *George Simmel on Individuality and Social Forms.* Chicago, IL: University of Chicago Press.

Smolensky, E. (2007) Children in the vanguard of the U.S. welfare state, *Journal of Economic Literature* 45, pp. 1011–1023.

Stegman, M., Quercia, R. & Davis, W. (2007) The wealth-creating potential of homeownership: A preliminary assessment of price appreciation among low-income home buyers, in: Willam M. Rohe & Harry L. Watson (eds), *Chasing the American Dream: New Perspectives on Affordable Homeownership*, pp. 271–292. Ithaca, NY: Cornell University Press.

Suttles, G. (1972) *The Social Construction of Communities.* Chicago, IL: University of Chicago Press.

Taub, R. Taylor, G. & Dunham, J. (1984) *Paths of Neighborhood Change.* Chicago, IL: University of Chicago Press.

Temkin, K. & Rohe, W. (1996) Neighborhood change and urban policy, *Journal of Planning Education and Research* 15, pp. 159–170.

Tu, Y. (2003) Segmentation, adjustment, and disequilibrium, in: T. O'Sullivan and K. Gibb (eds), *Housing Economics and Public Policy*, pp. 38-55. Oxford: Blackwell Publishing.

Vandell, K. (1995) Market factors affecting spatial heterogeneity among urban neighborhoods, *Housing Policy Debate* 6(1), pp. 103–139.

Van Kempen, E. (1997) Poverty pockets and life chances, *American Behavioural Scientist* 41(3), pp. 430–449.

Warren, D. (1975) *Black Neighborhoods: An Assessment of Community Power.* Ann Arbor, MI: University of Michigan Press.

Warren, D. (1981) *Helping Networks*. South Bend, IN: Notre Dame University Press.

Warren, R. & Warren, D. (1977) *The Neighborhood Organizer's Handbook*. South Bend, IN: Notre Dame University Press.

Weber, M. (1978) *Economy and Society*, 2 volumes. Berkeley, CA: University of California Press.

Weinberg, B., Reagan, P. & Yankow, J. (2004) Do neighborhoods affect work behaviour? Evidence from the NLSY79, *Journal of Labor Economics* 22(4), pp. 891–924.

Wilson, W. J. (1987) *The Truly Disadvantaged*. Chicago, IL: University of Chicago Press.

SECTION 2

Approaches

David Clapham

INTRODUCTION TO SECTION 2

The aim of Section 2 is to review the different approaches to the analysis of housing. The study of housing has been a multi-disciplinary enterprise and many (but not all) of the main approaches are reviewed here, including economics, sociology, politics, social policy, psychology and geography. There are two contributions in economics and sociology reflecting not only the size of the contributions from these disciplines but also the different approaches within them. All of the contributions reflect on the relationship between the different disciplines and some draw heavily from another discipline in their discussions. For example, the people–environment studies reviewed in Chapter 13 are based in psychology, but use insights from sociology. The behavioural economics tradition reviewed in Chapter 7 incorporates insights from psychology. Therefore, a key theme in the contributions is the desirability of inter-disciplinary analysis and the possibilities, strengths and weaknesses of such an approach.

The inter-disciplinarity shown in housing research may owe something to the small size of the field and its applied nature, which means that academics from different disciplines meet regularly and sometimes tackle the same topics, often from different directions. However, the nature of housing as a commodity/product/physical entity is complex and multifaceted (see Chapter 6 for a list of the factors that may contribute to the difference). Therefore, there is an important discussion about whether it requires different approaches and conceptual tools in order to understand it. For example, the debate in economics over the efficacy of neo-liberal as against behavioural approaches hinges to a large extent on the nature of housing as a different form of commodity than others which therefore requires a different approach. It is probably for this reason that housing is often used as an example by those authors at the forefront of behavioural economics who are seeking to amend the assumptions of the traditional neo-liberal approach.

Section 2 starts with a review of neo-liberal economics (Chapter 6). As Christine Whitehead argues, it has been a very influential approach in housing studies and has been the basis of the modelling that has dominated much work in this tradition. Whitehead asks us to judge the tradition not on whether it is based on an accurate view of how people behave and the market operates, but on whether the predictions derived are accurate and useful. One may think that the one would be dependent on the other, but it may be that the neo-liberal model is a good enough simplification of what actually happens. One of the criticisms of some alternative approaches is that they do not easily lend themselves to generalisation and predictive modelling. One of the heavily criticised elements of the neo-liberal approach is hedonic price modelling in which houses are divided into different attributes which are then priced individually and brought together into a bundle for specific houses. This approach forms the basis of house price models that underpin wider models of the macroeconomy. However, despite their influence there is little evidence that consumers behave in this way towards houses.

Whitehead links closely what she calls neo-liberal economics with neo-liberal philosophy and politics. She sees the economic philosophy and analysis underpinning the move towards privatisation in societies such as those in Eastern Europe. She also points to the move towards demand rather than supply subsidies and the deregulation of housing finance markets as being stimulated by neo-liberal ideas and analysis.

In Chapter 7, Kenneth Gibb takes up some of the criticisms of the neo-liberal approach and reviews the tradition of institutional economics, which sees markets as culturally formed and maintained and eschews the generalised analysis of markets enshrined in neo-liberal economics in favour of an approach based on the analysis grounded in specific times and locations. Gibb reviews a new resurgence of institutional economics that has examined the formal and informal rules that impact on markets. This emphasis has led to a focus on issues such as agency behaviour, transaction costs and property rights. New Institutional Economics (NIE) has been criticised by neo-liberal economists as lacking rigour and mathematical precision and by others as being too tied to neo-liberal assumptions of rationality, individualism and positivism. However, NIE has enabled economists to analyse the public sector in housing by examining issues such as contracting behaviour and the efficiency of different organisational forms.

In an interesting section, Gibb draws links between the institutional tradition and more recent work on the performativity of markets based on material sociology. This work sees markets as interactions between networks of people and material things. He argues that the material sociology approach fits well with an institutional economic approach, as they both focus on the institutional characteristics of the market. Gibb also reviews insights from behavioural economics and shows how it can help to overcome some of the unrealistic rationalistic assumptions about consumer behaviour inherent in the dominant approach. Behavioural economics draws on insights from psychology to illustrate how consumers simplify their search behaviour and tend to make systematic biases in their assessments of the value of properties. In Gibb's view it should be possible to integrate some of the insights from each of these approaches, and he outlines a research agenda to achieve this.

In Chapter 8, Tim Butler and Chris Hamnett take the question – Who lives where? – as the centrepoint of their review of the geographical tradition of housing research. They also pose the related question of how distinctive social and geographical areas come into being and are reproduced in space and time. The example they use for their discussion is that of gentrification – the process by which former working class areas of cities are 'improved' and become middle class enclaves.

They identify three strands of research on social and spatial differentiation – the sociological (based on the work of the Chicago School), the economic (focusing largely on demand preferences) and the geographical. They argue that the reasons for spatial segregation have been sought in the demand preferences of households or in the supply processes of the housing market. They argue for an integrated approach that combines the two approaches. On the supply side they use the work of Harvey and others to focus on the structure of housing supply in the profit-making activities of housing developers, financiers and builders. They use this analysis to explain the move to suburban development which is prevalent in many cities. However, they criticise many economic analyses of housing supply for their relative neglect of rented sectors and particularly the public rented sector. They argue that decisions on this sector require a different form of analysis than those in the housing market and do not lend themselves to traditional economic analysis (for a fuller discussion see Chapter 23).

Butler and Hamnett's analysis of demand issues goes well beyond the usual economic focus on the preferences of households. They use Bourdieu's concept of habitus to illustrate how different people have different ways of thinking and behaving in the housing system, but that these practices are class related and have status implications. They illustrate this with reference to Savage's work on what he calls 'elective belonging' where some middle class households weave their biography into a story of why they live in a particular place and how they relate to it. But Butler and Hamnett argue that housing outcomes are as much about the lack of choice as of the achievement of preferences. Social and spatial segregation can be explained partly from factors of housing supply in particular locations, partly from the preferences or habitus of particular groups, but partly also from the opportunities or lack of them available to households of different class, race and age.

Although, both the previous two chapters have argued for a holistic analysis of housing, there are difficulties with combining theories and concepts derived from disciplines with very different epistemological and ontological positions. For example, economic analysis has found it easier to engage with some psychological theories that share an individualist and positivist tradition than with sociology, which tends to adopt different underlying assumptions about the nature of the world and of the nature of knowledge within it. These tensions are highlighted by David Clapham in Chapter 9, which examines the social policy tradition of research in housing. Housing is an important feature of personal and community life and so it is the subject of political interest and concern and community action. Poor housing conditions can be seen as a problem that governments are urged to ameliorate. Therefore, there has been a tradition of research on housing that has examined housing problems associated with homelessness, poverty and poor health. Much of this research, whether by government, charities or pressure groups, has focused on practical problems and has been empirical and positivist in nature. It has started from what is defined as a social problem and has then gathered empirical material and used this through inductive processes to generate general laws or theories that can guide government action.

Clapham sees the nature of this approach fitting closely a cybernetic policymaking process that values 'neutral facts' and generalised statements or laws. The approach has been challenged by the rise of theoretical awareness in housing research, but will probably still prosper as long as it fits the government policymaking process that it feeds. The two major strengths of the tradition are its focus on practical social problems and the explicit moral stance that underpins some of the work, particularly that funded by pressure groups and voluntary organisations.

Chapter 10, also by David Clapham, examines the social constructionist approach that has underpinned much recent housing research. The approach is based on a disagreement with approaches that assume the objective status of knowledge; a focus on the construction of meaning through social interaction; and the importance of language and discourse in the carrying of meaning. Clapham identifies a number of strands of housing research using this perspective. Probably the most common has been the questioning of taken-for-granted assumptions about the nature of social problems, often through discourse analysis of policies. Another has been research that has focused on the social interactions that shape relationships such as those between landlords and tenants. The third has been international comparisons of housing policies examining the factors that have shaped the different definition of housing problems in different countries. The final strand is made up of the few studies that have used social constructionism as a base for the integration of other perspectives such as the structuration approach of Giddens. Despite the popularity of the social constructionist approach, it has been heavily criticised. Clapham identifies four major criticisms. The first criticism is the lack of a clear conceptualisation of the relationship between the social and the material world, which is particularly important in housing because of the material nature of the house and the embodied use of houses by people. The second criticism is the relative lack of an analysis of power and an incorporation of structural factors in any analysis. The third criticism is the relativist nature of social constructionism that precludes integration with positivist approaches. The fourth criticism is the lack of fit between social constructionism and the policymaking process. Clapham puts forward suggestions for ways of integrating these elements into social constructionist analysis.

If social constructionism can be said to focus on human agency, Chapter 11 by Julie Lawson focuses on the different ways in which social structures have been conceptualised and studied in housing studies. She traces the important work of Castells and Harvey in the 1970s and their impact on housing research. The structural body of work was particularly influential in international comparative housing research, leading to the formulation of the structures of provision thesis that sought to provide a framework to study the similarities and differences between national housing systems. This has been built on by concepts of chains of provision and welfare regimes that use concepts such as commodification to explain change and difference in national housing systems. Regulation theory has also been an influential approach to international comparative research (for a discussion of welfare regimes see Chapter 18).

Lawson also discusses the comparatively underdeveloped field of the application of class analysis to housing. More recent work in this area has been stimulated by the class theories of Bourdieu, which incorporated ideas of cultural capital and class identity in forms of housing consumption. Lawson ends her chapter with some criticisms of the structural tradition and looks towards critical realism as a way of bringing together structural analysis with elements of social constructionism.

In Chapter 17, Bo Bengtsson notes that many housing researchers have focused on government policy, but few have employed a politics perspective, analyzing the political institutions of relevance to housing provision and the games and processes of decision-making per se. His chapter takes a politics perspective and reviews research on housing that focuses on political institutions (state and non-state) and processes of interaction between political elite actors as well as between elite actors and citizens in general. It also discusses applications in housing studies of some normative political concepts like democracy, citizenship and social justice. Bengtsson concludes by calling for the incorporation of political studies approaches with others. For example, he notes the complementarity between 'path dependence' analysis and critical realism. Game theory can be utilized in studies of policy and policymaking alongside concepts such as democracy and power.

In Chapter 13, the final chapter in Section 2, Roderick Lawrence examines the contribution of people–environment studies. Although with a basis in environmental psychology, Lawrence argues that it is essentially a multi-disciplinary approach that focuses on the relationship between people and their domestic environment. He emphasizes the point that housing, dwelling and home are fundamental human constructs that are crucial components of human culture that partly define the condition and status of individuals and households in relation to others in their society. He sees domestic culture as consisting of material artefacts, social organisation (such as the family, etc.) and meanings associated with social and personal identity. He examines the substantial empirical and conceptual understanding generated through people–environment studies.

Lawrence continues with an analysis of ways of gauging the quality of human environments. He argues that housing quality can be interpreted as a relative concept by referring to sets of interrelated constituents and processes that concern not only the material conditions of residential environments but also social relationships (such as landlord and tenant rights and obligations), economic conditions (especially affordability in terms of household budgets) and ecological consequences (including the use of natural resources). This means that commonly used environmental health or other statutory yardsticks of housing quality give only a static and partial picture that is not related to the different and changing goals of individuals.

Lawrence ends his contribution with a discussion of the concepts of inter- and multi-disciplinarity and this is a theme which runs throughout Section 2. He defines multi-disciplinarity as the state of affairs when each discipline stays within its own boundaries and conceptual underpinnings. Inter-disciplinarity is where common or complementary topics may be chosen, and, although each discipline retains its own approach, there is an integration of concepts or findings. But Lawrence's clear goal is the achievement of trans-disciplinarity, which involves the bringing together and the transcendence of individual disciplines with the aim of using common approaches and concepts.

The contributions in Section 2 show the breadth and variety of approaches to the study of housing. In some cases they also show the desire and the perceived need to move towards inter-disciplinary and trans-disciplinary working. Examples may be the links between economics and psychology in behavioural economics, or the wish to bring together political theories of path dependence with critical realism. However, the variety of the contributions here also shows the great challenges involved in attempting fusion or transcendence. Behavioural economics has arisen because of the shared assumptions and approaches between the constituents. But attempts to build on this through the incorporation of other disciplines with different assumptions have proved more challenging. Nevertheless, many chapters also show that housing is a fertile field for attempting such endeavours, as its complexity highlights the constraints of the single-discipline approach.

The Neo-Liberal Legacy to Housing Research

Christine M.E. Whitehead

INTRODUCTION

Definitions of neo-classicism & neo-liberalism

The neo-classical tradition is one where the emphasis is on perfect markets and their outcomes in terms of the efficient use of resources. Distributional issues are seen as distinct to be addressed by government through the redistribution of income and wealth (Bator, 1957; Hicks, 1975).

Over the last decades the emphasis has been not so much on traditional neo-classicism but on a rather more politicised concept of neo-liberalism.

Neo-liberalism is a term which came to prominence in the 1960s and 1970s as a political/economic philosophy which focused on the free market and argued for a massive reduction in government intervention, the liberalisation of markets and particularly of trade. A general definition might be that it blends traditional liberal concerns for social justice with an emphasis on economic growth as a means of achieving that social justice (Harvey, 2005). It is strongly associated with the prevalent policy approach of Ronald Reagan in the United States and the economic and political stance taken by the International Monetary Fund (IMF) and the World Bank (Williamson, 1990). In the UK it is often regarded as synonymous with Thatcherism and particularly with the privatisation of the public realm (Evans, 1997; Clarke, 2004). It is also seen as the dominant principle underpinning the expansion of financial markets over the last decade and therefore at the core of the current global financial crisis.

These are grand political and ideological ideas which have influenced international and national policies across the world. However, they are also strongly grounded in the neo-classical models of efficient markets which form the intellectual basis for assessing the conditions under which privatisation and liberalisation can be expected to operate effectively. In the context of housing, therefore, the neo-liberal legacy comes as much from the pressures to develop these models in the context of housing markets as in the outcomes of the shift towards market-based approaches to housing problems observed across the world.

No one, or almost no one, argues that the market efficiently provides housing across the whole spectrum of requirements. Indeed, governments intervene through an enormous range of instruments covering everything from land supply to individual relationships between landlord and tenant and assistance to improve energy efficiency and ensure affordability. Even so, there is a very significant neo-liberal legacy which has impacted on all aspects of housing decisions and policy not only in countries such as the USA which are strongly market oriented but also in countries which regard housing as part of the welfare state or even the social wage. Indeed, it has framed the research agenda in relation to housing economics for at least the past 50 years.

The obvious positives of this neo-classical and neo-liberal legacy lie in the development of both simple and more sophisticated models that assume housing can be treated like any other good. The factors determining demand and supply can therefore, with carefully applied formal techniques and empirical evidence, be measured, as can the outcomes in terms of price and the quantity supplied. These relationships can then be used to help improve the operation of the housing system.

The neo-liberal legacy, in particular, has other, far less desirable, attributes. Most importantly it has been used to argue that government intervention in the housing market is usually undesirable and that market failures, if they exist, are small as compared to the administrative failures associated particularly with regulation and the direct allocation of housing resources.

It has further been used to suggest that it is never, or hardly ever, appropriate to provide housing specific subsidies, and particularly supply-side subsidies, as these will, in their terms, inherently be a less efficient means of improving income distribution than income and wealth transfers.

To address these issues, we look first at the basics of the neo-classical and neo-liberal approaches, and their antecedents in the economics literature; secondly, we examine the main predictions and relationships which can be attributed to neo-classical and neo-liberal analysis; and thirdly, we look at its impact on the relationship between the economics of housing and other disciplines and the implications of these findings for housing policy. Finally, we assess the likely legacy as economics and finance markets appear to be moving towards a stronger regulatory framework related more to a behavioural economics approach which aims to harness the perceived excesses of the market.

Positioning the neo-classical and neo-liberal approaches to housing

The basic neo-classical model sets out the necessary conditions under which markets operate efficiently and the issues of efficiency can be separated from those of distribution and equity. More generally, it helps to clarify the basic determinants of demand, supply and adjustment to change.

The conditions necessary for prices to allocate resources efficiently are extreme: all goods must be homogeneous and traded on the market; all consumers must maximise their own utility, while all firms maximise profit; there must be free entry and exit to all production and consumption; certainty and no transactions costs; and no externalities, either positive or negative. Were these assumptions to hold, it would then be possible to separate questions of efficiency from those of distribution and equity – so government could concentrate on ensuring all households are able to access adequate housing through income and wealth redistribution (Bator, 1957; Hicks, 1975).

Clearly these assumptions cannot hold in the real world for any good, let alone housing. Even so, in many circumstances frictionless, neo-classical models can have value because they point to the most important relationships and enable us to build models that help us better to understand how housing systems operate. In other words, neo-liberal models are not about process and it is not a valid criticism to say that 'people do not behave like that'. What matters is whether, as a result of these models, there are valid predictions about behaviour and outcomes. Assessing the neo-liberal legacy is therefore about whether these predictions help us to improve the allocation of resources to and within the housing system. That depends on two things: (1) whether the predictions reflect the evidence on outcomes and are robust and (2) whether there are other factors which must be taken into account because they are as (or more) important than the elements included in these highly abstract approaches.

There are many different attempts to provide a typology of the most important attributes of housing which clearly violate the basic assumptions of the neo-classical model (Charles, 1977; Smith, Rosen and Fallis,, 1988; Miles, 1994; Whitehead, 1998). A typology relevant to assessing the neo-liberal approach might include:

1 Any dwelling is made up of a complex bundle of multiple attributes, reflecting at the least the physicality of the dwelling, the quality of services within the dwelling, the neighbourhood and accessibility to activities.
2 Housing is a long-lasting asset which is locationally specific, indivisible and cannot be costlessly transformed to meet changing demands.
3 Because housing is a big costly indivisible asset, both consumers and producers are highly dependent on the finance market, which is itself imperfect.
4 The housing market involves a large number of individual relationships – e.g. between owner and occupier, occupier and neighbours, owner and financiers, and many others. All of these relationships are likely to be complex and to involve asymmetric information and relative power.
5 Both with respect to new investment and the use and maintenance of the property, housing and land markets are closely intertwined. In particular, much of the value of housing can be associated with land and location rather than specifically to dwelling, and land ownership structures affect the extent of competition in the market.
6 The housing market is typified by slow adjustment, with much more rapid response on the demand than on the supply side. The relationship between the market for new investment and that for existing dwellings is affected by all the complexities listed above.
7 More generally, taking an active part in housing and the related markets of land and finance involves significant transactions costs and risks, associated both with inadequate information and market asymmetries.
8 Because the market is inherently imperfect, the neo-liberal assumption that efficiency and distribution can be treated as separable issues is difficult to sustain. Moreover, because housing is a necessity but takes a large part of most people's incomes, the issues of equity and distribution are core to ensuring acceptable housing outcomes.
9 Because government intervention is so all-pervasive in housing systems, it is never possible to start from 'a clean sheet' when analysing behaviour or evaluating policy. Models of housing that can provide an evidence-based approach to policy change must therefore address not only the complexities of the market but also political and social as well as economic outcomes.

These, and many other equivalent typologies, would suggest that the housing good is certainly not homogeneous; by no means all of its value is traded on the market; consumers cannot be expected to maximise utility because of the complexity of the product; production similarly involves complexities both with respect to land and investment in the existing stock; there are many constraints on entry and exit notably with respect to land and finance; there are large, sometimes very large, transactions costs and uncertainties; and there are obvious social costs and benefits which accrue to neighbours and to society as a whole.

Given the extent to which housing contradicts the basic assumptions of the neo-liberal approach, at first sight it appears extraordinary that the neo-classical model that underlies the neo-liberal approach can have any significant value, let alone that it is the starting point for so much of research and thinking in the field. Indeed, commentators from other disciplines and paradigms sometimes do take the view that economists of this persuasion are too far away from reality to be relevant. Yet the reality is that a sophisticated version of neo-liberalism which addresses at least some of the complexities discussed above has increasingly dominated both theory and policy over the last few decades.

NEO-CLASSICISM, NEO-LIBERALISM AND HOUSING MARKETS

The starting point

Analysis of how markets work and the most important aspects of these markets go back far further than the formal models of the late 20th century. The economics of Adam Smith and Marshall concentrated on the role of price in determining the allocation of resources and the importance of marginality in optimising decisions. Equally, ideas of neo-liberalism are grounded in the political theory of the 18th and 19th century which concentrated on identifying the appropriate role of the state (Blaug, 1996).

Early urban housing systems were almost wholly privately organised, with only limited regulation to address public health and safety issues. The outcomes of these market decisions were highly undesirable in terms of the effective use of land, the quality of housing and infrastructure services provided, the allocation of available housing resources across income groups and many other obvious imperfections. The result was the much of the analytic interest in the 19th and early 20th century was on the one hand in how land markets operate in relation to residential development and on the other in both the efficiency and distributional problems associated with poor-quality housing in urban areas. These analyses were almost all quite partial, looking at specific relationships which were perceived as relevant to particular policy issues.

The policy outcomes, at least in the UK, involved increased regulation, notably of building standards but later also in the context of rents; the public provision of water sewerage and other urban utilities necessary for the provision of adequate housing; and increasing concerns about affordability. It was only in the immediate post-war period that housing came to be regarded as a central aspect of the welfare state, not only in the UK but in much of northern Europe. But this was, again, the outcome of political belief rather than economic analysis.

It is not really until the 1950s and 1960s that the detailed economic analysis of housing and related markets became important in research terms. This development was grounded in the neo-classical models of economics. It was also led almost entirely by American academics whose starting point was that the market should provide for all but the poorest.

Unless it is possible to abstract away from the complexities of housing, it is not possible to develop more general predictive models which must have mathematical tractability as well as practical relevance. It is this fundamental development that has enabled housing and urban economists to begin to contribute to these analyses by abstraction and simplification together with an increasing emphasis on empirical testing.

The starting point for this approach was undoubtedly the article by Muth in Harberger (1960) which redefined housing for the purposes of modelling as an unidimensional and divisible product. Here he identified the unit of measurement as 'that quantity of service yielded by one unit of housing stock per unit of time' (p. 32) where the stock is to be measured by its constant dollar value and price is determined for a standard unit. It is this approach which is carried forward into the seminal work by Muth (1969) in which he argues that 'my usage of the term price of housing is perfectly analogous to the meaning more readily attached to the term price of food, namely the expenditure required to obtain a given "market basket" of food and related items' (p. 32). This approach matched well with that of Alonso (1964), Mills (1967) and others working on the development of access/space models of urban areas. By assuming normal substitution effects between space and structure, and further assuming competition in the construction market, it was possible to develop predictions about the spatial relationships of density and price within the urban area, suggesting that both would decrease with distance from the city centre. The first comprehensive attempt at testing these relationships was that by Muth himself (1969) using data from 46 cities.

A very different but highly complementary approach to understanding and measuring the good housing was that grounded in the more general characteristic approach developed by Lancaster during the same period (Lancaster, 1966, 1979). With respect to housing, this emphasised the heterogeneity of the housing product but made it possible to evaluate different bundles of attributes within the same total expenditure package. The assumption here is that households value goods by their characteristics and that a well-operating market will generate different groupings of characteristics in relation to relative costs. The approach was described formally by Rosen (1974) who set out a model of demand, supply and competitive equilibrium. It is this approach that lies behind the use of hedonic price models which enable the complexity of housing to be encapsulated in a single price variable.

Although this approach makes the heroic and unrealistic assumption of fully adjusted market equilibrium for the housing overall, and for each element of the composite good that makes up the housing product, the results are generally seen as robust enough to be used across a wide range of housing decisions. They underpin housing valuation principles used for taxation purposes, and house price indices which are an essential element of macroeconomic policy. They provide a wealth of information about the relative value of different physical, neighbourhood and accessibility attributes which can be used by actors in the market place as well as planners and policymakers.

Understanding housing markets

The central elements of a neo-classical approach must be a clear understanding of the nature of demand, supply and price, both in the housing market itself and in the related land and finance markets (Buckley, 1982; Hansket, 1979; Quigley, 1982). Understanding these relationships has continued to be the core agenda for mainstream economic research in housing – and the most positive legacy of neo-classicism (see also Chapter 1).

The most fundamental assumption is that housing is a private good where the benefits go to the owner and/or the occupier of the dwelling. Undoubtedly the consumption of housing is both rival and excludable, the necessary attributes of a good that can in principle be provided by the market. Most importantly, because of different preferences, so that the utility of a particular dwelling depends significantly on the attributes of the household, the benefits of choice lies at the core of libertarian views that housing should be privately provided and allocated (Whitehead, 1991). Yet, this assumption is very much the opposite of the view held by governments in countries with significant welfare states, where housing was seen as having an important social value over and above the individual household's utility, and at the limit in socialist economies, where housing was regarded as an element in the social wage, allocated by government and charged at a nominal price.

Housing demand

The assumptions made in all housing market modelling is that private demand and supply make up that market; that government intervention, including non-market sectors, can be modelled by modifying the values of the variables determining demand, supply and price; and that issues associated with the social value of housing will be addressed using the outcome of these models rather than playing any integral part in their specification.

The positive neo-classical legacy is perhaps most obvious in the development of robust measures of income and price elasticities of demand for housing. These have come increasingly to recognise more complex attributes of housing demand notably with respect to the measures of income, price and quantity.

An important starting point was that by Reid (1962) in which, using Friedman's permanent income hypothesis and aggregate data, she found that the income elasticity of demand might be nearer two than the usually assumed value of unity or below. Starting with Lee (1964, 1968), much of the work thereafter was concentrated on refining both specification and testing, particularly to take account of the problem that what is observable is expenditure rather than price and quantity separately (de Leeuw, 1971, 1976). Household-level studies, which tended to result in far lower income elasticities, were the next breakthrough. In particular, Polinsky (1977) showed how separating out transitory income, interpreted as variance around aggregate estimates, allowed a better specification of permanent income, while Polinsky and Ellwood (1979) took account of spatial variations in measured prices to improve the estimates of both price and income elasticities.

One issue has been whether and how income elasticities vary with level of income. Ihlanfeldt (1982) suggested elasticities were higher for higher-income groups, while Hansen et al. (1996), using Lorenz curves, showed income elasticity to be less than unity at all income levels. These findings have clear implications for any economy where the distribution of income is widening – as is the case in most advanced economies at the present time – because it suggests that lower-income households will find it increasingly difficult to compete for scarce housing resources. Another finding has been on joint modelling of demand and tenure, which tends to suggest that permanent income is more important for tenure choice than the level of demand (Goodman, 1988).

Initial UK analyses tended to stress the importance of tenure: for instance, Byatt et al. (1973) suggested that income elasticities were higher for owner-occupation than for the private rented sector. A second area of analysis in the UK context was the impact of financial constraints on the individual household's capacity to adjust housing expenditure to desired levels. Mervyn King (now Governor of the Bank of England) for instance, showed that, while individually based measures of income elasticity were still inelastic, once financial constraints were taken into account income elasticities would be much closer to unity (King, 1980). Again, both these findings are relevant to policy and choice, suggesting that financial liberalisation and an emphasis on owner-occupation may better meet individual objectives. In this context, later work suggests income elasticities of unity or above (Muellbauer & Murphy, 1997; Pain & Westerway, 1997) (further details of results can be found in Whitehead, 1999 and Meen, 2001).

In the comparative context, the detailed work undertaken at the World Bank (Mayo, 1981; Jimenez & Keane, 1984; Mayo & Malpezzi, 1985) showed that income elasticities are reasonably constant across countries and, by implication, that different administrative systems did not significantly modify the underlying responsiveness of housing demand to economic growth. The research also showed differences in elasticities between rental and owner housing; and that governmental and other constraints were important in limiting adjustment. These findings supported the World Bank's policy of regularisation of housing property rights, reducing land constraints and particularly improving housing finance markets (Dunkerley, 1983; Chiquier & Lee, 2009).

Estimates of price elasticities followed a similar pattern. Early unit cost-based measures tended to generate estimates ranging from -0.3 to -0.7 in the United States (de Leeuw, 1971; Maisel et al., 1971). Estimates based on appraisal data suggested the upper end of the range (Polinsky, 1977; Polinsky & Ellwood, 1979). Using grouped data tended to increase both income and price elasticities in comparison to individual observations but still generated estimates of a similar order (Rosenthal, 1989).

An important question for policy and the construction industry is the extent to which income and price elasticities vary across different attributes (Kain & Quigley, 1975; King, 1976, 1977; Witte et al., 1979; Follain & Jimenez, 1985). Relevant studies use a range of approaches: for instance, Awan et al. (1982) and Parsons (1986), which estimated an Almost Ideal Demand System developed by Deaton and Muellbauer (1980) across a range of attributes; Ball and Kirwan (1975, 1977), which took account of space and structure; and Boehm (1982), which examined the demand for dwelling size and quality in relation to tenure choice. All these studies tend to suggest that income and price elasticities vary considerably across the ranges of attributes that have been identified, notably with respect to space, structure and environment, as do cross-elasticities of demand with respect to substitute and complementary attributes.

Later work has evaluated price and income elasticities within the wider analysis of urban areas. In the USA these differential estimates are crucial to the analysis of segmented markets (Rothenburg et al., 1991) – a necessary element in understanding segregation and exclusion (Galster, 2001). In the UK, Cheshire and Sheppard (1995, 1998), in an analysis of the impact of land-use planning on demand and house prices, suggested particularly high income elasticities of demand, as well as large price elasticities because of a capacity to adjust between attributes.

An area of particular concern with respect to demand is that of tenure choice (Henderson and Ioannides, 1986). The American literature tends to treat the decision as dependent simply upon economic and demographic variables, with particular emphasis on price differentials between tenures (Kain & Quigley, 1972; Struyk, 1976, McDonald, 1979; Megbolugbe & Linneman, 1993). The assumption has been that credit market constraints could either be priced or were irrelevant. Later developments have concentrated on how best to define the user cost of housing, taking account of both local and national taxation policies was well as inflationary expectations within the context of life-cycle models (Kearl, 1979; Hendershott, 1980; Follain, 1982; Wheaton, 1985; Goodman, 1988). Similar studies have been undertaken in Australia, where the inclusion of well-defined user costs have significantly improved goodness of fit (Bourassa, 1995).

In the European context, far more of the emphasis has been on constraints on tenure choice arising from financial restrictions and rent regulation as well as the relationship between the market and administratively allocated social housing. King (1980), for instance, stressed the nature of the joint decision between quantity and tenure in a system where there was rationing in both of the two main tenures. Meen (1989), in particular, modelled the impact of the ending of mortgage rationing, suggesting much greater responsiveness. Ermisch et al. (1996), using data for 1988 and 1989 when financial rationing for owner-occupation had almost disappeared, found aggregated price elasticities ranging from −0.35 to −0.44.

Finally, there is the question of the number of households in the market place. Over the last decade there has been considerable interest in this issue in the UK, particularly with respect to whether the number of households is endogenous to the housing market (Ermisch, 1999; Meen et al., 2005). The evidence suggests that demographic factors are quantitatively more important than economic factors in determining household formation; that the income elasticity is relatively low except for younger single-person households; and that housing cost/price elasticities are lower than income elasticities (Clark & Dielman, 1996; Bramley et al., 1997; Meen et al., 2005). These findings have enormous importance for projecting demand for housing and its impact on price into the longer term.

Housing supply

One of the most important attributes of housing is the fact that new supply forms only a very small proportion of the total supply of housing at any given time. Moreover, the overall supply of housing is modified not just by new building but also by improvement and conversion of the existing stock, on the one hand, and depreciation of that stock, on the other. Equally, new housing supply is made up of both land and structure, which means that the analysis of housing supply must be linked both to the operation of land markets and the organisation of the construction industry (see Chapter 2). It is perhaps not surprising therefore that, for both technical and data reasons, neo-classically based models of supply appear to have made relatively little progress as compared to those dealing with demand (Quigley, 1979; Olsen in Mills, 1987).

De Leeuw and Ekanem (1971) is the usual starting point for analysis of the responsiveness of supply to price. This study used cross-sectional data to estimate a reduced-form equation where the assumption was that long-run supply was in equilibrium. The results, which suggested very low price elasticities of supply, have been strongly criticised on both empirical and theoretical grounds (see, e.g., Follain, 1979; Quigley, 1979; Olsen in Mills, 1987). Later cross-sectional work by Stover (1986) and more formal modelling approaches by Smith (1989) suggested that the long-run supply elasticity is close to infinite, a result consistent with time series analyses by both Muth (1960) and Follain (1979).

Since then there has been an increasingly important empirical literature on housing supply elasticities in the USA relating to planning but also to other sources of constraint which can occur in market-oriented systems. Cross-metropolitan studies suggested that there were considerable differences between cities (Mayer & Somerville, 2000; Green et al., 2005). Later surveys have stressed the range from near-infinite elasticity in the sunbelt to considerable constraints in superstar cities (see, e.g., Glaeser, 2004; Gyourko, 2008).

British contributions to the literature on supply and housing markets tend both to give less emphasis to cross-sectional analysis (in part because of a paucity of the necessary locally based data) and more to the flow of new building, rather than the stock of housing services. The provenance of these models is usually that of estimating investment at the national level, as an input into wider macroeconomic analysis. Their emphasis is on stock adjustment towards equilibrium (Hendry, 1984; Meen, 1989).

Early econometric models tended to distinguish construction costs, credit availability and land costs as determinants of new supply (Whitehead, 1974; Hadjimatheou, 1976). They typically found that borrowing constraints and land prices were relatively insignificant in determining that supply, although this may in part have been a result of the quality of the aggregate data. Later models have incorporated formal optimisation decisions by builders as well as more appropriate error correction and forward-looking techniques which emphasise the importance of expectations (Tompkinson, 1979; Ericsson & Hendry, 1985; and particularly Tsoukis & Westaway, 1994). Dynamic models of economics with credit constraints have been used to explain cycles in durable asset investment, including residential property (Kiyotaki & Moore, 1997).

A particularly important issue has been the impact of land markets and planning regimes on the supply elasticity. In the USA there is a long tradition of analysis of the impact of zoning in land and housing markets (e.g. Grieson & White, 1981; Mark & Goldberg, 1986). The model by Mayo and Sheppard (1991, 1996) examines the effect of stochastic development controls and suggests that there may be situations in which increases in demand could impact more on the price of vacant land than on developed land, resulting in a reduction in current supply. In the UK context, Cheshire and Sheppard (1989) examined the impact of land-use controls on supply and access to housing to two areas – one with tight controls, the other less constrained – and found that constraints were important in both. Bramley (1993) estimated a cross-sectional model across local authorities, suggesting that land availability at the district level impacted significantly on housing output. Malpezzi and Maclennan (2001) show very considerable differences between supply elasticities in the more constrained UK as compared to the USA. Work by Meen for the Barker Review further supported the negative impact of land constraints, as did that by Hilber at the local level (Meen, 2005; Hilber & Vermeulen, 2010). In the Netherlands, Vermeulen and Rouwendal (2007) found elasticities as low as 0.2, again related to planning constraints.

International comparisons suggest that, unlike demand elasticities, supply elasticities vary enormously between countries and are dependent on each country's property rights and planning regimes (Malpezzi and Mayo, 1997). Mayo and Sheppard (1994), in particular, point to the negative impact in countries using traditional UK planning permission-based systems. All of the models introduce these constraints within neo-classical models, which assume constant construction costs.

House prices

The final area in positive economics where the neo-classical model has dominated is in the context of asset pricing and housing finance markets. The most influential model has undoubtedly been that by Poterba (1984, 1991 and 1992), which set out a two-equation stock flow rational expectations model to test for whether housing markets are efficient given that population movements are predictable. This suggested that demand shocks would be followed by supply adjustment, which might take decades even with relatively large elasticities. It also predicts overshooting but not cycles. Other research has concentrated on the relative importance of speculative bubbles and fundamentals. In the USA, Abraham and Hendershott (1966) find bubbles, but only in coastal regions. Muellbauer and Murphy (1997) suggest the existence of market frenzy arising from transactions costs. Meen (2008), on the other hand, sees fundamentals (including structural changes in determining variables) as central to house price determination, although there may have been some overvaluation in the UK after 2005.

NEO-LIBERAL INFLUENCES ON POLICY: PRIVATISATION

As has already been noted, much of post-war Europe was characterised by the growth of the welfare state (Esping-Anderson, 1990 and 1996). In the context of housing this involved large-scale government intervention in housing, particularly with respect to new building, rent regulation and the administrative allocation of housing. Most of Scandinavia, the Netherlands, France and the UK, in particular, saw massive growth in their social, as well as declines in their regulated private rented, sectors. In socialist countries the prevalence of government intervention and the lack of private property rights made public housing even more dominant, especially in urban areas where apartment blocks predominate.

It was in this context that the ideas of neo-liberalism started to take hold on public policy at the same time as finance markets in general and residential mortgage markets in particular were starting to be liberalised. The first depended on the second in Western Europe. In Eastern Europe, initial transfers after the fall of communism involved near-zero priced restitution as well as a concentrated effort to build new financial markets in line with IMF/World Bank policy (Doling, 2007).

Restitution

In Eastern Europe the rapidity and extent of privatisation through restitution was quite extraordinary. In all but one of the 18 countries included in the UN-ECE statistics, more than 50% of the public rental sector of 1990 had been privatised by 2000. The exception was Poland, at 49.1%. In 10 of the countries the proportion was over 70% and, within this group, six had privatised over 90% of the public stock. The reality was that there was very little choice, as institutional structures did not exist to maintain a social sector, given the extent of retrenchment of the state. There were, however, massive costs and inefficiencies involved, because of the poor condition of the dwelling stock, the state monopoly of management and maintenance companies and price controls of housing-related services remained in place. The consequences in terms of physical structures and the provision of utilities have been very costly (Hegedüs & Teller, 2004. In addition, the lack of well-operating finance markets has made it difficult to generate a second-hand market or the capacity to finance improvements, while the rapid decline of social housing, without a strong household-based subsidy system has left very few options for poorer and younger households. In addition, in some Eastern European countries there has been an increase in the numbers of mortgages denominated in foreign currencies – increasing risks very considerably (Lux, 2010; Hegedus & Sunega, 2010).

Privatisation in Western Europe

In Western Europe, the UK led the way in both the growth of owner-occupation and the privatisation of public housing:

- first, through the expansion of lending in the 1960s and then the liberalisation of the mortgage market in the 1970s and early 1980s;
- secondly, through the transfer of ownership to owner-occupation under the Right to Buy scheme;
- thirdly, through the introduction of private finance into social housing provision.

As a result, owner-occupation increased in England from under 50% in 1970 to almost 70% at the turn of the century, and public housing was restructured, so that by 2010 housing associations were the majority provider of a much smaller sector.

The economic rationale for the privatisation of housing had many facets. First, as incomes rose over the post-war years, housing standards for the vast majority of households were well above those necessary to ensure adequate minimum physical comforts (Whitehead, 1993; Lundquist, 1992). The numerical deficit had been overcome by 1971 – and, indeed, in that year there were more dwellings than households in almost all local authorities in England. The same was true across most of Northern Europe, except West Germany (which anyway had a relatively small public sector). Secondly, the case for housing as a private good of choice strengthened as the consumption of housing increased, so people were purchasing a wider range of attributes whose value depended on their own preferences – a home of any type anywhere was no longer the basis for provision. Privatising housing allocation could therefore almost certainly increase the overall value of a given housing stock. Thirdly, there was increasing evidence of the inefficiency of public sector providers, who faced few incentives to minimise costs and incomplete and costly monitoring processes.

More ideologically, housing was an ideal starting point for the implementation of the neo-liberal agenda to limit the role of the state and to 'sweat' public assets more effectively. The Right to Buy was an important – and extremely popular – policy in the Conservative Party's 1979 election manifesto and indeed the only element of their privatisation programme that had been spelled out before they were elected.

Even so, it could reasonably be argued that the main rationale was not ideological but simply to reduce the public spending borrowing requirement. Deregulation of the mortgage and finance markets provided the opportunity to enable assets to be transferred to their occupiers and later to refinance much of the existing social sector stock through transfers to non-profit housing associations. The sale of assets raised large-scale funds and was indeed the biggest privatisation programme up to the late 1980s. Equally, housing took 80% of the net cuts in public expenditure during the first two years of government (Whitehead, 1993).

Few countries implemented policies with such a clear-cut set of objectives as that found in the UK – but the general pressures were similar. During the following decade across Europe the need to cut public spending, and in particular to meet the new European budgetary requirements, dominated much of the housing agenda (Turner & Whitehead, 1993). Most countries experienced both cutbacks and targeting of general supply-side subsidies as well as an increasing use of private finance. Associated with these changes were increasing concerns about affordability among lower-income households.

Arguably, there were three distinct pressures to increase owner-occupation after 1980: continued growth in incomes, which favoured owner-occupation as the tenure of choice for more settled households; the continued deregulation of mortgage and finance markets, which made this possible; and specific government subsidies to support entry into owner-occupation. All these pressures were observed across Europe to a greater or lesser degree but were undoubtedly strongest in the UK, where the ideological basis for privatisation remained in place until 1997. An assessment of changes in England up to 1989 suggested that these three elements were of roughly equal weight. Even so, it was the liberalisation of mortgage and finance markets that facilitated all three (Kleinman and Whitehead, 1988). As a result, England moved from being in the lowest group of countries in terms of the proportion of households in owner-occupation to being in the middle group of countries that included most of the Anglo-Saxon world (Holmans et al., 1996). However, a similar pattern could be observed in many countries in Europe – with increases of over 10% over the period 1980 to 2002 in the proportion of owner-occupiers in Belgium, Greece, Italy, the Netherlands, Norway, Spain and Sweden as well as in the UK.

Overall, the results of privatisation have been seen to be desirable for the vast majority of those who were able to purchase – in part because they were often somewhat more established households who were able to pay but had been excluded from owner-occupation by the highly regulated finance market up to the 1980s and in part because they benefited from subsidies and tax advantages. The problems have been more in terms of the greater concentrations of poverty among tenants and of large mono-tenure estates in the social sector across much of Northern Europe (Whitehead & Scanlon, 2007). The second major problem, which has greatly worsened during the 21st century, has been the increasing difficulties of access and affordability for new entrants to the owner-occupied market and the inadequate response of the private rented sector to the needs of younger, more mobile and poorer households. To this extent, the neo-liberal legacy has clearly been to worsen the situation for those lower down the income scale – and to redistribute income and wealth to established owners at a cost to the next generation.

THE FAILURES OF NEO-LIBERALISM

The two most obvious areas where the neo-liberal legacy can be seen to have failed lie with the excesses of the finance market in the 21st century and the outcome of transferring subsidy from bricks and mortar to households. The first appears to be a failure of theory as well as of practice; the second can be interpreted as a failure of government to provide adequate demand-side subsidies and of markets to respond to demand- rather than supply-side incentives, associated with continuing emphasis on housing standards above those that individuals can afford in a world where the distribution of income is worsening.

Liberalisation of finance markets

The seminal work by Poterba (1984) was the first major approach to the use of asset pricing models in the context of housing. Since that time there have been many attempts to test for efficiency in housing markets (Case and Schuller, 1989). However, most commentators on both sides of the Atlantic doubt whether a full rational expectations framework is appropriate in the case of housing (Poterba, 1991; Barkham & Geltner, 1996; Clayton, 1996; Muellbauer & Murphy, 1997).

It is in the context of finance markets that the theoretical underpinning of neo-liberal economics has been particularly questioned (Malkiel, 1996; Shiller, 2003). The efficient market hypothesis which underlies most modern financial theory requires not just that agents are utility maximisers but they have rational expectations and that new information is always incorporated to update these expectations. As with other neo-classically based models, the theory does not require that all investors act correctly – rather, that their reactions are randomly distributed and follow a normal distribution. Thus, no one can outwit the market on the basis of publicly available information. As such, the model is an extreme extension of neo-classical assumptions that underscore all of the emphasis on liberalisation and globalisation of finance markets.

Behavioural economists, in particular, have argued against the efficient market hypothesis on both theoretical and empirical grounds. They suggest that the very significant imperfections, arising from cognitive biases from overconfidence, information bias and other human errors in reasoning and information processing, make the predictions unsafe (Frank & Bernanke, 2008). Empirical evidence tends to suggest that strong versions of the efficient market hypothesis are not upheld and that market behaviour favours growth – which, in turn, generates a propensity for speculative bubbles (Malkiel, 2010). (For a broader account of behavioural economics see Chapter 7.)

During the early years of mortgage liberalisation there was strong evidence that improved access to finance not only enabled large numbers of households who had otherwise been excluded to purchase but also that risks remained low and real interest rates fell even in the face of a large-scale growth in demand for mortgage market finance (Diamond & Lee, 1992; European Mortgage Federation, 2003). The situation changed in England during the later part of the 1980s when there was a massive expansion in available funds, in part because of the entry of centralised lenders in the market (Holmans et al., 2003). Competition among lenders led to high loan-to-value (often well over 100%) and loan-to-income ratios. When the economy turned and unemployment and inflation increased, there was a major crisis for many households – but the financial institutions survived almost unscathed (although there was direct help given to support insurance companies who bore the immediate losses) (Megalube & Whitehead, 1994; Whitehead & Gaus, 2007). This, however, was only a preliminary to the run-up to the major financial crisis, starting in 2007, which involved the global system (Miles, 2003; Girourd et al, 2006; Girmaud et al., 2006). Responses to the crisis have been very different across countries – but the clearest message has been that the belief in neo-liberal financial markets has been shattered (Edelstein et al., forthcoming; Priemus & Maclennan, forthcoming). One result has been a move towards basing decisions on the assumptions underlying behaviourism by policymakers and regulators – signalling greater regulation (Financial Services Authority, 2009, 2010).

Shifting from subsidy to demand-side subsidies

The logic of the neo-liberal approach to subsidies is that these will be more efficient if they are targeted at low-income households, who will then be better able to compete in the market place. This is based on a number of assumptions, including that price effects arising from the additional demand will be offset by expansion of supply; that incentives to work will not be reduced; and that there are no direct social benefits to housing standards above those provided by the market. In particular, it takes no account of the large literature on second best which suggests that, if the objective is to improve income distribution, in imperfect markets supply-side subsidies which ensure the provision of necessary goods may generate larger Pareto improvements than supporting demand. This is because the distortion arising from a below market price for the necessary good which would normally have a price-inelastic demand is less than distortions arising in both the labour market and the goods markets from the income subsidy (Bos & Seidl, 1986; Bos, 1991).

The related policy debate has been very much one between economists in the USA, where market solutions remain prevalent, and those in Europe, where institutional structures have favoured both a more welfare approach to housing and supply interventions (Whitehead and Scanlon, 2007) (for a detailed discussion of institutional economics, see Chapter 7). The discussion came to the fore again in the 1990s as governments across Europe both reduced the extent of supply subsidies and increased the relative emphasis on income-related benefits (Turner & Whitehead, 1993, 2002). The discussion has centred on the potentially effective role of movement between submarkets in supporting demand-side approaches, on the one hand, and the extent to which income-related benefits either fail to generate adequate supply and/or cannot ensure adequate standards while maintaining incentives, on the other (Galster, 1997; Yates & Whitehead, 1998; Kemp, 2008). More generally, the debate suggests that the neo-classical approach, while stressing the benefits of deregulation, is not in itself an acceptable basis for housing policy because of the importance of market failures and the importance of housing in welfare.

A rather different but equally relevant question lies in the reasons for supply inelasticity not only in highly regulated economies such as the UK and the Netherlands – as discussed above in the second section – but also increasingly in more market-oriented countries. Neo-liberals argue that variations between cities and countries are significantly the outcome of differential regulatory frameworks – and that liberalisation is necessary to improve the operation of housing systems. Many other more policy-oriented commentators, particularly those concentrating on political economy, argue that as incomes grow the implicit value to society – and particularly its richer members – of constraint increases resulting in lower supply responses (Barker, 2004, 2008).

CONCLUSIONS

Neo-classical models have undoubtedly been at the core of the economics of housing over the last half century. Without these models there would have been little capacity to predict behaviour and test these predictions. However, housing is always some way along the spectrum of market failure, and housing markets are always the subject of intervention to improve both market outcomes and the distribution of housing resources. No one, therefore, uses these models without noting the extent to which the results need to be treated with particular care (for a discussion of drawbacks of neo-classical legacy to housing research see Chapter 1).

In the context of positive economics, the principles of neo-classical economics have resulted in robust empirical analyses of some areas of housing markets, notably with respect to demand. But the fundamental that demand for housing adjusts far more rapidly than supply and that new supply is such a small part of the total makes it more difficult to explain supply and investment behaviour as well as to predict prices, supply and market volatility. Even so, it is difficult to believe that the neo-classical model will be superseded, as opposed to complemented, by other economic models. The new forms of behavioural economics help to explain process but ultimately rely on the principles of neo-classical economics – as indeed was the case in the earlier phase of behaviouralism led by Herbert Simon and others (Simon, 1957; Rubinstein, 1998).

The big problems emerge if neo-classical models are accepted as a full reflection of reality rather than as a valuable element in understanding. The use of extreme rational expectations models in the context of rapidly adjusting finance markets is the most obvious area of concern, mainly because of the massive negative impacts on world financial markets – and thus housing markets (Quiggan, 2010, Posner 2010).

The same applies to neo-liberalism in the context of housing policy. It is often said that economists only manage to persuade policy-makers of very simple economic principles – such as that poll taxes and, indeed, demand-side subsidies are economically efficient – and that the results are usually disastrous because they are implemented simplistically without account of institutional realities or path dependency. Housing is a complex good. To have a chance of success, policies to improve the allocation of housing resources require as much and more sophistication and patience as has been expended on positive economic modelling.

REFERENCES

Alonso W (1964) *Location and Land Use*, Harvard University Press, Cambridge, MA.
Abraham JM & Hendershott PH (1996) "Bubbles in metropolitan housing markets", *Journal of Housing Research*, 7(2): 191–207.
Awan, K, Odling-Smee JC & Whitehead CME (1982) "Housing attributes and the demand for private rented housing", *Economica*, 49: 183–200.
Ball M & Kirwan R (1975) *The Economics of an Urban Housing Market*, Bristol Area Study, Centre for Environmental Studies, London.
Ball M & Kirwan R (1977) "Accessibility and supply constraints in an urban housing market", *Urban Studies*, 14: 11–32.
Barker K (2004) *Review of Housing Supply: Delivering Stability – Securing our Future Housing Needs*, HM Treasury, London.
Barker K (2008) "Planning policy, planning practice, and housing supply", *Oxford Review of Economic Policy*, 24(1): 34–49.
Barkham RJ & Geltner DM (1996) "Price discovery and efficiency in the UK housing market", *Journal of Housing Economics*, 5(1); 41–63.
Bator F (1957) "The simple analysis of welfare maximisation", *American Economic Review*, 47(1): 22–59.
Blaug M (1996) *Economic Theory in Retrospect*, University of Cambridge Press, Cambridge.
Boehm (1982) "A hierarchical model of housing choice", *Urban Studies*, 19: 17–31.
Bourassa, SC (1995) "A model of housing tenure choice in Australia", *Journal of Urban Economics*, 37: 161–175.
Bos, D (1991) *Privatisation: A Theoretical Treatment*, Clarendon Press, Oxford.
Bos, D & Seidl, C (1986) *Welfare Economics and the Second Best*, Springer-Verlag, Berlin.
Bramley, G (1993) "The impact of land use planning and tax subsidies on the supply and price of housing in Britain", *Urban Studies*, 30: 5–30.
Bramley G, Munro M & Lancaster S (1997) *The Economic Determinants of Household Formation: A Literature Review*, Department of Environment, Transport and the Regions, London.
Buckley, RM (1982) "A simple theory of the UK housing sector", *Urban Studies*, 19(3): 303–312.
Byatt ICR, Holmes P & Laidlaw DW (1973) "Income and the demand for housing: some evidence for Great Britain", in JM Parkin (ed.), *Essays in Modern Economics*, Longman, London.
Case KE & Schiller R (1989) "The efficiency of the market for single family homes", *American Economic Review*, 79(1): 345–363.
Charles S (1977) *Housing Economics*, Macmillan, London.
Cheshire P & Sheppard S (1989) "British planning policy and access to housing", *Urban Studies*, 26: 469–485.
Cheshire P & Sheppard S (1995) "On the price of land and the value of amenity", *Econometrica*, 62: 247–267.
Cheshire P & Sheppard S (1998) "Estimating the demand for housing, land and neighbourhood characteristics" *Oxford Bulletin of Economics and Statistics*, 60(3): 357–382.

Chiquier L & Lea M (2009) *Housing Finance Policy in Emerging Markets*, The World Bank, Washington, DC.

Clark WA & Dielman FM (1996) *Households and Housing: Choice and Outcomes in the Housing Market*, Rutgers University Press, New Brunswick, NJ.

Clarke J (2004) "Dissolving the public realm? The logics and limits of neo-liberalism", *Journal of Social Policy*, 33: 27–48.

Clayton J (1996) "Rational expectations, market fundamentals and housing price volatility", *Real Estate Economics*, 24(4): 441–470.

Deaton A & Muellbauer J (1980) "An almost ideal demand system", *American Economics Review*, 70: 312–326.

de Leeuw F (1971) "The demand for housing: A review of cross-section evidence", *Review of Economics and Statistics*, 53: 1–10.

de Leeuw F (1976) "The demand for housing: A review of the cross-sectional evidence", *Review of Economics and Statistics*, 53: 1–10.

de Leeuw F & Ekanem NF (1971) "The supply of rental housing", *American Economic Review*, 61: 806–817.

Diamond D & Lee M (1992) "Housing finance in developed countries: An international comparison of efficiency", *Journal of Housing Research*, 3(1).

Doling J (2007) "Homeownership policies in Europe: Limits to growth", in D Czischke (ed.), *Current Developments in Housing Policies and Housing Markets in Europe*, CECODHAS, Brussels.

Dunkerley H (ed.) (1983) *Urban Land Policy: Issues and Opportunities*, Oxford University Press, Oxford.

Edelstein R, Bardham, A & Kroll, C (forthcoming) *One World, One Crisis, the Global Housing Market Meltdown*, University of California, Berkeley, CA.

Ericsson NR & Hendry DF (1985) "Conditional econometric modelling: An application to new house prices in the UK", in AC Atkinson & SE Feinberg (eds), *A Celebration of Statistics*, Springer-Verlag, Berlin.

Ermisch J (1999) "Prices, parents and young people's household formation", *Journal of Urban Economics*, 45(1): 47–71.

Ermisch J, Findlay J & Gibb K (1996) "The price elasticity of demand for housing in Britain: Issues of sample selection", *Journal of Housing Economics*, 5: 64–86.

Esping-Andersen O (1990) *The Three Worlds of Welfare Capitalism*, Polity Press, Cambridge.

Esping-Andersen O (1996) *Welfare States in Transition*, Sage, London.

European Mortgage Federation (2003) (Mercer Oliver Wymer) *Financial Integration of European Mortgage Markets*, EMF, Brussels.

Evans FJ (1997) *Thatcher and Thatcherism*, Routledge, London.

Financial Services Authority (2009) *Mortgage Market Review*, Discussion Paper 09/3, FSA, London.

Financial Services Authority (2010) *Mortgage Market Review: Responsible Lending*, Consultation Paper 10/16, FSA, London.

Follain JR (1979) "The price elasticity of the long-run supply of new housing", *Land Economics*, 55: 190–199.

Follain JR (1982) "Does inflation affect real behaviour? The case of housing", *Southern Economic Journal*, 48: 570–582.

Follain JR & Jimenez E (1985) "Estimating the demand for housing characteristics: a survey and critique", *Regional Science and Urban Economics*, 15: 77–107.

Frank RH & Bernanke BS (2008) *Principles of Economics*, 4th edn, McGraw Hill, Maidenhead.

Galster G (1997) "Comparing demand side and supply side housing policies: Market and spatial perspectives", *Housing Studies*, 12: 561–577.

Galster G (2001) "On the nature of neighbourhood", *Urban Studies*, 38(12): 2111–2124.

Girouard N, Kennedy M & André C (2006) *Has the Rise in Debt Made Households More Vulnerable?* OECD Working Paper No. 535, OECD website at http://www.oecd-ilibrary.org/economics/has-the-rise-in-debt-made-households-more-vulnerable_352035704305

Girouard N, Kennedy M, van den Noord P & André C (2006) *Recent House Price Developments in the Role of Fundamentals*, OECD Working Paper No. 475, OECD website at http://www.oecd-ilibrary.org/economics/recent-house-pricedevelopments_864035447847

Glaeser EL (2004) *Housing Supply*, NBER Reported Research Summary, NBER, New York.

Goodman AC (1988) "An econometric model of housing price, permanent income, tenure choice and housing demand", *Journal of Urban Economics* 23(1): 327–353.

Green RK, Malpezzi S & Mayo SK (2005) "Metropolitan-specific estimates of the price elasticity of supply of housing, and their sources", *American Economic Review*, 95(2): 334–339.

Grieson RE & White JR (1981) "The effects of zoning on structure and land markets", *Journal of Urban Economics*, 10: 27–85.

Gyourko J (2008) *Housing Supply*, prepared for the *Annals of Economics*, mimeo, Wharton School.

Hadjimatheou G (1976) *Housing and Mortgage Markets*, Saxon House, Farnborough.

Hansen JL, Formby JP & Smith WJ (1996) "The income elasticity of demand for housing: Evidence from concentration curves", *Journal of Urban Economics*, 39: 173–192.

Hanushek E & Quigley J (1979) "The dynamics of the housing market: A stock adjustment model of housing consumption", *Journal of Urban Economics*, 6: 90–111.

Hanushek E & Quigley J (1982) "The determinants of housing demand", in J Vernon Henderson (ed.), *Research in Urban Economics*, Vol. 2, JAI Press, Greenwich, CT, pp. 221–242.

Harvey D (2005) *Brief History of Neo-liberalism*, Oxford University Press, Oxford.

Hegedüs J, Lux, M and Sunega P "Decline and Depression: the impact of global economic crisis on housing markets in two socialist states". *Journal of Housing and the British Environment*, DOI 1-.1007/s 10901-011-9228-7.

Hegedüs J & Teller N (2004) "The social and economic significance of housing management", in *Housing in Eastern Europe (Solving a Puzzle of Challenges)*, World Bank and Council of Europe Development Bank, pp. 21–34.

Hendershott P (1980) "Real user costs and the demand for single-family housing", *Brookings Papers on Economic Activity*, 2: 401–144.

Henderson JV & Ioannides YM (1986) "Tenure choice and the demand for housing", *Economica*, 53: 231–246.

Hendry D (1984) "Econometric modelling of house prices in the UK", in DF Hendry & KF Wallis (eds), *Econometrics and Quantitative Economics*, Blackwell, Oxford.

Hicks (1975) "The scope and status of welfare economics", *Oxford Economic Papers*, 27(3): 307–326.

Hilber C & Vermeulen W (2010) *The Impact of Restructuring Housing Supply on Housing Prices and Affordability*, Final Report, Department of Communities and Local Government, London.

Holmans A, Freeman A & Whitehead C (1996) *Is the UK Different? International Comparisons of Housing Tenure Patters*, Council of Mortgage Lenders, London.

Holmans AE, Karley NK & Whitehead CME (2003) *The Mortgage Backed Securities Market in the UK: Overview and Prospects*, Council of Mortgage Lenders at www.cml.org.uk

Ihlanfeldt KR (1982) "Property tax incidence on owner-occupied housing: Evidence from the Annual Housing Survey", *National Tax Journal*, 35: 89–97.

Jimenez E & Keane D (1984) "Housing consumption and permanent income in developing countries: Estimates from panel data in El Salvador", *Journal of Urban Economics*, 15: 172–194.

Kain J & Quigley J (1972) "Housing market discrimination, home-ownership and savings behaviour", *American Economic Review*, 62: 263–277.

Kain JF & Quigley JM (1975) *Housing Markets and Racial Discrimination*, National Bureau of Economic Research, New York.

Kearl JR (1979) "Inflation, mortgages and housing", *Journal of Political Economy*, 87(5): 1115–1138.

Kemp P (ed.) (2008) *Housing Allowances in Comparative Perspective*, Policy Press, Bristol.

King AT (1976) "The demand for housing", in N Terleckyj (ed.), *Household Production and Consumption*, National Bureau of Economic Research, New York.

King AT (1977) "The demand for housing: A Lancaster approach", *Southern Economic Journal*, 43: 1077–1087.

King MA (1980) "An econometric model of tenure choice and the demand for housing as a joint decision", *Journal of Public Economics*, 14: 137–159.

Kiyotaki N & Moore JE (1997) "Credit cycles", *Journal of Political Economy*, 105: 211–248.

Kleinman M & Whitehead C (1988) "British housing since 1979: Has the system changed?", *Housing Studies*, 3: 3–19.

Lancaster KJ (1966) "A new approach to consumer theory", *Journal of Political Economy*, 74: 132–157.

Lancaster K (1979) *Variety, Equity and Efficiency*, Basil Blackwell, Oxford.

Lee TH (1964) "The stock demand elasticities of non-farm housing", *Review of Economics and Statistics*, 49: 82–89.

Lee TH (1968) "Housing and permanent income", *Review of Economics and Statistics*, 50: 480–490.

Lundqvist LJ (1992) *Dislodging the Welfare State? Housing and Privatisation of Four European States*, Delft University Press, Delft.

Lux M (2010) "The impact of the global economic crisis on housing markets in two post socialist states", paper presented at ENHR International Conference, July, Istanbul.

McDonald JF (1979) *Economic Analysis of an Urban Housing Market*, Academic Press, New York.

Maisel SJ, Burnham JB & Austin JS (1971) "The demand for housing: A comment", *Review of Economics and Statistics*, 53: 410–415.

Malkiel BG (1996) "Bubbles, rational expectations and financial markets" in *A Random Walk down Wall Street*, WW Norton.

Malkiel BG (2010) *Bubbles in Asset Prices*, CEPS Working Paper No. 200, January, Princeton.

Malpezzi S & Maclennan D (2001) "The long-run price elasticity of supply of new residential construction in the United States and the United Kingdom", *Journal of Housing Economics*, 10: 278–306.

Malpezzi S & Mayo S (1997) "Getting housing incentives right: A case study of the effects of regulation, taxes and subsidies on housing supply in Malaysia", *Land Economics*, 73(3), 372–391.

Mark JH & Goldberg MA (1986) "A study of the impacts of zoning on housing values over time", *Journal of Urban Economics*, 20: 257–273.

Mayer CJ & Somerville CT (2000) "Land use regulation and new construction", *Regional Science and Urban Economics*, 30(6): 639–662.

Mayo SK (1981) "Theory and estimation in the economics of housing demand", *Journal of Urban Economics*, 10: 95–116.

Mayo SK & Malpezzi S (1985) *Housing Demand in Developing Countries*, WP-733, The World Bank, Washington, DC.

Mayo S & Sheppard S (1994) "Housing supply under rapid economic growth and varying regulatory stringency: An international comparison", *Journal of Housing Economics*, 5(3): 274–289.

Meen G (1989) "The ending of mortgage rationing and its effects on the housing market: A simulation study", *Urban Studies*, 26: 240–253.

Meen G (2001) *Modelling Spatial Housing Markets: Theory, Analysis and Policy*, Kluwer Academic Publishers, Boston.

Meen G (2005) "On the economics of the Barker Review of Housing Supply", *Housing Studies*, 20: 949–971.

Meen G (2008) "Ten New Propositions in UK Housing Macroeconomics: an overview of the first years of the century", *Urban Studies*, Vol 45, No 13, pp. 2759–2781.

Meen et al. (2005) "Affordability targets: Implications for housing supply", ODPM Research Report and Technical Appendix, ODPM, London.

Megbolugbe I & Linneman P (1993) "Home ownership", *Urban Studies* 30: 659–682.

Megbolugbe I & Whitehead C (eds) (1994) "Understanding structural adjustment of the mortgage market in the US: Lessons from the protracted real estate recession in the UK", *Housing Policy Debate* Special Issue, 5(3): 219–230.

Miles D (1994) *Housing, Financial Markets and the Wider Economy*, Wiley, Chichester.

Miles D (2003) *The UK Mortgage Market: Taking a Longer Term View*, Interim Report December 2003 and Final Reports March 2004 at www.hm-treasury.gov.uk/miles

Mills ES (1967) "An aggregative model of resource allocation in a metropolitan area", *American Economic Review*, 57: 197–210.

Muellbauer J & Murphy A (1997) "Booms and busts in the UK housing market", *Economic Journal*, 107: 1701–1727.

Muth RF (1960) "The demand for non-farm housing", in: A Harberger (ed.), *The Demand for Durable Goods*, University of Chicago Press, Chicago, pp. 29–96.

Olsen EO (1987) "The demand and supply of housing service: A critical survey of the empirical literature", in ES Mills (ed.), *Handbook of Regional and Urban Economics*, North Holland, Amsterdam.

Pain N & Westaway P (1997) "Modelling structural change in the UK housing market: A comparison of alternative house price models", *Economic Modelling*, 14(4): 587–610.

Parsons GR (1986) "An almost ideal demand system for housing attributes", *Southern Economic Journal*, 53: 347–363.

Polinsky AM (1977) "The demand for housing: A study in specification and grouping", *Econometrica*, 45: 447–461.

Polinsky AM & Ellwood DT (1979) "An empirical reconciliation of micro and grouped estimates of the demand for housing", *Review of Economics and Statistics*, 61: 199–205.

Posner R (2010) "After the blow-up", *The New Yorker*, 11 January 2010.

Poterba JM (1984) "Tax subsidies to owner-occupied housing: An asset-market approach", *Quarterly Journal of Economics*, 99: 729–752.

Poterba JM (1991) "House price dynamics: The role of tax policy and demographics", *Brookings Papers on Economic Activity No 2*, 143–199.

Poterba JM (1992) "Taxation and housing: Old questions, new answers", *Papers and Proceedings of the American Economic Association*, May: 237–242.

Priemus, H & Maclennan, D (forthcoming) "The credit crunch and the resilience of housing systems", special issue of *Journal of Housing and the Built Environment*.

Quiggan J (2010) *Zombie Economics: How Dead Ideas Still Walk Among Us*, Princeton University Press, Princeton, NJ.

Quigley J (1979) "What have we learned about urban housing markets?", in P Mieszkowski & M Straszheim (eds), *Current Issues in Urban Economics*, Johns Hopkins Press, Baltimore, pp. 391–429.

Reid M (1962) *Housing and Income*, University of Chicago Press, Chicago, IL.

Rosen S (1974), Hedonic prices and implicit markets product differentiation – pure competition, *Journal of Political Economy*, 82, 34–55.

Rosenthal L (1989) "Income and price elasticites of demand for owner-occupied housing in the UK: Evidence poled cross-sectional and time series data", *Applied Economics*, 21: 761–775.

Rothenburg J, Galster GC, Butler RV & Pitkin J (1991) *The Maze of Urban Housing Markets*, University of Chicago Press, Chicago, IL.

Rubinstein A (1998). *Modeling Bounded Rationality*. MIT Press, Boston, MA.

Simon H (1957) "A behavioral model of rational choice", in *Models of Man, Social and Rational: Mathematical Essays on Rational Human Behavior in a Social Setting*. Wiley, New York.

Smith JW (1989) "A theoretical analysis of the supply of housing", *Journal of Urban Economics*, 26: 174–188.

Smith LB, Rosen KT & Fallis G (1988) "Recent developments in economic models of housing markets", *Journal of Economic Literature*, 26: 29–64.

Stover M (1986) "The price elasticity of supply of single family detached housing", *Journal of Urban Economics*, 20: 331–340.

Struyk RJ (1976) *Urban Home Ownership*, DC Heath, Lexington.

Tompkinson P (1979) "A model of housebuilder's supply behaviour", *Applied Economics*, 11: 195–210.

Tsoukis C & Westaway P (1994) "A forward looking model of housing construction in the UK", *Economic Modelling*, 11: 266–279.

Turner B & Whitehead CME (1993) *Housing Finance in the 1990s*, SB56, The National Institute for Building Research, Gävle.

Turner B & Whitehead C (2002) "Reducing housing subsidy: Swedish housing policy in the international context", *Urban Studies*, 39(2): 201–217.

Vermeulen W & Rouwendal J (2007) "On the price (in) elasticity of Dutch housing supply", paper presented at ENHR International Conference, Rotterdam.

Wheaton WC (1985) "Life-cycle theory, inflation and the demand for housing", *Journal of Urban Economics*, 18: 161–179.

Whitehead CME (1974) *The UK Housing Market: An Econometric Model*, Saxon House, Farnborough.

Whitehead CME (1991) "From need to affordability", *Urban Studies*, 8: 871–886.

Whitehead CME (1993) "Privatising housing: An assessment of UK experience", *Housing Policy Debate*, 4(1): 104–139.

Whitehead CME (1998) *The Benefit of Better Homes*, Shelter, London.

Whitehead (1999) "Urban housing markets: Theory and policy" in ES Mills & P Cheshire (eds), *Handbook of Regional and Urban Economics*, Elsevier Science, North Holland.

Whitehead C (2007) "Privatisation of housing in Europe: Challenges for social housing providers", in D Czischke (ed.), *Current Developments in Housing Policies and Housing Markets in Europe*, CECODHAS, Brussels.

Whitehead C & Gaus K (2007) *At Any Cost? Access to Housing in a Changing Financial Marketplace*, Shelter, London.

Whitehead C & Scanlon K (2007) *Social Housing in Europe I*, LSE, London.

Shiller R (2003) "From efficient market theory to behavioural finance", *Journal of Economic Perspectives*, 17(1): 83–104.

Williamson J (1990) "What Washington means by policy reform", in J Williamson (ed.), *Late American Adjustment: How Much has Happened?*, Institute for International Economics, Washington, DC.

Witte A, Sumko H & Erikson H (1979) "An estimate of a structural hedonic price model of the housing market: An application of Rosen's theory of implicit markets", *Econometrica*, 47: 1151–1174.

Yates J & Whitehead C (1998) "In defence of greater agnosticism: A response to Galster's comparing demand-side and supply-side housing policies", *Housing Studies*, 13(3): 415–423.

7

Institutional Economics

Kenneth Gibb

INTRODUCTION

Economics as a discipline has a long tradition of studying the nature and effects of institutions in terms of their consequences for economic systems and behaviour. This concern has fractured into different institutional schools which possess both overlapping and diverging features. Crudely, institutional economics (sometimes called 'old' institutional economics) is associated chiefly with the work of Veblen, Commons and Mitchell, but has (in part due to its inherent interdisciplinarity) retained considerable heft for a range of social scientists not least in the housing, planning and property fields (Hodgson, 1988, 1996, 1998; Ball et al., 1998; Guy and Henneberry, 2000, 2002; McMaster and Watkins, 2006; McMaster, forthcoming). At the same time, and more in tune with, though distinct from, mainstream economics, the new institutional economics – associated with Coase, Simon, Williamson, Demetz, Hart and Grossman – has developed a research programme concerned with the economic consequences of inter alia transactions costs, property rights and bounded rationality, and considered the implications for corporate governance and public policy. Again, though to a lesser extent, housing economists have embraced these issues and techniques (Marsh, 1995; Ball et al., 1998; Webster, 2003; Webster and Lai, 2003; Gibb and Maclennan, 2006; Gibb and Nygaard, 2006; Nygaard et al., 2007, 2008; Nygaard, forthcoming; Chen and Webster, forthcoming).

This chapter is concerned with the role of institutions and institutional economics and their application to housing phenomena. There are boundary issues here about what should be included and excluded from this chapter. Consequently, while most of the chapter emphasises the above 'traditions' in institutional economics, the penultimate section does introduce a number of related studies in the housing field which touch on institutional dimensions of housing markets and housing systems: the recent application of ideas of performativity to housing markets, and the potential application of behavioural economics to housing (possibly in conjunction with institutionalist ideas). Section 2 of the chapter reviews the main features, distinguishing points and controversies between the old and new institutional economics. Section 3 surveys the ways in which this body of work has been applied in the housing studies realm. Section 4 briefly considers possible extensions and new agendas that link institutions to housing systems. This includes a digression into behavioural economics (which is closely linked to the idea of bounded rationality) and considers its implications for housing analysis, including recent efforts to incorporate institutional factors within the behavioural framework – Marsh and Gibb, 2009; Gibb, forthcoming). Section 5 concludes the chapter and identifies a possible research agenda for future work in this area.

ECONOMICS AND INSTITUTIONS

Institutions have a long and rather complex history within the evolution of economics. Although this chapter makes no attempt to be comprehensive, it does emphasise three broad phases: the original wave of 'old' institutional economics (OIE) and its related ideas and arguments; the body of work now commonly known as new institutional economics; and more recent developments that hark back to older ideas, though these are often manifested outside of the economics discipline (and applied to housing, planning, urban studies and related subjects). In this section, there is a brief account of the principal features and controversies surrounding each of these developments, leaving most of the housing-related applications to the section thereafter.

The 'old' institutionalist approach to economics

One of the most useful definitions of an institution was provided by the institutional economist Walter Hamilton [*writing in 1932*]. He saw an institution as 'a way of thought or action of some prevalence and permanence, which is embedded in the habits of a group or the customs of a people' (Hodgson, 1998, p. 179).

The institutionalist work associated with Hamilton, Commons, Mitchell and Veblen was, for a brief period, dominant in North American university economics departments and the American Economics Association but declined after 1930 (Hodgson, 1998, p.166; McMaster and Watkins, 2006). Hodgson argues that while Commons and others did link institutionalism to key ideas in both evolutionary and behavioural economics, the theoretical framework was lacking in that there was no agreement over, or indeed any systematic treatment of, a 'theoretical core'.

The institutional economics school went into decline, in part reflecting wider scientific methodological trends embracing positivism rather than their pragmatism-based philosophy and in economics, in particular, the upsurge in the formal neo-classical methodology rooted, eventually, in utility-maximising rational self-interested individualism (Hodgson, op. cit.). However, in the period since broadly the mid-1980s, there has been a discernible increase in the adaptation of institutionalist approaches within the social sciences (Adams et al., 2005a, p. 37), particularly with respect to understanding state–policy relations, drawing on a range of social science disciplines. Institutional ideas have come to be bound up with and help reinforce important analytical frameworks such as structure–agency explanations of social and economic processes (including policymaking) and the institutional thickness of actor–network relationships. Adams et al. (p. 39), referring to Samuels (1995), argue that institutional economics indicates that markets 'both reflect and help to operationalise the institutional structure of society'. This also means that broader variables such as the distribution of power and cultural influences also help explain how markets work and allocate resources.

Going forward, Hodgson and others have sought to develop a programme of work linking institutionalism to evolutionary economics and also to broader political economy approaches that straddle different social science disciplines. This is also apparent in the more applied areas of housing, property and urban development (Adams et al., 2005a), where similar convergences are underway, as well as links to behavioural economics and uncertainty, which are discussed later in this chapter (Marsh and Gibb, 2009).

What are the key ideas associated with the older institutionalist perspective? Hodgson argues (1998, p. 168) that institutionalism does not seek to devise a single general model because inherently it seeks to develop time- and place-specific accounts based on habit, custom, agency and evolution. It is because of this essential contingency to empirical circumstances in real markets at a point in real time that makes the search for general theories of institutionalism so elusive and arguably misplaced. Moreover, Hodgson argues (p. 169) that the focus should be on not the general but the specific through the application of a range of non-economic social science accounts of behaviour: 'if institutionalism had a general theory, it would be a general theory indicating how to develop specific and varied analyses of specific phenomena' (op. cit.).

Habit, inertia and routine behaviour are central to the older institutionalist framework (Hodgson, 1997). This is closely related to the social dimension of consumption, harking back to Veblen (1899) but also Duesenberry. Partly this is explained by adherence to the consequences of Herbert Simon's bounded rationality (wherein economic agents may at best follow rules of procedural rationality rather than aspire to the unrealistic calculations required of substantive rationality in decision making in the face of imperfect knowledge and uncertainty), but also through support of the pragmatist philosophy of Peirce (McMaster and Watkins, 2006; McMaster, forthcoming). Hodgson (1998) contends that institutions, rules and habits are critical to society and create an interactive relationship between individuals and slowly changing institutions (p. 181). Adams et al. (2005a) emphasise the political economy aspects of institutional analysis: in particular, the importance of power relations and the functional role institutions play in providing stability in uncertain markets and economic systems much more characterised by disequilibria and shocks than the economic mainstream would suggest (p. 45).

The recurring criticisms of the old insititutionalist framework are readily described. As we have seen, it is often viewed as atheoretic or under-theorised or in danger of being excessive empiricism lacking conceptual rigour. There is also a sense, particularly for more mainstream economists that the OIE is a bit woolly, pragmatic to the extent of being ad hoc in the way that it bolts on useful ideas from other places when it sees fit. Hodgson (1998) provides a stout defence of this broader and more open approach to economic analysis but he does recognise legitimate criticisms of overly empiricist research. However, in taking head-on the criticism of where institutions come from (e.g. Ball et al., 1998) and whether in fact institutions are explainable ultimately from individual behaviour, he concludes that the resulting infinite regression has no satisfactory answer or rebuttal (p. 184). Clearly, institutionalism is in part about a fusion of economics and sociology, the individual and the social, and it is inherently hard to communicate between different schools with very different positions on the centrality of decision-making and behaviour with respect to individual or social primacy.

The new institutional economics approach

> Institutions are the humanly devised constraints that structure political, economic and social interaction. They consist of both informal constraints (sanctions, taboos, customs, traditions and codes of conduct) and formal rules (constitutions, laws, property rights) (North, 1991, p. 97).

New institutional economics (hereafter NIE to distinguish from the older tradition) is a very different though discernibly related school of economic analysis. More modern in its history, it too has been enjoying a resurgence and indeed wider recognition in economics and the social sciences, including its application to housing, property and land market research.[1] The NIE body of work begins with the singular contribution of Coase (1937, 1960) who developed and extended the key ideas of transactions costs as explanatory ideas indicating why organisations develop internal structures or instead subcontract with market suppliers; and, also the importance of property rights in terms of a theoretical solution to the problem of externalities. From these two papers has been spawned a massive and growing literature (see also Demetz, 1967; Williamson, 1975, 1985, 2000; Simon, 1982, 1984; Grossman and Hart, 1986; Furubotn and Richter, 1991; North, 1991; Hart, 1995; Chen and Webster, forthcoming; Nygaard, forthcoming).

Coase (1937, 1960) developed a theory of the minimisation of transactions costs as a way of optimising both the relationship of a firm with its wider market and the underlying governance of the firm (in Williamson's language where it was on the spectrum between a market-focused firm and a bureaucratic hierarchy in terms, for example, of the decision to outsource supplies and specialist services or to develop them in-house). In the later paper, Coase went on to link property rights to transactions costs, arguing that where such costs tended to zero, it would be possible to reassign property rights to overcome problems associated with the social cost of externalities, thereby theoretically undermining the standard market failure case for intervention in such cases. This view of the world has come to be seen as a precursor of the public choice and government failure scepticism about the state's capacity to efficiently intervene. However, as Williamson and others have indicated, the issues to do with property rights, transactions costs and contracts have to be understood in a world of bounded rationality, agency problems and information asymmetries: i.e. where markets are more or less imperfect and choices are often suboptimal. It is not state-bad or market-good – but a search for the best institutional arrangements in a flawed, complex and procedurally, if not substantively, rational world.

Williamson (2000) distinguishes between three broad levels of analysis (ignoring the informal institutions of customs, traditions, mores and embedded norms of what he calls social theory – which if course has a clear resonance with the older tradition in institutionalism). First, there is the economics of property rights and what he calls the formal rules of the institutional environment. Williamson argues (p. 599) that the economics of property rights has been greatly strengthened by focus on the enforcement of contracts and their governance. This is really his next level of analysis – governance and its alignment with transactions and the specific focus on transactions costs. While Williamson argues that these two levels are the primary domain of NIE, he does recognise a further level of analysis, wherein resource allocation takes place, which he sees as primarily the space for neo-classical economics, but this is also where problems of incentives and agency arise, both of which are important to the NIE story. It is this link or overlap with the neo-classical frame of reference that is central to non-mainstream critiques of the NIE (and we discuss this below).

Williamson identifies a number of 'good ideas' associated with the NIE body of work (2000, pp. 600–607). The first of these is the the notion of bounded rationality and consequent cognitive limits to optimisation, leading to, among other things, the likelihood of incomplete contracts. The impact of these ideas on economic behaviour becomes all the more significant when combined with other informational problems such as opportunism, adverse selection, moral hazard, etc. (p. 601). A second good idea concerns feasible alternative organisational structures. All such structures are costly and imperfect – the real issue is about identifying which is least costly and in that sense efficient (rather than deal in theoretical optimising ideals). A third idea concerns the distinction made between firms and bureaus – to understand the basis by which to prefer different governance structures comparing between complete markets and hierarchies through the analysis of which structure minimises transactions costs. Fourthly, Williamson considers the effective formalisation (within limits) of the theoretical development of these core ideas (and in this regard, overcomes the perceived weakness of the older institutionalism) to be a significant development within NIE. Finally, Williamson indicates (p. 607) that a substantial body of empirical analyses of these matters across a range of sectors and applications has now been assembled.

The critique of NIE comes from within and without the mainstream economics fraternity. Within the mainstream, NIE has been sometimes viewed as somewhat second class and lacking the rigour or mathematical formalism of neo-classical economics. At worst, it has been attributed as displaying 'worrying' tendencies to draw from other social sciences and to rely less heavily on formal testing. Ball et al. (1998, p. 116) note the practical problems found trying to measure accurately transactions costs. It is noteworthy, however, that in applied areas of economics such as public finance, health economics or urban economics, there has been a much greater willingness to embrace its 'good ideas'.

Ironically, the critique from outside of the mainstream argues that NIE is too close to neo-classical economics and all the problems associated by critics to its methodological positivism, individualism and rationality assumptions. Hodgson (1998) squarely views the NIE edifice as based on methodological individualism wherein rational economic behaviour is utilised to explain the emergence of economic institutions from a theoretical institution-free state of nature. We saw earlier that there is a case to say that the importance of bounded rationality to NIE softens this critique. Nonetheless, it remains reasonable to say that the analysis does work from neo-classical core presumptions such as fixed or exogenously given preferences (in the penultimate section of the chapter we consider allying institutional ideas to behavioural economics which does not necessitate given preferences on the parts of individuals, although it is still otherwise positivist, methodologically). Hodgson (op. cit.) focuses on the philosophical problem of imagining an institution-free world with which to develop economic institutions – we saw this infinite regress problem with the old institutionalists in a different respect but it clearly also applies to NIE so conceived.

APPLICATIONS TO HOUSING

> A simple word count of the current UK literature on property markets would suggest that institutions are enormously important, given the sheer scale of the number of books and articles devoted to analysing them and their effects (Ball et al., 1998, p. 108).

It should not be surprising that insitutional analysis has played a considerable role in housing studies, and related research in urban land and property markets. There are a number of reasons for this intersection. First, institutional themes have remained important outside of economics, and in recent decades sociologists, human geographers and others have drawn on concepts such as structure and agency, actor–networks, structures of provision and related frameworks with which to understand market processes and policy development in the built environment sphere. Secondly, these non-economic antecedents also overlap and communicate with the reformulation of institutional economics with evolutionary economics by Hodgson, as applied by Adams et al. (2005b) in what they call a political economy approach to state–market relations in the property sector. Thirdly, many economists interested in non-market housing and property research have found the NIE toolbox of transactions cost economics, property rights analysis and agency incentives helpful to better understand a wide range of questions stretching from the organisational form of not-for-profits and neighbourhood analysis to questions to do with political decisions over future ownership of landlord vehicles (e.g. Maclennan and More, 1997; Gibb and Maclennan, 2006).

Fundamentally, individual, social, economic, technical and legal relations with the housing commodity in its different guises lend themselves to different forms of institutional analysis. The durable and spatially fixed nature of housing, the possibility of separating ownership from consumption through rental tenures, the association of people with places and their connection to specific landlords, developments and neighbourhoods, and the pervasive impact of state intervention in the housing system all serve to create opportunities or spaces where habit and custom, power relations and institutions matter in both routine and more significant transactions involving housing and the community. At the same time, it seems likely that whatever the nature of the housing relationship to the market (or indeed non-market housing), questions of property rights, contractual relations, organisational design, agency problems and transactions costs minimisation will be relevant and can act as a lens on housing processes and policy debates. The multi-dimensional complexity of housing choice, and allied to it the rapid redundancy of knowledge of the market, also suggest the likely importance of bounded rationality on the part of individual economic agents.

In this section, an overview of housing and institutions research is organised. This builds on other earlier reviews (e.g. Ball et al., 1998; Adams et al., 2005a) but also casts the net a little wider to take account of other developments, particularly with respect to non-market housing and applications to neighbourhoods. This is not supposed to be comprehensive but rather to identify key themes and debates.

Moving beyond more mainstream approaches (including NIE and asymmetric information-based analysis), Ball et al. (1998), helpfully identify five clusters of relevant institutional theories applied to housing and property:

- Accounts based often on the role of individuals as opposed to wider markets and other institutions: these types of studies vary considerably and lack a core theoretical basis. They are to be found particularly in the commercial property literature, e.g. Scott (1996), and have little scope to generalise from (Ball et al., 1998, p. 120).
- Conflict institutionalism: by definition, much of the development process involves disputes between interested parties and the state, the local community, landowners, property developers, multiple local government and public agencies. These different parties have shifting and more or less distinct interests and objectives and may not be genuinely consistent or reducible to a clear platform (Fainstein, 1992). This pluralist perspective can be readily adapted to try to understand the resolution of conflict within, for instance, spatially based urban regeneration programmes and plans.
- Behavioural institutionalism challenges instrumentalist optimising assumptions within neo-classical economics by distinguishing them from the the 'real' observed motivations of particular actors in property markets. Institutions and culture are argued to lie behind the behaviour of key agents such as landowners, developers, housing consumers (suggesting, for instance, that homeownership may be itself an institution – see below). Ball et al. (1998) suggest that major landowners have been closely examined within this tradition, e.g. public ownership (Adams et al., 1988) and financial institutions (Guy and Henneberry, 2000). While this makes undoubtedly a valuable contribution that warns the analyst about overgeneralisation, Ball et al. (1998, p. 124), list several conceptual and practical shortcomings relating to causality, preference heterogeneity and sampling.
- Structure–agency institutionalism within urban development is associated with Patsy Healey, cojoining sociological, institutional and urban analysis (Healey and Barrett, 1990; Healey, 1992; Hooper, 1992). The structural elements are threefold: material resources such as the factors of production, including finance, political and organisational rules for using these resources, and ideas – all of which are, as it were, acknowledged by agents (Ball et al., 1998, p. 125). Property sector institutions exist within a broader

set of social, political and economic institutions. In research terms, this framework provides a basis by which to analyse specific development processes with much of the actual focus on agency relationships. Ball et al. (1998) argued that this comprehensive framework is both a strength but also a weakness because it remains often difficult to see how structural factors cause property market change (Ball et al., 1998, p. 126; and in Gore and Nicholson, 1991). There are also problems about the separating out of the independent nature and impacts of agency, as distinct from structural factors (op. cit., p. 129).

- Structure of building provision, associated with the work of Michael Ball, is an influential methodological theory which can be used with different economic perspectives to understand the 'contemporary network of relationships associated with providing particular types of building' (Ball et al., 1998, p. 129). The authors argue that the structure of provision is itself an institution helping to explain how property development operates – but herein there is no distinction between agency and structure. Organisational relationships are one of the institutions of the property sector but markets, organisations and institutions can all be part of the structure of provision. Because it is methodological in focus, it is not an explanation of property or housing phenomena in its own right but rather a way of organising how to go about examining institutions (Ball et al., 1998, p. 131). The framework would be expected to be dynamic and evolutionary. Ball has himself used this framework to analyse UK homeownership and the UK house-building industry.

Is homeownership an institution? One aspect of institutional existence, as it were, is capacity to withstand change, even when it may not make financial sense. Marsh and Gibb (2009) argue that the stubborn support for homeownership, as reported in tenure preferences in repeated surveys, and the unwillingness to contemplate renting alternatives even in the face of compelling evidence, suggests there may be a form of institutional rigidity at play that goes well beyond the conventional arguments about tax advantages and beliefs about wealth accumulation. Homeownership is viewed as inherently superior and this may help explain why households are less likely to switch to renting when financial arguments would suggest that this would be appropriate. Murie (1998) has argued that homeownership is now a 'badge of citizenship' and that those who rent are viewed as 'damaged' citizens (see also Gurney, 1999). Marsh and Gibb (2009) argue that so long as it is commonly believed that renting is throwing money away and that rising real house prices are fundamentally good things, there will continue to be a presumption in favour of owning that will persist even when it is out of step with the underlying economic 'requirements' of the British economy. Not only is it reasonable to argue that homeownership is an institution as suggested by this inertia but because institutions like homeownership evolve relatively slowly over time they inhibit wider functional change.

Turning to social or non-market housing, in the last two decades there has been comparatively little analysis of the emerging models of social housing in the UK. Exceptions to this 'rule' include Maclennan et al. (1989), Baker et al. (1993), Marsh and Walker (1998), Hills (2001), Whitehead (2003) and Gibb and Maclennan (2006). However, there is evidence that new institutional economics can bring different and useful insights (Gibb and Maclennan, 2006).

Ricketts (1994) applies NIE ideas to the non-profit sector in general in a way that resonates with social housing. Ricketts distinguishes between funding (state, voluntary or commercial) and governance, which can be vested in trustees (board members) as distinct from professional management, also stressing the importance of state regulation. Secondly, however, managers by definition cannot be incentivised to be paid in profit shares. Also, measuring performance may be inherently difficult because the not-for-profit sector is generally hard to measure in comparison with the market. There is often no takeover threat (other than in the case of UK housing associations, where there is wide scope for regulatory intervention and replacement of management and directors and even selling the association to another party). Managers in the not-for-profit sector can have considerable discretionary power. However, this may be lessened in the social housing sector because of possible managerial altruism, and there may be competition for tenants with other providers and trustees are responsible for monitoring management performance and service delivery. A third point is that there may be difficulties designing efficient contracts between the not-for-profit sector and their commercial suppliers (including private finance). Fourthly, state regulation may have a wide range of anticipated and unintended effects.

Applying these ideas further, Gibb and Maclennan (2006), following Maclennan and More (1997), argue that examining the economic interests, property rights and structures of social housing and how they impact on incentives and behaviour, can shed light on both the effectiveness of individual providers (and provider types) as well as the non-market system as a whole. This requires a clear sense of the structure of ownership and control within organisations, their market–hierarchy split (in Williamson's sense) and the impact of external regulation from the state and from loan finance. Maclennan and More (1997) argue that analysis should focus in on five dimensions of performance: competitiveness, the control of owner/manager discretion, internal incentive structures, hierarchy design and the setting the hierarchy–market boundary (1997, p. 542). In a recent paper, Gibb and Nygaard (2006) argue that there should be an explicit sixth dimension relating to the impact of regulation and governance on incentives and behaviour.

Motivation and purpose are core problems for understanding social housing systems, processes and outcomes. This is a general problem in not-for-profit and public sector systems but it is a critical complexity for mixed welfare or quasi-market systems – but it is too often glossed over. Contemporary UK social housing is a sector that increasingly includes actors with a range of for-profit and other more altruistic motivations, but in which not-for-profit providers currently dominate. This must have a significant impact upon the way in which the 'market' functions (Le Grand, 1997, 2003; Taylor-Gooby, 1999; Taylor-Gooby et al., 2000; Jones and Cullis, 2003).

Contracts and organisational hierarchies are standard features of the design of non-market organisations providing not-for-profit services. Bartlett and Le Grand (1993) highlight the insights that transactions cost analysis demonstrate for quasi-markets in the UK welfare state (including social housing), distinguishing between *ex ante* and *ex post* transactions costs. *Ex ante* costs are the costs of setting up an exchange, wherein complex exchanges are often contracts with legal and wider opportunity costs. *Ex post* transactions costs refer to the monitoring of these exchange agreements or contracts once in place. A lack of rigour in addressing the *ex ante* costs may mean high costs of enforcement and compliance later on. Bartlett and Le Grand (pp. 27–30) conclude that the efficient balance between market versus hierarchy or integrated versus contracted-out service delivery is highly contingent on the specifics of the sector in question. Secondly, where there are asset specificity issues – i.e. where the combining of human and physical capital is so embedded, such that the cost of replacement is very high or where there is no obvious alternate use – there will be generally advantages in keeping provision integrated in-house rather than based on market relationships. Thirdly, future uncertainty of demand is linked to issues of bounded rationality and the limited scope of individuals to make efficient decisions in the face of complexity and uncertainty. The more uncertain the operating environment, the more difficult it will be to agree an encompassing, efficient contract (Marsh, 1995).

Nygaard et al. (2007) analyse social housing from a property rights perspective. Commodities have multiple attributes and that the rights to these attributes can, in principle, be separated (Barzel, 1997; Webster and Lai, 2003; Nygaard, forthcoming). Separation of attributes occurs where the expected value of attribute ownership exceeds the transaction costs associated with establishing and protecting such value (Barzel, 1997; Webster and Lai, 2003). According to Nygaard et al., we can identify the attributes of social housing. It provides shelter for households. It is also an asset base, a source of revenue, a source of patronage or constituency building (Maclennan and More, 1997), a community asset and a resource for policy implementation. Ownership of social housing confers a degree of control over these attributes. As their relative value change over time and in response to political, economic and technological circumstances, the relative value of property rights change as well. Transfer of engagements, such as the stock transfer of UK council housing as a going concern to a housing association, can therefore be seen as a situation that allows an alternative owner to extract value that has hitherto remained uncaptured or that the original owner is believed cannot capture as efficiently (Nygaard et al., 2007). In related fashion, in a series of innovative contributions, Webster has applied property rights theory and club goods to issues such as neighbourhood management, urban policy and, to some effect, to the study of gated communities (e.g. Webster and Lai, 2003; Chen and Webster, forthcoming).

A further strand of work in recent years has been comparative research drawing on actor–network relationships in order to understand better the changing structures of non-market housing across different housing systems in Europe (see Mullins and Rhodes (2007). Interest in these models stems from the growing pluralism of non-market provision in many countries, the emerging enabling role of local government, the enhanced regulation of social housing, and partnerships with constriction and finance interests on the one hand, and with local communities and their interests, on the other.

In the UK and the Netherlands, for instance, this has allowed analysis of the housing association sector and in the UK, in particular, the increasingly significant arms-length management organisations that now run more than one million homes in England.

This section has reviewed just a flavour of the research that is available and inevitably reflects the author's immediate interests as an illustration of how institutions analysis is being applied on the broad area of housing (through an economics lens). The next section considers two further areas that may shed new light on housing phenomena still clearly linked to institutions.

EXTENSIONS, POSSIBLE DEVELOPMENTS AND AGENDAS

In a series of recent papers, Susan Smith and colleagues focus in on certain institutional features of micro housing markets (see Smith and Munro, 2008; Smith, 2009; Smith et al., 2006). In doing so, they have drawn on ideas from cultural geography, particularly the notion of performativity (Callon, 1998). Callon argues that there is 'as much to be gained by documenting the diverse features of actually existing markets, as there is by concentrating on the essentials, abstractions and universals that sometimes tie markets together' (Smith and Munro, 2008, p. 161).

There is a striking similarity with the methods and direction we saw earlier in Hodgson's account of the old institutionalists. Performative housing market research rests on the 'fundamental sociality of (housing) markets, or their hybrid form (the way they are constituted by affective relationships which attach people to the materials and meanings of *things* including house and home' (Smith and Munro, 2008, p. 160). They argue that the housing economy can be understood across three dimensions of materiality, cultural economy and the emotional economy. Markets are 'concrete entities as well as abstract concepts' (Smith and Munro, 2008, p. 160). Materiality is particularly associated with 'the bodily encounters, calculative practices, pricing technologies and "staging" strategies entangled within housing transactions' (op. cit.). The cultural economy of housing has a strong resonance with institutional ideas in that it suggests history, tradition, habit, geography and the fundamental social nature of the market also help shape and define the housing market. Empirically, these studies are essentially accounts of how individual and household behaviour is mediated by the above institutions. The emotional element of the framework is an attempt to recognise the authors' belief in the fundamental non-separability of the rational and the emotional.

Smith et al. (2006) assert that a better understanding of actual, as opposed to abstract, housing markets may also produce efficiency gains through better understanding of process and outcome, although a description of the implied empirical project to make sense of different local housing markets at different market stages is nowhere spelled out. In other words, we may ask what are the practical policy implications for planners, the private sector and communities of taking on board the strongly empirical slant of the performative paradigm? Would there not be a stage of diminishing returns from further work where one would seek to draw a line and generalise from the findings? However, more recently, Smith has gone further to suggest that projects such as Robert Shiller's plan to develop a house price futures index to reduce risk in local housing markets is precisely the sort of policy consistent with a richer understanding of the practices, culture and emotional dimensions of the housing market (Smith, 2009). It is here, as elsewhere in the emerging housing economy/performing markets literature, that there are several intersections with the behavioural economics and behavioural finance literatures. The latter also has resonance with institutional analysis and is explored further below.

Although the ideas of behavioural economics first made their mark in the 1970s and early 1980s with a series of papers by Kahneman and Tversky (e.g. 1979) and colleagues, and later developed by others such as Thaler (1992), Shleifer (2000) and Shiller (2005), they were initially fringing on the mainstream of microeconomics (see Poundstone, 2010, for an excellent review of the rise of behavioural economics). Particularly as a result of developments in financial economics, but increasingly also across the wider economics of consumer choices and public policy, behavioural economics has itself become mainstream and is approaching orthodoxy. It is not surprising, however, that the key ideas behind behavioural economics, which stem from the notion that there are empirical regularities that suggest situations where economics agents do not act in classical rational optimising ways, have now fed into housing and mortgage market analysis (Shiller, 2008; Wilkinson, 2008; Gibb, 2009; Marsh and Gibb, 2009; Gibb, forthcoming). Again, several of these ideas speak directly to institutional analysis of housing phenomena. (The discussion of behavioural economics below draws on Gibb, forthcoming.)

The behavioural approach is to identify a number of non-rational regularities in evidenced behaviour and then to reposition our understanding of markets and policy design as a result. Tversky and Kahneman developed heuristics, simpler methods for economic agents to cope better with decision-making complexity and uncertainty, but these devices lead to bias and systematic error when attempting to assess the probability of an event occurring or when seeking to calculate value. The principal heuristics and related concepts are summarised briefly below:

Representativeness. When asked to judge whether an outcome is representative of something else, the decision depends on the perception of how similar the one is to the other. This is often based on erroneous

comparisons and an intuitive overconfidence in how representative is the comparison made.
Availability. Familiarity with an event can lead to overestimation of the probability of its occurrence. Biased judgements can occur because, for instance, specific outcomes are more salient than others. The contexts within which we take decisions shape and filter the range of outcomes. Adopting rules of thumb as a result may assist those decisions but can readily arrive at inaccurate calculations.
Anchoring. A theme of behavioural economics is the importance of relative values (compared to a reference point) as opposed to absolute levels. Repeated evidence suggests that announcing arbitrary numbers can influence how agents then value or quantify real entities. – valuation is anchored to the initial arbitrary value. Moreover, valuations can be *framed* by the precise way questions are asked.
Endowment effects. The utility derived from a good or service is not independent of ownership (Wilkinson, 2008). Ownership seems to convey a higher value on an item compared to the valuation of an identical item by someone who does not possess it. This can lead to problems for sellers unwilling to accept, for instance, falling values of asset prices. There is a clear relevance here to housing.
Herd behaviour. Financial markets research (but alluded to in the housing market too) suggests that market volatility can be exacerbated by herd-like behaviour to follow fashion, but also the fear of missing out before the market turns. To the extent that these transactions are based primarily on price expectations, they can clearly constitute bubbles (see Levin and Pryce, 2008).

A second theme of the work by Kahneman and Tversky (1979) arose out of the development of their *prospect theory*, proposed as an alternative model of decision-making under risk. Wilkinson (2008) summarises prospect theory as a two-stage process wherein agents first edit the prospects (i.e. a range of possible outcomes, gambles or risky alternatives) into an ordered set, which is then evaluated.

In this second phase, in addition to the use of various heuristics, there are other important decision-making dimensions. First, the use of relative utility reference points, and gains and losses measured against that reference point. Secondly, the principle of *loss aversion* (i.e. sensitivity is greater to losses than equivalent gains). Thirdly, agents exhibit diminishing marginal sensitivity to value differences as they get larger (either as gains or losses) and this is associated with risk aversion. Prospect theory has been widely used by behavioural economists, and specific elements of it, particularly loss aversion, have appeared in many applied economics papers.

A third dimension of behavioural economics explores the extent to which and the circumstances when *altruism* or fairness is a better basis of actor motivation than pure self-interest. The behaviouralists do generally work in a self-interested motivational framework but they have tested for anomalies in the self-interested motivation theory, as well as examining more clear-cut versions of fairness. While the evidence appears to find many flaws in the standard model, which suggests simple self-interest breaks down as a motivator, it remains hard to pin down evidence of the converse – of decisions based around fairness and altruism (Wilkinson, 2008).

A fourth area of work is *mental accounting*, a direct application of prospect theory. Thaler (1999) describes mental accounting as the set of cognitive operations put in place by agents to monitor, evaluate and coordinate household finances – hence, the direct relevance to decision-making choices. Thaler (1999) argues that mental accounting rules are not neutral in that they influence the relative attractiveness of different choices. Wilkinson contends (2008, pp. 184–86) that several features of mental accounting alongside non-standard discounting of the future (creating problems for inter-temporal choices) can help explain international evidence on mortgage equity withdrawal, consumption and housing wealth impacts.

Northcraft and Neale (1987) conducted valuation experiments and combined their findings with actual housing market data from Arizona to confirm anchoring adjustment biases in valuation. Genovese and Mayer (2001) and Engelhardt (2003) both provide evidence of loss aversion where sellers in falling housing markets retain unrealistic values, slowing down the normal adjustment of the market. Marsh and Gibb (2009) conclude that the social nature of housing decision-making combined with bounded rationality and behavioural ideas may help develop a richer framework with which to conduct meaningful housing market analysis. Shiller (2008) argues that several policies could improve the mortgage market by directly tapping into the behavioural economics ideas surrounding mental accounting.

Behavioural economics is both popular and fashionable but not without its critics. It does not as yet provide an alternative conceptual basis to the mainstream, but rather operates from different empirical regularities about behaviour to greater or lesser extent than built on the mainstream edifice (not unlike NIE). It may present more acceptable assumptions about agent behaviour than rational utility maximisation and hence be a priori more agreeable to those outside of the mainstream but it does use conventional methods and the superstructure of mainstream economic analysis, it is firmly in the realm of positive science and it may be seen as a special case of the mainstream (Rabin, 2002, expects the mainstream to adapt to or otherwise subsume the key behavioural tenets over time).

DellaVigna (2009) has suggested that agents may learn from their mistakes and alongside normal competitive forces may tend towards more orthodox economic outcomes as time elapses. There is thus a need to argue and justify the idea that behavioural economics ideas can survive learning and market forces and remain relevant (a case which DellaVigna argues is borne out by the field evidence). So, while there is much of interest about behavioural economics, it would be fair to say that it is in many respects less radical, methodologically, than it may at first appear, and may actually be more comfortable with NIE than the older variant (with the exception of the social relativities and Veblen comparison effects on consumption). However, even so, it clearly has much to say of value about housing market analysis.

CONCLUSIONS

This chapter has taken a selective tour through the old and new institutional economics before indicating how these ideas of custom, habit, power and rules, on the one hand, and transactions costs, property rights and bounded rationality, on the other, might be usefully applied to a range of areas in the market and non-market sectors of the housing sector. The strong antipathy between the two views of institutionalism was brought out and rests in part on fundamentally different views about the place and role of individualism in economic methodologies. From my own point of view, just as there is much to be lost from ignoring the insights of old institutionalist thinkers with regards to social sciences generally and housing phenomena particularly, it would be very wasteful to dismiss and lose the considerable insights gleaned from the NIE, in particular as we saw in terms of the design of social housing organisations and non-market systems of organising housing. We also saw in the penultimate section that new strands of work relating housing to market making and performativity agendas, as well as the behavioural economics research agenda, apply directly to housing and can to more or less of an extent be synthesised with institutional ideas. These latter approaches challenge the central mainstream idea of the exogeneity of preferences and of substantive rational behaviour. In that sense, they speak more readily to the old institutionalist tradition.

Looking forward to new and emerging research agendas, there should be scope for a rich vein of work across several interesting dimensions of housing studies (all of these could be applied at an international comparative level):

- Actor–network relations applied to private housing development/land planning/mixed tenure development processes but also to social housing systems and relations with regulators and funders, etc.
- Political economy/institutionalist research on local policy processes and outcomes such as conflicts over tenure change, gentrification, stock transfer, regeneration and redevelopment, etc.
- Property rights research related to neighbourhoods, economic clubs and their financing, as well as further work on attributes of property rights as applied to private, club and social housing.
- Social housing provision and market–hierarchy/transactions costs analysis as tools towards designing more incentive compatible and efficient non-market forms of housing provision.
- NIE analysis of public policy design in a context of mixed economy of welfare models of housing.
- Performative housing economy research has only just begun and would seem to be ripe for extensions into the mortgage market, estate agency and property valuation as well as deepening one's understanding of local markets and making clearer how such cultural analysis might be developed alongside more conventional economic accounts of markets.
- Individual housing choice research on uncertainty and expectations, drawing on the huge potential of behavioural economics and bounded rationality.

NOTE

1 Oliver Williamson shared the 2009 Nobel Prize for Economics.

REFERENCES

Alchian, A. and Demsetz, H. (1973) 'The Property Right Paradigm', *Journal of Economic History*, Vol. 33, pp. 16–27.

Adams, D, Baum, A and MacGregor, B (1988) 'The Availability of Land for Inner City Development: A Case Study of Inner Manchester', *Urban Studies*, Vol. 25, pp. 62–76.

Adams, D, Dunse, N and White, M (2005a) 'Conceptualising State–Market Relations in Land and Property: The Growth of Institutionalism – Extension or Challenge to Mainstream Economics', in Adams et al. (eds), *Planning, Public Policy and Property Markets*. Blackwell RICS, Oxford.

Adams, D, Watkins, C and White, M (eds) (2005b) *Planning, Public Policy and Property Markets*. Blackwell RICS, Oxford.

Baker, R, Challen, P, Maclennan, D, Reid, V and Whitehead, C (1993) *The Scope for Competitive Tendering of Housing Management*. HMSO, London.

Ball, M, Lizieri, C and MacGregor, B (1998) *Economics of Commercial Property Markets*. Routledge, London.

Bartlett, W and Le Grand, J (eds) (1993) *Quasi-markets and Social Policy*. Macmillan, Basingstoke.

Barzel, Y. (1997) *Economic Analysis of Property Rights*, 2nd edn. Cambridge University Press, Cambridge.

Bines, W, Kemp, P, Pleace, N and Radley, C (1993) *Managing Social Housing*. HMSO, London.

Callon, M (ed.) (2007) *The Laws of Markets*. Blackwell, Oxford.

Chen, S and Webster, C (forthcoming) 'New Institutional Economics in Housing Studies 640', in S Smith (editor in chief), *International Encyclopaedia of Housing and Home*. Elsevier.

Coase, R (1937) 'The Nature of the Firm', *Economica*, Vol. 4, pp. 386–405.

Coase, R (1960) 'The Problem of Social Cost', *Journal of Law and Economics*, Vol. 3, pp. 1–44.

DellaVigna, S (2009) 'Psychology and Economics: Evidence from the Field', *Journal of Economic Literature*, Vol. 47, pp. 315–372.

Demetz, H (1967) 'Towards a Theory of Property Rights', *American Economic Review*, Vol. 57, pp. 347–359.

Engelhardt, G (2003) 'Nominal Loss Aversion, Housing Equity Constraints and Household Mobility: Evidence from the United States', *Journal of Urban Economics*, Vol. 53, pp. 171–195.

Fainstein, S (1992) *The City Builders*. Blackwell, Oxford.

Furubotn, E and Richter, R (1991) 'The New Institutional Economics: An Assessment', in E Furubotn and R Richter (eds), *The New Institutional Economics*. A&M University Press, Texas.

Genovese, D and Mayer, C (2001) 'Nominal Loss Aversion and Seller Behaviour: Evidence from the Housing Market', *Quarterly Journal of Economics*, Vol. 116, pp. 1233–1260.

Gibb, K (2005) *The Social Housing Quasi-Market*. CPPR Working Paper, University of Glasgow.

Gibb, K (2009) 'Housing Studies and the Role of Economic Theory: An (Applied) Disciplinary Perspective', *Housing, Theory and Society*, Vol. 26, pp. 26–40.

Gibb (forthcoming) 'Behavioural Economics Applied to Housing 609', in S Smith (editor in chief), *International Encyclopaedia of Housing and Home*. Elsevier.

Gibb, K and MacLennan, D (2006) 'Changing Social Housing: Economic System Issues', *Public Finance and Management*, Vol. 6, No. 1, pp. 88–121.

Gibb, K and Marsh, A (2007) 'The Economics of Regulating Social Housing: Implications for the Future Role of the Sector'. Paper presented at ENHR Housing Economics Workshop, Edinburgh, February.

Gibb, K. and Nygaard, C. (2006) 'Transfers, Contracts and Regulation: a New Institutional Economics Perspective on the Changing Provision of Social Housing in Britain', *Housing Studies*, Vol. 21, No. 6, pp. 825–850.

Gibb, K, Kintrea, K, Nygaard, C and Flint, J (2005) *The Transfer of Scottish Homes Houses into Community Ownership*, Research Report 50. Communities Scotland, Edinburgh.

Gore, T and Nicholson, D (1991) 'Models of the Land Development Process: A Critical Review', *Environment and Planning A* Vol. 23, pp. 705–730.

Green, R and Malpezzi, S (2003) *A Primer on US Housing Markets and Housing Policy*. AREUEA Monograph Series No. 3. The Urban Institute Press, Washington, DC.

Grossman, S and Hart, O (1986) 'The Costs and Benefits of Ownership: A Theory of Vertical and Lateral Integration', *Journal of Political Economy*, Vol. 94, pp. 691–719.

Gurney, C. (1999) 'Pride and Prejudice: Discourses of Normalisation in Public and Private Accounts of Home Ownership', *Housing Studies*, Vol. 14, No. 2, pp. 163–183.

Guy, S and Henneberry, J (2000) 'Understanding Urban Development Processes: Integrating the Economic and the Social in Property Research', *Urban Studies*, Vol. 37, pp. 2399–2416.

Guy, S and Henneberry, J (2002) (eds) *Development and Developers: Perspectives on Property*. Blackwell Science/RICS, Oxford.

Haack, S (2004) 'Pragmatism, Old and New', *Contemporary Pragmatism*, Vol. 1, pp. 3–41.

Hart, O (1995) *Firms, Contracts and Financial Structure*. Oxford University Press, New York.

Healey, P (1992) 'An Institutional Model of the Development Process', *Journal of Property Research*, Vol. 9, pp. 33–44.

Healey, P and Barratt, S (1990) 'Structure and Agency in Land and Property Development Processes: Some Ideas for Research', *Urban Studies*, Vol. 27, pp. 89–14.

Hills, J (2001) *Modernising Social Housing Finance*. IPPR, London.

Hodgson, G. (1988) *Institutions and Economics*. Basil Blackwell, Oxford.

Hodgson, G (1996) 'Institutional Economics', in M Warner (ed.), *International Encyclopedia of Business and Management*. Routledge, London.

Hodgson, G. (1997) 'The ubiquity of habits and rules', *Cambridge Journal of Economics*. 21: 663–684.

Hodgson, G (1998) 'The Approach of Institutional Economics', *Journal of Economic Literature*, Vol. XXXVI, pp. 166–192.

Hooper, A (1992) 'The Construction of Theory: A Comment', *Journal of Property Research*, Vol. 9, pp. 45–48.

Jones, P and Cullis, J (2003) Key Parameters in Policy Design: The Case of Intrinsic Motivation, *Journal of Social Policy*, Vol. 32, No. 4, pp. 527–547.

Kahneman, D and Tversky, A (1979) 'Prospect Theory: An Analysis of Decision under Risk', *Econometrica*, Vol. 47, pp. 263–291.

Le Grand, J (1997) 'Knights, Knaves or Pawns? Human Behaviour and Social Policy', *Journal of Social Policy*, Vol. 26, pp. 149–169.

Le Grand, J (2003) *Motivation, Agency and Public Policy*, Oxford University Press, Oxford.

Levin, E and Pryce, G (2008) 'Beyond Reason', *RICS Residential Property Journal*, August/September.

Maclennan, D et al. (1989) *The Nature and Effectiveness of Housing Management in England*. Department of the Environment, London.

Maclennan, D and More, A (1997) 'The Future of Social Housing: Key Economic Questions', *Housing Studies*, Vol. 12, pp. 531–547.

Marsh, A (1995) 'Organising Social Housing Management: What Can We Learn from Transaction Cost Economics?', Housing Studies Association conference, Edinburgh, September.

Marsh, A and Gibb, K (1997) *Uncertainty and Expectations in the Economics of Housing*. Centre for Housing Research and Urban Studies Working Paper 40. University of Glasgow, Department of Urban Studies.

Marsh, A and Gibb, K (2009) 'Uncertainty, Expectations and Behavioural Aspects of Housing Market Choices'. Paper presented at International Sociological Association Housing Assets Housing People Conference, Glasgow, September.

Marsh, A and Walker, B (1998) 'Control, Discretion and Evaluation: Economic Issues in the Organisations of Public Housing in England'. Paper presented to the European Network of Housing Research Conference, Cardiff Business School, September, mimeo.

McMaster, R (forthcoming) 'Institutional Economics: Traditional Approaches 641', in S Smith (editor in chief), *International Encyclopaedia of Housing and Home*. Elsevier.

McMaster, R and Watkins, C (2006) 'Economics and Under-Determination: a Case Study of Urban Land and Housing Economics', *Cambridge Journal of Economics*, Vol. 30, pp. 901–922.

Mullins, D and Rhodes. M (2007) 'Special Issue on Network Theory and Social Housing', *Housing, Theory and Society*, Vol. 24, pp. 1–13.

Murie, A (1998) 'Secure and Contented Citizens? Home Ownership in Britain', in A Marsh and D Mullins (eds), *Housing and Public Policy: Citizenship, Choice and Control*. Open University Press, Buckingham.

North, D (1990) *Institutions, Institutional Change, and Economic Performance*. Cambridge University Press, Cambridge.

North, D (1991) 'Institutions', *Journal of Economic Perspectives*, Vol. 5, pp. 97–112.

Northcraft, G and Neale, M (1987) 'Experts, Amateurs and Real Estate: An Anchoring and Adjustment Perspective on Property Pricing Decisions', *Organizational Behavior and Human Decision Processes*, Vol. 39, pp. 84–97.

Nygaard, C (forthcoming) 'Property Rights Approaches', in S Smith (editor in chief), *International Encyclopaedia of Housing and Home*. Elsevier.

Nygaard, C, Gibb, K and Berry, M (2007) 'Ownership Transfer of Social Housing in the UK: A Property Rights Approach', *Housing, Theory and Society*, Vol. 24, No. 2, pp. 89–110.

Nygaard, C, Berry, M and Gibb, K (2008) 'The Political Economy of Social Housing Reform – A Framework for Considering Decentralized Ownership, Management and Service Delivery in Australia', *Urban Policy and Research*, Vol. 26, No. 1, pp. 5–21.

Poundstone, W (2010) *Priceless: The Hidden Psychology of Value*. Oneworld, Oxford.

Rabin, M (1998) 'Psychology and Economics', *Journal of Economic Literature*, Vol. XXXVI, pp. 11–46.

Rabin, M (2002) 'A Perspective on Psychology and Economics', *European Economic Review*, Vol. 46, pp. 657–685.

Rabin, M (2004) 'Behavioural Economics', in M Szenberg and L Ramrattan (eds), *New Frontiers in Economics*. Cambridge University Press, Cambridge.

Ricketts, M (1994) *The Economics of Business Enterprise*, 2nd edn. Harvester Wheatsheaf, Hemel Hempstead.

Sah, R and Stiglitz, J (1988) 'Committees, Hierarchies and Polyarchies', *Economic Journal*, Vol. 98, pp. 451–470.

Samuels, W (1995) 'The Present State of Institutional Economics', *Cambridge Journal of Economics*, Vol. 19, pp. 569–590.

Scott, P (1996) *The Property Masters*. E&FN Spon, London.

Shleifer, A (2000) *Inefficient Markets: An Introduction to Behavioural Finance*. Oxford University Press, Oxford.

Shiller, R (2005) *Irrational Exuberance*, 2nd edn. Princeton University Press, Princeton, NJ.

Shiller, R (2008) *The Subprime Solution*. Princeton University Press, Princeton, NJ.

Simon, HA (1982) *Models of Bounded Rationality. Vol 2: Behavioral Economics and Business Organization*. MIT Press, Cambridge, MA.

Simon, HA (1984) 'On the Behavioural and Rational Foundations of Economic Dynamics', *Journal of Economic Behaviour and Organization*, Vol. 5, pp. 35–55.

Smith, S (2009) 'Housing Futures: A Role for Derivatives?' 'International Sociological Association Housing Assets, Housing People Conference, September, Glasgow.

Smith, S and Munro, M (2008) 'Guest Editorial: The Microstructures of Housing Markets', *Housing Studies*, Vol. 23, pp. 159–162.

Smith, S, Munro, M and Christie. H (2006) 'Performing (Housing) Markets', *Urban Studies*, Vol. 43, pp. 81–98.

Taylor-Gooby, P (1999) 'Markets and Motives: Trust and Egoism in Welfare Markets', *Journal of Social Policy*, Vol. 28, No. 1, pp. 97–114.

Taylor-Gooby, P, Sylvester, S , Calnan, M and Manley, G (2000) 'Knights, Knaves and Gnashers: Professional Values and Private Dentistry', *Journal of Social Policy*, Vol. 29, No. 3, pp. 375–395.

Thaler, R (1992) *The Winner's Curse: Paradoxes and Anomalies of Economic Life*. Princeton University Press: Princeton, NJ.

Thaler, R (1999) 'Mental Accounting Matters', *Journal of Behavioural Decision Making*, Vol. 12, pp. 183–206.

Tversky, A and Kahenman, D (1974) 'Judgment under Uncertainty: Heuristics and Biases', *Science*, Vol. 185, pp. 1124–1131.

Veblen, T (1899) *A Theory of the Leisure Classes*. Unwin, London.

Watkins, C (2008) 'Microeconomic Perspectives on the Structure and Operation of Local Housing Markets', *Housing Studies*, Vol. 23, pp. 163–177.

Webster C (2003) "The Nature of the Neighbourhood", *Urban Studies*, Vol. 40, pp. 2591–2612.

Webster, C. and Lai, L (2003) *Property Rights, Planning and Markets: Managing Spontaneous Cities*. Edward Elgar, Cheltenham.

Whitehead, C (2003) 'The Economics of Social Housing', in A O'Sullivan and K Gibb (eds), *Housing Economics and Public Policy*. Blackwell Science/RICS Foundation, Oxford.

Wilkinson, N (2008) *An Introduction to Behavioural Economics*. Palgrave Macmillan, Basingstoke.

Williamson, O (1975) *Markets and Hierarchies, Analysis and Anti-Trust Implications: A Study in the Economics of Internal Organisation*. Free Press, New York.

Williamson, O (1985) *The Economic Institutions of Capitalism*. Free Press: New York.

Williamson, O (2000) 'The New Institutional Economics: Taking Stock, Moving Forward', *Journal of Economic Literature*, Vol. XXXVIII, pp. 595–613.

Social Geographic Interpretations of Housing Spaces

Tim Butler and Chris Hamnett

INTRODUCTION

The organising theme of the chapter engages the question of 'who lives where' and how this and our understanding of it has changed over the last 50 years. We know that most, if not all, cities are divided, socially and spatially, into an often complex mosaic of social groups and residential areas differentiated by social class, income, race and ethnicity and religion. There are rich areas and poor areas, white areas and black areas, Protestant and Catholic areas, Shia and Sunni Muslim areas, Hindu and Muslim, Jewish and Christian areas, Wasp and Italian, Polish and Latino, etc. The list is nearly endless, but almost every city has its division into acceptable and unacceptable areas, the rough and the respectable, our side, and 'the other side of the tracks' inhabited by some nameless or fearsome 'other'. Place of residence is a very important social marker for many people. Not only is it very important in terms of quality of life (or the lack of it) but also it tells others a great deal about the sort of person that lives in an area. The images are pervasive: mention 'Beverley Hills' and a world is conjured up, however inaccurately, of movie stars, grand mansions and stretch limos. In New York, Park Avenue North provides an equivalent image of affluence and wealth, whereas Harlem conjures up a very different image of black residential concentration. Names with less internationally known connotations include the Shankhill and Falls Road areas of Belfast, Lakeshore Drive and its other – the South Side of Chicago, Kreutzberg in Berlin, Notting Hill or Chelsea in London or Belleville in Paris. Historically, the lower East Side in New York or the Gorbals in Glasgow carried a clear message of intense urban poverty. The residents of these cities know very well what such names signify in terms of their social composition and the names often have an international significance and circulation.

The questions we wish to try to address in this chapter are how such distinctive social and geographical residential areas come into being and are reproduced in space and time: in other words, we need to address what can be termed 'the (re)production of social space'. In order to examine the question it is necessary to examine the interrelationships between social structure, residential choice and constraint, the structure of the housing market, and the institutions which, directly or indirectly, control access to different types of housing and residential areas. As Robson (1975) observed over 30 years ago, 'Residential areas are made up of people, living in houses, distributed in space'. This superficially simple statement in fact highlights the fact that residential areas are made up of two distinct components – the distribution of housing types and of residents – and it is the concentration of different types of resident in different housing types in different areas which (re)produces different types of residential space and residential differentiation and segregation (for other discussions of segregation, see Chapters 22 and 23).

There have been three distinct traditions in this work – the sociological, the geographical and the economic. The first two can be seen to have emerged from the work of Park and Burgess and the Chicago School of urban sociology which attempted to grapple with the emerging social differentiation of American cities. Park examined the formation of urban social areas, many of which had a distinct ethnic character, while Burgess is remembered for his influential, migration-driven, zonal model of residential structure and change (Park and Burgess 1925).

The urban economic approach began with Hoyt's (1939) analysis of residential structure in American cities, and continued with Alonso's (1960, 1964) attempts to develop an economic model based on the idea of bid rent. Alonso's model was based on the idea of a trade-off between the cost of land, which was most expensive in the city centre owing to greater accessibility, and the desire for space. He argued that the dominant value system in the USA was a preference for space, which led to the majority of households opting for larger houses and more space in the suburbs and paying the cost of greater travel times. Although he recognised the existence of a group of high-income households who preferred to live in the city centre, preferring accessibility to space, he argued that this was a minority preference in the USA. He argued that low-income households who lived in the inner city did so because they could not afford the cost of commuting, and adjusted to high land values by living at high densities. He termed his theory 'the structural theory of land values' in contrast to what he saw as 'the historic theory' of Burgess and the Chicago School (Alonso, 1964)

The traditional geographical literature on urban residential segregation that developed during the 1960s and 1970s emerged out of the Chicago School and developed a variety of models of urban residential structure based on analysis of residential patterning in different cities. The accepted wisdom in the North American literature at this time was that there were three principal dimensions or axes of segregation: occupational class or income, family status and race. Whereas class was generally patterned sectorally, family status was zonal and race formed specific patterns (Shevky and Bell, 1955; Johnston, 1970; Hamnett, 1976). At this time in the late 1960s, when geographers had just discovered quantification, a great deal of attention was given to the construction of multivariate factorial ecologies, social areas and to examination of choice and preference (Murdie, 1969), particularly on the part of the middle classes, and a detailed picture was built up of the residential structure of different cities (Johnston, 1971).

In some extreme manifestations, notably the 'revealed preference' approach based on neo-classical economics, it was argued that the residential structure of the city simply reflected the residential preferences of different types of household. In retrospect, however, it is fair to say that the picture was very skewed towards the Anglo-American literature and the North American city formed the basic reference point for the analysis of residential patterns – with scarcely any discussion of European cities, which were seen as anomalous (Timms, 1971; Herbert, 1972). Not until the work of Robson (1969) on the residential structure of Sunderland was the major role of council housing in British cities taken seriously. But the quantitative multivariate factorial ecology approach began to peter out in the early 1980s as declining returns set in and the focus of attention shifted to what were seen as more productive and innovative areas of inquiry.

In the mid 1970s a sociological critique of the residential location literature developed, based in part on the work of Rex and Moore (1967), with far greater attention being given to the role of the housing market and to the significance of constraints on choice and the role of what Pahl (1971) termed urban 'gatekeepers' in controlling access to, and allocation in, the housing market. This 'institutional' approach focused on the idea that choice and preference were exercised in the context of a set of institutional arrangements, allocational criteria and access rules and procedures which directed different types of household to different types of area. This applied to both the public sector, in terms of the allocation criteria for public housing, and the private sector, in terms of who landlords accept as tenants, zoning by laws and mortgage availability for particular types of property and areas. An example of this work was Williams' (1976) analysis of gentrification in Islington.

This was followed in the mid 1970s, with publication of David Harvey's (1973) radical analysis *Social Justice and the City* which focused research attention on the differential resources available to households and the way in which they had to operate within an opportunity set and price structure, which inevitably limited choices for most households. Harvey's work prompted an upsurge in the political economy analysis of housing markets under capitalism, particularly in Britain. Harvey argued that capitalist cities rested on institutionalised inequality and the drive for profit maximization on the part of developers, landowners, landlords and others which generally forced low-income households into poor-quality accommodation in the least attractive areas of the city. The impact of directly Marxist-influenced work on the production of space continued with [Neil] Smith's (1979) pioneering analysis of gentrification which argued that choice and preference and demand-based approaches were both limited and misleading, and that gentrification needed to be understood via the analysis of the nature of housing production and supply.

The great majority of potential buyers are unable to buy a house out of income: they need to borrow to do so, and the most common form of borrowing is the mortgage. We are currently only too familiar with the dramatic consequences of subprime lending to poor households on low initial rates of interest, who cannot subsequently afford to keep up their repayments. But in the 1960s and 1970s, the principal problem facing households in poor areas was that mortgage lending institutions refused to lend in these areas: they were redlined – so-called because lending institutions drew red lines on maps around areas within which they were not prepared to advance money. Harvey (1974) examined some of the social consequences of this in Baltimore where, as in other American and British inner cities, whole areas were denied funding (Williams, 1976; Dingemans, 1979) with the result that some areas suffered dereliction and abandoned as prices declined.

The remainder of the chapter is organised as follows. In the next section we discuss the issues of choice and preference in very broad brush terms and then in relation to a number of different approaches that have been taken to explain this in the literature over the last 30 years. These approaches are not necessarily in conflict with each other, although they do draw on rather different disciplinary approaches and often make very different assumptions about behaviour. Following these introductory remarks, we consider the issues of choice in relation to the debates over the supply of housing; we then follow this with a discussion of literature about gentrification which explicitly raised these issues in relation to the 'urban seeking' and 'urban fleeing' middle classes and which contrasted two sets of explanations based around the supply of gentrified housing and the demand for it by a gentrifying 'new class'. Thirdly, we consider a more recent literature that focuses on the issue of choice through the concept of 'elective belonging' and challenges some of the assumptions of placelessness implicit in at least parts of the literature on globalisation.

CHOICE AND PREFERENCE

What is the relationship between the production of different types of housing in different areas and the social characteristics of their residents? The approach traditionally taken by many neo-classical economists is to look first at residential choice and preference, on the basis that market outcomes reflect the decisions that consumers make. Choice and preference are very important – many people prefer to live in the suburbs in a detached or semi-detached house, while others prefer to live in a house or flat in the centre or inner city. But the uncritical use of the term 'choice' is problematic: not only do different groups of people have different choices, based on different preferences and values, but also preferences and choices generally have to be made in terms of the structure, availability, cost and accessibility of supply. As Henry Ford memorably said of his model T cars – 'People can have any colour they want as long as it's black'. The structure of opportunities has varied considerably both over time and across societies. This was clearly seen in the communist states pre-1989 where housing supply was limited to what the state made available and allocated to different social groups on the basis of specified criteria. For the most part, the range of opportunities consisted of new apartment blocks, located on the periphery of the city, and the possibility of choosing a house was virtually non-existent (for other discussions of residential choice and preference, see Chapters 3 and 5).

The degree of choice is also very unequally distributed in capitalist or market-based societies in that choice is, to a large extent, based on income and ability to pay. At the top end of the income distribution, households have a very wide range of choice, whereas at the bottom, households have virtually no choice, and many are unable to buy in the market at any price – although they may make 'constrained choices' about, for example, where in the socially rented housing market to live. Choice is always constrained, particularly for those on low incomes or for groups subject to various forms of residential discrimination, and it is crucial to look at the structure of constraints as well as choices (Bassett and Short, 1980). What this means in practice is that there is a hierarchy of effective demand which is largely income related, though it can also be a product of racial and religious discrimination. At the bottom end, particularly in the social rented housing sector, many households simply have to take what they are offered or what they can afford. For such households the idea of choice is a misnomer. This was highlighted by Harvey (1973) in *Social Justice and the City* where he put forward the analogy of the urban housing market as a theatre with differentially priced seats. Those with highest incomes can choose from any seats, and are likely to choose the most expensive ones with the best views, whereas those with limited incomes can only afford the cheapest seats in the house, possibly with restricted views, while some cannot afford a seat at all. It follows that is also important to look at the seat structure of the theatre and the pricing policy of the box office. Whereas income and resources are undoubtedly the prime determinant of choice, we should not forget that preferences are also the outcome of complex patterns of associational preferences for being with people we like or identify with ('people like us': Butler, 1997).

There is a rich and long-standing social psychological literature on who people like to associate with and against whom they are likely to be prejudiced (e.g. Allport, 1954) and this has been documented in terms of religious and ethno-racial residential segregation by the work of Boal (1969), Frey (1995) and others. More recently, there have been attempts to understand how normative ideas of identification can mesh with the structural inequality in the allocation of resources, through reference to Bourdieu's work on 'habitus'. We return to this theme later in a discussion of Savage et al.'s (2005) notion of 'elective belonging'. To return to the theatre metaphor, it might be argued that sometimes even if people can afford a seat in the dress circle, they might sometimes choose to sit with people they know and like in the cheaper seats.

At this point, it is important also to note the influential work by Schelling (1971) on residential preference and racial segregation. Schelling formulated a simulation model based on individual agents and an assumption that individuals (white or black) would prefer to be located on a checkerboard (chess board) where half or more of adjacent neighbours were of similar colour. He showed that, from this starting point, complete segregation tended to rapidly follow. This has been confirmed in subsequent work by Zhang (2004), who showed that segregation is a stochastically stable state, and that segregation can occur through the process of residential tipping on the basis of slight asymmetries in preferences even when most people would prefer integrated neighbourhoods. This is supported empirically by research based on survey data on ethnic residential preferences (Clark, 2002; Clark and Fossett, 2008).

THE STRUCTURE OF HOUSING SUPPLY

It is clearly important in examining the production and reproduction of various types of residential and housing spaces to examine variations in the structure and history of housing supply, alongside the development of residential choice and preference, the existence of differential constraints and various allocation mechanisms and institutional barriers to access. Looking first at the structure of supply, some areas are initially built in the form of large, expensive, houses on large plots or luxury apartments with a specific group of buyers in mind. The cost of such properties will effectively debar many groups from access even if there are no social or legislative barriers to access. There are many examples of the role of developers and landed interests in the production of high-status residential areas from the 18th century onwards in Britain and the USA. Large areas of the West End of London were built on this basis by the landed estate owners and developers in the 18th and early 19th centuries and some had gated squares to control access – which was largely restricted to the gentry and aristocracy. On the other hand, many of the slum areas of the East End of London were built as low-quality housing for low-income groups, with the aim being to maximise the number of units on a given land area. The result was huge differences in the geography of income, social class and crowding (Steadman-Jones, 1971; Dyos and Reader, 1973). To a significant extent, therefore, the structure of supply and, in particular, its price structure, will influence or directly control the social status of residents (for a discussion of housing supply within the industrial organization approach, see Chapter 2).

In a number of cases, the high status of some residential areas declined over time as other high-status residential areas were developed, and residents left. In such cases, the status of the areas such as Islington and Notting Hill in London changed, as lower-income groups moved in, but in other areas such as the area around Boston Common, the high status of the area was retained over time (Firey, 1945). In the USA, as is well known, the social status of particular jurisdictions was historically maintained by zoning ordinances, which restrict housing plots to a minimum size, and also by the lack of public transport. This links to the production of suburbanisation and the resultant social segregation (Walker, 1981).

However, the rise and decline of areas is not simply a factor of 'market sentiment' whereby areas fall in or out of favour. As Harvey has shown, the built environment is produced in the same manner as any other commodity within an overall capitalist system. The built environment, according to Harvey, performs a critically useful function for capitalist accumulation of absorbing excess surplus during periods of boom and effectively devalorising such investments during subsequent 'busts'. Harvey argues that the shift of housing preferences from the inner city to the suburbs during the post-war period in North America and Britain (what Rex has referred to as the game of 'urban leapfrog') was precisely the consequence of such a shift in the investment cycle. Excess surplus was invested in suburban housing and shopping centres where land was relatively cheap and greater profits could be made than continuing to invest in relatively highly valued inner urban areas or in manufacturing industry. In addition, the state invested heavily in the supporting infrastructure of roads (the Interstate system in the USA) and public transportation (in Britain and especially elsewhere in Europe). In Britain, whose cities had had their infrastructure partly destroyed by a combination of enemy action and lack of maintenance during the Second World War, there was the additional attraction of building on green field sites where new infrastructure could be put in place cheaply and quickly by the state. Harvey thus explains how the structure of housing supply is largely determined by the larger macroeconomic environment of investment within the capitalist economy. The approach can be criticised, as we shall see below when we discuss the debate over gentrification, because it largely ignores the motivations and interests of individuals and social groups about where they might choose to want to live. The 'capital logic' approach of Harvey and others leaves a gap in the analytical trail, but this can be addressed by complementing the approach with a more sociological one (Hamnett 1991). Cultural differences and national economic and political contexts also matter; it is not only individual preferences that get marginalized, as we argue next. There are major differences in housing provision between free market economies, social democratic welfare states and former state socialist regimes.

It is important to understand the role of different housing market structures in different countries in influencing the intellectual approaches to the analysis of urban residential patterns. In North America, where there was limited public sector housing provision, most attention focused on the role of the market and residential choice. In Eastern Europe, pre-1989, attention was focused on the role of the state in housing allocation (Hegedüs and Tosics, 1992), whereas in European mixed economies, there was a focus on the interaction of both state and market and the growing segregation of different social classes and income groups in state and private market housing. The emergence of post-socialism in Eastern Europe led to a dramatic shift of approach, as urban analysts examined the role of newly emerged market economies in the creation of new forms of residential inequality and redistribution. We would argue that the literature on residential choice and housing market patterns in North America is, to a large extent, specific to that historical and social situation and needs to be placed in a more general social, political and historical context. A key example of this is the great importance of social housing in many European countries in the post-war period. In Britain this reached over 25% nationally, and in the Netherlands 40%, at its peak. In Amsterdam, social housing accounted for over 70% of the stock at its peak.

The geographical distribution of social housing and tenant characteristics

While the production of high-status residential areas is a good example of the importance of housing development and supply in production of residential space, it is also important to look at the production of social housing, which has also had a major effect on the residential structure of many European cities such as Amsterdam, Paris and Berlin. First, there is a very uneven geography to the distribution of social housing, which partly reflects the period and the politics of its construction. In Britain, for example, there are higher concentrations in large northern industrial cities and relatively less in more middle class southern cities. In the Netherlands, the greatest concentrations are in the major cities, particularly in Amsterdam and Rotterdam. Some South-east Asian cities such as Hong Kong and Singapore also have large social or subsidised housing sectors.

Secondly, there is often an uneven internal geography, with relatively little social housing in more middle class areas. The specific form of this differs from one country to another. In French and Swedish cities, much of the social housing is in large estates on the periphery, whereas in Britain there are many large inner-city estates. As Saunders (1976 and Young and Kramer (1978) have shown, in London, this was a result of strong political resistance on the part of conservative middle class suburban localities and a greater willingness for council housing in inner London areas of Labour control. Conversely, the level of homeownership increased in new-built Conservative-controlled suburban outer London compared to inner London. Thus, the changing tenure structure of the housing market has both reflected and influenced the social structure of residential areas. This parallels work in the USA on the exclusion of social housing and low-income groups from many jurisdictions.

One of the clearest examples of the role of tenure structure in housing supply is in the historic dominance of private rental in many inner-city areas where the majority of properties were generally built for rent. The growth of homeownership in the inter-war period was, to a large extent, a suburban phenomenon in London (Jackson, 1974) and private renting remained the dominant tenure in the inner city until 1961, when it accounted for over 60% of households, at which time housing in outer London was predominantly owner-occupied. The decline of private renting in the inner city from the late 1960s onwards was associated with both clearance and demolition of poor-quality housing and its replacement by large-scale social housing. The shift in tenures was also the result of sales to sitting tenants, the 'winkling out' of other tenants and the sale of the subsequently 'vacant' property to owner-occupiers (Hamnett and Randoph, 1984). The implications of this shift was that, whereas in 1961 council housing and homeownership each accounted for less than 20% of households in inner London, by 1981 council housing had become the single largest tenure at 42% while private renting shrank dramatically. Today, council housing and social landlordism accounts for less than 25% of all households in inner London, while homeownership accounts for 40%. This has a profound impact on the nature of housing choice. In the borough of Tower Hamlets (in inner East London), for example, social housing accounted for over 80% of households in 1981, whereas today the figure is 50% and falling and is distributed across a range of registered social landlords. Buying in Tower Hamlets was very difficult until a few years ago, simply because there was so little property available to purchase.

The result has been that council housing has tended to be concentrated in poorer, working class communities. Given that council housing was originally designated as housing for the working classes, the unsurprising result has been a high degree of social polarisation by tenure (Hamnett, 1984, 2003), which has increased in recent decades as a result of the 'Right to Buy' policy (enshrined in the 1981 Housing Act), which has led to the sale of many of the better-quality properties to sitting tenants (Forrest and Murie, 1984). Whereas the great majority of managerial and professional (about 80%) and a majority of skilled manual workers households are homeowners, this steadily decreases with social class and income, with only about 40% of the semi-skilled and unskilled in the owner-occupier category. There is also a marked divide by ethnic group, with the proportion of white homeowners (70%) matching the proportion of homeowners nationally, but the proportion of ethnic minority homeowners varyies from 80% of Indians to just 30% of Bangladeshis and black Caribbean families. The inverse also holds, with high proportions of social housing tenants among Bangladeshis and black Caribbean households. The degree of concentration of these groups in social housing in London increased between 1991 and 2001, even though ethnic minorities saw a substantial absolute and percentage growth in homeownership, particularly in suburban outer London (Hamnett and Butler, 2010). This seeming paradox is a result of the fact that the size of the ethnic minority population increased dramatically (57%) over this period. So, even though there was substantial growth of ethnic minority homeownership, the growth of social housing in these groups was even more marked.

When this is combined with the statutory housing allocation policies operated by most local governments, which have to give priority to homeless families, including single-parent families, refugees and asylum seekers, the result has been an increase in the proportion of the less skilled, the unemployed, the economically inactive and single-parent families, low-income groups, and some (but not all) ethnic minorities in social rented housing estates, which has reinforced their relative undesirability. As vacancies occur, they are allocated to the groups with the greatest need, of which homeless families top the list. This reinforces the social character of the neighbourhood, and a process of tenurial social residualisation has taken place which reflects the very limited level of effective choice most council residents have. They live where they do not out of choice, but because of their lack of effective choice. Many residents would, if they were able to, opt to live in a better area, but this is rarely a realistic option. Thus, as Taylor (1979) shows, some residential areas have the social characteristics they have as a result of the lack of choice: their residents are effectively trapped at the bottom of the housing market and find it difficult to escape. This has been intensified by the cuts in new council house building over the last 30 years. The sector is now much smaller than it was at its peak in 1980, and the groups with least choice have become increasingly concentrated within it, as has happened with social housing in the USA.

GENTRIFICATION AND SUBURBANISATION

The historical distinction between older inner-city terraced or row housing and suburban detached or (in Britain) semi-detached housing with larger gardens means that those households with some degree of choice are faced with the fundamental choice of whether to live in the inner city or suburbia. As Alonso (1964) argued, the dominant value system in the USA and in Britain has been for suburbia, and there has been a large degree of suburban growth and out-migration, particularly of more affluent households (Frey, 1995). However, as Ruth Glass (1964) observed in London 40 years ago, there has been a tendency for some middle class groups to move to the inner city in the process known as gentrification.

'One by one, many of the working class quarters of London have been invaded by the middle classes – upper and lower. Shabby, modest mews and cottages – two rooms up and two down – have been taken over, when their leases have expired, and have become elegant, expensive residences. Once this process of gentrification starts in a district, it goes on rapidly until all or most of the original working class occupiers are displaced and the whole social character of the district is changed' (Glass, 1964: xviii).

The discovery of gentrification in a number of cities (Ley, 1970, 1976; Hamnett and Williams, 1980; Gale, 1979) highlighted the fact that the process of outwards residential migration and inner-city decline was not necessarily general or inevitable, although this continued to be the dominant process in most North American cities (Frey, 1995; Beauregard, 1996). It also raised questions about the factors leading a specific fraction of the middle class to turn their back on the suburbs for the inner city.

The existence of this group was recognised in the 1950s in Greenwich Village in New York and the West End of Boston and they have been described as cosmopolitan centralists; Lockwood (1995) has commented that we can distinguish between an 'urban seeking' and an 'urban fleeing' middle class. Some of the former live in central and inner-city middle class residential areas such as Kensington and Chelsea in London, Edgbaston in Birmingham or Georgetown in Washington, some in formerly working class areas near the city centre, often with large minority populations, whereas the latter continue to seek single-class and ethnically homogenous suburban communities. In more recent times, particularly in the USA, it is this group that are identified as being the ones who are most actively populating gated communities. As Low (2004) showed, such communities are often finely sorted according to class, ethnic and stage of the life cycle.

Neil Smith (Smith 1979, 1996) explained gentrification in terms derived from Harvey's analysis of the processes of investment and disinvestment in the built environment and the ways in which 'switching mechanisms' have diverted investment from primary circuits of accumulation (manufacturing) to the built environment and infrastructure. Like Harvey, he points to a post Second World War process of 'disinvestment' in the urban environment in favour of the 'super profits' that could be made at the time by investing in the suburbs. He extended this analysis by arguing that this devalorisation of land in the inner city led to the emergence of a 'rent gap', which in the early 1970s encouraged investors to identify profitable opportunities and to begin to reinvest in the city or at least those parts near to the affluent downtown areas. As the subtitle of one his early papers notes, this was a return to the city 'by capital not people' and his account was focused on why capital should begin to reinvest in parts at least of the inner city. Smith (1979) would argue that questions about which particular class fractions choose to move into newly gentrified areas is largely a 'second order' concern – but in our view, this fails to deal with crucial aspects of urban social class change.

We have already noted that the emphasis on the demand for gentrified housing was the approach taken by David Ley, who began writing on gentrification at much the same time as Neil Smith. Ley noted, in the context of Vancouver, that the process of gentrification rests on the changing economic base of the city and the growth of service sector jobs, which created the basis for an expanded new middle class in some cities (Ley, 1996; Hamnett, 2003). This, however, is a necessary but not a sufficient condition for gentrification to occur; it also involved a specific fraction of the middle class with high levels of educational attainment, and a set of values which prioritised the aesthetic value of older, period, housing (Jager, 1986) and proximity to the cultural and entertainment facilities of the central city (Ley 1996, Butler and Robson, 2003). As has been shown in a variety of cities, this group has been strongly attracted to the mix of housing and cultural attractions of the inner city (Caulfield 1989; Hamnett and Whitelegg, 2007) and to proximity to work. As a group, they are therefore quite distinct from the households which tend to move to the suburbs (Warde, 1991; Butler and Hamnett, 1994; Lockwood, 1995). The ability to synthesise these two approaches to housing choice and constraint has been long noted, if not always achieved, in the study of gentrification (Hamnett, 1991; Lees, 1994, 2000; Atkinson, 2003).

Although gentrification has met considerable criticism in academic literature on the grounds that it involves the displacement of working class households (Smith, 1996; Atkinson, 2000; Slater, 2006, 2008; Lees et al., 2008; Watt, 2008), it is nevertheless generally accepted that gentrifying households normally move initially into socially mixed areas at least in the early years of the gentrifying process (Hackworth and Smith, 2001). This raises interesting questions about the motivations of such households and the trade-offs they are prepared to make. To what extent do they positively value social heterogeneity over social homogeneity and are they prepared to put up with concerns about safety and security? Are they effectively taking a gamble on the future social change of the areas concerned and see social mix as a necessary cost of the positive attractions of older housing and proximity to the centre (Butler, 1997).

Lees (2000) argued that the so-called third wave of gentrification that emerged out of the recession of the late 1980s and early 1990s extended the concept both in terms of the groups it embraced and its spatial context, giving it a more diverse geography than in its first and second stages. In particular, she argued that a distinctive 'geography of gentrification' was emerging and it was also spreading beyond its mono-ethnic origins in a few global cities. She identified new groups of senior professionals and managers who were pursuing a process that she termed 'super gentrification'; such groups were now able to buy up areas of the inner city that had become unaffordable to the original groups of gentrifiers – see Butler and Lees (2006) for an account of how this group has colonised parts of North London and has been replacing some of the original gentrifiers who have been 'cashing out'. Hamnett's (2009) analysis of the geography of house price changes in London from 1995 to 2006 links this to gentrification and outlines the concept of 'spatially displaced demand' to help explain the diffusion of house price increases across large swathes of the inner city. It is shown that while the ranking of mean borough house prices in London has remained broadly stable, with the most expensive and the lowest-price boroughs retaining their respective positions, there has been a marked catching-up process by the lower-priced boroughs, at least in terms of percentage house price change. It is argued that increased high-income housing demand has been partly spatially displaced downwards to less expensive boroughs, with consequent knock-on effects on prices in these boroughs.

It is possible to associate particular occupational and cultural characteristics with this group: they work in a few global industries such as the law and investment banking but are themselves often relatively immobile, coming from a restricted range of universities and working in a limited number of companies in the City of London (Butler and Lees, 2006). For them, residence matters: it needs to be near work and the social and cultural facilities of the inner city, and, to some extent, near people like themselves. In other words, there is a particular 'habitus' that is spatially as well as socially bounded and this is highly influential on their choice of where to live. This work has been subject to virulent critical appraisal by Slater (2006, 2008) and Watt (2008) who argue that it has served to de-radicalise the idea of gentrification and transform it into an understanding of the city which is viewed through middle class eyes and is seen as the new 'urban norm' (see Hamnett, 2009b for a critique).

Elective belonging

The process by which particular groups have sought out specific areas is still not well understood, although there are numerous examples of specific groups of people who tend to cluster together in self-defined neighbourhoods. These range from the well-known Jewish residential clusters in many big cities such as London and New York, the reason being partly cultural and the need to walk to the synagogue, to the deeply entrenched religious segregation of Catholics and Protestants in Belfast (Boal, 1969), and the religious segregation of Shia and Sunni Muslims in Baghdad, and religious segregation in Jerusalem and Beirut. Much of this segregation is not voluntary, but defensive and a search for safety in numbers. Similarly, it has been argued that a significant amount of black residential segregation is the result of discrimination rather than choice (Massey and Denton, 1993), although other work (Zhang, 2004) suggests that the process is more complex and that discrimination is just one factor.

More recently, there have been attempts by urban sociologists and human geographers to understand 'Who lives where?' through reference to the work of the French sociologist Pierre Bourdieu. As we have seen in relation to the work on gentrification, one strand of this has focused on the preferences of an 'urban seeking' middle class (Lockwood, 1995). Originally, this approach was associated with the work of Ley (Ley, 1996), who focused on the production of gentrifiers and the rise of a 'new class' of upper professionals and managers. This approach has been pursued by Butler (Butler, 1997; Butler and Robson, 2003) and Bridge (Bridge, 2001, 2006) who drew on Bourdieu's notion of habitus and field to understand the ways in which different middle class groups tended to associate together and also with particular inner-city neighbourhoods – giving rise to a series of 'mini habituses' in the gentrified inner city which attract particular social groups who feel comfortable with these areas and their fellow gentrifiers (Bridge, 2006) within an overall 'metropolitan habitus' (Butler, 2007). In some ways, this behaviour appeared contrarian in an age where the conventional wisdom appeared to be suggesting that loyalty to place was declining in the context of increasing globalization, which, in turn, might be thought to have most impact on the middle classes. Butler and Lees' (2006) study of 'super gentrification' in Barnsbury in London's gentrified district of Islington, however, suggested that many of the new professional elites were in fact tied to specific places of work and residence and exhibited very low levels of spatial mobility.

Savage (Savage et al., 2005) has developed the notion of 'elective belonging' in an attempt to understand the relations between social and physical space in how people reach decisions about where to live. In particular, he was interested in how some of the middle classes, who might appear to be the most likely to exhibit lack of loyalty to place and to be globally mobile, are amongst those displaying the highest levels of attachment to places populated by people like themselves. The findings that underpin this work are based on research undertaken in four areas in and around Manchester in the north west of England. Drawing on Bourdieu's concepts of 'field' and 'habitus', Savage and his co-authors argue that, within the differentiated social fields (work, leisure, residence, friendship) across which their respondents operate, 'residential space is a key arena in which respondents define their social position' (Savage et al., 2005: 207) – noting that it has the greatest fixity in relation to other fields in terms of defining one's sense of 'social location' and allows access to other fields (work, culture and crucially education). In a rather bold claim, they argue that:

> ... one's residence is a crucial, possibly the crucial identifier of who you are. The sorting processes by which people chose to live in certain places and others leave is at the heart of contemporary battles over social distinction. Rather than seeing wider social identities as arising out of the field of employment it would be more promising to examine their relationship to residential location. ... in all four areas there are striking congruences between the capitals of the residents and their sense of feeling at home. (Savage et al., 2005: 207)

It is argued that it is around the sense of place, and an often very local sense of place, that identities are forged and developed which may be ones of class but are rarely expressed in these terms. Savage argues that people make choices about where to live as a way of associating with their 'habitus' across a number of 'fields' (as outlined above). Each group, however, has its own habitus which, while in itself is a relatively fixed concept, operates across a series of 'fields' such as work, leisure and residence. Savage argues that Bourdieu's conception of the habitus is essentially spatial:

> people are comfortable when there is a correspondence between habitus and field, but otherwise people feel ill at ease and seek to move – socially and spatially – so that their discomfort is relieved ... mobility is driven as people, with their relatively fixed habitus, both move between fields ... and move to places within fields where they feel more comfortable. (Savage et al., 2005: 9)

The trick, as it were, is for people to triangulate these fields spatially so that they live with 'people like themselves'.[1] In Savage's study, it is those who exercise choice to move, 'the incomers', who are more socially integrated and at ease with their localities – which become their habitus of choice – than 'the born and breds' who often remain there precisely because of their lack of choice. This finding turns on its head the assumption of many years of community studies about the role played by middle class incomers in trying to become accepted (e.g. Pahl, 1965).

Interestingly, the same assumption about behaviour lies at the heart of geodemographic classifications, such as Mosaic in the UK or Claritas in the USA, which, on the basis of the cluster analysis of demographic characteristics, show that people with similar economic, social and ethnic characteristics tend to cluster together in the same neighbourhoods (Webber, 2007). The problem with the habitus and elective affinities argument, however, is that it arguably underplays the key role of social class and economic and financial constraints; those living in poor council housing estates may well do so not because they want to cluster with those similar to themselves, but because they have no other effective options and are largely trapped at the bottom end of the housing market (Taylor, 1979). Equally, those living in areas of low-cost homeownership are likely to do so because they can afford little else. They may have similar characteristics but it is likely that, in a market economy, limited ability to pay serves to cluster like with like. It is only when people have more economic resources that issues of choice and preference really come into play. This is highlighted by our work on ethnic residential location in London (Hamnett and Butler, 2011) which shows the growth of middle class ethnic minority suburbanisation driven, in part, by a desire to escape from poor living and social conditions in some parts of inner London and to achieve the markers of suburban homeownership. To this extent, the notions of choice and habitus may be simply restating some fundamental economic truths about class, income and housing affordability in cultural terms. Nevertheless, both the elective affinities approach, drawing on Bourdieuian concepts, and the empiricist approach of geodemographics, point to the fact that large numbers of people, whether from choice or constraint, tend to live with people like themselves at a quite fine-grained level in both social and spatial terms. The problem with the geodemographics approach is that it is simply a descriptive classification of residential social space, with no analysis of process or causation.

CONCLUSIONS

The debates over gentrification have symbolised dramatically the conflictual nature of our understanding of housing space: not only do different social classes compete for space but also so do our understandings of that competition. The debate has demonstrated dramatically the way in which causes and consequences have become entangled in our understanding of the allocation and control of urban space. Different and competing explanations draw on structural constraints and individual choice and appear reluctant to find common ground. Only with reluctance have the academic protagonists accepted that both have a role in understanding how the changes in the wider class and occupational structure have worked their way through into the distribution of housing places. These different interpretations of how housing space is allocated reflect a bigger debate around the socio-spatial consequences of social change. As Britain, along with other previously industrial economies, has deindustrialised, the size of its manual working class has declined dramatically. Thus, the early incidences of gentrification in London (but also in New York, Vancouver and Sydney) were to some extent the forerunners of the dramatic changes that have taken place in cities which can no longer be described as predominantly working class places. The decline in their working class populations has been matched by a rise both in the numbers of the middle classes and those who are economically inactive. These cities have also witnessed, for the most part, a huge increase in their minority ethnic populations (in the case of London, from something under 3% in 1961 to nearly a third in 2001 – an increase of over 50% over the previous decade). Until recently at least, the middle class population of gentrifying areas has been largely a white one, whereas the BME (black and minority ethnic background) population has often been overrepresented amongst those who are economically inactive and in the worst housing.

Over the 50-year time span we set at the outset of this chapter for understanding the question of who lives where, the nature of the question has not changed but the context in which it has been asked is very different. The relationship between choice and constraint, on the one hand, and structural and social divisions, on the other, remains as do the arguments within human geography, economics and sociology about their relative importance. The changing context has seen the continued rise of owner-occupied housing, the rise and then relative decline of public rented housing and the decline and subsequent rise of private rented housing (although to nothing like its post-war levels, where it accounted for something like two-thirds of all housing in Britain). At the same time, the relatively easy way in which we could assign owner occupation to the middle class and public rented to the working class has now long passed. With over two-thirds of households now in owner-occupation (albeit with heavy levels of mortgage debt), no such correlation is possible.

The picture has been further complicated by the large expansion of the middle classes, who have spearheaded the gentrification of the city as well as continuing to people the suburbs. More recently, the middle class have become significant occupants of private rented housing as a result of the rapid rise of house prices in the first years of the century and the increased availability of supply rental housing through the buy-to-let phenomenon. The working class has shrunk in size, particularly in the large conurbations it once dominated, and its share of the council housing sector has shrunk to be replaced by the growing proportion of households of the economically inactive.

The growing ethnic minority population has further complicated the picture, with some groups being strongly represented in owner–occupation, while others are concentrated in the social housing sector. Given this complexity of geography, class and ethnicity, it would be surprising if the picture had become clarified over time. On the other hand, the partial breakdown of the previous binaries (class, tenure and suburban/urban) has forced social scientists into acknowledging an accommodation with more complex explanations and away from monocausality. What we can learn from the research on gentrification – which focused specifically on who lived where and why – is that we can bring together structural and social explanations in ways such as demonstrated by Savage with his concept of 'elective belonging' in which choice – or lack of choice – about where to live now becomes one of the most important indicators of social position and identification. Thus, the focus on residential choice as an indicator of social position for those lucky enough to be able to choose is one of the most significant changes of the last half-century. The issue of lack of choice has in itself become a fascinating issue in terms of social policy. The New Labour government believed that you could deal with this by forcing the state to make choice available to all; what we now see is that this has simply confirmed a new polarity between places that people choose to live and those where those who have no choice live. This is summed up dramatically in the new geodemographic databases such as Acorn and Mosaic which, with unnerving accuracy, sum up individuals' preferences and constraints on the basis of where they live.

NOTE

1 We are grateful to Bill Clark for drawing some parallels here between the literature on preferences and elective belonging and a previous approach in social psychology and rational choice theory which we referred to earlier (Allport, 1954; Schelling, 1971).

REFERENCES

Allport, G. (1954) *The Nature of Prejudice*. New York: Anchor Books.
Alonso, W. (1960) 'A theory of the urban land market', *Regional Science Association, Papers and Proceedings* 6: 149–147.
Alonso, W. (1964) 'The historic and structural theories of urban form; Their implications for urban renewal', *Land Economics* 40: 227–231.
Atkinson, R. (2000). 'Measuring gentrification and displacement in Greater London.' *Urban Studies* 37(1): 149–165.
Atkinson, R. (2003) 'Introduction: Misunderstood saviour or vengeful wrecker? The main meanings and problems of gentrification', *Urban Studies* 40: 2343–2350.
Bassett, J. and Short, J.R. (1980) *Housing and Residential Structure*. London: Routledge.
Beauregard, R.A. (1996) *Voices of Decline*. New York: Routledge.
Boal, F.W. (1969) 'Territoriality on the Shankill Falls divide', *Irish Geography* 6: 30–50.
Bourdieu, P. (1984) *Distinction: A Social Critique of the Formation of Taste*. London: Routledge.
Bourne, L. (1981) *The Geography of Housing*. London: Edward Arnold.
Bridge, G. (2001) 'Bourdieu rational action and the time-space strategy of gentrification', *Transactions of the Institute of British Geographers NS* 26: 205–216.
Bridge, G. (2006) 'It's not just a question of taste: Gentrification, the neighbourhood and cultural capital', *Environment and Planning A* 38: 1965–1978.
Burgess, E.W. (1924) 'The growth of the City: An introduction to a research project', *Publics American Sociological Society* 18: 85–97.
Butler, T. and Hamnett, C. (1994) 'Gentrification class and gender: Some comments on Warde's 'gentrification of consumption', *Environment and Planning D Society and Space* 12: 477–493.
Butler, T. and Lees, L. (2006) 'Super-gentrification in Barnsbury, London: globalisation and gentrifying elites at the neighbourhood level', *Transactions of the Institute of British Geographers NS31*: 467–487.
Butler, T. (1997) *Gentrification and the Middle Classes*. Aldershot: Ashgate.
Butler, T. (2007) 'For gentrification?', *Environment and Planning A* 39: 162–181.
Butler, T. and Robson, G. (2003) *London Calling: The Middle Classes and the Remaking of Inner London*. Oxford: Berg.
Caulfield, J. (1989). 'Gentrification and desire', *Canadian Review of Sociology and Anthropology* 26: 619–632.
Clark, W.A.V. (2002) 'Ethnic preferences and ethnic perceptions in multi-ethnic settings', *Urban Geography* 23: 237–256.
Clark, W.A.V. and Fossett, M. (2008) 'Understanding the social context of the Schelling segregation model', *Proceedings of the National Academy of Sciences of the USA*, March.
Davis, J.T. (1965) 'Middle class housing in the central city', *Economic Geography* 41: 238–251.

Dingemans, D. (1979) 'Redlining and mortgage lending in Sacramento', *Annals of the Association of American Geographers* 69: 225–237.

Dyos, H.J. and Reader, D.A. (1973) 'Slums and suburbs', in H.J. Dyos and M. Wolff (eds), *The Victorian City: Images and Realities*. London: Routledge and Kegan Paul.

Firey, W. (1945) 'Sentiment and symbolism as ecological variables', *American Sociological Review* 10: 140–148.

Forrest, R. and Murie, A. (1984) *Selling the Welfare State*. London: Routledge.

Frey, W.H. (1995) 'Immigration and internal migration "flight" from US metropolitan areas: Toward a new demographic balkanisation', *Urban Studies* 32: 733–758.

Gale, D.E. (1979). 'Middle class resettlement in older urban neighbourhoods: The evidence and the implications', *Journal of the American Planning Association* 45: 293–304.

Glass, R. (1964). *London : Aspects of Change*. Centre for Urban Studies. London: MacGibbon & Kee.

Gordon, G. (1979) 'The status areas of early to mid-Victorian Edinburgh', *Transactions of the Institute of British Geographers NS4*: 168–191.

Hackworth, J. and Smith, N. (2001) 'The changing state of gentrification', *Tijdschrift voor Economische en Sociale Geografie* 92: 464–477.

Hamnett, C. (1984) 'Housing the two nations: Socio-tenurial polarisation in the housing market', *Urban Studies* 21: 389–405.

Hamnett, C. (1991) 'The blind man and the elephant: The explanation of gentrification', *Transactions of the Institute of British Geographers NS16*: 173–189.

Hamnett, C. (2003) 'Gentrification and the middle class remaking of inner London, 1961–2001', *Urban Studies* 40: 2401–2426.

Hamnett, C. and Whitelegg, D. (2007). "Loft Conversions and Gentrification: from Industrial to Post industrial Land Use." *Environment and Planning A* 39(1): 106–124.

Hamnett, C. (2009) 'Spatially displaced demand and the changing geography of house prices in London, 1995–2006', *Housing Studies* 24: 301–320.

Hamnett, C. (2009b) The New Mikardo? Tom Slater, gentrification and displacement', *City*, 13: 4, 476.

Hamnett, C. and Butler, T. (2010) 'The changing ethnic structure of housing tenures in London, 1991–2001', *Urban Studies*.

Hamnett, C. and Randolph, B. (1984) 'The role of landlord disinvestment in housing market transformation: An analysis of the flat break-up market in central London', *Transactions of the Institute of British Geographers* 9: 259–279.

Hamnett, C. and Williams, P. (1980) Social change in London: study of gentrification, *Urban Affairs Quarterly*, 15: 469–87.

Harvey, D. (1973) *Social Justice and the City*. London: Edward Arnold.

David Harvey (1974) Class-monopoly rent, finance capital and the urban revolution, *Regional Studies*, 1974, Vol. 8, 3–4, pages 239–255.

Hegedüs J. and Tosics, I. (1992) 'Conclusion: Past tendencies and recent problems of the East European housing model', in B.Turner, J. Hegedüs and I. Tosics (eds), *The Reform of Housing in Eastern Europe and the Soviet Union*. London: Routledge.

Herbert, D.T. (1972) *Urban Geography: A social perspective*. Praeger.

Hoyt, H. (1939) The structure and growth of residential neighborhoods in American cities, Washington D.C. Federal Housing Administration.

Jager, M. (1986). 'Class definition and the esthetics of gentrification: Victoriana in Melbourne' in P. Williams and N. Smith *Gentrification of the City*. London: Allen and Unwin: 78–91.

Johnston, R.J. (1970) 'On spatial patterns in the residential structure of cities', *Canadian Geographer*, XIV: 361–367.

Johnston, R.J (1971) *Urban Residential Segregation*. London: Bell.

Lees, L. (1994) 'Rethinking gentrification: Beyond the positions of economics or culture', *Progress in Human Geography* 18: 137–150.

Lees, L. (2000) 'A reappraisal of gentrification towards a "geography of gentrification"', *Progress in Human Geography* 24: 389–408.

Lees, L., Slater, T. and Wyly, E. (2008) *Gentrification*. New York: Routledge.

Ley, D. (1970) Liberal Ideology and the Post-Industrial City, Annals, *Association of American Geographers*, 70(2): 238–5.

Ley, D. (1976) Alternative Explanations for Inner-City Gentrification: A Canadian Assessment, *Annals of the Association of American Geographers Volume* 76, Issue 4, pages 521–535, December 1986.

Ley, D. (1996) *The New Middle Class and the Remaking of the Central City*. Oxford: Oxford University Press.

Lockwood, D. (1995). 'Marking out the middle classes' in T. Butler and M. Savage *Social Change and the Middle Classes*. London: UCL Press: 1–12.

Low, S. (2004). *Behind the Gates: Life, Security and the Pursuit of Happiness in Fortress America*. New York: Routledge.

Massey, D.S. and Denton, N.A. (1993) *American Apartheid: Segregation and the Making of the Underclass.* Cambridge, MA: Harvard University Press.

Olsen, D. (1976) *The Growth of Victorian London.* London: Penguin Books.

Park, Robert, Ernest W. Burgess and Roderick D. McKenzie (1925). *The City.* Chicago: University of Chicago Press.

Pahl, R. (1965) 'Class and community in English commuter villages', S*ociologia Ruralis: Journal of the European Society for Rural Sociology,* V 1: pp. 5–23.

Pahl, R.E. (1965) *Urbs in Rure: The Metropolitan Fringe in Hertfordshire.* London: Weidenfield and London School of Economics.

Pahl, R. (1971) *Whose City and Other Essays?* Harlow: Longman.

Pahl, R.E. (1975) *Whose City?* Harmondsworth: Penguin.

Rex, J. and Moore, R. (1967) *Race Community and Conflict: A Study of Sparkbrook.* Oxford: Oxford University Press.

Robson, B. (1969) *Urban Analysis: A Study of City Structure With Special Reference to Sunderland.* Cambridge. Cambridge University Press.

Robson, B. (1975) *Urban Social Areas.* Cambridge: Cambridge University Press.

Saunders, P. (1976) *Urban Politics: A Sociological Interpretation.* London: Heinemann.

Savage, M., Bagnall, G. and B Longhurst (2005) *Globalization and Belonging.* London: Sage.

Schelling, T. (1971) 'Dynamic models of segregation', *Journal of Mathematical Sociology* 1: 143–186.

Shevky, E. and Bell, W. 1955: *Social Area Analysis: Theory, Illustrative Application and Computational Procedures.* Stanford, CA: Stanford University.

Slater, T. (2006) 'The eviction of critical perspectives from gentrification research', *International Journal of Urban and Regional Research* 30: 737–757.

Slater, T. (2008) 'A literal necessity to be re-placed: A rejoinder to the gentrification debate', *International Journal of Urban and Regional Research* 32: 212–223.

Smith, N. (1979) 'Towards a theory of gentrification: A back to the city movement by capital, not people', *Journal of the American Planning Association* 45: 538–548.

Smith, N. (1996) *The New Urban Frontier: Gentrification and the Revanchist City.* London: Routledge.

Steadman-Jones, G. (1971) *Outcast London.* Harmondsworth: Penguin.

Taylor, P.J. (1979) '"Difficult-to-let", "difficult-to-live-in", and sometimes "difficult-to-get-out-of": An essay on the provision of council housing, with special reference to Killingworth', *Environment and Planning A* 11: 1305–1320.

Timms, D. (1971) *The Residential Mosaic: Towards a Theory of Residential Differentiation.* Cambridge: Cambridge University Press.

Walker, R. (1981 'A Theory of Suburbanization: Capitalism and the Construction of Urban Space in the United States.' Pp. 383–429 in M. Dear and A. Scott (eds), *Urbanization and UrbanPlanning in Capitalist Society.* London: Methuen.

Warde, A. (1991) 'Gentrification as consumption issues of class and gender', *Environment and Planning D Society and Space* 6: 75–95.

Watt, P. (2008). 'The only class in town? Gentrification and middle-class colonization of the city and the urban imagination.' *International Journal of Urban and Regional Research* 32(1): 206–211.

Webber, R. (2007) 'The metropolitan habitus: Its manifestations, locations and consumption profiles', *Environment and Planning A* 39: 182–207.

Williams, P. (1976). "The role of institutions in the inner London housing markets: the case of Islington." *Transactions of the Institute of British Geographers* 3(New Series): 72–82.

Young, K. and Kramer, J. (1978) *Strategy and Conflict in Metropolitan Housing.* London: Heinemann.

Zhang, J. (2004) 'A dynamic model of residential segregation', *Journal of Mathematical Sociology* 28: 147–170.

9

Social Policy Approaches to Housing Research

David Clapham

INTRODUCTION

When Jim Kemeny made his well-known plea for more theoretically aware housing research in 1992, he was implicitly criticising the dominant social policy paradigm in housing research at that time, which consisted extensively of empirical, policy-related research, often undertaken for government agencies. Kemeny (1992) considered this approach to lack an explicit research epistemology or ontology and to be isolated from the societal context within which the specific problem was situated. Furthermore, he argued that much research in this tradition adopted the problem definition of powerful agents – most notably governments. Housing research mirrored that in other social policy fields and Kemeny's criticisms were reflected in discussions within the social policy tradition triggered by attempts during the 1970s and 1980s to define a 'critical' social policy that was more theoretically oriented in opposition to the predominant approach (see, for example, Mishra, 1977). Despite Kemeny's and the other criticisms, the social policy tradition of research has continued to build on its long history and undoubtedly has many strengths, such as its strong relationship with the policy process and its commitment to rigorous empirical research. Also, the proposition that there is a lack of a coherent theoretical framework can be challenged, although it may be a framework that does not bring universal acceptance.

The aim of this chapter is to review the contribution of the social policy approach to the study of housing policies and problems, and to suggest ways in which the approach can be taken forward. The chapter begins with a brief review of the approach from its origins in the first poverty surveys up to the explosion in housing research in the 1970s and beyond. The character of the approach will then be outlined and its strengths and weaknesses considered. Particular issues addressed are the positivist nature of the approach, the links with the policy process and the moral dimensions of research. Finally, the chapter will ask whether the approach can survive the Kemeny critique and make a fruitful contribution to housing studies.

The form it should take to make a useful complement to other approaches will be considered.

First it is necessary to define some terms. Clapham, Kemp and Smith (1990: p. x) define social policy as 'those areas of consumption in which the state plays a central role, either by regulating the provision of services, underwriting the cost of their provision, or providing goods and services in kind.' The problem here is in defining consumption and identifying the aims of the intervention. Alternatively, social policy can be considered to be state intervention in any field designed to achieve social objectives. But what are considered to be social objectives? For example, policies designed to increase the provision of housing could be primarily related to economic or environmental objectives that may not be considered to be social. Housing policy constitutes a variety of aims and objectives that may relate to the economy, the environment, as well as social policy, and this probably accounts for the view that housing is 'the wobbly pillar' of the welfare state (Torgerson, 1987).

Therefore, the term 'social policy research' will be defined here in very wide terms. It is taken to cover research that is concerned with particular social problems that may be (or are thought to be) the role of government to ameliorate, prevent or otherwise deal with through the provision of services or other forms of intervention. Although it will be argued later that there are common elements to much research, it covers a wide field of different types of studies.

HOUSING AS SOCIAL POLICY

The nature of housing makes it amenable to a social policy approach (see Clapham, Kemp and Smith, 1990). Houses have a physical and material existence, which can be problematic when poor conditions can be associated with poor health. People with health problems may need special forms of housing. Examples may be older people or those with a physical disability. Therefore, it is likely that housing may be considered in policy debates on health and health services (see, for example, Smith, Knill-Jones and McGuckin, 1991).

Also, housing is a very expensive good in terms of personal income. Because the quality of housing tends to be closely related to its price, it is usual that those on low incomes inhabit the worst housing, which may be below the standards considered adequate in society (Murie, 1983). Therefore, housing is an important mechanism in transmitting income inequality into wider disadvantage (Le Grand, 1982). Housing has a physical location that can facilitate or hinder access to other goods and services such as shops, schools or employment. Also, housing is located in neighbourhoods that can be of similar quality or market position. This can result in social segregation that may be considered harmful to the life chances of low-income or disadvantaged people (Burrows and Rhodes, 1998). Policy concern with social exclusion tends to be focused on particular neighbourhoods where low-income people are concentrated.

The nature of shelter as a basic human need and its expense and its link to other key constituents of life chances mean that housing policies have been seen by many governments as elements of the state welfare provision. Debates on housing policy are often linked to those of health or poverty. Housing agencies have practical links to other state agencies in the fields of social services, health and education. Housing can be seen as an important instrument of social policy, both in its own right but also as a means of achieving objectives in areas such as health and poverty.

Nevertheless, housing has been termed the 'wobbly pillar' of the welfare state, in that it has rarely in any country been the subject of universal state provision in the way that education or health services have been in some places at some times. In most countries there is a substantial market in housing and widespread trends of privatisation and marketisation have seen this share grow in the last couple of decades. However, governments have intervened in the market to achieve their social objectives by, for example, making housing allowances available to low-income households, controlling rents, or using land-use planning or other mechanisms to influence the amount and type of new housebuilding. A common policy is for governments to subsidise the provision of new housing for low income people. So, although a 'wobbly pillar', housing is still a focus of state social policy in most countries, and the nature of the good means that this is likely to continue. Nevertheless, the preponderance of market relations has limited the extent of social policy research, which has tended to focus on the areas of state provision and where there has been overlap with social policy areas such as health, poverty or social work services.

THE SOCIAL POLICY TRADITION

In Britain what we would now call empirical research on housing issues was closely related to the first government interventions in housing in the 19th century. Edwin Chadwick in 1842 undertook the collection of evidence to show that, contrary to prevailing wisdom, 'low moral standards' were a consequence rather than a cause of poor housing conditions. The early public health reforms were backed by research on the spread of infectious diseases and the health consequences of an unsafe water supply (for reviews, see Wohl, 1977 and Gauldie, 1974). Poor health was shown to be linked to poor and overcrowded housing and a case made for slum clearance to improve health. Such calls for action were answered by governments which, although limited by their laissez-faire political ideologies, were concerned by the impact of crime and the spread of infectious diseases on the middle class voters.

The early studies of poverty by Seebohm Rowntree (see for example, Rowntree, 1902) involved the collection of data on the living conditions of urban dwellers. Another example is the work of Friedrich Engels (1891) in his *Condition of the Working Class in England* where he examined the living conditions and lifestyles of the working classes in the North of England. These studies drew attention to the links between poor housing and low income.

These studies show the long history of the social policy approach and illustrate some of its long-standing themes, such as the concern with 'social evils' including ill health and poverty and the situation of the poorest parts of the population. Also, the emphasis on systematic enquiry to uncover the 'facts' of the situation is evident. In addition, there is a clear focus on government policy intervention. Research is aimed at trying to bring about social change. Interestingly, given later criticisms of the government dominance in this type of research, many of the studies were undertaken by radical political activists trying to pressure governments to take action to achieve social change. Finally, much of the research was infused with implicit moral values of what was right. Poor health and poverty were clearly seen as immoral and unacceptable.

The focus on government action limited the scope and extent of research until the widening of the electoral franchise and the rise of the Liberal and Labour parties brought about the establishment of the Welfare State, with housing policy as one of its elements. Since the end of the First World War in 1918, government has become deeply involved in the mechanics of housing policy and practice, often acting through local government. This approach has chimed with different political philosophies. In particular, the Fabian socialist tradition associated with Sidney and Beatrice Webb gave an impetus to social policy research. The tradition placed emphasis on gradual change of state institutions and policies to achieve social change. The implicit assumption was of a neutral and powerful state that could be captured by the working classes to achieve their interests. The detail of policy is important because of the social ends it is required to serve. The state needs to know how to prevent and deal with social problems such as poverty or homelessness. The assumption is that it has the will and the means to solve these problems within the existing social order.

In Britain, housing research grew substantially during the 1970s when state involvement in housing reached a peak. There was a policy emphasis on building new public housing for low-income people, along with an increasing concern with the physical and social conditions on some existing public housing estates. These policy concerns led to the demand for research to inform policy and practice. At the same time, and largely for the same reasons, government became concerned with the trained staff available to local authorities to manage public housing estates. Therefore, it took the initiative to establish postgraduate training courses in many universities. This meant that a substantial number of academics existed to meet the demand for housing research from government and local authorities. The government interest in housing was matched by a growth in voluntary sector activity from bodies such as Shelter or the Joseph Rowntree Foundation, which were both the funders and the consumers of housing research.

From the 1980s onwards, government became increasingly concerned with 'value for money' in public services following the policy process adopted that will be considered further in a later section. The result was a growth in evaluation studies of public policies and services, based on the social policy tradition, in which the focus was on the cost-effectiveness of services. During the 1990s and up to 2010 (the time of writing), there was an emphasis on 'evidence-based policy' that also fuelled the amount of housing research and shaped its nature. Obviously, other countries have had different experiences, but the aim here has been to show the link between the growth of the social policy tradition of housing research and the philosophies and practices of government.

THE NATURE OF SOCIAL POLICY RESEARCH

In this section the social policy approach will be reviewed and categorised. Clearly this involves considerable generalisation over what is a substantial body of research. The review will not focus on individual research studies, but will attempt to generalise across the body of work. Therefore, the points made will be relevant to different degrees in each particular research study.

Positivism or empiricism?

It was noted earlier that the first social policy research was directed at the discovery of social facts about the conditions of (usually) poor people. A later emphasis was on 'evidence' on which to base policy. Most research has involved the use of semi-structured or structured interview schedules to large groups of people or the manipulation of large databases such as the census in order to ascertain the extent of social problems. This approach tends to indicate an empiricist or positivist philosophy of research, although this has been rarely articulated in individual studies. One of the criticisms of the approach from Kemeny was its lack of an explicit theoretical base.

The collection of social facts about a problem could be construed as empiricism. According to Bryman (2004), empiricism implies two things. First, empiricism shares with positivism the belief that ideas must be subjected to the rigours of testing before they can be considered knowledge: in other words, the belief that the 'natural science' approach can be applied to social phenomena. The second element, according to Bryman, is the belief that the accumulation of facts is a legitimate goal in its own right: this element he calls 'naïve empiricism'. Mishra (1977) criticises the social policy tradition as assuming that there is a broad social consensus concerning the aims and objectives of social policy and so believing that the display of empirical fact is the basis from which policy decisions flow. In this sense much social policy research has been empiricist, as the collection of data about a social problem has been a key element.

However, in my view, very few social policy studies of housing could be termed 'naïve empiricism' as they usually involve some form of deductive or inductive theory building. For example, studies of homelessness are based on the deductive approach in that they usually have an (often implicit) set of assumptions about the nature of the 'social problem', which is often expressed in terms of a hypothesis to be tested. There is also an element of inductive theory building, because findings are generalised into 'laws' that can be used as a basis for government action. Kemeny's major criticism is that housing research of this type was not integrated into the mainstream of social science theory, and into the overall society that this was attempting to describe. This criticism relates to the scale of the theory used in research. Most studies have used middle-range theories or concepts such as the concept of labelling theory or stigma to understand the disadvantage suffered by residents of some unpopular estates. These individual concepts or theories are rarely related to grand theories. In other words, the stigma associated with some estates is not related to wider societal processes of inequality and disadvantage that are deeply rooted in society and require grand theories to understand. The Fabian tradition may have been influential in reinforcing this emphasis. Therefore, in my view, the valid criticism concerns the level of theory employed rather than the lack of theory. Much social policy research is not solely empiricist, although there has been a clear commitment to the collection of empirical data as a core research aim.

It is more accurate to label the social policy approach as positivist rather than empiricist. Bryman (2004) identifies five features of positivism:

- only phenomena tested by the senses can be warranted as knowledge
- the purpose of theory is to generate hypotheses for testing (deductivism)
- the gathering of facts provides the basis for laws (inductivism)
- social science must be conducted in a way that is value-free and objective
- there is a clear distinction between scientific statements and normative statements, with only the former the true domain of the social scientist.

I have argued above that much housing research in the social policy tradition has employed deductive and inductive theory making with middle-range theories or concepts. But the problem in fitting the tradition into the positivist category is the question of objectivity. Much research commissioned by government has to espouse objectivity. But does it ever achieve it when the nature of the problem to be researched is often assumed in the hypothesis to be tested or the way the issue is defined? I will return to this issue in the later discussion of the nature of the policy process.

Another problem with the objectivity issue is that social policy research often seems to be underpinned by moral concepts. There is a clear commitment in much research to the solving of social problems such as homelessness or social deprivation and, indeed, many would argue that this is a major strength of the research tradition. Much research commissioned by pressure groups or voluntary organisations is used to create a moral outrage at the impact (or lack of it) of government policies. Of course, such research usually claims to be objective. If it is objective, then it should be repeatable in the sense that the same findings would be reached by different researchers undertaking the same research. This only happens where the second set of researchers share the paradigm of the first. What often happens is that schools of thought emerge on how to approach research on a particular topic and on the way to interpret findings. An example of this would be the different ways of approaching the phenomenon of homelessness (compare Fitzpatrick, 2005 and Clapham, 2003).

Clearly, one's view of positivism will vary according to the personal beliefs of the researcher and there is no logical or scientific way of choosing between different paradigms. But we can ask how plausible and useful the positivist tradition has been. The plausibility of positivism has been considered to be very low in sociology and geography but, in the disciplines of economics and psychology, positivism is still strong and dominant. In my view, the strengths of the positivist approach are its rigour and testability and its attempted objectivity, but the weaknesses are its lack of appreciation of the socially constructed and contested nature of reality. Both critical realism and social constructionism accept that there are competing versions of reality even though, in the case of critical realism, it is asserted that there is an underlying reality that may not be apparent to the people involved.

The lack of an appreciation of different constructions of reality is coupled with a belief in the objectivity of the researcher, which has been discarded in many fields. In psychology and in the health field, experiments are devised that can minimise the impact of researcher bias. One can think of the double-blind randomised clinical trial used in assessing medicines as being the best example of this. Of course, there are problems in this model, for example, in explaining the placebo effect, but at least it can be allowed for. Housing research rarely allows for this form of experiment, and so the interaction between researcher and subject cannot be ignored.

The positivist influence on much social policy research has influenced the research tools chosen, although there is not necessarily a direct link between epistemology and method. Nevertheless, as a generalisation, much research has adopted quantitative techniques, whether analysis of large secondary data sets such as the census, or the administration of structured questionnaire surveys. In some cases this has led to poor interpretation of results. For example, in the study by Saunders (1990) of attitudes to homeownership, differences of 10 or 20 percentage points in answers to questions on for instance, the feeling of 'home' by homeowners, on the one hand, and tenants, on the other, were taken as absolute differences in features of the tenures. Some social policy research has sacrificed understanding in the quest for extensive 'data', but generally, research studies have taken a very pragmatic approach to research methods with, often, a mix of qualitative and quantitative approaches. For example, a common model adopted by government in the research that it commissions is the use of focus groups at the beginning of a research study to clarify research aims and hypotheses and at the end to confirm findings. The concept of triangulation between different methods is often used. Triangulation of a mix of research methods aids the interpretation of research findings, but rarely moves beyond the confines of the positivist search for scientifically based 'truth'. The social constructionist search for different meanings held by different groups is usually ignored in favour of positivist generalisation and universal understandings uncovered by neutral researchers.

The same problems occur in the nature of the findings of social policy research. Positivism sees findings as laws that can be considered to lead to predictions of future behaviour. Can findings in one place about the nature of homelessness be considered to relate to different places at different times? Clearly, there are problems with this assumption. The meaning of homelessness has varied between different countries and times, because it is inextricably linked to a particular social setting, which frames the understanding and behaviour of actors. So positivism as an approach to the study of housing problems has flaws. But can social policy research exist without positivism? This is a crucial question we will return to later.

Research and the policy process

It was argued earlier that a major aim of the social policy tradition of research in housing has been to influence policy. Much research has been directly sponsored by government or by pressure groups aiming to influence some aspect of housing policy. Therefore, it is likely that the research will be shaped by the policy process it is attempting to influence. There are different approaches to understanding the policy process, which may be categorised as the cybernetic and the democratic (for a review of the policy process, see Chapter 12).

The cybernetic approach has been dominant since the 1960s and involves the application of a 'rational decision-making' approach to policymaking (for a review, see Hogwood and Gunn, 1984). The essence of rational planning is a policymaking process that follows a number of defined steps. The first step is an analysis of the environment of the decision-making organisation in order to identify and quantify problems and needs. The second step is the identification of goals or objectives in order to meet these needs. Different ways of meeting these objectives are then devised and the most cost-effective ones chosen with the use of techniques such as cost–benefit analysis. The policies are implemented and, finally, the impact of the policy is assessed with the use of cost-effectiveness techniques such as performance indicators. The process is said to be circular and continuous, with the results of impact analysis feeding back into the assessment of need.

This model has dominated policy planning in Britain since the 1960s in such guises as 'Best Value' and evidence-based policy. One important element of the model is that it shares the positivist assumption of the need for the objective assessment of social facts.

Research can be seen to play crucial roles in many stages of the process: for example, the analysis of problems and needs in the environment usually would require research. Much social policy research has been of this type: examples would be the analysis of the housing needs and conditions of certain groups such as (so-called) ethnic minorities or older people, or explorations of the extent and nature of homelessness. Cost-effectiveness analysis has also been a major element of social policy research: examples are studies designed to find the most appropriate intervention tools in dealing with and preventing rough sleeping. Analysis of the impact of policies is also well developed: an example would be the impact of the government's Rough Sleepers Initiative on the numbers of people sleeping on the streets.

Much of the research is commissioned by government and so the definition of the problem to be researched and the objectives of policy are usually set out in the research brief and have to be followed by the researchers. However, one role of research commissioned by pressure groups has been to question these and to suggest alternative objectives and values. The value-laden tradition in social policy research fits well with this role: an example would be research to challenge the policy emphasis on rough sleeping and to draw attention to other forms of homelessness.

Therefore, the cybernetic view of policymaking fits well with the social policy approach to research and, of course, this is no coincidence. Its claim to objectivity fits well with a government ideology of neutral administration through a professional civil service. Its rationality and focus on empirical data fits well with a policymaking process in which 'evidence' and testable findings are valued. It can be argued that the tradition has developed in a way that maximises its impact on policy, as this is one of its major goals. However, this does not imply that it has been very successful in making an impact on policy and this will be discussed later.

There are other ways of describing the policymaking process and some would argue that the rational approach is merely an aspiration that is rarely met. Alternative approaches to policymaking are usually based on a democratic or political model. The traditional example of this is Lindblom's account of 'muddling through' (Lindblom, 1959), which sees policymaking as a process of negotiation between competing interest groups. A good policy is one that stakeholders can agree on rather than one which is considered to be 'rationally' cost-effective. He sees this negotiation and bargaining as being allied to an administrative process that values incrementalism and avoids radical change and makes choices based on successive limited comparisons: essentially, try a little and see what happens.

Other political processes of decision making stress the deliberative aspects. For example, a number of authors associated with ideas of collaborative planning have stressed the importance of discussion in turning different perceptions and attitudes of social groups into a consensus (Fischer and Forrester, 1993; Healey, 1997). The role of research in such a policymaking process would be very different from the rational model. Rather than searching for an objective 'solution', research would be aimed at exploring different perceptions and attitudes. It would be imbued with the values and meanings of the stakeholders rather than seeking objectivity. Some pressure group research may fall under this heading.

The major strength of the social policy approach is its link to the policymaking process. There are a number of advantages here. The first is the focus on policy issues in the research aims. In other fields it is usual for the research question to be derived from theory, but in the social policy tradition it is usually derived from a policy problem. Secondly, the positivist nature of the research fits well with the rational or evidence-based approach to the policy process. One element of this is the provision of findings that are generalised into 'laws' that can form the basis for policy decisions. In contrast, the moralistic tradition of social policy research links in more closely to the political decision-making process.

Given its emphasis on policy impact, it is valid to ask how successful social policy-oriented research has been in influencing housing policy. There has been no systematic study that would answer this question in a rigorous way. My own personal experience has included examples of research challenging government policy that has been completely ignored, such as the evaluation of the GEAR urban renewal project (see Donnison and Middleton, 1987) or the evaluation of housing cooperatives (see Clapham and Kintrea, 1992, which was based on government-sponsored research). Where research has been more successful is in fine tuning areas where there is political commitment. A personal example was research into housing for older people in Scotland that resulted in a change of funding away from sheltered housing and towards alternative forms of provision (Clapham and Munro, 1988).

An interesting recent example of the relationship between research and policy is the Housing Market Renewal Programme in the UK (for a critical review, see Allen, 2009). Government was committed to spending large sums of money on new build housing in the economically growing areas of the South of England. Politicians from the North of England picked up on research pointing to the abandonment of some areas in the North and used this to argue for investment there. This campaign was supported by some committed academics and was successful in seeing the implementation of a market renewal programme. Success seems to be possible where research fits with political priorities.

Other traditions of research have had a more difficult task in influencing policy. One of the criticisms of social constructionist research is that it has been seen as unhelpful to policymakers because of its critical nature (see Chapter 15). Critical realism has concentrated on macro analysis in the housing field and has contributed little to policy debates. Therefore, the social policy tradition has an important niche in a field which is defined by its orientation to a specific area of life that is the subject of extensive policy intervention.

The moral dimension

Some social policy research has taken an explicitly moral stance on social problems. Concepts such as 'citizenship' (Marshall, 1950) have been used to emphasise the rights (and obligations) that people are deemed to have. For example, the right for public sector tenants to be consulted on housing management issues that affect them (Cairncross et al., 1997) or the rights of homeless people to be provided with accommodation. The moral dimension has entered debates about poverty and poor housing conditions. The description of conditions on certain estates or of homelessness has been used to shock or to encourage politicians to take a problem seriously. The power of 'scandal' in creating pressure for political action to deal with problems is well known in analyses of policymaking. Although not a research study, an example in housing would be the television programme *Cathy Come Home* that led to the formation of the charity Shelter and publicisation of homelessness. Some research has taken a similar line in bringing to light conditions deemed to be unacceptable or government action held to be unfavourable to low-income groups. Examples would be studies of slum clearance activity in the 1960s and 1970s (Dennis, 1970; Davies, 1972). This approach can be seen as an alternative way of influencing policy by attempting to influence political decision makers, either directly, or through the force of public opinion.

It was argued above that an important element of the social policy approach to housing research has been its moral dimension. It was shown earlier that the earliest research was driven by a concern for the conditions of the poorest sections of the population and employed religious or other moral values to judge these. Later research has used the formulations of Rawls (1971) and others to provide an explicit moral framework by which to evaluate policy. An important feature of the research in housing has been the challenge of commonly accepted beliefs. A good example is the review of the cycle of deprivation in the 1970s that challenged the politically dominant view that disadvantage was culturally transmitted (Rutter and Madge, 1976). The social policy tradition has been at the forefront in challenging gender and ethnic prejudice by researching the behaviour and attitudes of disadvantaged people. This is a unique contribution in comparison with other major frameworks. But this element of the tradition has not been as well developed recently, probably because of its contrast with the rational policy process.

CONCLUSION: THE FUTURE OF THE SOCIAL POLICY APPROACH IN HOUSING STUDIES

The social policy tradition has evident strengths in its policy focus and pragmatic research design. However, it has been challenged by trends in social science research. In particular there has been a move away from positivism, with sociological research generally dividing into social constructionist or critical realist traditions. What place does social policy research have in this new climate? (For a detailed discussion, see Chapter 10.)

It was argued earlier that the strengths of the social policy approach are its focus on policy and its moral dimension. Both of those elements are clearly worth keeping. But the key question is whether the social policy approach can overcome the criticisms of the positivist orientation? But first, the question is whether the approach has itself changed. Following the criticisms of the approach by Kemeny and others in the 1990s there is no doubt that housing research has been more theoretically aware (see Chapters 15 and 16 for a review of some of this research). However, the social policy tradition lives on in the form of policy-oriented, empirical research, often funded by government or by pressure groups such as the Rowntree Foundation.

There is clearly a real value in research which takes its starting point as a particular social or policy problem and produces evidence that is of use to the policy process. If the drawbacks of positivism are to be overcome there needs to be an awareness of the limitations of a reliance on 'facts'. This would involve both taking into account the meaning dimension of human action, but also being aware of the social situational aspects of the social problem. The former is easily incorporated through the use of qualitative research techniques, and most studies are now designed in this way. But there needs to be a realisation that qualitative data is not just a way of 'triangulating' with other data to establish the 'facts': rather, it is a way of entering the assumptive worlds of individuals in order to establish how they see the world and what influences their behaviour. Without this knowledge it is difficult to design effective policy mechanisms. The outcome of policies is the result of interaction between individual households and the policy agents within the 'action space' delimited by the policy mechanism. For example, the result of the 'Right to Buy' mechanism is dependent on the propensity for tenants to buy their rented house on particular terms. Also, the outcome of housing allocation policies is determined by the interaction between households and the housing managers implementing the devised policy. Therefore, successful policy design is dependent on an understanding of the motivations and behaviour of individuals. But this behaviour may be dependent on social meanings that may change. Therefore, research needs to be aware of the limitations on the generalisability of its findings. The social laws expected from the positivist approach need to be carefully limited in their applicability and extent. The understanding of meaning and behaviour needs to be situated in the particular, relevant social setting which influences it. Therefore, social policy research needs to be wide in its scope and cannot be too tightly focused around the details of policy interventions without taking into account the wider setting.

The second major strength of the social policy tradition is its engagement with political and moral philosophy through concepts such as citizenship, inequality and poverty. The application of these concepts to the field of housing has drawn attention to the conditions faced by the poorest in society and to their rights over their housing situation such as in terms of their relationship to their landlord or their status and treatment as homeless people. Clearly, this is a very valuable approach to the field of housing studies which is complementary to other approaches discussed in this volume. It can speak in the same language as political discourse and therefore can be accessible to politicians, although many may not share the moral stance taken in particular studies.

Therefore, the tradition shows the value of research that starts from social issues and problems, and adopts a rigorous method and a clear moral position to engage with the policy process. However, this research needs to be situated within the context of the wider society and to be aware of the meaning dimensions of human action.

REFERENCES

Allen, C. (2009) 'The Fallacy of housing studies', *Housing, Theory and Society 26*.1 pp. 53–79.

Bryman, A. (2004) *Social Research Methods*, 2nd edn. Oxford: Oxford University Press.

Burrows, R. and Rhodes, D. (1998) *Unpopular Places? Area Disadvantage and the Geography of Misery*. Bristol: The Policy Press.

Cairncross, L., Clapham, D. and Goodlad, G. (1997) *Housing Management, Consumers and Citizens*. London and New York: Routledge pp. 212.

Clapham, D., Kemp, P. and Smith, S. J. (1990) *Housing and Social Policy*. Basingstoke: Macmillan

Clapham, D. and Kintrea, K. (1992) *Housing Co-operatives in Britain: Achievements and Prospects*. Harlow: Longman.

Clapham, D, and Munro, M. (1988) *A Comparison of Sheltered and Amenity Housing for Older People*. Edinburgh: Scottish Office.

Clapham, D. (2003) 'A Pathways Approach to Homelessness Research' *Journal of Community and Applied Social Psychology* vol 13 pp. 1–9.

Davies, J. G. (1972) *The Evangelistic Bureaucrat*. London: Tavistock.

Dennis, N. (1970) *People and Planning*. London: Faber and Faber.

Donnison, D. and Middleton, A, (eds) (1987) *Regenerating the Inner City*. London: Routledge.

Fischer, F. and Forrester, J. (eds) (1993) *The Argumentative Turn in Policy Analysis and Planning*. London: UCL press.

Fitzpatrick, S. (2005) 'Explaining homelessness: a critical realist approach' *Housing, Theory and Society*, 22.1 pp. 1–17.

Gauldie, E. (1974) *Cruel Habitations: A History of Working Class Housing 1780–1918*. London: George, Allen and Unwin.

Healey P. (1997) *Collaborative Planning: Shaping Places in Fragmented Societies*. London: Macmillan.

Hogwood, B. and Gunn, L. (1984) *Policy Analysis for the Real World*. Oxford: Blackwell.

Kemeny, J. (1992) *Housing and Social Theory*. London: Routledge.

Le Grand, J. (1982) *The Strategy of Equality: Redistribution and the Social Services*. London: Allen and Unwin.

Lindblom, C. (1959) 'The science of muddling through' *Public Administration Review* 19 pp. 79–88.

Marshall. T. H. (1950) *Citizenship and Social Class*. Cambridge: Cambridge University Press.

Mishra, R. (1977) *Society and Social Policy*. London: Macmillan.

Murie, A. (1983) *Housing Inequality and Deprivation* London: Heinemann.

Rawls, J. (1971) *A Theory of Justice*. Oxford: Blackwell

Rowntree B. Seebohm. (1902) *Poverty: A Study of Town Life*. London: Macmillan.

Rutter, M. and Madge, N. (1976) *Cycles of Disadvantage*. London: Heinemann.

Saunders, P. (1990) *A Nation of Home Owners*. London: Unwin Hyman.

Smith, S. J., McGuckin, A. and Knill-Jones, R. (eds) (1991) *Housing For Health Harlow*. Longman.

Torgersen, U. (1987) *Housing: The Wobbly Pillar of the Welfare State*, in Turner, B., Kemeny, J. & Lundqvist, L. J., (eds), *Between State and Market: Housing in the Post-Industrial Era*. Scandinavian Housing and Planning Research, Supplement 1.

Wohl, A. (1977) *The Eternal Slum: Housing and Social Policy in Victorian London*. London: Edward Arnold.

10

Social Constructionism and Beyond in Housing Research

David Clapham

INTRODUCTION

Since Jim Kemeny's call in 1992 for a more theoretically informed housing research (Kemeny, 1992), there has been a substantial body of work claiming social constructionism as its theoretical foundation. Indeed, Kemeny himself used social constructionism in his research on comparative national housing policy (see, for example, Kemeny and Lowe, 1998). The aim of this chapter is to review the social constructionist approach in housing research and to assess its strengths and weaknesses. Despite its generally worthwhile contribution to research on housing, the weaknesses of the approach have become increasingly apparent. These range from an abstract difficulty of dealing with a 'material world' to the divorce that has been created with policymakers. Therefore, the chapter examines the attempts to build on or to move beyond the tradition of social constructionism. In particular, the possibility of using it as a base for interdisciplinary research will be explored. The chapter is written from the standpoint of someone who is an exponent of the social constructionist approach and some of the work being examined is my own. However, I argue that social constructionism by itself is a limited paradigm within which to work but one that lends itself to adaptation and extension.

The chapter begins with a brief description of the origins and central tenets of social constructionism. It is argued that it is not just one approach but has different referents and emphases from symbolic interactionism to discourse analysis. The way that social constructionism has been used in housing research is then examined. Most research has fallen into four categories, which will be described: the social problems tradition; interactionism; comparative national housing policy; and holistic analyses of housing. The conclusion to this section will focus on research outside these categories that has used social constructionism as a building block and tried to develop from it. This leads in the next section to a focus on the strengths and weaknesses of the social constructionist approach. Four areas are examined here. The first area is the embodied nature of humans and the impact this has on meaning, which is important in understanding the relationship between people and their home. The second related issue is the 'problem' of dealing with a 'material world', which impacts on social constructionist housing research in understanding the relationship between people and the material fabric of a house. A third problem is the relativism of social constructionism, which has been the focus of many critics of the overall paradigm. In the wider literature this has led to divisions into *strong* and *weak* constructionism. In housing research the relativism has led in a practical sense to a perception that social constructionists are always critical of policy but have little to help in a policy-making process wedded to the concept of 'objective knowledge'. Relativism is one of the factors that make it difficult to incorporate social constructionism into interdisciplinary research. Most research on housing is based on a positivist approach, either because of its roots in policy-sponsored work or in economic or psychological analysis. A fourth problem comprises the perceived lack of a structural element to constructionism and its neglect of concepts such as power. Constructionist housing research has been useful in identifying and interpreting policy discourses, but has added little to the understanding of why one discourse has dominated others.

The chapter then examines the potential for amending or adding to constructionism in illuminating housing questions. The section examines social constructionist research that has strained at (or breached) perceived conceptual or disciplinary boundaries and also research from other traditions that seems to offer a way forward for social constructionism. In particular, the focus is on research in psychology and economics that offers potential for useful incorporation and collaboration.

In conclusion, the chapter offers an assessment of the contribution to housing research made by the social constructionist paradigm and offers thoughts on how it can be fruitfully developed and applied in the future.

SOCIAL CONSTRUCTIONISM

Most sociological paradigms are an amalgamation of different strands of work that have different emphases, although they may share the same fundamental assumptions. Social constructionism is perhaps an extreme example of this. Much housing research has uncritically accepted an approach that has many roots and different traditions without making clear on which branch it is based. The *Handbook of Social Theory*, a comprehensive overview of social theory edited by Ritzer and Smart (2000), does not allocate one of its 39 chapters to social constructionism. However, there are chapters on symbolic interactionism, phenomenology, ethnomethodology and post-modernism that cover authors that are regularly quoted by social constructionist housing researchers. Most housing research has started from the work of Berger and Luckmann (1967), who, in the handbook are discussed under phenomenology, despite themselves acknowledging their debt to George Mead (1934), who is discussed in the handbook under symbolic interactionism. Of course this is only one way of arranging a wide dispersion of conceptual approaches, and other editors may have chosen another way. Nevertheless, the main point here is that some housing researchers have tended to accept and adopt uncritically a dispersed body of work that they have misleadingly expressed and used as a coherent and unified whole.

However, there is considerable agreement on the basic tenets of the approach adopted by most housing researchers, which accords with the three premises identified by Blumer for symbolic interactionism:

> The first premise is that human beings act toward things on the basis of the meanings those things have for them. ...The second premise is that the

meaning of such things is derived from, or arises out of, the social interaction that one has with one's fellows. The third premise is that these meanings are handled in, and modified through, an interpretive process used by the person in dealing with the things he (or she) encounters (Blumer, 1969, p. 2, quoted in Sandstrom, Martin and Fine, 2000, p. 218).

Sandstrom, Martin and Fine (2000) identify six implicit assumptions of the approach which expand on Blumer's premises. These are that, first, people are unique in their use of symbols to generate meaning. The major system of symbols is language, which enables the generation and communication of meaning to occur through social interaction. Therefore, much research in this tradition focuses on the use and meanings of language as it mediates in the social construction of the 'reality' of the way that people see the world. Secondly, there is the belief that, although people are born with a biological make-up, they become human and develop a sense of self through social interaction. These socialisation processes are a major focus of research. Thirdly, people are self-reflexive beings that shape their own behaviour despite the influence of a variety of social factors that may constrain them. Therefore, people are neither viewed as dupes of structural forces beyond their control nor as completely free agents. Fourthly, people are purposive in their behaviour and determine what meaning to give to a situation and how to act through taking into account the unfolding intentions, actions and expressions of others. Therefore, processes of negotiation and interaction are crucial in understanding behaviour. Fifthly, human society consists of people engaging in symbolic interaction. The emphasis on interaction means that the approach is different from the psychological belief that society exists primarily in people's heads or some sociologists' view that society exists independently of individuals and has its own dynamic. Finally, the major aim of social research is to understand the worlds of meaning that people generate through interaction in order to understand how social actors define, construct and act towards the 'realities' that constitute their everyday worlds.

Berger and Luckmann (1967) offer a similar view of the basis of social constructionism. In their view the fundamental tenet is that social life is constructed by people through interaction. It is through interaction that individuals define themselves and the world they inhabit and so it is through interaction that the nature of individuals becomes apparent to themselves and to others. Much emphasis in social constructionism is on face-to-face interactions where an individual's subjectivity becomes available to themselves and to others through what they say and their body language. A key element in this interaction is the use of language, which is defined as a system of vocal signs. Berger and Luckmann argue that language is important because it enables interaction to be detached from the subjective 'here and now' of face-to-face interaction to become objectively available. Language allows interaction about individuals or objects that are not present and enables a vast accumulation of experiences and meanings to be available in the here and now:

> Language is capable not only of constructing symbols that are highly abstracted from everyday experience, but also of bringing back these symbols and presenting them as objectively real elements in everyday life. In this manner, symbolism and symbolic language become essential constituents of the reality of everyday life and the commonsense apprehension of this reality. I live in a world of signs and symbols every day (Berger and Luckmann, 1967, pp. 40–41).

Language is capable of building up zones of meaning that serve as a stock of knowledge that individuals use in everyday life and which can be transmitted from generation to generation. These systems of meaning or discourse represent or describe the nature of the world or reality and become taken for granted. They tend to be seen as having an independent, objective reality which is above the subjectivity of individuals. This is partly because they are transmitted from generation to generation through socialisation and so people perceive that they are the reality of the world into which they are born. They become reified – that is seen as being other than human products – although social constructionists argue that they are merely the product of and are only sustained by human interaction. These discourses play an active part in people's construction of their worlds. Meaning is produced, reproduced, altered and transformed through language and discourse. Social objects are constantly constructed, negotiated and altered by individuals in their attempts to make sense of happenings in the world. In this way language and knowledge are not copies of reality, but constitute reality, each language constructing specific aspects of reality in its own way. The focus is on the linguistic and social construction of reality, on interpretation and negotiation of the meaning of the lived world.

Discourses are built up into 'sub-universes of meaning' that define the taken-for-granted reality and include institutionalised codes of conduct which define and construct appropriate behaviour. With the establishment of sub-universes of meaning, a variety of perspectives on the total society emerges, each viewing the latter from the angle of one sub-universe. Each perspective will be related to the concrete social interests of the group that holds it, although it will not necessarily be a mechanical reflection of those interests, as it is possible for knowledge to attain a great deal of detachment from the biographical and social interests of the knower. The nature of social order in the society will depend on the ability of people to be able to sustain a particular version of reality as being the objective truth. This depends on the sub-universe of meaning being legitimated through being available to people and being plausible. Therefore, it will not merely contain a description of the world, but also explanations and justifications of why things are as they are and why people should act in a certain way.

Social constructionist researchers in housing have also drawn on strands of other traditions: for example, in phenomenology, the work of Schutz (1967) in championing a 'subjective sociology' where there are no objective facts and the world consists exclusively of interpreted behaviour in which the task of the sociologist is to investigate the 'lifeworld' of our ordinary, everyday understandings; in ethnomethodology, the work of Garfinkel (1967) in illuminating the way that people manage their everyday lives in settings such as the home; and also the work of Strauss (1978), who used the term 'negotiated order' to describe and explain the power relations between professionals and patients in hospital settings.

As well as these subjectivist traditions, social constructionism has been influenced by the work of Foucault (1972) with his focus on the construction of knowledge and the role it plays in the regulation of humans and populations and the assignment of normalised identities and subjectivities. He was centrally concerned with the exercise of power, which he viewed as multiple and relational. In his work there is no single source of power, but it is pervasive, present in all forms of social interaction, and is exercised in a multiplicity of forms. This formulation of power adds a crucial and missing dimension to social constructionist work in which the concept is rarely discussed. Also, it has reinforced the focus on discourse and language in the construction of knowledge and the enforcement of power.

More recent influences have been of 'postmodern' writers such as Bauman with his argument for the dissipation of objectivity. 'The post-modern perspective reveals the world as composed of an infinite number of meaning generating agencies, all relatively self-sustained and autonomous, all subject to their own respective logics and armed with their own facilities of truth validation' (Bauman, 1992, p. 35). The compatibility of social constructionism with some postmodern theorists has increased its popularity over recent years and has allowed the incorporation of some concepts and ideas, most notably those of Giddens (1984).

The main point here is that social constructionism is not a clear unified tradition of thought with an agreed research modus operandi: by contrast, it is a dispersed field that draws on different traditions and in which there are many differences of approach. What is generally shared can be summarised as: a disagreement with approaches that assume the objective status of knowledge; a focus on the construction of meaning through social interaction; and the importance of language and discourse in the carrying of meaning. Housing research has tended not to engage with the theoretical debates about method and focus. Rather, research has either been based on the general shared assumptions, or the analysis has been based on one particular author or approach. This will be discussed further in a later section.

SOCIAL CONSTRUCTIONIST HOUSING RESEARCH

Although there are many strands in social constructionism, housing research has largely been confined to four areas. The most popular has been what has been termed the 'social construction of social problems'. This follows a long tradition of social constructionist research that derived from labelling theory and was given an impetus by Spector and Kitsuse (1977). (For a review, see Kemeny, 2004.) The emphasis has been on trying to understand different definitions of social problems, such as homelessness, by examining policy narratives. These problems are perceived not to have 'objective' foundations, but are 'constructed on shifting sands of public rhetoric, coalition building, interest group lobbying and political expediency' (Jacobs, Kemeny and Manzi, 2004, p. 5). An example of the approach is Jacobs, Kemeny and Manzi's (1999) description of the minimalist and maximalist discourses of homelessness policy in the UK. However, the quotation could describe a 'political science approach' to policymaking, but most social constructionist research in housing has not examined in detail the actions of individuals and agencies in the policymaking process: rather, it has focused on the content of policy discourses through an examination of policy documents. Therefore, social problems research has often consisted largely of discourse analysis. (For a review of discourse analysis in housing, see Hastings, 2000.) This form of analysis has been applied in a number of fields such as urban renewal, housing management and tenure. The strength of the approach is in its questioning of existing ways of thinking in policy. One can think of this as opening the eyes of policymakers to question existing assumptions of policy. In social constructionist terminology it is making explicit the reification of certain ways of seeing the world, the viewing of these ways as objective facts. The popularity of this type of research is one of the reasons why social constructionism has often been perceived as being unhelpful to policymakers. Who takes kindly to their assumptions being questioned and criticised, without often any constructive thoughts about how to do things differently?

The focus on discourse is one that is shared with other perspectives. For example, critical realists would accept the importance of discourse in framing policy and discourse analysis can be undertaken with many different theoretical approaches. So an important question is what is different about social constructionist discourse analysis? This is a question to which we will return, as it is difficult to discern any difference in much housing research, and social constructionist researchers have 'incorporated' critical discourse analysis (Fairclough, 1995) and the approach of Foucault (1972) with his emphasis on the mechanisms of governmentality through discourse.

Kemeny (2004) criticises much housing research in the social problems tradition as being too focused on discourse and not enough on the power relations that underpin its creation. Following Spector and Kitsuse (1977), Kemeny argues that social problems are better understood in terms of process rather than as static conditions. This formulation places emphasis on the claims-making process: that is, the different definitions (or claims) made by different groups and the process by which pressure groups seek to impose their definition on public discourse and ultimately the policy-making process above those of others. This formulation harks back to the interactionist tradition of social constructionism. Kemeny calls for more housing research that examines the way that housing policies are constructed in terms of the institutional arrangements that are put in place to deal with particular definitions of housing problems and the practices through which they are implemented. He looks for more studies of 'doing' housing policymaking, and understanding these as processes and achievements of interaction. The possible links with political science approaches to policymaking and governance are easy to see, but have seldom been grasped. Social constructionism can bring to the table the focus on subjectivity and the importance of discourse. Traditional political science approaches can bring ways of conceiving of the networks or patterns of interaction around policymaking and governance.

The second tradition of social constructionist housing research has focused on interaction, but is much less developed than the social problems tradition. For example, the work on the social construction of housing management (Clapham, Franklin and Saugeres, 2000; Darcy and Manzi, 2004) has taken an explicitly interactionist stance. This field of research is highlighted because of its difference from any other form of social constructionist housing research. The research studies in this field have shared the usual focus on discourse as expressed in policy documents and written procedures. However, they have moved further and examined the social interaction between housing officers and tenants. Of course this type of research has a long pedigree in other fields, such as the doctor–patient relationship, but is unique in housing terms. What are being socially constructed in the housing management research are a relationship and an occupational role. This is different from the social problems tradition as it is not a social problem that is being constructed but a small part of social reality as constructed through interaction between individuals in different positions in social space. In this way the analysis is uniquely social constructionist in a way that other research, as epitomized in discourse analysis, may not be.

A third area of social constructionist housing research is in international comparative research. This can be seen as a variation on the social problems tradition outlined earlier. The emphasis is on how and why social problems are defined differently in different countries. Kemeny has examined the social construction of tenures and their relationship to general political cultures. This approach has led to a questioning of theories of national housing policy that have emphasised the convergence of policy and instead posited a thesis of continuing divergence (Kemeny and Lowe, 1998). Kemeny has used the concept of culture to argue that countries retain an individual housing structure that accords with political structure and, in particular, the form of welfare policy pursued. This approach builds on the ideas of Esping-Andersen (1990) who identified what he saw as the three worlds of welfare. Much research has sought to place housing within this framework and to map the relationship between housing and other elements of the Welfare State (see chapter 15 for a fuller discussion). There has also been a discussion of the factors contributing to the dominance of owner-occupation in some countries.

Haworth, Manzi and Kemeny (2004) claim that a social constructionist approach to international comparative housing research can combat the ethnocentrism inherent in much research of this kind. The strength of the social constructionist approach has been the questioning of taken-for-granted assumptions about housing institutions and problem definitions. For example, research has shown the different meanings attached to owner-occupation in different countries (Mandic and Clapham, 1996). Social constructionism has also led to the questioning of structuralist conceptions of change in housing systems, and to the emphasis on political choice and cultural norms in creating and sustaining housing institutions. However, there has not been a reconciliation between the social constructionist approach emphasising agency and the structuralist emphasis. Therefore, there has not been any integrationist model (although, see Clapham, 2006 for a discussion of the discourse of globalisation).

Also, the symbolic interactionist strand of social constructionism places emphasis on uncovering the lifeworlds of individuals and groups and describing the world as they see and experience it. When applied to international comparative research, the emphasis would be on uncovering the way that housing experiences were perceived by those experiencing them in the countries concerned in the tradition of ethnographic studies of different societies. Comparative housing research has not been developed in this direction, with most social constructionist analyses focusing on the national level of social problem construction.

The fourth category of social constructionist research has been in developing a holistic view of the housing field. Most social constructionist housing research has been directed at particular research topics rather than attempting to describe a social constructionist view of the housing field and its relationship to other fields. The only attempt here has been by the present author in the pathways approach (Clapham, 2005). However, although this approach was based on social constructionism, it did draw on concepts from outside, such as the Giddens' concept of structuration. This raises the question of whether social constructionism has been developed enough to provide a way forward in housing analysis or whether further work is needed if the approach can be used to give a coherent and comprehensive view of the housing field.

SOCIAL CONSTRUCTIONISM – SOME PROBLEMS

There are many general criticisms of social constructionism, reflecting the many other sociological approaches. Four important issues will be mentioned briefly here because they help to define and understand the approach. However, all will be considered in more detail later as they impact on the actuality and potential of housing research.

The first general criticism of social constructionism is its relativism. King (2004) repeats the common criticism of authors such as Nozick (2001) that there is a fundamental contradiction at the heart of the approach. If all discourse is socially constructed and there is no such thing as objective truth, then social constructionism itself is only one discourse among many and cannot claim superiority over any other approach. It is difficult to disagree with the criticism, but most social constructionists would not make claims of superiority, but would accept that theirs was just one way of looking at the world that had no special claims above any other. Much social constructionist research is concerned with describing peoples' lifeworlds and contrasting them with other peoples' realities. It is concerned with why certain discourses or versions of reality become accepted and others not, without imposing its own reality. However, if social constructionism was to stop at this point, its value would be limited. Is it possible to generalise from findings in any way or to provide clues to future actions and events? The problem of relativity is at the heart of the perceived inadequacy of social constructionism in offering anything for the policymaking process.

A second general criticism is the assumption described in the discussion of symbolic interactionism that humans only achieve their humanity through social interaction. King (2004) argues that social constructionism sees individual subjects as 'empty vessels filled up through discourse' (p. 43). However, recent literature has stressed the embodied nature of human action (see, for example, Shilling, 2003) and there has emerged a social constructionist sociology of the body. In research on the meaning of home there has been an understanding of the importance of emotions in influencing the relationship between people and their physical environment. However, there has not emerged a persuasive synthesis of the different factors of body, mind and discourse. How do our physical bodies and minds influence our subjective meanings? Within some topics in the housing field this lack could be very important. For example, people may have a strong emotional relationship with home. People's relationship to the physical fabric of the house is mediated through their physical characteristics – it is embodied. The obvious issue is the meaning and use of housing by older or physically disabled people, but the general point is valid for all. Without an understanding of the influence of embodiment on meaning, social constructionism can offer only partial explanations.

The criticism of social constructionism can be widened out to make a third general point that the 'material world' is viewed only as a passive conductor of meaning. Social constructionism does not deny the existence of a material world, but argues that our access to it is mediated through language and discourse. Jacobs, Kemeny and Manzi (2004) quote Collin (1997, pp. 2–3) 'our perception of the material world is affected by the way we *think* or *talk* about it, by our *consensus* about its nature, by the way we *explain* it to each other, and by the *concepts* we use to grasp it'. This is in contrast to some versions of actor–network theory that imbue material objects with agency conceptually on a par with human action. (For a review in housing, see Gabriel and Jacobs, 2007). This debate is a crucial one for housing studies because of its impact on the theorisation of the relationship between an individual and his house. Much of the literature on the meaning of home has treated the built structure as an empty vessel into which meaning is poured. Does the built form influence the meaning? And, if so, how and to what extent?

Advocates of social constructionism in housing research have responded to the above criticisms by arguing that they do not adhere to the positions ascribed to the approach. They follow Sayer (2000) in drawing a distinction between *strong* and *weak* constructionism and argue that the criticisms only apply to the strong version whereas most researchers ascribe to the weak version (see, for example, Fopp, 2008 for a discussion). However, there is no clarity about what a weak variety of social constructionism consists of. Sommerville and Bengtsson (2002) report Sayer as arguing that strong social constructionism views objects or referents of knowledge as nothing more than social constructions. In contrast, weak social constructionism merely emphasises the socially constructed nature of knowledge and institutions and is primarily a reaction to and an antipathy to positivism. Fopp (2008) argues that the anti-positivism has been the primary impetus in social constructionist housing research.

There seem to be two different aspects to the weak version of social constructionism. The first is to emphasise that there is a material world of objects that have an existence beyond the socially constructed meanings ascribed to them by people. In other words, a house can fall down as a consequence of natural laws of physics and chemistry. However, social constructionists argue that our understanding of the phenomenon of the house falling down is socially constructed through the language and concepts we use to understand it. This version would seem to be eminently sensible and defensible. However, as we shall argue later, in a field such as housing research, the relationship between a person and the material world of the body and the house are very important topics. Therefore, although this version of weak social constructionism does overcome some of the criticisms of the strong version, it places an obligation on its adherents to theorise the relationship between the world of meaning and the material world. We shall return to this point later.

The second version of weak social constructionism put forward by Jacobs and

Manzi (2000) is more difficult to sustain. They argue that the weak position 'maintains that reality is socially constructed, but does not entirely reject the notion of an objective understanding of "truth"' (p. 38). They continue by making a distinction 'between ideas and concepts that are socially constructed and the social and spatial processes which have a material existence' (p. 38). As King (2004) observes: Why are some things socially constructed and others not? How does one make a distinction between the two elements of reality? What exactly is socially constructed and what is not and how are the two elements related? This version of weak social constructionism is logically flawed and demands much further theorising if it is to be acceptable.

The fourth general criticism of social constructionism concerns the relationship between the individual and society. Social constructionist writers have differed in their emphasis on individual agency and societal structures. Travers (2004) emphasises the difference between Schutz and Berger and Luckmann. Schutz (1967) places stress on the pre-existence of a social world that we are born into and which will survive us. He is interested in how we make sense of this world and view it is an objective reality. By contrast, Travers argues that Berger and Luckmann (1967) suggest that society can be changed without too much difficulty. It is perhaps indicative that Berger and Luckmann do not discuss the nature of power. Later influential writers such as Foucault (1972) emphasise the way that discourses are framed within power relations and are integral to them. The agency/structure debate has been one of the key ones in recent sociology. However, it is unclear how social constructionism relates to this debate. (For a review of structuralist approaches, see Chapter 11.)

BEYOND SOCIAL CONSTRUCTIONISM

It may be argued that social constructionism is a useful paradigm that helps us to question the dominant definitions of social problems and this is the extent of its value. However, I would argue that social constructionism has a much wider value as a paradigm to guide all aspects of housing research. However, the criticisms of social constructionism are important to ensure its future as an acceptable framework for the analysis of housing issues. As we have argued earlier, most social constructionist research in housing has been either partial, in the sense that it has just focused on particular issues (such as the social problems strand), or has sought to incorporate other theories and concepts (such as some discourse analysis and the pathways framework). As a result, social constructionism has not been incorporated into the mainstream of housing research.

Before proceeding, it is worthwhile taking a slight digression into another debate. In his appeal to housing researchers to move beyond the empirical and positivist approach of much work, Kemeny argued for the application of social theory to housing. His view was that there should not be housing theory because housing was not a field that should be separated from a wider analysis of the social world. The assumption here was that housing could be adequately analysed using theoretical concepts and approaches from the general social science disciplines. Social constructionism is such an approach. However, others, for example King (2009), have argued that the experience of housing was unique enough to require its own set of concepts and approaches which, he argued, should be drawn from the experience of consuming and using housing. I have argued elsewhere for a mixed approach that starts from the relationship between an individual and their house but broadens out from this base (Clapham, 2009). The basic approach should be taken from the general social sciences, but there may be a need for specific concepts to understand housing, or general concepts may need to be amended or adapted to fit this particular application. Clearly, social constructionism could be such a general approach. The questions then concern its value in furthering the understanding of housing and the value of general concepts to the specific application to housing. Also, it has been argued earlier that social constructionism has needed supplementation with concepts from other approaches when applied to housing questions. The key questions here relate to the appropriate concepts to incorporate, but also whether the incorporation is justifiable in terms of complementarity. In other words, are the additional concepts compatible with the tenets of social constructionism or built on other foundations that are opposed to them? Any amalgamation of concepts needs to be justified and not be just a mishmash of incompatible ideas.

King (2009) has suggested a theoretical approach to housing that starts from the use of a dwelling and expands from that base. Social constructionism has much value as a base for such a theoretical exercise because of its focus on subjective meaning and much valuable research has been undertaken on the meaning and use of dwellings. However, two of the major criticisms of social constructionism need to be overcome if it is to be useful as a base. The first is the embodied nature of the meaning and use of housing.

The assumption of social constructionism – that people are made through social interaction – is an easy one to question, but a difficult one to build upon. What the assumption may lack in realism, it makes up for in consistency. Any attempt to add on to this an idea of embodiment needs to confront the logical inconsistency involved and answer difficult questions about the relationship between body and meaning.

The second major problematic area is the relationship between people and material objects such as houses. It was argued earlier that social constructionism has tended to deal with material objects as existing solely in terms of the meaning that is projected onto them by people. They are signs, usually interpreted through the language, we use to describe them. Social constructionists do not deny that objects have a material existence, but argue that, to understand human action, we only need to be concerned with the meanings that the objects have, because it is this which influences people.

This justification has been increasingly seen as inadequate and it is easy to see that housing is a field where this inadequacy is important, because of the relationship that people have with the built structure of their houses as well as with the built form of the neighbourhood and material possessions within the house. There are a number of traditions of research on the relationship between people and their environment. Perhaps the most developed is what has been termed people–environment studies based around the discipline of psychology (see Chapter 13). However, this approach has shared the social constructionist focus on meaning and identity and has paid little attention to the physical attributes of a house or material possessions. One way forward is offered by the concept of 'affordances' coined by Gibson (1986). The basic concept is that the physical structure of houses does not just have symbolic meanings, but also allows or hinders different uses. The physical structure has a material existence that can facilitate or hinder particular uses. Therefore, different houses may offer different mobility possibilities for disabled people. The concept of affordances is a good starting point for a dual analysis of meaning and use, but it has not yet been developed to put some flesh on the basic idea. It is also not clear what the relationship is between the use and meaning dimensions. What is the relative impact of the two and how do they influence each other?

Another more recent approach to the people–environment interface is provided by actor–network theory (ANT; see Chapter 11). Writers in this tradition have stressed the need to decentre the human subject as the nucleus of social life and have called for greater recognition of non-human actors (such as animals, technology and material artefacts). The emphasis is on the temporary and fluid assemblage of things or networks that bring together human and non-human actors. Rather than the social constructionist focus on discourse, actor–network theorists seek to illuminate the 'socio-technical' construction work that is involved in making some truth claims more durable in particular contexts than others (Gabriel and Jacobs, 2007 p. 529).

Latour (1996; quoted in Gabriel and Jacobs, 2007, p. 530) identifies the three ways in which material objects have been considered in social science: as 'invisible and faithful tools' of human subjects; the fixed material terrain on which human activity is staged; and as projection screens for human meaning. All of these assume objects to be passive recipients of human action and meaning. ANT emphasises the agency potential of networks consisting of both objects and humans. Gabriel and Jacobs (2007) argue that ANT has been criticised for its notion of symmetry in the equal treatment of the agency of humans and objects. However, this criticism, if valid, can be easily overcome. Equality of treatment as an a priori assumption open to challenge through empirical enquiry would seem to offer a way of keeping an open mind to all possible relationships. It must also be noted that agency is vested in a network or a relationship rather than in material objects per se.

This formulation seems to capture the essence of the relationship between people and their houses. Houses are not just passive tools of use or conveyors of meaning, but in their built form influence use (through their affordances) and influence meaning through their design and appearance. Focus on the two-way relationship between people and their houses is the key to understanding the nature of the dwelling experience. Therefore, what remains for housing studies is to study the different forms that this relationship can take. This focus of research has been a very unfashionable one in the last 40 years or so. In the 1960s there was research jointly undertaken by architects and social scientists into the impact of particular design features in houses, but this seems to have ceased as architects became more interested in aesthetics as the criteria of good design and social scientists became mired in debates about environmental determinism and focused more on structural levels of analysis. The need now is for a return to the former tradition, but armed with the insights that ANT has given us.

Structure and agency

It was argued earlier that social constructionism has been criticised for a lack of connection with concepts of power. Clearly, the approach does not owe any debt to structural theories and can be argued to emphasise human agency. However, there have been attempts to engage with power using this framework. For example, the work of Strauss (1978) on negotiated order stresses the differential ability of different groups to have their definition of reality accepted. The 'social problems' approach outlined earlier focuses on the struggles around different definitions of any problem. Comparative housing research in this tradition has placed emphasis on the political factors that have shaped the definition of housing issues in different countries. Social constructionist writers have used the writings of Foucault to ground their discussions of the power around the construction and use of discourses. Others have made use of the structuration theory of Giddens (1984) and the power approach of Clegg (1989) to explain the differential ability of different people to 'set the agenda'. This work shows that the gap in the original formulation of the approach can easily be filled. Social constructionism does not fit easily with theories that stress the structural forces of change. However, it can be integrated with theories that see power invested in human agency and the differential ability of different groups to exercise it.

Positivism and relativism

It was argued earlier that social constructionism has been criticised by adherents of other approaches for its relativism. Economists and psychologists have collaborated in fields such as behavioural economics, but social constructionism has been isolated from such inclusion because of its perceived relativism, in contrast to their positivist orientations. The lack of integration has hindered housing studies and in particular hindered the application to housing policy. Therefore, the key question posed by Clapham (2009) is whether social constructionism can be adapted to share insights with positivist approaches. Social constructionism takes as its basic premise the social construction of reality through social interaction. It alerts the researcher to the different perceptions of reality that may be held by individuals or groups. However, a key element of social constructionism is that knowledge of the world often becomes reified or objectified in that people view the world as they see it as an objective 'fact'. It is only by doing this that people can manage their everyday lives by accepting its reality. In many or most situations there is general agreement over what is reality between the different actors. Of course social constructionism would have a lot to say about how the dominant conception of reality was constructed and the discourses that underpinned it. It would also be concerned with the power structures that led to one particular version of reality being accepted rather than another. However, within a particular 'reality' it may be possible to forge a common conception of how actors would behave. Of course social constructionists would stress the limited extent of the 'reality' over both time and space, which would limit the generality of the conclusions that could be drawn.

It would be interesting (and extremely challenging) to work through the conditions under which an agreed position of what may be termed 'limited positivism' or 'fixed constructionism' could be derived. Social constructionists would have to accept that social institutions could become reified in certain situations where it could be accurate to talk about social facts. The key factor would be to ascertain the boundaries in time and space of such situations.

HOUSING POLICY

One of the often-stated drawbacks of social constructionism is its perceived inability to contribute to the policymaking process. (For a detailed discussion, see Clapham, (chapter 9 in this volume). Undoubtedly, the nature of social constructionist analysis that has sought to question the accepted definitions of problems can be viewed as unhelpful by policymakers, who may see this as critical without offering an alternative. The aim of research has been to understand why things are as they are rather then to offer advice on how to change things. The relativism of social constructionism may be perceived as unhelpful as it does not deliver 'an answer' as much positivist research offers to do. It is unlikely that social constructionism can add much to a policymaking process if the people involved are wedded to a positivist orientation. In this case, social constructionism may be perceived as not delivering 'real knowledge' in the form of facts or figures or evidence. However, if a relativist paradigm was accepted in policy circles, then social constructionist knowledge could be perceived as useful. For example, much research is focused on uncovering the way that certain groups of people perceive themselves and their world. This form of research could be perceived as important in allowing politicians to judge the acceptability of policies. Many politicians employ advisors whose job is to do precisely this and there are many examples of legislation designed to change people's perceptions and meanings rather than to achieve particular actions. Social constructionism can also help to tailor policy interventions so they have the required impact on perceptions or action. Clapham (2005) has argued that policy interventions may fail if implementers do not share the aims of the policymakers, or if those receiving policy intervention do not perceive the situation as intended and do not deliver the required action: an example of the former may be homelessness officers who interpret intentionality provisions in a different way than intended by the policymakers; an example of the latter may be homeless people perceiving a particular intervention as unhelpful and refusing to be subject to it.

The argument here is that the perceived difficulties of social constructionism in contributing to policy debates is not inherent in the approach, but is related to the lack of fit between relativist researchers and positivist policymakers. There are policy approaches that would fit well with a social constructionist research framework. Examples are Lindblom's (1959) classic model of muddling through in which the policy process is one of negotiation and bargaining between concerned groups. Concepts of deliberative planning also fit here (Healey, 1997).

CONCLUSION

The chapter has sought to draw out the strengths and weaknesses of a social constructionist approach to housing studies. It has been argued that social constructionism has delivered many insights into housing phenomena, particularly in the fields of policy definitions and in international comparisons of housing policies and outcomes. However, there are limitations to the scope of research undertaken and this relates in part to the limitations of the social constructionist tradition. The tradition can be criticized as being broadly based and encompassing a wide number of individual paradigms of research. However, this breadth could be a virtue, given the need to incorporate other traditions and concepts if the scope of research is to be broadened. This chapter has reviewed a number of areas where development is needed and possible. Some of these are more challenging than others. It has been argued that theories of power can be easily incorporated and the contribution to policymaking can be achieved with an appropriate policy paradigm. More difficult issues are the relationship with the material world of the dwelling which could undermine the fundamental tenets of constructionism and where new concepts are needed to ensure progress. Perhaps the most daunting challenge is the possible interface with positivist disciplines such as economics and psychology. However, it is in this area that the potential benefits are the greatest.

REFERENCES

Bauman, Z. (1992) *Intimations of Post-modernity*. London: Routledge.
Berger, P. and Luckmann, T. (1967) *The Social Construction of Reality*. Harmondsworth: Penguin.
Blumer, H. (1969) *Symbolic Interactionism: Perspective and Method*. Englewood Cliffs, NJ: Prentice Hall.
Clapham, D. (2005) *The Meaning of Housing*. Bristol: Policy Press.
Clapham, D. (2006) 'Housing policy and the discourse of globalization', *European Journal of Housing Policy* 6(1): 55–76.
Clapham, D. (2009) 'A theory of housing: Problems and potential', *Housing Theory and Society* 26(1): 1–9.
Clapham, D., Franklin, B. and Saugeres, L. (2000) 'Housing management: The social construction of an occupational role', *Housing Theory and Society* 17(2): 68–82.
Clegg, S. (1989) *Frameworks of Power*. London: Sage.
Collin F. (1997) *Social Reality*. London: Routledge.
Darcy, M. and Manzi, A. (2004) 'Organisational research: Conflict and power within UK and Australian social housing organisations', in K. Jacobs, J. Kemeny and A. Manzi (eds), *Social Constructionism in Housing Research*. Aldershot: Ashgate.
Esping-Andersen, G. (1990) *Three Worlds of Welfare Capitalism*. Cambridge: Polity Press.
Fairclough, N. (1995) *Critical Discourse Aanalysis: The Critical Study of Language*. London: Longman.
Fopp, R. (2008) 'Social constructionism and housing studies: A critical reflection', *Urban Policy and Research* 26(2): 159–175.
Foucault, M. (1972) *The Archaeology of Knowledge*. London: Tavistock.
Gabriel, M. and Jacobs, K. (2007) 'The post-social turn: Challenges for housing research', *Housing Studies* 23(4): 527–540.

Garfinkel, H. (1967) *Studies in Ethnomethodology.* Englewood Cliffs, NJ: Prentice Hall.

Gibson, J. (1986) *The Ecological Approach to Visual Perception.* Mahwah, NJ: Erlbaum.

Giddens, A. (1984) *The Constitution of Society.* Cambridge: Polity Press.

Hastings, A. (2000) 'Discourse analysis: What does it offer housing studies', *Housing Theory and Society* 17(3): 131–138.

Haworth, A., Manzi, A. and Kemeny, J. (2004) 'Social constructionism and international comparative housing research', in K. Jacobs, J. Kemeny and A. Manzi (eds), *Social Constructionism in Housing Research.* Aldershot: Ashgate.

Healey, P. (1997) *Collaborative Planning: Shaping Places in Fragmented Societies.* London: Macmillan.

Jacobs, K. and Manzi, A. (2000) 'Evaluating the social constructionist paradigm in housing research', *Housing, Theory and Society* 17(1): 35–42.

Jacobs, K., Kemeny, J. and Manzi, A. (1999) 'The struggle to define homelessness: A constructivist approach', in D. Clapham and S. Hutson (eds), *Homelessness: Public Policies and Private Troubles.* London: Cassell, pp. 11–28.

Jacobs, K., Kemeny, J. and Manzi, A. (eds) (2004) *Social Constructionism in Housing Research.* Aldershot: Ashgate.

Kemeny, J. (1992) *Housing and Social Theory.* London: Routledge.

Kemeny, J. (2004) 'Extending constructionist social problems to the study of housing problems', in K. Jacobs, J. Kemeny and A. Manzi (eds), *Social Constructionism in Housing Research.* Aldershot: Ashgate.

Kemeny, J. and Lowe, S. (1998) 'Schools of comparative housing research: From convergence to divergence', *Housing Studies* 13(2): 161–196.

King, P. (2004) 'Relativism, subjectivity and the self: A critique of social constructionism', in K. Jacobs, J. Kemeny and A. Manzi (eds), *Social Constructionism in Housing Research.* Aldershot: Ashgate.

King, P. (2009) 'Using theory or making theory: Can there be theories of housing?', *Housing Theory and Society* 26(1): 41–52.

Latour, (1996) *On inter-objectivity. Mind, Culture and Activity 3* pp.228–245.

Lindblom, C. (1959) 'The science of muddling through', *Public Administration Review* 19: 79–88.

Mandic, S. and Clapham, D. (1996) 'The meaning of home ownership in the transition from socialism: The example of Slovenia', *Urban Studies* 33(1): 83–97.

Mead, G. (1934) *Mind, Self and Society.* Chicago, IL: University of Chicago Press.

Nozick, R. (2001) *Invariance: The Structure of the Objective World.* Cambridge, MA: Harvard University Press.

Ritzer, G. and Smart, B. (eds) (2000) *Handbook of Social Theory.* London: Sage.

Sandstrom, K., Martin, D. and Fine, G. (2000) 'Symbolic Interactionism at the End of the Century' in G. Ritzer and B. Smart (eds), *Handbook of Social Theory.* London: Sage pp. 217–231.

Sayer, A. (2000) *Realism and Social Science.* London: Sage.

Schutz, A. (1967) *The Phenomenology of the Social World.* Chicago, IL: North Western Press.

Shilling, C. (2003) *The Body and Social Theory.* London: Sage.

Sommerville, P. and Bengtsson, B. (2002) 'Constructionism, realism and housing theory', *Housing, Theory and Society* 19: 121–136.

Spector, M. and Kitsuse, J. (1977) *Constructing Social Problems.* New York: Aldine de Gruyter.

Strauss, A. (1978) *Negotiations: Varieties, Contexts, Processes and Social Order.* San Francisco, CA: Jossey-Bass.

Travers, M. (2004) 'The philosophical assumptions of constructionism', in K. Jacobs, J. Kemeny and A. Manzi (eds), *Social Constructionism in Housing Research.* Aldershot: Ashgate.

A Review of Structurally Inspired Approaches in Housing Studies – Concepts, Contributions and Future Perspectives

Julie Lawson

WHAT IS STRUCTURE AND HOW DOES IT INFORM HOUSING ANALYSIS?

Structuralist theories assume that individuals coexist, not as isolated atoms, but as people bound by interdependent social relationships which may form a relatively coherent system, albeit subject to crises adaptation over time. Modes of housing provision and consumption can be viewed objects for research that embody cross-cutting and complex social, economic, political and cultural relationships. Indeed, I have argued that housing can be viewed as a unique and concrete expression of inter-related social arrangements such as class, property relations, tenure, labour relations, gender and kinship (Lawson, 2006).

However, while social structures pertinent to housing have an enduring quality, they are nevertheless malleable, evolving differently over time and space. Furthermore, these structures are both carried and mediated by individual actors, who are propelled and motivated by their own class position, power and social identity (compare to Clapham, in this volume).

Claims about social structures and their causal powers, however, remain highly contestable. Since the 1960s competing and conflicting theories have emerged, each making assertions about the nature and role of social structures. These include theories debating the relative power of structure over individual agency, the role of class and social movements, the level of consciousness held by agents and the pervasiveness and endurance of structures over time and space. These debates have been particularly influential in urban and housing analysis, pushing housing researchers into the realms of political economy, radical geography and urban sociology. Thus, the concept of structure in housing studies is not only multifaceted but also contested, generating not only a rich body of debate but also counter movements such as post-structuralism and post-modernism. This chapter examines the role of structures in housing studies since the 1960s, with a focus on contemporary developments.

TRACING THE HISTORY OF STRUCTURAL IDEAS

The concept of interdependent elements belonging to a system actually originated from the study of languages but has since metamorphosed across the social sciences via French sociology to Marxism, influencing the way we analyse housing phenomena such as residential markets and housing tenure.

During the late 19th century, the Swiss linguist Ferdinand Saussure proposed a new way of ordering the analysis of different languages based on relations between signs, signifiers and referents. After spending some time teaching in Paris, Saussure's ideas also inspired French sociologist Levi-Strauss, who put forward that an influential system of laws shaped patterns of human thought. This spurred an intellectual movement that also influenced Marxist debates and developments. Philosopher Louis Pierre Althusser argued that society was not merely a product of economic determinism, but an outcome of interdependent relations between the economic base of a capitalist system and its political and cultural superstructure, which, together, influenced day-to-day practices. He claimed that ideology played an ever-present and often repressive role mediating individual agency.

While a broad analysis of structural concepts in social research can be found in Lawrence (1989, 1987), this chapter narrows the field to focus on those which were employed by neo-Marxist social scientists since the late 1960s. More than any other school of thought, Marxist structural concepts of class, land rent and historical materialism has influenced research endeavours and perspectives in the field of housing research. This chapter reviews their contribution since the 1970s, when widely read authors such as Castells and Harvey directed our attention towards the relative power of human agency in structures influencing the production, consumption, commodification and extraction of surplus value of housing and provided a critique of more benign policy research and market processes.

This chapter reviews the influence of structuralist ideas which have influenced urban political economy, radical geography and sociology, generating particular schools of thought such as locality studies, regulation theory and comparative historical analysis. The chapter also reviews some of the criticisms of political economy and the structural movement, as well as political and professional forces which have generated an era of post-structuralism and post-modernism in housing research.

More recently, critical realist ontology has provided the philosophical underpinnings for the existence of social structures and today – independent of Marxism – explicitly inspires explanatory research on housing studies. Both Castells and Harvey continue to inspire housing researchers, generating critical analysis of the US mortgage market crises, gentrification and housing inequality.

An introduction to structural concepts and approaches

In general terms, structural theorists claim that there are underlying social relationships which are likely to have a causal effect on social phenomena such as modes of housing provision or the housing 'system'. However, these interdependent social relations are contingent upon spatially and historically specific circumstances and must therefore be derived from concrete historical analysis.

A structurally inspired research strategy aims to abstract from case study research the causal features of particular housing systems to test and revise explanatory theory using appropriate methods, in order to reveal the nature of the causal process. The logic of the research process is not inductive, but informed by preceding explanatory developments and debates and should aim to generate explanations of causal processes. In this way the epistemological strategy employs justified concepts in the development of a postulated model or theory and revises this via concrete research, towards a more competitive explanation. It combines elements of deductive and inductive logic, which can be considered as *retroductive* (Blaikie, 1993; Sayer, 2000; Danermark et al., 2002).

Structural theorists attempt to explain causal processes underlying housing phenomena by using methods such as comparative historical analysis and process tracing of concrete reality. This approach contrasts and sometimes conflicts with other approaches with more inductive and deductive approaches, such as 'bottom up' or conversely anthropological studies theories that build (mathematical) models or games which build on certain assumptions of human or market behaviour, such as rational choice theory and game theory which assume certain types of human interactions and their choices.

A key difference between structural and actor-centred explanations is the claim by the former that objects and events are embedded in key social relations. In housing studies, such theories focus upon the definition of specific social relations pertinent to housing provision. These include the relations of savings and investment, the exploitation of land, materials and labour relations in the formal work place and their (gendered) reproduction in the home, as well as circuits of capital accumulation throughout the production, consumption and exchange process. As agents produce and reproduce relations their behaviour remains integral to causal explanation (Lawson, 2006).

Contemporary 'relationists' also argue that particular, context-defined sets of social relations have different types of causal tendencies, which can explain the existence of very different forms of housing provision. These causal tendencies or mechanisms, in combination with contingent relations and other necessary relations, help to explain the nature and development of housing-related events and experiences (Dickens et al., 1985; Terhorst and van de Ven, 1997; Lawson, 2006).

Housing outcomes can be considered as being generated in part by a system of provision, which comprises different but interdependent parts. The functional terminology of structural theory (necessary relations, causal mechanisms, etc.) appears to imply a certain rigidity of roles and relationships and has indeed generated a number of important criticisms – the diminution of individual agency; the focus on economic relations; the universality of causal claims; and their broad-brush insensitivity to more fine-grained explanation – which have led to a number of responses (Bourdieu, 1990, 2005) and in turn partially shaped ongoing research in this field, which is reviewed in this chapter.

Indeed, the growing body of international and comparative housing research clearly demonstrates the diversity of forms of housing provision amongst capitalist societies and their change over time. Few researchers, inspired by structural concepts, have ventured to specify even the 'essential' components of a housing system, without reference to a specific contingent context (Dickens et al., 1985; Ball and Harloe, 1992; Ambrose, 1994; Doling, 1997; Lawson, 2006).

Nevertheless, efforts to build a more general theory of difference and change can be found in Lawson (2006, 2010), where the contingent nature of emergent relations and the cumulative development of institutions underpinning systems of housing provision are stressed. There are limits to this generalisation, as explanatory theories require abstraction from concrete social relations which underpin local forms of housing provision, such as their property relations and their submarkets, financial circuits of savings and assets affecting investment in housing and the capacity of households to pay for housing services underpinned by labour and welfare arrangements and conditions. This approach is returned to in the final part of this chapter.

Historical materialism and structuralist housing research

A variety of social theories that emphasise different structural dimensions inspire housing studies (Lambert et al., 1978; Basset and Short, 1980; Ball, 1983; Dickens et al., 1985; Lawrence, 1989; Kemeny, 1992; Paris, 1993). Basset and Short (1980), in *Housing and Residential Structure: Alternative Approaches*, provide a broad list of structural dimensions, describing housing as:

- a heterogeneous, durable and essential consumer good
- an indirect indicator of social status and income differences
- a map of social relations within the city
- an important facet of residential structure
- a source of profit to different institutions and agents involved in the production, consumption and exchange of housing (Basset and Short, 1980: 1–2).

This last dimension has been associated with structurally inspired housing research generated by the social theories of Marx in the late 20th century, which has provided both a foil and spur for theories of explanation for change and difference in forms of housing provision.

Researchers inspired by Marx's theory of historical materialism generated a rich body of urban and housing analysis in the 1970s and 1980s. This work centred round the evolving and often conflicting relationship between the economic base of different societies and their political and cultural superstructure. Researchers examined the role of class struggle in forms of housing provision, differential land rent and the extraction of surplus value from land development, construction, allocation and exchange and emphasised the rights and obligations attached to forms of housing tenure.

Marxist housing research tended to view housing from the perspective of uneven and often unequal capitalist relations that were embedded in the process of dwelling production, consumption and exchange. Prominence was given to the notion of housing as an exploitable commodity, often produced and distributed by labour-employing, profit-seeking capitalist firms. Moreover, while housing services were considered essential to the reproduction of labour, workers also had to be able to pay adequate rents for these services. Finally, given that housing was a fixed asset occupying land and had to compete with other land uses that may be more or less profitable for different market parties, analysis of housing tenure and the spatial patterns of urban forms must therefore examine how profit is extracted from different processes of land development, finance, construction, allocation and exchange and how competitive or monopolistic practices, land use and building regulation and the delivery of ancillary services combined to influence the market for housing, its allocation amongst different households and patterns of investment, ultimately shaping the form and composition of residential development (Harvey, 1973; Castells, 1977; Berry, 1983a: 91–92).

KEY TEXTS IN STRUCTURALISM INFLUENCING HOUSING STUDIES

The Marxist movement in housing studies emerged in France during the late 1960s. Students and academics began to challenge dominant social theories of post-war Europe, such as orthodox economics and modernism. They raised sharp questions about the role of class in urban development and questioned benevolent relations between the state and capital, which they argued generated social inequality and polarised living conditions. Neo-classical economic theories were also criticised for their atomistic view of society, their mechanistic and ahistorical analysis of officially recorded facts and their ignorance of underlying social relations shaping ideology and power. These arguments undermined the conservative cold war political consensus which had pervaded academia and policy realms in capitalist countries since the 1950s.

Emerging from these criticisms, housing studies (alongside urban social theory and geography) took a more radical turn and a more critical stance towards relationships between the state, labour and capital emerged. According to Basset and Short (1980), this critical turn also coincided with academic aspirations to chart alternative theoretical territory, leading some researchers and social activists to rediscover Marxism (Pickvance, Walker, Harloe and Castells), promoting a historical macro-sociological perspective of social-structural determinants of social inequality and conflict (Berry, 1983b: 8). This shift was greatly influenced by the work of David Harvey and Manuel Castells during the 1970s, which became a focus and launch pad for a structuralist paradigm in housing studies.

The Urban Question by Manuel Castells (1977) introduced Marxist concepts to urban analysis and emphasised the importance of a historically contingent definition of class relations emergent from social structures underlying each urban system. Thus, cities and their social structures, including their housing systems, must be historically understood within the 'rhythms of capital accumulation' of uneven global expansion of capitalism, which has generated different and uneven forms of development (Berry, 1983b: 16). This theme remains central to Boyer's variety of capitalism thesis, which is employed by economic geographers to this day (Heiden and Terhorst, 2007). Castells used the term 'structure' to refer to the interrelation of economic, political/juridical and ideological levels of society, which had a relatively autonomous rather than deterministic relationship with each other. Productive enterprises in the private for-profit sphere were sustained by collective forms of consumption, including housing, which enabled the reproduction of labour power. Castells also argued that from time to time housing conditions would deteriorate – either in terms of availability, affordability or quality – undermining the reproduction of labour power and leading to a crisis of collective consumption. The role of social class in this process was a puzzle for Castells during the 1970s, who examined the role of conflict, contradiction and social movements through comparative case study research.

The structured operation of land markets, essential to forms of housing provision, were also a key focus of historical materialist research. David Harvey's landmark text *Social Justice and the City* (1973) critically examines the extraction of rent by landowners from productive processes, distinguishing monopoly from absolute rent and creation of value through manipulating supply to promote scarcity to increase rents and thus profit margins. Class monopoly rent refers to owners of housing resources able to release units when profitable rents can be extracted. For Harvey, housing markets were a complex of submarkets with different modes of extraction differentiated by their levels of monopoly rent. These filtered access to housing and divided the city into spatially segregated residential environments. Filtering is a process derived from a number of generative relations: labour market specialisation; consumption lifestyles; authority relations at the workplace; housing ideologies; and intergenerational barriers compounding residential divisions and fragmenting class awareness and solidarity (Basset and Short, 1980: 196).

Critics of structurally focused housing studies have stressed the importance of agency and consequently, gone on to deepen our understanding of the role of individual agents in forms of housing provision and consumption. In doing so, they have promoted concrete research using ethnographic methods, discourse analysis (Saugeres, 1999) and employed concepts such as contextualised rational action (Somerville and Bengtsson, 2002) and contingent action within institutionalised housing pathways (Clapham, 2004). These efforts have greatly embellished our understanding of housing differences and encouraged far more sensitive empirical analysis than overtly structural explanations which sometimes rode roughshod over careful historical analysis.

Today, unlike the 1970 and 1980s, there is no dominant theory of social structure, such as historical materialism, which pervades contemporary housing studies. However, a number of tributary streams emerging from the urban political economy of Harvey and Castells continue to flow though housing research. Concepts such as inequality, uneven development, the role of (and relations between) state/capital, structure and agency, the variety of capitalism thesis, monopoly rent and exploitation, processes of glocalisation, commodification, modes of capital accumulation and capital switching continue to inspire researchers. Other themes, such as Castells' urban social movements, have receded from contemporary focus. Despite many criticisms of structuralism, the subordination of class relations to accumulation processes and a cultural post-structural turn in social science, many themes from Castells and Harvey early work continues to influence researchers more than four decades later, as will be reviewed below.

Re-examining housing and urban history

During the 1980s, historical urban and housing studies, informed by theoretical Marxism and political economy, emphasized the importance of property relations, the timing and unique forms of capital accumulation and the differing role of complex state arrangements which funded urban infrastructure, mediating the pace and form of urban expansion and housing consumption. This approach spurred a wave of historical analysis using concepts such as reproduction, modes of capital accumulation and land rent theory. This movement was particularly influential within Australian housing research but also in the UK, France and to a much lesser degree Germanic countries where Weberian sociology and Elias (the civilising process) had taken a stronger hold (Mullins, 1981; Sandercock and Berry, 1983a and b; Badcock, 1984; Williams, 1984; King, 1986; Daly, 1988; Hayward, 1992; Terhorst and van de Ven, 1997). According to Ball et al. (1988):

> The determination of changes in housing provision is a complex historical process whose explanation can only be investigated through detailed empirical analysis (Ball et al., 1988: 32).

Berry later provided a typology of the states' role in housing and urban development as either market supporting, market supplementing or market replacing (Berry, 1983; Dalton, 1999). Although many rich cases were produced, there remained an interest in more overarching theories of provision.

Frameworks to examine difference

During the 1980s, Ball undertook a detailed examination of the homeownership in Britain (1983) and devised the structure of housing provision thesis, promoting concrete empirical research to reveal the unique relations of production over time and space (Ball, 1983, and Harloe, 1992, 1998; Ball et al., 1988). Ball argued that, in capitalist societies, some aspects of housing production, exchange and consumption can become highly commodified, while others remain decommodified. Exploitation of surplus value may occur within land transactions; when securing development rights; exploiting the use of labour and materials; in the exchange of dwellings; and ongoing housing maintenance. Furthermore, consumption of certain forms of housing may demand participation in the paid labour market and (re)enforce certain modes of domestic labour exploitation (i.e. unpaid, gendered and unevenly shared) (Lawson, 2006). Ball assumed, in the first instance, that that these relations were 'an historically given process of providing and reproducing the physical entity, housing' and recommended that researchers focus on the social agents essential to the process of housing provision and the relations which exist between them in time and space (Ball, 1986: 158). Thus, intensive case study research is required to identify the social agents involved in production, allocation, consumption and reproduction relations of housing (Ball, 1986: 160) and their interlinkages (Ball et al., 1988):

> Actual structures of housing provision, however, are empirical constructs and cannot be theoretically deduced, although obviously theory has to be applied in their analysis. (Ball et al., 1988: 29)

Another descriptive framework includes the chain-of-provision framework developed and applied by Ambrose (1991, 1994) which emphasises the wide variety of state, private and voluntary configurations of agents engaged in the interconnected stages of housing promotion, investment, construction, allocation and maintenance (Ambrose, 1991: 41), which has also inspired a number of evaluations. Ambrose (1994) later proposed a model of state–market–civil society relations that underpins any chain-of-housing provision. In his book *Urban Process and Power* he analyses the shift in power balance between the state and the market and the influence of these shifts upon the built environment (Ambrose, 1994: 12–13). A polarised characterisation of the state and market is proposed: on the one hand, the state is perceived as democratic, responsive to need and allocating on this basis; and on the other hand, the market is undemocratic, responsive to effective demand and allocating on the basis of capacity to pay. This abstraction 'floats' beneath the chain of provision (Lawson, 2006). Doling has also proposed the commodification–decommodication continuum in housing processes. Both offer a useful framework, rather than a theory, which must be grounded in concrete case study research.

Theories of change across housing systems

Theories of change in housing systems have been put forward debating convergence and divergence; explaining differences and similarities; linking powerful phases of economic development to the role of the state in housing and the changing role of housing consumption in daily life and its relationship with the development of different welfare states. As mentioned earlier, large-scale comparisons overlook locally embedded causal mechanisms generating national housing systems.

More overarching theories of change in housing systems have been put forward by Harloe, linking powerful phases of economic development to the role of the state in housing and the changing role of housing consumption in the development of different welfare states. Harloe's theory of converging phases of housing provision perceives systems of housing provision as oscillating between mass and residual forms of housing provision, linked to normal and abnormal phases in capitalist development (Harloe, 1995). These phases are briefly summarised as follows:

- Pre 1914 – social housing began in most European countries to assist the least well off
- After 1918, the mass model dominates during post-war recovery
- From the 1920s to 1939, the residual model was reasserted
- From 1945 to the mid 1970s – the golden age of social housing
- Since the mid 1970s – when the mass model was challenged and retreated as residualism advances (Harloe in Malpass 2008: 4)

Countering Harloe's theory of converging phases of housing provision linked to economic development is Kemeny's less deterministic divergence thesis, focusing upon the financial position of social landlords and the state's role in shaping competition between private and non-profit landlords. For Kemeny (1995), divergent systems emerge partly as governments role in and respond to different types of rental markets (dual, integrated, unitary), where different rental models (cost rent, market rent, etc.) and competitive market conditions are of strategic explanatory significance. Several researchers have attempted to ground these interesting concepts via empirical case studies (Kemeny et al., 2005 on the Netherlands, Switzerland and Sweden and Elsinga et al., 2008 on the Netherlands).

There have, of course, been numerous efforts to identify key phases in the development of housing systems across Europe (Matznetter, 2006), some linking these to factors beyond Harloe's phases in capitalist development or Kemeny's financial maturation phase of landlords, often focusing on the role of the state at various spatial scales. This work includes Boelhouwer and van der Heijden's (1993) attempt to discern phases in policy development between 1945 and 1990 across seven Western European countries, defined by policy emphasis and degree of state involvement. Yet while a typology can assist a parallel description of nominated policy phases, it cannot explain their differences. However, the danger has also been that large-scale, albeit historically informed comparisons can downplay the locally embedded nature of causality affecting national housing systems and overlook important differences in the development of housing 'solutions'.

Housing and the nature and role of the state

One of the central projects of housing research inspired by urban political economy has been the development of a theory of the capitalist/state relations as they apply to regions, cities and systems of housing provision and these efforts go back to the 1970s when locality studies (Massey, 1978; Gregory and Urry, 1985; Urry, 1986) and structuration thesis (Giddens, 1984), regulation theory (Boyer, 1990; Jessop, 1990; Goodwin, 2001) and most recently structural–relational theory (Jessop, 2007) have all emerged as theoretical frameworks to inspire explanation of housing provision and its differences (Lawson, 2006 on difference and change, Aalbers, 2009 on the unique geography of mortgage markets, Becker and Novy, 1999 on the interaction between nation and city states in Austria, Berry, 1998 on Australian urban history and Marcuse, 1986 challenging simplistic views of the benevolent or meddling state).

Beyond explanations for difference between so-called 'national' housing systems, researchers inspired by structural concepts have also paid attention to dynamic state structures at the urban scale in the development of long-term housing solutions using a variety of ideas emanating from the locality studies movement from Lancaster in the 1970 and 1980s (Urry, 1986, Massey, 1978) as well as the glocalisation movement (Swyngedouw, 2004) and variety of capitalism thesis. Indeed, while national-level analysis predominates comparative housing research there are critics of this approach, especially amongst political and economic geographers, who argue for the recognition of the regional and local origins of national housing policies (Lawson, 2006, 2008, 2010; Matznetter, 2007).

Regulation theory seeks to account for differences in social phenomena via concrete contexts of specific social practices. Rather than universalizing propositions, such as the convergence of housing provision, it seeks to provide explanations for differences. Analysis compares the regulatory systems and their outcomes according to critical interactions between modes of social regulation (MSR) and regimes of capital accumulation (RCA).

It implies that explanations for change in forms of social housing provision must *not* be seen in functional economic terms but as an interaction between MSR and RCA. Lawson and Nieboer (2009) take a more considered look at the concept of regulation and investment strategies of social housing organisations, drawing on the literature from institutional economics, sociology and geography. According to Cloke and Goodwin:

> A key notion…is the idea that the expanded social reproduction of capitalism is never guaranteed, but has to be continuously secured through a range of social norms, mechanisms and institutions. Together these help to stabilize relations between production and consumption within a particular regime of accumulation. (Cloke and Goodwin, 1992: 322)

Regulation theory has inspired a body of housing and urban research (Florida and Feldman, 1988; Gertler, 1988; Harvey and Scott, 1988; Cooke, 1989; Sayer, 1989; Schoenberger, 1989; Chouinard, 1990; Dunford, 1990) but has been criticised for its neglect of class relations in social phenomena (Allen, 2008).

Most recently, Jessop (2007) has promoted a strategic–relational approach for understanding and explaining different state forms, which acknowledges its gendered selectivity, the hollowing out of the nation-state, its temporal sovereignty and the relevance of multi-scalar meta-governance in Europe for the more general future of the state. It is too early to say what influence this theory is likely to hold for housing research, but it certainly places city-based research on the housing agenda, a theme which has been recently re-embraced by the ENHR social housing working group (Scanlon and Whitehead, 2008).

Class and structural theories

A less prominent stream in structural studies has been the role of class in housing systems. Structural theorists have tended to examine social class through the window of labour relations: the reproduction of labour power and the production of surplus value through housing production and consumption and the commodification of housing (Lambert et al., 1978). The strong emphasis on economic relations tended to overshadow the role of other social systems of influence such as patriarchy, political processes and the creation of ideological norms and the role of cultural preferences in supporting alternative market arrangements (Kemeny, 1992).

Nevertheless, an important breakthrough in the appreciation of social class in housing studies was provided by the French social theorist Pierre Bourdieu (1990, 2005). He argued for a much broader interpretation of social class and housing markets. Class analysis should examine the role of cultural capital and class identity in forms of housing consumption. Allen's (2008) critical and extensive review of the treatment of class in housing and urban studies also provides valuable reading, which argues for a more prominent analysis of identity and being in class formation and patterns of housing consumption.

Housing markets, consumption and production

Alongside a re-conceptualisation of class, Bourdieu (2005) also argued that forms of housing provision, comprising numerous submarkets with overlapping patterns of demand and supply, had been analysed by economists and sociologists using utopian theories that bore no resemblance to reality. Earlier, Bourdieu (1990) had argued that markets and state roles were rather fluid and socially constructed historical processes and questioned the inherent rationality of agents participating in markets, as claimed by both Marxist and orthodox economists. Later, Bourdieu (2005) analysed the role, economic dispositions and resources of agents in the supply of single-family houses and the influential role of the state in establishing particular market conditions which guided both financial and emotional investment toward various forms of housing provision. He argued that research should focus on the:

> structure of the field of production and the mechanisms that determine its functioning (instead of being content with mere recording, which would itself require explanation, of statistical co-variations between variables and events) and also the structure of the distribution of economic dispositions and, more especially, of tastes in respect of housing, not forgetting to establish, by a historical analysis, the social conditions of the production of this particular field and of the dispositions able to find more or less complete fulfilment in it. (Bourdieu, 2005: 17)

Bourdieu has reinstated structural thinking in housing research – striking a chord with critics of neo-liberalism and neo-classical economics and those disenchanted by historical materialism's focus on economic demands of capital to the neglect of class identity and relations mediating individual agency (Allen, 2008).

Globalisation and glocalisation

Another important dimension of housing studies inspired by the notion of structures and systems, is the pervasive globalisation thesis. This is based on the increasing mobility of (manufacturing) capital and financial markets across international boundaries and the undermining of national rules of regulation and their capacity to steer investment. It has influenced comparative housing research and critical perspectives on investment flows and housing outcomes (Sassen, 2001; Smart, 2003).

Focusing on financial markets, a primary object of globalisation, Sassen (2009) recently explains how housing has become a new channel for extracting household incomes, via mortgage instruments that are packaged and sold internationally as RMBS (residential mortgage-backed securities), with profit extracted from the sale of financial products, rather than fulfilment of mortgage obligations. Wainwright (2009) and Aalbers (2008) return to the work of Harvey (1982) concerning capital switching, not only to explain this process of financialisation but also the very foundations of the global financial crises. Recent developments in comparative political science and economic geography concerning the 'variety of capitalism thesis' (Goodwin, 2001; Hall and Soskice, 2001; Brenner, 2004) have also been used to argue why some mortgage markets have been more resilient to the problem of default and repossession than others (Aalbers, 2009).

A weak globalisation variant, giving more autonomy to national governments and welfare regimes, has informed comparative research on the rise of homeownership across Europe, using statistical data and qualitative case studies (HOSE project, Doling and Ford, 2003). It has also inspired other European research on the security and insecurity aspects of this tenure (OSIS, see http://www.osis.bham.ac.uk) and the role ownership plays in securing social welfare (DEMHOW, see http://www.demhow.bham.ac.uk/).

Theoretically informed and empirically grounded research has been undertaken by a multidisciplinary team of researchers using a range of methods to explain the targeting and exploitation of racial and ethnic minorities by predatory lenders in the USA (Wyly et al., 2009). Their outstanding work draws inspiration from the early work of Harvey (1974) concerning class monopoly rents, localised structures mediation with national banking systems, as well as more recent work concerning accumulation by dispossession (Harvey, 2003).

Path dependence and institutional layering

The concepts of path dependence and institutional layering (Mahoney and Rueschemeyer, 2003) complement and enrich the emergence approach to comparative historical analysis, by strengthening the critique of convergence in forms of provision amongst nation-states and demanding more careful consideration of local regimes and causal processes (Heijden and Terhorst, 2007). This has led to the development of theories explaining the very different housing regimes present in five Nordic countries (Bengstsson et al., 2006) and a special journal issue on path dependence in housing edited by Bengtsson and Ruanovarra (2010).

Lawson (2006, 2008, 2009, 2010) has explored the issues of how key social relationships underpinning forms of housing provision were contingently defined and packaged together over time. Cumulative phases of coherence, crises or adaptation were defined by the contingent definition of property, finance and consumption underpinning open and vulnerable forms of housing provision (Lawson, 2006: 88). Coherence is defined as 'historically contingent ensembles of complementary economic and extra-economic mechanisms and practices which enable relatively stable accumulation to occur over relatively long periods' (Jessop, 1997: 503 in Goodwin, 2001). It is contended that *coherence* in housing provision occurs when the contingent definition of property rights, circuit of savings and investment and the mode of housing consumption are able to sustain a particular form of housing provision, such as cost-rent LPH (limited-profit housing), homeownership or private rental.

Yet, structural coherence can be undone amidst open and dynamic housing markets, in which monopolies, misinformation, opportunism, material constraints, ideological shifts and changes in policy constantly threaten. These changes may generate a *crisis* in provision, in which actors, with varying degrees of agency, may struggle to establish new norms, practices and institutions, leading to the development of new, revised or reformed solutions to moderate (or exacerbate) a crisis of housing provision (Lawson, 2006: 83–86). *Adaptation* may occur via the adoption of new land-use regulations, establishment of financing guarantees and the revision of demand assistance programmes, drawing on the institutional foundations and reflections of the past.

Welfare regimes as social structures

Some housing researchers have turned away from traditional political economy, with its emphasis on accumulation regimes, towards different arrangements of labour and welfare provisions and conditions for answers, largely inspired by Esping-Anderson's work on welfare regimes (1990) and Kemeny's concept of residence (1992). The concept of welfare regimes has influenced new perspectives in comparative housing research (Kleinman, 1996 and Hoekstra, 2005, 2003 on the Netherlands; Matznetter, 2002 on Austria) and consideration of less-examined regions of Europe (Allen et al., 2004) as well as the investigation of familial-based welfare models (for a review, see Chapter 18). In addition to more nuanced categorisation of cases, theoretical progress has attempted by combining welfare regime theory with other types of development regimes (Matznetter, 2002; Lee, 2002 in Lawson et al., 2009).

There are recent comparative studies which have attempted to comprehensively apply ideas encompassing market structures and contingent dynamics, historical processes of industrialisation (Fordist, post-Fordist, regimes of accumulation), evolving state roles (market promoting, regulating or replacing) and welfare regimes (bismarkian, Beveridge, conservative, neo-liberal, social democratic) (Smart, 2003; Hoekstra, 2005; Schröder, 2008; Dalton, 2009).

Beyond state-focused research, there have been valiant attempts to investigate other structures influencing housing provision: namely, gender and labour relations and challenge conceptions of the nature of capitalist relations mediating these realms of social life. This work has examined not only the nature of work (causal, paid, permanent, gendered, professional, skilled, etc.)

but also its location and influence on home life and the nature of housing services consumed. This includes research by Hayden (1982), Allport (1983), Allen and Hamnett (1991), Randolph (1991) and Fincher and Nieuwenhuysen (1998). Housing consumption is greatly influenced by access to credit and the separation of home from the workplace – and this unequally affects men and women. Watson (1991: 136–154) stresses the importance of the changing nature of home and work arguing for a feminist approach to labour and work relations that recognises the complex interplay of culture, gender and class (Lawson, 2006). This point is returned to in the conclusion of this chapter.

THE ROLE OF CRITICAL REALISM AS UNDER-LABOURER IN THE FRAGMENTED FIELD OF HOUSING STUDIES

Housing researchers, inspired by notions of underlying structural causes, have to confront a plurality of influential relations that have generated change and differences in forms of housing provision. These influences are not easy to isolate, observe or measure. Critical realism (CR) is helpful in this regard, as it provides an ontological theory for abstracting causal mechanisms that can emerge from the realm of dominant ideas, material resources and social relations, which are contended to underlie forms of housing provision.

Thus, cultural belief systems and ideologies, such as those embedded in housing aspirations, state-promoted individualistic ideals of the 'property owning democracy', asset-based welfare, or the solidarity of social housing or the self-sufficient cooperative, are acknowledged to have causal influence upon institution building and policymaking. Furthermore, influences can be generated from actual material conditions, such as the stability of investment in the built environment or the technical capacity of the building industry, and availability and market suitable sites for development are materially important when explaining difference and change in forms of provision.

Furthermore, causes can also be embedded in long-established and institutionalised power relationships or 'ways of doing', which mediate the agency of urban planners and landowners, borrowers and lenders of housing finance and tenants and landlords. Attention to these different realms of reality (experience, actual events and social relations) and their contingent definition (Bergene, 2007) can provide a rich source of causal explanation.

Finally, towards more nuanced and accurate explanations for difference and change, historical research should be alert to the scalar nature of shifting state structures operating within dynamic and often vulnerable housing markets and critically aware of the weak social construction of cultural norms and aspirations influencing class identity, social action and pattern of housing consumption.

Yet CR is not a sociological, urban or housing theory: it is a philosophical theory of ontology that can inspire research strategies which aim to explain social phenomena in the housing field. It cannot replace sound empirical research or robust conceptualisation.

To date, CR theory of ontology has inspired explanations for differences in housing 'solutions' in Australia, the Netherlands, Korea, Austria and Switzerland (Lawson, 2006, 2008, 2009) and the causes of homelessness in the UK (Fitzpatrick, 2005) (see Chapter 19). It has also inspired analysis of urban differences, including very thorough explanations for differences in the housing and urban development of Amsterdam and Brussels (Terhorst and van de Ven, 1997). In terms of methodology, it has also generated lively debate within housing studies, particularly from social constructionists, political economists and sociologists (Somerville 1994; Lawson, 2001, 2002, 2006; Fitzpatrick, 2002; Manzi, 2002; Somerville and Bengtsson, 2002; Fopp, 2008), which is discussed in part below.

FINDING THE 'EXPLANATORY EDGE' AND PLACING 'CRITICAL' ON CENTRE STAGE

There are certainly criticisms of structural approaches within political economy. This section outlines these and the need for more focused efforts in conceptualizing housing phenomena, which necessarily demands an adequate empirical understanding of housing practice, interdependent processes subject to change and their sustaining ideologies. It also outlines an agenda driven by much stronger and more explicit commitment to critical explanation, however fallible.

In 2006, I argued that researchers should aim to make a contribution to real social knowledge, be concerned with *contributing towards answers* to identified social problems and strive for *progress in explanation*. This implies a commitment to seek the most plausible, competitive explanation. Of course any knowledge claims a research makes will always be partial, fallible and contestable. Arguing about the quality of explanation strengthens the rigour of scientific progress in housing research.

On the topic of 'answers to social problems', Sayer (2000) and Jessop (2007) argue that researchers should not only continue to strive for objectivity in their work but also engage more closely with moral and political philosophy which can underpin arguments concerning basic needs for shelter, sociable and safe living environments, equality, democracy, fairness and tolerance. To progress beyond the confines of benign policy studies and commissioned research (Donnison and Stephens, 2003: 257), critical housing studies, informed by an awareness of social structures, should interact with these disciplines to strengthen their normative standpoint when dealing with more neo-liberal perspectives emanating from other domains. Having sought explanations for housing problems, such as scarcity, homelessness, inequality and housing-related poverty, researchers should be able to suggest appropriate and feasible alternatives, which may require different structures and mechanisms to achieve more desirable outcomes.

There have been a number of important criticisms of structural approach in housing research which have promoted alternative post-structural approaches: deconstructionism, aesthetics and versions of social constructionism. In the 1990s geographers shifted their analytic focus to 'deconstruct' urban narratives (Soja, 1989), often employing a far more literary style such as Davis' dramatic account of Los Angeles (1990), disenfranchising some geographers and social theorists used to more strategic–relational prose and argument (Davidson and Fincher, 1998: 172; Sayer, 2000). While they can be grouped together as the post-structuralists, their ontological approaches, claims and prescriptions for the future are very different (contrast Sommerville, 2000 with Davis, 1990 and Gibson-Graham, 1996).

Other criticisms have stressed, particularly, kinds of structures – concerning the power of agency (Sommerville, 2000), patriarchy (Watson, 1988; Fincher, 1990) – and promoted alternative representations of society, space and the home (Gibson-Graham, 1996: 3 in Davidson and Fincher, 1998: 192). There have also been alternative arguments stemming from the nature of societal risk, claiming that greater uncertainty, flexibility and change in social and economic relationships (in the workplace, home and social networks) are shifting risks along new societal lines. As societies modernise, old processes are subject to increasing scrutiny and modification. Traditions fall rapidly by the wayside and old structures and collective institutions recede (Beck et al., 1994). These researchers shifted their conceptual focus from political economy of class to gender, environment, technology, aesthetics and identity formation. Thus, the critical thinkers of the 1980s and 1990s, unlike those of the 1970s, formed closer alliances with cultural studies rather than political economy, taking their feminist and green interests to post-structural pastures, applying more linguistic and cultural concepts and methods.

These debates have been very important in shaping structurally inspired debates, research strategies and methods. Indeed, the debate generated by Sommerville and Bengtsson's article in *Housing Theory and Society* (2002) (and the response by Fitzpatrick and Lawson in the same issue), as well as the recent contribution by Fopp (2008), attest to the lively interchange in which there is common ground to be found between critical realists' conception of structure, causality and open systems (Sayer, 2000: 12) and social constructionists' interests in experience and meaning. I have argued that there is certainly room for both (Lawson, 2002) within realist ontology.

Reflecting on the competing debates above, this chapter has tried to bring together coherent elements into a research ontology which moves beyond the descriptive devise of structures of housing provision. This approach incorporates weak social constructionism, recognizing the influence (but not determinism) of meaning and dominant ideologies that influence the perception of different housing actors in their material and socially constructed contexts. It recognises the uneven position of different actors in housing provision and their coalitions that may form to promote more commodified or decommodifed forms of provision. It recognizes the different and related elements of housing provision, each subject to its own institutional network, competing ideologies, economic relations and power coalitions (Lawson, 2006).

Given the slow and sluggish nature of housing provision (Bengtsson, 2008), explanations for difference and change need a historical, in-depth case study approach rather than a static outcomes-level correlation of similarities and differences. It must be sensitive to the embedded interdependencies of structures of housing provision and, in particular, the dynamic and open nature of state structures operating within open markets, as well as housing consumption norms and aspirations of key agents, in order to produce more nuanced and accurate explanations for difference. Towards this end, this chapter agrees with the arguments of Mahoney and Rueschemeyer:

> comparative historical studies can yield more meaningful advice concerning contemporary choices and possibilities than studies that aim for universal truths but cannot grasp historical details. (Mahoney and Rueschemeyer, 2003: 9).

REFERENCES

Aalbers, M. (2008) The financialization of home and the mortgage market crisis, *Competition and Change*, 12 (2): 148–166.

Aalbers, M.B. (2009) *Geographies of the Financial Crisis*, Area 41 (1): 34–42.

Allen, C. (2008) *Housing Market Renewal and Social Class*, Routledge, London, 2008.

Allen, C. and Hamnett, S. (1991) *Housing and Labour Markets: Building the Connections*, Unwin Hyman, London.

Allen, J., Barlow, J., Leal, J., Maloutas, T., & Padovani, L. (2004). *Housing and Welfare in Southern Europe*, Blackwell, Oxford.

Allport, C. (1983) Women and suburban housing, in P. Williams (ed.), *Social Process and the City*, Allen and Unwin, Sydney, pp. 64–87.

Ambrose, P. (1991) The housing provision chain as a comparative analytical framework, *Scandinavian Housing and Planning Research*, 8 (2): 91–104.

Ambrose, P. (1994) *Urban Process and Power*, Routledge, London.

Badcock, B. (1984) *Unfairly Structured Cities*, Basil Blackwell, Oxford.

Ball, M. (1983) *Housing Policy and Economic Power: The Political Economy of Owner Occupation*, Methuen, London.

Ball, M. (1986) Housing analysis: Time for a theoretical refocus? *Housing Studies*, 1 (3): 147–165.

Ball, M. (1988) *Housing Provision and Comparative Housing Research*, pp. 7–39.

Ball, M. (1998) Institutions in British property research: A review, *Urban Studies*, 35: 1501–1517.

Ball, M. and Harloe, M. (1992) Rhetorical barriers to understanding housing provision: What the 'provision thesis' is and is not, *Housing Studies*, 7 (1): 3–15.

Ball, M., Harloe, M. and Martens, M. (1988) *Housing and Social Change in Europe and the USA*, Routledge, New York.

Basset, K. and Short, J. (1980) *Housing and Residential Structure*, Routledge and Kegan Paul, London.

Beck, U., Giddens, A. and Lash, S. (1994) *Reflexive Modernization: Politics, Tradition, and Aesthetics in the Modern Social Order*, Polity and Stanford University Press, Oxford.

Becker, J. and Novy, A. (1999) Divergence and convergence of national and local regulation: The case of Austria and Vienna. *European Urban and Regional Studies*, 6 (2): 127–141.

Bengtsson, B., Annaniassen, E., Jensen, L., Ruonavaara, H., and Sveinsson, J. (2006) *Varför så olika? Nordisk bostadspolitik i jämförande historiskt ljus* (Why so Different? Nordic Housing Policies in Comparative Historical Light), Égalité, Malmö.

Bengtsson, B. (2008) Why so different? Housing regimes and path dependence in five Nordic countries, ENHR Conference Shrinking Cities, Sprawling Suburubs, Changing Countrysides, Dublin, July 6–9.

Bengtsson, B. and Ruanovarra, H. (2010) Special Issue: Path dependence and housing, *Housing Theory and Society*, 27 (3): 193–203

Bergene, A. (2007) Towards a critical realist comparative methodology, *Journal of Critical Realism*, 6(1): 5–27.

Berry, M. (1983a) Posing the housing question, in L. Sandercock and M. Berry (eds), *Urban Political Economy: The Australian Case*, George Allen and Unwin, Sydney.

Berry, M. (1983b) The Australian city in history, in L. Sandercock and M. Berry (eds), *Urban Political Economy*, Allen and Unwin, Melbourne.

Berry, M. (1998) Unravelling the Australian housing solution: The post war years, Presented to the 8th International Planning History Conference, University of New South Wales, Sydney, Australia, 15–17 July.

Blaikie, N. (1993) *Approaches to Social Enquiry*, Polity Press, Cambridge.

Boelhouwer, P. and Heijden, H. van der (1993) Methodological trends in international comparative housing research, *Netherlands Journal of Housing and the Built Environment*, 8 (4): 371–382.

Bourdieu, P. (2005) *Social Structures of the Economy*, Polity Press, Cambridge.

Bourdieu, P. (1990) Structures, habitus, practices, in P. Bourdieu (ed.), *The Logic of Practice*, Stanford University Press, Stanford, CA, p. 54.

Boyer, R. (1990) *The Regulation School: A Critical Introduction*, Columbia University Press, New York.

Brenner, N. (2004) *New State Spaces: urban governance and the rescaling of statehood*, Oxford University Press, Oxford.

Castells, M. (1977) *The Urban Question*, Arnold, London.

Chouinard, V. (1990) The uneven developments of capitalist states: 1. Theoretical proposals and an analysis of post-war changes in Canada's assisted housing programme, *Environmental Planning A*, 22: 1291–1308.

Clapham, D. (2004) Housing pathways – A social constructionist research framework, in K. Jacobs, J. Kemeny and A. Manzi (eds), *Social Constructionism in Housing Research*, Ashgate, Aldershot.

Cloke, P. and Goodwin, M. (1992) Conceptualizing countryside change: From post-Fordism to rural structured coherence, Transactions of the Institute of British Geographers, *New Series*, 17 (3): 321–336.

Cooke, P. (1989) Critical cosmopolitanism: Urban and regional studies into the 1990's, *Geoforum*, 20: 240–245.

Dalton, T. (1999) Making housing policy in Australia: Home ownership and the Disengagement of the State, unpublished PhD thesis, RMIT, Melbourne.

Dalton, T. (2009) Housing policy retrenchment: Australia and Canada compared, *Urban Studies*, 46 (91): 63–91.

Daly, M. (1988) The Australian city: Development in an open world, in R. Heathcote (ed.), *The Australian Experience: Essays in Australian Land Settlement and Resources Management*, Longman, Cheshire, Melbourne.

Danermark, B., Ekstrom, M., Jacobssen, L. and Karlssom, J.C. (1997/2002) *Explaining Society: Critical Realism in the Social Sciences*, Routledge, London.

Davidson, G. and Fincher, R. (1998) Urban studies in Australia: A road map and ways ahead, *Urban Policy and Research*, 16 (3): 183–197.

Davis, M. (1990) *City of Quartz*, Verso, London and New York.

Dickens, P., Duncan, S., Goodwin, M. and Gray, F. (1985) *Housing, States and Localities*, Methuen, London and New York.

Doling, J. (1997) *Comparative Housing Policy: Government and Housing in Advanced Industrialized Countries*, Macmillan, Basingstoke/St. Martin's Press, New York.

Doling, J. and Ford, J. (eds) (2003) *Globalisation and Home Ownership Part 1*, IOS Press, Amsterdam.

Donnison, D. and Stephens, M. (2003) The political economy of housing research. In: A. O'Sullivan and K. Gibb (eds.) *Housing Economics and Public Policy. Series: Real estate issues*, Blackwell Science, Oxford, pp. 248–267.

Dunford, M. (1990) Theories of regulation, *Environment Planning D: Soc. Space 8*: 297–322.

Elsinga, M., Haffner, M. and Van der Heijden, H. (2008) Threats to the Dutch unitary rental market, *European Journal of Housing Policy*, 8 (1): 21–37.

Esping-Anderson, G. (1990) *Three Worlds of Welfare Capitalism*, Polity Press, Cambridge.

Fincher, R. (1990) Women in the city, *Australian Geographical Studies* 28: 29–37.

Fincher, R. and Nieuwenhuysen, J. (eds) (1998) *Australian Poverty: Then and Now*, Melbourne University Press, Melbourne.

Fitzpatrick, S. (2002) A timely critique – with reservations, *Housing Theory and Society*, 19, (3–4): 137–138.

Fitzpatrick, S. (2005) Explaining homelessness: A critical realist perspective, *Housing, Theory & Society*, 22 (1): 1–17.

Florida, R. and Feldman, M. (1988) Housing in US Fordism, *International Journal of Urban and Regional Research*, 12: 187–210.

Fopp, R. (2008) From weak social constructionism to critical realism in housing theory – exploring issues, Paper presented to the Australian Housing Researchers Conference, RMIT, Melbourne.

Gertler, M.S. (1988) The limits to flexibility: Comments on the post-Fordist vision of production and its geography, *Trans. Inst. Br. Geogr. NS* 13: 419–432.

Gibson-Graham, J. (1996) *The End of Capitalism (As We Knew It): A Feminist Critique of Political Economy*, Blackwell Publishers, Oxford.

Giddens, A. (1984) *The Constitution of Society: Outline of the Theory of Structuration*, Polity Press, London.

Goodwin, M. (2001) Regulation as Process: Regulation Theory and Comparative Urban and Regional Research, In: *Netherlands Journal of Housing and the Built Environment*, 16(1).

Gregory, D. and Urry, J. (1985) *Social Relations and Spatial Structures, Critical Human Geography*, Macmillan, London.

Hall, P. and Soskice, D. (2001) *Varieties of Capitalism: The Institutional Foundations of Comparative Advantage*, Oxford University Press, Oxford

Harloe, M. (1995) *The People's Home: Social Rented Housing in Europe and America*, Blackwell, Oxford.

Harvey, D. (1973) *Social Justice and the City*, London, Edward Arnold.

Harvey, D. (1974) Class-monopoly rent, finance capital and the urban revolution, *Reg. Studies* 8: 239–255.

Harvey, D. (1982) *The Limits to Capital*, University of Chicago Press, Chicago.

Harvey, D. (2003) *The New Imperialism*, Oxford University Press, Oxford.

Harvey, D. and Scott, C. (1988) The practice of human geography: theory and empirical specificity in the transition from Fordism to flexible accumulation, in W. Macmillan (ed.), *Remodelling Geography*, Blackwell, Oxford, pp. 217–239.

Hayden, D. (1982) *The Grand Domestic Revolution: A History of Feminist Designs for American Houses, Neighbourhoods and Cities*, Cambridge, MA, MIT Press.

Hayward, D. (1992) Reconstructing a dream: An analysis of home ownership in Australia, unpublished PhD thesis, Department of Anthropology and Sociology, Monash University, Melbourne.

Heiden, van der N. and Terhorst, P. (2007) Varieties of glocalisation: the international economic strategies of Amsterdam, Manchester and Zurich compared, *Environment and Planning C: Government and Policy*, 25: 341–356.

Hoekstra, J. (2003) Housing and the welfare state in the Netherlands: An application of Esping-Anderson's typology, *Housing Theory and Society*, 20: 58–71.

Hoekstra, J. (2005) Is there a connection between welfare state regime and dwellings type? An exploratory statistical analysis, *Housing Studies*, 20 (3): 475–495.

Jacobs, K., Kemeny, J. and Manzi, T. (eds) (2004) *Social Constructionism in Housing Research*, Ashgate, Aldershot.

Jessop, B. (1990) *State Theory: Putting Capitalist States in their Place*, Polity Press, Cambridge.

Jessop, B. (1997) A neo-Gramscian approach to the regulation of urban regimes: Accumulation strategies, hegemonic projects and governance, in: M. Lauria (ed.), *Reconstructing Urban Regime Theory: Regulating Urban Politics in a Global Economy*, Sage, Thousand Oaks, CA.

Jessop, B. (2007) *State Power: Strategic–Relational Approach*, Polity Press, London.

Kemeny, J. (1992) *Housing and Social Theory*, Routledge, London.

Kemeny, J. (1995) *From Public Housing to Social Renting: Rental Policy Strategies in Comparative Perspective*, Routledge, London.

Kemeny, J., Kersloot, J. and Thalmann, P. (2005) Non-profit housing influencing, leading and dominating the unitary rental market: Three case studies, *Housing Studies*, 20 (6): 855–872.

King, R. (1986) Housing policy, planning practice, in J.B. McLoughlin and M. Huxley (eds), *Urban Planning in Australia: Critical Readings*, Longman and Cheshire, Melbourne.

Kleinman, M. (1996) *Housing, Welfare and the State in Europe: Comparative Analysis of Britain, France and Germany*, Edward Edgar, Cheltenham.

Lambert, J., Paris, C. and Blackaby, B. (1978) *Housing policy and the state : allocation, access, and control*, Macmillan Press, London

Lawrence, R.J. (1989) Structuralist theories in environment-behavior-design research: Applications for analyses of people and the built environment. In E. Zube & G. Moore (eds.) *Advances in Environment, Behavior and Design*, volume 2, pp. 37–70. Plenum Press, New York.

Lawson, J. (2001) Comparing the causal mechanisms underlying housing networks over time and space, *Housing and the Built Environment*, 16(1) 29–52.

Lawson, J. (2002) Thin rationality, weak social constructionism and critical realism: The way forward in housing theory?' *Housing, Theory and Society*, 19: 142–144.

Lawson, J. (2006) *Critical Realism and Housing Research*, Routledge, London and New York.

Lawson, J. (2008) Transformation in and challenges to the Korean housing solution, *Journal of Asian Public Policy*, 1 (3): 313–327.

Lawson , J. (2009) The transformation of social housing provision in Switzerland mediated by federalism, direct democracy and the urban/rural divide, *European Journal of Housing Policy*, 9 (1): 45–67.

Lawson, J. (2010) Path dependency and emergent relations: explaining the different role of limited profit housing in the dynamic urban regimes of Vienna and Zurich, *Housing Theory and Society*, 26 (3): 204–220.

Lawson, J., Haffner, M. and Oxley, M. (2009) Comparative housing research in the new millennium: Methodological and theoretical contributions from the first decade, presentation to Australasian Housing Research and APNHR Conference Sydney August 5–7.

Lawson, J. and Nieboer, N. (2009) The regulation of social housing outcomes: a micro examination of Dutch and Austrian social landlords since financing reforms, Presented to ENHR Conference, Changing Housing Markets: Integration and Segmentation, 1–22, Prague.

Lee, J.K. (2002) *Comparing Asian housing systems: Implications on the link between housing and social welfare*, The Symposium on Social Development in East Asia, School of Social Welfare, University of California, Berkeley, CA, 11–14 December.

Mahoney, J. and Rueschemeyer, D. (eds) (2003) *Comparative Historical Analysis in the Social Sciences*, Cambridge University Press, Cambridge.

Malpass, P. (2008) Histories of social housing: a comparative approach, in K. Scanlon and C. Whitehead, *Social Housing in Europe II*, LSE, London, pp 15–30.

Manzi, T. (2002) Constructionism, realism and housing theory, *Housing, Theory and Society*, 19: 144–145.

Marcuse, P. (1986) Housing policy and the myth of the benevolent state, in R. Bratt, C. Hartman and A. Meyerson (eds), *Critical Perspectives on Housing*, Temple Press, PA.

Massey, D. (1978) Capital and locational change: The UK electrical engineering and electronics industries, *Review of Radical Political Economics*, 10, (3): 39–54.

Matznetter, W. (2002) Social housing policy in a conservative welfare state: Austria as an example, *Urban Studies*, 39 (2): 265–282.

Matznetter, W. (2006) Quo vadis, comparative housing research? Paper presented to ENHR conference Housing in an expanding Europe, Ljubljana, 2–5 July.

Mullins, P. (1981) Theoretical perspectives in Australian urbanisation: material components in the reproduction of Australian labour power, *Australian and New Zealand Journal of Sociology*, 1 (1 and 3).

Paris, C. (1993) *Housing Australia*, Macmillan, Melbourne.

Randolph, B. (1991) Housing markets, labour markets and discontinuity theory, in: J. Allen and C. Hamnett (eds), *Housing and Labour Markets: Building the Connections*, Unwin Hyman, London, pp. 16–51.

Sandercock, L. and Berry, M. (1983) *Urban Political Economy: the Australian Case*, George Allen and Unwin, Sydney.

Sassen, S. (2001) *The Global City: New York, London, Tokyo*, Princeton University Press, Princeton, NJ.

Sassen, S. (2009) When local housing becomes an electronic instrument: The global circulation of mortgages – a research note, *International Journal of Urban and Regional Research*, 33 (2): 411–426.

Saugeres, L. (1999) The social construction of housing management discourse: Objectivity, rationality and everyday practice, *Housing Theory and Society*, 16 (3): 93–105.

Sayer, A. (1989) Post-Fordism in question, International *Journal of Urban and Regional Research*, 13: 666–695.

Sayer, A. (2000) *Realism and Social Science*, Sage, London.

Scanlon, K. and Whitehead, C. (2008) *Social Housing in Europe II*, LSE, London

Schoenberger, E. (1989) Thinking about flexibility: a response to Gertler, *Transactions of the Institute of British Geographers. NS* 14: 98–108.

Schröder, M. (2008) Integrating welfare and production typologies: How refinements of the varieties of capitalism approach calls for a combination of welfare typologies, *Journal of Social Policy*, 38(1): 19–43.

Smart, A. (2003) Housing and regulation theory: Domestic demand and global financialization, with J. Lee, in R. Forrest and & J. Lee (eds), *Housing and Social Change: East West Perspectives*, Routledge, London, pp. 87–107.

Soja, E. (1989) *Postmodern Geographies*, Verso, London.

Somerville, P. (1994) On explanation of housing policy, *Scandinavian Housing and Planning Research*, 11: 211–230.

Somerville, P. (2000) *Social Relations and Social Exclusion: Rethinking Political Economy*, Routledge, London.

Somerville, P. and Bengtsson, B. (2002) Constructionism, realism and housing theory, *Housing, Theory and Society*, 19: 121–136.

Swyngedouw, E. (2004) *Social Power and the Urbanization of Water – Flows of Power*, Oxford University Press, Oxford.

Terhorst, P. (2008) Comments to the author in response to Lawson (2009) 30 December.

Terhorst, P. and J Van de Ven, J. (1997) Fragmented Brussels and Consolidated Amsterdam: A Comparative Study of the Spatial Organisation of Property Rights, *Nederlandse Geografische Studies*, University of Amsterdam, Amsterdam.

Urry, J. (1986) Locality research: the case of Lancaster, *Reg. Studies* 20: 233–242.

Wainwright, T. (2009) Laying the foundations of the crises: Mapping the historico-geographical construction of residential mortgage backed securitization in the UK, *International Journal of Urban and Regional Research*, 33 (2): 372–388.

Watson, S. (1988) *Accommodating Inequality: Gender and Housing*, Allen & Unwin, Sydney.

Watson, S. (1991) The restructuring of work and home: Productive and reproductive relations, in J. Allen and C. Hamnett (eds), *Housing and Labour Markets: Building the Connections*, Unwin Hyman, London.

Watson, S. and Gibson, K. (eds) (1995) *Post-Modern Cities and Spaces*, Blackwell, Cambridge.

Williams, P. (1984) The politics of property: Home ownership in Australia, in J. Halligan and C. Paris (eds), *Australian Urban Politics: Critical Perspectives*, Longman Cheshire, Melbourne.

Wyly, E.K., Moos, M., Kabahizi, E. and Hammel, D. (2009) Cartographies of race and class: Mapping the class-monopoly rents of American subprime mortgage capital, *International Journal of Urban and Regional Research* 33 (2): 332–354.

12

Housing Politics and Political Science

Bo Bengtsson

INTRODUCTION

It has often been claimed that the academic field of housing studies is dominated by a *policy perspective*, i.e. an ambition to make relevant and useful contributions to political, administrative and professional decision-making (see Clapham, in this volume). More seldom, researchers in the field employ a *politics perspective*, analysing the political institutions of relevance to housing provision and the games and processes of decision-making per se.

This chapter takes a politics perspective and reviews research on housing that focuses political institutions (state and non-state) and processes of interaction between political elite actors as well as between elite actors and citizens in general. The argument is related to three societal levels: national housing systems; local urban governance; and estate management and resident participation. The main emphasis is on the national level. The review encompasses work by political scientists as well as by researchers from other disciplines. The focus on *housing politics* means that both research on the macro-social prerequisites of political power and on the concrete substantial outcome of political decision-making are left out.[1]

The outline of the chapter is as follows. In the next section the modest position of political science in the field of housing studies is discussed, together with some possible explanations to this deficit. This is followed by a short conceptual discussion on housing policy and housing politics, leading up to the outline of a more elaborate political perspective on housing provision. On the basis of previous research it is claimed that the specific policy theory of housing provision prescribes central roles to markets and informal networks. The review of empirical research, which is the main part of the chapter, builds on this theoretical background and consists of two sections: the first focusing research on the national level, and the second highlighting some research on the more local levels of region, city, neighbourhood and individual estate. The concluding section sums up the argument, evaluates the potential of various approaches and points out some promising lines of development.

THE POLICY ORIENTATION OF HOUSING STUDIES AND THE MODEST ROLE OF POLITICAL SCIENCE

Political science is about policy and politics. Since housing research, according to many observers, is (too) policy-oriented (e.g. Kemeny 1992, Bengtsson & Kemeny 1995, Kemeny 1999, Allen 2005; cf. Allen & Gurney 1997), one might perhaps expect a rich body of political research on housing. However, somewhat paradoxically, the discipline of political science has a rather modest position in the field, both when it comes to empirical contributions and theoretical influence. Few researchers with a background in political science are active in the housing studies community, and the discipline has not left many traces in the scientific housing discourse.[2] When studies of housing policy, or indeed of politics, power and governance in housing, are carried out, this is mainly done by scholars from other disciplines, e.g. economics, geography and, in particular, sociology.

The limited role of political science in the field has been verified quantitatively by a search of articles in the four leading European multidisciplinary housing journals, *European Journal of Housing Policy*, *Housing Studies*, *Housing, Theory and Society* and *Journal of Housing and the Built Environment*. Political science is far less visible in these journals than the disciplines of economics, geography and sociology (Bengtsson 2009b).

None of the more obvious explanations to this deficit seem to be valid. The central concepts of political science ('power', 'democracy', 'citizenship', 'social justice', etc.) are definitely of relevance to housing, and housing issues are still generally considered to be of political interest. A more plausible explanation is based on the historical traditions of political science – its macro orientation and its emphasis on analysing the state, while housing policy is mainly implemented on micro levels and through non-state institutions (cf. below). It is true that modern political science, with its interest in informal institutions, networks and governance, does not overlook such broad societal perspectives. However, academic inertia and path dependence may also be part of the explanation, affecting negatively the status within the political science community of micro-level and non-statist studies. More important, and perhaps related to this, the economic incentives and the institutional support for doing housing research seem to be weaker in political science than in other disciplines, again, somewhat paradoxically, due to the policy orientation in the field (Bengtsson 2009b).[3]

Due to these findings, the main point of departure of this chapter is not the discipline of political science, but the subject of *housing politics*. There is no consensus about how to define the general concept of *politics*. What is needed here is, however, not a precise but a broad definition that generally corresponds to the prevailing understanding of the concept within political science, and at the same time makes a clear distinction to *policy*.[4] I claim that these two criteria are met by the following definition, which will be used in the chapter:

> Politics concerns the processes by which groups of actors make binding decisions, in particular in relation to governments. Such processes involve authority, power and co-operation, and include the enforcing of goals and interests, and the settling of conflicts, both in designing political institutions and in formulating and applying policy.

This definition also gives an indication of what could be meant by 'housing politics' – in contrast to 'housing policy'. It focuses on process, action and interaction rather than outcome, on the formulation and application of policy rather than on substantial contents. Moreover, the definition features power and, though it highlights government, it also includes non-state institutions. Most important, it emphasises the games between political actors, and the institutional rules and outcomes of these games, rather than the substantial outcome of political decision-making. While *housing policy* is about housing-related decision-making, its substance and outcome, *housing politics*, is about conflict and cooperation between actors with interests in housing provision and about the effects of such interaction in terms of policy, implementation, institutions, power and legitimacy.[5]

The chapter reviews theoretical and empirical research on housing politics on the 'macro', 'meso' and 'micro' levels, corresponding to politics of national housing provision, local governance and planning and direct supply of housing, respectively.[6] Following the tradition of political science the emphasis is on the national level, though some interesting studies of housing politics on the meso and micro levels will also be discussed.

One obvious speciality of political science, tentatively the theoretical core of the discipline, can be summarised in the slogan 'taking elite actors seriously'. The action and interaction of individual and collective elite actors and the effects on policy and institutions are often in focus and problematised in political science research, typically based on some implicit assumption of bounded (Simon 1957) or thin rationality (Elster 1983).[7] Paraphrasing Mills (1959) about the 'sociological imagination', the open-ended analysis of political action and interaction, based on ideology, self-interest and social norms, may be where the *politological imagination* is at its best and can give its richest contributions.[8]

Such approaches often imply an interest in *middle-range theorizing* (Merton 1957) and in more or less rationalistic or intentional *social mechanisms* (Elster 1989, Hedström & Swedberg 1998, cf. Coleman 1990). In some of the classics of political science and political sociology, perspectives like these have been fruitfully used to discuss, among other things, political and social dilemmas (Ostrom 1991), actor-based versions of 'power over' (Lukes 1974), political opportunity structures (Tilly 1978), path dependence (Collier &

Collier 1991), welfare state development (Korpi 2001) and retrenchment (Pierson 1994).[9]

In political theory, concepts like power, democracy and citizenship are also typically related to actors and institutions, whereas sociologists more often tend to define them in terms of structures and discourses (again there is certainly no clear-cut line of demarcation).[10]

A POLITICAL PERSPECTIVE ON HOUSING PROVISION

What distinguishes the politics of housing provision from the politics of other welfare state sectors – and from welfare state politics in general? The discussion about the *policy theory of housing provision* may well be the scientific discourse where political science as a discipline has made its most distinct contribution to our understanding of housing policy and politics.[11]

The relation between type of policy and type of politics was discussed in the 1970s by the political scientists Theodore J. Lowi and James Q. Wilson. The general idea was that the specific characteristics of a certain policy field (i.e. the policy theory) should have an impact on the political process related to the sector. Lowi (1972) makes the distinction between policies which are regulative, redistributive, distributive and constituent, depending on the applicability and the likelihood of coercion. He relates each type of policy (and each mode of state coercion) to a distinctive process of political activity and interaction. Criticising Lowi's model, Wilson (1974) suggests another typology based on the distribution of (1) the benefits and (2) the costs of a policy. Both benefits and costs may either be concentrated to a few members of society or distributed among many, which would give four types of policy with different impacts on coalition building and power relations within a policy sector.

Lowi's and Wilson's models are both based on the distributive patterns of different policies, in economic and regulatory terms. The state is seen as a redistributing mechanism, which collects taxes from citizens and allocates public goods. For reasons examined below, however, it is difficult to apply such distributive welfare models to housing provision.[12] Instead, the corresponding academic discourse on housing has focused on the mode of implementation and not the outcome.[13] What make housing policy special are the well-known economic and social specificities of housing markets: on the 'supply side' the longevity and physical sluggishness of the housing stock (Stahl 1985, Arnott 1987), and on the 'demand side' the social importance of dwelling and the 'attachment costs' (Dynarski 1986) associated with a household's transfer from one dwelling in another area.

As explicated by Bengtsson (2001), the socially and politically dominant policy theory of housing provision as welfare state policy defines housing as being at the same time an individual market commodity and a public good demanding state involvement. This makes analogies with other welfare sectors, where state allocation is the main distributive mechanism, misleading. Since housing should, as far as possible, be distributed in accordance with individual consumer preferences, the politically defined 'needs' cannot be fulfilled by direct state allocation.[14] Instead, voluntary market contracts between buyer and seller or between landlord and tenant serve as the main mechanism for distributing housing, while state intervention typically has the form of *correctives*, defining the economic and institutional setting of those market contracts.[15]

Another Scandinavian political scientist who has discussed the specificity of housing policy and politics is Ulf Torgersen, who in a short seminal article describes housing as 'the wobbly pillar of the welfare state'. Other welfare sectors, e.g. pensions, schooling and health, have a number of common characteristics. Fairly clear standards have been extracted from the vague concept of need, standards that define when the institutions in charge are responsible to take action, and lack of conformity to those standards is subject to legal action from the prospective recipient. Those responsible for implementing the policies in other sectors are typically trained bodies of professionals, within a fairly unified institutional complex with well-defined borders, a certain esprit de corps and a national director. Even though some of those elements may sometimes be discerned in housing provision as well, what is striking is the contrast in these respects between housing and other welfare sectors (Torgersen 1987, pp. 116–118).

These deviations in how housing policy is implemented are all expressions of the policy theory of market correctives. In such a policy theory the politically defined 'needs' of housing must include manifest or latent individual consumer preferences as an important ingredient, which means that a formal and bureaucratic mode of implementation would represent too strong an intrusion on consumer sovereignty.[16]

The specificities of housing provision as a policy field have theoretically important implications for *politics* on different levels.[17] On the *macro level*, the policy theory of market correctives means that political decisions on tenure forms and other types of market regulations are crucial. Such decisions may concern market regulations constraining the bargaining room for seller and buyer, or economic support to certain types and forms of housing by means of subsidisation, financial security or tax relief. The dominant policy theory says it is not for the state to decide how citizens should be housed, but it may be for the state to set up guarantees that citizens have a real opportunity to find decent housing in the market at a reasonable cost.

This is why *housing tenures* should be seen as the most important political institutions of housing provision as welfare state policy. Forms of tenure are vital to housing policy and implementation at all levels because they define the formal position of residents in their capacities as owners, co-owners and users of their dwellings, and thus set up the rules of the games between actors in the housing market. 'Housing tenures are institutions, sets of practices and rules that regulate a particular field of human action and interaction' (Ruonavaara 2005, p. 214).[18] Thus, tenure forms, defined widely and including how housing estate ownership is organised, are crucial both to housing policy and politics. Housing (tenure) policy on the macro level defines housing politics on lower levels – and, through institutionalisation, on the macro level as well.[19]

In the traditional ideal-type form of state allocation of public goods the *meso level* consists of national, regional or local state agencies in charge of the distribution, or responsible for organising, financing, recruiting and supervising the administrative activities on the micro level. Agencies on the meso level provide the link between political decisions and the ultimate provision to citizens, typically by interpreting, translating and implementing policies and evaluating results. Meso-level politics often has to do with games and institutions of steering, implementation and evaluation or with power relations and power games between different administrative levels, e.g. between central and local government.

In housing provision the meso level is more difficult to define since it consists not only, and not primarily, of public bodies:[20] rather, it consists of several, formally independent, though in practice interdependent, actors and institutions: local authorities, contractors, housing companies, non-governmental organisations (NGOs), etc. Furthermore, and again due to the specific policy theory of market correctives, the main political instrument on the meso level is not direct allocation to citizens, but physical, economic and social *planning*, aiming at securing, among other things, that citizens' housing needs are fulfilled in the longer term. In this context, housing is only one element of urban politics – though undeniably an important one. As a consequence, the meso level of housing provision is typically organised in planning networks where broader issues than just housing needs are negotiated.[21]

The political *micro level* in general is where citizens ultimately acquire the public good. Here, political scientists often study the meeting between citizens and 'street-level bureaucrats' and professionals, be they teachers, police officers or social workers. In practice these civil servants often have considerable discretion in the delivery of services, so they are not only neutral implementers but also exercisers of political power (cf. Lipsky 1980). In housing provision, in contrast, this final delivery is normally not executed by state (or state-regulated) officials, but by market actors following a completely different logic of implementation. In owner-occupation this is typically a one-time transaction – though of long-lasting importance. In the rental sector the relation is more permanent, and the 'street-level bureaucrat' of housing policy is the public or private landlord. Here things are complicated by the landlord's potential market power over tenants due to Dynarski's attachment costs.[22]

Thus, the deviant policy theory of housing provision has important implications for the scientific analysis of housing politics on the macro, meso and micro levels. We now turn to some examples of such analysis.[23]

STUDIES OF HOUSING POLITICS ON THE MACRO LEVEL

The dominance of policy perspectives

There is a rich, almost abundant literature about *housing policy* on the national level, both comparative and single-country studies. Even though the policy theory of market correctives is seldom highlighted, tenure policy, in the wide meaning discussed above, regularly has a central position in the accounts and analyses – which corroborates

Bengtsson's and Torgersen's theses about the distributive logic of housing provision.

One category of comparative studies contrasts 'housing systems', 'housing regimes' or 'structures of housing provision'[24] (see Chapter 18). Other studies compare policies directed towards specific tenures: private renting (e.g. Harloe 1985, Danermark & Elander, eds, 1994), social rented housing (e.g. Clapham & English, eds, 1987, Emms 1990, Harloe 1995), and sometimes both rental sectors together (e.g. Kemeny 1995, Oxley & Smith 1996). There are also several comparative studies of homeownership (e.g. Kemeny 1981, Kurz & Blossfeld 2004), at least one about cooperative housing (Andrusz 1999) and one about conversions from rental tenure to homeownership (Lundqvist 1986). Most work in this genre has a focus on policy and only considers politics in brief, without theorising.[25]

Numerous studies investigate the housing regime and housing policies of one single country: in the English language mainly on the UK, the USA, and to some extent other English-speaking countries.[26] There is also a large stock of evaluations of specific policy instruments (rent regulation, planning, mortgage systems, housing allowances, etc.) or housing reforms, mainly those launched by British governments. The UK bias is not surprising and mirrors both the strong British housing studies community and the general dominance of the English language in social science publication. In particular, the housing privatisation reforms initiated by the Thatcher governments in the 1980s have left deep traces in the international housing literature.[27]

Both the comparative and the single-country studies are often descriptive in their nature. Typically they describe the historical development of housing, the main institutions in terms of tenure forms, systems of finance, land and estate regulation, the characteristics of the existing stock and the recent production. If power and politics are discussed it is often in a narrative mode rather than in universal terms. The perspective may be macro-sociological and related to social or discursive structures, or microeconomic and related to outcomes on the housing market in terms of efficiency or distribution. Sometimes these studies are, overtly or covertly, critical to current government policies, often on rather obscure normative grounds.[28]

In a critical review of comparative housing research Kemeny and Lowe (1998) make a distinction between 'juxtapositional', 'convergence thesis' and 'divergence thesis' studies.[29] Using instead their alternative terms ('particularistic', 'universalistic' and 'middle-range' approaches), a similar categorisation can be applied to single-country studies as well. Undoubtedly, most studies of housing policy are of the particularistic type, i.e. detailed descriptions of a kind criticized already by Oxley (1991, p. 67). Kemeny and Lowe make the important point (pp. 163–164) that there is actually an unexplicated theoretical perspective informing this type of analysis, one of central governments having important formative influence, almost a capacity to pick and choose between different housing systems. The other side of this implicit government omnipotence is, of course, that the institutional context is disregarded – and that actors other than government and political parties also tend to be ignored. This also makes such studies less interesting in terms of housing *politics*.

Case studies and comparative studies of housing policy are often based on some theory, used as a taxonomy or a conceptual framework to organise the presentation and make comparison possible. Several studies have been based on Esping-Andersen's three models of welfare regimes: liberal, corporatist and social democratic (Esping-Andersen 1990; e.g. Balchin 1996 and, more ambitiously, Barlow & Duncan 1994 who also include 'rudimentary welfare states'; cf. also Hulse 2003, Hoekstra 2003, 2005 and Stamsø 2009).[30] Other, more housing-specific, theories that have been used as basis for comparison are Ball's concept of 'structure of housing provision' (Ball 1986, Ball, Harloe & Martens 1988, van der Heijden 2002;

cf. Lundqvist 1992), and Kemeny's distinction between unitary and dualistic rental markets (Kemeny 1993, 1995, 2006, Balchin 1996 and van der Heijden 2002).[31]

The importance of middle-range theorising

The descriptive application of theory as taxonomies may indeed be a fruitful approach to interpreting and comparing *housing policy* – e.g. it is open for conclusions in terms of convergence and divergence. In contrast, the scientific study of *housing politics*, in the meaning used in this chapter, is typically middle range in its nature.

In the grand universalistic social theories, political actors and institutions at the most serve as ripples on the surface of the structural waves of convergence. On the other hand, we may learn a lot about political actors and institutions in particularistic and juxtapositional texts on housing policy and housing systems, not least in the descriptions and analyses of historical backgrounds.[32] However, what we get is often non-theoretical narratives about what policies specific governments, commissions, parties and political leaders have supported. And the institutions described (not seldom in detail) are often rather myopically presented in terms of formal organisation, official functions, etc., and without the theoretical relief necessary to draw any general conclusions.

In contrast, the challenge to academic students of housing politics is to analyse political actors, institutions and discourses in general terms by replacing their specific 'proper names' and specific characteristics with theoretical concepts and perspectives that allow some form of generalisation beyond the empirical cases studied. In the tradition of middle-range theorising, the aim should be to identify and analyse logics, patterns and mechanisms in one empirical context that may also be recognisable in other similar contexts. This would make it possible to combine open-endedness with an ambition to generalise beyond the individual case without assuming actors to be neither what Garfinkel dubbed 'cultural dopes' (Garfinkel 1967), nor utility-maximising – and also fully predictable – 'rational dopes'.[33]

Studies of housing politics and policy

Headey (1978) is an early work that relates differences in housing policy to politics and ideology in a comparison between Sweden, Britain and the USA. Headey tries to go beyond particularism by introducing a conceptual framework based on the incentives of housing sector actors and the 'political and operational feasibility' of sequences of policy development. This is definitely an example of middle-range theorising on housing politics. Still, the empirical analysis is rather voluntaristic and, as pointed out by Marcuse (1982) in a review article, the application of the framework does not add much to the historical account but rather makes it more superficial.

Gustavsson (1980a) investigates the coalitions and conflicts leading up to the formative political decisions on Swedish housing policy in 1974. Though his empirical evidence on the actor level is surprisingly thin, Gustavsson's analysis can still serve as an illustration of how this type of rationalistic reconstruction of policy alternatives, preferences and strategies on elite level could be carried out in the specific context of housing provision.

Along similar lines, another Swedish political scientist, Lundqvist (1992), carries out an empirically more ambitious exploration of elite politics and housing policy in a comparison of housing and privatisation in four European countries. He applies a perspective of policy networks and power resources in an analysis of the positions and actions taken by political parties in relation to welfare state retrenchment in the housing sector. Backed by empirical data, this frame of reference proves to give a plausible interpretation of the course of events and outcomes in the cases studied, in particular the continued economic support to mortgaged owner-occupation even in a period of general financial cutbacks.

Studies of housing politics and institutions

The three studies discussed above mainly explore the impact of politics on *policy*. Other investigations focus on the relation between politics and *institutions*.[34] The early and exemplary comparison between housing provision in Britain and Sweden by Dickens et al. (1985) is actually a two-level analysis on the national as well as – in the case of Britain – the local level.[35] Differences in the relation between capital, labour and land ownership are seen as crucial to understanding the variability over time and between the two countries, whereas local differences are found to be the result of varying economic and political strategies within these general institutional conditions (Dickens et al., 1985, pp. 242–244). Notwithstanding this 'open-ended Marxian' framing, the case studies on both levels identify patterns of interaction between elite and mass actors that should be of relevance to the analysis of housing politics regardless of institutional differences over time and place.[36]

Harloe's book on social rented housing (Harloe 1995) is probably the most comprehensive individual contribution to comparative housing. Applying the general concept of 'structure of housing provision', Harloe investigates the historical development of social rented housing in six countries in the 20th century. The study is organised in five historical phases and is based to a large extent on secondary sources. Despite the number of cases and the long time period covered, the empirical analysis is both broad and deep, and it encompasses both politics and policy, and social structures as well as political actors and institutions. Though Harloe's theoretical model emphasises agents and power, only a subordinate role is conceded to actors and interaction in the housing arena. The main strength of the book is how the development of social housing in each country is placed in the context of the general social and political evolution in each country. Harloe's conclusions are more structural than political, drawing out universal lines of development related to political economy (cf. discussion in Kemeny & Lowe 1998, pp. 167–168). Nevertheless, his rich material would also lend itself to a more actor-oriented and open-ended discussion of housing politics and institutional design of social housing.

Kemeny (1995), analysing national rental systems, makes a distinction between an 'Anglo-Saxon' dualist rental market with a residual public rental sector, and a 'European' unitary model based on the integration of profit and non-profit renting systems. Both actors and institutions are in focus in Kemeny's case studies, and the development of the different market systems is seen as a result of an interaction between political actors, state and market institutions, economic development and housing discourse. Kemeny himself describes his approach in this study as 'policy constructivism', which appears to have some similarity to an actor-based analysis of housing politics (cf. Somerville & Bengtsson 2002 and response by Kemeny 2002).

Studies of housing corporatism

Corporatism is a theoretical perspective which highlights actors, bargaining and institutions in a manner that represents a challenge to the politological imagination. A corporatist political system is characterised by close and stable ties between some privileged organisational actors and the state (see Schmitter 1974 and Williamson 1989 for formal definitions). Corporatist analysis should be of particular relevance to housing, with its dominant policy theory of state correctives to the market.[37] In the 1980s a number of studies were published that applied theories of corporatism to housing provision (e.g. Flynn 1986, Heclo & Madsen 1987, Boddy 1989 and the theoretically and empirically sophisticated article Lundqvist 1988; cf. also Saunders 1986, Schmidt 1989).

The general literature on corporatism often investigates the tripartite relation between state, capital and labour (or in empirical research, government, business organisations and labour unions). In housing politics, with its orientation towards consumption, other organised interests may also acquire corporatist relations to the state, e.g. housing companies, building worker unions and mortgage lenders (Clapham, Kemp & Smith 1990, pp. 10–13, Doling 1997, pp. 71–72). In the Scandinavian countries, with their well-organised residents, even consumer organisations have been granted a bargaining position regarding housing policy with clear corporatist elements, in Sweden represented by the National Union of Tenants and in Denmark by the National Federation of Non-Profit Housing Associations.[38] This, still surviving, consumer-oriented housing corporatism has recently been examined in a perspective of path dependence (Bengtsson 2004, Jensen 2006; cf. also below under Historical institutionalism).[39]

With these Scandinavian exceptions, studies of housing and corporatism have been fewer in the recent period of privatisation and marketisation. However, with the growing impact of European Union (EU) institutions on housing provision and policies and the growth of internationally active NGOs we may be witnessing a revival of corporatist perspectives – although this time at the European level (cf. Elsinga, Haffner & van der Heijden 2008, Ghékière 2008, Gruis & Priemus 2008).

Historical institutionalism and housing politics

Theories of *historical institutionalism* and *path dependence* appear to be fruitful for studying the interplay between political action and institutional conditions in housing.[40] The typical case of path dependence in a perspective of politics is where actors more or less deliberately design institutions at point A, institutions which at later point B serve as restraints to political decision-making, and thus make some policy alternatives impossible or implausible.[41] The mechanisms of path dependence may be summarised as efficiency, legitimacy and power, implicating that events at point A would make some alternatives appear to be either more efficient, more legitimate or more powerful at point B (North 1990, Hall & Taylor 1996, p. 945, Thelen 1999, pp. 394–396, Pierson 2000).[42]

Perspectives of historical institutionalism are not new in housing studies.[43] An early application of path dependence is Kleinman (1996), who compares the development of housing provision in Britain, France and Germany from the mid-1970s. In all three countries he identifies a 'bifurcation', which has led to different policies regarding the middle mass of households and the impoverished minority. However, the economic, political and social forces of change in all three countries are mediated through very different institutions and political structures, which leaves profound marks on both the policy and its implementation (Kleinman 1996, pp. 180–181).

Lowe (2004, chap. 6) chooses a more politics-oriented approach to path dependence when he analyses the sometimes dramatic historical development of the British housing tenure structure. His key questions are why the country, by the end of the 20th century, became a nation of owner-occupiers, why it has developed such a large state rental sector, largely owned by local councils, and what happened to the 19th century private landlordism. Lowe identifies some critical junctures and highlights in particular the impact of the two world wars. Although modest in size, the study is a good example of how the politological imagination can contribute to our understanding of housing history.[44]

A more comprehensive attempt is Bengtsson et al. (2006), who compare the development of the – surprisingly different – housing regimes of five Nordic countries in a perspective of path dependence.[45] In the formative period of the Nordic housing regimes, between the turn of the century 1900 and the Second World War, different solutions were chosen in each country in order to deal with the specific housing problems that occurred at different points of time. When more comprehensive programmes of housing policy were introduced after the Second World War, it was often seen as efficient (or even taken for granted) by political actors that the already existing, if still undeveloped, organisations and institutions should be utilized to implement the new programmes. With the massive production of new housing between 1950 and 1980, the respective national housing regimes were successively consolidated and institutionalised.

In a historical comparison between housing in Australia and the Netherlands, Lawson (2006) applies a perspective of path dependence and relates it to a consistent ontology and epistemology of critical realism. Her two cases represent divergent housing trajectories, one dominated by sprawling homeownership, the other with social rental housing playing a significant role. Unlike Bengtsson et al. 2006, who compare tenure policy and politics, Lawson focuses on the historical and spatial definition of property rights, saving and investment, and on labour and welfare relations (Lawson 2006, pp. 2–3). Her geohistorical approach, however, gives only limited room to the role of politics.[46]

Path dependence is often contrasted to retrenchment. Lindbom analyses interestingly how the radical state budget cuts of the 1990s in Swedish housing policy could be carried out with very little resistance. He explains the 'successful' retrenchment by the difficulty for political actors as well as the general public to observe financial cuts in a policy area that is so complex and non-transparent (Lindbom 2001, pp. 520–521). This complexity and unclear political responsibility is another important aspect of the policy theory of state correctives to the market.

STUDIES OF HOUSING POLITICS ON THE MICRO AND MESO LEVELS

This section will comment on some studies of housing politics on lower levels, both the micro 'street level', where citizens/consumers meet public, private and semi-private providers of housing, and the meso 'community level', which represents the link between national housing policy and final outcomes in terms of individual and collective housing consumption. As already discussed, with reference to Torgersen (1987) and Bengtsson (2001), the dominant policy theory of state correctives to the market means that the implementation of housing provision differs from that of other sectors. Summarised briefly, citizens as residents are not welfare clients with formal rights as they are in the roles of, for example, school pupils (and their parents), hospital patients, pensioners or recipients of social care.

The British exception

To some extent Britain represents an exception to this, which should be kept in mind considering the strong position of British perspectives in housing research. Here the management of social rented housing has been entrusted to local authorities as a direct responsibility. In other countries the corresponding functions were carried out largely by other agencies, with only arms-length municipal influence (cf. Emms 1990, pp. 2–4). There are a number of interesting investigations of housing bureaucracies (e.g. Houlihan 1988) and in particular housing management in Britain (e.g. Clapham 1997, Somerville & Steele 1999, Franklin 2000, Clapham, Franklin & Saugères 2000).[47]

They all cover problems associated with the fair implementation of state allocation of a welfare state utility, but are not readily translated to a context of implementation by voluntary market contracts.

This deviation can be related to Kemeny's distinction between the Anglo-Saxon 'command economy' dualist rental system and the continental model of unitary rental markets (Kemeny 1995). However, other dualist rental systems tend to have only a minor means-tested rental sector with a more definite residual role than the British, which should make issues about housing bureaucracy and allocation less prominent. Lately, with the ongoing residualisation of council housing and the expansion of housing associations in Britain, the institutional conditions of housing politics may be converging towards other European countries.[48] According to Power (1993, p. 9), this will also make the European housing history of single-purpose independent landlords more relevant to Britain than it has been. One example of such converging interests may be the relatively young discourse on *hybrid organisations* in housing, i.e. organisations with both economic and non-economic goals (e.g. Priemus 2003, Mullins & Walker 2009; cf. Powell 1987).

In principle a clear distinction can be made between the micro level of direct provision where tenants meet management on markets and pseudo-markets and the meso level where the conditions of future implementation on the micro level are planned and negotiated. The political practice, however, is often more fluid, and some actors and institutions have an impact on both levels. The following discussion will move from the micro level towards the meso level.[49]

Tenant participation, citizenship and urban movements

Arguably the most important micro-level issue of housing politics has to do with power and collective action on the individual estate: i.e. questions related to tenant participation and other forms of local cooperation. Such questions can be analysed in terms of local resident politics.[50] In their broad empirical study from the late 1980s and early 1990s, Cairncross, Clapham and Goodlad identify three different models of participation: traditionalism, consumerism and citizenship. The relation between the three models is described as a 'battle of ideas', so the approach is primarily constructionist. However, the 'political' interaction between tenants, housing managers, councillors and tenants' associations is also analysed and related to the institutional arrangements of participation. The authors discuss their findings with reference to Clegg (1989) and his concept of 'circuits of power', where resources (including legitimacy), tactics and rules of the game are key elements (Cairncross, Clapham & Goodlad 1997).

Cairncross, Clapham and Goodlad relate their analysis of tenant participation to theories about *citizenship*, and so does Jensen (1995) in her study of Danish social housing. This social, ultimately normative, understanding of citizenship has also been taken as a point of departure in housing studies on other levels, often related to Marshall's ideas about civil, political and social rights (Marshall 1950). For example, a perspective of citizenship has been applied to issues about universal and selective national housing regimes (Bengtsson 2001), urban governance (García 2006), tenure security and homelessness (Mullen et al. 1999), the inclusion of ethnic minorities in housing markets (Bowes, Dar & Sim 2000) and post-apartheid ethnic segregation (Lalloo 1998).

Bengtsson (2000) reanalyses earlier Swedish studies on collective action in housing estates, applying a model of a potentially virtuous 'cooperative circle' moving from norms of cooperation via actual participation and local power resources to collective influence and then back to norms of cooperation. For cooperation to be successful and sustainable, tenants must have some real collective influence on the conditions in their estate, and at least some of the tenants must also be moved by some social norm of cooperation. An analysis based on thin rationality indicates that the crucial mechanism underlying local institutionalisation may be a norm of local utilitarianism ('I take part if it is needed and if I can contribute to the collective good in my estate'). In some estates, where residents share higher and more demanding ambitions of cooperation, more contract-like norms of reciprocity ('If others cooperate, why shouldn't I?') also play an important role. 'Reproductive activities', such as information to tenants, study courses and common leisure activities, are crucial in defining an estate as an arena where tenants do things together.

These studies focus on actors and institutions, so it is plausible to say that they have a perspective of housing politics, though at a very local level. This brings to the fore the concept of *democracy*. The socio-geographic concentration of local resident organisations, and the fact that members residing in the same area share a broad common interest in a defined territory should make housing an empirical field well suited for the study of the social mechanisms of small-scale democratic interaction. Nevertheless the concept of democracy – essential to all political scientists – is surprisingly seldom used in housing studies on the micro level, not even to shed light on and evaluate evident phenomena of participatory and deliberative democracy like tenant participation and housing cooperatives.[51]

The formal contracts and the continuous social interaction between the owner of an estate and its residents provide institutionalised rules of the game in a specific local housing area, which makes it plausible to define a local 'demos'. However, collective action, cooperation and conflict over local politics and housing are not always confined to formal boundaries. The study of urban protest and *urban social movements*, inspired by Castells (1977, 1983), embraces both the micro and meso levels. Grayson (1997) discusses social movements in Britain with a special focus on housing, and Cooper and Hawtin (1997) outline a conceptual framework for analysing community involvement in housing. However, the theoretically and empirically most impressive demonstration of politological imagination in this genre may still be Michael Lipsky's case studies of rent strikes in New York City, and other forms of protest in American cities in the 1960s (Lipsky 1968, 1970). Lipsky's conclusions about the, typically limited, prospects of success, when groups with scarce resources go out in protest, point out a number of tangible and symbolic aspects, which should be of general relevance. One important strategy in such cases is to appeal to other actors with more political power; however, this dependency on the responsiveness of other groups tends to make actions vulnerable and short-lived.

Urban governance as meso-level housing politics

Moving up in scale takes us to the theme of urban planning and urban governance, where the political goals of housing policy are supposed to be implemented. This is certainly a vast field of practice and research, where political science overall has contributed more than in housing politics (see, e.g. the contributions in Judge, Stoker & Wolman 1995 and Davies & Imbroscio 2009). An approach confined to housing provision is not always fruitful in this broader context – though the early local studies by Dunleavy (1981) and Dickens et al. (1985) prove that a primary focus on housing may sometimes be.

More generally, at least one important aspect makes housing critical in urban governance and gives housing actors a special role in the games of planning and negotiation. In a perspective of democratic theory, the residents of an urban area are the closest we get to a local 'demos'. They are the citizens who are directly affected by the 'interdependent and autonomous' negotiations, networks and partnerships where political and professional stakeholders are involved.

Bearing this in mind, the relation – and possible tension – between local governance and democracy, which is an important subject in modern political science (e.g. Pierre 2000, Stoker 2000, Klijn & Skelcher 2007), is seldom explored in housing studies on the meso level. Some interesting, mainly theoretical, articles informed by empirical findings seem to represent the main exceptions (e.g. Somerville 1998, 2005, Burns 2000). Tenure policy on the national level has an impact here as well, since a 'demos' consisting of owner-occupants typically can be expected to have stronger veto power than rental tenants – provided that they can agree on goals and strategies, as in some NIMBY (not in my back yard) cases, where opposing groups of homeowners have succeeded in blocking the development of local infrastructure and care centres. (This is also an illustration of the links between housing provision and other aspects of urban politics.)

There is certainly no lack of sociological and geographical studies of poor and deprived housing estates.[52] However, the academic interest in the local games of politics in these contexts has been weaker.[53] One interesting example carried out with praiseworthy political imagination is Hertting's investigation of local governance networks in area renewal (Hertting 2003, 2007). He interprets network governance in urban renewal in thinly rationalistic terms as a 'battle of the sexes' game, where key actors have a preference for more cooperation, although they are repeatedly frustrated by both processes and outcome. Hertting's analysis clearly reveals how the network organisation of urban renewal offers a generous supply of social mechanisms of power, cooperation, conflict and negotiations, where the characteristics of local governance are more visible than in most other political contexts.

Concluding discussion

This chapter has discussed, and to some extent, evaluated empirical research on housing politics on different levels, together with some relevant conceptual contributions. This concluding section considers which approaches and lines of research are the most promising and how they could be further developed.

The *conceptual discourse* on the social and political definition of housing policy is one field where political scientists have made important contributions. This discourse would clearly stand to gain from a stronger empirical attachment. However, in recent years it has attracted less interest than it used to, despite the fact that housing policies and institutions have gone through considerable change in most countries. So far, it seems, this development has not made the policy theory of state correctives to the market obsolete; rather, the ideas of new public management (NPM) may have moved other policy fields closer to housing provision in this respect. The recent EU interventionism in the national systems of housing provision (see Ghékière 2008) also indicates that the socio-political construction of housing policy may indeed be a discourse worth revisiting. The policy theory of housing provision in different national and international contexts, and its impact on housing politics, should be investigated both at citizen and elite levels, and using both qualitative and quantitative methodology.

In housing studies on the *macro level*, perspectives of housing politics have definitely been less common than analyses and empirical studies of housing policy. This can be seen as only one of many aspects of the general policy orientation in the field; however, to some extent it may also be explained by the modest role of political science in housing studies.

The development in the EU may lead to a revival of approaches based on the concept of *corporatism*, now in the study of EU and national housing politics – and the relation between them. This can be combined with *historical institutionalism* and path dependence, which appears to be a particularly promising approach to housing with its generally high degree of sluggishness.

Another theoretical perspective that could be of particular relevance in housing studies is *framing analysis* (e.g. Goffman 1974, Stone 1989, Benford & Snow 2000, Fischer 2003). Some variations of framing theory combine (in an interesting way) actor-based and discourse analysis. Such theoretical integration should be fruitful to the study of housing policy and politics. The specific policy theory of state correctives to the market is often complemented with, more or less symbolic, discursive frames of the type 'housing is a social right' (Sweden), 'owning other people's homes is no legitimate line of business' (Norway), 'the home-owning society', and 'an Englishman's home is his castle'. Such subjects have been fruitfully covered by housing sociologists, but the more actor-related aspects, including the impact of this type of ideas on political institutions, have so far been less investigated. Framing is also of importance to the very local housing politics where professional providers and managers meet individuals and groups of residents.[54]

Approaches of historical institutionalism and framing analysis could also be used to shed more light on the complexities of housing politics on the *micro and meso levels* (see Bengtsson 2009a for some examples of path dependence analysis on these levels). One interesting possibility would be to examine theories of urban governance empirically by means of historical process tracing and open-ended path dependence analysis – if this should be labelled housing or urban studies is no big concern. A renewed interest in *urban movements* and urban protest can also be predicted. As pointed out by Pickvance (2003), the writing in this field should relate more to general social movement theory and its theoretical frameworks such as resource mobilization and political opportunity structure.[55] Empirically, there is still a lot to be learned from Lipsky (1968, 1970) and his studies of protest in American cities.

Moving towards the micro level, the analysis of *hybrid organisations* as political actors and institutions is a relatively young branch of housing studies, which should be of great importance for our understanding of the conditions of housing politics, policy and implementation. In contrast to other sectors, the geographical concentration of the residents brings to the fore issues of participative and deliberative democracy, which further complicates the internal goal conflicts of hybrid organisations.

More generally, the concept of *democracy* should be applied – and problematised – more consistently than before in housing studies on the micro and meso levels. The discourse on models of democracy is a well-developed theoretical speciality in political science, which should be of relevance to several lines of housing research, e.g. the analysis of tenant participation and local governance. Both these applications have to do with 'democracy in small scale' (cf. Dahl & Tufte 1973), which also deserves to be given more attention in political science.

Should the modest role of political science in housing studies be deplored?[56] As mentioned now and then in the chapter, the politological imagination could sometimes contribute to a more penetrating and theory-based interpretation of housing actors and institutions and to open-ended middle-range theorising in terms of thinly rationalistic logics, patterns and mechanisms. Again, this type of imagination is neither an inherent nor an exclusive quality of political scientists.

Political scientists could definitely contribute to the application of central political concepts to housing. Even though 'democracy' and 'citizenship' (and 'social justice') are often used well in housing studies, a stronger involvement of political scientists would link these applications more firmly to the broad discourses on these concepts in the discipline.

Conversely, political science should take more advantage of applications in housing studies. Jim Kemeny has often pointed out that theory development in the disciplines stands to gain from such applications (Kemeny 1992). In political science, more specifically, conceptual and empirical studies of housing politics could contribute to the development of concepts like power, democracy and citizenship, in particular on the small scale and on local levels. Furthermore, micro-, meso- and macro- level studies of housing politics could contribute to politological theorising about local governance, hybrid organisations and market-oriented politics and policies more generally.

NOTES

1 These aspects are discussed in several other chapters in this Handbook.

2 The Scandinavian countries appear to represent a minor deviation from this general picture – even allowing for this author's observation post in Sweden. The single best-known work on housing written by a political scientist is probably still Patrick Dunleavy's book on the political process behind mass housing and the boom of high-rise construction in Britain after the Second World War (Dunleavy 1981). Dunleavy's research career may also illustrate political scientists' limited interest in housing studies; he has not returned to the field since.

3 Since political scientists are typically more interested in political actors, processes and institutions than in social and economic outcomes, their contributions may be less relevant to policy recommendations than those of economists, sociologists or geographers.

4 Two of the most cited suggestions are David Easton's 'authoritative allocation of values for a society', and Harold Lasswell's 'who gets what, when, and how'. Both definitions are too narrow – and too close to 'policy' – for the purpose of this chapter. It should be noted that several European languages, including German and French, do not make a distinction between 'policy' and 'politics' (cf. Heidenheimer 1986).

5 'Housing policy' has been defined as 'any sustained course of action designed to affect housing conditions' (Donnison & Ungerson 1982, p. 13). In practice, the demarcation line between housing policy and housing politics is not clear-cut, and much empirical work actually includes both. The balance between the two perspectives in housing studies is illustrated by the fact that in the period 2000–2008 no less than 185 articles in the four journals mentioned above had the word 'policy' in their titles, whereas only 10 article titles included the word 'politics' (Bengtsson 2009b, p. 7). This balance – or imbalance – is another side of the modest role of political science in the field.

6 Higher and lower levels have been left out, mainly due to lack of space, e.g. the household level and the international and transnational levels. Housing-related issues on these levels could also be analysed in terms of housing politics (cf. for example Somerville 2000, chap. 2, and Smith 2002, respectively).

7 An assumption of thin rationality means that social action (and interaction) is interpreted as being to some extent consistent in the pursuit of individual actors' goals, whereas the nature of those goals is not assumed a priori but seen as context-dependent (cf. Somerville & Bengtsson 2002).

8 Of course political scientists have neither monopoly on nor precedence to this type of imagination – as will be clear from the empirical review below. Dunleavy's case study of British mass housing politics (Dunleavy 1981) is a good empirical example of how politological imagination can be used to make theoretically relevant interpretations of housing politics and power. (If written today, Dunleavy's case studies would no doubt have been related to modern political theories, e.g. about institutionalisation.)

9 See Somerville and Bengtsson (2002) and Bengtsson and Somerville (2002) for an outline of such a perspective of 'contextualised rational action' and a discussion of how it can be applied in studies of tenant participation, housing management and comparative housing policy. Perspectives based on thin rationality can also help us understand why policymakers do not always consider ambitious evaluations, nor implement well thought-out policy proposals from housing researchers (cf. Scharpf 1997, pp. 10–12, Bengtsson 2009b).

10 The normative discussion about justice, democracy and citizenship is also more explicit in political science than in other disciplines. These issues are certainly crucial in housing studies. Such lines of research are, however, left out from this chapter as being of relevance to housing policy rather than housing politics.

11 'Policy theory' can be defined as 'the total of causal and other assumptions underlying a policy' (Hoogerwerf 1990).

12 Another, and more general, problem is that the very classification of a policy in Lowi's or Wilson's terms is often part of what is politically contested (cf. Fischer 2003, pp. 64–66).

13 Gustavsson (1980b) is an interesting exception. He boldly combines Lowi's and Wilson's models and makes an attempt to apply an integrated model to the political and academic debate on Swedish housing policy.

14 If housing is basically a private good, why is its provision seen as a matter of political concern at

all? One answer is that the specificities of the housing market, if left alone, may result in strong fluctuations and in heavy imbalances in market power between suppliers and consumers (cf. Bengtsson 2001).

15 Oxley and Smith (1996, pp. 2–3) make a similar observation about the role of the state in housing provision, though not related to a discussion on policy theory; cf. also Lund (2006, pp. 1–2). Lundqvist (1992, pp. 4–6) also takes the policy theory of state correctives to the market as the implicit point of departure in his model of possible state interventions into the housing sector, which relates such interventions to either consumption (affecting household purchasing power) or production (affecting dwelling prices).

16 Harloe, who refers to Torgersen, explains the difference by the fact that housing, unlike other spheres of provision for human needs, provides profitable opportunities for capitalism, and so '... anything more than a limited and partial decommodification is likely to provoke intense resistance' (Harloe 1995, pp. 2–3). Of course, Bengtsson's and Torgersen's interpretations of the political and normative discourse are not inconsistent with Harloe's structural explanation.

17 Certainly the mode of implementation of each welfare state sector has its specific features, but in most cases they only represent variations within a general logic of state allocation, as outlined by Torgersen. The critical role played by the market, together with the specificities of this market, makes the policy theory of housing provision different in kind from this ideal-type model of welfare state provision.

18 See Ruonavaara (1992) for a discussion on types and forms of tenure. Scott suggests a useful and inclusive general definition of institution: 'Institutions consist of cognitive, normative, and regulative structures and activities that provide stability and meaning to social behaviour' (Scott 1995, p. 33).

19 Several authors have claimed that the concept of housing tenure has been used too widely and too abstractly in housing research (e.g. Ball, Harloe & Martens 1988, p. 30, Barlow & Duncan 1988, 1994). Hulse (2008, p. 217) suggests that '…the position of housing tenure as the key explanatory concept in housing research is at best inflated and at worst can obscure the relationships between households and housing'. Actually what these authors warn against seems to be a simplified analysis where e.g. owner-occupation is tacitly taken to represent the same thing in different housing regimes. Always keeping in mind the important distinction suggested by Ruonavaara (1992) between (ideal) types and (specific) forms of tenure should actually take care of that problem. Regardless of this general debate, precisely in the analysis of housing politics and institutions the concepts of tenure and tenure policy are not only useful but absolutely crucial.

20 To some extent Britain has been an exception, with its large state-owned social rental sector; cf. below.

21 Recent trends of new public management (NPM) and network governance in welfare state implementation have made other sectors more similar to housing in this respect. In housing, network implementation is nothing new but an integrated aspect of the policy theory of state correctives to the market. Again, Britain is an important exception here, which will be discussed below.

22 This is not to say that local bureaucrats have no power over citizens: actually, their power position is precisely the point that Lipsky makes. But administrative power and market power have different logics and should be analysed accordingly.

23 The distinction between the three levels is analytical and, as we will see, they often overlap empirically.

24 Some of the best-known works in this genre are Donnison 1967 (and Donnison & Ungerson 1982), Headey 1978, Pugh 1980, McGuire 1981, Dickens et al. 1985, Ball, Harloe & Martens 1988, Boelhouwer & van der Heijden 1992, Lundqvist 1992, Power 1993, Barlow & Duncan 1994, McCrone & Stephens 1995, Balchin (ed.) 1996, Donner 2000 and Lawson 2006. There are also some comparative books on housing in Eastern Europe, e.g. Turner, Hegedüs & Tosics (eds) 1992, Clapham et al. (eds) 1996 and Donner 2006.

25 Some exceptions are discussed below.

26 On Britain, see e.g. Cullingworth 1979, Dunleavy 1981, Clapham, Kemp & Smith 1990, Birchall (ed.) 1992, Balchin 1995, Malpass & Murie 1999, Somerville (ed.) 2005, and Mullins & Murie 2006.

27 Cf. Kemeny (1992, chap. 2) for a critical discussion of 'the Anglo-Saxon bias in comparative rental research'. US policies seem to be less prominent in studies of housing than in many other sectors, probably due to the strong market-orientation and the residual and privatised character of US housing (cf. Bratt, Stone & Hartman 2006, Doling 1997, pp. 17–19). Of course, numerous studies of housing policy and politics have been published in other languages than English. They have not been reviewed for this chapter – with the only exception of three Scandinavian projects which have been published in English only summarily or in parts. Another delimitation of the chapter is that studies of housing politics in the Third World are not included.

28 More seldom are they related to the universal politico-philosophical discourse about justice, freedom and natural rights, with contributions from scholars like John Rawls, Robert Nozick and Ronald Dworkin. One important exception is the work of Peter King, who has consistently deliberated the

implications for housing of these concepts, often from a libertarian point of view (e.g. King 1996, 1998, 2003). As mentioned, this normative discourse on social justice and natural rights is more relevant to housing policy than housing politics and in consequence it is not reviewed in this chapter. In contrast, 'citizenship' and 'democracy', two ultimately normative political concepts with more bearing on housing politics, will be discussed.

29 'Convergence thesis studies' see all countries as being subject to the same universalistic imperatives, be it the logic of capitalism, industrialism, privatisation, or something else. 'Divergence thesis studies', instead, attempt to discern patterns and typologies of housing systems, and to develop theories of the middle range, drawing on wider social sciences to generate contextualised explanations (Kemeny & Lowe 1998).

30 As pointed out by Kemeny (2001), many applications of Esping-Andersen's welfare regime model, both on the macro level and specifically on the housing sector, use it only as a typology, without considering the underlying social theory about power structures and class-based constellations.

31 Kemeny's model is presented below. Different variants of Titmuss' (1968) distinction between residual and institutional welfare state arrangements have also been applied to housing (e.g. Heidenheimer, Heclo & Adams 1975, Donnison & Ungerson 1982); cf. also Chapter 18.

32 Somerville (1994) labels some of the particularistic studies 'explanations in terms of systems of actors' – adding that this type of explanation is more often implied than discussed.

33 This of course only touches upon what is really a wide-ranging methodological discussion – far beyond the scope of this chapter. See Elster (2007) for a comprehensive discussion of this form of theorising, and Somerville and Bengtsson (2002) for a brief discussion of how it can be applied to housing studies.

34 Bearing in mind that housing policy is largely about correctives to the market, i.e. institutions, which blurs the distinction empirically.

35 Dunleavy (1981) is another two-level case study, including both the national and local political processes behind mass housing in Britain.

36 The authors relate their approach to critical realism, though only in the last chapter and not in a very elucidating manner (cf. criticism by Somerville 1994 and Lawson 2006, p. 57).

37 Quoting Kemeny:

Because housing straddles both state and market, it is probable that vested market interests are more prominent in housing than in other welfare sectors. For this reason the housing market is likely to reflect the power balance between different interest groups particularly clearly, especially in comparison with other welfare sectors where the market still plays a much more limited role (Kemeny 2006, p. 1).

38 The Danish housing associations are to a large extent controlled by the tenants.

39 Bengtsson (1995) discusses in general terms how a perspective of thin rationality can be applied to the political role of housing organisations in terms of collective action, market power and corporatism. By analysing over time the interaction between housing organisations and other actors in the political arena, the market arena and the organisational arena, a historical web of critical junctures and resulting institutional and market development can be reconstructed – what Tsebelis (1990) calls 'games of institutional design'.

40 Historical institutionalism takes time seriously, 'specifying sequences and tracing transformations and processes of varying scale and temporality' (Pierson & Skocpol 2002, pp. 695–696). This does not necessarily imply covering long historical periods of time.

41 Critics of path dependence have claimed that the concept says little more than 'history matters'. To avoid this it has been suggested that path dependence should be defined rather strictly as 'historical sequences in which contingent events set into motion institutional patterns or event chains that have deterministic properties' (Mahoney 2000, pp. 507–508). In a more open-ended perspective, path dependence can be seen as a historical pattern where a certain outcome can be traced back to a particular set of events on the basis of empirical observation and guided by some social theory (cf. Bengtsson 2009a).

42 The specificities of housing as a good, and of housing tenures as institutions, seem to make path dependence perspectives particularly relevant in housing studies. One way to elaborate on the power mechanism is to apply Steven Lukes' well-known 'three faces of power' (Lukes 1974), and distinguish between different forms of power-based path dependence. Earlier more 'contingent' events at point A may at point B have an effect on either decision-making, agenda-setting or perceptions (cf. Bengtsson 2009a).

43 Besides Power's book (Power 1993), which could just as well have been framed in terms of path dependence, in particular the work by Peter Malpass on the history of British housing provision deserves to be mentioned here (e.g. Malpass 2000, 2005). In a recent article Malpass stresses how history can help to explain current differences and similarities in social housing provision, 'in terms of the size of the social sector, its trajectory to change (growth or decline), organisational forms, methods of financing and role in the housing system as a whole' (Malpass 2008,

pp. 15–16), i.e. some of the key questions of path dependence applied to housing.

44 See Daunton (1987) for a more traditional historical account related to similar questions.

45 See Bengtsson and Ruonavaara (2010) for a brief presentation of the approach and the main results in English.

46 Some other examples of path dependence analysis of housing politics are Kemp (2000) on the housing benefit system in Britain, Kay (2005) on rent-setting in social housing, and Lévy-Vroelant, Reinprecht & Wassenberg (2008) on social housing in Austria, France and the Netherlands (cf. review in Bengtsson 2009a).

47 British housing managers are arguably the actors closest to Lipsky's street-level bureaucrats we find in housing.

48 Thus, the ideas of new public management (NPM) have left clear traces in the British housing sector (cf. Walker 1998), whereas in other countries the implementation of housing provision has for long been seen as the responsibility mainly of market actors, and consequently the impact of NPM has been less evident in housing than in other welfare state sectors.

49 The micro level of the individual housing estate allows more clear-cut analysis in terms of housing actors and institutions. When we move towards larger geographical units a more differentiated set of actors and institutions are involved, e.g. representing social services, schools, culture and local business.

50 They can also be part of a national housing policy, as (in the last few decades) has been the case in Britain (cf. Langstaff 1992).

51 Important exceptions – and good examples – are Birchall (1988) on housing cooperatives in Britain and Jensen (1995, 1997) on Danish social housing governance. Glasze (2005) analyses gated neighbourhoods in a perspective of 'shareholder democracy'. Birchall (1997) is a useful conceptual discussion of the micromechanisms of participative democracy in housing.

52 Analyses in a perspective of social capital (Putnam 1993, 2000) may be seen as representing a middle ground between sociology and politics. In housing studies the concept has so far been applied in the analysis of social relations rather than micro- and meso-level politics (e.g. Forrest & Kearns 2001; Middleton, Murie & Groves 2005; cf., however, Dekker 2007, who analyses local social capital and neighbourhood participation in distressed urban areas).

53 Keating, Krumholz & Star (1996) is one largely housing-oriented volume, where political analysis has been given some space.

54 Framing analysis has to some extent been applied to the study of homelessness and affordable housing (e.g. Schön & Rein 1994, chap. 6, Croteau & Hicks 2003, Goetz 2008), but it should also be fruitful in the analysis of housing politics more generally. Similar perspectives have been used in constructionist discussions on macro-level housing policy (e.g. Kemeny 1995); however, an explicit liaison with the framing discourse should add more precision to this type of analysis of symbolic politics. Ideational and ideological institutionalism are other related approaches (Blyth 2003, Hay 2004).

55 Political opportunity structure has been defined as '… consistent – but not necessarily formal or permanent – dimensions of the political environment that provide incentives for people to undertake collective action by affecting their expectations for success or failure' (Tarrow 1994, p. 85). A perspective of political opportunity structure emphasises conditions like the openness of the political system, the stability of elite alignments and the state's capacity and propensity for repression (McAdam 1996, p. 27).

56 This is discussed in more detail in Bengtsson (2009b).

REFERENCES

Allen, C. (2005) Reflections on Housing and Social Theory: An Interview with Jim Kemeny, *Housing, Theory and Society*, 22(2), pp. 94–107.

Allen, C. & Gurney, C. (1997) Beyond 'Housing and Social Theory', *European Network for Housing Research Newsletter*, 3(97), pp. 3–5.

Andrusz, G. (1999) *The Co-operative Alternative in Europe: The Case of Housing*. Aldershot: Ashgate.

Arnott, R. (1987) Economic Theory and Housing, in Mills, E. S., ed., *Handbook of Regional and Urban Economics, Vol. II. Urban Economics*. Amsterdam: North-Holland.

Balchin, P. ([1983] 1995) *Housing Policy. An Introduction*, 3rd edn. London & New York: Routledge.

Balchin, P., ed. (1996) *Housing Policy in Europe*. London & New York: Routledge.

Ball, M. (1986) Housing Analysis: Time for a Theoretical Refocus? *Housing Studies*, 1(3), pp. 147–166.

Ball, M., Harloe, M. & Martens, M. (1988) *Housing and Social Change in Europe and the USA*. London and New York: Routledge.

Barlow, J. & Duncan, S. (1988) The Use and Abuse of Housing Tenure, *Housing Studies*, 3(4), pp. 219–231.

Barlow, J. & Duncan, S. (1994) *Success and Failure in Housing Provision*. Oxford: Elsevier.

Benford, R. D. & Snow, D. A. (2000) Framing Processes and Social Movements: An Overview and Assessment, *Annual Review of Sociology*, 26, pp. 11–39.

Bengtsson, B. (1995) Housing in Game-Theoretical Perspective, *Housing Studies*, 10(2), pp. 229–243.

Bengtsson, B. (2000) Solving the Tenants' Dilemma: Collective Action and Norms of Co-operation in Housing, *Housing, Theory and Society*, 17(4), pp. 175–187.

Bengtsson, B. (2001) Housing as a Social Right: Implications for Welfare State Theory, *Scandinavian Political Studies*, 24(4), pp. 255–275.

Bengtsson, B. (2004) Swedish Housing Corporatism – A Case of Path Dependence? Paper presented at the ENHR Conference 'Housing: Growth and Regeneration', Cambridge, July 2004.

Bengtsson, B. (2009a) Applying Path Dependence Perspectives in Housing Studies – Review and Discussion. Paper presented at the ENHR Conference 'Changing Housing Markets: Integration and Segmentation', Prague, June–July 2009.

Bengtsson, B. (2009b) Political Science as the Missing Link in Housing Studies, *Housing, Theory and Society*, 26(1), pp. 10–25.

Bengtsson, B. & Kemeny, J. (1995) Encouraging Theory in Housing, *European Network for Housing Research Newsletter*, 4(95), p. 3.

Bengtsson, B. & Ruonavaara, H. (2010) Introduction to the Special Issue: Path Dependence in Housing. *Housing, Theory and Society*, 27(3), pp. 193–203.

Bengtsson, B. & Somerville, P. (2002) Understanding Contextualised Rational Action – Authors' Response, *Housing Theory and Society*, 19(3–4), pp. 148–152.

Bengtsson, B., ed., Annaniassen, E., Jensen, L., Ruonavaara, H. & Sveinsson, J. R. (2006) *Varför så olika? Nordisk bostadspolitik i jämförande historiskt ljus* [Why so Different? Nordic Housing Policy in Comparative Historical Light], Malmö: Égalité.

Birchall, J. (1988) *Building Communities the Co-operative Way*. London: Routledge & Kegan Paul.

Birchall, J., ed. (1992) *Housing Policy in the 1990s*. London and New York: Routledge.

Birchall, J. (1997) The Psychology of Participation, in Cooper, C. & Hawtin, M., eds, *Housing, Community and Conflict: Understanding 'Resident Involvement'*. Aldershot: Arena.

Blyth, M. (2003) Structures Do Not Come with an Instruction Sheet: Interest, Ideas, and Progress in Political Science, *Cambridge Journals*, 1(4), pp. 695–706.

Boddy, M. (1989) Financial Deregulation and UK Housing Finance: Government-Building Society Relations and the Building Society Act, 1986, *Housing Studies*, 4(2), pp. 92–104.

Boelhouwer, P. & van der Heijden, H. (1992) *Housing Systems in Europe: Part 1. A Comparative Study of Housing Policy*. Delft: Delft University Press.

Bowes, A., Dar, N. & Sim, D. (2000) Citizenship, Housing and Minority Ethnic Groups: An Approach to Multiculturalism, *Housing, Theory and Society*, 17(2), pp. 83–95.

Bratt, R. G., Stone, M. E. & Hartman, C., eds (2006) *A Right to Housing. Foundation for a New Social Agenda*. Philadelphia, PA: Temple University Press.

Burns, D. (2000) Can Local Democracy Survive Governance?, *Urban Studies* 37(5–6), pp. 963–973.

Cairncross, L., Clapham, D. & Goodlad, R. (1997) *Housing Management, Consumers and Citizens*. London & New York: Routledge.

Castells, M. (1977) *The Urban Question. A Marxist Approach*. London: Arnold.

Castells, M. (1983) *The City and the Grassroots*. London: Arnold.

Clapham, D. (1997) The Social Construction of Housing Management Research, *Urban Studies*, 34(5–6), pp. 761–774.

Clapham, D. & English, J., eds (1987) *Public Housing: Current Trends and Future Developments*. London, Sydney and Wolfeboro, NH: Croom Helm.

Clapham, D., Franklin, B. & Saugères, L. (2000) Housing Management: The Social Construction of an Occupational Role', *Housing, Theory and Society*, 17(2), pp. 68–82.

Clapham, D., Kay, H., Hegedus, J, Kintrea, K. & Tosics, I. (with Mark, K.), eds (1996) *Housing Privatization in Eastern Europe*. London: Greenwood Press.

Clapham, D., Kemp, P. & Smith, S. J. (1990) *Housing and Social Policy*. Basingstoke & London: Macmillan.

Clegg, S. (1989) *Frameworks of Power*. London: Sage.

Coleman, J. S. (1990) *Foundations of Social Theory*. Cambridge, MA: Harvard University Press.

Collier, R. B. & Collier, D. (1991) *Shaping the Political Arena: Critical Junctures, the Labor Movement, and Regime Dynamics in Latin America*. Berkeley, CA: University of California Press.

Cooper, C. & Hawtin M. (1997) Concepts of Community Involvement, Power and Democracy, in Cooper, C. & Hawtin, M., eds, *Housing, Community and Conflict: Understanding 'Resident Involvement'*. Aldershot: Arena.

Croteau, D. & Hicks, L. (2003) Coalition Framing and the Challenge of a Consonant Frame Pyramid: The Case of a Collaborative Response to Homelessness, *Social Problems*, 50(2), pp. 251–272.

Cullingworth, J. B. (1979) *Essays on Housing Policy. The British Scene*. London: George Allen & Unwin.

Dahl, R. & Tufte, E. (1973) *Size and Democracy*. Stanford, CA: Stanford University Press.

Danermark, B. & Elander, I., eds (1994) *Social Rented Housing in Europe: Policy, Tenure and Design*. Delft: Delft University Press.

Daunton, M. J. (1987) *A Property-Owning Democracy? Housing in Britain*. London: Faber & Faber.

Davies, J. S. & Imbroscio, D. L., eds (2009) *Theories of Urban Politics*, 2nd edn. London, Thousand Oaks, CA, New Delhi and Singapore: Sage.

Dekker, K. (2007) Social Capital, Neighbourhood Attachment and Participation in Distressed Urban Areas. A Case Study in The Hague and Utrecht, the Netherlands, *Housing Studies*, 22(3), pp. 355–379.

Dickens, P., Duncan, S., Goodwin, M. & Gray, F. (1985) *Housing, States and Localities*. London & New York: Methuen.

Doling, J. (1997) *Comparative Housing Policy: Government and Housing in Advanced Industrialized Countries*. Basingstoke and London: Macmillan and New York: St. Martin's Press.

Donner, C. (2000) *Housing Policies in the European Union. Theory and Practice*. Vienna.

Donner, C. (2006) *Housing Policies in Central Eastern Europe*. Vienna.

Donnison, D. V. (1967) *The Government of Housing*. Harmondsworth: Penguin.

Donnison, D. & Ungerson, C. (1982) *Housing Policy*. Harmondsworth: Penguin.

Dunleavy, P. (1981) *The Politics of Mass Housing in Britain 1945–1975: A Study of Corporate Power, and Professional Influence in the Welfare State*. Oxford: Clarendon Press.

Dynarski, M. (1986) Residential Attachment and Housing Demand, *Urban Studies*, 23(1), pp. 11–20.

Elsinga, M., Haffner, M. & van der Heijden, H. (2008) Threats to the Dutch Unitary Rental Market, *European Journal of Housing Policy*, 8(1), pp. 21–37.

Elster, J. (1983) *Sour Grapes. Studies in the Subversion of Rationality*. Cambridge: Cambridge University Press.

Elster, J. (1989) *Nuts and Bolts for the Social Sciences*. Cambridge: Cambridge University Press.

Elster, J. (2007) *Explaining Social Behavior. More Nuts and Bolts for the Social Sciences*. Cambridge: Cambridge University Press.

Emms, P. (1990) *Social Housing. A European Dilemma?* Bristol: School for Advanced Urban Studies.

Esping-Andersen, G. (1990) *The Three Worlds of Welfare Capitalism*. Cambridge: Polity Press.

Fischer, F. (2003) *Reframing Public Policy. Discursive Politics and Deliberative Practice*. Oxford and New York: Oxford University Press.

Flynn, R. (1986) Cutback Contradictions in Dutch Housing Policy, *Journal of Social Policy*, 15(2), pp. 223–236.

Forrest, R. & Kearns, A. (2001) Social Cohesion, Social Capital and the Neighbourhood, *Urban Studies*, 38(12), pp. 2125–2143.

Franklin, B. (2000) Demands, Expectations and Responses: The Shaping of Housing Management, *Housing Studies*, 15(6), pp. 907–927.

García, M. (2006) Citizenship Practices and Urban Governance in European Cities, *Urban Studies*, 43(4), pp. 745–765.

Garfinkel, H. (1967) *Studies in Ethnomethodology*. Englewood Cliffs, NJ: Prentice-Hall.

Ghékière, L. (2008) Social Housing as a Service of General Interest, in Scanlon, K. & Whitehead, C., eds, *Social Housing in Europe II. A Review of Policies and Outcomes*. London: London School of Economics and Political Science.

Glasze, G. (2005) Some Reflections on the Economic and Political Organisation of Private Neighbourhoods, *Housing Studies*, 20(2), pp. 221–233.

Goetz, E. G. (2008) Words Matter: The Importance of Issue Framing and the Case of Affordable Housing, *Journal of the American Planning Association*, 74(2), pp. 222–229.

Goffman, E. (1974) *Frame Analysis: An Essay on the Organization of Experience*. New York: Harper Row.

Grayson, J. (1997) Campaigning Tenants: A Pre-History of Tenant Involvement to 1979, in Cooper, C. & Hawtin, M., eds, *Housing, Community and Conflict: Understanding 'Resident Involvement'*. Aldershot: Arena.

Gruis, V. & Priemus, H. (2008) European Competition Policy and National Housing Policies: International Implications of the Dutch Case, *Housing Studies*, 23(3), pp. 485–505.

Gustavsson, S. (1980a) Housing, Building, and Planning, in Lewin, L. & Vedung, E., eds, *Politics as Rational Action*. Dordrecht: Reidel.

Gustavsson, S. (1980b) Types of Policy and Types of Politics, *Scandinavian Political Studies*, 3(2), pp. 123–142.

Hall, P. A. & Taylor, R. C. R. (1996) Political Science and the Three New Institutionalisms, *Political Studies*, 44(5), pp. 936–957.

Harloe, M. (1985) *Private Rented Housing in the United States and Europe*. London and Sydney: Croom Helm.

Harloe, M. (1995) *The People's Home? Social Rented Housing in Europe and America*. Oxford and Cambridge, MA: Blackwell.

Hay, C. (2004) Ideas, Interest and Institutions in the Comparative Political Economy of Great Transformation, *Review of International Political Economy*, 11(1), pp. 204–226.

Headey, B. (1978) *Housing Policy in the Developed Economy. The United Kingdom, Sweden and the United States*. London: Croom Helm.

Heclo, H. & Madsen, H. (1987) *Policy and Politics in Sweden. Principled Pragmatism*. Philadelphia, PA: Temple University Press.

Hedström, P. & Swedberg, R. (1998) Social Mechanisms: An Introductory Essay, in Hedström, P. & Swedberg, R., eds, *Social Mechanisms. An Analytical Approach to Social Theory*. Cambridge: Cambridge University Press.

Heidenheimer, A. J. (1986) Politics, Policy and Policey as Concepts in English and Continental Languages: An Attempt to Explain Divergencies, *The Review of Politics*, 48(1), pp. 3–30.

Heidenheimer, A., Heclo, H. & Adams, C. T. (1975) *Comparative Public Policy. The Policy of Social Choice in Europe and America*. New York: St Martin's Press.

Hertting, N. (2003) *Samverkan på spel: Rationalitet och frustration i nätverksstyrning och svensk stadsdelsförnyelse* [Games Local Actors Play: Rationality and Frustration in Network Governance and Swedish Neighbourhood Renewal]. Stockholm: Égalité.

Hertting, N. (2007) Mechanisms of Governance Network Formation – A Contextual Rational Choice Perspective, in Torfing, J. & Sorensen, E., eds, *Theories of Democratic Network Governance*. Basingstoke and New York: Palgrave Macmillan.

Hoekstra, J. (2003) Housing and the Welfare State in the Netherlands: An Application of Esping-Andersen's Typology, *Housing, Theory and Society*, 20(1), pp. 58–71.

Hoekstra, J. (2005) Is There a Connection between Welfare State Regime and Dwelling Type? An Exploratory Statistical Analysis, *Housing Studies*, 20(3), pp. 475–495.

Hoogerwerf, A. (1990) Reconstructing Policy Theory, *Evaluation and Program Planning*, 13(3), pp. 285–291.

Houlihan, B. (1988) *Housing Policy and Central–Local Government Relations*. Aldershot and Brookfield, VT: Avebury.

Hulse, K. (2003) Housing Allowances and Private Renting in Liberal Welfare Regimes, *Housing, Theory and Society*, 20(1), pp. 28–42.

Hulse, K. (2008) Shaky Foundations: Moving beyond 'Housing Tenure', *Housing, Theory and Society*, 25(3), pp. 202–219.

Jensen, L. (1995) Challenges to Citizenship, *Scandinavian Housing and Planning Research*, 12(4), pp. 177–194.

Jensen, L. (1997) *Demokratiforestillinger i den almennyttige boligsektor* [Images of Democracy in the Danish Social Housing Sector]. Copenhagen: University of Copenhagen, Department of Political Science.

Jensen, L. (2006) *Danmark – lokal boendedemokrati och nationell korporatism* [Denmark – Local Housing Democracy and National Corporatism], in Bengtsson, B., ed., Annaniassen, E., Jensen, L., Ruonavaara, H. & Sveinsson, J.R. *Varför så olika? Nordisk bostadspolitik i jämförande historiskt ljus* [Why so Different? Nordic Housing Policy in Comparative Historical Light]. Malmö: Égalité.

Judge, D., Stoker, G. & Wolman, H., eds (1995) *Theories of Urban Politics*. London, Thousand Oaks, CA and New Delhi: Sage.

Kay, A. (2005) A Critique of the Use of Path Dependency in Policy Studies, *Public Administration*, 83(3), pp. 553–571.

Keating, D., Krumholz, N. & Star, P., eds (1996) *Revitalizing Urban Neighbourhoods*. Lawrence, KS: University Press of Kansas.

Kemeny, J. (1981) *The Myth Of Home Ownership: Public versus Private Choices in Housing Tenure*. London: Routledge and Kegan Paul.

Kemeny, J. (1992) *Housing and Social Theory*. London and New York: Routledge.

Kemeny, J. (1993) The Significance of Swedish Rental Policy: Cost Renting Command Economy versus the Social Market in Comparative Perspective, *Housing Studies*, 8(1), pp. 3–15.

Kemeny, J. (1995) *From Public Housing to the Social Market. Rental Policy Strategies in Comparative Perspective*. London: Routledge.

Kemeny, J. (1999) Editorial, *Housing, Theory and Society*, 16(1), pp. 1–2.

Kemeny, J. (2001) Comparative Housing and Welfare: Theorising the Relationship, *Journal of Housing and the Built Environment*, 16(1), pp. 53–70.

Kemeny, J. (2002) Re-Inventing the Wheel? The Interactional Basis of Constructionism, *Housing, Theory and Society*, 19(3–4), pp. 140–141.

Kemeny, J. (2006) Corporatism and Housing Regimes, *Housing, Theory and Society*, 23(1), pp. 1–18.

Kemeny, J. & Lowe, S. (1998) Schools of Comparative Housing Research: From Convergence to Divergence, *Housing Studies*, 13(2), pp. 161–176.

Kemp, P. A. (2000) Housing Benefit and Welfare Retrenchment in Britain, *Journal of Social Policy*, 29(2), pp. 263–279.

King, P. (1996) *The Limits of Housing Policy: A Philosophical Investigation*. London: Middlesex University Press.

King, P. (1998) *Housing, Individuals and the State. The Morality of Government Intervention*. London and New York: Routledge.

King, P. (2003) Housing as a Freedom Right, *Housing Studies*, 18(5), pp. 661–672.

Kleinman, M. (1996) *Housing, Welfare and the State in Europe*. Cheltenham: Edward Elgar.

Klijn, E.-H. & Skelcher, C. (2007) Democracy and Governance Networks: Compatible or not? *Public Administration*, 85(3), pp. 587–608.

Korpi, W. (2001) Contentious Institutions: An Augmented Rational-Action Analysis of the Origins and Path Dependency of Welfare State Institutions in Western Countries, *Rationality and Society*, 13(2), pp. 235–283.

Kurz, K. & Blossfeld, H.-P., eds (2004) *Home Ownership and Social Inequality in Comparative Perspective*. Stanford, CA: Stanford University Press.

Lalloo, K. (1998) Arenas of Contested Citizenship: Housing Policy in South Africa, *Habitat International*, 23(1), pp. 35–47.

Langstaff, M. (1992) Housing Associations: A Move to Centre Stage, in Birchall, J., ed., *Housing Policy in the 1990s*. London and New York: Routledge.

Lawson, J. (2006) *Critical Realism and Housing Research*. London and New York: Routledge.

Lévy-Vroelant, C., Reinprecht, C. & Wassenberg, F. (2008) Learning from History: Changes and Path Dependency in the Social Housing Sector in Austria, France and the Netherlands, in Scanlon, K. & Whitehead, C., eds, *Social Housing in Europe II. A Review of Policies and Outcomes*, London: London School of Economics and Political Science.

Lindbom, A. (2001) Dismantling Swedish Housing Policy, *Governance*, 14(4), pp. 503–527.

Lipsky, M. (1968) Protest as a Political Resource, *American Political Science Review*, 62(4), pp. 1144–1158.

Lipsky, M. (1970) *Protest in City Politics: Rent Strikes, Housing and the Power of the Poor*. Chicago, IL: Rand McNally and Company.

Lipsky, M. (1980) *Street-Level Bureaucracy: Dilemmas of the Individual in Public Services*. New York: Russell Sage Foundation.

Lowe, S. (2004) *Housing Policy Analysis. British Housing in Cultural and Comparative Context*. Basingstoke and New York: Palgrave Macmillan.

Lowi, T. J. (1972) Four Systems of Policy, Politics and Choice, *Public Administration Review*, 32(4), pp. 298–310.

Lukes, S. (1974) *Power. A Radical View*, Basingstoke and London: Macmillan.

Lund, B. (2006) *Understanding Housing Policy*. Bristol: Policy Press.

Lundqvist, L. J. (1986) *Housing Policy and Equality. A Comparative Study of Tenure Conversions and their Effects*. London: Croom Helm.

Lundqvist, L. J. (1988) Corporatist Implementation and Legitimacy: The Case of Privatisation in Swedish Public Housing, *Housing Studies*, 3(3), pp. 172–182.

Lundqvist, L. J. (1992) *Dislodging the Welfare State? Housing and Privatization in Four European Nations*. Delft: Delft University Press.

McAdam, D. (1996) Conceptual Origins, Current Problems, Future Directions, in McAdam, D., McCarthy, J. D. & Zald, M. N., eds, *Comparative Perspectives on Social Movements*. Cambridge: Cambridge University Press.

McCrone, R. G. L. & Stephens, M. (1995) *Housing Policy in Britain and Europe*. London: UCL Press.

McGuire, C. C. (1981) *International Housing Policies*. Lexington, MA: D. C. Heath and Company.

Mahoney, J. (2000) Path Dependency in Historical Sociology, *Theory and Society*, 29, pp. 507–548.

Malpass, P. (2000) *Housing Associations and Housing Policy*. Basingstoke: Palgrave Macmillan.

Malpass, P. (2005) *Housing and the Welfare State. The Development of Housing Policy in Britain*. Basingstoke: Palgrave Macmillan.

Malpass, P. (2008) Histories of Social Housing: A Comparative Approach, in Scanlon, K. & Whitehead, C., eds, *Social Housing in Europe II. A Review of Policies and Outcomes*, London: London School of Economics and Political Science.

Malpass. P. & Murie, A. ([1982] 1999) *Housing Policy and Practice*, 5th edn. Basingstoke: Palgrave Macmillan.

Marcuse, P. (1982) Building Housing Theory. Notes on Some Recent Work, *International Journal of Urban and Regional Research*, 6(1), pp. 115–120.

Marshall, T. H. (1950) Citizenship and Social Class, in Marshall, T. H., ed., *Citizenship and Class and Other Essays*. Cambridge: Cambridge University Press.

Merton, R. K. ([1948] 1957) *Social Theory and Social Structure*. New York: The Free Press.

Middleton, A., Murie, A. & Groves, R. (2005) Social Capital and Neighbourhoods that Work, *Urban Studies*, 42(10), pp. 1711–1738.

Mills, C. W. (1959) *The Sociological Imagination*. New York: Oxford University Press.

Mullen, T., Scott, S., Fitzpatrick, S. & Goodlad, R. (1999) Rights and Security in Housing: The Repossession Process in the Social Rented Sector, *Modern Law Review*, 62(1), pp. 11–31.

Mullins, D. & Murie, A. (2006) *Housing Policy in the UK*. Basingstoke: Palgrave Macmillan.

Mullins, D. & Walker, B. (2009) The Impact of Direct Public Funding for Private Developers on Non-Profit Housing Networks in England: Exploring a Research Agenda, *European Journal of Housing Policy*, 9(2), pp. 201–222.

North, D. C. (1990) *Institutions, Institutional Change and Economic Performance*. New York: Cambridge University Press.

Ostrom, E. (1991) *Governing the Commons. The Evolution of Institutions for Collective Action*. Cambridge: Cambridge University Press.

Oxley, M. (1991) The Aims and Methods of Comparative Housing Research, *Scandinavian Housing and Planning Research*, 8(2), pp. 67–77.

Oxley, M. & Smith, J. (1996) *Housing Policy and Rented Housing in Europe*. London: E. & F. N. Spon.

Pickvance, C. (2003) From Urban Social Movements to Urban Movements: A Review of the Field and Introduction to a Symposium, *International Journal of Urban and Regional Research*, 27, pp. 102–109.

Pierre, J., ed. (2000) *Debating Governance: Authority, Steering, and Democracy*. Oxford and New York: Oxford University Press.

Pierson, P. (1994) *Dismantling the Welfare State?* Cambridge: Cambridge University Press.

Pierson, P. (2000) Increasing Returns, Path Dependency and the Study of Politics, *American Political Science Review*, 94(2), pp. 251–267.

Pierson, P. & Skocpol, T. (2002) Historical Institutionalism in Contemporary Political Science, in Katznelson, I. & Milner, H., eds, *Political Science: The State of the Discipline (III)*. New York and London: Norton and Company.

Powell, W. W. (1987) Hybrid Organizational Arrangements: New Form or Transitional Development? *California Management Review*, 30(1), pp. 67–87.

Power, A. (1993) *Hovels to High Rise. State Housing in Europe since 1850*. London and New York: Routledge.

Priemus, H. (2003) Dutch Housing Associations: Current Developments and Debates, *Housing Studies*, 18(3), pp. 327–351.

Pugh, C. (1980) *Housing in Capitalist Societies*. Farnborough, Hampshire: Gower.

Putnam, R. S. (1993) *Making Democracy Work. Civic Traditions in Modern Italy*. Princeton, NJ: Princeton University Press.

Putnam, R. S. (2000) *Bowling Alone. The Collapse and Revival of American Community*. New York: Simon & Schuster.

Ruonavaara, H. (1992) Types and Forms of Housing Tenure: Towards Solving the Comparison/Translation Problem, *Scandinavian Housing and Planning Research*, 10(1), pp. 3–20.

Ruonavaara, H. (2005) How Divergent Housing Institutions Evolve: A Comparison of Swedish Tenant Co-operatives and Finnish Shareholders' Housing Companies, *Housing, Theory and Society*, 22(4), pp. 213–236.

Saunders, P. ([1981] 1986) *Social Theory and the Urban Question*, 2nd edn. London: Routledge.

Scharpf, F. W. (1997) *Games Real Actors Play. Actor-Centered Institutionalism in Policy Research*. Boulder, CO and Oxford: Westview Press.

Schmidt, S. (1989) Convergence Theory, Labour Movements, and Corporatism: The Case of Housing, *Scandinavian Housing and Planning Research*, 6(2), pp. 83–101.

Schmitter, P. (1974) Still the Century of Corporatism? *Review of Politics*, 36(1), pp. 85–131.

Schön, D. A. & Rein, M. (1994) *Frame Reflection. Toward the Resolution of Intractable Policy Controversies*. New York: Basic Books.

Scott, W. R. (1995) *Institutions and Organizations*. Thousand Oaks, CA, London and New Delhi: Sage.

Simon, H. (1957) *Models of Man*. New York: John Wiley.

Smith, N. (2002) New Globalism, New Urbanism: Gentrification as Global Urban Strategy, *Antipode*, 34(3), pp. 427–450.

Somerville, P. (1994) On Explanations of Housing Policy, *Scandinavian Housing and Planning Research*, 11(4), pp. 211–230.

Somerville, P. (1998) Empowerment through Residence, *Housing Studies*, 13(2), pp. 233–257.

Somerville, P. (2000) *Social Relations and Social Exclusion. Rethinking Political Economy*. London and New York: Routledge.

Somerville, P. (2005) Community Governance and Democracy, *Policy and Politics*, 33(1), 117–144.

Somerville, P. & Bengtsson, B. (2002) Constructionism, Realism and Housing Theory, *Housing, Theory and Society*, 19(3–4), pp. 121–136.

Somerville, P. & Steele, A. (1999) Making Oneself at Home: The Mediation of Residential Action', *International Journal of Urban and Regional Research*, 23(1), pp. 88–102.

Stahl, K. (1985) Microeconomic Analysis of Housing Markets: Towards a Conceptual Framework, in Stahl, K., ed., *Microeconomic Models of Housing Markets*. Berlin and Heidelberg: Springer-Verlag.

Stamsø, M. A. (2009) Housing and the Welfare State in Norway, *Scandinavian Political Studies*, 32(2), pp. 195–220.

Stoker, G. (2000) Urban Political Science and the Challenge of Urban Governance, in Pierre, J., ed., *Debating Governance: Authority, Steering, and Democracy*. Oxford and New York: Oxford University Press.

Stone, D. A. (1989) Causal Stories and the Formation of Policy Agendas, *Political Science Quarterly*, 104(2), pp. 281–300.

Tarrow, S. (1994) *Power in Movement*. Cambridge: Cambridge University Press.

Thelen, K. (1999) Historical Institutionalism in Comparative Politics, *Annual Review of Political Science*, 2, pp. 369–404.

Tilly, C. (1978) *From Mobilization to Revolution*. Reading, MA: Addison-Wesley.

Titmuss, R. (1968) *Commitment to Welfare*. London: Allen & Unwin.

Torgersen, U. (1987) Housing: The Wobbly Pillar of the Welfare State, in Turner, B., Kemeny, J. & Lundqvist, L. J., eds, *Between State and Market: Housing in the Post-Industrial Era*. Scandinavian Housing and Planning Research, Supplement 1.

Tsebelis, G. (1990) *Nested Games: Rational Choice in Comparative Politics*. Berkeley, CA: University of California Press.

Turner, B., Hegedüs, J. & Tosics, I. (1992) *The Reform of Housing in Eastern Europe and the Soviet Union*. London: Routledge.

van der Heijden, H. (2002) Social Rented Housing in Western Europe: Developments and Expectations, *Urban Studies*, 39(2), pp. 327–340.

Walker, R. (1998) New Public Management and Housing Associations: From Comfort to Competition, *Policy and Politics*, 26(1), pp. 71–87.

Williamson, P. (1989) *Corporatism in Perspective. An Introductory Guide to Corporatist Theory*. London: Sage.

Wilson, J. Q. (1974) The Politics of Regulation, in McKie, J. W., ed., *Social Responsibility and the Business Predicament*. Washington, DC: The Brookings Institution.

13

People–Environment Studies

Roderick Lawrence

INTRODUCTION

Housing environments can be characterized by their complexity, their variety and change over time. An increasing number of people are living in mass-produced housing constructed by either the private or public sector rather than customer-designed housing units. Too often, the providers of housing do not account for the culture, socio-economic status and lifestyle of the residents. This shortcoming was clearly identified in the 1960s and 1970s (Habraken, 1972; Turner, 1976). Much housing research has been implemented since then. Unfortunately, the results of this research have not been applied systematically in housing design, construction and policy definition. There are several reasons for this, one being that much research was not explicitly related to housing policies and professional practice. This chapter will re-examine the interdisciplinary contribution of people–environment studies to the vast field of housing research, and it will discuss why and how innovative approaches are necessary in the immediate future.

'People–environment studies' is a term that refers to a broad multidisciplinary field of theoretical and applied research stemming from a concern about the relations between people and their immediate surroundings. The term 'immediate surroundings' refers to the internal and external conditions of housing units, from the scale of rooms to residential neighbourhoods. During the 1960s, architects and psychologists played a crucial role working at the micro scale of habitable rooms, buildings and neighbourhoods. These contributions were labelled architectural psychology (Lawrence, 1987). They were meant to identify how people perceive and use their immediate surroundings in terms of their personal traits and the physical fabric of buildings. In recent decades, the term 'architectural psychology' has largely been replaced by 'environmental psychology' and many empirical studies have not only considered buildings but also neighbourhoods and rural landscapes (Bechtel & Churchman, 2002). However, this chapter shows that the term 'environmental psychology' does not reflect the broad scope and multidisciplinary concepts that have been applied especially to study housing and residential neighbourhoods. These contributions are from disciplines and professions such as anthropology, architecture, epidemiology, ergonomics, human ecology, environmental and social psychology, geography, sociology and town/urban planning.

The field of people–environment studies gathered momentum in the 1960s and it has been represented by the International Association for People–Environment Studies (IAPS), formally founded in 1981 after a number of international conferences. The Environmental Design Research Association (EDRA) and other regional associations have served a similar purpose. This chapter begins with a presentation of some key definitions and interpretations used in the field of people–environment studies to reconsider the relations between residents and their housing. Then it presents a review of numerous contributions that have studied the design, the furnishing and the use of housing units in relation to cultural variables, sociodemographic variables and psychological variables.

The innovative findings of theoretical and empirical research in the field of people–environment studies have been instrumental in promoting broader, interdisciplinary interpretations of several subjects in housing research, including home, housing demand, housing quality, residential mobility and housing preferences. Whereas some of these subjects continue to be studied narrowly by housing economists, policy scientists and housing sociologists, this chapter argues that the contribution of people–environment studies is complementary to them. The enlarged interpretation of housing quality is an example of the fertile integration of knowledge from several disciplines that is included later in this chapter after a presentation of some key findings of people–environment studies in relation to housing.

RETHINKING HOUSING–PEOPLE RELATIONS

Housing is meant to provide shelter and security by ensuring protection against climatic conditions – excessive heat and cold – and unwanted intrusions from insects, rodents and environmental nuisances such as noise and air pollution. These may be harmful for health and quality of life (Lawrence, 2002). Housing contains household activities and material possessions. Housing is also an economic good that can be rented and exchanged in housing markets. Beyond functional and monetary values, housing also has aesthetic, symbolic and cultural values. Studies show that housing is an indicator of cultural identity, a sign of social status and a catalyst for the expression of individual preferences (Sommerville, 1997; Aragones, Francescato & Gärling, 2002).

Turner (1976) made the important distinction between housing as a noun and housing as a verb. According to Turner, an architect, housing can be considered simultaneously as a **product** (from an individual housing unit to the housing stock in a neighbourhood or city) and as a **process**, by referring to the provision and maintenance of residential buildings by either public authorities or private initiatives. Turner's interpretation is particularly pertinent for people–environment studies of housing because it enables researchers and practitioners to consider the multiple interrelations between housing conditions and human processes in specific localities (Lawrence, 1987). An illustration of this interpretation is the long-standing custom of lay people collaborating to construct and maintain their housing.

In England, for example, Hardy and Ward (1984) present case studies of owner-builder housing that illustrate how the labour of residents transformed basic materials and marginal plots of land into property with a relatively high capital value. These residents moved from the formal to the informal sector in order to own makeshift accommodation that was gradually modified and improved over an extended period of time, despite the caustic opposition between public and private interests. In general, the authors show that conflicting interpretations of societal and individual rights concerning land use have become stronger during the 20th century in tandem with the enactment and the enforcement of land and housing legislation. In this study, many residents indicated that one of the main reasons for residing in housing of this kind was its 'health-giving qualities', whereas there is also ample evidence to show that Medical Health Officers were severe critics of this kind of housing owing to rudimentary water supplies and sewerage disposal. Furthermore, the authors indicate that public officials decried the visual disorder of this kind of housing, whereas such aesthetic considerations were unimportant for the residents, especially in relation to health and economic parameters.

Hardy and Ward (1984) show that housing practices in the informal sector can be compared with housing provision in the formal sector. The latter is often regulated by 'objective' housing standards and normative regulations. Such comparisons indicate that beyond differences between the designs of housing units in each of these sectors, the inhabitants also have quite different means of expressing their aspirations, lifestyles and values in the domestic realm. For example, there is now ample evidence to show that the design, the meaning and the use of housing differ when viewed from 'the bottom up' and 'the top down' (Hamdi, 1991). It is necessary to distinguish between the explicit knowledge of professionals (including architects and housing administrators) and the tacit know-how of diverse groups of lay people. The responsibilities of the public and private, and the formal and informal sectors should be examined bearing these principles in mind. Moreover, questions concerning individual's rights and societal responsibilities, short- and long-term planning perspectives, and intended and unintended consequences, ought to be addressed. Consequently, the informal sector may not be the panacea for the implementation of land and housing policies. Nonetheless, there is evidence today which confirms that the contribution of this sector can help to bridge the chasm between the goals, values and economic means of low-income households and affordable housing.

Statistics and household surveys in many countries show the increasing numbers of different types of households in specific urban neighbourhoods and large-scale housing estates (Arias, 1993; OECD, 1996). These households differ according to their ethnic origin, their nationality, their socio-professional status and their culture, especially their domestic lifestyle. In-depth studies of the layout, furnishing and use of housing units provide a large amount of information that contradicts generalizations that have characterized the interpretation of housing by architects, professional planners and policymakers (Kron, 1983; Putman & Newton, 1990). These contributions show how specific features of the housing environment can express and communicate cultural and social identities as well as personal preferences by the manifest consumption patterns of specific social groups.

The built environment of housing projects and residential neighbourhoods should serve multiple functions and uses for an increasingly diverse population (Franck & Ahrentzen, 1989). However, requirements for visual and auditory privacy, or social contacts with neighbours, or gender differences in the use of collective and public spaces, or domestic practices for the preparation and eating of food, may not be met in a large residential building or housing project with a standardized floor plan, kitchen equipment and interior finishes (Cooper, 1975; Andrews, 1979). When requirements prescribed by cultural and social conventions cannot be accommodated, then conflicts between **the intended use of housing** (by the architect, housing manager or property owner) and **the actual use of housing** (by individuals, households and specific population groups) can have several consequences (Ravetz, 1974, 1980; Prak & Priemus, 1985). The possibilities offered or prohibited by the built form of housing to accommodate different kinds of household activities are largely related to the inherent/implicit or the structural/explicit adaptability of housing units. Certain ethnographic studies provide detailed information about **why** residents have made changes to housing (Vernez Moudon, 1986; Arias, 1993). The reasons for changes extend beyond functional adjustments that are often made in order to accommodate new circumstances during the life span. Housing research shows that motives for change might include the wish to comply with new social trends (in house decorations, for example), which indicate that the household adheres to a specific social group (Duncan, 1981; Kron, 1983; Putman & Newton, 1990).

The incompatibility between different domestic cultures can be another source of conflict between households. This incompatibility can be expressed by conflicting lifestyles, meanings and values about housing (Ravetz, 1974, 1980; van Kempen, 1994). For example, different households in the same large residential building or housing project may not share the same opinion about what should be accessible or inaccessible, what should be visible or not seen, or what should be heard or unheard, and whether prescriptions about these aspects of household activities change according to the status of the individual as well as at different times. For example, household surveys in several European cities indicate that disturbance by noise stemming from road traffic is a significant cause of sleep disturbance which does affect health and well-being (Berglund & Lindvall, 1995). However, disturbance by noise from the activities of neighbours using their housing unit can be an even greater cause of concern to residents, irrespective of the objective measure of sound (Halpern, 1995).

Accumulated evidence from numerous housing surveys shows that disagreements about the appropriate uses of housing, and different values attributed to social relations between neighbours, reflect different social identities at the micro scale of residential buildings and neighbourhoods (Altman & Werner, 1985; Cooper Marcus & Sarkissian, 1986). Therefore, it is appropriate to study the interrelations between increasingly diverse domestic cultures. This raises the key question of how the knowledge about the human dimensions of housing can be used effectively in housing design, housing management and housing policies (Lawrence, 1987). Too often, researchers in the field of people–environment studies have not addressed the empirical findings of their research to housing managers, housing designers or other professionals.

It is increasingly recognized that the reciprocal relations between the design, meanings and uses of housing units ought to be considered in terms of architectural, cultural, social and psychological variables. This holistic and systemic framework ought to be applied bearing in mind the following principles. First, the specific characteristics of the location of housing, including site orientation, microclimate and availability of construction materials, and the characteristics of the immediate surroundings should be identified and analysed. Secondly, alone, these physical and material characteristics do not explain housing and domestic lifestyles; in addition, social norms and conventions as well as personal preferences need to be studied because they are transmitted in the layout, furnishing and use of domestic space. Thirdly, beyond economic and political factors that influence the availability and affordability of housing, an in-depth understanding of cultural, social and psychological variables is necessary to analyse domestic processes including the cultivation of the private domestic domain, the residential biography of individuals and households and residential satisfaction (Clark & Dieleman, 1996). Fourthly, there is a non-deterministic dialectical relationship between people and the built form of housing owing to the influence of numerous implicit and explicit codes; given that these codes act as mediators in dwelling processes, they need to be identified and analysed.

The following paragraphs report the findings of numerous empirical studies of housing by researchers in the field of people–environment studies. These findings are considered in terms of the cultural, the socio-demographic and the psychological dimensions of housing.

Cultural dimensions of housing

Culture refers to characteristics of human societies that involve the acquisition and transmission by non-genetic means (from one person to another, between human groups and societies as well as over generations) of shared beliefs, customs, information, institutions, language, rules, symbols, technology and values. Although culture was often interpreted by anthropologists to be a monolithic and static concept, today it increasingly designates a relativistic and pluralistic concept within and between human groups, societies and nations (Kent, 1990).

Housing cultures are complex and diverse but they are too often taken for granted. Housing, dwelling and home are fundamental human constructs that are crucial components of human culture that partly define the condition and status of individuals and households in relation to others in their society (Altman & Werner, 1985; Waterson, 1990). Cultures of domestic life explicitly concern three attributes. First, the artefacts and techniques of human groups (housing units, infrastructure and services). This can be considered as the material culture of domestic life that may express and communicate cultural and social/group identities. The second attribute is the social organization of human groups according to norms about marriage, kinship, household composition and social relations (Clark & Dieleman, 1996). The residential environment not only expresses social conventions but also social differentiation by differences in architectural style, the size of housing units and site location (Duncan, 1981). The third attribute is the meanings attributed to the physical and non-material components of human habitats and how these are expressed by language: for example, a housing unit, a dwelling, a domicile, or home, as discussed in Benjamin (1995).

There are numerous theoretical and empirical studies that analyse the cultural conventions, rules and values that are expressed in or attributed to the spatial layout, the furnishing and the use of housing units. These cultural dimensions of housing and everyday life are transmitted by the cultural predispositions of residents (Lawrence, 1987). Ethnographies by cultural and social anthropologists and human ecologists in diverse countries confirm that although the internal organization and use of housing units can be described according to orientation, climate and the availability of construction materials, this description does not include the shared meanings and values attributed to domestic space unless cultural dimensions are considered (Kent, 1990; Waterson, 1990). These cultural dimensions are reflected in the preparation and consumption of food, the nomenclature of domestic space and household activities, customs about receiving family, friends and neighbours, and rituals and religious practices for special occasions, including birth, marriage and death.

Other contributions in Western countries show that several cultural variables ought to be considered if more than explicit and manifest functions of housing in urban areas are to be understood. Given the demographic diversity of contemporary urban societies in the larger capital cities of many countries, it is pertinent to identify which cultural variables influence the design, meaning and uses of housing units in precise localities. Housing surveys have been completed in order to achieve this objective (Després & Piché, 1995). Other contributions have used the participant observation method in residential neighbourhoods, especially large-scale housing estates (Andrews, 1979). In both cases follow-up studies have rarely been completed in order to identify constancy and change in the furnishing and use of housing units, or in the meanings and lifestyles of the residents.

Social and demographic dimensions of housing

People–environment studies not only focus on individuals but also social groups who comprise individuals that may or may not share ideas, meanings and values about housing and domestic life. A housing unit, specific rooms and household objects can be attributed a number of functions and values that may be manifest and intentional, or latent and unintended. In general, manifest functions alone do not explain the furnishing, appliances and services inside housing units. Many studies show how socio-demographic variables such as age, gender, social class, household composition and housing tenure can be related to the design, the meaning and uses of housing units (Low & Chambers, 1989). For example, some studies show that the housing unit is a physical fabric that expresses social status and the identification of the residents with a social group (Kron, 1983; Sommerville, 1997). These values may be conservative and traditional, progressive and innovative, or a mixture of both. Some values may be expressed by residents in the decoration and use of some rooms, whereas other rooms are quite different.

The preparation and eating of food is a common characteristic of housing in all societies, and the variability of how it is accommodated by domestic space provides an interesting topic for the study of social and cultural diversity. A limited number of studies show that the domestic activities and routines, in general, and those related to the preparation and eating of food, in particular, are prescribed by the significance of a specific meal in the total food system. Daily breakfast can have a different meaning to an evening meal, and this meal will not have the same significance if it is meant to celebrate a birthday of a household member. In principle, there are social and cultural codes that indicate what food is eaten, how it is embellished, when it is eaten, who is present, and where the meal is served (Lawrence, 1987). This implies that a household may wish to eat some meals, such as breakfast on weekdays, in the kitchen, whereas the evening meal on those days is served and eaten in a dining or living room. Whether or not the housing unit permits both possible locations for the consumption of food is a crucial question that challenges normative approaches to housing design so commonly applied during the 20th century.

Identity commonly refers to properties of individuality, the essential characteristics that make a person distinct from others (self-identity). Identity has also been interpreted as the qualities of sameness between an individual and others (Duncan, 1981). The most common categories for comparisons are education, ethnicity, gender, place of residence, nationality, profession and religion. In this chapter, identity refers to the common characteristics of individuals and groups in prescribed residential environments. An individual's housing environment, especially the social and cultural context of daily life, is a structured framework for the expression and transmission of personal and social identities (Franklin, 1996). Contributions in the field of people–environment studies show the interrelations between numerous dimensions of domestic life, how these dimensions are defined by individuals and different groups, and whether or not they evolve over time (see Chapter 17).

Psychological dimensions of housing

A housing unit and all its content is a medium for non-verbal communication between household members, family, friends and strangers. Contributions by psychologists have confirmed that domestic space and household possessions not only have monetary and use values. In addition, they become objects with psychological dimensions that express the self, because they convey information about the personal identity, group identity and values of the resident (Altman and Werner, 1985). For example, domestic objects express private/personal and public/shared meanings and values, because a housing unit is both a haven for withdrawal from the public realm of society and a stage for the expression of respect by members of the local community. Hence the concept of **privacy** can be interpreted not only in terms of the dialectical relations between spaces and activities inside the housing unit but also in terms of individuality and communality (Lawrence, 1987; 1992). Studies show that residents prefer to have some personal control over the access that others have to them in their private domain by regulating the boundaries between the inside of the housing unit and the immediate surroundings. These surroundings are not just physical but also social and they include neighbours and strangers.

Other contributions show that the design and furnishing of housing units is also related to past residential experience, known as the **residential biography**. Some of these contributions have adopted a phenomenological and developmental interpretation of housing conditions during the resident's life (Altman & Low, 1992). These qualitative studies often use in-depth interviews with residents to decipher the meaning of housing and domestic life. They have been instrumental in developing new interdisciplinary concepts, including appropriation, place attachment and place identity (Altman & Werner, 1985).

Cultivation is a multi-dimensional process in which implicit cognitive structures, individual and group practices, social rules and conventions, institutional structures, and human consciousness are purposely interrelated. The intentional use of space, time and resources for housing construction implies that a part of the world is appropriated psychologically and physically. The term **appropriation** has etymological roots in the Latin word *appropriare*, which means 'to make one's own.' Cultivation processes may be conducted to express and communicate adherence to cultural traditions, or new social trends, or to express individualism rather than collectivism. Rituals, roles and a wide range of conventional practices are commonly used during the construction of housing units, especially collective or communal housing types, in order to express and transmit cultural codes and social identities (Altman & Werner, 1985; Altman & Low, 1992; Lawrence, 2005). Housing is one of the main forums for the application of cultivation during the life cycle.

Cultivation implies that researches and practitioners should identify and understand the active, perhaps mobile interrelations between individuals and their habitat. It can also account for the cognitive and symbolic interrelations between individuals, groups and their past and present. Cultivation also stresses the importance of intentionality within the ongoing practices of domesticity, especially the way that individual, social and cultural identities are expressed and communicated (see chapter 3).

BUILT ENVIRONMENT OF HOUSING

Housing units should be reinterpreted not only in terms of their material components but also according to the goals, priorities and values of those who design and build, those who manage and maintain, and those who live in them. The decision to construct housing offers two approaches for the analysis of people–environment studies. The first approach involves consulting the future residents (or their representatives) before or during the design and construction process. This approach is a way for those who make decisions about a future housing project to become aware of the point of view of the residents about different options for the physical fabric of the new residential environment (Sanoff, 1999). This approach has been used to define behavioural criteria for the design of new housing units in a wide range of localities. The second approach involves the observation of a housing project during its use either at a precise time or over an extended period. Repeated observations of occupied housing can enable those responsible for it to test assumptions about the interrelations between the residents and their domestic environment (Després & Piché, 1995). Empirical studies of buildings in use are known as post-occupancy evaluations (Preiser, Rabinowitz & White, 1988). Often this second approach uses housing survey tools such as checklists for observational records, interview schedules and questionnaires. It has been argued that the findings of housing surveys can be reapplied in other localities, but this kind of generalization should be considered carefully as Lawrence (2003) has discussed.

A number of architectural research methods and design tools have been used to incorporate the needs of residents in housing design since the 1960s (Lawrence, 2003). These tools include:

- Architectural checklists, standards and specifications, usually descriptive texts, that present norms or regulations, sometimes linked to government housing loans or subsidies (Department of the Environment, 1983).
- Design, including principles, rules or patterns, presented often as texts and drawings such as model floor plans (Cooper, 1975; Cooper Marcus & Sarkissian, 1986).
- Design games that present step-by-step decision-making processes that lead to the selection of one amongst several options (Sanoff, 1999).

In these approaches aesthetic, functional and ergonomic criteria are assessed in terms of client or user satisfaction, sometimes in conjunction with cost/benefit analysis using monetary values.

Some research has considered the mismatch between the intended outcomes of housing designers and policymakers and the effective meaning and uses of residential environments: how the design and layout of housing units and urban neighbourhoods can enhance or impede social interaction between residents or prevent antisocial behaviour, including criminal offences. There have been a small number of contributions that have considered the impacts of housing and residential environments on the health and well-being of residents.

The residential context of health and well-being

Housing units and residential environments are known to be an important determinant of quality of life and well-being following the empirical results of numerous studies (Burridge & Ormandy, 1993). The multiple components of housing units and outdoor areas need to be considered in terms of their potential and effective contribution to physical, social and mental well-being. In general, the domain of housing and health has been considered in relation to the following eight topics:

1. The characteristics of the site in ensuring safety from 'natural' disasters, including earthquakes, landslides, flooding and fires, and protection from any potential source of natural radon.
2. The residential building as a shelter for the inhabitants from the extremes of outdoor temperature, as a protector against dust, insects and rodents, as a provider of security from unwanted persons and as an insulator against noise.
3. The effective provision of a safe and continuous supply of water that meets standards for human consumption, and the maintenance of sewage and solid waste disposal.
4. Ambient atmospheric conditions in the residential neighbourhood and indoor air quality both of which are related to emissions from industrial production, transportation, fuels used for domestic cooking and heating, as well as the local climate and ventilation inside and around buildings.
5. Household occupancy conditions, which can influence the transmission of airborne infections such as pneumonia and tuberculosis, and the incidence of injury from domestic accidents.
6. Accessibility to community facilities and services (for commerce, education, employment, leisure and primary healthcare) which are affordable and available to all individuals and households.
7. Food safety, including provision of uncontaminated fresh foods that can be stored with protection against spoilage.

8   The control of vectors and hosts of disease outdoors and inside residential buildings which can propagate in the building structure, the use of non-toxic materials and finishes for housing and building construction and the use and storage of hazardous substances or equipment in the residential environment.

Contributions of people–environment studies during the 1990s confirm that the relations between residential environments and health are not limited to the above eight topics (Hartig & Lawrence, 2003). Housing environments have also been analysed in terms of their capacity to nurture and sustain social and psychological processes (Bistrup, 1991): for example, the capacity of the resident in her/his home environment to alleviate stress accumulated at school or in the workplace, and whether this capacity is mediated by views of nature or being in natural surroundings such as urban parks. The multiple dimensions of housing that circumscribe the resident's capacity to use her/his domestic setting for restorative processes is a subject that has been studied by a limited number of scholars during the last two decades. In addition, there is little doubt that the physical condition of housing units should be examined with respect to forms of housing tenure, household composition and income, the availability and cost of building materials, infrastructure and services, the levels of education and the employment status of residents. These dimensions of housing environments and the health of residents should not be isolated from their diet, lifestyle, type of employment and the availability of healthcare. Hartig and Lawrence (2003) have used the term 'the residential context of health' to refer to all those dimensions that define the interrelated nature of housing, health and well-being.

CRITIQUE OF RECENT ARCHITECTURAL AND PSYCHO-SOCIOLOGICAL CONTRIBUTIONS

There are numerous published studies that evaluate residential environments from the point of view of the residents. These studies were commonly conducted using sociological and psycho-physiological models of aesthetics, ergonomics and human comfort. The objective of the majority of these contributions has been to make design professionals accountable for the 'anonymous users'. The most common way of meeting this goal has been the formulation of design checklists or guidelines about 'user needs' (Cooper, 1975). These contributions, especially the studies by architects and urban designers, evaluate housing environments largely in terms of aesthetic and functional parameters. However, little consideration has been given to the conflicting values and goals of different groups of people (for example, building owners, administrative officials, residents and professional designers). Moreover, ecological factors related to the costs of consuming resources and energy-saving measures have commonly been ignored, although these were debated publicly from the 1970s.

This kind of approach has recurred consistently during the last four decades. It reflects an underlying belief of many professional designers and social scientists who maintain that there is 'an empirically-based ability to create and/or modify the design of residential environment(s) to provide for greater residential satisfaction' (Michelson, 1980, p. 137). An underlying assumption of this interpretation is that there is a law-like, mechanistic relationship between the degree of satisfaction with the built environment and its physical configuration which is studied in terms of aesthetic response, functional efficiency, human behaviour and stress. Michelson (1977, 1980) relates this custom to the approach of those academic and professional designers, and social scientists, who maintain that if 'user needs' are identified they can serve as guidelines for architectural design (Alexander, Ishikawa & Silverstein, 1977).

In contrast to interpretations of this kind, which assume a direct relationship between the physical features of residential environments and resident's satisfaction, selection and use of them, Michelson (1980) and

Lawrence (1987) show that there is no law which prescribes the interaction between how satisfied people are with their residence or whether they will move elsewhere. Rather, both argue for the application of a contextual analysis. According to Michelson (1980, pp. 144–145), the relativity of an individual's evaluation of the quantitative and qualitative characteristics of residential environments should be acknowledged in housing research. Furthermore, in view of advances in the building and environmental sciences since the 1970s, which have identified relationships between global environmental issues and building construction practices, housing quality can no longer be narrowly defined in terms of aesthetics, ergonomics or space standards. Today, it is necessary to consider housing quality in relation to environmental quality using an integrative perspective that not only includes economic, material, social and psychological factors but also ecological and political ones. This reorientation can identify those basic principles underlying the means and measures that can enable and sustain a quality of housing that is acceptable to individuals, households and social groups.

HOUSING QUALITY: AN INTERDISCIPLINARY AND HUMANISTIC PERSPECTIVE

Housing quality can be interpreted in many ways (Lawrence, 1987). Diverse approaches reflect the rationale and objectives of those who conduct or sponsor research and policy formulation. For example, studies on housing quality may be intended for the formulation and the implementation of government housing policies, or academic research, or the dissemination of information to professional groups (such as architects or building contractors) and to the public. The purpose of defining housing quality may concern one or more of the following objectives:

1 The assessment of aesthetic and/or use values of residential buildings.
2 The identification of targets for upgrading or replacing the existing housing stock.
3 The allocation of housing loans and subsidies by consideration of effective occupancy conditions, household income and expenditure.
4 Concern about the health and well-being of the residents in relation to the internal and external conditions of housing neighbourhoods.

Given that there is a wide range of contributions on this subject, it is not surprising that there has been little consensus about those concepts, means and measures used to define and assess housing quality. Following a bibliographical survey, the three main classes of contributions can be summarized in the following way:

1 Those approaches that focus on the point of view of the individual, be it that of an architect, a building contractor, a housing administrator, or a resident. By this approach, people are meant to evaluate a specific residential environment using one or more sociological and/or psychological research methods.
2 Research about the material/quantifiable characteristics of housing, especially in terms of the external appearance of residential buildings and functional, technical and construction components. Calculations of net habitable floor area per person and of acoustic and thermal insulation provided by internal and external walls are commonly included. These approaches often ignore the fact that ergonomic, technical and physical standards of housing are dependent on cultural values, social conventions and individual preferences which may vary over time.
3 Studies of the supply of housing (annual construction output), of the cost of new residential buildings, of the rationale, and outcomes of housing construction grants to public authorities and private firms, and of housing subsidies and allowances to households.

Each of these approaches examines a number of factors related to housing quality. However, it is rare for contributions to address or define a broad, integrated definition of housing quality, which accounts for the three sets of approaches simultaneously. There appears to be no methodological reasons for this lack of integration. Nonetheless, academics, professionals and politicians have created conceptual and institutional barriers that hinder advances. Some of these barriers have been discussed in Lawrence (2002). There is an urgent need for an integrated definition of housing quality in which sets of architectural, demographic, economic, ecological and political factors are explicitly interrelated.

The preceding sections of this chapter suggest that it is necessary to redefine what is commonly meant by housing quality, which has frequently been measured in terms of physical standards and regulations. Contributions from people–environment studies show that housing quality can be interpreted as a relative concept by referring to sets of interrelated constituents and processes that concern not only the material conditions of residential environments but also social relationships (such as landlord and tenant rights and obligations), economic conditions (especially affordability in terms of household budgets) and ecological consequences (including the use of natural resources). From this perspective, housing quality is no longer defined only in terms of static, objective measures but also according to the opportunities that people have in choosing, appropriating and modifying their residence and its surroundings in order to meet and sustain individual, household and communal aspirations, goals and requirements that change over time. These objectives concern both the short and the long term, and they are relevant to one or more geographical scales. This has still not been widely recognized in contributions about housing quality.

All housing and residential land-use projects generate a range of costs and benefits that vary according to the evaluation criteria used as well as the point of view of the assessor. The relativity of any evaluation should not be seen as an obstacle, but rather as an opportunity for professional designers and housing administrators to explicitly account for the point of view of lay people. However, one of the significant anomalies of the architecture and town planning professions (as they are and have always been conducted) is that buildings or larger projects are rarely evaluated with any rigour once they have been constructed and occupied. It has been argued by Lawrence (1987) that this custom must change and that lay people should be included in the evaluation process.

The reinterpretation of housing quality requested in this chapter can be used by accounting for lessons learned from the findings of people–environment studies. This requires a shift away from the formulation of prescriptive principles in order to identify and apply those proscriptive principles that enable and sustain a quality of life that is acceptable to individuals, households and communities. It is noteworthy that contemporary environmental, housing and public health regulations are usually prescriptive principles. They specify what ought to be achieved. This approach means they decrease the capacity of autonomous environmental control that each party can exercise. In contrast, earlier paragraphs of this chapter have argued that environmental control by individuals or households ought to be increased. In order to achieve this goal it is suggested that proscriptive principles replace prescriptive ones. Proscriptive principles state what not to achieve or do; they imply that what is not forbidden is permitted, and may engender a wide range of solutions to housing requirements, as many studies including that by Hardy and Ward (1984) mentioned earlier have shown.

INTERDISCIPLINARITY AND TRANSDISCIPLINARITY: A WAY FORWARD

Today, we know that most housing subjects are not structured within traditional disciplinary and professional boundaries. This is the main reason to propose a shift from disciplinary to interdisciplinary contributions in housing research, in general, and for people–environment studies, in particular. This shift can provide the foundation for innovative research and professional practice.

In this chapter, disciplinarity has referred to the specialization of academic disciplines that became strong during the 19th century (Lawrence & Després, 2004). Each discipline has its own concepts, definitions and methodological protocols for the study of its precisely defined domain of competence. Multidisciplinary refers to research in which each specialist remains within her/his discipline and makes a contribution using only his/her disciplinary concepts and methods. Interdisciplinary contributions involve the bringing together of several disciplines; each discipline retains its own concepts and methods that are applied to a mutually agreed subject. In these studies one contributor will usually coordinate the research process and seek integration. This integration may provide a synergy for the development of new concepts; for example, in the field of people–environment relations, as already noted earlier, the disciplinary concepts of cultural identity (in anthropology), personal space and identity (in psychology), social status and position (in sociology) and space/place (in geography) have been interrelated to create the new concept known as **place identity**.

In contrast to interdisciplinary contributions, transdisciplinary collaboration involves a fusion of disciplinary knowledge together with the knowledge of lay people (Somerville & Rapport, 2000). This creates a new hybrid. This interpretation means that transdisciplinarity is not an automated process that stems from the bringing together of people from different disciplines or professions. In addition, it requires an ingredient that some have called 'transcendence.' This implies the giving up of sovereignty over scientific knowledge and professional information. It involves the generation of new insights and knowledge by collaboration, and the capacity to consider the expertise of professionals and lay people as being as equally important as scientific knowledge.

Collectively, transdisciplinary contributions enable the cross-fertilization of ideas and knowledge from different contributors that leads to an enlarged vision of a subject, innovative concepts and concrete proposals to deal with societal problems, such as affordable housing accessible to all (Somerville & Rapport, 2000).

Transdisciplinarity is a way of achieving innovative goals, enriched understanding and a synergy of new methods that has been effectively applied to housing in order to promote quality of life (Lawrence & Després, 2004). Multidisciplinarity, interdisciplinarity and transdisciplinarity are complementary rather than being mutually exclusive. It is important to stress this principle because without specialised disciplinary studies there would be no in-depth knowledge and data. This is essential for complex subjects, including the interrelations between research on housing culture and the definition of housing policy (Jones & Seelig, 2004). Applied research on these interrelations ought to be more systematic than it has been (Jones & Seelig, 2005). The dominant mode of housing research and housing policy has undoubtedly been disciplinary contributions. Today, there still is too little cross-disciplinary collaboration.

CONCLUSION

Following the significant contribution of people–environment studies, it is pertinent to question recurrent interpretations of housing design and housing quality. First, it is necessary to challenge the common interpretation of design as either a product (for example, the material composition of housing units) or as a process (for example, furnishing activities of households). This dual interpretation of design hinders the application of more integrated concepts. In contrast, housing design can be reconsidered to refer to the intentional organization of housing units, a setting for household activities and a longer-term project to achieve desired objectives. This integrated definition of housing design underlines the principle that housing always occurs in a human context. It also highlights the principle that housing is intentional not haphazard. It involves choosing between ranges of options in order to achieve preferred outcomes. Therefore, housing design is not simply the art of aesthetic and spatial composition. It also has a political dimension, if politics is interpreted as the ordering of the activities and intentions of people who seek to obtain a defined goal.

People–environment studies are multidisciplinary and sometimes interdisciplinary and transdisciplinary. Given that the interrelations between people and their housing are not structured within traditional disciplinary and professional boundaries, more interdisciplinary and transdisciplinary contributions are necessary. They ought to apply a broad integrated perspective which recognizes that architectural, behavioural, cultural, economic, social, physical and political factors need to be considered simultaneously if a comprehensive understanding of people and their housing is to complement disciplinary and professional interpretations.

REFERENCES

Alexander, C., Ishikawa, I. & Silverstein, M. (1977). *A Pattern Language: Towns, Buildings, Construction.* New York: Oxford University Press.

Altman, I. & Low, S. (eds) (1992). *Place Attachment: Human Behavior and Environment.* New York: Plenum Press.

Altman, I. & Werner, C. (eds) (1985). *Home Environments: Human Behaviour and Environment. Advances in Theory and Research*, Volume 8. New York: Plenum Press.

Andrews, C.L. (1979). *Tenants and Town Hall.* London: Her Majesty's Stationery Office.

Aragones, J., Francescato, G. & Gärling, T. (eds.) (2002). *Residential Environments: Choice, Satisfaction and Behavior.* Westport, CT: Bergin and Garvey.

Arias, E.G. (ed.) (1993). *The Meaning and Use of Housing: International Perspectives, Approaches and Their Applications.* Aldershot, UK: Avebury.

Benjamin, D. (ed.) (1995). *The Home: Words, Interpretations, Meanings and Environments.* Aldershot, UK: Avebury.

Berglund, B. & Lindvall, T. (1995). *Community Noise.* Stockholm: Archives of the Center for Sensory Research.

Bechtel, R. & Churchman, A. (eds) (2002). *Handbook of Environmental Psychology.* New York: John Wiley.

Bistrup, M.L. (1991). *Housing and Community Environments: How They Support Health.* Copenhagen: National Board of Health.

Burridge, R. & Ormandy D. (eds) (1993). *Unhealthy Housing: Research, Remedy and Reform.* London: E. & F.N. Spon.

Clark, W. & Dieleman, F. (1996). *Households and Housing: Choice and Outcomes in the Housing Market.* New Brunswick, NJ: Center for Public Policy Research.

Cooper, C.C. (1975). *Easter Hill Village: Some Social Implications of Design.* New York: The Free Press.

Cooper Marcus, C.C. & Sarkissian, W. (1986). *Housing as if People Mattered.* Berkeley, CA: University of California Press.

Department of the Environment (1983). *Housing Appraisal Kit.* London: Her Majesty's Stationery Office.

Després, C. & Piché, D. (eds) (1995). *Housing Surveys: Advances in Theory and Methods.* Quebec: Laval University, CRAD.

Duncan, J.S. (ed.) (1981). *Housing and Identity: Cross-Cultural Perspectives.* London: Croom Helm.

Franck, K.A. & Ahrentzen, S. (eds) (1989). *New Households, New Housing.* New York: Van Nostrand Reinhold.

Franklin, B. (1996). A new dimension to housing: Context and meanings in the built form, *Environments by Design*, 1, 163–184.

Habraken, J. (1972). *Supports: An Alternative to Mass Housing.* London: Architectural Press (first edition in Dutch in 1961).

Halpern, D. (1995). *Mental Health and the Built Environment: More Than Bricks and Mortar.* London: Taylor and Francis.

Hamdi, N. (1991). *Housing Without Houses: Participation, Flexibility, Enablement.* New York: Van Nostrand Reinhold.

Hardy, D. & Ward, C. (1984). *Arcadia For All: The Legacy of a Makeshift Landscape.* London: Mansell.

Hartig, T. & Lawrence, R. (eds) (2003). The residential context of health, *Journal of Social Issues*, 59, 455–650.

Jones, A. & Seelig, T. (2004). *Understanding and Enhancing Research-policy Linkages in Australian*

Housing: A Discussion Paper. Melbourne: Australian Housing and Urban Research Institute.

Jones, A. & Seelig, T. (2005). *Enhancing Research-policy Linkages in Australian Housing: An Options Paper.* Melbourne: Australian Housing and Urban Research Institute.

Kent, S. (ed.) (1990). *Domestic Architecture and the Use of Space: An interdisciplinary cross-cultural study.* Cambridge: Cambridge University Press.

Kron, J. (1983). *Home-psych: The Social Psychology of Home and Decoration.* New York: Clarkson N. Potter.

Lawrence, R.J. (1987). *Housing, Dwellings and Homes: Design Theory, Research and Practice.* Chichester, UK: John Wiley.

Lawrence, R.J. (1992). Collective and co-operative housing: A multi-dimensional view. *Open House International*, 17(2), 1–86.

Lawrence, R.J. (2002). Healthy residential environments. In R. Bechtel & A. Churchman (eds), *Handbook of Environmental Psychology*. New York: John Wiley, pp. 394–412.

Lawrence, R.J. (2003). Methodologies in contemporary housing research: A critical review. In D. Vestbro, Y. Hurol & N. Wilkinson (eds), *Methodologies in Housing Research*. Gateshead, UK: The Urban International Press, pp.1–16.

Lawrence, R.J. (2005). Learning from the vernacular: Basic principles for sustaining human habitats. In L. Asquith & M. Vellinga (eds), *Vernacular Architecture in the Twenty-first Century: Theory, Education and Practice*. London: Taylor and Francis, pp. 110–127.

Lawrence, R.J. & Després, C. (eds) (2004). Transdisciplinarity. *Futures*, 36, 397–526 (special issue).

Low, S.M. & Chambers, E. (eds) (1989). *Housing, Culture and Design: A comparative perspective.* Philadelphia, PA: University of Pennsylvania Press.

Michelson, W. (1977). *Environmental Choice, Human Behavior and Residential Satisfaction.* New York: Oxford University Press.

Michelson, W. (1980). Long and short range criteria for housing choice and environmental behavior. *Journal of Social Issues*, 36, 135–149.

Organization for Economic Co-operation and Development (OECD) (1996). *Strategies for Housing and Social Integration in Cities.* Paris: Organization for Economic Co-operation and Development.

Putman, T. & Newton, C. (1990). *Household Choices.* London: Futures Publications.

Prak, N. & Priemus, H. (eds) (1985). *Post-war Housing in Trouble.* Delft: Delft University Press.

Preiser, W., Rabinowitz, H. & White, E. (1988). *Post-occupancy Evaluation.* New York: Van Nostrand Reinhold.

Ravetz, A. (1974). *Model Estate: Planned Housing at Quarry Hill, Leeds.* London: Croom Helm.

Ravetz, A. (1980). *Remaking Cities: Contradictions of the Recent Urban Environment.* London: Croom Helm.

Sanoff, H. (1999). *Community Participation Methods in Design and Planning.* New York: John Wiley.

Somerville, M. & Rapport, D. (eds) (2000). *Transdisciplinarity: Recreating Integrated Knowledge.* Oxford: EOLSS Publishers.

Sommerville, P. (1997). The social construction of home, *Journal of Architectural and Planning Research*, 14(3), 226–239.

Turner, J. (1976). *Housing by People: Towards Autonomy in Building Environment.* New York: Pantheon Books.

Van Kempen, E.T. (1994). High-rise living: The social limits of design. In B. Danermark & I. Elander (eds), *Social Rented Housing in Europe: Policy, Tenure and Design*. Delft: Delft University Press, pp. 159–180.

Vernez Moudon, A. (1986). *Built for Change: Neighbourhood Architecture in San Francisco.* Cambridge, MA: MIT Press.

Waterson, R. (1990). *The Living House: An Anthropology of Architecture in Southeast Asia.* Kuala Lumpur: Oxford University Press.

SECTION 3

Context

William A.V. Clark

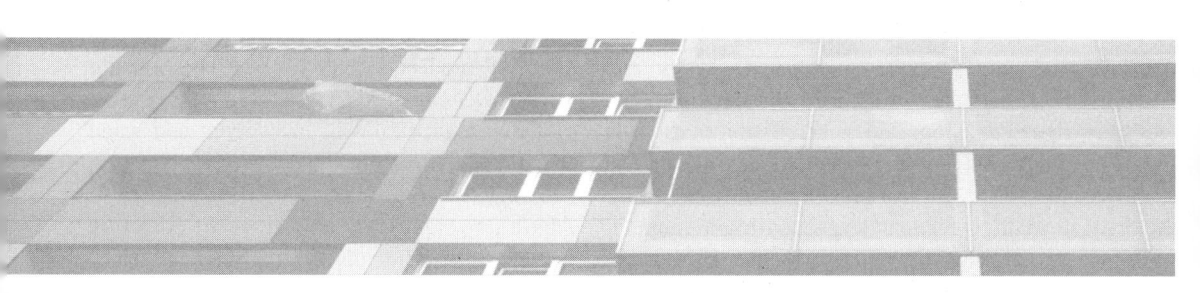

INTRODUCTION TO SECTION 3

Houses and housing do not exist in a vacuum: they are connected to local, regional and national infrastructures and even to the global economy. What happens in local housing markets can truly be said to have international repercussions as we have seen in the recent turbulence in housing markets in the United States and other Western economies. Thus, understanding the context in which housing is situated is a crucial part of understanding housing and its role in both national and local situations. The five chapters in Section 3 focus on questions of context and form a continuum from the macro scale of the national economy and the organization of the nation-state to the very local, the house itself (but also with implications for issues at the global scale.

The first two chapters in Section 3 focus on housing in the context of the national economy and the intersection of housing evolution in Europe and the growth of the welfare state. Meen reminds us that until recently housing was not central in economic concerns and Matznetter and Mundt examine the way in which privatization is changing housing in the European welfare state. Until recently housing provision and the welfare state were inextricably linked. What will the future bring? But while aggregate economic policies have important implications for housing other contexts down to the house itself are equally important. Indeed, there is growing interest in the house itself as part of the urban context. The mass production of housing has not changed significantly in the last half-century, but now, with growing concerns about climate change and energy use, there is significant interest in how housing might be built to better address the growing concerns of energy conservation and urban sustainability more broadly. The chapter by Philip Jones takes up this issue, with a discussion of both energy use and carbon emissions. But beyond the physical structure of the house, there are concerns with how it facilitates social contacts and social interactions. Where we live, and what we live in, is a critical part of structuring our wider social network and that is the theme of Ray Forrest's chapter on housing and social life. People, of course, do not spend their whole life in one house or one location; mobility and migration are fundamental processes of housing market operation. How migration affects housing markets, as people move through them, is taken up in chapter 16 by David Plane and Christopher Bitter on housing markets, life cycles and migration. The Plane and Bitter chapter is in the nature of a bridge between the more macro concerns in the first two chapters (Chapters 14 and 15) and more micro concerns of Jones and Forrest (Chapters 17 and 18). Together, the five chapters provide a discussion of the role of housing and households in it, at the varying scales from the national to the local.

With the expanding baby-boom population after the Second World War the concern in the United States was to build new communities of single-family housing for the growing baby-boomer families. In Europe, by contrast, much of the initial concern with housing construction revolved around reconstructing the swaths of housing that had been damaged or destroyed during the war and in providing affordable housing across the income scale. In the US context the private developer held sway while in Europe there was a strong link between government and housing providers – two different paths which still reverberate through these contrasting housing markets.

The period of the 1950s and 1960s in the United States saw the emergence of large building companies who constructed new mass-produced housing on relatively inexpensive suburban land. The long period of rising affluence after the Second World War and into the 1970s and early 1980s was the underpinning for increasing homeownership, an increase which was fueled by increases in income and wealth, which was spent on mobility and houses rather than apartments. Car ownership increased by 21 million between 1950 and 1960 and in the same period the number of owner-occupied homes almost doubled (Levy, 1998). The car opened up new areas for construction and cheap land with mass home construction techniques revolutionizing the availability of the ownership society. The US economy grew and housing expenditures along with it.

In the opening chapter in the section Meen examines the role of housing in the national economy. He emphasizes that until very recently housing was almost peripheral in discussions of macroeconomic behavior – certainly it was not central. This was at least in part because housing investment was typically a modest 3% or 4% of GDP, housing was often merely viewed as a minor facet of the larger issues of investment and wage and price concerns. It was thought that changes to housing would need to be large to have any significant impact on the economy as a whole. But, the recent financial crisis, the credit crunch, and the massive wave of housing foreclosures along with the very slow financial recovery has brought discussions of housing and housing markets to the center of policy discussions. The chapter sets the discussion of household expenditures and house prices in an historical perspective, especially in relationship to household savings ratios, as a way of entering into an evaluation of housing and aggregate demand. The review and discussion take us through how mortgages affect the ability of young households and low-income households to enter the housing market. Not surprisingly, the chapter wrestles with the recent housing price dislocation in the United States and its global implications but, more generally, Meen asks: 'What traditional transmission mechanisms exist to explain the observed positive correlation between consumers' expenditure and house prices'? Most of the suggested explanations still lack empirical validation, but there is evidence that that potential first-time buyers have been hurt by the rise in household debt, and that the young have typically not gained from the rise in household prices. It is existing homeowners, particularly those at the latest stage of their life cycles, who are the real beneficiaries. Does this mean yet further inequality in society?

The chapter reiterates, and it is worth repeating, that housing (the housing stock) is unusual in its spatial fixity and its longevity. In turn, these characteristics are enhanced by the nature of property rights and the planning system. Changes occur slowly, over decades. Neighborhoods often preserve their characteristics through succeeding generations of residents. This, in turn, affects the ability to intervene with housing policies. There may be a need for government intervention and regulation but such interventions are far from straightforward, and they may have competing objectives. There are conflicts between macro housing objectives, and social objectives, conflicts between national budgetary requirements and the design of optimal taxation. Clearly, policies about housing are increasingly interlinked with international mortgage markets, and it will be difficult to design policies which are effective at both local and national scales. Given the increasing globalization of international mortgage markets, the chapter concludes that there is a developing need for research on housing and finance and that these research areas will converge more closely over the coming years. Even though the chapter still privileges the rational agent, neo-classical model, Meen recognizes that even if these approaches still dominate housing economics, there is growing evidence that the rational expectation assumptions may not always be appropriate. Already there is a developing literature which questions the assumption of rationality and financial and housing markets (see Clark, 2011 for a review and discussion).

How housing and housing markets will evolve and change in the coming decades is also related to the political structures within which they exist. In Europe, where the welfare state has been central in the relationship between families and society, the main focus was on health, education and social security, with housing a less important focus. Now, even the modest interest by the state in housing is being challenged by the push to privatization of housing and housing markets. How should housing be provided and who should provide it? The increased pressure for housing privatization has brought to the fore the complex issue of just how housing should be situated within socio-political structures. Chapter 15 examines housing and welfare regimes in mainly European contexts and demonstrates the complexity of these conflicting policies on housing. Clearly, the rise of ownership and the commitment to ownership across diverse socio-political formats has changed both those structures and the nature of housing within the nation-state. Certainly it appears that the heyday of the nation-state as the organizer at the national level for the provision of social housing is under challenge, if not over. While some suggest that housing privatization has increased the divisions in society, there is a contradictory perspective that points to the fact that most homeowners (across a diverse range of countries) show higher levels of housing satisfaction than renters as support for the shift to a private ownership market.

As the reduction in social spending across the welfare economies of Europe accelerates and the need for social spending is no longer accepted unequivocally, social programs including housing are undergoing increased scrutiny for their relevance in the economic growth models in European welfare states. The debate around welfare regimes and housing brings to the fore the issue of how housing will be provided in 21st-century societies. The new competitive global economy has fundamentally changed political responses to housing and other welfare provisions too.

People and households do not stay in just one location and their moves change and modify housing markets. During much of the 20th century households and people were highly mobile: more so in the United States and Australia and New Zealand than in Europe but nonetheless mobility has been high for several of the past decades.

That mobility fueled housing growth in the suburbs generally, but in the West and South of the US particularly. What does this mobility mean for households and housing markets in the coming decades? Because the baby-boom generation is finally on the cusp of retirement, there have been suggestions that there will be significant impacts of the aging population on the housing market. While that may be so, in Chapter 16 Plane and Bitter emphasize that the real question is not simply the impact of aging but rather how aging and migration in combination will differentially impact different housing markets. The affects are likely to be localized, with bigger impacts in some housing markets than others. The key is how housing demand intersects with both the life course, and with interregional migration. We know that housing demand varies with age, and perhaps most critically, that housing demand increases significantly with younger cohorts as they move out of apartments and into houses and then later begins to decline after the initiation of retirement. Now, with demographic changes, the population of young adults, who represent the principal source of new housing demand will grow much more slowly in the coming decades, and the aging baby boomers will become net home sellers over the next several decades. These two intersecting processes and the accompanied moves across the urban hierarchy will create continuing demand in some markets and housing surpluses in others.

In the end the implications for the nation's housing markets will depend on where the people of various ages choose to live. Thus, movement up and down the urban hierarchy and the associated housing markets will be an important piece of understanding the puzzle of housing market outcomes. Clearly, affordability is going to play an important role for individual households and will affect the propensity to migrate up and down the urban hierarchy, but overall, the outflows we have seen previously from the largest metro areas to smaller metro locations in the South and Southwest are likely to accelerate. The previous analyses of age-related migration up and down the urban hierarchy emphasize how sensitive housing markets are to age-related migration. As amenity migration continues to the South and South-west of the United States we can expect continued growth in these housing markets and slower or even negative growth in the large housing markets of the eastern cities. The recent returns of the 2010 US census, which emphasize the considerable gains in electoral seats in Texas, illustrate the importance, beyond housing, of these changes.

Housing markets are made up of houses of course and the context of the house has implications for the life of individuals and by extension their communities. How the house structures the wider social life of individuals and communities is taken up in Ray Forrest's chapter on housing and social life. Chapter 17 asks just how does the house and its location structure our social life. As he points out, choosing a home and location is also choosing a neighborhood and, to that extent, the choice makes a statement about the kind of social life we wish to have. The choices are in a sense a reflection of aspirations as well as simply choices of space and place. Invariably, the chapter engages with the issues: What is the neighborhood and what does the neighborhood mean for individuals and families? There are other chapters which take up the important issue of neighborhoods (see Chapters 5, 22 and 23), but here the questions are more specifically focused on issues of social relationships in localized spaces. Much of the chapter focuses on the issue of neighborly activity, and how much we interact with people nearby.

A central issue is whether or not the dwelling and the associated localized social interaction has changed from one in which there was considerable face-to-face contact to one in which there is greater fluidity, individualism and reliance on electronics and technology, rather than proximate behavior. In this latter context we may have more contact with far-flung acquaintances than with the people next door, which in turn raises the question of whether the interest in neighboring and good neighbor schemes is somewhat at odds with social trends. Still, as Forrest points out, the literature suggests that the local arena still plays an important role. But, that role is quite variable depending on whether we view the relationship from the perspective of a working young professional, a young child, a retired person or someone who is part of an ethnic or religious minority. There are complicated relationships, which can and do occur within local spaces, and much still needs to be done to uncover the nature of those interactions.

In the rush to build housing in the 1960s and 1970s in the US there was little if any concern with environmental issues, as large areas of land were given over to housing development. Moreover, the houses were constructed with little attention to issues of energy efficiency, either in the house itself or within the urban structure. Now, with the rise of concerns about long-term urban sustainability, how we design a building to be physically sustainable in relation to energy, water and material use is a central and critical issue of housing development in the 21st century. It is this issue which is at the heart of Chapter 18 by Phil Jones on low energy and zero carbon. But the implications go well beyond the construction of the house itself. As he points out, in the United Kingdom, energy use in buildings accounts for nearly half of the UK's total energy consumption and housing accounts for about two-thirds of that. It is also an important contributor to the UK's carbon dioxide emissions. The chapter provides an important window on how government and building regulations have approached the issue of achieving both low energy use and reduced carbon dioxide emissions, in new housing, and in the refurbishment of the existing housing stock. The changes which have occurred during the last decade are a precursor to changes which will continue to occur as housing's role in urban sustainability continues to evolve.

Housing is fiscally, socially and emotionally central in our lives. It is the *context* in which we raise our families and from which we structure social relations in the surrounding neighborhood and community. It is the location which defines our commute, where children attend school and our access to urban services. Some have suggested that we are defined by our houses and neighborhood and certainly marketing companies are adept at using the socio-economic characteristics of the places we live to market goods and services. Housing is also increasingly connected to our sense of fiscal stability as it is the house which is a formidable context for our financial well-being as well as our social and emotional wellbeing. The chapters in this section are focused on the context and setting of housing, but invariably they have touched on issues beyond the context of housing specifically.

REFERENCES

Clark, William A. V. (2011) Prices, expectations and the changing housing market: A commentary and discussion, *Housing Theory and Society*.

Levy, F. (1998) *The New Dollars and Dreams*. New York: Russell Sage Foundation.

14

Housing and the Economy

Geoffrey Meen

INTRODUCTION

Only recently have mainstream economists considered housing to be of importance for the macro economy. In most developed economies, housing investment typically comprises a modest 3–4% of gross domestic product (GDP). Therefore any changes to housing would need to be very large to have a major direct impact. But four events have altered the perspective. First, in the UK in the late 1980s, consumers' expenditure grew faster than implied by traditional consumption functions. Although still controversial, some analysts argued that the observed positive correlation between strong house price and consumption growth at that time was, in fact, a causal relationship, operating as a form of wealth effect. Second, in 2003, structural housing market differences between the UK and the rest of Europe were one of the reasons why the UK did not join the Economic and Monetary Union (EMU). Third, in the early years of this century, the strength of US house prices was a factor limiting the downturn in the US economy. Again, this was seen as a form of wealth effect, supporting consumers' expenditure. Fourth, each of these events has been dwarfed by the fallout from the credit crunch, which has housing at its foundations, although arguably housing merely provided the trigger to more fundamental problems in capital markets. All these events stress the indirect rather than direct effects of housing on the economy.

This chapter is concerned, therefore, with the relationship between housing and the macroeconomy and brings together the existing theoretical and empirical knowledge. This sheds light on the four events above and highlights further ways in which housing can affect the economy. The chapter has five substantive sections: Section 2 considers the relationship between housing and aggregate demand; Section 3 the relationship between housing and supply; Section 4 considers the credit crunch in more detail; and Section 5 turns to the role of policy. The final section is more speculative and considers possible future research directions.

HOUSING AND AGGREGATE DEMAND

Since consumers' expenditure constitutes approximately 60% of GDP in the UK, with similar values for other advanced countries, this section concentrates on the relationship between housing and consumption. Indeed, this comprises the main focus for both theoretical and empirical research in the literature. Since most work is based on the standard neo-classical framework, this approach receives most attention, although the section also comments on recent approaches that relax the assumption of rational economic agents and stress the role of irrational exuberance.

The starting point, therefore, is the standard neo-classical housing and consumption model, set in a life-cycle framework under conditions of perfect and imperfect credit markets (see Chapters 1 and 6). This approach demonstrates the expected relationship between housing and consumption and shows how the relationship changes according to credit conditions. The model provides insights, therefore, into both the relationship between housing and consumption and into the expected effects of the credit crunch. But, first, in order to provide a feel for what is to be explained, graphs in Figure 14.1 show the growth in real household expenditure and real house prices. Figure 14.2 shows the aggregate household savings ratio. From Figure 14.1, for the period 1969–2008, there is a strong correlation between the growth in consumption and house prices (correlation coefficient = 0.74). Of course, correlation does not imply causality, but it might be noted that the correlation rose to 0.81 between 1982 and 1999 – a sample covering the period of mortgage deregulation – but fell to 0.65 from the turn of the century. The fall in the correlation has been highlighted in the recent literature as evidence that increasing prices are not a cause of consumption growth. Perhaps, equally interesting is the fact that the correlation between 1969 and 1981 was 0.76. Given that this early period was one where mortgage rationing was the norm, there is no obvious transmission mechanism available whereby an increase in housing wealth could be converted into higher consumption. Indeed, concentrating on the price boom of the early 1970s, it can be seen that the rise in consumption was modest compared to the rise in house prices. Figure 14.2 shows a fall in the savings ratio during the 1980s as financial deregulation took place. This could be consistent with a bringing forward of consumption by previously credit-constrained households and a reduction in the need to save for housing as deposit requirements became less binding.

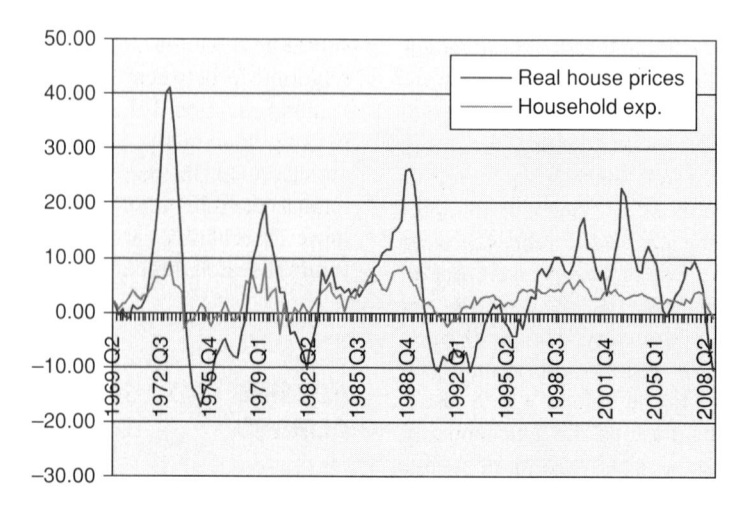

Figure 14.1 Household expenditure and real house prices

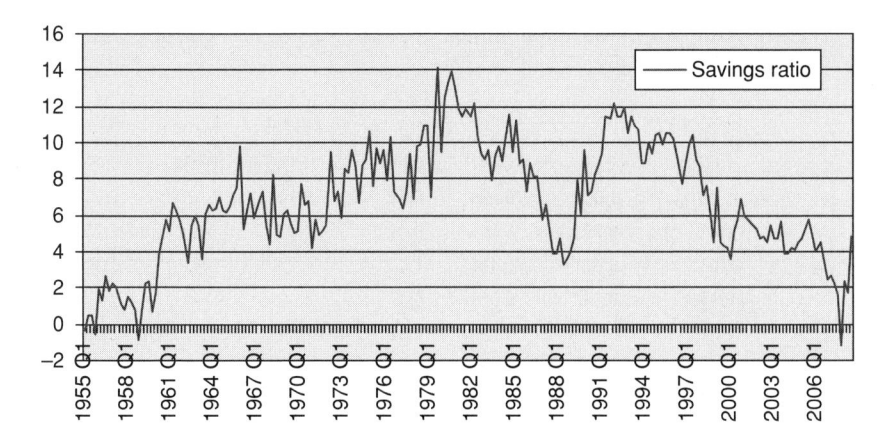

Figure 14.2 Household savings ratio

Although savings rose again in the early 1990s recession, the ratio has subsequently been on a downward trend.

Table 14.1 adds an international dimension and compares the annual growth rates in real house prices for a selection of major countries. The sample, which begins in 1972, is split at the beginning of the most recent house price boom, taken to be 1996. It might be expected that the move towards internationalisation of credit markets would lead to a higher correlation in house prices in the later period. Although there is some evidence that the cycles have become more highly correlated, the patterns are, by no means, uniform.

The standard model begins with a multi-period consumer utility maximisation problem (1) where there are two goods – housing services (for simplicity assumed to be proportional to the housing stock, H) and an aggregate consumption good (C). The model can be extended to include leisure or labour supply (see Meen and Andrew 1998) in which case income becomes endogenously determined. Here, income is treated as predetermined; (β) is the discount rate in (1).

$$\int_0^\infty e^{-\beta t} \mu(H(t), C(t)) \, dt \quad (1)$$

This representation has a long history: see, for example, Dougherty and Van Order (1982). Equation (1) is maximised with respect to the period-to-period budget constraint (2) and technical constraints (3) and (4) which describe the evolution of asset stocks (housing and financial) over time:

$$g(t)X(t) + S(t) + C(t) = (1-\theta)RY(t) \\ + (1-\theta)i(t)A(t) \quad (2)$$

$$\dot{H}(t) = X(t) - \delta H(t) \quad (3)$$

$$\dot{A}(t) = S(t) - \pi A(t) \quad (4)$$

where:

$g(t)$ = real purchase price of dwellings
$X(t)$ = new purchases of dwellings
$S(t)$ = real savings net of real new loans
θ = household marginal tax rate
$RY(t)$ = real household income
$i(t)$ = market interest rate
$A(t)$ = real net non-housing assets
δ = depreciation rate on housing
π = general inflation rate
$(.)$ = time derivative
δ, π, θ are assumed to be time invariant

Maximisation leads to Euler equations for consumption (5) and the ratio of the marginal

Table 14.1 Correlation in international annual growth rates of real house prices

1996–2008

	Germany	Spain	France	GB	Ireland	Italy	Neth	USA
Germany	1.00	−0.26	−0.07	0.05	0.14	0.03	0.49	−0.21
Spain	−0.26	1.00	0.79	0.57	0.14	0.75	−0.34	0.75
France	−0.07	0.79	1.00	0.41	0.05	0.85	−0.25	0.73
GB	0.05	0.57	0.41	1.00	0.37	0.52	0.24	0.44
Ireland	0.14	0.14	0.05	0.37	1.00	−0.11	0.53	0.45
Italy	0.03	0.75	0.85	0.52	−0.11	1.00	−0.26	0.58
Neth	0.49	−0.34	−0.25	0.24	0.53	−0.26	1.00	0.00
USA	−0.21	0.75	0.73	0.44	0.45	0.58	0.00	1.00

1972–1995

	Germany	Spain	France	GB	Ireland	Italy	Neth	USA
Germany	1.00	0.03	0.37	0.12	0.61	0.35	0.04	0.16
Spain	0.03	1.00	0.51	0.33	0.20	0.36	0.38	0.44
France	0.37	0.51	1.00	0.41	0.20	0.43	0.26	0.32
GB	0.12	0.33	0.41	1.00	0.06	−0.06	−0.06	0.58
Ireland	0.61	0.20	0.20	0.06	1.00	0.22	0.21	0.30
Italy	0.35	0.36	0.43	−0.06	0.22	1.00	−0.05	−0.16
Neth	0.04	0.38	0.26	−0.06	0.21	−0.05	1.00	0.52
USA	0.16	0.44	0.32	0.58	0.30	−0.16	0.52	1.00

Source: OECD house price database.

utility of housing to that of the consumption good, $\mu_h(H(t) / \mu_c(C(t)))$, (6).

$$\mu_c(C(t)) = (1+\beta)^{-1}/(1+r)\mu_c(C(t+1)) \quad (5)$$

$$\mu_h(H(t))/\mu_c(C(t)) = g(t)[(1-\theta)i(t)$$
$$-\pi + \delta - \dot{g}^e/g(t)] \quad (6)$$

where $r = [(1 − \theta)i − \pi]$ and is the post-tax real interest rate.

Equation (5) is equivalent to the standard Hall (1978) Rational Expectations consumption rule. If the market interest rate equals the discount rate, lifetime consumption, under perfect capital markets will be constant. If the market rate exceeds the discount rate, consumption will rise over time. The right-hand side of (6) is the unit price of owner-occupied housing services, known as the housing user cost of capital. Versions of this equation have been used extensively in both the theoretical and empirical housing literatures. The model can easily be extended to incorporate transactions costs, e.g. stamp duty, property taxes and maintenance expenditures.

The model above assumes perfect credit markets. However, the user cost is modified if credit constraints are binding. If there is an absolute constraint on the amount of borrowing for housing purposes, as was generally the case in the UK prior to the early 1980s, then the user cost is defined by (7), where the expression takes into account the shadow price of the rationing constraint, $\lambda(t)$. Therefore, credit restrictions raise housing costs faced by households. This is one way in which the effects of the credit crunch can be incorporated formally. Notice that, in this representation, the constraint is imposed on mortgage markets alone rather than on consumption. But consumption liquidity constraints can also be added (Muellbauer 1983) and, as discussed below, the role of housing in acting as collateral for consumption loans is a key strand of the recent literature.

$$\mu_H(H(t))/\mu_c(C(t)) = g(t)[(1-\theta)i(t)$$
$$-\pi + \delta - \dot{g}^e/g(t) \quad (7)$$
$$+\lambda(t)/\mu_c(C(t))]$$

The set of equations (5)–(7) provided a good way of analysing UK housing and mortgage markets until the early 1980s, because mortgage rationing was a fundamental feature of the UK housing system up to that time. Arguably, it can still be used as a basis for modelling in countries, where mortgage constraints currently bind, although there are no examples in the literature. Furthermore, the model was still capable of capturing the effects of deregulation of mortgage markets in the UK in the 1980s, which can be represented by setting $\lambda(t) = 0$. A central feature of deregulation captured by the model is that monetary policy becomes more powerful. For example, under rationing, the length of the mortgage queue acts as a buffer in response to a cut in interest rates, by choking off the rise in effective demand. This constraint disappears in deregulated markets.

The model can also be used as a basis for analysing the effects of the credit crunch, since a central feature is an absolute constraint on the volume of funds available. This implies that the record cuts in interest rates during 2008 have only limited effects in this model unless they are also accompanied by an increase in the volume of lending. Figure 14.3 shows the sharp fall in nominal net mortgage advances during 2008.

But the literature also provides an alternative, although related, approach, which stresses the importance of down payment or deposit requirements. Even in the absence of credit shortages, deposits are still typically required, because of asymmetric information on credit risk between borrowers and lenders. Much of this literature is US-based, where down payments are required to ensure that securitised mortgages meet minimum lending criteria. But the central messages carry over to other developed economies. Figure 14.4 shows the average deposit for first-time buyers in the UK, which reached 28% in 2009.

In this version of the model, the lender imposes down payment requirements (see Brueckner 1986, Plaut 1987, Nakagami and Pereira 1991, 1993, Engelhardt 1994), so that each borrower has to pay a percentage of the property value (plus any transactions costs) up-front. If the borrower cannot meet the

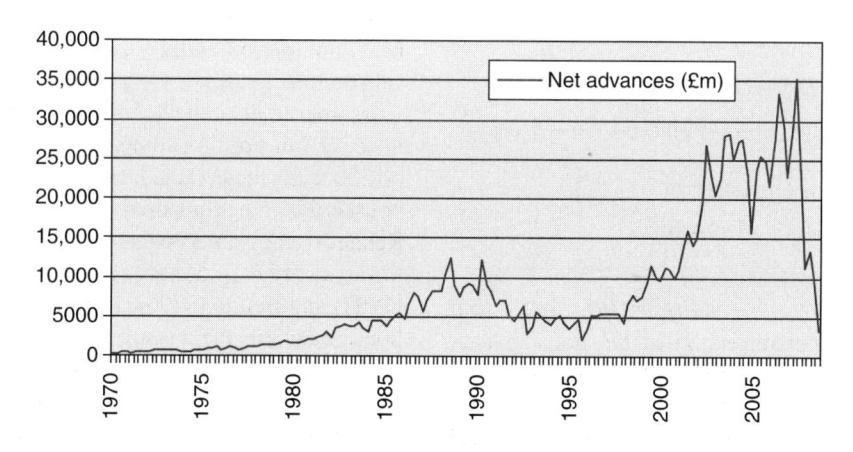

Figure 14.3 Net mortgage advances (1970–2008)

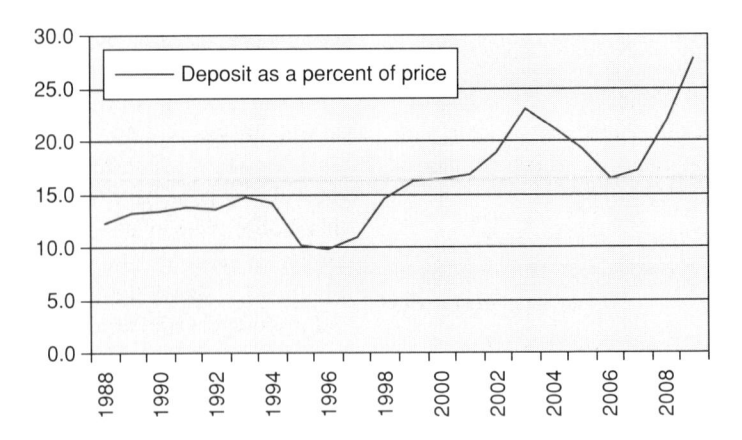

Figure 14.4 Average deposit for first-time buyers (%, 1988–2009)

down payment, she has to delay moving until sufficient equity has been accrued. Actual housing consumption may, therefore, deviate from the unconstrained optimum and the length of time spent in disequilibrium will be positively related to the down payment percentage. Furthermore, housing paths will experience discrete jumps and credit-unconstrained households will, typically, have smoother housing profiles than constrained households. To take an example (see Meen 2001 for further details), if the utility function takes the additive form $U(C_t, H_t) = [C_t^{1-\gamma} + H_t^{1-\gamma}]/(1-\gamma)$, (now expressed in discrete time) utility maximisation leads to housing (8), and consumption (9) demand functions:

$$H_t = (1-D_t)*H_{t-1} + D_t$$
$$*[e(\ln(C_t) - (1/\gamma)\ln(1+UCC_t))] \quad (8)$$

$$\ln(C_t) = \ln(C_{t+1}^e) - (1/\gamma)$$
$$\ln[(1+r_t)/(1+\beta)] \quad (9)$$

where $UCC_t = (i_t - \dot{PH}_t)*(PH_t/PC_t)$ and is a simplified version of the housing user cost of capital; PH is the nominal house price; PC is the price of the consumption good, so that $PH/PC = g$ above; r is the real interest rate $(i - \dot{PC})$. Equation (8) captures the down payment constraint, through a dummy variable (D), which takes a value of one if the household is able to meet the down payment and can move. But, if the constraint is binding, the household cannot move and housing consumption is the same as in the previous period. The second part of the equation is the standard housing consumption rule. The ratio of housing to composite consumption depends on the housing user cost, which represents the relative price of housing. Once again, if the relative price is unchanging, then the consumption ratio will also be constant over time. Equation (9) is, again, the standard Hall (1978) consumption rule under rational expectations where C_{t+1}^e is expected consumption in the next time period and $1/\gamma$ is the elasticity of substitution.

In order to illustrate the discontinuities that arise in housing consumption profiles, the positions for constrained and unconstrained households are compared in Figure 14.5. Related issues are considered by Artle and Varaiya (1978), Miles (1992), Patterson (1993) and Benito (2006). For unconstrained households, if the user cost of capital is constant over time and the discount rate equals the real interest rate, the solid line in Figure 14.5 shows desired housing demand. In the absence of unexpected shocks, for

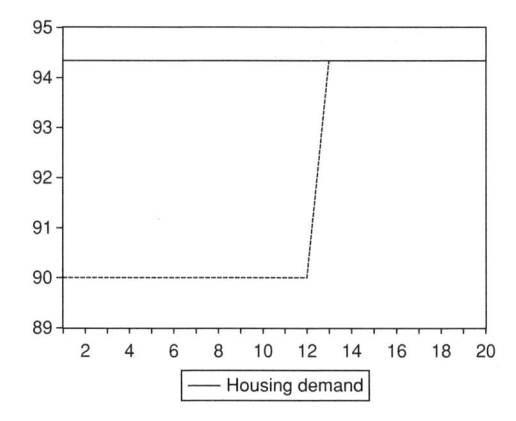

Figure 14.5 Housing demand: unconstrained (solid line) and constrained (dashed line) households

example to income, both the housing and consumption paths will be constant over time. Under perfect foresight, having reached the desired position in the first time period, the household has no need to move, even if (expected) income rises over the household's lifetime.

But the dashed line in Figure 14.5 reflects the position for constrained households, facing a down payment requirement. If the constraint is binding, then the household, initially, has to under-consume owner-occupied housing or rent or remain in the parental home. For the first part of the period housing consumption is suboptimal. However, over time, as the household accumulates assets, the constraint is no longer binding so that housing consumption jumps to the optimal path.

The model is consistent with recent trends in homeownership rates amongst the young in the UK summarised in Table 14.2. Here 'young' households are defined as those where the age of the head is under 30. Young adult homeownership rates rose in the second half of the 1980s and fell in the 1990s and in the current decade, with large falls in both groups identified in the table. The reductions in their homeownership rates coincided with increases in private renting. Thus, the figures imply a switch away from owner-occupation to private renting at an early stage of a person's life cycle. As shown in Figure 14.4, an important feature of UK housing markets in recent years has been the increasing deposit requirements for first-time buyers, leading to a fall in the proportion of loans to this group.

Furthermore, the model suggests that lower-income groups are more likely to consume housing suboptimally for longer periods of time. Indeed, the deposit constraint may bind permanently, leading to permanent residence in private or social renting, despite the fact that surveys suggest most households would prefer ownership. The model also suggests that household mobility is impeded in that households cannot readily move from low- to high-priced areas because of the inability to meet the deposit. Low-income households are also more likely to be affected by variations in national policy, such as interest rate changes, than high-income groups. This arises from a front-end loading problem. The rich can borrow against purely nominal interest rate changes, leaving lifetime wealth unchanged; the poor cannot. Finally, deposit requirements are also likely to generate persistence in house price changes, since the constraint prevents all households from responding equally to market shocks.

One of the central concerns of policy is whether house price changes cause variations in consumers' expenditure. There is little doubt that the two are correlated in many countries, although, as noted above, the correlation has weakened in recent years in the UK. But, there are alternative explanations and the micro evidence, in particular, is far from clear. But neither (5) and (6) nor (8) and (9) suggest a direct relationship between prices and consumption, unless either housing wealth adds to household lifetime resources or price rises are able to relax deposit constraints. As shown below, there are strong theoretical arguments why housing wealth cannot be considered in the same way as human capital and it is unlikely that deposit constraints are reduced. In the basic

Table 14.2 Trends in housing tenure among young adults

Year	Owner-occupied (%)	Social rented (%)	Private rented (%)
Aged 20–24			
1984	35	33	33
1988	41	28	30
1991	38	27	35
1993/4	34	31	35
1996/7	28	28	44
1997/8	26	29	44
1998/9	25	32	43
1999/00	27	28	45
2000/1	26	30	44
2001/2	25	30	44
2002/3	28	30	42
2003/4	25	29	46
2004/5	19	28	53
2005/6	20	28	52
Aged 25–29			
1984	60	24	16
1988	64	23	13
1991	63	21	16
1993/4	59	21	19
1996/7	54	23	23
1997/8	55	22	23
1998/9	52	23	24
1999/00	54	20	26
2000/1	54	21	26
2001/2	50	21	28
2002/3	51	21	28
2003/4	50	20	30
2004/5	49	18	33
2005/6	46	19	34

Source: DCLG Survey of English Housing.

model, the time paths for consumption and housing are determined by relative prices and the discount rate.

Given the basic model, therefore, the question arises what additional transmission mechanisms may exist to explain the observed positive correlation between consumers' expenditure and house prices in many other developed economies? Furthermore, even if there are theoretical possibilities, is there any supporting evidence? The following have been suggested (see Benito et al. 2006):

(i) There is no causal influence, but movements in both prices and consumption are related to a common third factor.

(ii) Consumption increases are caused by rises in housing wealth in a similar manner to changes in financial wealth.
(iii) Housing acts as collateral for loans to be used for consumption purposes.

In general, it is difficult to distinguish between different explanations from time-series information alone. In the UK, both consumers' expenditure and house prices rose sharply in the late 1980s (see Figure 14.1) and, as noted in the Introduction, traditional consumption functions failed to predict the rise in the former. At the time, many commentators attributed the rise to a housing wealth effect not incorporated into standard consumption functions. But King (1990) pointed to the problems with this view. An alternative explanation for the rise in both variables can be found in terms of a rise in income expectations, given the improvement in labour market conditions and possible rises in productivity at that time. From the model above, a rise in permanent income raises both consumers' expenditure and housing demand. But it is most unlikely that time-series information will be able to distinguish between a housing wealth and an expectations effect.

The UK is not alone in finding a strong association between consumers' expenditure and house prices. A significant number of empirical studies of the relationship between consumption and house prices have recently been conducted, commonly in a VAR or VECM framework, for both the USA and Europe (see Iacoviello 2000, 2003, Giuliodori 2004, Case et al. 2005, Chen 2006). The studies generally find a significant relationship between consumption and the housing market, although of considerably varying strengths. A further issue is whether housing wealth is expected to have a stronger or weaker effect on consumption than financial wealth. Case et al. (2005) find considerably stronger propensities for consumption from housing wealth than from stock market wealth. A justification is that house prices are less volatile and changes are more likely to be considered permanent. Other studies are less supportive of this view; for example, since housing is less liquid and has high transactions costs, the effect of housing wealth might be small. In a review of the empirical results, Mishkin (2007) finds the evidence for differential effects is inconclusive. It is also not clear that empirical estimates of the housing wealth coefficient in consumption functions are stable over time. For the UK, Benito et al. (2006) conduct recursive coefficient tests and find the coefficient falls over time.

In addition, housing cannot be treated as a form of wealth in the same way as financial assets (see Buiter 2008). Although rises in house prices may make existing owners better off, the position of renters worsens, both because rents are related to house prices and because many renters wish to become owners at a later stage of their life cycles. Therefore, although there will be distributional consequences, it is not clear that there are aggregate effects, unless the consumption propensities differ between the two groups. It may be argued that in the UK, since owners constitute approximately 70% of households, this group dominates, but this fails to take account of intergenerational effects. The behaviour of current owners may be influenced by the housing requirements of their offspring. Tatch (2006) finds that in 2005, almost 50% of first-time buyers under the age of 30 were receiving deposit assistance.

The issues can be related to the models above. Figure 14.3 showed the build up in net mortgage advances since the mid 1990s until the collapse in 2008. Rather than flows, Figure 14.6 shows the corresponding mortgage stock expressed as a ratio to household disposable income. The figure demonstrates three phases: (i) strong growth following deregulation in the 1980s; (ii) stagnation in the slump of the early 1990s; and (iii) a further strong period of growth from 1996. However, despite this rise, Table 14.2 showed that the owner-occupation rate of the young has fallen sharply since the mid 1990s.

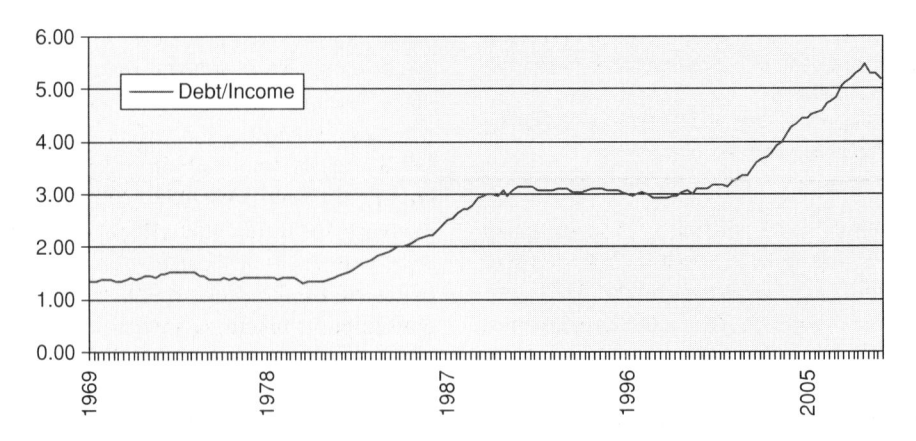

Figure 14.6 Household mortgage debt to income

Furthermore, the aggregate homeownership rate in England has fallen during the current decade. This suggests that potential first-time buyers have not benefitted from the rise in household debt. Indeed, Figure 14.4 showed that deposit requirements have risen and greater parental support has been required. The young have typically not gained from the rise in house prices and would be expected to increase savings rather than consumption. Rather, the main gainers have been existing homeowners, particularly those at later stages of their life cycles, not supporting children, and considering moving down market to cheaper properties. For this group, credit constraints are not binding and the potential for increasing consumption or accumulating financial assets is greater.

These distributional differences cannot be tested from aggregate time-series data and, therefore, a further strand of research has concentrated on micro-household data (see Attanasio and Weber 1994, Attanasio et al. 2005, Campbell and Cocco 2005). Micro data allow research to concentrate on household differences, particularly between age and tenure groups. If housing wealth is the true explanation of rises in consumers' expenditure, then consumption of owners should rise relative to renters. If income expectations are the explanation, then both groups should be affected in a similar manner, assuming no changes in the income distribution. Similarly, under the housing wealth hypothesis, consumption of older households is expected to rise relative to the young, since the latter are less likely to have accumulated housing equity. By contrast, under the expectations view, the young are likely to increase consumption relative to the older groups because they have a greater number of years in future employment. The evidence in Attanasio and Weber (1994) and Attanasio et al. (2005) suggests that consumption of renters and owners has risen at similar rates, implying the income expectations hypothesis is more likely than the housing wealth view. Furthermore, the consumption of the younger groups has risen faster than older age groups. However, the evidence supports strong consumption growth by older households in Campbell and Cocco (2005).

Even if housing is not considered as a form of wealth directly, it may still act as collateral for loans. Using a financial accelerator approach, Aoki et al. (2002) indicate that an increase in housing wealth raises credit worthiness and, therefore, reduces the external finance premiums that households face under asymmetric information. From (5) or (9) this would be expected to affect consumption. However, these equations also show that the effects are on the time path of consumption rather than on the total life-cycle level. In general, the relaxation of credit constraints has its primary effects on timing. This is also true in terms of tenure, as in Figure 14.5. Furthermore, any relationship between housing collateral and consumption is expected to be non-linear. If collateral is low, then the effect of an increase in house prices may be strong; but when collateral reaches a threshold, further reductions in the cost of credit are unlikely. This is potentially consistent with the weakening influence of housing wealth in recursive tests. Benito et al. (2006) suggest, therefore, that this channel is not now strong.

A final link between housing and consumption may occur because of the requirement for new white goods on moving home. It is, indeed, the case that the relationship between consumers' expenditure and prices is stronger for durables than for non-durables. Therefore, since house prices and property transactions are positively correlated (see Berkovec and Goodman 1996 for the underlying theory), consumption and prices will also be correlated.

All the arguments above are based on the rational agent, neo-classical model. Although such models are powerful and still dominate housing economics, there is evidence that the rational expectations assumption is not always the most appropriate. At one level, doubts have been raised because housing markets do not appear to meet the requirements of the efficient markets hypothesis in that current house prices are partly predictable on the basis of past prices. Under the efficient markets view, this should not be possible, because all past information should already have been capitalised into current prices. However, a wide range of studies have rejected efficiency (see Englund and Ioannides 1997, for example) and find that house price changes are autocorrelated. Furthermore, time-series econometric studies of house prices always find lagged price changes to be an important determinant. But, from the models above, this is unsurprising; in the context of (8) and (9) deposit requirements and other forms of transactions costs imply that households consume housing suboptimally for periods of time, which generates persistence in price movements. Therefore, in contrast to the financial markets literature (where such constraints are, arguably, less severe), autocorrelation in price movements is not sufficient evidence of market inefficiency. More appropriate tests require a comparison of the 'excess returns to housing' with the transactions costs in order to examine whether any inefficiencies are exploitable.

A more fundamental criticism arising from some strands of recent research has begun to challenge the assumptions of rationality in financial and housing markets, because irrational exuberance may be a better representation of human behaviour. Examples across a range of different markets are given in Akerlof and Shiller (2009), who stress the importance of human psychology and animal spirits in determining outcomes, which may well not fully match the rationality assumption. The existence of animal spirits implies that freely operating markets do not necessarily lead to optimal outcomes and there may be greater need for government intervention: for example, through greater regulation of financial markets. This point appears to have been accepted in the Turner Review – the UK Financial Services Authority's Regulatory Response to the Global Banking Crisis (2009). But no academic study appears to have introduced animal spirits directly into joint housing/consumption models, although to the extent that they generate price bubbles, they have been considered in housing markets independently. Therefore, under this view of the world, it is not entirely clear what the relationship between housing and consumption should be. It might be speculated that links would be stronger than neo-classical theory might suggest, since Akerlof and Shiller show that money illusion is more likely to occur; this, in turn, leads to a greater role for nominal rather than real interest rates in determining outcomes. But this is an area for further research (see Chapters 1 and 7).

HOUSING AND AGGREGATE SUPPLY

This section contains two parts. In the first part, models of housing supply are discussed. Together with the model of housing demand set out in the last section, the standard stock adjustment model commonly employed in the literature is derived. Extensions to the model are also considered, including the determination of housing market turnover. In the second part, the effects of housing on economy-wide aggregate supply are discussed. As in the last part, there are a number of potential channels through traditional routes such as migration and labour markets to the more recent consideration of housing in growth models.

Housing supply

The section begins by deriving the two-equation Poterba (1984) model, versions of which underlie much quantitative research on housing construction; the model yields powerful insights even in its simplest form. Equation (7) can be written in a slightly different form as a market efficiency condition or an arbitrage relationship. If $R(t)$ represents the real imputed rental price of housing services, arbitrage requires:

$$g(t) = R(t) / [(1-\theta)i(t) - \pi + \delta \\ - \dot{g}^e / g(t) + \lambda(t) / \mu_c(C(t))] \quad (10)$$

Therefore (10) is an equation of fundamental value, where prices are the discounted value of the rental stream, although the discount rate is different from standard financial asset pricing models, since it allows for both real capital gains on housing and potential credit constraints. Furthermore, note that the equation implies that only real interest rates affect prices; if front-end loading exists, due to credit market imperfections, nominal rates can still play an important role (see, for example, Meen 2008).

Writing $a_1 = (1 - \theta)i - \pi + \delta + \lambda/\mu_c(C))$ which, here, is assumed to be constant and, therefore, excludes time subscripts, (10) can be expressed as (11). This is the first equation of the model and is a *stock* equilibrium condition. The rental is assumed to be determined by conditions in the market for housing services and, hence, is related to the size of the housing stock (H), population (POP), and income (RY), with the responses summarised in a_2.

$$\dot{g} = a_1 g - a_2 R(H, POP, RY) \quad (11)$$

$$\dot{H} = b_1 g - \delta H \quad (12)$$

The second equation, (12), represents *flow* housing supply and is positively related to the real house price (as a proxy for profitability) and negatively to the size of the existing stock through depreciation. The link between the two equations comes from this contribution of new supply to the stock and from the responsiveness of new supply to the level of prices. Therefore, if, for example, government provides a demand subsidy, according to the model, initially prices will rise as the subsidy is capitalised into prices, but then, over time, supply begins to respond, increasing the stock of dwellings and pushing prices back towards their original position.

Even this simple model has a number of implications. First, in the short run, the main impact of demand subsidies is to increase prices. Second, although over time the subsidy may increase supply, because new construction is a small part of the housing stock, the total effect may take many years to occur. Third, the final outcome depends on the price responsiveness of supply (the price elasticity). If this is low, even the long-run effects are primarily on prices, rather than on output. Fourth, if there are planning controls, which affect the price elasticity, then the final impact will be on house and land prices rather than output. Fifth, the dynamics of adjustment following the policy change depend on the form of expectations (see DiPasquale and Wheaton 1996). Typically, with forward-looking expectations, adjustment to the long-run equilibrium is smoother than under backward-looking expectations, which may exhibit cycles.

For macroeconomic policy, the key implication is that low elasticities are likely to imply a long-run upward trend in real house prices, whereas high elasticities suggest price stationarity. In the latter case, any housing wealth effects on consumption are eliminated. This is one of the issues that lay behind the UK government's attempts to increase construction in response to the 2004 Barker Review of Housing Supply. Strong supply elasticities remove one of the channels through which housing affects the economy, although the possible greater volatility in construction introduces other issues.

In the UK, the price elasticity of supply, captured in b_1, is typically found to be low – certainly well below one (see, for example, Bramley and Leishman 2005, Meen 2005).[1] Furthermore, even though national estimates of the elasticity are higher in the USA (Topel and Rosen 1988), local estimates show considerable variation, e.g. Green et al. (2005). Both Goodman and Thibodeau (2008) and Glaeser et al. (2008) argue that the areas of the USA that experience the strongest supply responses are less prone to bubbles and the areas that experience the strongest planning controls have the lowest price elasticities.

In (12), the *level* of house prices, or more precisely profitability, affects construction, as an approximation to the Q investment model. In empirical research, profitability is measured by the ratio of house prices to construction costs. The model, therefore, implies that new construction continues until the house prices are driven to equality with construction costs. At this point, the market value equals the replacement cost. However, this condition may never be met in the presence of land supply constraints. Indeed, UK data suggest only a limited relationship between house prices and construction costs. In constrained markets, therefore, excess profits are removed by a rise in land prices. In empirical research, this implies that the *change* in house prices rather than the *level* of prices is the more important determinant of new construction (see the US studies of Blackley 1999, Mayer and Somerville 2000a, 2000b, Riddel 2000, 2004, Hwang and Quigley 2006).

Importantly, both US and UK research suggest that the responsiveness of supply to price changes is much larger than the response to price levels. Given the volatility of house prices, this can account for a large proportion of the variation in construction over the business cycle. Furthermore, empirical research on new construction in both the UK and the USA finds interest rates, as a measure of the cost of capital, to be highly significant.[2] Consequently, the stability of monetary policy has been an important factor in the relative stability of construction since the mid 1990s until the credit crunch.

The previous section highlighted the potential *indirect* effects of housing through consumers' expenditure, but housing construction also contributes directly to GDP. As noted in the Introduction, housing investment typically adds 3–4% to GDP (although there is considerable international variation). Although the share is modest,[3] the contribution to business cycles is larger, since construction has historically been one of the most volatile sectors of the economy. For example, in the USA, Mishkin (2007) argues that the fall in single-family starts from the peak in January 2006 to mid 2007 reduced GDP by 1% over the previous four quarters. Added to the effects on industries servicing construction, the effects are substantially larger.

However, it does not necessarily follow that increases in (public) housing construction can be used to stimulate the economy by generating positive multipliers. The idea that public housing may crowd out private housing construction, when demand pressures are high, has been tested in a number of countries. Meen (1995) considered the effect of a £500 million per annum increase in UK public housing investment, using a full macroeconomic simulation model. He argued that, although the stimulus to GDP was initially positive, most of the gains had disappeared by the fourth year through crowding out as construction costs and interest rates started to rise. Furthermore, private starts were crowded out. However, the simulation was conducted in a boom and, arguably, similar crowding out would not occur under conditions of less than full employment. Most international studies indicate that only partial crowding out occurs from public housing programmes (see Murray 1999, Malpezzi and Vandell 2002, Sinai and Waldfogel 2005, Nordvik 2006, Lee 2007).

The model above concentrates on house prices and construction and, indeed, these are the main variables to impact on the economy and the main focus of research. However, market turnover provides a further strand and is particularly important as a determinant of mortgage market activity. Furthermore, DiPasquale and Wheaton (1996), and Topel and Rosen (1988), argue that new construction is heavily dependent on the expected sales time, which is negatively related to market turnover. An important issue in the literature is the finding that turnover and house prices are positively correlated. In a fully efficient market, changes in demand should be reflected immediately in a change in prices with little effect on transactions. The positive correlation may reflect price stickiness (Berkovec and Goodman 1996). Using UK data, Andrew and Meen (2003) construct a joint model of prices and turnover in which both variables respond to market disequilibrium, but transactions react more quickly than prices. Therefore, at times of excess housing supply, the length of time properties are on the market rises. More micro-based approaches, using hazard models, have examined the relationship between the probability of sale for individual properties, the length of time that they have already been on the market and the state of the cycle (see Pryce and Gibb 2006, for an analysis on Scottish data).

Housing and aggregate supply

Just as housing has indirect effects on aggregate demand, it may also affect aggregate supply, by influencing both the human and physical capital stocks. In addition to national effects, housing also contributes to regional disparities, which have been a long-standing feature of the UK economy. Overall, the literature identifies a number of routes through which housing influences aggregate supply and its spatial distribution:[4]

- migration, earnings, employment and wages
- spatial lock-in through existing land use
- collateral for business start-ups
- growth and crowding out.

Although a considerable volume of evidence exists on the impact of housing market variables on migration, the other routes are more subtle and speculative.

High rates of migration are usually considered necessary for an efficiently functioning labour market, moving resources from areas of excess supply to excess demand, although this ignores the social consequences of the break up of local communities. In fact, housing is probably not the main factor affecting long-distance moves (but has a stronger influence on short-distance relocation). Research on migration, using both aggregate time-series and micro data sets, considers a large class of variables, covering individual characteristics as well as housing and labour market influences. For the UK, studies by Cameron and Muellbauer (1998) and Böheim and Taylor (2002) are particularly relevant. Amongst housing market influences, the following appears to hold internationally:

(i) Private renters move more frequently than owners.

(ii) Social tenants have low rates of migration.
(iii) Negative equity reduces rates of mobility amongst owners.
(iv) High relative house prices discourage migration into an area, but this may be offset by expectations of capital gains.
(v) Migration into an area is deterred by housing shortages, but equally areas that experience excessive levels of vacancies are unattractive because they indicate decline.
(vi) Aggregate rates of homeownership are correlated with high rates of unemployment.

There is strong evidence that private renters have higher rates of migration than households in other tenures. It might, therefore, be concluded that a vibrant private rental sector is a necessary prerequisite for a mobile labour force. However, it is also the case that the young, who are more mobile (perhaps because they change job more frequently or have less attachment to place), are more likely to be in the private rented sector and, therefore, some care needs to be taken with the interpretation of the tenure effect. Nevertheless, since the moving costs in the private rented sector are much lower than in owner-occupation, it would be surprising if tenure did not have some independent influence.

Studies also, generally, find social tenants to have low rates of moving. The early studies of Hughes and McCormick (1981, 1985, 1987, 1990) were particularly influential in the UK. But, Böheim and Taylor (2002) argue that social tenants have higher moving probabilities than owners with mortgages and there appear to be two possible causes. First, their study period was one where owners were facing negative equity, which locks households into their homes and reduces spatial mobility. Henley (1998) finds strong support for the lock-in hypothesis. In the USA, Chan (2001) also provides evidence that negative shocks to house prices generate reductions in mobility through spatial lock-in.

At first sight, the view that high housing costs reduce in-migration appears uncontroversial. The work of Bover et al. (1989) and Cameron and Muellbauer (2001), for example, both provide support. In this case, high house prices are seen as a key factor in preventing labour market adjustment through migration. Strong regional differences also contribute to increases in real wages, lower employment and higher unemployment. More generally, behaviour depends on expectations of relative capital gains between the regions, a point stressed by Cameron and Muellbauer (1998). Households currently based in Southern England may be unwilling to move, despite higher prices, if they expect faster capital gains in the future.

Again it would seem uncontroversial that housing shortages limit inflows into an area. Böheim and Taylor find a significant relationship between inflows and the local vacancy rate, but, arguably, the response may be asymmetric. A rise in vacancies may free up properties for new migrants in high-demand areas, but in low-demand areas, high vacancies can act as an indicator of cumulative processes of urban decline (Keenan et al. 1999, Power and Mumford 1999) (for a discussion of the socio-spatial results of migration see Chapter 8).

Perhaps the most controversial finding is Oswald's (1996) conjecture that high rates of homeownership are associated with high rates of unemployment. The results were found to be robust to data for the UK regions as well as developed countries and the US states. The argument centres on labour mobility and the finding that homeowners are less mobile than renters, because of the transactions costs. Results on micro data are less supportive of Oswald's findings (see Coulson and Fisher 2002, Green and Hendershott 2001).

As noted above, the remaining potential routes are more speculative. The key characteristics of the housing stock are longevity and spatial fixity. These physical features are enhanced by the nature of property rights and the planning system. This implies that spatial structures in any area, typically, change only slowly – areas are locked into patterns that only vary significantly over decades or even centuries. Therefore, history matters and has an effect on both migration and on the ability to change the physical structure of urban areas. Furthermore, households often exhibit an attachment to their current location, because they are unwilling to disrupt ties with family and friends. Most household moves are, therefore, short distance. Given the combination of spatial fixity of area structures and household immobility, it is scarcely surprising that patterns of wealth and deprivation are difficult to change through policy.

Although empirical evidence is inconclusive, it can be argued that housing affects the physical capital stock of industrial and commercial companies; in principle, either crowding out or crowding in could take place. The traditional view is that tax subsidies to housing lead to a market distortion and to under-investment in so-called productive capital. But more recent work stresses the role of housing wealth as collateral for business start-ups and the attraction of high-quality neighbourhoods and housing to skilled workers. By generating agglomeration economies, these factors can generate increasing returns. De Meza and Webb (1999) argue that capital market imperfections prevent low-wealth individuals from starting new businesses. However, housing equity can overcome the constraint.[5] Black et al. (1996) find empirical support.

Two sector growth models – housing and the rest of the economy – shed further light on the crowding-out question. Theoretical research by Turnovsky and Okuyama (1994) demonstrates that crowding out of business investment only occurs if housing subsidies affect the marginal productivity of capital: for example if the subsidy is financed by a tax on profits or leads to a rise in interest rates. But Brito and Pereira (2002) introduce the idea that housing may even have a positive effect on the production of non-housing goods, rather than generating crowding out. Housing may improve the underlying productivity of the economy. But growth models of this form are theoretical and there is no evidence of the quantitative importance of housing from this direction of research. But arguably, improved housing quality from regeneration schemes increases social capital and may lead to increasing returns. Pryce (2004) points to the fact that an increase in new housing supply may have two effects: first, a conventional direct negative effect on prices in the area where the construction takes place; and, second, a positive effect in neighbouring areas, which experience spillovers. He suggests that the neighbourhood effect depends on the nature of the submarket. Although the effects are likely to be small in areas that are already wealthy, they have the potential to be strong in deprived areas.

HOUSING AND THE CREDIT CRUNCH

The previous sections have already highlighted the importance of credit markets for housing. In principle, there are a number of transmission mechanisms through which the credit crunch may operate:

(i) Absolute constraints on the volume of mortgage funds ($\lambda(t)$ in (7)).
(ii) Through changes in required deposits under conditions of asymmetric information.
(iii) Through the availability of collateral; this affects the interest rate at which households borrow and changes the user cost of capital.
(iv) Through the effects on house price expectations; again, this influences the user cost of capital.
(v) By increasing the importance of nominal interest rates relative to real interest rates as a determinant of housing demand and house prices.
(vi) By affecting income expectations and, therefore, lifetime resources.
(vii) By disruptions to the operation of the financial system in general.

Points (v) and (vii) need further explanation. Equation (10) implies that, under perfect capital markets, only real interest rates influence house prices. Any change in nominal interest rates, which in turn generate a rise in nominal mortgage repayments, can be compensated by an increase in borrowing, leaving the total real value of repayments over the lifetime of the loan unchanged. But, in the presence of borrowing constraints, front-end loading occurs and housing decisions are affected by current nominal interest rates. Certainly in the UK there is strong evidence that nominal interest rates matter empirically in addition to real rates (see, for example, Meen 2008). Arguably, point (vii) is already captured under (i). However, it is possible that the disruption arising from the credit crunch is on such a scale as to invalidate the nature of previous relationships. For example, the coefficients of housing demand and consumption functions may be changed by the extreme disruption that has been caused to financial markets.

Although there is little doubt that the credit crunch has affected housing markets, the transmission mechanism to the wider economy, notably consumers' expenditure is less clear-cut, given the models above. Nevertheless, there are a number of possibilities.

First, although questions have been raised about the role of housing wealth as a determinant of consumers' expenditure, it would be premature to reject any linkage on the basis of current evidence. If valid, the house price reduction is expected to reduce consumption. In fact, UK household consumption fell through 2008 and the first half of 2009. Of course, as in earlier cycles, the fall in consumption is consistent with other explanations, including a fall in income expectations.

Second, using (5), consumers' expenditure is affected if the covariance between housing market rationing and the availability of credit for consumers' expenditure is non-zero. Given the disruption to financial markets, it would be surprising if housing credit and other sources of credit were independent, particularly since most mortgage loans are provided by banks rather than by the specialist mortgage providers that were in operation before the 1980s, i.e. building societies.

Third, the fall in house prices reduces available collateral and, therefore, raises r.

However, at the end of 2009, real house prices were still 50% higher than in 2000. Prima facie, there still appears to be significant equity available.

Fourth, the slump in the economy as a result of the credit crisis affects income expectations, reducing consumers' expenditure. This channel is uncontroversial, but raises the question whether housing was the underlying cause of the slump or whether the sub-prime crisis was merely the trigger to more deep-rooted problems running throughout the financial system.

Finally, Figure 14.6 indicates that, despite the steep decline in net advances, the mortgage debt *stock* as a percentage of household income has changed little. This is the result of the long-term nature of mortgage debt contracts and the indivisibility of housing; in a downturn, households cannot easily reduce debt by moving, because both prices and the volume of transactions are typically lower. But, at high debt levels, the probability of default and market crashes in general rise (see Reinhart and Rogoff 2009). The possibility, therefore, remains that the underlying causes of the credit crisis in terms of indebtedness have yet to be resolved.

HOUSING POLICY AND THE ECONOMY

Although macroeconomic policies for housing are not generally explicit, the effects of housing on the economy are likely to be minimised where real house prices and construction activity are stable. However, there are many reasons why the design of policies for achieving these aims is not straightforward:

First, there are competing objectives. Notably, the required level for interest rates to meet general inflation targets is not necessarily the same level required to stabilise the rate of house price inflation, particularly if the supply of housing is price inelastic. Meen (2000) suggests that general inflation targets can increase volatility in house prices.

Post-1996, there was considerable debate across the developed world whether the authorities should act in response to the asset price boom. However, as Mishkin (2007) argues, the question was not whether the authorities should act at all, but whether they should undertake measures above those necessary to stabilise the general rate of inflation and unemployment. Maintaining higher levels of interest rates in order to pop any potential bubble runs the risk of deflating the economy more than necessary. In any case, UK short-term rates were significantly higher than European levels over the boom period. With exceptions, central banks have not favoured special treatment for house prices. For policy to be effective requires that central banks can identify the causes of the price hike, in particular whether the rise is due to fundamentals or to a bubble. Considerable controversy still exists over the causes of the 1996–2007 boom. Although popular perception is that the rise in prices was due to a bubble, for the US, Himmelberg et al. (2005) provide convincing evidence that fundamentals can account for a large part of the rise. Case and Shiller (2003) provide an alternative perspective. Both Meen (2008) and Cameron et al. (2006) favour explanations in terms of fundamentals for the UK. But the appropriate policy responses differ according to cause. For example, a sustained long-run rise in prices coupled with price volatility may be consistent with fundamental housing supply shortages and the appropriate policy may involve relaxing planning regulations, as advocated in the Barker *Review of Housing Supply* (2004) or, as a second best solution, imposing controls on mortgage credit, since changes in supply cannot quickly be used as a tool of short-term demand management. But if the cause of the boom is a bubble, the appropriate policy response is far from clear since the effects of monetary policy on bubbles are uncertain. By their nature, since bubbles depend on expectations, standard econometric estimates are likely to provide only limited guidance and house price based policies could do more harm than good.

Second, there is a potential conflict between macro housing objectives and social objectives. For example, tenure subsidies recognise the value of housing as a merit good, but non-neutral subsidies distort the relative returns on different assets, particularly if the subsidies are capitalised into house prices. As argued above, the distortion in returns can promote housing at the expense of investment in business plant and machinery.

Third, there may be conflict between national budgetary requirements and the design of optimal taxation (see Andrew et al. 2003). For example, the yield on residential stamp duty rose from £675 million in 1996/97 to £6,445 million in 2006/7, primarily because increasing prices took purchasers into higher tax bands, rather than from higher levels of transactions. But despite the fact that the increase in yield arose from fiscal drag, was spatially biased towards the southern regions of the country and potentially leads to inefficiencies, there was an understandable reluctance by the Treasury to lose revenue at a time of a weakening budgetary position.

Fourth, conflicts arise because of the distributional consequences of taxation. For example, local authority property taxes in the UK (the Council Tax) are regressive because of the structure of the tax bands. The distortionary impacts of the property taxation system, have received particular attention in Muellbauer and Cameron (2000) and Muellbauer (2005). As a percentage of property values, council tax is lower in the most expensive parts of London than in the poorest areas of the North. Muellbauer and Cameron argue for a tax more closely related to property values, re-assessed every two to three years. However, such a policy could discriminate against households – generally the elderly – who are property rich, but income poor.

Fifth, the increasing inter-linkages in international mortgage markets and the use of securitisation change the nature of the monetary transmission mechanisms. On the one hand, securitisation allows greater use of fixed rate mortgages since banks are able to fund them through the issue of fixed-coupon mortgage-backed securities. However, UK households have shown only limited appetite for long-term fixed-rate loans (see Miles 2004). On the other hand, securitisation links housing into more general capital markets, increasing the responsiveness to wider market volatility. In the UK, only a limited amount of securitisation of mortgage debt took place until the early years of this century and the financial institutions that have experienced the greatest financial difficulties have been most heavily involved in wholesale markets as a source of funds.

FUTURE DIRECTIONS FOR RESEARCH

The potential areas for further research in theoretical and empirical housing economics remain large, despite the progress made in recent years; this section concentrates, therefore, on future directions in macroeconomic housing research.

First, given the increasing globalisation of international mortgage markets under securitisation, it is perhaps inevitable that research in housing and finance will converge even more closely. This has already been a trend for a number of years. Nevertheless, such research needs to recognise more clearly than has been the case so far, the distinctive characteristics of housing, for example spatial fixity, the importance of transactions costs and market imperfections. These are usually set out at the start of housing textbooks, but are generally neglected by macroeconomists or finance specialists. Equation (10) illustrates; at first sight, this is a simple discounting formula, equally applicable to financial assets. But the discount rate is different from conventional financial models. Furthermore, empirical implementation requires the incorporation of credit constraints and the relationship is unlikely to hold in all periods since households consume sub-optimally for lengthy periods of time as demonstrated in the models of the second section.

Arguably, the use of inappropriate pricing models was a factor contributing to the mispricing of mortgage-backed securities and added to market risk. But a more general class of research issues arises in the design of optimal housing policies – both fiscal and monetary – to reduce market volatility in a globalised credit system, when household debt levels are high. This is likely to require difficult general equilibrium approaches and needs to recognise the competing objectives outlined in the previous section and the paucity of available policy instruments. In addition, research needs to consider the distributional consequences of such policies.

Second, completely different approaches to asset pricing are now available, based on models of complex systems. Arthur et al. (1997), for example, construct an artificial stock market with heterogeneous agents who continually adapt their expectations, based on the latest information, discarding rules that do not work. The models generate both bubbles and crashes and prices exhibit GARCH behaviour consistent with observed time-series properties of the data. To our knowledge, such approaches have yet to be applied to house prices, but this would appear to be a valuable line of enquiry to compare with existing econometric models. The models are also likely to be valuable as stress tests for policy, since they exhibit highly non-linear behaviour and power laws in the manner that conventional models do not.

Third, there appears to be an acceptance that international securitised mortgage markets are the most efficient. However, this assumption can be challenged and there is considerable scope for research on optimal institutional structures for mortgage markets, perhaps adopting a new institutional economics perspective (see Chapter 7). For example, the need for securitised mortgages arose from a particular set of institutional structures in the US in the 1930s and as a response to the Great Depression (see Green and Wachter 2005), In particular, the system of localised banks meant that there was no ready way of channelling mortgage funds from areas of excess supply to areas of excess demand. Securitisation of mortgages provided a good way of overcoming the problem. But the UK has never had local banks and no significant shortage of mortgage funds since the early eighties. Although securitisation may provide the opportunity for cheaper funds, there is a cost in terms of increasing openness to international markets. Under conditions of asymmetric information, where local knowledge matters, there may be a case for greater reliance on local finance. There have already been calls for a return to specialist mortgage providers, relying more heavily on retail deposits. In other words, the same institutional model is not necessarily suitable for all countries. One size fits all policies are not necessarily appropriate. But this is highly controversial.

Fourth, the influence of housing markets on consumers' expenditure cannot be considered resolved. There remains a conflict between the evidence from aggregate time-series data and from micro household surveys. The size of the 2008–2009 market collapse may help to distinguish between different hypotheses, but it needs to be recognised that this is a difficult issue to resolve.

Finally, the effects of housing on aggregate supply are equally important as the effects on aggregate demand. As noted above, influences can occur through wages, unemployment, productivity, business collateral, and migration. Although quantitative research has been conducted on all these issues, there is still not a consensus on the size of any effects.

NOTES

1 Meen (2001) argues that the price elasticity in the UK would need to be approximately 12 to achieve long-run real price stationarity.

2 The literature suggests that nominal interest rates are more important than real rates.

3 This also does not allow for the large inter-industry linkages to real estate services.

4 The quality of housing may also affect the resident labour force through its influence on health and education, but these routes are not discussed in this chapter.

5 See the parallel discussion on the use of housing wealth as collateral for consumption loans in the previous section.

REFERENCES

Akerlof, G.A. and R.J. Shiller (2009), *Animal Spirits; How Human Psychology Drives the Economy and Why it Matters for Global Capitalism.* Princeton University Press, Princeton, NJ.

Andrew, M. and G. Meen (2003), "House Price Appreciation, Transactions and Structural Change in the British Housing Market: A Macroeconomic Perspective", *Real Estate Economics* 31(1): 99–116.

Andrew, M., Evans, A., Koundouri, P. and G. Meen (2003), *Residential Stamp Duty: Time for a Change*, CML Research, London.

Aoki, K., Proudman, J. and G. Vlieghe (2002), "House Prices, Consumption, and Monetary Policy: A Financial Accelerator Approach", *Bank of England Working Paper No. 169.* London.

Arthur, W.B., Holland, J.H., LeBaron, B., Palmer, R. and P. Taylor (1997), "Asset Pricing Under Endogenous Expectations in an Artificial Stock Market", in W.B Arthur, S.N. Durlauf and D.A. Lane (eds), *The Economy as an Evolving Complex System II*. Perseus Books. Reading, MA.

Artle, R. and P. Varaiya (1978), "Life Cycle Consumption and Home-Ownership", *Journal of Economic Theory* 18: 38–58.

Attanasio, O., Blow, L., Hamilton, R. and A. Leicester (2005), "Booms and Busts: Consumption, House Prices and Expectations", *Institute for Fiscal Studies Working Paper W05/24.*

Attanasio, O.P. and G. Weber. (1994), "The UK Consumption Boom of the Late 1980s: Aggregate Implications of Microeconomic Evidence", *Economic Journal* 104(427): 1269–1302.

Barker, K. (2004), *Review of Housing Supply: Final Report – Recommendations.* HMSO.

Benito, A. (2006), "The Downpayment Constraint and UK Housing Market: Does the Theory Fit the Facts?" *Journal of Housing Economics* 15(1): 1–20.

Benito, A., Thompson, J., Waldron, M. and R. Wood (2006), "House Prices and Consumer Spending",

Bank of England Quarterly Bulletin Summer, 142–154.

Berkovec, J.A. and J.L. Goodman. (1996), "Turnover as a Measure of Demand for Existing Homes", Real Estate Economics 24(4): 421–440.

Black, J., de Meza, D. and D. Jeffreys (1996), "House Prices, the Supply of Collateral and the Enterprise Economy", Economic Journal 106: 60–75.

Blackley, D.M. (1999), "The Long-Run Elasticity of New Housing Supply in the United States: Empirical Evidence for 1950 to 1994", Journal of Real Estate Finance and Economics 18(1): 25–42.

Böheim, R. and M. Taylor (2002), "Tied Down or Time to Move? Investigating the Relationships between Housing Tenure, Employment Status and Residential Mobility in Britain", Scottish Journal of Political Economy 49(4): 369–392.

Bover, O., Muellbauer, J. and A. Murphy (1989), "Housing, Wages and UK Labour Markets", Oxford Bulletin of Economics and Statistics 51(2): 97–136.

Bramley, G. and C. Leishman (2005), "Planning and Housing Supply in Two-Speed Britain: Modelling Local Market Outcomes", Urban Studies 42(12): 2213–2244.

Brito, P.M.B. and A.M. Pereira (2002), "Housing and Endogenous Long-term Growth", Journal of Urban Economics 51: 246–271.

Buiter, W.H. (2008), "Housing Wealth Isn't Wealth", CEPR Discussion Paper DP6920.

Brueckner, J. (1986), "The Downpayment Constraint and Housing Tenure Choice: A Simplified Exposition", Regional Science and Urban Economics 16: 519–525.

Cameron, G. and J. Muellbauer (1998), "The Housing Market and Regional Commuting and Migration Choices", Scottish Journal of Political Economy 45: 420–446.

Cameron, G. and J. Muellbauer (2001), "Earnings, Unemployment, and Housing in Britain", Journal of Applied Econometrics 16: 203–220.

Cameron, G, Muellbauer, J. and A. Murphy (2006), "Was There a British House Price Bubble? Evidence from a Regional Panel", Department of Economics, University of Oxford mimeo.

Campbell, J.Y. and J.F. Cocco (2005), "How Do House Prices Affect Consumption? Evidence from Micro Data", Harvard Institute of Economic Research Discussion Paper Number 2083.

Case, K.E. and R.J. Shiller (2003), "Is there a Bubble in the Housing Market?", Brooking Papers on Economic Activity 2: 229–362.

Case, K.E., Quigley, J.M. and R.J. Shiller (2005), "Comparing Wealth Effects: The Stock Market versus the Housing Market", The B.E. Journal of Macroeconomics 5(1): Article 1.

Chan, S. (2001), "Spatial Lock-in: Do Falling House Prices Constrain Residential Mobility?", Journal of Urban Economics 49: 567–586.

Chen, J. (2006), "Re-evaluating the Association between Housing Wealth and Aggregate Consumption: New Evidence from Sweden", Journal of Housing Economics 15(4): 321–348.

Coulson, N.E. and L.M. Fisher (2002), "Tenure Choice and Labour Market Outcomes", Housing Studies 17(1): 35–50.

de Meza, D. and D. Webb (1999), "Wealth, Enterprise and Credit Policy", Economic Journal 109: 153–163.

DiPasquale, D. and W. Wheaton (1996), Urban Economics and Real Estate Markets. Prentice Hall, Englewood Cliffs, NJ.

Dougherty, A. and R. Van Order (1982), "Inflation, Housing Costs and the Consumer Price Index", American Economic Review 72(1): 154–165.

Engelhardt, G. (1994), "House Prices and the Decision to Save for Down Payments", Journal of Urban Economics 36: 209–237.

Englund, P. and Y. Ioannides. (1997), "House Price Dynamics: An International Empirical Perspective", Journal of Housing Economics 6(2): 119–136.

Financial Services Authority (2009), The Turner Review: Regulatory Response to the Global Banking Crisis. London.

Giuliodori, M. (2004), "Monetary Policy Shocks and the Role of House Prices Across European Countries", DNB Working Paper No. 15.

Glaeser, G.L., Gyourko, J. and A. Saiz (2008), "Housing Supply and Housing Bubbles", Journal of Urban Economics 64: 198–217.

Goodman, A.C. and T.G. Thibodeau (2008), "Where are the Speculative Bubbles in US Housing Markets?", Journal of Housing Economics 17: 117–137.

Green, R.K. and P.H. Hendershott (2001), "Home-Ownership and Unemployment in the US", Urban Studies 38(9): 1509–1520.

Green, R.K. and S.M. Wachter (2005), "The American Mortgage in Historical and International Context", Journal of Economic Perspectives 19(4): 93–114.

Green, R.K., Malpezzi, S. and S.K. Mayo (2005), "Metropolitan-Specific Estimates of the Price Elasticity of Housing, and their Sources", American Economic Review Papers and Proceedings 95(2): 334–339.

Hall, R.E. (1978), "Stochastic Implications of the Life Cycle–Permanent Income Hypothesis: Theory and

Evidence", *Journal of Political Economy* 86: 971–987.
Henley, A. (1998), "Residential Mobility, Housing Equity and the Labour Market", *Economic Journal* 108(447): 414–427.
Himmelberg, C., Mayer, C. and T. Sinai (2005), "Assessing High House Prices: Bubbles, Fundamentals and Misperceptions", *Journal of Economic Perspectives* 19(4): 67–92.
Hughes, G.A. and B. McCormick (1981), "Do Council House Policies Reduce Migration between Regions?", *Economic Journal* 91(364): 919–939.
Hughes, G.A. and B. McCormick (1985), "Migration Intentions in the UK. Which Households want to Migrate and Which Succeed?", *Economic Journal* 95(Suppl): 113–123.
Hughes, G.A. and B. McCormick (1987), "Housing Markets, Unemployment and Labour Market Flexibility in the UK", *European Economic Review* 31(3): 615–645.
Hughes, G.A. and B. McCormick (1990), "Housing and Labour Market Mobility", in J. Ermisch (ed.), *Housing and the National Economy*. Avebury, Aldershot, UK.
Hwang, M. and J.M. Quigley (2006), "Economic Fundamentals in Local Housing Markets: Evidence from U.S. Metropolitan Regions", *Journal of Regional Science* 46(3): 425–453.
Iacoviello, M. (2000), "House Prices and the Macroeconomy in Europe: Results from a Structural VAR Analysis", European Central Bank, Working Paper No. 18.
Iacoviello, M. (2003), "Consumption, House Prices, and Collateral Constraints: A Structural Econometric Analysis", *Journal of Housing Economics* 13: 304–320.
Keenan, P., Lowe, S. and S. Spencer (1999), "Housing Abandonment in Inner Cities – The Politics of Low Demand for Housing", *Housing Studies* 14(5): 703–716.
King, M. (1990), "Discussion of J. Muellbauer and A. Murphy. Is the UK Balance of Payments Sustainable?", *Economic Policy* 11: 383–387.
Lee, Chul-In (2007), "Does Provision of Public Rental Housing Crowd Out Private Housing Investment? A Panel VAR Approach", *Journal of Housing Economics*, 16: 1–20.
Malpezzi, S. and K. Vandell (2002), "Does the Low-Income Tax Credit Increase the Supply of Housing?", *Journal of Housing Economics* 11: 360–381.
Mayer, C.J. and C.T. Somerville (2000a), "Residential Construction: Using the Urban Growth Model to Estimate Housing Supply", *Journal of Urban Economics* 48: 85–109.
Mayer, C.J. and C.T. Somerville (2000b), "Land Use Regulation and New Construction", *Regional Science and Urban Economics* 30: 639–662.
Meen, G.P. (1995), "Is Housing Good for the Economy?", *Housing Studies* 10(3): 405–424.
Meen, G.P. (2000), "Housing Cycles and Efficiency", *Scottish Journal of Political Economy* 47(2): 114–140.
Meen, G.P. (2001), *Modelling Spatial Housing Markets: Theory, Analysis and Policy*. Kluwer Academic Publishers, Boston, MA.
Meen, G.P. (2005), "On the Economics of the Barker Review of Housing Supply", *Housing Studies* 20(6): 949–971.
Meen, G.P. (2008), "Ten New Propositions in UK Housing Macroeconomics: An Overview of the First years of the Century", *Urban Studies* 45(13): 2759–2781.
Meen, G.P. and M. Andrew (1998), "On the Aggregate Housing Market Implications of Labour Market Change", *Scottish Journal of Political Economy* 45(4): 393–419.
Miles, D. (1992), "Housing Markets, Consumption and Financial Liberalisation in the Major Economies", *European Economic Review* 36(5): 1093–1136.
Miles, D. (2004), *The UK Mortgage Market: Taking a Longer-Term View*. HM Treasury, London.
Mishkin, F. (2007), "Housing and the Monetary Transmission Mechanism", Finance and Economics Discussion Series, Divisions of Research & Statistics and Monetary Affairs, Federal Reserve Board. Washington, DC.
Muellbauer, J. (1983), "Surprises in the Consumption Function", *Economic Journal* 93(Suppl): 34–49.
Muellbauer, J. (2005), "Property Taxation and the Economy after the Barker Review", *Economic Journal* 115(502): C99–C117.
Muellbauer, J. and G. Cameron (2000), "Five Key Council Tax Reforms and Twelve Reasons to Enact them", *New Economy* 7(2): 88–91.
Murray, M.P. (1999), "Subsidized and Unsubsidized Housing Stocks 1935 to 1987: Crowding Out and Cointegration", *Journal of Real Estate Finance and Economics* 18(1): 107–124.
Nakagami, Y. and A.M. Pereira (1991), "Housing Appreciation, Mortgage Interest Rates and Homeowner Mobility", *Journal of Urban Economics* 30: 271–292.
Nakagami, Y. and A.M. Pereira (1993), "Uptrading and the Macroeconomic Environment", *Journal of Urban Economics* 31: 1–23.

Nordvik, V. (2006), "Selective Housing Policy in Local Housing Markets and the Supply of Housing", *Journal of Housing Economics* 15: 279–292.

Oswald, A. (1996), "A Conjecture on the Explanation for High Unemployment in the Industrialised Nations: Part 1", *Warwick University Economic Research Papers No. 475*.

Patterson, K. (1993), "The Impact of Credit Constraints, Interest Rates, and Housing Equity Withdrawal on the Intertemporal Pattern of Consumption – A Diagrammatic Analysis", *Scottish Journal of Political Economy* 40(4): 391–407.

Plaut, E. (1987), "The Timing of Housing Tenure Transition", *Journal of Urban Economics* 21: 312–322.

Poterba, J.M. (1984), "Tax Subsidies to Owner-Occupied Housing: An Asset Market Approach", *Quarterly Journal of Economics* XCIX(4): 729–752.

Power, A. and K. Mumford (1999), *The Slow Death of Great Cities?* Joseph Rowntree Foundation, York.

Pryce, G. (2004), *The Micro and Macro Effects of the Location of New Housing Supply*. Final Report to the Office of the Deputy Prime Minister.

Pryce, G. and K. Gibb (2006), "Submarket Dynamics of Time to Sale", *Real Estate Economics* 34(3): 377–415.

Reinhart, C.M. and K.S. Rogoff (2009), *This Time is Different: Eight Centuries of Financial Folly*. Princeton University Press, Princeton, NJ.

Riddel, M. (2000), "Housing Market Dynamics under Stochastic Growth: An Application to the Housing Market in Boulder, Colorado", *Journal of Regional Science* 40(4): 771–788.

Riddel, M. (2004), "Housing-Market Disequilibrium: An Examination of Housing-Market Price and Stock Dynamics", *Journal of Housing Economics* 13: 120–135.

Sinai, T. and J. Waldfogel (2005), "Do Low-Income Housing Subsidies Increase Housing Consumption?", *Journal of Public Economics*, 89: 2137–2164.

Tatch, J. (2006), *Will the Real First-Time Buyers Please Stand Up?* CML Housing Finance, London.

Topel, R. and S. Rosen (1988), "Housing Investment in the United States", *Journal of Political Economy* 96(4): 718–740.

Turnovsky, S.J. and T. Okuyama (1994), "Taxes, Housing and Capital Accumulation in a Two-Sector Growing Economy", *Journal of Public Economics* 53: 245–267.

15

Housing and Welfare Regimes

Walter Matznetter and Alexis Mundt

THE CONCEPT OF WELFARE REGIMES

In his seminal publication of 1990, Gøsta Esping-Andersen introduced the term 'welfare-state regimes', to classify 'qualitatively different arrangements between state, market, and the family' (1990: 26). Before, comparative public policy research tended to rely on one-dimensional rankings of social policy, e.g. the share of social expenditure, measured against the state budget or gross domestic product (Wilensky & Lebaux, 1958; Wilensky, 1987). Measured over time, the upward trend of such scores lends itself to interpretations of a general convergence of social policies, depending on socioeconomic development.

A housing variant of the convergence thesis can be found in the book by Heidenheimer et al. (1983), where Carolyn Teich Adams suggested a universal trend towards the privatisation of housing, at least in Western Europe and North America. With further growth, private construction, private finance, and private ownership of housing would become the norm.

By contrast, Esping-Andersen's typology was multi-dimensional. For a limited set of social policies – health insurance, unemployment insurance, and pension system – and a limited set of 18 OECD (Organisation for Economic Cooperation and Development) countries, he measured the decommodification of services, and their effect upon stratification. Three types of welfare state regimes emerged from his analyses: the liberal welfare state, the conservative–corporatist welfare state, and the social-democratic welfare state. These were '*The Three Worlds of Welfare Capitalism*' alluded to in the book title. In this respect, he follows another founding father of comparative public policy, Richard Titmuss, who discriminated between a residual welfare model, an industrial achievement model, and an institutional-redistributive model, all carrying on along their divergent paths (1974: 30f). In their characteristics, these models bear resemblance to the liberal, the conservative, and the social-democratic welfare state, respectively (cf. Abrahamson, 1999: 396).

In the liberal welfare state, social policy focuses on those in current need. Entitlement to (typically modest) subsidies is controlled on a regular basis, and is lifted as soon as income limits are exceeded. Market supply of welfare services is regarded as the norm that should be upheld as long as possible. The outcomes of such policies can be called residualist – due to their focus on strictly circumscribed groups.

The social-democratic welfare state pursues quite opposite goals. Much of its social policies address the population as a whole, without many restrictions. Such a kind of welfare provision does not follow market principles – what we are observing is the universal delivery of decommodified goods and services. As a corollary, taxes and budget costs are highest in the social-democratic welfare state, but welfare services are typically of good to very good quality.

The conservative–corporatist welfare state is neither residualist nor universalist, but it supplies most of the population with graded welfare goods, graded along class, status, and gender. It is strong in reproducing income and wealth differentials. In many fields of policy, this regime relies upon welfare provided by the family, women within families in particular. This is argued with the principle of subsidiarity, a prominent feature of Catholic social thinking.

It is generally accepted that Esping-Andersen's typology brought progress into comparative social policy, by moving beyond the one-dimensional spectrum between welfare provision either by state or by market institutions. There are many more players involved in the provision of welfare goods and services, intermediate organisations, formal and informal groups, nuclear and extended families. Such a variety of providers is explicitly acknowledged in the concept of *'welfare pluralism'*, put forward by Adalbert Evers (1988, 1996) and illustrated by means of a welfare triangle, with the market, the state, and households as its corners (Figure 15.1).

All kinds of welfare organisations can be positioned within the triangle, with each country having its particular arrangement. In Evers' figure, designed before 1989, North-Western European countries tend to have a welfare mix close to the market; in North-Eastern (then communist) Europe, the welfare mix is provided mainly by the state; in Southern Europe, households and informal economies are strong. At about the same time, Esping-Andersen suggested a similar typology – that of three welfare-state regimes.

In empirical terms, however, families, households, and the informal economy are missing from Esping-Andersen's calculations. His 'three worlds of welfare' are based on data for state social policy alone, and the corresponding role of the formal

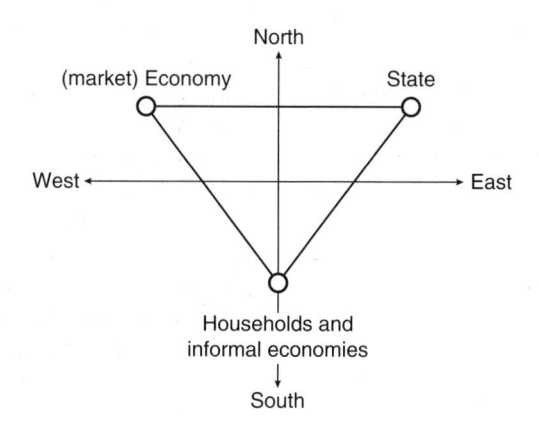

Figure 15.1 Countries' different position with respect to their welfare mix

Source: Evers, 1988.

market: decommodification scores are earned for old-age pensions, sickness benefits, and unemployment payments; stratification effects are measured by number of distinct pension schemes, by budget costs of civil servant pensions, by share of private pensions and private health, and share of universal entitlements, by the spread of social benefit payments.

Much critique has centred on the neglect of the micro level, the informal, the private, the household and family corner of the welfare triangle in Esping-Andersen's analyses. As a concept, it was there in his original publication (1990), but it took other comparative researchers to draw the connections with gender regimes (Duncan, 1995) and family regimes (Hantrais & Letablier, 1996) across Europe. Findings ranging from the social care for children or the elderly, to gender divisions in income and taxation, to family obligations have shown a great variety of both overlap with and cutting across welfare regimes. Regarding family policies, conservative welfare regimes come in two variants, following either a pronatalist model or a traditional model, while an egalitarian model coincides with social-democratic regimes and a non-interventionist model with the liberal regime (Gauthier, 1996: 205). By contrast, social care is being organised in different ways even within the same welfare state cluster, and further complicated by discrepancies between care for children and care for the elderly (Sainsbury, 1999: 246). Quite obviously, any welfare regime typology has to pay attention to the organisation of social services, as opposed to the organisation of cash benefits, on which the 'three worlds' are based (Bambra, 2005).

In his later writings, Gøsta Esping-Andersen accepted this stream of critique, stating that the

> ...lack of systematic attention to households is painfully evident in my own Three Worlds of Welfare Capitalism. It starts out by defining welfare regimes as the interaction of state, market, and family and subsequently pays hardly any notice to the latter (1999: 47 fn.1).

The change of name, from 'welfare state regimes' to 'welfare regimes', is another tribute to the change in focus, from formal institutions at the macro level to formal and informal institutions at the meso and micro levels of society. The debate about additional types of welfare regimes, such as a Mediterranean type of a familialist, 'rudimentary' welfare regime (Leibfried, 1992), is related to that critique of being blind to gender and household arrangements for welfare provision.

From the point of view of housing research, it is interesting to know that housing policy is rarely considered in the welfare regime literature. This is surprising insofar as it figures prominently in comparative Scandinavian studies, as the fourth, but *'wobbly pillar of the welfare state'* (Torgersen, 1987), besides social security, education and healthcare. Only in difficult times, such as post-war reconstruction, the housing agenda was taken over by other European welfare states. With prosperity, much of public housing fell victim to state retrenchment, and only hybrid forms of limited-profit housing survived. In comparative social policy research, housing is rarely included, but there are exceptions (Castles, 1998; Clasen, 1999; Hills, 1998). Within rental housing, groupings of distinct housing regimes have been observed. In Section 4 (*Housing Systems and Welfare Regimes*) below, their relationship with welfare regimes will be further discussed.

Conceptionally, Esping-Andersen is following the concept of power resources (cf. Kemeny, 1995b), whereas earlier typologies of the welfare state have been based on the socioeconomic concept. Four other concepts of comparative policy research are portrayed in Manfred Schmidt's textbook on the welfare state (Schmidt et al., 2007): the theory of party differences (including Hicks et al., 1995), institutionalist theories (including Obinger & Wagschal, 1998), an internationalist hypothesis (including Leibfried, 1992), and a path dependency school (including Pierson, 2001; cf. Section 2 below).

In the following sections, the original concept of 'welfare state regimes' will be expanded in several dimensions that have guided the debate ever since, and their relevance for housing research will be highlighted. Section 2 (*Path Dependency and Path Changes of Welfare Regimes*) will look at the history of welfare regimes and elaborate on the point that the classical trilogy is based on a specific period, before and until 1980, which has been changing since, and which had been the result of a long evolution of welfare policies then. Section 3 (*Three and More Welfare Regimes*) will question the original classification, also by looking at countries that had not been covered by the original study. Section 4 (*Housing Systems and Welfare Regimes*) is on typologies of comparative housing research and how they relate to welfare regimes. Section 5 (*Homeownership and Welfare*) elaborates on the specific role housing wealth is playing in welfare regimes with widespread homeownership. In Section 6 (*Rescaling Welfare and Housing*), the question about the appropriate scale of analysis will be raised, both concerning national welfare regimes, and national housing regimes, and whether comparative typologies should not rather be based on regional and urban findings. Section 7 (*Evaluation of Housing Systems*) will draw a preliminary conclusion of the welfare regime and housing debate that has informed and enriched housing research since the 1990s, by looking at some comparative studies evaluating the outcomes of different housing and welfare regimes. We summarise our findings in a brief *(Outlook)* in Section 8.

PATH DEPENDENCY AND PATH CHANGES OF WELFARE REGIMES

Esping-Andersen's classification of welfare-state regimes puts a strong focus on structure and stability. Although in his later work Esping-Andersen (1996, 1999, 2002) delves into the particular strategies of how different welfare regimes adapt to changing environments and internal shocks, his overall view is that in most countries 'what we see is not radical change, but rather a "frozen" welfare state landscape (1996: 24).' This picture of intrinsically different characters of welfare states arising from one important and irreversible turning point in history can be seen as an example of strong path dependency. Other categorisations such as the Bismarck–Beveridge divide also come under this concept: that crucial past decisions decisively curtail the options for future development.

The Bismarck–Beveridge distinction is particularly widespread in French academia. According to Bonoli (1997: 357), old Bismarckian social policies are based on social insurance and provide earnings-related benefits for employees; entitlement is conditional upon a satisfactory contribution record and financing is mainly based on employer/employee contributions. The new Beveridgean model, on the other hand, is characterised by universal provision, where entitlement is based on residence and/or need, benefits are typically flat rate and are financed through general taxation. While the main aim of the Bismarckian model is income maintenance for employees, Beveridgean social policy mainly addresses the prevention of poverty.

Historically, Bismarckian social policy developed in the 1880s and was tightly oriented towards the position of workers in the market economy. By granting basic work-related insurance, Bismarck aimed for the allegiance of workers to secure political stability. The Beveridgean concept of social security is named after the report of William Beveridge initiating the post World War II social security reforms in Great Britain. These reforms included the expansion of national insurance and the creation of the universal National Health Service. Social policy measures were aimed at the prevention of poverty and addressed the whole population, not just parts of it. Beveridgean welfare states differentiated into more universal Scandinavian welfare states and more means-tested residual welfare states, mainly in Anglo-Saxon countries.

The Bismack–Beveridge distinction thus blurs the difference between universal and means-tested social services that, however, is of great importance in analysing the elements of housing policy, such as the social rented sector and the rise of housing allowances. Maybe for this reason it has not been taken up in housing research so far. Beveridge himself preferred contribution financing and had an aversion to means-testing (Bonoli, 1997: 357).

Jens Borchert (1998) criticised the excessive path dependency of Esping-Andersen's approach. According to Borchert, Esping-Andersen's classification of welfare regimes arises from too strong a focus on the 'Golden Age' of welfare in the 1970s and 1980s. When adding dynamics to Esping-Andersen's rather static regimes, and when considering a much longer time period from the end of the 19th century to the 1990s, several stages of welfare-state development and regime changes can be distinguished. These phases are connected by 'critical junctures' at which path changes were frequent in some countries. During the second phase of welfare-state development in the 1960s there was a much larger variety of welfare states than in the early beginnings and also after the crisis of the 1970s.

Hicks et al. (1995) examined the consolidation of income-security programmes during the formation of the welfare state around 1880 to 1920. Besides the Bismarckian development path, they describe a second path, the Lib–Lab route, which centres on the strategic incorporation of Labour parties and/or unions into governing Liberal coalitions. They suggest common Lib–Lab roots for some 'social democratic' and some 'liberal' welfare states. Some of these states were recipient for universalist, Beveridge-type reforms after World War II. All in all, however, the findings of Hicks et al. support Esping-Andersen's fundamental socio-political explanation for the development of differing welfare regimes: the concept of working-class mobilisation and class coalitions. They find that all paths to welfare-state consolidations are 'manifestations of working-class pressures for social amelioration even prior to extensive entry of social democratic parties into government during the 1930s' (Hicks et al., 1995: 344).

In a European context, there is an extensive literature on the process of transformation to the welfare-state models in response to fundamental economic, demographic, social and technological changes (e.g. Kuhnle, 2000; Ferrara & Rhodes, 2000; Esping-Andersen, 2002; Taylor-Gooby, 2006; Pierson, 2007; Seeleib-Kaiser, 2008). The lack of housing as an element of the welfare state is particularly striking for these investigations.

Following the economic crisis of the mid 1970s, which fostered the end of the 'Golden Era' of the welfare state, a large part of the literature is dominated by a crisis discourse. The retrenchment of the welfare state is one version of a convergence explanation that sees the European welfare state on the defence and in need of a radical reorientation. The reduction of social spending is seen as necessary, for one part, as it is supposed to be an impediment to economic growth, and for another part, as high taxes needed for social spending are (per se) deemed as a disadvantage in a competitive global economy. Others are alarmed about the ageing of the population and the stress this poses on the future financing opportunities for social measures (Pierson, 2007). There is a strong nexus between an increasingly globalised economy and the Europeanisation that is argued to curtail the political competency and ability to act of the national welfare states. Therefore, the question of a 'qualitative dysfunctionality' (Schubert et al., eds 2009: 7) of the welfare state arises.

Addressing a possible convergence of welfare regimes, most authors therefore identify changes towards the liberal regime.

THREE AND MORE WELFARE REGIMES

A major strand of criticism of Esping-Andersen's welfare regime classification concerns the range of different welfare regimes (Leibfried, 1992; Castles & Mitchell, 1993; Castles & Ferrera, 1996; Ferrera, 1996; Bonoli, 1997; Trifiletti, 1999).

The most fruitful variant of this criticism has been the proposition of a fourth group of countries with a specific welfare state design emerging in southern Europe (Portugal, Spain, Italy and Greece). Esping-Andersen had either not considered these countries or seems to include them in the conservative–corporatist welfare regime. Out of a discussion with Bernd Schulte, Stephan Leibfried developed and coined their classification as 'rudimentary' welfare states (Leibfried, 1992: 253), situating them geographically in the 'Latin Rim' of Europe. According to this classification, southern European welfare states are lagging behind other European welfare states because not all classical social policy areas are covered by state services. These 'rudimentary' welfare states, according to Leibfried, are characterised by a lack of a right to welfare and the lack a full employment tradition, being influenced by older traditions of welfare (connected to the Catholic Church). Other commentators have also added the southern European welfare states to Esping-Andersen's trilogy, focussing, however, on other criteria than Leibfried (Ferrera, 1996; Bonoli, 1997; Trifiletti, 1999; for an overview, see Abrahamson, 1999; Arts & Gelissen, 2002; Bambra, 2005). For example, Trifiletti (1999) classifies welfare states according to Esping-Andersen's concept of decommodification, extended by an index of gender discrimination, of the way the state considers women as wives and mothers, or as workers. The peculiarity of southern Europe is the fact that the state does not support the families' normal functioning, as usually happens in etatist conservative countries, and likewise forms problematic expectations on the role of women. Trifiletti (1999: 56) also mentions the fact that owner-occupied housing is widespread in the southern European welfare regimes, in order to cope with risks in old age (cf. Section 5).

This nexus of the southern European welfare regime with housing is of particular interest for the present overview. Already in 1996, Castles and Ferrera posed the question 'Is southern Europe different?' when they analysed the tenure structure throughout Europe and tried to explain the extreme owner-occupation rates in southern Europe by stressing the overriding importance housing plays there in overall social policy. This concept was later on taken up by many scholars (Castles, 1998; Allen et al., 2004; Kemeny, 2005). Hoekstra (2005) confirms that only the southern European welfare-state cluster proves special when testing empirically the difference in dwelling type and tenure structure in the four different welfare regimes.

In 'Welfare Regimes, Welfare Systems and Housing in Southern Europe' Judith Allen (2006) also poses the question of how far housing provision systems in southern Europe are different from those in northern Europe. She thinks that the analysis of northern European housing systems dominates housing theory to such an extent that the particularities of the four southern European welfare states (Portugal, Spain, Italy and Greece) are lost within the discussion. While resembling conservative welfare regimes on the grounds of Esping-Andersen's main theoretical focus – namely, income maintenance programmes – southern European welfare states show specific traits in the field of housing. The first out of four such particularities is the dominance of the support for owner-occupation, which, according to Allen (2006: 252), is due to the fact that:

> ... political decision making was dominated by the need to prevent the growth of what was perceived, in the cold War, as 'communism'. There was no need, even if governmental resources had been available, to develop extensive social rented sectors outside of a few areas where some Fordist industry was located.

This helps to explain why southern European countries combine high levels of owner-occupation with very low levels of social rented housing. As a second attribute of southern European housing, Allen mentions the very high levels of secondary housing, especially purpose-built second homes and tourist developments, a high percentage of which are vacant throughout most of the year. Third, the extended family plays a crucial role in housing provision, such as in all other areas of social protection. Mobilising the assets of both families of origin is crucial for securing housing for young couples entering the housing market. These assets might take the form of financial help such as the down payment on a mortgage or of assistance in self-promotion and self-provision. Excepting Spain, the large diffusion of self-promotion is the fourth important trait in southern Europe housing. Allen concludes, that:

> ... within a non-Weberian welfare state which relies heavily on income maintenance schemes within the formal sector, and within economies characterised by large informal sectors and segmented labour forces, the southern extended family is the most significant institution mediating access to housing for its member households (Allen, 2006: 272).

Allen also identifies some problems of using welfare regime theory for analysing housing provision, especially in southern Europe. First, the welfare regimes are a synthetic concept combining empirical analysis and theorizing in order to establish three ideal-typical welfare states, none of which is realised in the real world. Also, southern European welfare states were not included in the primary investigations. Second, welfare regime analysis is designed to explore the relationship between state and market in income maintenance programmes and was never meant to be applied to a different field (housing), in a different region (southern Europe), drawing on a different element in the provision of social services (family). The most important factor constricting the application of welfare regime theory is its deep rooting in a modernist narrative which '…assumes a Weberian-rational civil administration, a more or less Fordist labour market [...] and the attenuation of extended affective kinship ties beyond the immediate household' (Allen, 2006, 274).

There is also an ongoing debate about the liberal welfare regime and the countries subsumed in it. Within the liberal group outlined by Esping-Andersen, Castles and Mitchell (1990, 1993) identify a 'radical' welfare regime to include Australia, New Zealand and the UK. Liberal welfare regimes have an institutionalised pattern of dualism in power relations that shapes means-tested welfare provision for a minority while providing strong support for private market solutions for the majority. The three countries identified to pertain to the 'radical' variant, on the other hand, show a strong influence of organised labour which has resulted in polices that rely more strongly on state intervention, progressive taxation, and wage regulation. The application of means-tested measures, with relatively generous replacement ratios, lead to the denomination as 'radical' welfare states, 'in terms of the equalizing potential of a given policy instrument' (Castles & Mitchell, 1993: 105). These 'radical' welfare states seem to achieve a certain level of redistribution and equality by means other than social expenditure, i.e. pre-tax, pre-transfer income and income-related benefits.

Behind the Iron Curtain, Central and Eastern Europe (CEE) welfare states were still absent from Esping-Andersen's original analysis. Nowadays, these post-socialist welfare states all belong to the Bismarckian low-spending type, but there are those who claim a unique welfare model in the CEE (Brusis, 1999; Aidukaite, 2004; Sykes, 2005). In fact, these welfare states show a similar past and face similar challenges that are often addressed by the provision of similar institutional arrangements. The new EU member states show a list of key attributes such as (1) the return to the Bismarckian social insurance system established before World War II in the early transition period as a primary common element of the welfare state in the market economy and (2) the defence of the socialist welfare state as far as full access to old age pension, disability payments, and health protection are concerned (Zukowski, 2008: 29). There are also some similarities to be identified in housing and housing policy in the region (see Section 4). Nevertheless, there are strong differences in welfare-state provision within the group of CEE welfare states, and, on the other hand, there are strong similarities with the southern European type. Therefore, the existence of a specific CEE welfare regime remains unclear.

The most comprehensive and up-to-date empirical comparison of European welfare provision (Schubert et al., 2009) will come as a major challenge to welfare regimes theorists. Comparing all 27 EU member states concerning the provision of welfare state services and analysing factors such as the spending priorities, the funding, the actors, and the 'leitmotifs' of social policy in the member states, this study negates the existence of a European welfare model and, more than that, concludes that 'it is neither possible to ratify any of the existing groupings we know from the relevant literature nor to identify clear-cut new clusters' (Bazant & Schubert, 2009: 533). Arguably, the factors used for the classification of welfare models differ considerably from Esping-Andersen's approach, yet the very controversial findings of the *Handbook of European Welfare Systems* will add oil to the flames of the 'welfare modelling business' in Europe.

In 1999, Abrahamson (p. 395) predicted that 'with the ongoing discourse on globalisation, the welfare typologizing business is bound, as a tendency, to be applied worldwide [...].' As a matter of fact, by 2009 the interest in welfare-state classifications had spread worldwide, especially to Latin America and East Asia. In Gough et al. (2004), for example, a group of social scientists are testing the applicability of the welfare regime approach on welfare provision in low- and middle-income countries in Latin America and East Asia.

Here, Esping-Andersen's focus on the state–market nexus of welfare in OECD countries leads to a lack of emphasis of other forms of welfare provision by family, kinship, and community.

The interest in the application of welfare regime analysis is particularly widespread in East Asia, or as Linda Low puts it: 'With literature on the Western construction and regime of welfare states produced *ad nauseam*, the new-kid-on-the-block is Confucian welfare.' (Low, 2006: 393). Confucian cultural heritage that underpins welfare states in East Asia stresses the importance of family and community-based mutual support. Respect for authority, self-help, education, and diligence are key themes that have promoted a high level of welfare without 'the state' (Walker & Wong, 2006).

Lee and Ku (2007) apply an empirical analysis on the question of whether there might be a further type of welfare regime in East Asia. They develop a set of 15 indicators on welfare-state systems and analyse 20 countries by applying a cluster analysis. They find that Taiwan and South Korea might be considered representatives of a new model of welfare that shows similarities with Esping-Andersen's conservative regime in respect of welfare stratification, while according to the non-coverage of welfare entitlements it is similar to the liberal regime. Japan, on the other hand, does not belong to the East Asian welfare model, but rather remains a composite of various regime types. Peng (2008), on the other hand, is critical towards the idea of applying the welfare regime analytical framework to quickly changing East Asian welfare provision. She describes the profound normative and institutional changes affecting social policy in Korea and Japan, especially the ability of the extended family to provide individual personal care.

Looking at these tendencies, the export of welfare regime theory from European and OECD countries to developing welfare states throughout the world has renewed some of the criticism (amongst others) that already in

Europe was applied to Esping-Andersen's approach: the overestimation of state and market provision of welfare in contrast to other institutions (family, kinship, community) and the absence of housing in the analysis.

HOUSING SYSTEMS AND WELFARE REGIMES

When trying to group different approaches to comparative housing research, it is possible to differentiate at least three (Kemeny & Lowe, 1998) or four (Matznetter, 2006). While the so called juxtapositional approach stresses the particularities of national housing systems and is more descriptive than analytical (Donner 2000, 2006; Schubert et al. 2009), the more influential approaches are the convergence and the divergence approaches as well as, more recently, the studies focussing on micro-scale comparisons (Section 6).

Early country comparisons of housing policy and housing outcomes focused on the similarities of housing policies and outcomes at national levels and therefore supposed housing systems to grow more alike over the post-war decades. Similar to early investigations of European welfare states, these theories distinguished phases of development, especially concerning the social housing sector and implied modernisation (Donnison, 1967; Donnison & Ungerson, 1982). The convergence approaches came under different names, be it recommodification (Harloe, 1981, 1995), decollectivization (Harloe & Paris, 1984), privatisation (Adams, 1987) or transition-to-the-market (Clapham, 1995), but the message remained the same: while post-war housing needs decreased in quantitative and, later, also qualitative terms, housing subsidies are being reduced and shifted from the supply side to the demand side of the housing market. Additionally, the social rental sector is increasingly superseded by owner-occupation. European integration, the aim to cut public spending, the (in)direct influence of EU competition legislation, and the transition of former communist states to the market fuels the impression of increasing convergence of housing policies across Europe and still determines research output to a large extent (Whitehead & Scanlon, 2007, Scanlon & Whitehead, 2008).

As in comparative welfare research, the distinction between independent 'housing systems' or housing regimes entered comparative housing research at a later stage. In 1992, Jim Kemeny published his book *Housing and Social Theory*, where he developed a strong case to apply a divergence thesis in comparative housing research. The influence of Esping-Andersen's (and maybe others') typology of welfare states also started in the 1990s.

One can distinguish three strands of approaches on the relationship between typologies of welfare regimes and housing systems:

- one approach focuses on the systematic application of Esping-Andersen's concept on a more or less specific field of housing policy (Matznetter, 2002; Hoekstra, 2003; Hulse, 2003)
- one approach is on the structure of housing production (Barlow & Duncan, 1994; Arbaci, 2007)
- and a third approach centres on housing tenures (Harloe, 1995; Kemeny, 1995a, 2005; Balchin, 1996; Castles & Ferrera, 1996; Castles, 1998; Allen, 2006).

Walter Matznetter (2002) explored the applicability of Esping-Andersen's concept to the field of housing policy in a particular country. By abstracting from Esping-Andersen's categories of decommodification and stratification, Matznetter identifies four aspects, typical for a conservative welfare state, and identifies them within Austrian housing policy in the 1990s. Austria, by unanimity amongst researchers, is firmly placed in the conservative–corporatist regime cluster and also in the field of housing shows typical traits of 'conservative' housing policy: fragmentation (between types of tenure, developer, and building cohorts and between the nine provinces); corporatism (corporatist, party-related networks mediating interests between developers and policymakers); familiarism (mutual help amongst relatives in self-developed housing, family-friendly subsidies); and immobilism (coherence to basically post-war structures of supply-side housing subsidies and funding).

Joris Hoekstra (2003) applies Esping-Andersen's theory to housing policy in the Netherlands in the 1980s and 1990s. By abstracting deductively from Esping-Andersen's concepts, Hoekstra relates the characteristics of welfare-state regimes with particular aspects of housing systems: (1) the concept of decomodification is linked to housing subsidisation (both demand side and supply side) and price regulation; (2) the concept of stratification is connected with housing allocation; and (3) the state, market, and family mix is related to the production of newly built dwellings. In a second step, these housing aspects are differentiated among the three welfare-state regimes proposed by Esping-Andersen. The fiscal treatment of housing is not very convincingly excluded from the analysis (Hoekstra, 2003: 60). After searching for elements of the social-democratic, the corporatist, and the liberal 'housing' welfare elements in the real-life housing policy of the Netherlands, Hoekstra confirms the Netherlands' hybrid nature between social-democratic and corporatist traits in the 1980s. Taking a closer look at the 1990s, however, Hoekstra shows that housing policy in the Netherlands increasingly lost its social-democratic traits and became more 'conservative' in character.

Kath Hulse (2003) explores the relevance of the concept of liberal welfare regimes to housing provision by analysing the rental housing sectors and the housing allowance schemes in Australia, New Zealand, Canada, and the United States. Hulse concludes that the welfare regime concept has some relevance in explaining dualism in rental markets, especially in Australia and New Zealand, where social housing sectors are smaller and the separation of support between social and private rental segments is more clear-cut than in the United States and Canada.

Barlow and Duncan (1994) abstracted from Esping-Andersen's welfare regime theory in order to apply it to the field of housing production and housing provision. Focusing on the experience in Britain, Sweden and France, they find that specific forms of land supply and housing promotion correspond with the four clusters of European welfare regimes. Liberal welfare regimes, for example, tend to have larger developers that rely more on speculative development gains than on building profits. In social-democratic welfare regimes, on the other hand, land supply is tightly regulated by the state and therefore developers have to rely more on building profits than on land speculation.

Another example for applying welfare regime typologies and housing system classification on special policy areas and outcomes is Sonia Arbaci's (2007) analysis of ethnic and social segregation across European cities. This study investigates the ways in which the diverse housing systems, embodied in three wider welfare regimes (expanded by the fourth southern European cluster), influence and reflect different principles of segregation. Arbaci finds that there is an important relationship between welfare arrangements and socio-spatial stratifications of European cities, as can be seen in three factors (Arbaci, 2007: 429):

1 The scale of housing production is essential in explaining the diverse degrees of ethnic and socio-spatial segregation across European cities, according to the principle of stratification embedded in the welfare regime.
2 The planning system directly affects segregation processes, especially by the degree of public ownership and control of the land supply.
3 In southern Europe low levels of spatial segregation recorded among the most vulnerable social and foreign groups are at the same time associated with high levels of social segregation.

Welfare arrangements are therefore critically important to understand the scale, design, and process of segregation. The concept thereby helps to explain the diversity of segregation patterns and counterbalances the widespread negative association of spatial segregation with social exclusion and deprivation.

> Arbaci concludes that '[t]he emphasis on welfare regimes, as an ideal-typical analytical tool, has proven instrumental in building an overarching comparative framework and showing how housing systems and land supply differently organise the socio-spatial hierarchy of the city, whilst reflecting macro-scale principles of stratification' (Arbaci, 2007: 430).

As a third strand of connecting the welfare-state regime debate with housing there is the differentiation of housing systems according to tenure. According to Malpass (2008), these approaches vary considerably according to the role housing is seen to play within the welfare-state structure. While some researchers (Harloe, 1995; Somerville, 2000) consider housing to be of less importance to the welfare state as a whole, other researchers see in it a cornerstone and stress the importance tenure arrangements play in the configuration and development of the welfare state (Castles, 1998; Kemeny, 2001).

Kemeny (Kemeny, 1995a; Kemeny et al., 2001, 2005) has developed a theoretical framework where the structure of the rental sector is the fundamental variable for analysing housing policies in welfare states. According to this theory, differences in the rental sector developed out of differences in the social and political structures between countries and the degree of privatism as opposed to collectivism. Some countries have dual rental markets, where the state successfully shields the private rental market from competition out of the social sector. The social sector is reserved for low-income households and functions purely as a residual safety net. The providers of social housing are closely controlled by the state and strict means-testing is applied. The private market, on the other hand, is characterised by high rents and insecure rental contracts. Therefore the two segments composing the dual rental market do not compete with each other.

In contrast to countries with dual rental markets, other countries have built up unitary rental markets. A unitary rental market – characterised by the absence of regulatory barriers to competition between profit and non-profit providers – is the precondition for the social rental market to enter into competition with the commercial rental market and thereby have a rent-dampening influence on the overall rent level. In countries with unitary rental markets, the social housing segment plays a large role in overall rental housing, is financed by state or federal subsidies, is open to broad classes of the population, and is often provided by semi-private or private limited-profit providers. If non-profit renting is allowed to compete with for-profit renting in a unitary rental market, and if high-quality rental housing can be provided at a lower price, for-profit landlords will have to lower their rents in order to stay competitive: 'This is the main channel through which the non-profit sector is able to act as a dampener on the general level of rents' (Kemeny et al., 2005: 858).

Later on, Kemeny et al. (2005) have shown how a unitary rental market may develop into a truly integrated rental market over time, passing through phases where the non-profit rental sector first influences, then leads, and finally dominates the market. At a final stage, an integrated rental market may emerge out of a unitary rental market if the supply of non-profit housing is competitive, provides good market coverage, and reaches a sufficient magnitude (Kemeny et al., 2005: 861). The evolution into an integrated rental market may be measured by the role non-profit housing providers play in the rental market. In this process, solidity plays a key role. The solidity of a housing association may be measured by the share of its own equity-to-market value: the higher this proportion, the lower is dependence on dept capital on the financial markets, which may lead to lower financing costs. Through this process of maturation, limited-profit providers will grow more and more able to set lower rents than for-profit providers because they only need to cover their costs. Solidity is supposed to increase over time, as both outstanding dept is paid back and the market value of a housing association increases.

Unitary rental markets can be found in European countries that have shown a strong commitment to social market policies, the employment of limited-profit or non-profit providers of social services, and where German cultural influence has been traditionally strong such as in Austria, Denmark, Germany, the Netherlands, Sweden, and Switzerland.

Kemeny's distinction of unitary versus dual rental market countries has shown itself to be difficult to combine with Esping-Andersen's welfare-regime thesis, the main stumbling block being that both apply different concepts of 'corporatism' to their analysis (Kemeny, 2006; Lennartz, 2010). Nevertheless, there is a strong empirical connection between social-democratic and conservative welfare states and the existence of unitary rental markets, Norway being a prominent exception. Southern European and the liberal welfare regimes, on the other hand, are characterised by dual rental markets.

Since Kemeny's theoretical distinction of different rental markets, there have been a few empirical applications of the concept, taking a look at housing policies and outcomes in European welfare states (Hoekstra, 2005; Kemeny et al., 2005; Elsinga et al., 2008; Amann & Mundt, 2009). Drawing on the European Community Household Panel, in Hoekstra (2009) there is empirical evidence that integrated rental systems and dualist rental systems do indeed exist. Yet, there are signs of increasing convergence between the two models.

Of course, Kemeny's distinction of different housing models is not the only tenure-related concept of comparative housing research. We have already mentioned the strand of research that analyses housing policy and the extent of owner-occupation within the structure of southern European welfare states (Section 3). Of increasing interest is also the analysis of the Eastern European housing policy and the intent to explain links with social policy changes (Lux, 2003; Hegedüs & Teller, 2005; Tsenkova, 2009). According to Hegedüs and Teller (2005: 205), the main trend in CEE countries is that the 'housing system seems to move towards a housing and welfare regime in which the state plays less and less role, the safety net puts more and more burden on the families, and it provides help only to the neediest families.' They conclude that these housing policy guidelines are close to a combination of the liberal and the rudimentary welfare regimes, but that the institutional structure of the welfare regime in CEE countries is still in the process of change.

Of particular interest in this context is a book on different kinds of housing systems in Scandinavian countries that supposedly belong to the same welfare regime. This book, unfortunately still only in Swedish (Bengtsson, 2006), shows how the institutional legacy of the different Scandinavian countries had an impact on tenure structures. It applies the concept of path dependency on housing in order to describe the persistence of differences and identify possible historical turning points or 'critical junctures'.

HOMEOWNERSHIP AND WELFARE

Throughout his academic career Kemeny has reflected on the meaning of homeownership within a welfare state (Kemeny, 1980, 1981, 2001, 2005). These reflections often took the form of clear opposition to high homeownership rates, up to the point that in some passages one 'can feel Kemeny's hostility dripping off the page' (O'Neill, 2008: 168). In Kemeny's reasoning, the rise of homeownership in industrialised nations was not due to the relationship between a variety of consumer preferences and the supply of different housing tenures, but was the outcome of systematic discrimination against other forms of tenure, in particular social rental housing. For that reason Kemeny sees the rise of homeownership as equivalent to the privatisation of one of the four great pillars of a welfare society. Back in the 1980s, Kemeny's overall argument was that

> ...high rates of home ownership impacted on society through various forms of privatisation, influencing urban form, public transport, lifestyles, gender roles, systems of welfare and social security as well as other dimensions of social structure. I argued that an overwhelming emphasis on home ownership created a lifestyle based on detached housing, privatised urban transport and its resulting 'one-household' (increasingly 'one-person') car ownership, a traditional gendered division of labour based on female housewifery and the full-time working male, and strong resistance to public expenditure that necessitated the high taxes needed to fund quality universal welfare provision (Kemeny, 2005: 60).

Kemeny argued that in societies with low public retirement pensions and poor public welfare provision for the elderly, households are forced to make private provision for their old age. Put shortly, in countries where policy encourages homeownership, paying for a home will act as a strong deterrent to welfare and social security funding. Kemeny confirmed this relationship between homeownership and welfare spending by conducting a very rudimentary statistical analysis of six countries (Kemeny, 1980).

Only around 20 years later was Kemeny's proposition tested with more refined methods by Castles (1998), including 18 OECD countries and covering the period of 1960–1990. Castles concluded that, except for the public health findings, Kemeny's basic proposition could be supported. Yet, the relationship between homeownership and privatisation of welfare had been weakening since 1980. Furthermore, Castles (1998: 17) suggested that the relationship between homeownership and welfare privatisation might have the opposite causality as proposed by Kemeny:

> There is no a priori reason why the relationship may not be entirely the other way around, with a weak welfare state providing an incentive to home ownership as a means of life cycle saving or a well developed state tax crowding out the possibility of saving for private home ownership.

The Kemeny and Castles versions of the causality do not have to exclude one another: rather, there might be an interesting dynamic at work between the two explanations.

At the OTB Institute in Delft there has been a recent research focus on these issues, testing the causality of welfare privatisation and owner-occupation and applying qualitative methods on the meaning of homeownership as opposed to renting in several European countries (Boelhouwer et al., 2005; Doling & Elsinga, 2006; Horsewood & Neuteboom, 2006; Elsinga et al., 2007; see also Behring & Helbrecht, 2002). In Toussaint and Elsinga (2009), there is support for the consideration that homeownership plays an increasing role in households' financial planning in European countries, especially where welfare levels are low or decreasing. In the UK, homeownership functions as a financial asset to meet welfare needs, especially in old age. This can also be seen in the rise of mortgage equity release products.

Allen (2006: 271) supports Kemeny's version of the relationship between strong state support for homeownership and a trend to privatisation of welfare services when she refers to southern Europe:

> High home ownership sets up a political constituency among the young which is opposed to extending the welfare state through taxation, because it would interfere with saving for home ownership, and in favour of private pensions, health care and schools because this allows a more flexible pattern of expenditure.

In the current economic and financial crisis there is increasing interest in the relationship between housing markets, financial markets, and the economy. There is abundant literature on the effects of homeownership and housing prices on consumption and household savings (for overviews, see Leung, 2004; Case & Quigley, 2008; Goodhart &

Hofmann, 2008; Muellbauer & Murphy, 2008). Less attention is still paid to the linkage between housing market dynamics and welfare, even though there can be no doubt about the effects of skyrocketing repossessions and negative equity, especially in high ownership countries such as the UK, the United States, and Spain, on the distribution of incomes and the ability of welfare systems to cope with housing-related risks. Furthermore, 'increases in the average real price of housing change the distribution of welfare towards the old, who tend to be owners, and away from the young, who tend not to be owners and may not even be old enough to vote' (Muellbauer & Murphy, 2008: 27). To investigate these topics, it is necessary to apply a very broad view on the interrelation of housing markets, welfare systems, and social policy (cf. Schwartz & Seabrooke, 2009).

RESCALING WELFARE AND HOUSING

As for most of comparative policy research, the concept of welfare regimes is deeply interwoven with the nation-state. Independent of size and internal divisions, this is the basic unit of analysis, for which data are collected and compared. When housing policy and outcomes are related to welfare regimes, this is done with national data, despite better knowledge that both welfare policies and housing markets operate at subnational, regional levels.

For the conservative welfare regime, the devolution of powers and the fragmentation of entitlements are considered typical features of welfare provision. Even in theses cases, average values are collected and analysed for the whole territory of the nation-state. Only in recent years has reasoning about the welfare state been embedded in supranational developments and broken down into urban and regional studies of welfare and housing.

Perhaps it is the traditional focus on cash benefits (cf. Bambra, 2005) in health insurance, unemployment insurance, and the pension system that has contributed to the long-term neglect of other, non-national, levels of welfare provision. More often than not, cash benefits are regulated on a nation-wide basis, but welfare-regime studies should also pay attention to the actual provision of welfare services, and these tend to be organised on the level of cities and regions. From the viewpoint of housing research, and social housing in particular, the debate on the 'rescaling of statehood' and the critique of 'methodological nationalism' (Brenner, 2004: 38) seem to be very pertinent, but rarely debated in the welfare regime and housing literature.

In housing research, the core argument is that the withdrawal of national housing policies and the ongoing commodification of housing do contribute to greater regional variations in house prices and other housing indicators. Regional and urban housing policies are called for to react to the specific problems encountered in different markets. For the Netherlands, Manuel Aalbers (2003) has elaborated on the very different problems encountered in regional housing markets across an otherwise balanced national housing market. While a number of regional markets have followed the national shift from suction (and shortage) to pressure (and vacancies), others have remained sellers' markets in short supply. Within regional housing markets, shortages in one market sector may be compensated by sufficient supply in another (e.g. social vs private renting vs owner-occupation). Even in a densely populated country with advanced transport systems, substitution is rarely possible between regional housing markets. Despite national balance, very demanding tasks remain for regional housing policies within the Netherlands, depending on where the regional housing market stands in the suction–pressure spectrum. And Aalbers concludes that 'There is no – and will not be a – national housing market with pressure' (2003: 64).

For the UK, Ian Cole (2003) has explored the development of housing policy at the regional level in a nation that used to be known for its 'nationalised' housing policy. Again, the core argument is the growing differentiation of local and regional housing markets, which calls for a multi-level governance of housing. New Labour made some steps towards stronger regional government, but in 'housing and urban policy (the creation of regional structures and processes) has been disjointed and ad hoc' (2003: 232). More recently, Cole and Etherington (2005) have added a comparative analysis of neighbourhood renewal policy in England and Denmark, criticizing the dominance of comparative analysis at the national level.

Within housing research, Aalbers and Cole are amongst the few proponents of comparative research at various scales or multi-scalar housing research. Beyond housing studies, there has been a substantial debate about the rescaling of public policies in recent years, with surprisingly little repercussion in the welfare-regime debate, so far. In Brenner's book, on the other hand, social housing is only a topic in his lengthy treatment of the Keynesian Welfare National State (KWNS) of the late 1950s to late 1970s, and does not show up in his chapters on the contemporary Rescaled Competition State Regimes (RCSR), where the focus shifts from social to technical infrastructure. For the political economist, social housing seems to have drifted outside the realm of the post-Keynesian state, and 'welfare regimes' are not mentioned at all.

For housing research, such a view from outside is neither new nor surprising. In the Golden Age of Welfare, housing policy was regarded a pillar of the KWNS – to use Brenner's terminology. Since the 1980s, state budget figures for housing have come down considerably and political saliency has decreased accordingly in most countries. On the national scale, some observers have spoken of the collapse of housing policy, while pointing to simultaneous trends of devolution and decentralisation (Kleinman, 1998: 249).

What the rescaling debate tells us about housing research is that the heyday of the nation-state as the organisational level for the provision of welfare and social housing is definitely over. Welfare provision has either been privatised or rearranged on lower levels, such as the urban or the regional. This scale is not new for housing policy; on the contrary, in many European countries there was a phase of experimental housing policy prior to the 'nationalisation' of housing policy after 1945, as part of the KWNS. In the interwar period, in some places even before World War I, there was a flurry of housing projects with public involvement, often by local and regional governments who were more exposed to grass-roots demands. In many cases, not only the pioneering architecture of early modernism survives to the present day but also part of the organisation of early social housing, be it cooperatives, non-profit societies, charities, or government agencies. As with welfare regimes, path continuities can be observed in housing, both at the national and the subnational (regional/urban) levels.

So far, only downward processes of rescaling have been addressed. In welfare, as well as in housing, responsibilities and powers of the KWNS have also been shifted upwards, to the EU and other supranational institutions. These issues are discussed in the most recent and comprehensive *Handbook of European Welfare Systems*, where part of the introductory chapter is devoted to the consequences of EU enlargement, EU consolidation, and supranationalism upon (formerly purely national) welfare systems (Schubert et al., 2009).

EVALUATION OF HOUSING SYSTEMS

Many research approaches see homeownership as an ideal – Kemeny's theory does the contrary. A lot about the differentiation of housing regimes has to do with the implicit appraisal or criticism of homeownership. Not surprisingly, there is a strand of research that tries to connect housing outcomes with the performance of different welfare regimes or housing systems.

Doling (1999) operationalises the concept of decommodification in the field of housing policy and shows that a meaningful application of de-ommodification has to go beyond the equation with state provision and, therefore, tenure structures have to be analysed in more detail before any conclusions on the ability of a housing system to protect from reductions in income can be drawn. By defining an (admittedly very crude and subjective) index of decommodification for housing provision in Britain, West Germany and Sweden, Doling found that, surprisingly, one may consider Britain's housing system to be more decommodifying than Sweden's, owing to 'the combined effect of the absence of an imputed rent tax facing the large group of outright owners, amounting to about 25 per cent of total households, and of a housing allowance system for tenants that is able to meet their rental payments in full' (Doling, 1999: 162). Doling's approach is meant as a provocative investigation into the possibilities of evaluating housing outcomes within the welfare-state debate and making use of the concepts of Esping-Andersen and Kemeny.

Considering homeownership and household housing satisfaction, there is an interesting conundrum here that still remains unsolved. While homeowners in most countries usually show a *higher* level of housing satisfaction than renters (Elsinga & Hoekstra, 2005), countries with a high rate of homeownership usually show a *lower* general level of housing satisfaction than countries with large rental segments (Czasny et al., 2008). In the first study, Elsinga and Hoekstra use ECHP (European Community Household Panel) data from 2001 to analyse household satisfaction according to tenure in six European countries, pertaining to different housing regimes (English-speaking high ownership, continental high rental, southern European high ownership). After controlling for tenure-related differences in housing quality, household characteristics, and housing costs, the coefficients for the variable 'type of tenure' (rental, owner-occupied) remain positive and statistically significant in all countries of the sample (except for Austria). As a conclusion, the quality of housing and the subjective perception of the dwelling size explain a large part of the differences in housing satisfaction between renters and owner-occupiers, but some explanation arises from the type of tenure itself.

Czasny, on the other hand, compares EQLS 2003 and Eurobarometer 2004 household data on satisfaction with dwelling, area you live, standard of living, and other indicators, by compiling country groups according to welfare regimes and ownership shares (nine EU15 high-ownership countries, six EU15 low-ownership countries, 10 new member states with high ownership shares). The EU countries with low ownership shares correspond to the conservative and social-democratic welfare regimes and likewise only include countries (except France) that Kemeny included in the group of countries with a unitary rental market. The old EU member states with high (>60%) ownership rates include both liberal and southern European welfare regime associated countries. Czasny finds that the EU15 low-ownership countries on average perform much better in terms of household satisfaction with dwelling and living area than new member states, and fairly better than EU15 high-ownership countries. Only concerning satisfaction with family life, high- and low-ownership countries perform equally well.

These two studies show that there is rising interest in analysing housing outcomes and housing conditions, as well as satisfaction with these, in a context of different housing or welfare regimes. This strand of research is not developed very thoroughly yet, but might in the future help to add another aspect to the housing modelling business that might also function as assistance to policymakers.

OUTLOOK

For housing research, the debate around welfare regimes has been and continues to be an inspiring exchange. In any state and region, there is a specific arrangement of welfare provision, drawing on varying contributions by formal state and market institutions and on informal economies and households. These arrangements can be grouped into a number of types of welfare regimes, with particular features that have grown over time and are difficult to change.

In the post-war European welfare state, the provision of housing was part and parcel of welfare provision, and housing policy was well integrated with other social policies (and economic policy). In health provision, schooling, pension systems, and social housing similar values prevailed, and similar organisational principles were followed. In a number of countries, a large stock of decommodified housing was built up over the decades, and has remained in the hands of non-market landlords. This is the case in unitary rental markets, where the social rented sector is either informing, leading, or dominating the rental market as a whole (cf. Kemeny et al., 2005). It takes a long time to construct such a large housing stock, and it seems that only social-democratic and conservative–corporatist welfare regimes have offered the habitat for such a stock to mature; hence, the overlap between welfare regimes and housing regimes is not a direct link but an outcome of shared values and principles in the past.

These are the lessons learned from the welfare regime and housing exchange, and the debate has only started. Twenty years after the original publication, there are many more points of reference than just Esping-Andersen (1990): data have to be updated, welfare providers have to be added, and country coverage has to be dramatically expanded. There is a lively debate in comparative policy research on these issues, but still without any reference to (or better, inclusion of) housing – with a few exceptions such as Castles' (1998) 'really big trade-off', also echoed in Behring & Helbrecht (2002). Here are important avenues for future research.

REFERENCES

Aalbers, M.B. (2003) Pressure and Suction on Housing Markets. *European Journal of Housing Policy*, Vol. 3 (1), pp. 61–81.

Abrahamson, P. (1999) The Welfare Modelling Business. *Social Policy and Administration*, Vol. 33 (4), pp. 394–415.

Adams, C.T. (1987) The Politics of Privatization. *Scandinavian Housing and Planning Research*, Supplement, No. 1, pp. 127–155.

Aidukaite, J. (2004) *The Emergence of the Post-Socialist Welfare State, the Case of the Baltic States: Estonia, Latvia and Lithuania*, Stockholm: Södertörns högskola.

Allen, J. (2006) Welfare Regimes, Welfare Systems and Housing in Southern Europe. *European Journal of Housing Policy*, Vol. 6 (3), pp. 251–277.

Allen, J., Barlow, J., Leal, J., Maloutas, T. & Padovani, L., (eds) (2004) *Housing and Welfare in Southern Europe*. Oxford: Blackwell.

Amann, W. & Mundt, A. (2009) Indicators of a Unitary Rental Market in Austria. Paper presented at the ENHR Conference Prague, July.

Arbaci, S. (2007) Ethnic Segregation, Housing Systems and Welfare Regimes in Europe. *European Journal of Housing Policy*, Vol. 7 (4), pp. 401–433.

Arts, W. & Gelissen, J. (2002) Three Worlds of Welfare Capitalism or More? A State-of-the-Art Report. *Journal of European Social Policy*, Vol. 12 (2), pp. 137–158.

Balchin, P., (ed.) (1996) *Housing Policy in Europe*. London: Routledge.

Bambra, C. (2005) Cash Versus Services: Worlds of Welfare and the Decommodification of Cash Benefits and Health Care Services. *Journal of Social Policy*, Vol. 34 (2), pp. 195–213.

Barlow, J. & Duncan, S. (1994) *Success and Failure in Housing Provision, European Systems Compared*. Oxford, New York & Tokyo: Elsevier Science Ltd.

Bazant, U. & Schubert, K. (2009) European Welfare Systems. Diversity beyond Existing Categories. In: K. Schubert, S. Hegelich & U. Bazant, (eds) *The Handbook of European Welfare Systems*. London & New York: Routledge, pp. 513–534.

Behring, K. & Helbrecht, I. (2002) *Wohneigentum in Europa* [Homeownership in Europe]. Ludwigsburg: Wüstenrot Stiftung.

Bengtsson, B., (ed.) (2006) *Varför så olika? Nordisk bostadspolitik i jämförande historisk ljus* [Why so different? Scandinavian Housing Policy in a Comparative Historical Perspective]. Malmö: Égalite.

Boelhouwer, P., Doling, J. & Elsinga, M., (eds) (2005) *Home Ownership. Getting in, Getting from, Getting out.* Delft: Delft University Press.

Bonoli, G. (1997) Classifying Welfare States: A Two-dimension Approach. *Journal of Social Policy*, Vol. 26 (3), pp. 351–372.

Borchert, J. (1998) Zur Statik und Dynamik wohlfahrtsstaatlicher Regime [Statics and Dynamics of Welfare State Regimes]. In: S. Lessenich & I. Ostner, (eds) *Welten des Wohlfahrtskapitalismus. Der Sozialstaat in vergleichender Perspektive.* [Worlds of Welfare Capitalism. The Welfare State in Comparative Perspective]. Frankfurt/Main: Campus, pp. 137–176.

Brenner, N. (2004) *New State Spaces. Urban Governance and the Rescaling of Statehood.* Oxford: Oxford University Press.

Brusis, M. (1999) Residuales oder europäisches Wohlfahrtsmodell? Die EU und die sozialpolitischen Reformen in Mittel- und Osteuropa [Residual or European Welfare Model? The EU and Sociopolitical Reforms in CEE]. *Prokla Zeitschrift für Sozialwissenschaft*, Vol. 114 (1), pp. 73–94.

Case, K. & Quigley, J. (2008) How Housing Booms Unwind: Income Effects, Wealth Effects, and Feedbacks through Financial Markets. *European Journal of Housing Policy*, Vol. 8 (2), pp. 161–180.

Castles, F.G. (1998) The Really Big Trade-Off: Home Ownership and the Welfare State in the New World and the Old. *Acta Politica*, Vol. 33 (1), pp. 5–19.

Castles, F.G. & Ferrera, M. (1996) Home Ownership and the Welfare State: Is Southern Europe Different? *South European Society and Politics*, Vol. 1 (2), pp. 163–184.

Castles, F.G. & Mitchell, D. (1990) Three Worlds of Welfare Capitalism or Four? Australian National University, Graduate Program in Public Policy, Discussion Paper No. 21.

Castles, F.G. & Mitchell, D. (1993) Worlds of Welfare and Families of Nations. In: F.G. Castles, (ed.) *Families of Nations: Patterns of Public Policy in Western Democracies.* Aldershot: Dartmouth, pp. 93–128.

Clapham, D. (1995) Privatisation and the East European Housing Model. *Urban Studies*, Vol. 32 (4–5), pp. 679–694.

Clasen, J., (ed.) (1999) *Comparative Social Policy. Concepts, Theories and Methods.* Oxford: Blackwell.

Cole, I. (2003): The Development of Housing Policy in the English Regions: Trends and Prospects. *Housing Studies*, Vol. 18 (2), pp. 219–234.

Cole, I. & Etherington, D. (2005) Neighbourhood Renewal Policy and Spatial Differentiation in Housing Markets: Recent Trends in England and Denmark. *European Journal of Housing Policy*, Vol. 5 (1), pp. 77–97.

Czasny, K., Feigelfeld, H., Hajek, J., Moser, P. & Stocker, E. (2008) *Wohnzufriedenheit und Wohnbedingungen in Österreich im europäischen Vergleich* [Housing Satisfaction and Housing Conditions in Austria in a European Comparison]. Vienna: SRZ.

Doling, J. (1999) De-commodification and Welfare: Evaluating Housing Systems. *Housing, Theory and Society*, Vol. 16 (4), pp. 156–164.

Doling, J. & Elsinga, M., (eds) (2006) *Home Ownership. Getting in, Getting from, Getting out. Part II.* Delft: Delft University Press.

Donner (2000) *Housing Policies in the European Union.* Vienna: Donner Eigenverlag.

Donner (2006) *Housing Policies in Central Eastern Europe.* Vienna: Donner Eigenverlag.

Donnison, D. (1967) *The Government of Housing.* Harmondsworth: Penguin Books.

Donnison, D. & Ungerson, C. (1982) *Housing Policy.* Harmondsworth: Penguin Books.

Duncan, S. (1995) Theorizing European Gender Systems. *Journal of European Social Policy*, Vol. 5 (4), pp. 263–284.

Elsinga, M. & Hoekstra, J. (2005) Homeownership and Housing Satisfaction. *Journal of Housing and the Built Environment*, Vol. 20, pp. 401–424.

Elsinga, M., De Decker, P., Teller, N. & Toussaint, J., (eds) (2007) *Home Ownership beyond Asset and Security.* Delft: Delft University Press.

Elsinga, M., Haffner, M. & van der Heijden, H. (2008) Threats to the Dutch Unitary Rental Market. *European Journal of Housing Policy*, Vol. 8 (1), pp. 21–37.

Esping-Andersen, G. (1990) *The Three Worlds of Welfare Capitalism.* Princeton, NJ: Princeton University Press.

Esping-Andersen, G. (1996) *Welfare States in Transition. National Adaptions in Global Economies.* London: Sage.

Esping-Andersen, G. (1999) *Social Foundations of Postindustrial Economies.* Oxford University Press: Oxford.

Esping-Andersen, G. (2002) *Why We Need a New Welfare State*. Oxford: Oxford University Press.

Evers, A. (1988) Shifts in the Welfare Mix – Introducing a New Approach for the Study of Transformations in Welfare and Social Policy. In: A. Evers & H. Wintersberger, (eds) *Shifts in the Welfare Mix*. Vienna: European Centre for Social Welfare Training and Research, pp.7–30.

Evers, A. & Olk, T. (1996) Wohlfahrtspluralismus – Analytische und normativ-politische Dimensionen eines Leitbegriffs [Welfare Pluralism – analytical and normative-political dimensions of a guiding theme]. In: A. Evers & T. Olk, (eds) *Wohlfahrtspluralismus*. [Welfare Pluralism] Opladen: Westdeutscher Verlag, pp. 9–60.

Ferrera, M. (1996) The 'southern Model' of Welfare in Social Europe. *Journal of European Social Policy*, Vol. 6 (1), pp. 17–37.

Ferrera, M. & Rhodes, M., (eds) (2000) *Recasting European Welfare States*. London: Frank Cass.

Gauthier, A.H. (1996) *The State and the Family. A Comparative Analysis of Family Policies in Industrialized Countries*. Oxford: Clarendon Press.

Goodhart, C. & Hofmann, B. (2008) House Prices, Money, Credit, and the Macroeconomy. *Oxford Review of Economic Policy*, Vol. 24 (1), pp. 180–205.

Gough, I., Wood, G., Barrietos, A., Bevan, P., Davis, P. & Room, G. (2004) *Insecurity and Welfare Regimes in Asia, Africa and Latin America*. New York: Cambridge University Press.

Hantrais, L. & Letablier, M.-T. (1996) *Families and Family Policies in Europe*. London: Longman.

Harloe, M. (1981) The Recommodification of Housing. In: M. Harloe & E. Lebas, (eds) *City, Class and Capital*. London: Edward Arnold, pp. 17–50.

Harloe, M. (1995) *The People's Home: Social Rented Housing in Europe and America*. Oxford: Blackwell.

Harloe, M. & Paris, C. (1984) The Decollectivization of Consumption: Housing and Local Government Finance in England and Wales, 1979–1983. In: I. Szelenyi, (ed.), *Cities in Recession*. London: Sage, pp. 70–98.

Hegedüs, J. & Teller, N. (2005) Development of the Housing Allowance Programmes in Hungary in the Context of CEE Transitional Countries. *European Journal of Housing Policy*, Vol. 5 (2), pp. 187–209.

Heidenheimer, A.J., Heclo, H. & Adams, C.T. (1975, 1983, 1990) *Comparative Public Policy. The Politics of Social Choice in Europe and America*. New York: St. Martin's Press.

Hicks, A., Misra, J. & Ng, T. (1995) The Programmatic Emergence of the Social Security State. *American Sociological Review*, Vol. 60 (3), pp. 329–349.

Hills, J. (1998) Housing: A Decent Home within the Reach of Every Family? In: H. Glennerster, & J. Hills, (eds) *The State of Welfare. The Economics of Social Spending*, 2nd edn. Oxford: Oxford University Press.

Hoekstra, J. (2003) Housing and the Welfare State in the Netherlands: An Application of Esping-Andersen's Typology. *Housing, Theory and Society*, Vol. 20 (2), pp. 58–71.

Hoekstra, J. (2005) Is There a Connection between Welfare State Regime and Dwelling Type? An Exploratory Statistical Analysis. *Housing Studies*, Vol. 20 (3), pp. 475–495.

Hoekstra, J. (2009) Two Types of Rental System? An Exploratory Empirical Test of Kemeny's Rental System Typology. *Urban Studies*, Vol. 46 (1), pp. 45–62.

Horsewood, N. & Neuteboom, P., (eds) (2006) *The Social Limits to Growth. Security and Insecurity Aspects of Home Ownership*. Delft: Delft University Press.

Hulse, K. (2003) Housing Allowances and Private Renting in Liberal Welfare Regimes. *Housing, Theory and Society*, Vol. 20 (1), pp. 28–42.

Kemeny, J. (1980): Homeownership and Privatisation, *International Journal of Urban and Regional Research*, Vol. 4, pp. 372–388.

Kemeny, J. (1981) *The Myth of Homeownership*. London: Routledge and Kegan Paul.

Kemeny, J. (1992) *Housing and Social Theory*. London: Routledge.

Kemeny, J. (1995a) *From Public Housing to the Social Market: Rental Policy Strategy in Comparative Perspective*. London: Routledge.

Kemeny, J. (1995b) Theories of Power in 'The Three Worlds of Welfare Capitalism'. *Journal of European Social Policy*, Vol. 5, pp. 87–96.

Kemeny, J. (2001) Comparative Housing and Welfare: Theorising the Relationship. *Journal of Housing and the Built Environment*, Vol. 16, pp. 53–70.

Kemeny, J. (2005) The Really Big Trade-Off between Homeownership and Welfare: Castles' Evaluation of the 1980 Thesis and a Reformulation 25 years on. *Housing, Theory and Society*, Vol. 22, pp. 59–75.

Kemeny, J. (2006) Corporatism and Housing Regime. *Housing, Theory and Society*, Vol. 23, pp. 1–18.

Kemeny, J. & Lowe, S. (1998) Schools of Comparative Housing Research: From Convergence to Divergence. *Housing Studies*, Vol. 13 (2), pp. 161–176.

Kemeny, J., Andersen, H.T., Matznetter, W. & Thalmann, P. (2001) Non-Retrenchment Reasons for State Withdrawal: Developing the Social Rental Market in Four Countries. Working Paper 40, Institute for Housing and Urban Research, Uppsala University, Uppsala.

Kemeny, J., Kersloot, J. & Thalmann, P. (2005) Non-Profit Housing Influencing, Leading and Dominating the Unitary Rental Market: Three Case Studies. *Housing Studies*, Vol. 20 (6), pp. 855–872.

Kleinman, M. (1998) Western European Housing Policies: Convergence or Collapse? In: M. Kleinman, W. Matznetter & M. Stephens, (eds) *European Integration and Housing Policy*. London: Routledge, pp. 242–255.

Kuhnle, S., (ed.) (2000) *Survival of the European Welfare State*. London: Routledge.

Lee, Y. & Ku, Y. (2007) East Asian Welfare Regimes: Testing the Hypothesis of the Developmental Welfare State. *Social Policy & Administration*, Vol. 41 (2), pp. 197–212.

Leibfried, S. (1992) Towards a European Welfare State? On Integrating Poverty Regimes into the European Community. In: Z. Ferge & J. Kolberg, (eds) *Social Policy in a Changing Europe*. Frankfurt/Main: Campus, pp. 245–279.

Lennartz, C. (2010) Typologies of welfare state and housing regimes: Why do they differ? Working Paper presented at the Conference Comparative housing research: approaches and policy challenges in a new international era, Delft University of Technology, March 24th – 25th, 2010.

Leung, C. (2004) Macroeconomics and Housing: A Review of the Literature. *Journal of Housing Economics*, Vol. 13, pp. 249–267.

Low, L. (2006) Book Review: East Asian Welfare Regimes in Transition: From Confucianism to Globalisation. In: A. Walker & C. Wong, (eds) *ASEAN Economic Bulletin*, Vol. 23 (3), pp. 393–395. UK: The Policy Press.

Lux, M., (ed.) (2003) *Housing Policy: An End or a New Beginning*. Budapest: Open Society Institute.

Malpass, P. (2008) Housing and the New Welfare State: Wobbly Pillar or Cornerstone? *Housing Studies*, Vol. 23 (1), pp. 1–19.

Matznetter, W. (2002) Social Housing in a Conservative Welfare State: Austria as an Example. *Urban Studies*, Vol. 39 (2), pp. 265–282.

Matznetter, W. (2006) Quo Vadis, Comparative Housing Research? Paper presented at the ENHR Conference, Ljubljana, July.

Muellbauer, J. & Murphy, A. (2008) Housing Markets and the Economy: The Assessment. *Oxford Review of Economic Policy*, Vol. 24 (1), pp. 1–33.

Obinger, H. & Wagschal, U. (1998) Drei Welten des Wohlfahrtsstaates? Das Stratifizierungskonzept in der clusteranalytischen Überprüfung. [Three Worlds of the Welfare State? Testing the Stratification Concept with Cluster Analysis] In: S. Lessenich & I. Ostner, (eds) *Welten des Wohlfahrtskapitalismus. Der Sozialstaat in vergleichender Perspektive* [Worlds of Welfare Capitalism. The Welfare State in Comparative Perspective], Frankfurt/Main & New York: Campus Verlag, pp. 109–136.

O'Neill, P. (2008) The Role of Theory in Housing Research: Partial Reflections of the Work of Jim Kemeny. *Housing, Theory and Society*, Vol. 25 (3), pp. 164–176.

Peng, I. (2008) Welfare Policy Reforms in Japan and Korea: Cultural and Institutional Factors. In: W. van Oorschot, M. Opielka & B. Pfau-Effinger, (eds) *Culture and Welfare State*. Cheltenham (UK) & Northampton, MA (USA): Edwar Elgar, pp. 162–182.

Pierson, C., (ed.) (2001) *The New Politics of the Welfare State*. Oxford: Oxford University Press.

Pierson, C., (ed.) (2007) *Beyond the Welfare State? The New Political Economy of Welfare*. Cambridge: Polity.

Sainsbury, D., (ed.) (1999): *Gender and Welfare State Regimes*. Oxford: Oxford University Press.

Scanlon, K. & Whitehead, C. (2008) *Social Housing in Europe II*. London: LSE.

Schmidt, M., Ostheim, T., Siegel, N. & Zohlnhöfer, R., (eds) (2007) *Der Wohlfahrtsstaat. Eine Einführung in den historischen und internationalen Vergleich.* [The Welfare State. An Introduction into Historical and International Comparison] Wiesbaden: VS Verlag für Sozialwissenschaften.

Schubert, K., Hegelich, S. & Bazant, U., (eds) (2009) *The Handbook of European Welfare Systems*. London & New York: Routledge.

Schwarz, H. & Seabrooke, L., (eds) (2009) *The Politics of Housing Booms and Busts*. Basingstoke & New York: Palgrave Macmillan.

Seeleib-Kaiser, M., (ed.) (2008) *Welfare State Transformations*. Basingstoke: Palgrave Macmillan.

Somerville, P. (2000) *Social Relations and Social Exclusion: Rethinking Political Economy*. London: Routledge.

Sykes, R. (2005) Crisis? What Crisis? EU Enlargement and the Political Economy of European Union Social Policy. *Social Policy & Society*, Vol. 4 (2), pp. 207–215.

Taylor-Gooby, P. (2006) *Ideas and Welfare State Reform in Western Europe*. New York: Palgrave Macmillan.

Titmuss, R. (1974): *Social Policy*. London: George Allen & Unwin.

Torgersen, U. (1987) Housing: The Wobbly Pillar under the Welfare State. In: B. Turner, J. Kemeny and L. Lundqvist, (eds) *Between State and Market: Housing in the Post-industrial Era*. Stockholm: Almqvist and Wicksell International, pp. 116–126.

Toussaint, J. & Elsinga, M. (2009) Housing Asset-Based Welfare. Can the UK be Held Up as an Example for Europe? *Housing Studies*, Vol. 24 (5), pp. 669–692.

Trifiletti, R. (1999) Southern European Welfare Regimes and the Worsening Position of Women. *Journal of European Social Policy*, Vol. 9 (1), pp. 49–64.

Tsenkova, S. (2009) *Housing Reforms in Post-Socialist Europe: Lost in Transition*. Heidelberg: Springer-Verlag.

Walker, A. & Wong, C., (eds) (2006) *East Asian Welfare Regimes in Transition: From Confucianism to Globalisation*. UK: The Policy Press.

Whitehead, C. & Scanlon, K., (eds) (2007) *Social Housing in Europe*. London: LSE.

Wilensky, H. (1987) Comparative Social Policy: Theories, Methods, Findings. In: M. Dierkes & A. Antal, (eds) *Comparative Policy Research: Learning from Experience*. Aldershot: Gower.

Wilensky, H. & Lebaux, C. (1958) *Industrial Society and Social Welfare*. New York: Russell.

Zukowski, M. (2008) Social Policy Regimes in the European Countries. In: S. Golinowska, P. Hengstenberg & M. Zukowski, (eds) *Diversity and Commonality in European Social Policies: The Forging of a European Social Model*. Warsaw: Wydawnictwo Naukowe Scholar, pp. 23–32.

16

Housing Markets, the Life Course, and Migration Up and Down the Urban Hierarchy

Christopher Bitter and David A. Plane

INTRODUCTION

During the past several decades the US population has been aging due to declining fertility rates, longer life expectancies, and the progression of the vast Baby Boom cohorts toward their elderly years. At least since the 1980s, housing prognosticators such as Mankiw and Weil (1989) have been warning of dire consequences of the aging population for the US housing market. As the recent housing boom illustrates, these predictions have not yet come to pass. Now the large Baby-Boom generation is finally on the cusp of retirement. What does this portend for the future of the US housing market? We argue that such national scale issues may not be the most relevant to ask. Housing markets are local and the consequences of aging will play out differently in various locales. The American population is highly mobile. Migration has highly age-articulated patterns and thus exerts strong influences on local

housing supply and demand conditions. The more relevant question, then, is what spatially differentiated implications does population aging have for the nation's local housing markets?

In order to accurately assess the future effects of population aging on the nation's housing markets, we need to understand not only how demand for housing varies with age but also where people will choose to live at various ages. Like housing demand, migration propensities, motivations, and outcomes vary widely across the distinct stages of life. Housing itself plays an important role in mobility decisions, so changes in housing affordability will feed back into migration decisions, hence impacting future migration flows. Thus, housing demand, interregional migration, and the life course are intricately intertwined (see Chapter 3).

Given the unprecedented housing market boom and ensuing bust that have occurred during the first decade of the 21st century, as well as the changes in age composition that will play out over the next several decades, it is perhaps more important than ever to understand the linkages between migration, housing markets, and the life course. Changing geographic patterns of migration and housing affordability have important implications for households, cities, and the housing industry.

This chapter examines the literature linking age, housing markets, and interregional migration. In particular, we use the concept of movement up and down the urban hierarchy as a way of linking migration and housing market outcomes with stage of life. We begin by surveying the literature and empirical evidence linking interregional migration and housing markets, of which there is surprisingly little. We then discuss how the propensities to move up and down the urban hierarchy differ with age. This is followed by a section documenting how housing prices, tenure, and characteristics vary across the urban hierarchy. Next, we present the results of a study examining the changing importance of housing prices in migration decisions as householders age. The chapter concludes by discussing implications for future housing demand and affordability across the urban hierarchy.

AGE AND HOUSING DEMAND

There is a voluminous literature linking the life course with housing tenure and housing types (Myers 1990; Clark and Dieleman 1996) (see Chapters 3 and 4). Young 'emerging' adults (Arnett 2004) demand relatively little housing, have minimal or no savings, move frequently, and as Table 16.1 indicates, almost always rent apartments rather than buying homes. As households age into their late twenties and early thirties, many begin to form families and have children. The demand for single-family housing accelerates, and homeownership rates increase rapidly during these years as rising household incomes

Table 16.1 Homeownership rate by age of householder

Home Ownership rate by age of householder (2000)

Age	Rate (%)
Less than 25 years	21.7
25 to 29 years	38.1
30 to 34 years	54.6
35 to 39 years	65.0
40 to 44 years	70.6
45 to 49 years	74.7
50 to 54 years	78.5
55 to 59 years	80.4
60 to 64 years	80.3
65 to 69 years	83.0
70 to 74 years	82.6
75 years and over	77.7
Total	67.4

Source: U.S. Census Bureau.

make ownership more affordable. While space demands may decrease as households reach their fifties and the empty-nester stage, homeownership continues to increase as retirement nears because it provides a vehicle for wealth generation and retirement savings. Households in this stage of life also have the highest rates of second-home ownership. It is not until after retirement that homeownership rates peak and begin to decline.

Given these strong relationships, the aging of the US population will have important repercussions for housing demand. Based on an analysis of census data, Myers and Ryu (2008) detail how the propensity to buy versus sell homes varies with age. Their analysis suggests that individuals in their twenties and early thirties have a much greater propensity to buy homes than sell them, as most are purchasing for the first time. The difference between rates of buying and selling begins to narrow among those in their forties and fifties, and by the time individuals reach their early sixties, buying and selling is roughly balanced. Individuals first become net sellers of homes when they reach their late sixties. Net selling accelerates rapidly during the seventies, and skyrockets during the eighties, as mortality rates increase and the elderly move into homes and facilities where they can be cared for by others.

Myers and Ryu's analysis suggests that the aging Baby Boom generation will become net sellers of homes over the next several decades. The population of young adults, who represent the principal source of new housing demand, will grow much more slowly. This growing imbalance between buyers and sellers clearly has important implications for the US housing market and may have similar implications for European housing markets. These impending imbalances will be magnified at the local scale. The implications for the nation's local housing markets will also depend upon where people of various ages choose to live. Thus, interregional migration constitutes an important piece of the puzzle. In the next section, we review the literature pertaining to the linkages between migration and housing markets.

MIGRATION AND HOUSING MARKETS

There are dramatic variations in the level of housing prices and across the United States. For example, the median price of homes sold during 2006 in San Jose, CA was $750,000, more than eight times the median value of $95,000 in Buffalo, NY (National Association of Realtors, 2007). Rates of appreciation also vary widely over time. US Census data on median housing values indicated that between 1970 and 2000 nominal housing values in the San Francisco Bay area increased more than 15-fold, while those in Buffalo grew only four-fold. Differential rates of appreciation have caused a widening geographic dispersion of house prices over the past several decades. In 1980, median values in the 20 most expensive metropolitan statistical areas (MSAs), located primarily in the Northeast and along the West Coast, averaged roughly three times those of the 20 least expensive. By 2000, this gap had increased by 50 percent, and the recent housing boom has driven the differential to an astounding seven times. Clearly, these vast differences in housing prices have the potential to influence interregional migration decisions, but interregional moves also have the potential to influence housing prices.

The demand for housing in a local market is driven by both the number of households and their characteristics. Interregional migration is an important source of household change, and it thus has important implications for housing markets. Interregional moves entail leaving a housing unit at the origin and occupying a different one at the destination. Large influxes of migrants into or out of a local housing market have important repercussions for housing demand. Equally important are the characteristics of the migrants themselves, as the propensity to buy versus rent, preferences for different types of housing, and the ability to pay for it vary with characteristics such as age and income.

The linkage between interregional migration and housing demand is straightforward (see Chapters 3, 4 and 5). However, the effect of interregional migration on house prices is more ambiguous because it depends upon the elasticity of housing supply. As Glaeser et al. (2006) articulate, exogenous economic shocks will play out differently depending on the elasticity of housing supply, which varies widely between metropolitan areas due to factors such as land constraints and the regulatory environment. For example, in regions such as San Francisco and New York, buildable land is limited and the local regulatory environments are arduous. In such constrained markets it is difficult for builders to expand the stock of housing in the face of rising demand. In other housing markets, such as Dallas or Atlanta, land is more plentiful and builders face fewer regulatory constraints. Thus, new housing is developed rapidly in response to growing demand, keeping purchase prices low.

Because local milieux can dramatically affect market conditions, areas experiencing strong net in-migration will not necessarily experience rapid housing price growth. Large influxes of migrants into areas with elastic housing supply may result in relatively little appreciation in housing prices. For example, the population of Las Vegas nearly tripled between 1980 and 2000 as a result of rapid in-migration, yet house price appreciation was modest. During this same period, median housing values in Las Vegas increased by approximately 4 percent per year, which is less than the national average of 4.8 percent, and not much higher than inflation, which was averaging 3.3 percent.

While migration clearly has implications for local housing demand and affordability, housing market conditions also have the potential to influence interregional migration decisions, as differences in housing costs account for the lion's share of the variation in cost of living across the country. Given the dramatic variation in house price levels and rates of appreciation across regions described earlier, one would expect housing prices to play a role in both the decision to move between regions and destination choice.

Housing is a complex commodity because it has not only a use value but also an investment value. For many Americans their home is far and away their largest source of wealth; therefore price differentials may not be the only facet of housing markets that influence interregional migration decisions. Rates of housing price appreciation, too, may be important. Households may be willing to pay a higher cost for housing if they expect housing prices to appreciate rapidly in the future. Thus, high prices may actually draw migrants who expect continuing rapid price appreciation. Rapidly escalating prices may also depress out-migration because existing homeowners don't want to lose out on future appreciation. Falling housing prices, too, may depress interregional migration, as homeowners may find themselves under water, owing more to their mortgage lender than the home is worth. A move would entail realizing this loss; thus, moving decisions may be put off. Negative equity has been shown to depress mobility rates in general (Stein 1995; Henley 1998; Engelhardt 2003).

The role that housing markets play in intraurban mobility has been amply demonstrated (Clark and Dieleman 1996). One might expect the relationship between housing markets and interregional migration to be well documented in the migration literature, but in fact there has been surprisingly little empirical work done in this area. The differential effects of shorter versus longer distance intraurban job-change triggers on residential location choices have been the subject of inquiry (Clark and Withers 1999; Clark, Huang, Withers 2003), but generally most focus has been given to job market and migration linkages rather than those between housing markets and migration. This may be due, at least in part, to the dominance of the 'equilibrium' perspective on migration, which has been favored by the regional economic modelers.

Research on the determinants of interregional migration has typically been couched within a utility-maximizing framework in which households compare utility as a function of economic opportunity and amenities evaluated at their present location versus that attainable in alternative locations. If the differential is great enough to overcome the costs of moving – both monetary and psychic – migration is postulated to occur.

Within the utility-maximization paradigm, two main theoretical perspectives dominate the US migration literature. The disequilibrium perspective sees migration as largely a response to regional wage differentials that reflect opportunities for utility gains (Greenwood and Hunt 1989). Conversely, the equilibrium perspective argues that regions adjust quickly to economic shocks and are never far from equilibrium. From this perspective, wage and rent differentials do not reflect opportunities for utility gains, but, rather, they compensate for differences in place-specific amenities. Migration thereby represents a response to changing preferences for amenities, which may arise due to factors such as rising incomes (Graves 1980, 1983; Mueser and Graves 1992, 1995).

Much of the empirical research on interregional migration from these perspectives has focused on isolating the relative roles of jobs versus amenities, while the role of housing markets has clearly been a secondary consideration (Graves 1980; Porell 1982; Greenwood and Hunt 1989; Greenwood et al. 1991; Mueser and Graves 1995). The issue of interregional equilibrium has an important bearing on understanding the relationship between housing markets and migration. From the equilibrium perspective, house price differentials compensate for location-specific amenities, so they should only affect migration decisions to the extent that preferences for housing versus amenities are changing through time (Graves 1983). Empirical studies in this vein may include measures of rents (Graves 1983) or housing prices (Clark and Hunter 1992), but they are conceptualized as controls for omitted place-specific characteristics, rather than as shapers of migration themselves. The disequilibrium perspective, although concerned foremost with wage differentials, leaves more latitude for house price differentials to represent real utility differentials, which may be arbitraged through moving.

The interregional hedonic valuation literature provides some evidence for amenity capitalization into housing prices, although capitalization in the labor market appears to be more prevalent (Gyourko and Tracy 1991; Bloomquist et al. 1992; Carruthers and Mulligan). But the literature on interregional house price dynamics makes an equally strong case that housing markets, at least in some parts of the country, have strong tendencies toward disequilibrium. This literature finds that housing markets tend to be highly cyclical and prone to boom-and-bust cycles that may drive housing prices far from their equilibrium or fundamental value (Case and Shiller 1989; Shiller 1990; Abraham and Hendershott 1993 & 1996). This is due to both construction cycles and to expectations of future price growth, as buyers respond speculatively to rapid price increases by bidding prices even higher, until the bubble eventually bursts. Conversely, housing prices may over-correct on the way down as expectations of further losses drive prices below their fundamental value.

Thus, housing market cycles themselves appear to be an important driver of interregional disequilibrium. The recent housing boom illustrates this point. Between 2003 and 2005, median housing prices expanded by nearly 70 percent in Las Vegas; those in Austin, Texas grew by less than 5 percent. In a period of just two years, the price of housing in Las Vegas relative to that in Austin rose from 114 percent to 186 percent. This rising differential cannot be explained based on local economic conditions or changing preferences for amenities alone. Indeed, speculation is known to have been an important driver of Las Vegas's rapid appreciation, but it was relatively absent in Austin. Because housing prices are driven not only by changes in local economic fundamentals but also by speculative forces, geographic house price differences at times may reflect opportunities for utility gains through migration.

Despite the demonstrated tendency of housing markets to stray from equilibrium, relatively few studies have explicitly addressed the role that housing markets play in interregional migration within the United States. Berger and Bloomquist (1992) examined the respective roles of economic opportunities, amenities, and housing prices in a study of interregional migration between 253 large urban counties. They found that when housing characteristics and quality of life are held constant, housing cost differentials were not important determinants in the decision to move. Housing costs did appear, however, to exert a significant influence on destination choice.

Responding to the growing dispersion in regional house prices during the housing boom of the late 1980s, Gabriel et al. (1992) analyzed migration flows among the nine broad Census Divisions. They investigated several different measures of housing prices, including user costs, which incorporate appreciation expectations. Their empirical results generally found that high destination prices deterred migration while origin prices had little discernible effect. However, the coarse scale of analysis and failure to control for amenities suggests caution in applying the study's findings more generally.

Potepan (1994) investigated the relationship between gross migration and housing prices in 38 metropolitan areas during the 1970s, arguing that housing prices and migration are jointly determined. Employing a simultaneous equations framework, his results indicated that high levels of in-migration had a positive and statistically significant influence on housing price growth, while out-migration had a negative and significant influence. However, he did not find housing prices to have a statistically significant effect on either in-migration or out-migration rates.

Withers and Clark (2006) examined the linkages between family migration decisions, migration outcomes, and housing costs. They argue that the motivations for and benefits from migration can not be assessed without considering the housing market context. They find that families who move to more affordable housing markets generally benefit financially. Moreover, housing costs influence labor force participation on the part of wives. Wives are more likely to leave the labor market when they move to a more affordable housing market. Conversely, they are more likely to enter the labor market upon a move to a more expensive housing market. Thus interregional migration, housing prices, and labor force participation are intricately intertwined.

While our review focuses on the US literature, several additional studies have examined the linkages between migration and housing markets within the European context (Jackman and Savouri 1992; Johnes and Hyclak 1994; Cameron and Muellbauer 1998; Hämäläinen and Böckerman 2004).

As our literature review indicates, the case for a relationship between interregional migration decisions and housing markets is strong, but this has not yet been well documented in the literature. One clear shortcoming in the work to date is a failure to consider the different role that housing considerations play at the various stages of life. Housing demand and migration are intricately intertwined with age, as well as with one another. We suggest that it is critically important to tie interregional migration and housing markets together within an explicit life-course approach in order to understand impending changes in migration patterns and housing markets associated with population aging.

MIGRATION AND HOUSING MARKETS: A LIFE-COURSE PERSPECTIVE

The linkages between migration and housing markets are tightly intertwined with age. While the migration literature has generally been approached from an age-aggregate perspective, the propensity to migrate varies widely over the stages of life, and radically different factors shape migration outcomes at different ages. Thus a life course perspective is imperative to understanding how population aging will influence both future migration patterns and their housing market outcomes. One way of linking migration, housing markets, and stage of the life course is through the concept of age-articulated migration up and down the urban hierarchy.

Age-articulated migration up and down the urban hierarchy

As the well-known 'age schedule' of migration illustrates, migration propensities also vary in a regular manner as individuals progress through the various stages of life. Mobility rates peak during the footloose stage of young adulthood and family formation and decline slowly thereafter as households move into their forties and fifties due to cumulative inertia as household's rear children, buy homes, and focus on their careers. A slight uptick in mobility occurs later in life as households achieve empty-nester status or move in association with impending retirement.

The reasons that households move also shift throughout the life course, as do the weightings they assign to various factors such as housing, labor market opportunities, and place-specific amenities in their migration decisions. This leads to regularities in the migration outcomes of households within different stages of the life course. Plane and Jurjevich (2009) find a strong relationship between stage in the life course and the propensity to move to settlements of various size classes within the urban hierarchy.

Two extended periods of many people's life courses are particularly salient both for housing and migration analysis. These are the two stages of life when location decisions are relatively 'footloose' in the sense that family ties do not bind as strongly as at other ages. The period of emerging adulthood from the late teens to around age 30 is the first of these stages. This is an age range beginning with the completion of high school and, in many cases, the leaving of the parental home. A series of moves may then ensue in rapid succession. It is a stage of exploration – of career choices, living arrangement, and geographical options. The traditional characteristic end of this extended stage involves family formation, settling into long-term careers, and home purchases.

The second stage is also one of exploration, greater footlooseness, and multiple moves. At an advanced stage of adulthood, ties to family, careers, and locations are lessened compared to the middle-adult years. Often triggered first by 'empty-nesting,' when children leave the household, and then by the investigation and implementation of retirement decisions, this second extended period of mobility has been made possible by the lengthening of life spans and the increase in the number of years the elderly can anticipate engaging in relatively healthy, active lifestyles.

Plane and Heins (2003) investigated the commonalities across metropolitan areas in terms of the age schedules of areas' in- and out-migration streams. A typology of the age-articulated fields of intermetropolitan migration was developed, and it was seen that among the discriminating factors seemed to be the population sizes of metropolitan origins and destinations.

The relationships between migration, the life course and the urban hierarchy critically depend on two key extended periods of life. During these two age spans, very different characteristic patterns of movement take place upward and downward within the urban hierarchy. To examine these patterns we shall make use of the seven-category, size-based classification of Core-Based Statistical Areas (CBSAs) employed in Plane and Jurjevich (2009), which is shown in Table 16.2.

As shown in Table 16.3 (and detailed in Plane et al. 2005), the overall direction of recent US migration has been *down* the national urban hierarchy, with the 12 Mega

Table 16.2 Seven-level Core-Based Statistical Area (CBSA) population size hierarchy

	Population size range
Mega Metropolitan	4,000,000 or more
Major Metropolitan	1,000,000–3,999,999
AAA-Metropolitan	500,000–999,999
AA-Metropolitan	250,000–499,999
A-Metropolitan	50,000–249,999
Micropolitan	Urban cluster of 10,000–49,999
Non-CBSA County	No urban cluster ≥ 10,000

Source: Hierarchy adapted from Plane, Henrie and Perry (2005). Note: The Major, AAA, AA, A nomenclature follows the custom of baseball league classifications. The federal government's Office of Management and Budget did not adopt official size classes when approving post-2000 metropolitan definitions. The metropolitan population classification scheme previously in effect involving levels D through A had proven unpopular with local officials unhappy with their areas being assigned to lower than "A" level categories.

Table 16.3 Net migration between CBSA hierarchy levels by age group at the time of move, 1995–2000

Level	All ages	15–24	20–29	55–64	75–84
Mega Metro	−1,834,821	−203,745	202,805	−158,553	−15,882
Major Metro	912,161	177,335	270,034	−6,347	11,123
AAA-Metro	−15,610	34,680	−43,828	−5,011	2,663
AA-Metro	357,034	106,811	−67,756	31,603	8,487
A-Metro	356,310	236,555	−211,322	28,473	7,086
Micropolitan	215,423	−63,901	−135,430	55,324	−974
Non-CBSA	9,503	−287,735	−14,503	54,511	−12,503

Source: Calculated by the authors from special county-to-county tabulation of Census 2000 migration data.

Metropolitan areas losing more than 1.8 million people through internal migration to counties at the lower levels. Major Metros – those with populations of more than a million but less than four million – experienced the largest gains. With respect to housing markets, however, it should be noted that a number of the Mega MSAs continue to gain population both through foreign immigration and natural increase, thereby offsetting their net losses of internal migrants.

Note in Table 16.3, the patterns of net internal migration gains and losses differ greatly when we break the flows down into key population age groups. In terms of the two emerging adult age groups, 15–24 and 20–29,[1] there were large net outflows of the younger, parental-home-leaving group from the levels at both extremes of the hierarchy – Mega Metro and non-CBSA counties. The smallest, A-level metropolitan areas, which include many college towns, military bases, and prisons, had very sizeable population gains for persons of this age. Note, however, that for those in the post-college, military-leaving 20–29-year-old age group, most of the A-Metro population gains at the youngest adult ages are lost. The only two hierarchy levels posting significant net migration gains among the somewhat older '20-somethings' are the Major and Mega Metro areas (see Franklin 2003).

By the time the empty-nesting, early-retirement ages of 55–64 are reached, downward movement becomes strongly entrenched, with massive out-movement from the Mega Metros by young-elderly cashing in their home equity to move to less congested smaller settlements. The two smallest metropolitan size categories, plus Micropolitan areas, and non-CBSA counties, all gain significant population through the internal migration patterns of this age group. One final thing to note in Table 16.3 is the last column. It shows that the older-elderly, although smaller in number, exhibit yet another pattern of net redistribution within the hierarchy: net outflow from both the largest and the smallest size categories with net inflow into the middle levels. For a significant portion of such golden-age migrants, 'return' migration to live closer to adult children may be the motivation (Litwak and Longino 1987; Rogers 1992; McHugh et. al. 1995; Warnes and Williams 2006; van der Meer 2006). Figure 16.1 gives a finer scale picture of how the origin–destination-specific streams of age-articulated migration play out differentially up and down the urban hierarchy. The lines on the graph trace the demographic effectiveness of the net migration exchanges of persons across 17 age groups. Shown are such measures for four from among the 21 total possible combinations of CBSA hierarchy levels. Demographic effectiveness of migration exchange between two hierarchy levels is calculated as:

$$E_{ija} = 100(N_{ija}/T_{ija})$$
$$= 100(M_{ija} - M_{jia})/(M_{ija} + M_{jia})$$

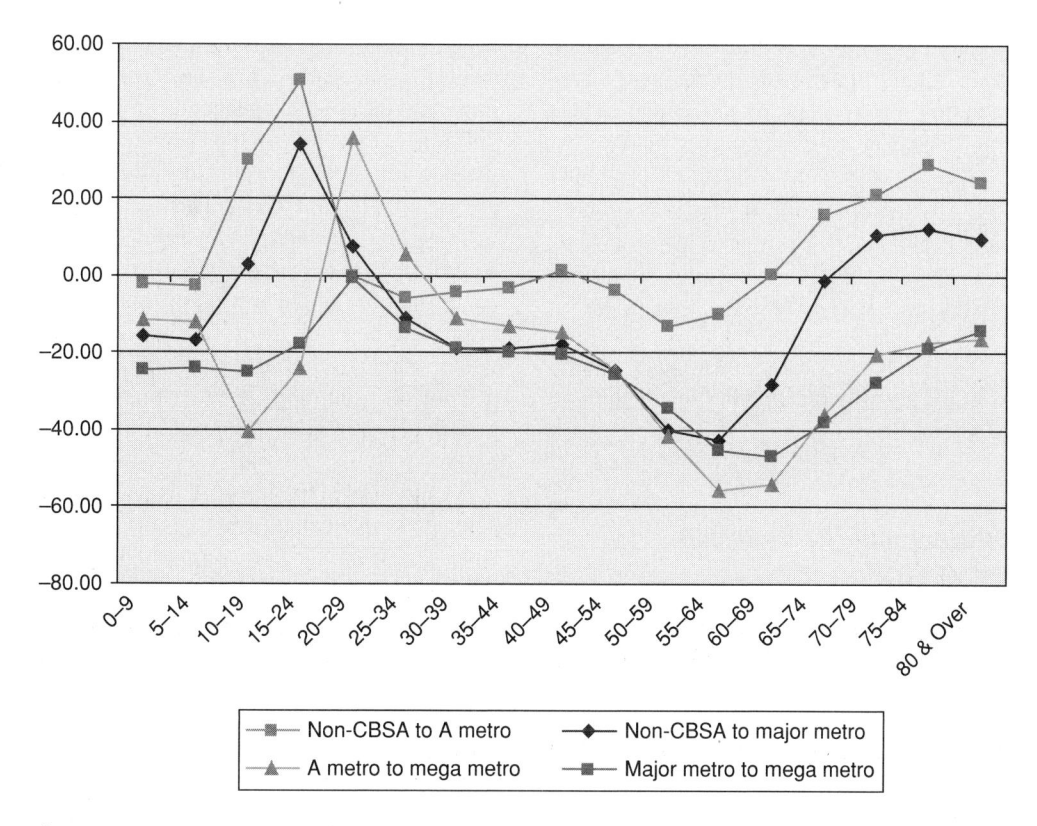

Figure 16.1 Demographic effectiveness of migration between CBSA hierarchy levels by age at time of move

Here N_{ija} is the net exchange of age group a migrants between a lower level of the CBSA hierarchy, i, and a higher level j, found as the difference between the gross upward flow of such migrants, M_{ija}, and the gross downward flow, M_{jia}; T_{ija} is the total exchange of age group a migrants found as the sum of the gross upward and downward flows.

Demographic effectiveness of 0 percent would indicate that there were equal amounts of gross movement upward and downward between the pair of levels. Under the convention we adopt, positive demographic effectiveness values are obtained if more migrants move upwards than downwards: i.e., the aggregate gross movements from areas at the lower level to those at the higher level exceed the gross movements from areas at the higher to those at the lower level. Negative demographic effectiveness, conversely, indicates a relative predominance of downward movement. The larger the values of demographic effectiveness, the more the flows in one direction exceed those in the counter direction. The limiting value of 100 percent would indicate that all flow was from the lower to the higher level of the hierarchy, whereas a value of −100 percent would mean that all flow was from the higher to the lower level.

Note in Figure 16.1 the exodus of the parental home-leavers from non-CBSA counties to both A-Metros and Major Metros. Note, conversely, the gain of young people by A-level counties from Mega Metros, but then the subsequent population losses back up to the highest level of the hierarchy among the early working ages of 20–29.

Late in the traditional working ages through the primary retirement years, the lines for all four of the selected inter-level combinations exhibit significant dips – meaning strongly downward movement corresponding, on average, to movement to less congested, lower-priced housing markets.

Over the oldest age groups, all four lines rise. The two involving non-CBSA counties have positive effectiveness values, meaning that net movement is up the hierarchy, whereas the two involving Mega Metros – while rising – remain negative, indicative of the tendency of the later-stage elderly to move towards the middle tier of the size hierarchy.

Housing and the US urban hierarchy

Varying propensities to migrate up and down the urban hierarchy during different stages of life are likely motivated by a variety of factors. Housing markets may be a particularly important part of the explanation as profound differences exist in both the characteristics of the housing stock and housing affordability across the urban hierarchy. This section summarizes housing data drawn from the 2007 American Housing survey by settlement size. As of the time of the writing of this chapter, these data had only been released for areas with a population of at least 60,000, so they do not include non-CBSA counties, and potentially a few small MSAs or Micropolitan areas.

As the data in Tables 16.4 and 16.5 indicate, both the composition of the housing stock and housing costs vary widely across the urban hierarchy. Detached single-family housing units comprise the majority of the housing stock at all levels of the hierarchy,

Table 16.4 Housing characteristics by CBSA hierarchy level

	Type of Strucure						Percent Vacant	Persons Per HH
Class	SF Det	SF Att	2_9 Units	10_49 Units	50 + Units	Mobile		
MEGA	51.5%	8.7%	16.5%	12.1%	8.9%	2.3%	9.8%	2.8
MAJOR	62.4%	6.8%	13.7%	9.0%	4.2%	3.9%	10.2%	2.6
AAA	64.2%	5.2%	13.7%	6.6%	3.4%	6.8%	11.5%	2.5
AA	66.1%	4.9%	12.3%	6.5%	2.5%	7.6%	11.7%	2.6
A	67.0%	3.5%	12.0%	5.4%	2.1%	9.9%	12.9%	2.6
MICRO	67.4%	3.0%	10.2%	3.2%	1.4%	13.0%	15.7%	2.5

SF Det, single-family detached; SF Att, single-family attached; HH, household.

Table 16.5 Housing occupancy and costs by CBSA hierarchy level

							Cost as a Percent of Household Income	
Class	Owner Occupied	Median Rent ($)	Median Value ($)	Value to income Ratio	Price Change 1995–2007	Montly Housing Cost	Owners	Renters
MEGA	65.1	845	339,821	5.5	155.9	1250.6	24.7	30.7
MAJOR	67.3	671	225,300	4.1	109.4	1001.6	21.9	29.6
AAA	68.4	641	208,188	3.5	90.2	937.7	21.6	30.1
AA	68.2	602	200,440	4.1	100.7	863.4	20.6	30.0
A	69.1	531	153,646	4.0	107.8	751.7	19.6	29.6
MICRO	72.0	492	151,847	3.4	n.a.	704.7	19.3	28.1

Source: OFHEO.

but the proportion of this type of housing declines markedly with settlement size. Single-family homes represent just over half of all housing units in Mega MSAs, but more than two-thirds of housing units in Micropolitan areas. Conversely, Mega Metro areas tend to have a much greater proportion of large housing complexes of more than 50 units. Mobile homes are much more prevalent in smaller-sized communities. While structure types vary widely across the urban hierarchy, the ACS data suggest that differences in other housing characteristics such as age and average number of rooms are much less significant.

The proportion of vacant housing units also increases in a regular manner with settlement size. Nearly 16 percent of housing units in Micropolitan areas were vacant in 2007, as compared to only 10 percent in Mega Metros. This is due in large part to the prevalence of seasonal housing units in smaller areas. In Mega and Major MSAs, respectively, 13 and 17 percent of vacant housing units were used only seasonally, while nearly 37 percent of vacant units in Micropolitan areas fell into this category.

There are also vast differences in median housing values and rents across the urban hierarchy. As Table 16.5 indicates, both median rents and values increase with settlement size. The high price of housing in Mega Metros is particularly evident, as median values in the Mega Metros are 50 percent higher than those in Major Metros and more than double those in Level-A MSAs and Micropolitan areas. Rents generally follow the same pattern, but the differences are not nearly as pronounced. Higher housing costs in Mega MSAs are partially offset by higher incomes, but the ratio of median housing value to median household income is still substantially higher, which indicates that housing is much less affordable. Indeed, Mega Metro homeowners spend nearly 25 percent of their income on housing, while those in A-Metros and Micropolitan areas spend less than 20 percent. Renters in Mega Metros also spend a greater proportion of their income on housing than do those in smaller-sized settlements, but the differences are less pronounced.

Variations in housing affordability across the urban hierarchy are clearly related to differences in housing tenure and household size. Despite their greater average incomes, fewer residents in the Mega Metros own their own homes. Homeownership increases steadily for each successive level down the urban hierarchy. Moreover, the lack of affordable housing likely contributes to larger household sizes found in the Mega Metros.

It is also important to highlight that the gap between housing values in the largest metropolitan areas and other settlement types has widened during the recent housing boom. We calculated housing appreciation over the period of 1995 to 2007 for the six metropolitan settlement categories based on the OFHEO repeat sales housing price index data.[2] These figures indicate that during the recent housing boom housing prices appreciated approximately 50 percent faster in the Mega Metros than in the other types of settlements. Nominal appreciation in the Mega Metros averaged more than 150 percent over this period, as compared to a range of 90–110 percent for smaller metropolitan areas (see also Shiller 2005).

The data presented above indicate that there are important differences in housing affordability and the composition of the housing stock across the various levels of the urban hierarchy. However, it is also important to note that there is significant variability in housing structure within these categories. Within the Mega Metro category, for instance, homeownership rates range from 52 percent in Los Angeles to 74 percent in Detroit. The proportion of detached single-family homes varies even more widely, from 36 percent in New York, to nearly 70 percent in Detroit. Similarly, median housing prices in Dallas and Houston are only about one-fifth of those in San Francisco. Settlement size is clearly only one of a multitude of factors that influence the structure of local housing markets. While it is beyond the scope of this chapter, a hierarchical settlement classification scheme based explicitly on housing market characteristics might reveal additional insights into the relationship between migration and housing markets.

Housing prices, age and net migration: an exploratory analysis

The distinct migration patterns associated with age clearly have important implications for local housing demand and affordability across the urban hierarchy. But the vast differences in housing affordability that exist across settlements of different sizes surely also play an important role in the observed propensity to migrate up and down the urban hierarchy at various stages of the life course. If housing costs are drivers of these outcomes, then changing patterns of housing affordability will inevitably feed back into migration decisions themselves.

Little is currently known regarding how house-price differentials influence interregional migration outcomes across the various stages of the life course. Yet such mechanisms are essential elements for understanding how national population aging will affect local housing markets. In this section we present some empirical evidence to fill this gap in the literature.

Table 16.6 depicts data pertaining to metro-to-metro migration flows by age during the period 1995–2000. We tabulate the number of movers within each age category that moved from higher- to lower-cost MSAs based on the median housing value from Census 2000. There is clear evidence that the propensity to move to lower-cost areas varies with age. Young adults aged 20–29 are more likely to move to higher-cost MSAs. However, as individuals reach their thirties, moves to lower-cost metropolitan areas begin to dominate. The proportion of these types of moves increases steadily with age, and it peaks at 63 percent for individuals in their late sixties. The propensity of moves to lower-cost areas for individuals near retirement would undoubtedly be stronger if Micropolitan and rural areas were included in these data. Finally, Table 16.6 also indicates that moves involving

Table 16.6 Age and the propensity to move to lower-cost metropolitan areas

Age Cohort	Total Movers	Movers to Lower Price MSA	Movers to Higher Price MSA	Precent Moves to Lower Price MSA
5–9	1,543,745	843,798	699,947	54.7
10–14	1,218,320	663,468	554,852	54.5
15–19	1,495,704	806,344	689,360	53.9
20–24	2,778,305	1,357,446	1,420,859	48.9
25–29	2,857,610	1,327,383	1,530,227	46.5
30–34	2,313,327	1,176,552	1,136,775	50.9
35–39	1,961,648	1,039,592	922,056	53.0
40–44	1,479,554	794,702	684,852	53.7
45–49	1,061,282	570,830	490,452	53.8
50–54	834,723	465,060	369,663	55.7
55–59	599,912	352,933	246,979	58.8
60–64	448,778	278,875	169,903	62.1
65–69	369,905	232,987	136,918	63.0
70–74	280,581	165,203	115,378	58.9
75–79	225,101	124,652	100,449	55.4
80–84	171,652	89,440	82,212	52.1
85+	181,033	90,134	90,899	49.8
Total	19,821,180	10,379,399	9,441,781	52.4

children are more likely to end in lower-cost metropolitan areas.

While the data presented above do suggest that the relationship between migration and housing prices varies with age, there are clearly many other factors that influence migration decisions. In order to control for these factors we estimated a simple OLS regression model, disaggregated by five-year age cohort. Our data consist of 232 US metropolitan area observations. We calculated age-specific rates of 1995–2000 net migration for each MSA based on the special county-to-county migration tabulation of Census 2000.

We model age-specific net-migration rates as a function of economic opportunities, housing prices, and place-specific amenities. Our housing price variable is based on the Census 2000 median housing value for each MSA, which is adjusted by the OFHEO constant quality house price index to reflect mid-period housing prices. This is clearly an imperfect measure of housing prices because it represents the homeowner's estimate of value and does not control for differences in housing quality. Nonetheless, we believe it to be a reasonably accurate measure of housing price differentials. The independent variables are described in Table 16.7. In addition to measures of amenities and economic opportunity, we include Census Division dummies to control for unspecified regional influences. While this is clearly not an exhaustive list of migration determinants, the results of our models should provide a reasonable picture of how the influence of housing prices varies with stage of life.

We first estimated an aggregate net migration model including all age groups. In this model, the house price estimate is insignificant, which implies that housing prices did not influence overall net migration rates. This is not surprising as this period was one of relatively balanced housing market conditions across much of the nation. Thus, house price differentials likely reflect amenity compensation to a greater extent than disequilibrium in housing markets. However, regional housing prices reflect average preferences for place-specific amenities. If preferences for place-specific characteristics vary at different ages, then housing price differentials may still be important despite the lack of overall significance.

Next, we estimated separate net-migration rate models for each of the 15 five-year age cohorts. The results of these models, presented in Table 16.8, do indeed suggest that the relationship between housing prices and net-migration rates varies over the life course.

Table 16.7 Variable descriptions

Variable	Description	Source
ADJVAL	Median housing value, third quarter, 1997	2000 Census, OFHEO
PTAX	Per capita property tax collections	2000 Census
POP	Population	2000 Census
RENT	Median rent, 1999	2000 Census
IMMIGRATE	Proportion of residents who lived in foreign country, 1995	2000 Census
UNEMPLOY	Unemployment rate	2000 Census
MFG	Proportion of employees engaged in manufacturing	2000 Census
INCOME	Per capita income	BEA
PRJOBS	Places rated jobs score	1997 Places Rated Almanac
PRCLIMATE	Places rated climate score	1997 Places Rated Almanac
PRCRIME	Places rated crime score	1997 Places Rated Almanac
PRREC	Places rated recreation score	1997 Places Rated Almanac
DIV	Census Division (8) - East South Central is omitted	2000 Census

Table 16.8 Age-disaggregated net-migration model results

	Summary Statistics			House-price Coefficients		
	R^2	Adj R^2	Std Err	Beta	T-stat	Sig
15–19	0.33	0.27	0.09	0.42	2.61	0.01
20–24	0.38	0.33	0.14	0.31	2.00	0.05
25–29	0.46	0.40	0.13	−0.39	−2.68	0.01
30–34	0.46	0.41	0.06	−0.48	−3.33	0.00
35–39	0.42	0.37	0.04	−0.20	−1.34	0.18
40–44	0.44	0.39	0.03	−0.14	−0.95	0.34
45–49	0.49	0.44	0.03	−0.12	−0.84	0.40
50–54	0.50	0.45	0.03	−0.23	−1.70	0.09
55–59	0.54	0.50	0.04	−0.26	−1.99	0.05
60–64	0.55	0.51	0.05	−0.34	−2.57	0.01
65–69	0.59	0.56	0.04	−0.35	−2.79	0.01
70–74	0.50	0.45	0.03	−0.37	−2.66	0.01
75–79	0.39	0.34	0.02	−0.44	−2.90	0.00
80–84	0.31	0.25	0.03	0.15	0.93	0.35
85+	0.21	0.14	0.05	0.02	0.10	0.92

N=232

Our basic OLS regressions explain between 40 and 60 percent of the variance in net-migration rates for most age groups. The explanatory power is weakest for the youngest and oldest.

The coefficients and significance levels of the house-price coefficients vary widely with age. Our results indicate that those between the ages of 15 and 24 appear to be attracted to MSAs with high housing prices. This is not surprising as emerging adults tends to rent rather than buy housing. They may be attracted by other factors associated with more expensive MSAs, such as educational opportunities or a vibrant night life, that are not captured in our model. In contrast, the house price coefficients are negative and highly significant for persons in their late twenties and early thirties. Thus, housing prices appear to play an important role in their migration decisions, although economic opportunities appear to be more important. This likely reflects growing demand for housing associated with family formation coupled with income and equity constraints, which may impede access to homeownership in more costly MSAs.

Our regressions indicate that the influence of house prices on net-migration rates wanes during middle age: the house price estimates are insignificant for 35–54 year olds. These individuals have higher incomes, have had more time to save for housing down payments, or may have already accrued housing equity.

Housing prices become progressively more important as individuals near and enter retirement. The house price coefficients are negative and significant for all age groups from 55 to 79. At these later stages in life, our regression results indicate that climate is the single most important migration determinant, but population size and housing prices are also significant. Thus, the moves of younger elderly down the urban hierarchy may reflect opportunities both to improve their quality of life as well as to cash out housing equity to be preserved for retirement. Finally, we find housing prices to be unimportant to persons older than 79, which is not surprising as moves during the late stages in the life course often reflect return migrations to former places of residence or moves to be in closer proximity to family members.

IMPLICATIONS FOR HOUSING DEMAND AND AFFORDABILITY ACROSS THE URBAN HIERARCHY

In this section we outline some potential implications of age-articulated migration up and down the urban hierarchy for future housing market conditions. The impending retirement of the Baby Boom generation will clearly have an important impact on the national housing market. The repercussions for housing demand and prices will be magnified at the local scale by the retirement migration decisions of the Baby Boomers. But we also argue that any associated changes in housing affordability will feed back into migration patterns themselves.

During the next 10 years, the vast Baby Boom generation will age into their fifties and sixties, a period of life during which the preceding generation demonstrated a strong tendency to move down the urban hierarchy, particularly to the warm, sunny climates of the Sunbelt and other smaller communities with abundant natural amenities. If this tendency prevails for the Baby Boom generation we can expect an acceleration of outflows of retirees and pre-retirees from the largest metropolitan areas into the nation's Micropolitan areas and smaller retirement communities. While only a small proportion of these households will likely desert the Mega MSAs, their impact on the housing market will be important because the vast majority of these future migrants now own homes. This should lead to a significant increase in the supply of homes available for sale in the nation's largest MSAs, and a growing imbalance in such markets between sellers and buyers. This imbalance may be particularly acute in the older Megas of the Northeast and Midwest, which have been losing older migrants at a much faster rate than the newly emerging Megas of the Sunbelt.

Does this spell doom for the Mega Metros housing sector? The effects will clearly be negative, and we expect the differential in housing prices between the Mega and smaller-sized settlements to narrow. But we also argue that narrowing house price differentials will feed back into migration patterns. As the differentials narrow, many Baby Boomers may remain in their Mega Metro homes, as the opportunity to capitalize on housing differentials diminishes. Moreover, the quality of life improvements in major American cities vis-à-vis earlier decades, such as lower crime rates and stronger cultural amenities, may reduce the propensity to leave and may even attract empty-nester/retirement-stage in-migrants.

Much also depends on the migration decisions of the Baby Boom Echo generation, which includes individuals born between approximately 1982 and 1995. They will swell the ranks of individuals in their late twenties and early thirties over the next decade, a stage in life when many purchase homes for the first time. Individuals in their late twenties have shown a tendency to migrate up the urban hierarchy. Indeed, this is the only age cohort that the Mega Metros have been attracting on net. However, there has also been a strong tendency for young adults to depart the Mega Metros during their early thirties. If this trend prevails, housing demand in Mega Metros could take a double hit. However, as our analysis in the last section suggests, this movement is in part due to high housing costs. Thus, improving housing affordability in the Mega Metros may impel more of the Baby Boom Echo generation to stay put and purchase homes, ameliorating some but not all of the loss of Boomer homeowners.

While beyond the scope of this chapter, immigration patterns will also play a pivotal role in the fate of the Mega Metro housing markets (Clark 1998). Despite currently changing patterns of initial immigrant settlement and of foreign-born population redistribution (Massey 2008, Plane and Hoffman 2009) many of the Mega Metros remain important immigration gateways. As the points of entry of much of the country's new population, congestion and the bidding up of supply-constrained housing markets have played a role in fueling the redistribution of recent immigrants away from the Mega Metros. More affordable housing in the future may impel this group, in particular, to stay due to earlier established social ties.

While the consequences of the impending retirement of the Baby Boomers has ominous implications for the Mega housing markets, the outlook for the major retirement destinations and smaller, amenity-rich communities that are their primary destinations are much more sanguine. The majority of retiree and pre-retiree in-movers are likely to initially purchase homes at their new destination. Wealthy Baby Boomers who remain in their Mega Metro homes may also purchase second homes in these same destinations. While Engelhardt (2006) argues that the Baby Boomers have not shown a stronger propensity to purchase second homes than their parents, the sheer growth in their numbers should lead to a significant increase in second home purchases.

These developments will surely bolster population growth and housing demand in the favored retirement metros and smaller, amenity-rich places. Indeed, the prior movements of the Baby Boom Generation have had significant impacts on non-metropolitan growth dynamics (Nelson et al. 2004). The impact on housing prices will hinge on the elasticity of supply in the destination housing markets. However, as our regressions indicate, retirees are also relatively sensitive to housing prices. Thus, we expect that, as the traditional retirement destinations in Florida and Arizona become pricier, the Baby Boomers will increasingly eschew them for lower-cost areas such as Texas or the Carolinas. Anecdotal evidence suggests that such a trend is already beginning to happen.

In sum, while the retirement of the Baby Boomers will have important repercussions for housing markets across the urban hierarchy, migration is an equilibrating mechanism that will help to even out demand as differences in housing affordability narrow across the urban hierarchy. Many of the Mega Metros have both vibrant economies and amenities. While many Baby Boomers may still choose to sell their homes and depart for smaller, amenity-rich communities, younger households will be attracted by more affordable housing.

While this chapter has focused on only one aspect of the impending Baby Boomer retirement and its consequences for housing markets across the urban hierarchy, there are many other interrelated issues that must be considered. For example, how will the recent stock market decline affect the Baby Boomer's retirement plans? Will the homes offered for sale by the Baby Boomers meet the housing requirements of the younger generations? Will the sprawling, automobile-reliant suburbs of the Baby Boomers be attractive to tomorrow's home buyers in an age of energy scarcity and growing environmental awareness? Finally, how will changes in household composition, such as the rapid growth of single-person and non-family households, influence migration patterns and housing demand? These issues are equally important for understanding future changes in housing demand and affordability within the United States.

NOTES

1 Note that the age groups used here overlap. The special tabulation of Census 2000 data used report age at the time of enumeration and the question asked was about place of residence five years earlier. Thus, the actual age at the time of the move could have been as much as five years younger than the age recorded on the census date.

2 Comparable data are not released for Micropolitan areas.

REFERENCES

Abraham, J. & Hendershott, P. (1993). Patterns and determinants of metropolitan housing prices 1977–1991, in L.E. Browne & E.S. Rosengren (eds), *Real Estate and the Credit Crunch*. Boston, MA: Federal Reserve Bank of Boston, pp. 18–42.

Abraham, J. & Hendershott, P. (1996). Bubbles in metropolitan housing markets. *Journal of Housing Research*, 7(2), 191–207.

Arnett, J. J. (2004). *Emerging Adulthood: The Winding Road from the Late Teens through the Twenties*. New York: Oxford University Press.

Berger, M.C. & Blomquist, G.C. (1992). Mobility and destination in migration decisions: the role of earnings, quality of life, and housing prices. *Journal of Housing Economics*. 2, 37–59.

Blomquist, G., Berger, M. & Hoehn, J. (1988). New estimates of quality of life in urban areas. *American Economic Review*, 1, 89–107.

Cameron, G. & Muellbauer, J. (1998). The housing market and regional commuting and migration choices. *Scottish Journal of Political Economy*, 45, 420–446.

Case, K. & Shiller, R. (1989). The efficiency of the market for single-family homes. *American Economic Review*, 79(1), 125–137.

Clark, D. & Hunter, W. (1992). The impact of economic opportunity, amenities, and fiscal factors on age-specific migration rates. *Journal of Regional Science*, 32, 349–365.

Clark, W.A.V. (1998). *The California Cauldron: Immigration and the Fortunes of Local Communities*. New York: Guilford Press.

Clark, W.A.V., & Dieleman, F. (1996). *Housing and Households: Choice and Outcomes in the Housing Market*. New Brunswick: Center for Urban Policy Research.

Clark, W.A.V., Huang, Y. & Withers, S. (2003). Does commuting distance matter?: Commuting tolerance and residential change. *Regional Science and Urban Economics*, 33, 199–221.

Clark, W.A.V., & Withers, S. D., 1999. Changing jobs and changing houses: Mobility outcomes of employment transitions. *Journal of Regional Science*, 39, 653–673.

Engelhardt, G. (2003). Nominal loss aversion, housing equity constraints, and household mobility: Evidence from the United States. *Journal of Urban Economics*, 5, 171–195.

Engelhardt, G. (2006). *Housing Trends Among Baby Boomers*. Washington, DC: Research Institute for Housing America, Mortgage Bankers Association.

Franklin, R. (2003). *Migration of the Young, Single, and College Educated: 1995 to 2000*. Census 2000 Special Reports, CENSR-12. Washington, DC: US Government Printing Office.

Gabriel, S., Shack-Marquez, J. & Wascher, W. (1992). Regional house-price dispersion and interregional migration. *Journal of Housing Economics*, 2, 235–256.

Glaeser, E., Gyourko, J. & Saks, R. (2006). Urban growth and housing supply. *Journal of Economic Geography*, 6, 71–89.

Graves, P. (1980). Migration and climate. *Journal of Regional Science*, 20, 227–237.

Graves, P. (1983). Migration with a composite amenity: The role of rents. *Journal of Regional Science*, 23, 541–546.

Greenwood, M. & Hunt, G. (1989). Jobs versus amenities in the analysis of metropolitan migration. *Journal of Urban Economics*, 25, 1–16.

Greenwood, M.J., Hunt, G.L., Rickman, D.S., & Treyz, G.I. (1991). Migration, regional equilibrium, and the estimation of compensating differentials. *American Economic Review*, 81(5), 1382–1390.

Gyourko, J. & Tracy, J. (1991). The structure of local public finance and the quality of life. *Journal of Political Economy*, 91, 774–806.

Hämäläinen, K. & Böckerman, P. (2004). Regional labor market dynamics, housing, and migration. *Journal of Regional Science*, 44(3), 543–568.

Henley, A. (1998). Residential mobility, housing equity and the labour market. *The Economic Journal*, 108, 414–427.

Jackman, R. & Savouri, S. (1992). Regional migration in Britain: An analysis of gross flows using NHS central register data. *The Economic Journal*, 102, 1433–1450.

Johnes, G. & Hyclak, T. (1994). Housing prices, migration, and regional labor markets. *Journal of Housing Economics*, 3, 312–329.

Litwak, E. & Longino Jr., C. (1987). Migration patterns among the elderly: A developmental perspective. *The Gerentologist*, 27, 266–272.

Mankiw, N.G. & Weil, D. (1989). The baby boom, the baby bust, and the housing market. *Regional Science and Urban Economics*, 19(2), 235–258.

Massey, D.S. (ed.) (2008). *New Faces in New Places: The Changing Geography of American Immigration*. New York: Russell Sage Foundation.

McHugh, K., Hogan, T. & Happel, S. (1995). Multiple residences and cyclical migration: A life-course perspective. *The Professional Geographer*, 47, 251–267.

Mueser, P. & Graves, P. (1995). Examining the role of economic opportunity and amenities in explaining population redistribution. *Journal of Urban Economics*, 37, 176–200.

Myers, D. (1990). *Housing Demography*. Madison, WI: The University of Wisconsin Press.

Myers, D. & Ryu, S. (2008). Aging baby boomers and the generational housing bubble. *Journal of the American Planning Association*, 74(1), 17–33.

Nelson, P.B., Nicholson, J.P. & Stege, E. H. (2004). The baby boom and nonmetropolitan population change, 1975–1990. *Growth and Change*, 24, 526–544.

Plane, D.A. & Heins, F. (2003). Age articulation of US inter-metropolitan migration. *The Annals of Regional Science*, 37, 107–130.

Plane, D.A. & Hoffman, L. (2009). Immigration in the United States: Evolving demographic contexts, geographies and policy, in Manie Geyer (ed.), Debates, issues in the developed world, *International Handbook of Urban Policy, Volume 2*: Occidental issues and controversies. Cheltenham, UK: Edward Elgar, pp. 340–362.

Plane, D.A. & Jurjevich, J.R. (2009). Ties that no longer bind? The patterns and repercussions of age-articulated migration. *Professional Geographer*, 61(1), 4–20.

Plane, D.A., Henrie, C.J. & Perry, M.J. (2005). Migration up and down the urban hierarchy and across the life course. *Proceedings of the National Academy of Sciences*, 102, 15313–15318.

Plane, D. A., & Hoffman, L. (2009). Immigration in the United States: Evolving demographic contexts, geographies and policy, pp. 340–362 in Manie Geyer (editor), *Debates, Issues in the Developed World, International Handbook of Urban Policy, Volume 2: Occidental issues and controversies*. Cheltenham, UK: Edward Elgar, in press.

Plane, D. A. & Jurjevich, J. R. (2009). Ties that no longer bind? The patterns and repercussions of age-articulated migration. *Professional Geographer*, 61(1), 4–20.

Porrel, F. (1982). Intermetropolitan migration and quality of life. *Journal of Regional Science*, 22, 137–158.

Potepan, M. (1994). Intermetropolitan migration and housing prices: Simultaneously determined? *Journal of Housing Economics*, 3, 77–91.

Rogers, A. (1992). Ed. *Elderly Migration and Population Redistribution: A Comparative Study*. London: Belhaven Press.

Shiller, R. (1990). Speculative prices and popular models. *Journal of Economic Perspectives*, 4(2), 55–65.

Shiller, R.J. (2005). *Irrational Exuberance* (2nd Edition). Princeton, NJ: Princeton University Press.

Stein, J. (1995). Prices and trading volume in the housing market: A model with down-payment effects. *The Quarterly Journal of Economics*, 110(2), 379–406.

Van der Meer, M. (2006). *Older Adults and Their Sociospatial Intergration in The Netherlands*. Netherland Geographical Studies 345, AMID-Studies Amsterdam: Amsterdam University.

Warnes, A. & Williams, A. (2006). Older migrants in Europe: A new focus for migration studies. *Journal of Ethnic and Migration Studies*, 32, 1257–1281.

Whisler, R., Waldorf, B., Mulligan, G., & Plane, D. (2008). Quality of life and the migration of the college educated: A life-course approach. *Growth and Change*, 39, 59–94.

Withers, S., & Clark, W.A.V. (2006). Housing Costs and the Geography of Family Migration Outcomes. *Population, Space and Place*, 12, 273–289.

17

Housing and Social Life

Ray Forrest

INTRODUCTION

In such a wide-ranging Handbook it is difficult to maintain clear boundaries between areas. The connections between 'housing' and 'social life' are numerous and multifaceted. *Where* we live and in *what* we live have major impacts on *how* we live. Residential location impacts on the journey to work, how we use our leisure time, where our children go to school and so on. Where we live affects our sense of identity and belonging (see Chapter 13).

Housing is pivotal to our social life on many levels and dimensions. However, its significance will vary for different groups in the population and for different individuals over their lifetime. Most of us spend as much, if not, more time at home than at work. Admittedly, a large part of that time may be spent inert, inactive and asleep. We tend to take this aspect of our life for granted, but social life falls apart rapidly and dramatically if we experience homelessness (for a fuller discussion, see Chapter 19). As Donnison (1967) observed in a relatively early contribution to the housing literature , 'House and home stand at the centre of people s lives, providing a shelter for sleep and for half their waking activities, a shield against the elements and the world....' (p. 9).

Some of us may also frequently work at home (as I am doing now), so that our social, work and home life are closely connected. The point is that at different stages in the life course, through choice or constraint, we spend a considerable amount of time in or around the dwelling. This is certainly the case for infants, for mothers, home workers, the unemployed and for many elderly households. Moroever, as demographic structures shift towards more elderly populations, and as retirement becomes increasingly stretched through earlier retirement (for some) and greater longevity, the residential sphere takes on a renewed importance.

In this chapter we shall restrict our view to focus on the social life in and around the dwelling – the local neighbourhood. Is neighbourhood still important to us? Is it more important to some than others? In particular, what about neighbouring? Do we still talk to our neighbours – and does it matter? Does a neighbourhood need active neighbouring? In discussing these issues, the chapter will seek to avoid encroaching on closely related literatures that are addressed elsewhere in this

Handbook – most notably, the substantial research output on neighbourhood effects in relation to issues such as health and educational outcomes (see Chapters 5, 22 and 23), and work on the meaning of home which has come more to the fore in housing studies in recent years (see Chapter 13).

HOUSING, SOCIAL LIFE AND THE NEIGHBOURHOOD

A key aim of this chapter is to reflect on the relationship between dwellings and the local area or neighbourhood: the underlying assumption is that there *is* a relationship – or at least there was. In other words, a neighbourhood is more than simply an aggregation of dwellings and other local amenities which may include places of work and recreation as well as residence (compare to discussions of neighbourhood change: see Chapters 4 and 5). The assumption is that the whole is greater than the sum of the parts and involves elements of social interaction which are distinctively and meaningfully local. There is something recognizable as the social life of the neighbourhood, which retains some contemporary significance. Given the volume of writings on this subject we could devote a sizeable part of this Handbook to exploring this question, given its continuing salience to fundamental questions of social cohesion, social structure and ideas of community. Moreover, despite the voluminous literature, it remains the case that the definition of 'neighbourhood' continues to be a challenging question for anyone involved in research in this field.

Galster (2001) captures these conceptual difficulties when he observes that 'Urban social scientists have treated "neighbourhood" in much the same way as courts of law have treated pornography: as a term that is hard to define precisely, but everyone knows it when they see it' (p. 2111). Kallus and Law-Yone (2000), similarly, emphasise the elusive and rather slippery nature of the term and distinguish between the way in which the neighbourhood is operationalised as a planning device and more humanistic interpretations – in other words the planning of neighbourhoods as normative and conscious attempts at social engineering as opposed to conceptions of a more spontaneous neighbourhood as one expression of the human need and desire for social interaction.

In one of the most detailed and nuanced recent studies of changing social relations at the local level, Blokland (2003) suggests that 'Quite simply, a neighbourhood is a geographically circumscribed, built environment that people use practically and symbolically' (p. 213). She continues, 'Over the course of seventy-five years, neighbourhood use has diminished in the overall range of the roles that a population assumes (that is, the role inventory), as we have observed in studying the Rotterdam neighbourhood of Hilleslius.' (p. 213). In her study of this older, inner-city neighbourhood, she demonstrates *inter alia* how the coincidence between social life and neighbourhood has changed historically and how it varies by social group. For some, neighbourhood use is extremely limited. For others, it retains significant practical and symbolic importance. As regards the 'modern city dweller', according to Blokland, they have 'few contacts with neighbours and do not view themselves as members of an imagined community. They use the neighbourhood to express their lifestyle in their own social circles' (p. 215).

It is this latter group, *the modern city dweller*, which is the main focus of this chapter. But as Blokland clearly shows, in the contemporary city the relationship between people and place is the product of a subtle layering of local historical factors amidst the more general influences and impacts of wider societal change. Savage et al. (2005) offer an equally subtle analysis of place attachment in the contemporary city in which they assert strongly the critical role of residence, as 'possibly *the* crucial identifier of who you are' (p. 207), but in a world in which social networks and 'fields of practice' are becoming more differentiated.

In one chapter, therefore, we cannot hope to capture all the variations in the practical and symbolic role of housing in social life even among societies which are ostensibly relatively similar in terms of economic and social development. It would also risk even greater superficiality to attempt serious comment on the interface between housing and social life in more traditional cultural settings: for example, in societies which remain predominantly rural and where poverty rather than relative affluence is prevalent. In the main, therefore, the chapter concentrates on what be most appropriately termed the 'modern' city in (post) industrial societies.

NEIGHBOURLY ACTIVITY

So, do we still interact with our neighbours? We certainly care who our neighbours are to the extent that we probably don't want 'difficult' neighbours or to live in a neighbourhood where norms of social behaviour are at odds with our own – although some of us may well want to live among a mix of lifestyles. Others may seek the comfort and security of a gated community. But whether we prefer to live among 'people like us' or not– Do we actually want to have much to do with them?

The nostalgic image of the neighbourhood is of conversations over the garden fence and of fleeting but friendly chats on the way to and from work. In the past this was also a strongly gendered image – with the men off to work in the morning, leaving their wives to tend the children during the day. The social life of the residential neighbourhood had strong temporal dimensions focusing around the school and other child-centred activities in the daytime and the more male-centred domains of pubs and clubs in the evening. This was the social life of suburbia, superseding the traditional occupational communities and dense, mixed-use inner-city neighbourhoods.

It seems, however, that despite the regular theoretical dismissals of the contemporary relevance of the neighbourhood in everyday life, many of us still crave this latter kind of environment. Indeed, it seems to be an important ingredient of contemporary gentrification – the classic village in the city. This emerges in studies such as that of Robson and Butler (2001) on Telegraph Hill in London. They quote Tina, describing her feelings about her local community in 1999:

> I love it here. I had a rootless childhood, and I love the very strong sense of community that the children have. It's like a village in the centre of London, it has that kind of support system. And the kids feel they belong here. I love the idea of their friendships carrying on over time…. I wouldn't move away from here to anywhere else in England (p. 80).

Among other things, this quote draws attention to the fact that, for some at least, contemporary urban life may be less rootless and nomadic than it was in the past. This runs somewhat counter to popular views, but, as Phillipson et al. (1999) have suggested, the relationship between people and place may well have been stronger at the end of the 20th century than it was at the beginning. Equally, sense of local belonging may now be constructed in very different ways, associated with social difference and social distinction and a process in which people 'elect' to put down roots in a particular place at a particular moment in their biographies (Savage et al., 2005). That sense of contemporary local belonging is, however, embedded within a network of places and people. Indeed, it is that diffusion of experiences and memories over time and space which gives 'the local' its distinctive meaning.

It is also the case that the growth of homeownership and more stable employment patterns contrasts with the more itinerant lifestyles associated with the earlier industrial period and an era of private renting (see, for example, Pritchard, 1976).

Thinking about this in a broader context, there are parts of the world where interregional and international migration are occurring on an unprecedented scale, most notably China. On the other hand, there are places where what were refugee cultures have become stable, settled communities. Cities such as Singapore and Hong Kong are prime examples. This is not to suggest that the relationship between housing and social life is necessarily closer in such cities, but that there is a higher proportion of the population living there now, than in the past, which have experienced relatively immobile residential histories.

But if many now live more settled lives, at least in terms of residential movement, does that mean we necessarily spend much time with our neighbours? It is popularly believed that neighbours in most contemporary societies are less important than they used to be. However, even if neighbouring activity continues to be important, it may be that its form and content have changed. For example, Fukayama (1999), engaging with Putnam's (2000) thesis on the decline of local associational activity, suggested that people still associate locally but perhaps more for negative than positive reasons. The kind of contrast he drew was between a local activity club (say, drama or football) and a neighbourhood watch committee. Perhaps there was just as much neighbouring activity in contemporary society, but it was more likely to be the kind of associational activity which was defensive and introverted and rooted in feelings of suspicion rather than trust. Of course, whether neighbouring is positive or negative, whether it is friendly or hostile, it still constitutes social interaction and is thus part of local social life. No doubt, conflict between neighbours has always been prevalent but is now rather lost behind the rosy glow of images of a supposed pervasive mutuality and reciprocity of an urban past – leaving aside deeply entrenched ethnic or religious divides which in some contexts remain a dominant feature of neighbourhood life.

A key distinction has also to be made between evident patterns of socialising and the shared feelings or attributes among residents which may underpin such activities. Thus, when asked, people may express a strong sense of community and belonging to their neighbourhood but they may not actually do much neighbouring. For example, Skjaeveland et al. (1996) distinguished between research on neighbouring and research on the psychological sense of community. The former they regarded as *manifest* neighbouring: namely, 'observable social interaction and exchange of help and goods' (p. 415). Although people may express a strong feeling of local community, in practice they may have little face-to-face contact with neighbours, indulge in limited socializing with them and rarely offer or receive any help from them. It is this manifest neighbouring, or neighbourhood sociability (Warren 1986), which we are concerned with, mainly because it is observable and measurable.

Neighbouring and being neighbourly tend to be associated with poorer, working-class neighbourhoods and elderly people and have rather anachronistic overtones. The dominant image of everyday life in the contemporary city is one of greater fluidity and individualism, heavy on electronics and technology, virtual rather than proximate, in which new generations have little inclination, or need, to get to know their neighbours. We have spatially diffuse social networks in which our friendships and acquaintances extend over national and international space. Much of the time spent in the dwelling involves interaction via Skype, Facebook or whatever. We may have more intimate contacts with far-flung acquaintances than with the people next door. The dwelling has simply become one site for transmission and reception of these electronic interactions. Local social life seems to have progressively diminished in terms of scale and social significance. If that is the case, it could seem that social policies aimed at encouraging more neighbouring, good neighbour schemes, building community and such like are somewhat at odds with the contours of contemporary urban life. If we don't need neighbours any more, or at least not to the same extent, is there any purpose in building policy interventions around assumptions which may have little contemporary resonance?

It may be, however, that we do still interact with neighbours but in a more socially uneven way and for more specialised reasons. The work by Savage et al. (2005) on globalization and belonging would seem to be consistent with this formulation and echo the earlier views of Castells (1997):

> People socialize and interact in their local environment, be it in the village, in the city, or in the suburb, and they build social networks among their neighbours. On the other hand, locally based identities intersect with other sources of meaning and social recognition, in a highly diversified pattern that allows for alternative interpretations (p. 60).

In other words, local neighbouring may remain important as a source of social identity and informal assistance but there are also, and increasingly, many other sources. A similar picture emerged from Spencer and Pahl's (2006) research on contemporary forms of friendship. For the geographically mobile, friendships are scattered across a wide area. However, there are still those with very local housing histories and with family and friendship networks rooted in particular locales. However, even among the more typical mobile group, the local neighbourhood was still an important source of 'fun, support and intimacy'. Spencer and Pahl continue,

> Where people have not been very geographically mobile this is perhaps not so, surprising but where people's lives and relationships have been disrupted by their own and others' moves, it is even more reassuring to discover that they have formed a range of attachments within their local community, in particular where this has involved starting afresh in a new area without any close family around (p. 194).

There are, of course, different levels of intimacy with our neighbours. We may not regard a neighbour as a close friend but we may exchange the odd pleasantry each morning on our way to work. Does that carry much social significance or is it pretty trivial in the overall scheme of things? A study in Sweden in 1993 by Henning and Lieberg (1996) made some interesting observations on this issue. Drawing on Granovetter (1973), they explored the role of what they referred to as 'unpretentious everyday contacts in the neighbourhood' (p. 6). They were particularly concerned to contrast the significance of these weak ties with strong ties outside the neighbourhood. Their findings indicated a continuing class dimension in the nature and significance of social networks in terms of strong ties. The local arena played a more important role for their blue-collar workers than for those from a white-collar background. For the middle classes, the local arena was just one of many. In general, people tended to have more strong ties outside the neighbourhood, but, they argued, if weaker ties were included the picture changed:

> When mapping people's *weak ties*, our findings from 1993 show that people meet their neighbours and other people in the residential area fairly often but on a more superficial basis. Thus the concept of weak ties becomes important. The number of weak ties in the neighbourhood are (sic) three times greater than strong ties if one compares the mean values for the total number of contacts. The significance of weak ties was underlined by the inhabitants who stated that these contacts meant a 'feeling of home', 'security' and 'practical as well as social support'. Only 10 per cent stated that these contacts were of little or no importance (p. 22).

For Henning and Lieberg, therefore, the significance of this aspect of local social life was partly as an arena for the development and maintenance of weak ties. These kinds of contacts ranged from a nodding acquaintance to modest levels of practical help (taking in a parcel). They suggested that these contacts were not only an important source of general well-being but also could provide important bridges between networks of strong ties.

IS NEIGHBOURING IN DECLINE?

But are even these casual interactions in decline? Do we indulge in mutual help on any significant scale? Do we actually socialise with our neighbours as friends – go to the pub with them, have them round for dinner and so on? The answers to these questions will obviously vary according to cultural norms and we can only offer some limited empirical evidence on these questions. Moreover, few systematic studies provide a longitudinal perspective that is sufficient to map trends.

In Britain, the growth of policy interest throughout the 1990s in building local social capital and the emphasis on neighbourhood renewal have been responsible for generating some new survey data. These provide snapshot pictures of contemporary neighbouring activity but offer little or no comparison over time. What do they show? The British Household Panel Study (BHPS) in 2002 asked how often people talked to their neighbours? Some 37% said 'on most days' and a similar percentage said 'once or twice a week'. The General Household Survey (GHS) in 2000/2001 asked a similar question at a slightly more detailed level, differentiating for example between those who said they did so every day as opposed to those who did so on most days of the week. In aggregate, around half of those interviewed spoke to their neighbours at least three or four days per week (28% said every day). And well over two-thirds of those questioned in the GHS stated that they had done a favour for a neighbour in the previous 6 months.

Taking in parcels is one thing, but would we borrow money from the person next door? It seems that most of us would find that kind of favour less acceptable. Rather quaintly, and perhaps reflecting assumptions about the kinds of neighbourhoods where such reciprocity survives, the British Attitude Survey in 2000 asked people if they would consider asking a neighbour to lend them £5 to pay the milkman if they were short of cash. Some two-thirds of those questioned said they would feel uncomfortable doing so. However, the vast majority would have no problem asking to borrow a plunger from a neighbour if their sink was blocked.

These findings do not, unfortunately, tell us anything about social trends in relation to neighbouring or, indeed, whether they indicate relatively high or low levels of social interaction. If the same questions had been asked of people in Britain 20 years ago would the figures have been substantially higher? It seems that the only systematic source of longitudinal data in this area comes from a USA study. Guest and Wierzbicki (1999) analysed data from the US General Social Survey from 1974 to 1996. The US GSS is a survey covering a wide range of topics and thus it includes only a few directly relevant questions. Nevertheless, two questions were asked in 15 of the 20 surveys over that period which allowed some analysis of trends in relation to neighbouring activity. People were asked how often they spent 'a social evening' with someone from the neighbourhood. A further question then asked how often they spent 'a social evening' with friends who live outside the neighbourhood.' As Guest and Wierzbicki emphasise, neighbouring in the GSS is quite explicitly defined in terms of socializing. What the GSS offers, therefore, is a longitudinal measure of the relative importance of socialising with neighbours compared with socialising beyond the neighbourhood. Although the questions are limited in scope, their analysis offers some clear answers as to whether neighbourly activities have declined, whether extra local socializing has grown in relative importance and differences in these patterns among particular subgroups.

In summary, the Guest and Wierzbicki study did indicate a slow but continuous decline in socializing with neighbours. It also found an increase in socializing beyond the neighbourhood and confirmed, therefore, the perception that social networks were increasingly extralocal. It also showed that elderly people, those with large families and the least educated tended to have more local ties. However, the overall picture which emerged was slightly more complex and cautioned against a simple dichotomous interpretation – that social life around the home is decreasing as our social networks become more spatially diffuse. Whereas the evidence did support an increasing dissociation between local and non-local socializing and a growing contrast between 'locals' and 'cosmopolitans', there was a degree of overlap between the two domains. In other words, active non-local socializers were also active local socializers. The most gregarious people were promiscuously rather than exclusively sociable. As they concluded,

> How can we reconcile the evidence that neighbouring and extra-neighbouring roles are becoming increasingly independent in the general population with the finding that the extent of specialization is somewhat ambiguous? What seems possible is that neighbouring is a more voluntaristic activity chosen only by some (p. 109).

Guest and Wierzbicki acknowledged that the data from the US General Household Survey only provided one measure of local social life and in one society. It may well be that other forms of local social interaction are increasing, such as political or caring activities, and this could involve significant variation among different subgroups. This would be consistent with the findings from studies such as Spencer and Pahl's (referred to above) in which more local and home-centred activities and relationships are not necessarily diminished by the growth of more spatially diffuse social networks.

WHOSE HOME? WHOSE SOCIAL LIFE?

As has been stressed throughout, the relationship between the home and social life has a number of dimensions and is subject to a number of influences. We are likely to get a very different picture if we view the relationship from the perspective of the working, young professional as opposed a young child, a retired person, someone experiencing long-term unemployment or through the lens of an ethnic or religious minority. The nature of the built environment and the extent to which it is mixed use or exclusively residential are also likely to impact on the scale and nature of local social interaction. These are all relatively complicated linkages and there is insufficient space in this chapter to provide a detailed assessment. However, we can address some of these issues.

First, and not surprisingly, we are more likely to know our neighbours and to socialize with them if we are long-standing residents. The classic study by Sampson (1988) found that the longer someone had lived in an area the more local friends they were likely to have. This seems hardly surprising. There could, however, be situations where the opposite can be the case, but this depends on the extent to which everyone in the neighbourhood is in a similar situation. For example, the studies of early social life in the British New Towns in the post-war period provide various accounts of how young families uprooted from familiar environments in London adapted to their novel surroundings (see, for example, Schaffer, 1970). The unfamiliar can bring people together in a pioneering spirit. Early residents of the New Towns were faced with recreating entirely new social networks in completely new residential settings. In such circumstances there are no distinctions between newcomers and locals and people come together to share experiences and information and to cope with the inevitable difficulties of establishing new lives.

Housing and social life can be particularly closely intertwined in newly built estates, particularly when people are at a similar stage in the life course as young families. In the more mature European urban environments these are now relatively unusual situations. The neighbourhoods of older, established cities include a wide variety of residents in terms of life-course stage and length of residence. In other parts of the world, however, such as in contemporary China, urbanization is proceeding on a new and rapid scale and it is not unusual for people to find themselves in precisely such circumstances.

It is important also to acknowledge the distinction between neighbourly contact and intimacy. For example, although the evident social interaction around the home may be more prevalent when residents face the common challenge of moving to a new estate or having to cope with some common threat, contact may be relatively superficial, instrumental and short lived. Similarly, those with limited resources outside their neighbourhood may be more reliant on their local area for help and support. However, a simple count of frequency of contact with neighbours may indicate little about the intensity of these contacts and the degree to which they have any deep social significance.

Gender and ethnicity are also important in the relationship between housing and social life as is the simple variable of time spent in and around the home. Some people have more time to get to know their neighbours than others. Not surprisingly, there seems to be a curvilinear pattern in relation to age. The young and old tend to have more leisure time and spend more of that time in their local area (Campbell and Lee, 1992). This study also suggested that women maintained larger social networks in their neighbourhood than men. This was associated with the higher proportion of women out of paid employment or in part-time work during child-raising years and the pivotal position of the local school as a meeting point for neighbours. It is women rather than men who tend to be active in and around the school.

The relationships between housing and social life may also be mediated in distinct ways among ethnic minorities. Ethnic minorities are often concentrated in particular parts of cities and have more 'defensive' and intense social networks. Language and cultural differences may structure and constrain their social contacts in ways which make the residential area more of a focal point of social interaction than among the ethnic majority. Neighbours may be more likely to be friends or acquaintances, or close relatives – what Mesch and Manor (2001) refer to as a *compression* of social relationships. Equally, however, while the dwelling may represent a site of intense social interaction in a multi-generation household, where close kin are living nearby or where there are frequent visitors from outside the neighbourhood, social contact with neighbours more generally may be quite limited in multi-ethnic areas. Mesch and Manor (2001) found that fear of crime, lack of trust and heterogeneity tended to constrain social interaction in residential settings. The pattern of social contact may be further skewed when other differentiating characteristics are overlain on ethnic differences, notably when housing tenure (renting/homeownership) distinguishes ethnic groups.

Perhaps the way we construct our social life in relation to where we live is also influenced by where we have come from. In other words, our propensity to local conviviality is a product of our personal history and upbringing as well as our present residential setting and circumstances. A study of two ethnic minorities with dispersed settlement patterns raised some interesting issues in this regard. Studies of ethnic minorities, their housing circumstances and patterns of social interaction typically focus on groups which cluster for a variety of reasons, positive and negative. In contrast, Martinez et al. (1991) looked at Spanish and German immigrants in Toronto who tended to be scattered within the general population. It is in these kinds of situations that language and cultural barriers are likely to create more difficulties of neighbourly interaction. Without going into the psychology literature drawn on by Martinez et al., they showed (and explained why) it was the German immigrants and those from more rural areas who were the most neighbourly. Among the Spanish immigrants, education and command of English were more predictable influences of the intensity of their local social life.

What about children? Besides the fact that children spend more time in and around the home, the mainstream literature on housing and neighbourhood tends not to delve into how children perceive and use space in their everyday lives. This aspect can, however, be touched upon briefly. Children experience space in a different way from adults. Space has a different institutionalised structure from adults, involving mainly home, school and some recreational setting. Rasmussen (2009) refers to this as an 'institutional triangle' with three corners. After home and school, the recreational facility 'is at the third corner, and the route from this place to home is the last leg' (p. 157). As Rasmussen stresses, these places are to a great extent constructed (literally) by adults and are places of contact between children and professional adults (such as teachers and social workers). He observes that 'it should come as no surprise that "children's places" are located in and around the areas where children live' (p. 165). When children refer to play 'at home', they subsume the outdoor places around their dwelling. For children living in flats, the common courtyard is a key site for their young social life. For suburban children, it is the garden.

The significance of the house and its immediate surroundings as a site for the social life of children is not surprising. What about teenagers? Here our expectations might be different. Personal experience and popular perceptions would suggest that, for teenagers, the house becomes more of a convenient dormitory, or indeed a place of confinement, from which they plan and execute their forays into the world beyond their residential environment. Excitement is elsewhere. The modern adolescent would seem to be tenuously attached to home and to be at the sharp end of social transformations associated with global consumerism and technological change. Abbot-Chapman and Robertson's (2001) research on school-age adolescents in rural Tasmania is at least suggestive of a more complex reality in the everyday lives of young people and of the ways they construct their social identity and sense of belonging. Their interviews about 'favourite places' produced responses

> which conflict with popular media images about young people's need for noisy music, non-stop entertainment, activity and stimulation, mainly within urban and usually crowded places... . For respondents largely chose 'local' (particularistic) rather than 'global' (universalistic) places ... places and activities in and around the home and in the natural environment near to home (p. 492).

Indeed, some 28% chose their home, a relative's home or a friend's home as their favourite place. Qualities of privacy, space, peacefulness and friendliness were highly valued. Abbot-Chapman and Robertson (2001) stress that it would be foolish to generalise their exploratory findings to the youth of more cosmopolitan urban settings. They merely claim that their findings in which adolescents stress many of the traditional qualities of home and neighbourhood ('the importance of friends and neighbours as accessible and helpful') suggest 'identification with "traditional" community values, despite the societal and global changes wrought by technological change, consumerism and commodification associated with development of attenuated "global" communities' (p. 501).

LIFESTYLE CHOICES

So far we have focused on the issue of social life and housing mainly in terms of neighbouring activity. The chapter has not touched upon social life *in the home* other than tangentially. This would take us into the sociology of the family and related discussions and stray into areas covered elsewhere in this Handbook. Similarly, there has been limited discussion of mobility choices, other than in relation to issues of turnover and its impact on the socialising in neighbourhoods (for a fuller discussion see Chapter 4).

However, some reference to locational choice is essential in any discussion of the relationships between social life and housing. When we choose housing, within whatever constraints we may have, we are not simply choosing a dwelling. We are to varying degrees making a statement about the kind of social life we wish to have – or to put it another way, we are making some kind of statement about the kinds of people we are, our aspirations and lifestyles. For example, some of us may actively seek to live somewhere where people will keep to themselves. For some, street parties, resident association meetings and other neighbourhood-based activities are precisely what they do not want. Although we may refer to our neighbourhood being 'friendly', it may be friendship at a distance where neighbours rarely encroach on our everyday life.

There is a common assumption that 'successful' neighbourhoods have a vibrant social life. I recall being involved in research in one of the more exclusive residential enclaves in Bristol, an area of large detached houses sitting in large, leafy gardens. One respondent remarked, 'the only thing that connects these houses is the sewers' (Forrest and Murie, 1987). Not much social life there then, but hardly an 'unsuccessful' neighbourhood. Similarly, Baumgartner's (1988) study of a middle-class suburban neighbourhood described a highly private existence with residents driving off to work in the morning with little social interaction. This dissonance between idealised prescriptions for the kinds of communities we should be creating and the aspirations of affluence is further highlighted in Talen's (1999) examination of new urbanist doctrines. Social life in the past may have revolved more around housing and neighbourhood because of scarcity and constraint. With greater wealth it seems we may prefer to escape these limitations of 'residential propinquity'. Talen refers to research by Fried (1986) which found that neighbourhood decreases in importance with increasing social status: 'More specifically, high-income groups deem the proximity of goods and services and interaction with neighbours as essential to a much lower degree than low and moderate income groups'(p. 1374).

In more affluent, technologically advanced and information-rich societies, we are also now able to approach residential choice with a substantial amount of information about the kind of area we may be moving to. What kinds of people live there? What kinds of cars do they drive? What do they read? What are the crime rates? Are the schools any good? All these data are available at an increasingly disaggregated level. In the USA and the UK, market research organisation such as Claritas and Experien combine numerous large data sets to provide online information on a wide range of variables. The website Upmystreet for example, tells me that people in my area enjoy

> ... the arts, including theatre, classical music, opera and the cinema. The most widely read newspapers are The Guardian, Independent, The Times and Observer. Foreign travel and skiing are popular leisure activities (http://www.upmystreet.com/local/neighbours-in-bs8-4tb.html).

Not entirely me but probably true of my neighbours! The same site can provide information for prospective residents on the house price histories of dwellings sold in the street over the previous 10 years, on school catchment area and exam performance, crime rates and so on. Or perhaps I am looking to move to the USA and fancy a Young and Rustic area. There I would apparently find somewhere

> ... composed of middle age, restless singles. These folks tend to be lower-middle-income, high school-educated, and live in tiny apartments in the nation's exurban towns. With their service industry jobs and modest incomes, these folks still try to fashion fast-paced lifestyles centered on sports, cars, and dating (http://www.claritas.com/MyBestSegments/Content/tabs/filterMenuFrameWork.jsp?page=../Segments/snapshot.jsp&menuid=91&submenuid=911)

Residential areas are increasingly packaged and sold as lifestyle areas that offer a particular brand of social life. With older housing areas, this may be a more subtle and informal process as areas go in and out of fashion, as demographic profiles change and as social norms or economic contingencies affect choices. The real estate sector will reinforce and reflect these developments through their property descriptions or even with the renaming of entire neighbourhoods. Buying a house as part of a whole lifestyle package is, however, most explicit in new developments. This is particularly evident in societies experiencing rapidly rising affluence and urbanisation and/or where there is less to differentiate in terms of dwelling type or location. In upscale, high-rise developments in Hong Kong there will almost always be a Clubhouse and restaurant, a pool, a sauna, a space for various recreational activities and a free shuttle bus to take children to school or residents downtown or to the nearest shopping mall. There may be squash or tennis courts.

It is, however, in the development of so-called gated communities where social life and housing appear most integrated. There is a substantial literature on these developments and what they represent and occasion in terms of the evolving spatial structure of cities (see, for example, Blandy et al. (2003) for a useful review; Atkinson and Flint, 2004). For the purposes of this chapter, the point is merely to highlight these kinds of developments as offering an explicit link between the home and social life. They represent, for some, a social life protected from a perceived higher-risk and more hostile urban environment beyond the gates. For others, the reasons may be rooted more in the attractions of a water-based lifestyle or golf. These residential enclaves also increasingly include the most advanced technology to communicate globally and protect locally. Canyon Gate in Houston has a security system in which 'Each resident is scanned into the community's hand geometry reader, which in turn takes a 3-dimensional view of the hand in order to determine the geometry and metrics around the finger length, height and other details' (http://www.canyongate.com/locations/). Residents are also assured of cutting-edge technology for their home entertainment and global networking.

In a rather different vein, growing environmental awareness is adding a new dimension to social life and the home. Recycling can involve collective community effort. Disposing of waste becomes a more time-consuming process where neighbours are more likely to meet up. Informal and implicit sanctions develop in which we do not want to offend through irresponsible behaviour. The planned association between lifestyle and home is most explicit with the development of eco-villages or eco-cities. The website of EcoVillage in Loudoun County in Virginia asks,

> Are you interested in living in a place where you know your neighbours and take care of the environment while also living in a healthy home? Then EcoVillage of Loudoun County, Virginia, is the place for you! (http://www.ecovillages.com/families.php – last accessed 26.11.10).

The creation of eco-towns on a relatively large scale imagines an urbanism in which work and residence are much more closely related than in the recent past. New technology not only applies to sophisticated energy-saving devices but also to the creation of lifestyles which do not necessitate long journeys to work or any journey at all. More futuristic visions of the impact of technology on urban social life have been invoked by authors such as Mitchell (1999) in which a process of disintermediation occurs in which face-to-face contact with neighbours increases in parallel with an expansion of global networking. In *E-topia*, in a chapter focusing on homes and neighbourhoods, Mitchell examines the implications of technology for physical planning and city zoning, residential architecture and the geography and content of primary and secondary relationships. He talks of 'a clustering of the new-style live/work dwellings in twenty-four hour neighbourhoods that effectively combines local attractions with global connections' (p. 78). A new relationship between home and work could mean suburbs that no longer empty out in the morning and central cities which can retain a larger residential population. Moreover, a zoning of cities which separated the residential and non-residential in the industrial age is, he argues, increasingly inappropriate in an environment in which much of the new employment is small scale, high tech and clean. His most interesting observations, however, concern the changing sociology and spatial patterning of social networks. For Mitchell (1999), they simultaneously involve an intensification of remoteness and co-presence.

> In the emergent twenty-four-hour neighbourhoods of the digital electronic era, patterns will be transformed yet again, and the net effect will be complex. Some secondary social relationships will simply be eliminated as electronic systems replace bank tellers, retail clerks, and the like. But others will be regenerated at the neighbourhood level, as social life revitalizes: more of the people that you get to know will be nearby residents. And others will be formed and maintained at a distance through combinations of electronic interaction and occasional face-to-face meetings (p. 80).

This view of the future is also echoed by Fukayama (1999) when he refers to the historically peculiar nature of the relationship between home and work which has been the hallmark of the industrial age. What we have taken to regard as normal, he suggests, is something of an anomaly compared to what preceded industrialisation and what may follow. He argues that

> It is if anything more natural and more in keeping with the experience of human beings throughout history that home and work should be co-located. It may be that technology, which has infinite capabilities of alienating us from our natural desires and inclinations, may in this instance be able to restore something of the wholeness and integration of life that industrialism took away from us (p. 277).

CONCLUDING DISCUSSION

Let's return to where we came in. This chapter has necessarily drawn fairly strict parameters around the exploration of the relationship between housing and social life. It has focused on neighbouring, as a particular form of social interaction, which is defined by where we live. It has also emphasised that the nature and pattern of that aspect of our social life will vary by our position in the life course, social status and according to factors such as gender, age and ethnicity. In discussing housing and social life it is impossible to separate that relationship from more general discussions of neighbourhood, since this is the shorthand term for the domain in which these social interactions occur. There may be continuing conceptual debates about what neighbourhood is and its significance for the contemporary urban dweller, but it continues to delineate a segment of our everyday life which is not (for most people) where they work, take their holidays or do much of their socializing.

In considering the connection between housing and social life, there would appear to be different, and potentially, contradictory perspectives. On the one hand, concerns about safety in the contemporary city, combined with the ever-expanding infrastructure of 'home' entertainment and the ability to access services online, suggest a retreat into the home environment, with echoes of Lasch's (1977) 'haven in a heartless world'. As Kumar (1997) observes, 'As the focus of private life, the home – especially one's privately owned home – emerges as a consecrated place. More than ever, it is regarded as the principal source of identity and fulfilment' (p. 206). This view echoes some elements of earlier arguments by Saunders (1989) about the role of homeownership in bolstering a sense of ontological security and the importance of home generally in shaping contemporary social life.

On the other hand, our social lives and social networks are becoming more spatially diffuse. This would seem to indicate a 'hollowing out' of neighbourhood use as our lives become simultaneously more home centred and cosmopolitan, a version of Mitchell's disintermediation. From this perspective, 'housing use' increases while 'neighbourhood use' diminishes – or, perhaps, our local domain of social interaction becomes more restricted to our immediate neighbours. We know the people around us very well but have little or no contact with those a few houses or a street away. Then, there are the issues of lifestyle and the marketing of neighbourhood types enabling a supposedly finer-grained choice of neighbours and lifestyles. This suggests an accentuation of place of residence in the construction of social identities and social status – although it does not necessarily involve any intensification of local socialising.

It is, however, essential to caution against some linear version of urbanisation which predicts an inevitable shift towards less parochial social lives and where the house becomes simply a receptacle for more sophisticated consumption and little more than a dormitory. The forces which have shaped the relationship between housing and everyday life in the recent past have reflected a particular relationship between the built form, demographics, changes in the labour market and lifestyles of ever-expanding possibilities for travel and general consumption. It was a world of suburban development, young and growing families, private transport, commuting and planning for single-use neighbourhoods. The emerging relationships between home and social life will be affected by very different demographics, growing concerns with social cohesion as the march of the middle classes grinds to something of a halt and a likely shift towards higher-density living and mixed-use neighbourhoods. Population ageing will be a key factor, as will concerns about environmental and social sustainability. The carbon-constrained city would seem to require a reordering of strategic priorities and individual aspirations with uncertain implications for urban morphologies. Resource constraints will involve the reshaping of residential choice, the reassertion of residential propinquity and new tensions around the relationship between social life, social status and housing.

REFERENCES

Abbot-Chapman, J. and Robertson, M. (2001) 'Youth, leisure and home: Space, place and identity', *Society and Leisure* 24(2), 485–506.

Atkinson, R. and Flint, J. (2004) 'Fortress UK? Gated communities, the spatial revolt of the elites and time–space trajectories of segregation', *Housing Studies* 19(6), 875–892.

Baumgartner, M. (1988) *The Moral Order of the Suburbs*. Oxford: Oxford University Press.

Blandy, S., Lister, D., Atkinson, R. and Flint, J. (2003) *Gated Communities: A Systematic Review of the Evidence*, Available online at: http://york.academia.edu/RowlandAtkinson/Papers/272572/Gated_Communities_A_Systematic_Review_of_the_Research_Evidence. Last accessed November 14, 2010.

Blokland, T. (2003) *Urban Bonds*. Cambridge: Polity Books.

Campbell, K.E. and Lee, B. (1992) 'Sources of personal neighbor networks: Social integration, need, or time?' *Social Forces* 70(4), 1077–1100.

Castells, M. (1997) *The Power of Identity*. Oxford: Blackwell.

Donnison, D.V. (1967) *The Government of Housing*. Harmondsworth: Penguin.

Forrest, R. and Murie, A. (1987) 'The affluent home owner: Labour market position and the shaping of housing histories', *Sociological Review* 35(2), 370–403.

Fried, M. (1986) 'The neighborhood in metropolitan life: Its psychological significance', in R. Taylor (ed.), *Urban Neighbourhoods*. New York: Praeger.

Fukayama, F. (1999) *The Great Disruption: Human Nature and the Reconstitution of Social Order*. London: Profile Books.

Galster, G. (2001) 'On the nature of neighbourhood', *Urban Studies* 38(12), 2111–2124.

Guest, A.M. and Wierzbicki, S.K. (1999) 'Social ties at the neighbourhood level. Two decades of GSS evidence', *Urban Affairs Review* 35(1), 92–111.

Granovetter, M. (1973) 'The strength of weak ties', *American Journal of Sociology* 78, 1360–1380.

Henning, C. and Lieberg, M. (1996) 'Strong ties or weak ties? Neighbourhood networks in a new perspective' *Scandinavian Housing and Planning Research* 13, 3–26.

Kallus, R. and Law-Yone, H. (2000) 'What is a neighbourhood? The structure and function of an idea', *Environment and Planning B* 27, 815–826.

Kumar, K. (1997) 'Home: The promise and predicament of private life at the end of the twentieth century', in J. Weintraub and K. Kumar (eds), *Public and*

Private Thought in Practice, Perspectives on a Grand Dichotomy. Chicago, IL: University of Chicago Press.

Lasch, C. (1977) *Haven in a Heartless World. The Family Beseiged*. New York: Basic Books.

Martinez, M., Felka, S., Simpson-Housley, P. and De Man, A. (1991) 'Neighbourliness, socializing and residential satisfaction in urban settings: Two studies of German and Spanish immigrants', *International Journal of Comparative Sociology* 32(3–4), 310–315.

Mesch, G. and Manor, O. (2001) 'Ethnic differences in urban nieghbour relations in Israel', *Urban Studies* 38(11), 1943–1952.

Mitchell, W.J. (1999) *E-topia: Urban Life, Jim, But Not as We Know It*. Cambridge, MA: MIT Press.

Phillipson, C., Bernard, M., Phillips, J. and Ogg, J. (1999) 'Older people's experiences of community life: Patterns of neighbouring in three urban areas', *Sociological Review* 715–739.

Pritchard, R.M. (1976) *Housing and Spatial Structure of the City: Residential Mobility and the Housing Market in an English City since the Industrial Revolution*. Liverpool: Liverpool University Press.

Putnam, R. (2000) *Bowling Alone*. London: Simon and Shuster.

Rasmussen, K. (2009) 'Places for children – children's places', *Childhood* 11, 155–171.

Robson, G. and Butler, T. (2001) 'Coming to terms with London: Middle-class communities in a global city', *International Journal of Urban and Regional Research* 25(1), 70–86.

Sampson, R. (1988) 'Local friendship ties and community attachment in mass society', *American Sociological Review* 53, 766–779.

Saunders, P. (1989) 'The meaning of home in contemporary English culture', *Housing Studies*, 4(3), 177–192.

Savage, M., Bagnall, G. and Longhurst, B. (2005) *Globalization and Belonging*. London: Sage Publications.

Skjaeveland, O., Garling, T. and Maeland, J.G. (1996) 'A multidimensional measure of neighboring,' *American Journal of Community Psychology* 24(3), 413–435.

Schaffer, F. (1970) *The New Town Story*. London: Granada.

Spencer, L. and Pahl, R. (2006) *Rethinking Friendship: Hidden Solidarities Today*. Princeton, NJ: Princeton University Press.

Talen, E. (1999) 'Sense of community and neighbourhood form: An assessment of the social doctrine of new urbanism, *Urban Studies* 36(8), 1361–1379.

Warren, D.I. (1986) 'The helping roles of neighbours: Some empirical patterns,' in R.B. Taylor (ed.), *Urban Neighbourhoods: Research and Policy*. New York: Praeger, pp. 310–330.

18

Housing: From Low Energy to Zero Carbon

Phillip Jones

INTRODUCTION

The subject of sustainable housing design is wide ranging. It includes how we design a house to be physically sustainable in relation to energy, water and material use, and to be resilient, for example, to be able to adapt to change of use or climate change. It also includes issues of how we design to support 'well-being' and a healthy lifestyle for people and how we design a building to be part of a socially and economically enlivening community. Sustainable housing is not only about the more readily quantifiable physical attributes but also about the 'softer' design aspects of creating place, and responding to a regional aesthetic and cultural identity. The design and construction of the house itself is not the end point; a sustainable building must also encourage a sustainable lifestyle for its occupants and its surrounding community.

All this points to a holistic approach to sustainable design, which is generally accepted as a 'good thing', but often difficult to achieve in practice. It may therefore be pragmatic to lead with the more quantifiable aspects of design and, in particular, its energy performance, or what is now considered important, the reduction of carbon dioxide emissions associated with fossil fuel energy sources. This approach is not meant to ignore the other aspects of sustainability.

Reducing carbon dioxide emissions in the built environment is high on the agenda for most governments as they attempt to deal with climate change, security of supply and the continual increase in demand for energy. As the majority of emissions in the built environment are associated with housing, this has become the prime target for regulations and incentives. In the UK, energy use in buildings (residential and commercial) accounts for about 40% of the UK's total energy consumption, with housing accounting for 28.5%, 62% of which is used for space conditioning (Pérez-Lombard et al., 2008)[1]. The design and construction of new housing and the refurbishment of the existing housing stock is a main priority area for achieving the UK government's target carbon dioxide emission reductions[2].

Using the low carbon agenda to drive sustainable design has provided a clear political message, with the aspiration to achieve 'zero carbon' new buildings within a relatively short time period. The Code for Sustainable Homes[3] in England covers a range of sustainability factors, and sets out a route map for reducing carbon dioxide emissions of new housing to be zero carbon by 2016. The current definition of 'zero carbon' might be considered to relate to political rather than technical correctness, and, as such, it is likely to continue to change in relation to how much is achieved for the building development and how much is achieved by some form of carbon 'offsetting' or 'allowable solution', yet to be fully resolved. In Wales, the Welsh Assembly Government set a target of zero carbon by 2013 (originally 2011) for all new buildings, although again the definition of zero carbon is under discussion, and recent announcements have suggested that only housing will be included. Current values suggested for housing are 55% reduction in England (2016) and in Wales (2013), in relation to 2006 standards (however, these values are continually changing).

Of course, target setting for new housing is only part of the solution, because up to 75% of buildings that will exist in 2050 already exist today (Ravetz, 2008). Therefore, if the UK and other countries are to achieve the necessary reductions in carbon dioxide emissions in the built environment, attention must also include the existing stock, where the giant share of savings will take place. Even, in the revision of the UK Building Regulations (Part L1: 2002), over 40% of the saving was predicted to come from improvements in the existing housing stock, through controlled services: namely, boiler replacement and window replacement[4].

Although there has been a growing interest in reducing carbon dioxide emissions in recent years, in an attempt to mitigate against climate change, attention to reducing energy use in housing is not new. Research into improving the energy efficiency of housing is now in its fourth decade of activity: it began in response to the oil crises of the mid 1970s, continued with passive design through the 1980s and into sustainable design and zero carbon design over the last two decades. Figure 18.1 locates the various periods of housing design since the 1970s in relation to the growing awareness of environmental issues. It also shows how global carbon dioxide levels and average global temperatures have increased over the same period. It is interesting to note that the Brundtland definition of sustainable development (Our Common Future, 1987), 'development that meets the needs of the present without compromising the ability of future generations to meet their own needs', is now over 20 years old. Earlier still, Alex Gordon's phrase 'long life, loose fit, low energy', coined while he was president of the RIBA in the early 1970s, is still very much relevant today in relation to the concepts of resilience and sustainability in the built environment.

So what has been achieved in the built environment and in particular in relation to reducing housing energy use and carbon dioxide emissions? We will now review developments in 'low energy' housing over the last four decades, referring to specific research and design activities carried out at the Welsh School of Architecture.

REGULATIONS AND OTHER GOVERNMENT DRIVERS

At the time of the energy crises of the 1970s there were very little thermal insulation requirements for walls and roofs for UK housing. Many homes were inadequately heated and 'whole house heating' was a relatively new concept for much of the housing stock. Figure 18.2 traces the changes in building regulations over the period from 1965, when the building regulations were first introduced in their present form, to the recent 2006 release of Part L 'conservation of fuel and power'. The 2010[5] and subsequent building regulations have further

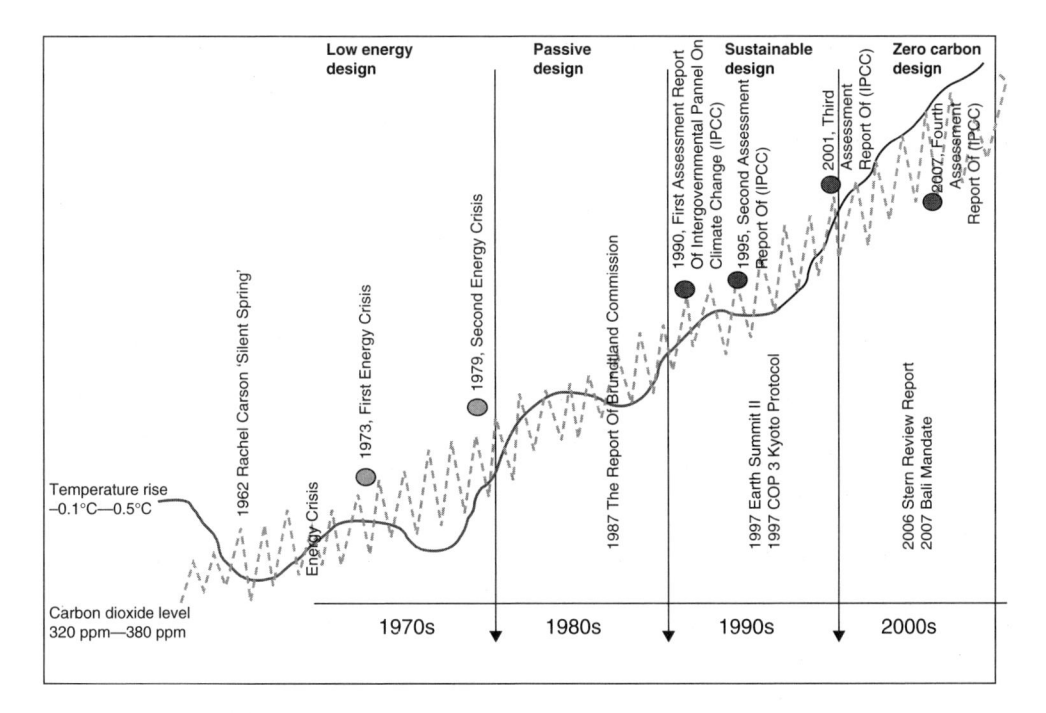

Figure 18.1 From low energy to zero carbon design

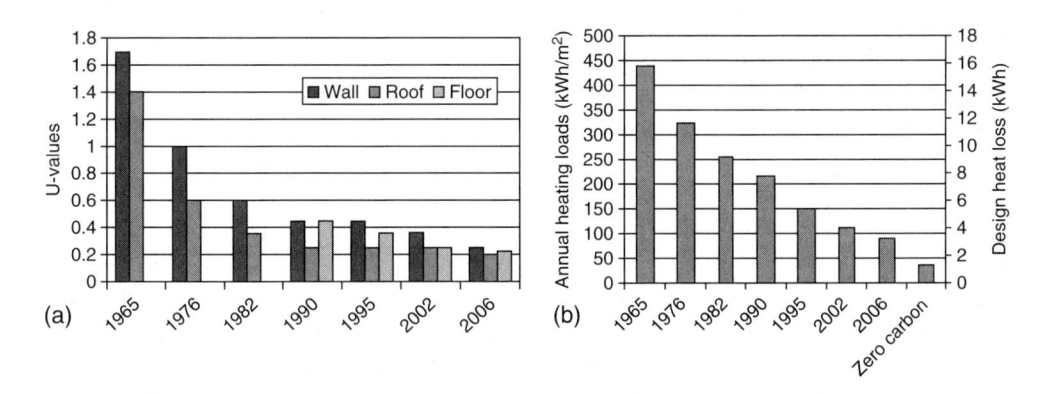

Figure 18.2 (a) UK Domestic U-values since 1965. (b) Annual heating load and design heat loss

improved energy efficiency in steps to achieve zero carbon performance by 2016.

Recent UK new housing (based on 2006 building regulations) has a typical design heat loss of just over 4 kW compared to about 12 kW in the 1970s, and an annual heating demand of about 100 kWh/m²/annum compared to a value of around 300 kWh/m² in the 1970s and 1980s. So, considerable improvements to the energy performance of new housing have been achieved, over this period, and in the main, without a great deal of innovation, but simply by increasing levels of thermal insulation, reducing air leakage and using more efficient heating systems. Future housing designed to a zero carbon performance might have a design heat loss of as low as 1 kW, which for the main part can be met by incidental heat gains from occupancy and solar heat gains. The energy supply will be from renewable energy systems, such as solar photovoltaic (PV), solar thermal, biomass and wind. This move to zero carbon will likely be technically more advanced and more costly relative to achievements so far. So, whereas in the past improvements have been achieved by a series of progressive modifications, in future we will probably need to design differently, both in terms of the technical solutions used and also in relation to the processes of planning, design and construction.

One of the main drivers for reducing energy demand in the built environment is the directive 2002/91/EC of the European Parliament and Council on energy efficiency of buildings ('Energy Performance of Buildings Directive', EPBD), which was passed in December 2002 and came into force in January 2003[6]. The official deadline for the 25 member states to turn the directive into national law was 2006. One of the main requirements of the directive is to establish calculations of energy performance to comply with national targets. Other requirements, for energy certification and regular inspection of boilers and air conditioning equipment, had an additional period of grace before implementation, until January 2009, mainly to give industry preparation time. There have been some delays in the implementation of the directive for some countries but a recent study, the European COST C23 Action titled, Low Carbon Urban Built Environments (LCUBE), reported that most countries had implemented all the requirements by 2009 although there were many difficulties and variations in approach (Jones et al., 2009). A number of countries have set a series of targets over time to reduce carbon dioxide emissions, typically by some 25% reduction every five years.

An increasing number of European countries are seeking to encourage higher performance standards for energy efficiency and reducing carbon dioxide emissions than what are the mandatory requirements through building regulations. There are an emerging range of schemes, including the Minergie Standard for Buildings in Switzerland[7], which sets an upper limit of 42 kWh/m^2/annum for new housing, and the Code for Sustainable Homes in the UK. The German Passivhaus (Passive House) standard has been adopted voluntarily as criteria for low energy design across Europe[8]. Some countries have introduced grant aid and tax incentives to encourage energy efficiency, and fuel tariff structures for encouraging the use of renewable energy supply systems.

Although new build has been a priority in terms of regulations, there has also been increasing attention to reducing the carbon dioxide emissions associated with the existing housing stock. The introduction in the UK of the 'sustainability and security bill' (the Stunnel Bill 2004) provided government with the powers to capture more of the existing stock in building regulations, requiring the application of energy efficient measures during refurbishment or extension work, in addition to those directly related to the refurbishment work itself. However, ensuring compliance in this area is fraught with difficulties and the full powers of this Act have yet to be taken up by government.

In the current Retrofit for the Future programme the UK government are funding demonstration refurbishments, predicted to achieve up to 80% reduction in carbon dioxide emissions for at least 50 existing social housing case studies throughout the UK[9]. Although the cost of such high reductions is likely to be considerable, typically £70,000, the programme will point the way to future solutions and cost reductions

DESCRIBING ENERGY EFFICIENT HOUSING

In the previous sections a number of units have been introduced to describe energy performance. This can be confusing, as varying definitions are often used. The energy demand for a building is usually described in terms of its annual energy use in kWh/m²/annum, which is the energy used per square metre of floor area per year. It may refer to just the heating demand, which for housing might also include heating for domestic hot water. Sometimes, and especially for other building types, it might include energy used for cooling and ventilation, and sometimes lighting and appliances. This energy is often described as the 'delivered energy' to the building, which is the energy metered at the building, from all fuel types: for example, gas and electricity supply.

Typical annual heating loads for recent UK housing would be around 100 kWh/m²/annum, for houses designed to 2006 Building Regulations, and 55 kWh/m²/annum for new housing (say to Sustainable Housing Code Level 3), and as low as 15 kWh/m²/annum to meet the Passivhaus standard. This lower value would equate to a design heat loss of about 1 kW for a standard size house of say about 100 m² floor area. However, although the unit of kWh/m²/annum is useful in comparing the energy performance of buildings, it does not give a true representation of energy use, which will vary with floor area. In some countries average floor area is increasing and so, even though our housing is getting more energy efficient (per m²), the size is also increasing, and the overall energy use might rise. In addition, the balance of energy use is changing, with less being used for heating and more used for electrical appliances. Future building regulations should therefore be extended to incorporate appliance energy use.

The 'design heat loss' is the rate of energy use needed in kilowatts to provide heat during the coldest weather conditions. In the UK, the design heat loss is usually calculated with reference to an external air temperature of −1°C. The design heat loss is traditionally used to 'size' the capacity of the heating system and so it is based on the typical extreme weather condition: i.e. the average coldest condition. The seasonal energy use is based on typical average weather conditions or actual measured data for the heating season.

However, to get a measure of energy that relates more to environmental impact, energy use can be represented in 'primary energy' units, which is a measure of the energy use in raw fuels, for example, the energy content of gas, coal or oil, that is converted to electricity at power stations. This relates closely to carbon dioxide emissions.

The energy use can be converted to carbon dioxide emissions if the fuel factors for specific fuels are known. Usually these are given as average values for a country. For electrical power, they can vary considerably, depending on the type of fossil fuel used at power stations in relation to the percentage of renewable and nuclear energy supply. Typical values are presented in Table 18.1 for the UK, compared to France and Norway, where the proportion of nuclear and renewable energy supply is higher. The use of electricity in these countries for heating would result in less carbon dioxide emissions, as would the use of electricity in the production of construction materials and components, the so-called embodied energy, which is discussed later.

These above definitions should prove useful in the following sections, which discuss the progression from the low energy housing of the 1970s to the zero carbon housing currently proposed. The discussion will focus on specific research and design projects.

Table 18.1 Typical fuel factors[10]

Country	Fuel factor
UK	0.59
France	0.04
Norway	0.02

Fuel factor in kg CO^2eq/kWh.

LOW ENERGY HOUSING DESIGN: ABERTRIDWR BETTER INSULATED HOUSING PROJECT, 1978 TO 1984

In response to the energy crises of the 1970s a series of research projects were set up by, what was then, the UK Department of Environment: Housing Development Directive (HDD) to investigate the energy performance benefits resulting from higher levels of thermal insulation and increased airtightness in housing, together with more efficient heating systems. The purpose was to inform government about measures that could be applied, possibly through building regulations, to reduce domestic energy use. The Abertridwr Better Insulated Housing project was carried out from 1978 to 1984, involving the detailed energy and environmental monitoring of 39 houses of which 20 'test' houses had higher levels of thermal insulation and reduced heating system size compared to the 19 'control' houses. The project also provided a test bed for assessing the use of Titon trickle ventilators (O'Sullivan and Jones 1982, Jones and O'Sullivan 1986) and Pilkington's low emissivity glazing (Jones et al., 1988). Figure 18.3 shows plans and elevations for a house.

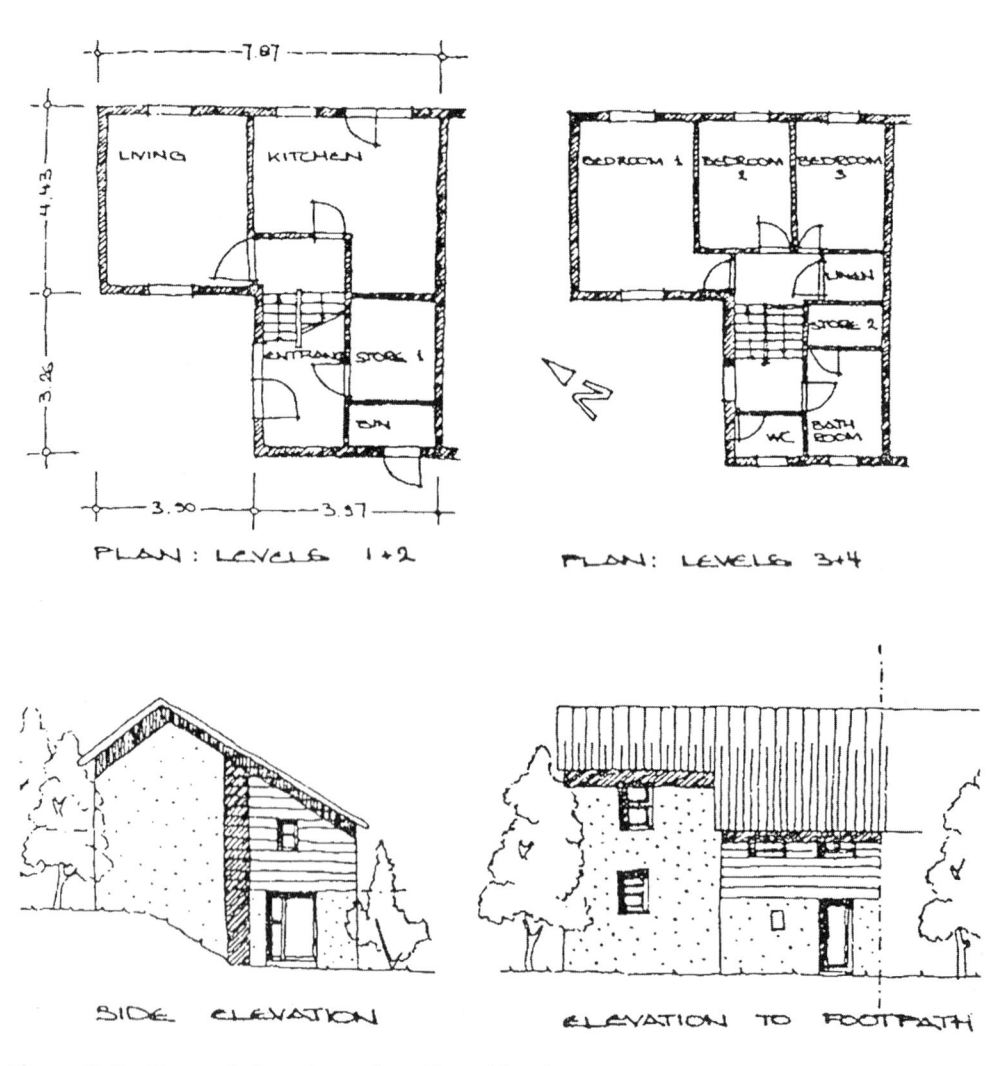

Figure 18.3 Plan and elevations of an Abertridwr house

The houses are terraced with a north-east, south-west aspect. The U-values for the control house were 1.0, 0.5 and 0.6 W/m^2/°C for the walls, roof and floor, respectively. The U-values for the test house were 0.5, 0.3 and 0.45 W/m^2/°C for the walls, roof and floor, respectively. The wall insulation in the test houses was in the form of dry lining, which was considered appropriate for the high exposure site. The roof insulation was 60 mm and 120 mm for the control and test houses. The test houses had 1 m of perimeter slab insulation. Both house types had single glazing at the start of the project, double glazing not being required by building regulations at that time. The boiler sizing in the control and test houses was 14.7 Kw and 8.3 Kw, and the estimated design heat losses were 10 kw and 6.5 kw.

All 39 houses were intensively monitored and a meteorological station constructed on site to measure weather conditions. Data was collected every 5 minutes and a social scientist was based in one of the test houses on site to observe the impact of the house design on the occupants' perception of comfort.

The average space heating energy use over a year is shown in Figure 18.4a. Energy use over the heating season was measured to be 37% less in the test houses compared to the control houses (Jones et al., 1982). The measured internal temperatures were slightly lower in the test houses in the heating season (Figure 18.4b), probably due to only one

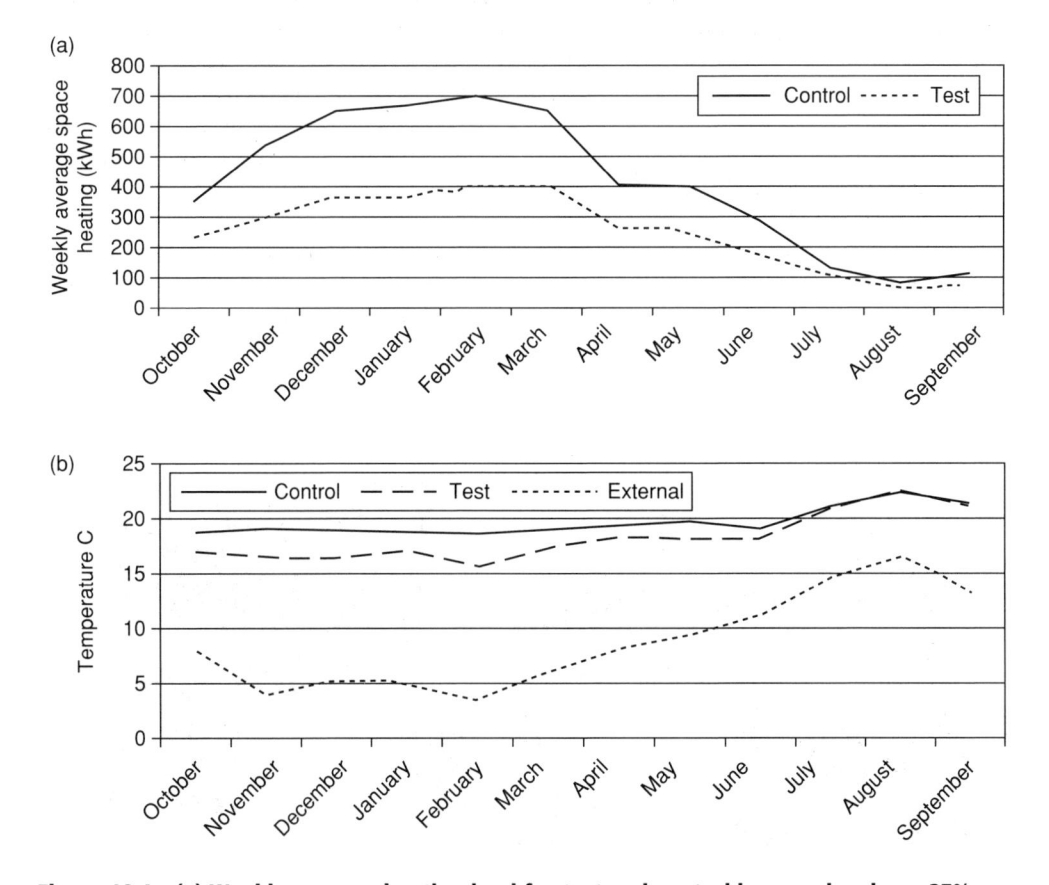

Figure 18.4 (a) Weekly average heating load for test and control houses showing a 37% energy saving. (b) Seasonal internal and external temperatures

radiator being installed on the first floor. The social survey found that this did not compromise comfort. The combined heat gain from incidental occupancy heat and solar energy was estimated to have contributed between 20 and 30% of the heating load, although a proportion of this was considered to have resulted in higher temperatures rather than a reduced heating demand. The internal dry lining thermal insulation in the test houses will reduce the impact of the thermal mass of the construction to stabilise the internal temperature. This may increase the risk of overheating in summertime, which has become a major concern for low energy housing design.

Measurements of boiler efficiencies in both test and control houses indicated that, for the test houses, efficiencies were on average 80% at high loads (above 6 kW) and 50–60% at lower loads (typically 2 kW), while for the control houses they were 75% at high loads (above 8 kW) and 50–60% at lower loads (typically 3 kW) (O'Sullivan and Jones, 1981).

In addition to measuring the heating energy performance of the housing, a number of tests were carried out to assess the thermal integrity of the house construction and, although these methods are fairly commonplace nowadays, they were considered to be pioneering when the housing at Abertridwr was built. Thermography surveys were carried out to check the installation of thermal insulation. They showed up a number of problems due to deficiencies in both construction and design: for example, discontinuity of insulation at eaves detail (Figure 18.5), and no insulation in walls between the stairway and roof space. Air infiltration and leakage measurements were carried out which showed that the houses were constructed to be relatively airtight, with infiltration rates of between 3.6 and 5.5 ac/h at 50 Pa. This corresponded to air leakage rates of about 5.6 to 8.5 $m^3/h/m^2$ on completion of construction. However, further tests performed two years later showed air leakage rates rising to 8.6–14 $m^3/h/m^2$, implying that houses had lost their airtightness during the first year after completion [16]. These can be compared with recent acceptable air leakage values of around 10 $m^3/h/m^2$.

The main programme of investigation was followed by two other highly significant trials:

1 Titon trickle ventilators were installed in half of the test and control houses to investigate potential energy savings due to reduced window

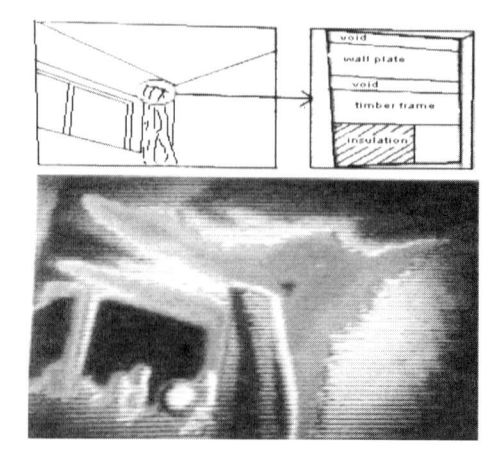

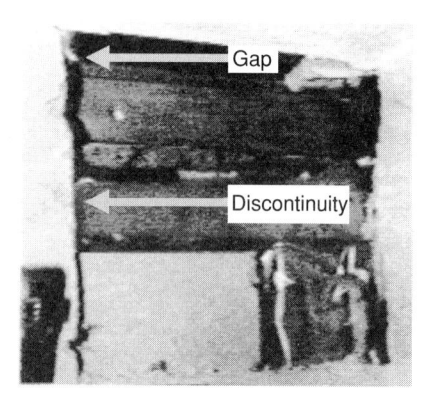

Figure 18.5 An example from the themography survey showing discontinuity of insulation at the eaves detail and a gap in insulation in the raked ceiling

opening [16]. However, no significant savings were identified, and window opening was only marginally reduced in the houses with trickle ventilators. What became apparent was the reduction in condensation in houses with trickle ventilators. Air leakage measurements showed that without trickle vents, infiltration rates were about 0.5 ac/h with vents and windows closed. In particular, bedrooms had low infiltration rates whereas the hall and bathroom had higher rates. The trickle ventilators, when open, increased the air leakage at 50 Pa by about 10%. This was not considered to be a large increase in overall ventilation, but it provided a better distribution of background ventilation throughout the house without incurring a significant energy penalty.

2 Pilkington's low emissivity double glazing units were installed in about half of the houses (Jones et al., 1985). Energy savings of about 14% were achieved, thermal comfort was slightly improved and condensation at window reveals eliminated.

The results of the Abertridwr programme played a major role in defining UK housing energy performance and component design, and informing the development of building regulations at the time. The project demonstrated that heating energy could be significantly reduced. It demonstrated the additional benefits of trickle ventilation and double glazing, not only to reduce energy demand but also to reduce the risk of condensation. The project introduced what are now commonplace measurements such as thermographic surveys and air leakage tests, to help understand performance aspects of low energy design and as a check on building performance on completion of construction.

PASSIVE DESIGN: ENERGY PERFORMANCE ASSESSMENTS (EPAS), 1988–1994

The Abertridwr houses were typical of houses built immediately following the energy crises of the 1970s. They were better insulated, airtight, with relatively small windows, and could generally be termed as 'climate rejecting' buildings. Any heating benefits derived from solar energy through glazing were fortuitous and not designed for, and the same could be said for daylighting and other aspects of what might be associated with 'good design' to take advantage of the climate of the location. During the 1980s greater attention was given to the concept of 'passive design' houses. These still used the basic concepts of low energy design, but were also designed to use solar energy as part of their heating and ventilation strategy, often combined with internal 'thermal mass' for heat storage and internal temperature stability. They were predominantly naturally ventilated and maximised the use of daylight.

The investigation of passive solar design through the Environmental Performance Assessment (EPA) programme, 1988–1994 (funded through the UK Energy Technology Support Unit (ETSU)) was aimed at investigating the potential for passive design, mainly through the use of solar heat gains. A series of passive solar design houses were monitored to assess their energy saving potential, environmental performance and costs. They were also modelled using computational dynamic thermal modelling to help understand their energy performance characteristics. The Welsh School of Architecture collaborated with the company DataBuild to monitor a number of individual houses each over a one-year period[11]. The wall and roof U-values of these houses were as good as, or better than, the test houses of Abertridwr described in the previous section, typically 0.3–0.5 and 0.2–0.35, respectively. The annual heating loads varied from 45 to 132 kWh/m^2, with an estimated useful solar contribution to heating load of between 10 to 30%. Measurements showed that not all the passive solar heat gains were useful and a proportion of them resulted in higher indoor air temperatures, sometimes causing overheating discomfort. This demonstrated that as houses become more 'passive' they need more responsive environmental control, not only through heating system controls but also using the thermal mass of the building construction to reduce extremes of internal temperature.

The monitoring programme was helpful in identifying particular performance characteristics of passive solar design. For example, Figure 18.6 presents a daily profile of temperatures and solar gains for the Spinney Garden housing, showing the solar gains displacing heating energy[12]. This illustrates the need for heating system controls to be able to respond to the occurrence of heat gains, not only from the sun but also from internal sources. We begin to appreciate that the heating system in low energy housing is not required to operate for a long period of time and when it is required the heat output often needs to be relatively low.

The estimated additional cost associated with the passive solar measures over the range of EPA projects was between 2% to 46%, with the higher costs resulting from considerable design additions in the form of glazing systems and sunspaces, and the lower values mainly associated with redistribution of glazing and improved thermal insulation. The EPA programme drew attention to the costing procedures for passive design buildings. When the cost analysis is based on an additive approach, that is, starting with a standard design and adding passive design features, the cost of the passive house will always be more expensive than a standard design. However, when the whole building costs for the passive houses were looked at in relation to typical 'non-passive design' houses, cost differences were often not that obvious. The cost analysis often ignored cost savings associated with passive design, for example, through reducing heating system capacity, and the benefits of a holistic approach to design.

The EPA houses could be considered to have an improved low energy performance relative to the Abertridwr 'test' houses. They demonstrated that a significant amount of this reduced energy demand could be provided through solar heat gains, although responsive control was required to avoid overheating. However, they generally required a greater understanding by the occupants of the way the house is controlled, and a more active participation by the occupants in controlling the environmental conditions.

The EPAs also indicated areas of conflicting design strategies: for example, the passive use of a sunspace versus the increased heating loads when occupants choose to heat them[13]. They demonstrated the need for a holistic approach to design and a clear statement of design aims with continuity throughout the design and construction processes. The success of such developments in housing design rely as much upon establishing robust design and construction processes as they do on technical innovation. They also require an

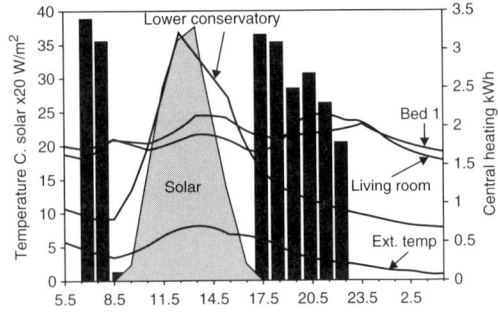

Figure 18.6 Daily temperature and solar gain profile for Spinney Garden with its double height sunspaces

appreciation of how occupants respond to, and use passive design housing.

THE DEVELOPMENT OF PASSIVE DESIGN IN EUROPE

During this period a number of larger-scale projects were developed based on passive solar design strategies, including the Linz Solar City in Austria, the Albertslund in Denmark and the Pefki Solar Village in Greece. These used plan layouts that provided solar access at a whole-site scale, as illustrated in Figure 18.7 for the Linz Solar City (Jones et al, 2009). They demonstrate how the success of passive design is very much dependent on initial planning decisions about site layout and solar access.

Towards the end of the 1980s and in the early 1990s the concept of Passivhaus (See note 8) was developed in Germany, with its standards for total energy demand for space heating and cooling to be less than 15 kWh/m^2/annum of floor area, and a total primary energy use for all appliances, domestic hot water and space heating and cooling of less than 120 kWh/m^2/annum. To achieve this performance standard, heating is normally combined with ventilation using a mechanical ventilation heat recovery system where, typically, heated fresh air is supplied to the main living spaces and air is extracted from kitchen and bathrooms spaces. Passivhaus walls are superinsulated with U-values of 0.10–0.15 W/(m^2.K) and triple glazing with U-values typically 0.85–0.70 W/(m^2.K). For some houses air is passed through underground pipes to preheat (or pre-cool) the intake air for the ventilation system (Figure 18.8). The Passivhaus method can typically cost up to 15% more, although costs can potentially be reduced if a holistic approach is used.

SUSTAINABLE HOUSING

The previous sections have focused mainly on energy efficiency as the design driver. However, there are other aspects of design which impact on the environment, perhaps at a more local level than the global impacts of energy use, and also in relation to the conditions in the house, which affect occupants, health, comfort and well-being. The Code for Sustainable Homes recognises environmental parameters other than energy use and carbon dioxide emissions, including water and material use. In 2004 the WWF set a target for 1,000,000 sustainable homes in the UK[14]. As part of this initiative, the Welsh School of Architecture produced a design strategy for sustainable housing for Wales, which aimed to tackle all aspects of sustainability through planning, design and construction[15]. It defines a sustainable house as follows:

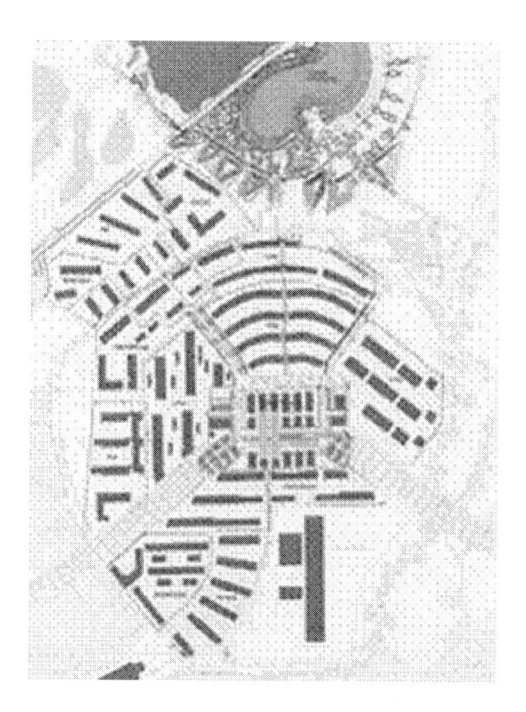

Figure 18.7 Linz Solar City, indicating site planning for solar access (Jones, et al 2009)

- To have *low to zero carbon emissions*, associated with heating, cooling and ventilation, and to

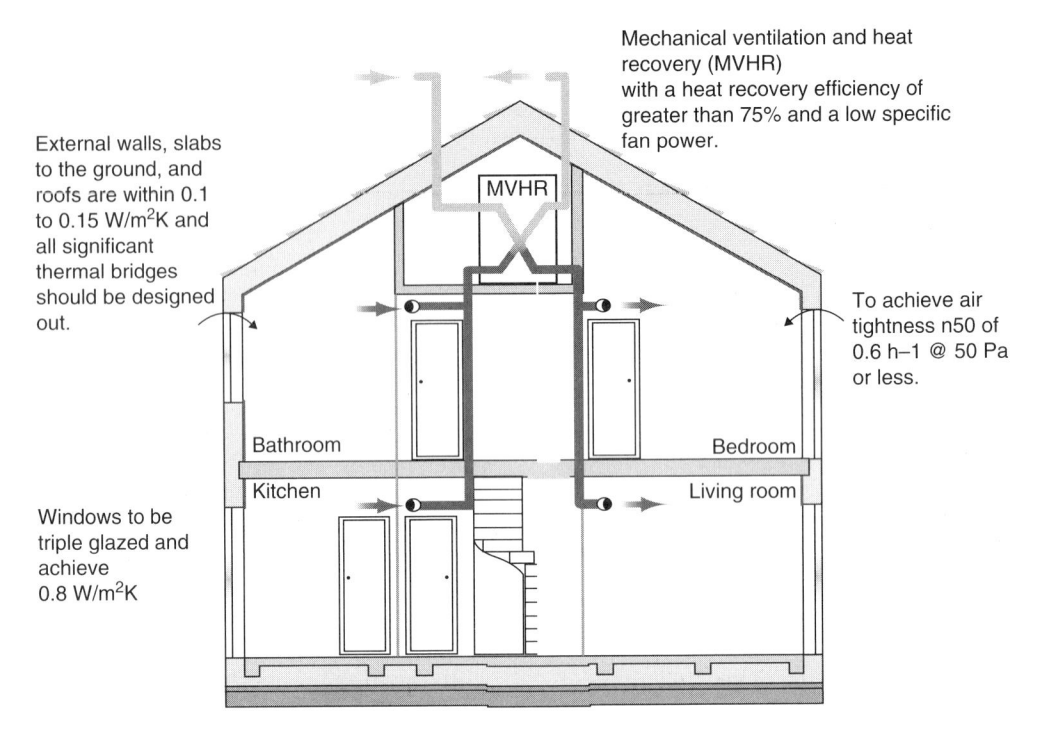

Figure 18.8 Summary of the Passivehaus design elements (Jones, et al 2009)

Labels on figure:
- External walls, slabs to the ground, and roofs are within 0.1 to 0.15 W/m²K and all significant thermal bridges should be designed out.
- Mechanical ventilation and heat recovery (MVHR) with a heat recovery efficiency of greater than 75% and a low specific fan power.
- To achieve air tightness n50 of 0.6 h−1 @ 50 Pa or less.
- Windows to be triple glazed and achieve 0.8 W/m²K

encourage low energy lighting and small power use. Design should maximise the use of passive design features and the use of renewable energy and low energy equipment.
- To select *environmentally friendly materials* and *use materials efficiently* incorporating reclaimed materials and waste minimisation during construction, operation and eventual disposal.
- To *use water efficiently* through water sensitive design and where possible to harvest rainwater.
- To *provide a good quality of life* for the occupants and provide internal conditions that promote health, comfort and a general feeling of well-being. This should include the provision of warmth in winter, minimise overheating in summer and good indoor air quality all the year round.
- To provide a house that is *easy and economic to maintain and to adapt* as a 'lifetime home' and future-proofed to be able to adapt for occupant disabilities and climate change.
- To *enhance the local built environment* in terms of its aesthetic appearance and contribute, and be part of, a safe and supporting neighbourhood.
- To be located where possible to encourage the *use of sustainable transport systems* and be *integrated with green areas* for leisure and food production and to enhance outdoor air quality.
- To have *easy access* to social, health, leisure and retail services.

One of the best examples of a holistic approach to sustainable housing development is the Beddington Zero Energy Development (Dunster et al., 2007), or BedZED, by the architect Bill Dunster of Z-Factory. Completed in 2002, it set out to be a zero carbon, high density urban redevelopment, promoting community involvement, and a zero energy lifestyle. The BedZED development consisted of 100 homes, community facilities and workspaces for 100 people. Figure 18.9 illustrates the layout of workspaces and dwellings. The workspaces are north-lit for good daylighting, without solar overheating, while the houses are south-facing, making use of passive solar heat gain

Figure 18.9 BedZED (BioRegional) (Dunster, et al 2007)

and solar PV. Sustainable design features include thermal mass, passive ventilation stacks with heat recovery, water saving devices and the use of reclaimed materials. The sustainability concept was extended into the community, addressing issues such as food supply, green travel planning and community facilities.

So, sustainable housing design expanded on the earlier concepts of low energy design and passive design, but with additional aspects of material use, building integrated renewable energy supply and socio-economic factors. However, developments such as BedZED, although hugely influential amongst the supporters of sustainable design, and generally successful in terms of its performance in use, were probably considered as an inconvenient challenge to the largely conservative nature of the mass housing industry. They pointed to the fact that in the future housing might be 'different' and involve new processes. Industry's 'pattern book' approach to new housing would generally find such innovation difficult to deal with.

ZERO CARBON HOUSING

Although there has been a growing interest in low energy buildings since the 1970s it is only in recent years that the pace has quickened. In response to the concerns over climate change, governments throughout the world have identified sustainability in the built environment as a high priority. This has resulted in a step change in the construction industries' approach to the low carbon agenda, with zero carbon or carbon neutral buildings set to play a major role in mitigating against further climate change. Also, industry has probably found it easier to deal with the emphasis on the single issue of 'zero carbon design', than the more holistic and multi-parameter nature of 'sustainable design'. In the UK there has also been the benefit of clear signals from government about its aspirations and targets for zero carbon housing and how this will be achieved through a progressive ramping up of standards through future building regulations.

So what is a zero carbon building? A 'low energy' building has its operating energy demand reduced, for example, through more efficient heating, lighting and ventilation, using the 'low energy' and 'passive design' approaches discussed above. A zero carbon building will have further energy demand reductions, for example, achieving the German-based Passivhaus standard, and then using renewable energy supply to meet this reduced demand. This renewable energy supply can either be integrated into the building design or be located 'near-to' as part of a community system. Generally speaking, the renewable energy system should be part of the development and not, for example, be assumed to come from existing green energy sources. Figure 18.10 illustrates the transition from what might be called a standard building (built to say 2002 UK building regulations with a delivered energy demand of around 100 kWh/m^2/annum for heating) to a low energy building (say built to about 50 kWh/m^2/annum) to a zero carbon building (with a heat demand of around 15 kWh/m^2/annum). It is also interesting to note the potential increasing significance of embodied energy as the operating energy is reduced. For a zero carbon building, the embodied energy may now be of a similar size to the operating energy over a typical lifetime, depending on the type of construction used. As a result of the transition to zero carbon, the embodied energy may even increase as a result of using more materials and renewable energy systems.

A zero carbon building will have a net fossil fuel energy demand, so the carbon dioxide emissions to the atmosphere will be zero, or neutral. Neutral means that it may import energy from the grid when there is no renewable energy available and then it will export back to the grid when there is a surplus of renewable energy generated by the building. In this way the grid can be thought of a means of energy storage.

The need for storage of energy is probably the main challenge associated with the use of renewable energy systems. The local supply of renewable energy is not always available, for example, due to the variation of wind and solar. Thermal energy can be stored in the building fabric, surrounding ground, or in specific fluids, sometimes incorporating

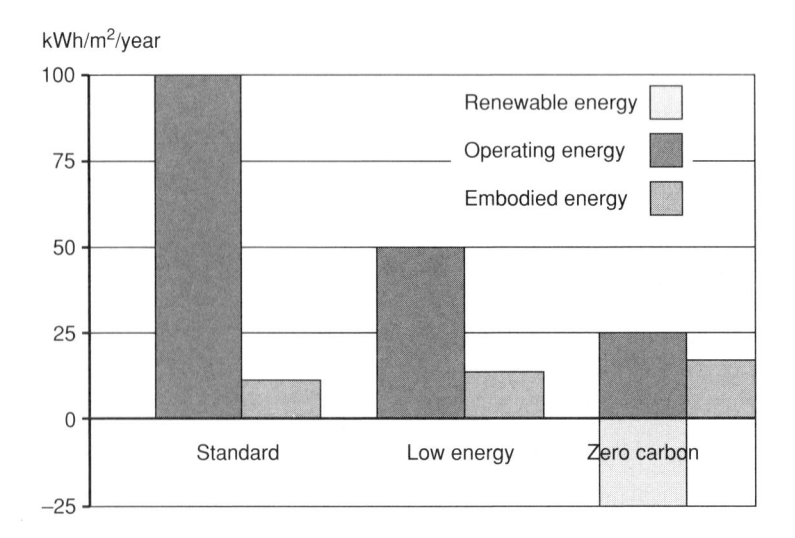

Figure 18.10 Zero carbon design: reduced energy demand, renewable energy supply, and the increasing significance of embodied energy

phase change properties. Figure 18.11 presents the concept of a seasonal thermal storage design, where a large underground water storage system is used to store solar heat gains from the summer to be used during the winter heating system (Schmidt et al., 2003). So there is the potential for thermal energy to be stored 'short term' in the building fabric, or up to 'seasonal' in ground or water storage systems.

Electrical power, however, is more difficult to store, and needs batteries or conversion to high temperature storage systems: for example, to be able generate steam for driving a turbine. Such systems are still relatively expensive, may be high in embodied energy, or may use materials that are difficult to dispose of. Therefore the carbon neutral concept of effectively using the grid as an electrical storage system is currently the preferred option. One solution to deal with the variation in supply from renewable energy systems is to vary the demand for heat or power to meet the availability of supply: for example, controlling electrical appliances such as washing machines and refrigerators to operate when the supply is available. Introducing greater diversity in the

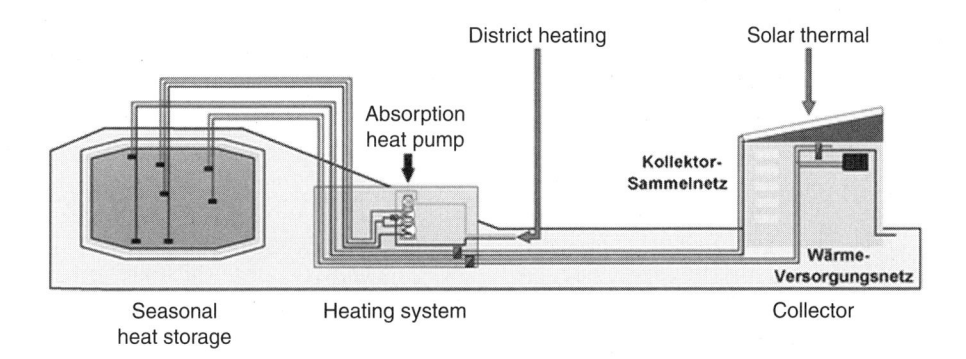

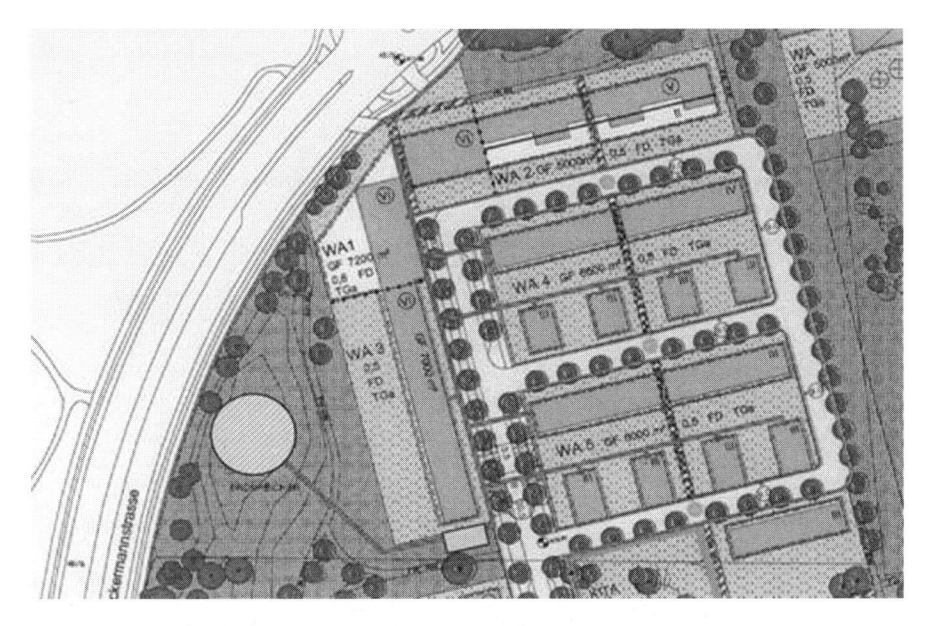

Figure 18.11 Solar Thermal Storage System in Germany (Schmidt et al 2003)

demand side may be more appropriate than local storage or relying on diversity in the supply side.

The drive towards zero carbon housing presents a big challenge, and although there are few truly zero carbon buildings to date, there are some good examples of how they might be achieved in future.

A typical application of a holistic approach to a zero carbon design strategy is the 'project house' designed by the Welsh School of Architecture for Gwalia Housing Association (Figure 18.12). It was designed to provide a zero carbon performance using sustainable materials with innovative off-site construction methods. In the UK, modern methods of construction (MMC) have been explored as a means of delivering sustainable buildings, using either a panel or volumetric system (or a combination of the two). The balance of energy demand reduction and renewable energy supply was explored using passive design features. The house was not built because of its estimated high cost at the time (2002). The figure shows the predicted time, varying results for heat load and internal air temperature, indicating a design heat loss of just over 1 kW, which is similar to a Passivehaus performance [12]. The building is heated using a mechanical ventilation heat recovery system which supplies air preheated in winter through the south-facing double-skin facade. The air is supplied to the living spaces on the south side of the house and air is extracted through the service zones on the north side. There is provision for photovoltaics and solar thermal water heating on the roof.

European case studies from the recent Low Carbon Urban Built Environment European COST C23 Action (Jones et al., 2009) include some autonomous buildings and a number of buildings where typically up to 75% savings have been achieved over current standards. They demonstrate a mix of technical innovation together with high standards of good passive design. Figure 18.13 shows an example from Italy where ground source pre-heating and pre-cooling of ventilation air have reduced the need for more energy intensive systems for heating, cooling and ventilation. Such examples demonstrate that a simpler approach to design is needed as opposed to using more complex systems and controls, which are difficult to maintain and often confusing for occupants to use.

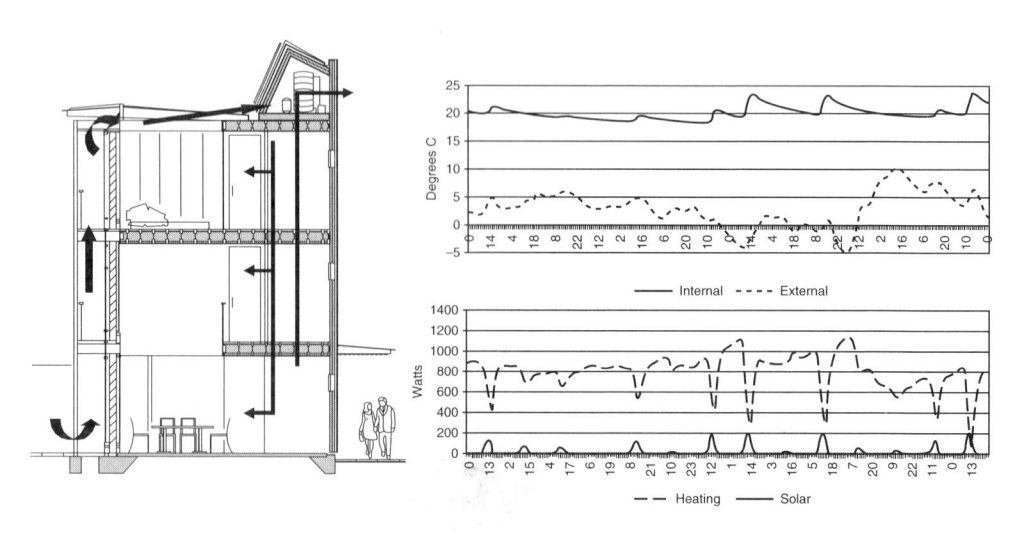

Figure 18.12 WSA project house, indicating winter ventilation, with simulation data for internal and external air temperature, heating energy and solar total horizontal

Figure 18.13 An example of a low carbon house from Italy: the Vieider House (See note 16)

Figure 18.14 presents a zero carbon house recently completed in Ebbw Vale, in South Wales. It uses a panel-based timber system designed specifically to use local timber, and therefore reduce embodied energy. It uses a mechanical ventilation heat recovery system, underfloor heating, and has solar thermal and the potential for the future fitting of solar photo-voltaic energy.

Currently a zero carbon building is defined as a building whose operating energy, for heating, cooling, ventilating and lighting, is carbon neutral. However, these are not the only energy uses that may give rise to carbon dioxide emissions. There is an increasing use of consumer goods in housing, which could be offset by renewable energy systems. These so-called 'non-regulated' appliance energy uses are not currently considered in building regulations in the UK although they are flagged for future consideration.

ZERO CARBON AND BUILDING REGULATIONS

The UK government's approach for achieving zero carbon housing will be staged through regular increases in performance standards specified through building regulations. In England zero carbon will be achieved by 2016 as outlined in the Code for Sustainable Homes [4], which has five 'Code levels'. Although the Code includes attention to aspects of sustainability, reducing carbon emissions is the main driver, and there are some indications that these other aspects may fall by the wayside as the carbon agenda increasingly dominates government thinking. The original aspiration was for a 25% improvement compared to 2006 by 2010 (Code level 3), 44% by 2013 (Code level 4) and zero carbon by 2016 (Code level 5). The improvements cover carbon dioxide emissions associated with heating, ventilation and lighting. There is not yet a clear date fixed for Code level 6, which includes energy use associated with appliances, the so-called 'non-regulated' energy uses. In Wales the zero carbon target (Code level 5) is currently 2013, or soon after, depending on how long it takes to devolve the building regulations to Wales to support the Welsh Assembly Government's aspiration.

However although the goal of zero carbon is still very much on the political agenda, the definition of zero carbon is changing. It now appears that the original definition of zero carbon (Code level 5) may be softened. Figure 18.15 illustrates the most recent definition of zero carbon relating to energy efficiency, carbon compliance and allowable solutions[16].

Figure 18.15 identifies three components of zero carbon performance. The first component, energy efficiency, is related to reducing the energy demand of the building through energy efficiency measures applied through the building design, including its thermal insulation and air tightness. The second component, termed carbon compliance, is related to a more efficient heating and lighting system and renewable energy supply systems. The third component relates to the non-regulated energy uses for which the government plans to identify a number of 'allowable solutions' that can be applied, some of which are summarised in Table 18.2[17].

The original definition of Code 5 was that a 100% improvement, compared to 2006

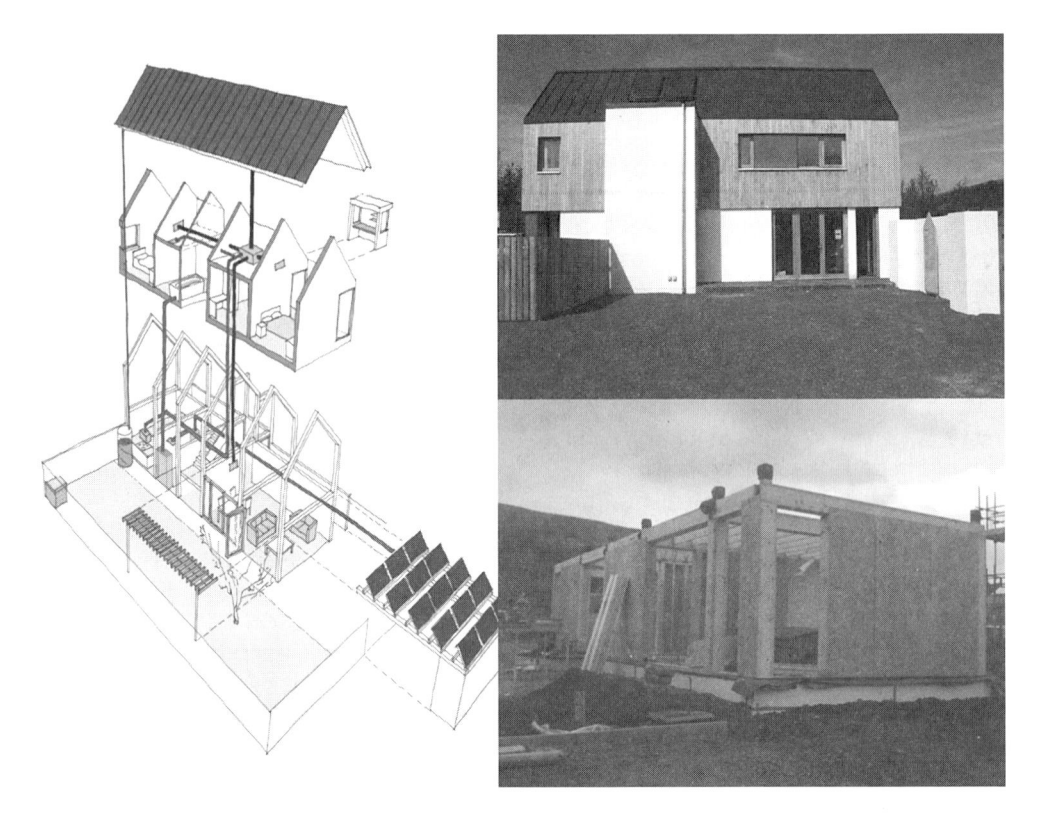

Figure 18.14 Ebbw Vale zero carbon house based on the 'Ty Unos' timber panel construction system

standards, was achieved through only components 1 and 2, i.e. energy efficiency and renewable energy supply. The softening of the Code level 5 definition now allows some 'allowable solution' measures to be included.

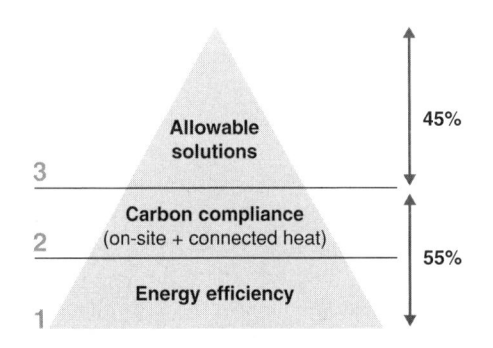

Figure 18.15 Zero carbon balance between energy efficiency, carbon compliance and allowable solutions (see note 16)

First, it was suggested that only 70% of the improvements are achieved through components 1 and 2. However, recently, this has been reduced to 55%, to be achieved on the building development, and the remaining 45% to be achieved through allowable solutions. In hindsight, it might be considered to be politically naive to have suggested that zero carbon performance could be achieved so quickly, given the current available technology and its apparent high cost. However, on the other hand, it did provide the stimulus to industry to seriously engage with the low carbon agenda and begin to innovate.

There are concerns that the proposed system of allowable solutions is too complicated, would be difficult to administer and could lead to double-accounting. However, there could be considerable cost savings for developers: for example, delivering zero carbon purely using on-site means has been

Table 18.2 Allowable solutions

Allowable solution	Description (See note 17)
Carbon compliance beyond the minimum standard	Towards or all the way up to mitigating 100% of regulated emissions plus emissions from cooking and appliances. There may be circumstances (e.g. larger sites) where going further on carbon compliance costs less than other allowable solutions
Energy efficient appliances / building control systems	Such as smart systems installed by the housebuilder, which automatically adjust energy settings if the home is unoccupied and reduce the anticipated energy demand from the home
Exports of low carbon or renewable heat (or cooling) to surrounding developments	As a result of the development, low carbon or renewable heat is exported from the development itself, or from an installation that is connected to the development, to existing properties that were previously heated (or cooled) by fossil fuels; then credit will be given for the resulting carbon savings.
S106 Planning Obligations	S106 Planning Obligations provide a potential mechanism through which decentralised and renewable or low-carbon energy infrastructure might be delivered, paid for by the developer (The Planning Policy Statement: Planning and Climate Change)
Retrofitting of existing buildings in the locality	Retrofitting works undertaken by the developer to transform the energy efficiency of existing buildings in the vicinity of the development: for example, a whole house approach to energy measures in existing homes to transform the energy efficiency of a home
Investments in LZC energy infrastructure	Any investment by the developer in low and zero carbon energy infrastructure (limited to the UK and UK waters) where the benefits of ownership of that investment are passed to the purchaser of the home, so there is a tangible benefit from owning a zero carbon home.
Offsite renewable electricity connected via direct physical connection	Where offsite renewable electricity is connected to the development by a direct physical connection, a credit for any carbon savings relative to grid electricity
Any other measures announced by Government	

estimated to cost up to an additional £30,000, or even higher for a single detached home (Figure 18.16), whereas with a definition that requires a 70% on-site reduction in carbon emissions, the construction cost premium would be about £16,000 (or less if a 55% target instead of 70% is agreed), with a further estimated £800 to £3,500 associated with adopting allowable solutions (McAlister, 2009).

The cost implications of achieving zero carbon performance are uncertain and there is often a 'high risk' cost premium applied to the application of new technologies and design solutions. The passive design element has already been estimated to be typically between 0 to 15%, although these costs can probably be reduced through a more holistic approach to design: for example, offsetting increased levels of insulation against reduced sizing of heating systems. Figure 18.16 illustrates the predicted cost increases against Code levels 1 to 5[18], with the major increase between levels 4 and 5 mainly due to the inclusion of renewable energy systems. However, these are likely to be reduced as economies of scale are applied – for example, to the production of renewable energy systems. In addition, cost savings can be achieved through the greater integration of renewable energy systems into the building design, such as Solar PV and thermal systems integrated into roofs, solar walls, etc.

The cost implications of going from 'near zero' to 'total zero' may prove excessive, and there is also the risk of increasing the embodied energy as more materials and equipment are used. Figure 18.17 (not to scale)

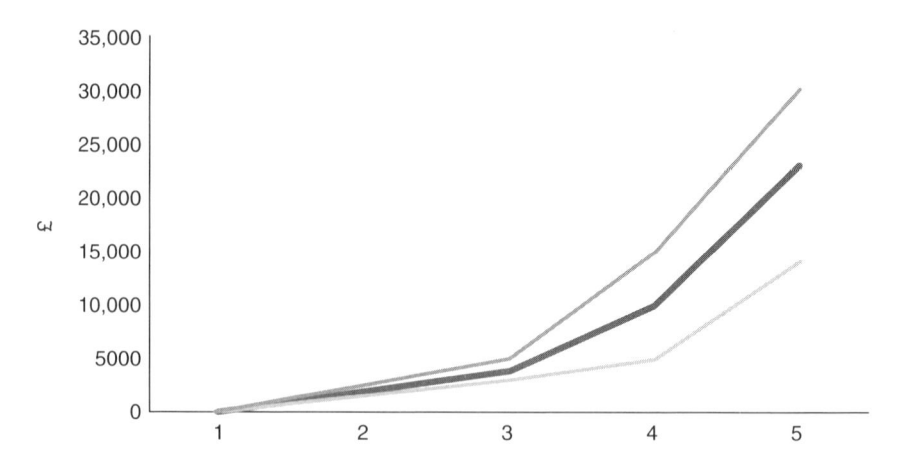

Figure 18.16 Increasing cost of low carbon designs with Code level (solid line: mean, light lines:range)

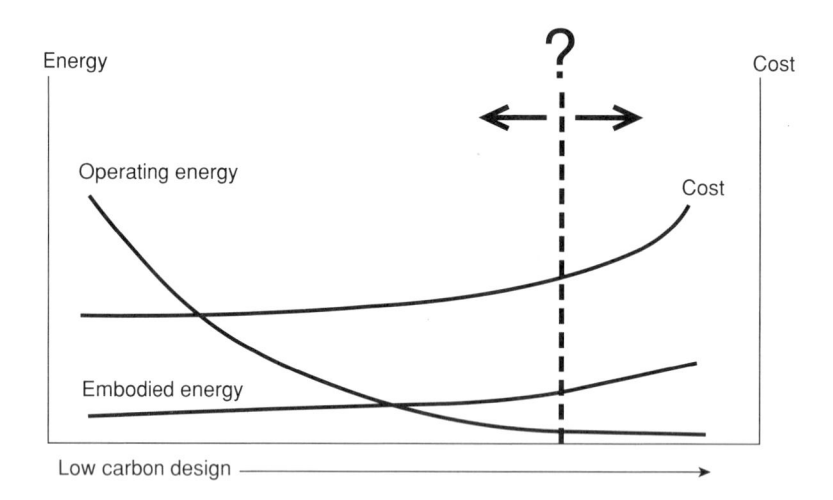

Figure 18.17 Balance of reducing emissions versus cost and embodied energy increases

illustrates the potential relationship between operating energy, embodied energy and cost, in progressing towards zero carbon performance. This relationship might be considered to support the UK government's current softening of the definition of zero carbon and the adoption of 'allowable solutions'.

New housing should not be considered in isolation, and any overall solution should include attention to the existing housing stock, and indeed the built environment as a whole. It will be practically impossible to achieve zero carbon for our existing housing and they will have to rely to some extent on decarbonising their energy supply, possibly through large-scale renewable energy systems, or some other 'allowable solution' to achieve zero carbon status. The current allowable solutions listed in Table 18.2 include some offsetting between new and existing housing, and it may be that this type of approach will be expanded in future: for example, if large-scale renewable energy supply systems are needed to deal with the existing stock, then why not extend them by what is probably a relatively small amount to include new build.

So the drive towards zero carbon continues, with attention not only to reducing heating (space and domestic hot water), ventilating and lighting, and renewable energy sources but also beginning to look at reducing appliance energy use and embodied energy. Thus, the level of carbon dioxide emissions can in some respect be considered as a good indicator of sustainable performance.

THE EXISTING HOUSING STOCK

It is generally accepted that there has been too much emphasis on reducing carbon dioxide emissions on the design of new buildings. Of course it is important to design new buildings to a high standard because they will be around for a long time. However, it is the existing building stock, at an individual building and urban scale, where the main effort will eventually need to be applied. As stated earlier, some 80% of the houses that will be present in the UK in 2050 have already been built. Therefore, the performance of the existing housing stock must be dramatically improved to meet the UK's target of an 80% reduction in carbon emissions by 2050.

There are many good examples of how to reduce the carbon dioxide emissions of existing buildings. Case studies from the Low Carbon Urban Built Environment COST C23 (Jones et al., 2009) countries include examples of carbon dioxide emission reductions ranging from 60% to 90% for existing buildings. Measures typically include increasing levels of thermal insulation, new highly insulated glazing and new efficient heating systems. Some have more advanced solutions such as introducing a glazed double skin to wrap the building and, in one Austrian case, integrating solar PV into the external glazed skin (Figure 18.18).

Figure 18.18 Retrofit for low carbon: Austrian case of integrating solar PV into the external glazed skin (Jones et al 2009)

Many countries have major social housing problems where energy use is high and often residents are in a situation of fuel poverty: i.e. when a significant amount of their income is spent on energy for the home (in the UK, greater than 10%). There are large-scale schemes, for example in Neath Port Talbot in Wales, where 60,000 houses were surveyed and relatively low-cost measures applied to reduce energy use on average by about 10% and take people out of fuel poverty [36].

In order to tackle the problem of upgrading the performance of existing housing, an energy and environmental prediction (EEP) model has been developed by the Welsh School of Architecture (Jones et al., 2007). This 'geographical information system' (GIS)-based model is able to contain information on all housing within a local authority area and can quickly predict their energy performance and assess the results of carrying out energy conservation measures, using embedded sub-models for predicting domestic energy use (and also non-domestic energy use, traffic flow and health impacts). It has been applied in Neath Port Talbot DBC to identify ways of managing the energy efficiency of the existing housing stock in the local authority. Figure 18.19 shows an example of EEP output in the form of a thematic map of annual energy use and carbon emissions and a menu of energy conservation measures that can be applied to a selected group of houses and the impact predicted.

As with new build, cost is an issue for retrofitting existing housing. The EEP model can help local authorities identify the highest energy use housing and determine the most appropriate and cost-effective set of energy saving measures to apply to them.

There are currently a number of retrofit demonstration projects in the UK, funded by government. One example of a low carbon retrofit project located in Newport, Wales (Figure 18.20) includes installation of, thermal insulation, a solar space extension, ground source heat pump, solar thermal and solar PV. The predicted carbon dioxide emissions will be reduced from 103 kg/m^2/annum to 17 kg/m^2/annum. This 83% reduction has incurred a cost of about £70,000. This demonstration project, and others like it, will provide much needed information not only on the performance of low carbon technologies but also on issues associated with carrying out refurbishment and costs.

Another example of retrofitting existing houses has been lead by the Building Research Establishment (BRE) in Pentrceiber in Wales (Figure 18.21). This has involved the refurbishment of a terrace of five houses. The dwellings would be considered 'hard to treat' due to their solid stone wall construction. Measures undertaken included new windows and doors (U-value 1.2), 30 mm of PUR internal solid wall front and back insulation (U-value walls reduced from 1.0 to 0.28), floor insulation (U-value 0.23), a warm roof (U-value 0.20), increased air tightness (5 m^3/hour/m^2), a new 90% efficient boiler and 4 m^2 solar thermal hot water heating. The project targeted 60% reductions in carbon dioxide emissions, for a cost of between £20,000 and £25,000. The current

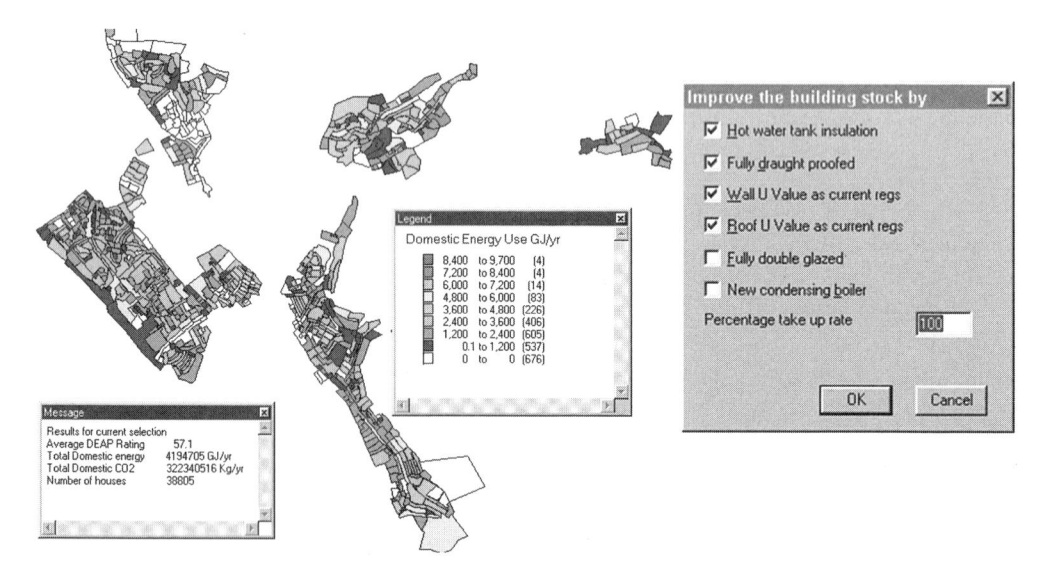

Figure 18.19 An example of EEP output in the form of a thematic map of annual energy use and carbon emissions and a menu of energy conservation measures that can be applied to a selected group of houses and the impact predicted

Figure 18.20 Low carbon retrofit project located in Newport, Wales

Measures for 60% reduction in CO_2
30 mm internal solid wall insulation U-value walls 0.28
Floor U-value 0.23; Warm roof U-value – 0.20
New windows U-value 1.2; New doors U-value 1.2
Increased air tightness to 5 m^3/hour/mm^2
New 90% efficient boiler
4 m^2 SHW

Figure 18.21 Low carbon retrofit project: the Building Research Establishment (BRE) in Pentrceiber in Wales

annual fuel bills were in the range £1,000–1,500 and most of the residents were in fuel poverty. The project also involved the complete refurbishment of the interior of the houses to a high standard.

On an individual building level, as with new build, the cost increases associated with low energy refurbishment are potentially high as zero carbon performance is approached. Figure 18.22 provides some initial cost predictions (Patterson 2008; 2010). The figure indicates that as the energy savings are increased for retrofitting existing houses, the costs increase exponentially, with typically 10–15% savings from an investment of about £5,000–10,000, 60% savings from an investment of about £20,000–25,000, with 80% savings needing an investment of typically £70,000. It is interesting to note that the target for the current UK Retrofit for the Future programme is around 80%. It again begs the question: Should zero carbon performance be achieved on an individual building level or at an urban (or rural) scale?

HOUSE OF THE FUTURE

So how will this trend over the past three to four decades, from low energy to zero carbon, extend into the future, and what are the emerging technologies and processes that will be applied to the house of the future?

The zero carbon performance target is likely to continue to be a driving force behind planning, design, construction and operation, and probably the definition of zero carbon will change over time as the industry becomes more confident in its ability to deliver. It is possible that in future the concept of zero carbon might develop into 'carbon positive', where the building becomes a net generator of energy, to cover not only the currently 'non-regulated' energy uses associated with electrical appliances, etc., but also to generate energy for the householder's transport, and to offset carbon emissions associated with food, holidays and other lifestyle activities. In the current definition of zero carbon, the emphasis is shifting from further energy

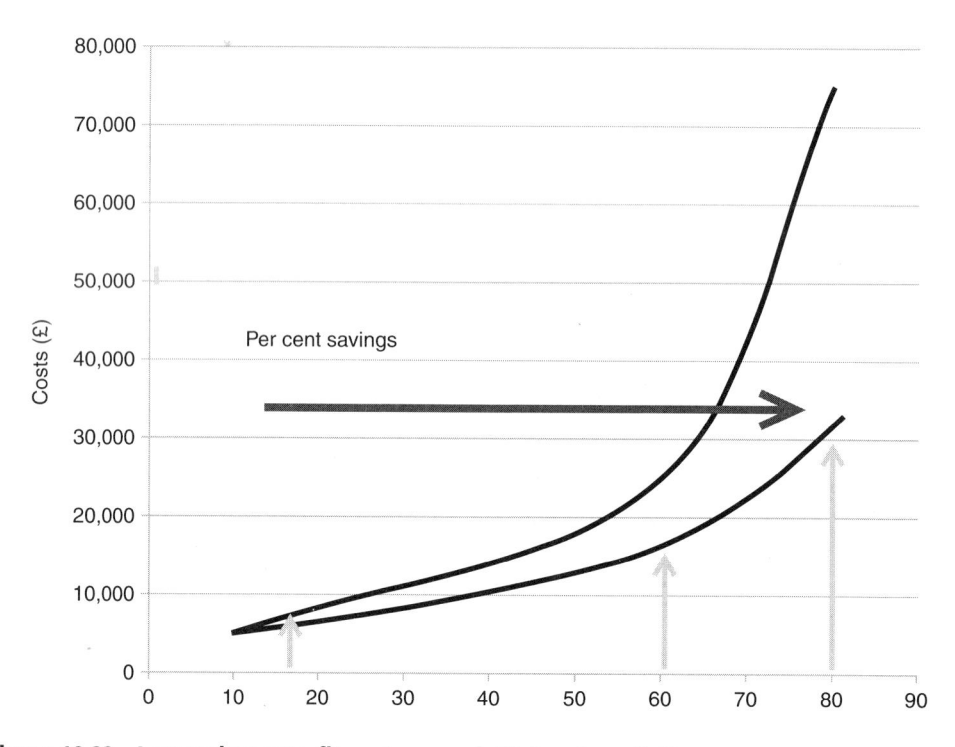

Figure 18.22 Low carbon retrofit costs: some initial cost predictions

efficiency measures (to reduce demand), to the application of renewable energy supply. It is therefore likely that energy efficient design, in relation to operating energy for heating and power, will not go much beyond the Passivhaus standard for the near future, and there will be more activity on the supply side.

Houses in future are more likely to be considered in groups or communities, where energy is shared locally and contributions are made from new developments to offset energy use in existing buildings – for example, through new community-based generation systems. Energy storage technologies will need to be developed both for thermal and electrical energy, as will systems that introduce greater diversity of demand. New feed-in tariff structures in the UK and elsewhere in Europe have the potential to drive innovation in these areas, providing investment opportunities for both individuals and companies.

As embodied energy becomes equivalent to operating energy over a building lifetime, this will become an area of development. There are already databases emerging for embodied energy of materials, and industries are already looking at how to decarbonise their products, Future designs may have an embodied energy value in kWh/m^2 associated with the whole building performance. Of course the 'low hanging fruit' for reducing the embodied energy is the reduction of waste. Waste is becoming a major concern not only in the volume of waste produced during construction and refurbishment but also in the nature of the materials being used as part of energy efficient design, many of which might be considered poisonous and difficult to deal with in terms of construction, refurbishment and eventual demolition. The Cradle to Cradle approach (McDonough and Braungart 2002) suggests that all products should be able to become 'natural waste' even if they go through a recycling process, because eventually they will end up in the natural environment. A zero pollution approach would require that no poisonous material should be used in the building construction, fit-out and appliances. We might therefore expect to see interesting developments of new and more 'environmental friendly' materials for house construction in future.

Modern methods of construction are now considered to be a means of delivering sustainable buildings, through reducing waste and providing a better-quality product. This is likely to result in a more integrated, rather than add-on, approach to design, which should contribute to cost reductions over time. A recent example of MMC is the Ty Unnos project developed by Coed Cymru and the Welsh School of Architecture, which uses Welsh timber in a panel-based system. Figure 18.23 shows this being demonstrated as part of the Wales in Washington event at the Smithsonian in 2009. The timber used in the house is able to 'lock in' carbon, and therefore provide a potentially low embodied energy building. This system was also used in the Ebbw Vale house described above (see Figure 18.20).

Sustainability is as much about process as technology, and new technologies cannot be applied without changing the way buildings are planned, designed and constructed. Also, the building is not the end point in itself, but rather, it is part of the process to support peoples' living. The 'one planet' approach that was applied to BedZED (Dunster et al., 2007) includes consideration of food supply, car sharing, work/live opportunities, etc., as a basis for how communities become more sustainable in addition to individual households. The ultimate aim for sustainable housing is to enable a good quality of life and provide health and well-being for people and communities, in a way that does not harm the environment

At the beginning of this chapter a holistic approach to housing was identified as being important. However, the approach should not be too deterministic. There is a need to be flexible and allow change to take place. In addition to buildings being able to respond to the usual 'changes in use', future buildings will also need to adapt to the climate change that will happen as a result of past carbon

Figure 18.23 Ty Unnos timber housing system demonstrated at the Washington Smithsonian in 2009

dioxide emissions, since the beginning of industrialisation. Future housing will therefore need to be resilient to these changes.

As we have seen – the development from low energy, through passive design, sustainable design, and now low carbon design – the process has been additive (Figure 18.24). We must be aware of this, and the current focus on zero carbon performance should not lose touch with these previous concepts, thereby maintaining the holistic approach.

FUTURE RESEARCH AGENDA

In order to achieve these ambitions for zero carbon sustainable housing, we have to work over a relatively short timescale. It is therefore important that we *measure the performance of new and retrofit housing projects*, and feed this back into the planning/design/construction process. The assessment should not only be concerned with the more quantifiable aspects of performance, such as energy

Low energy design:	Passive design:	Sustainable design:	Zero carbon design:
• Energy efficient design	• Solar	• Materials	• Reduce energy demand
• Thermal insulation	• Daylight	• Renewable energy	• Renewable energy supply
• Airtightness	• Natural ventilation	• Socio-economic	• Appliance energy
• Efficient HVAC	• Thermal mass		• Low embodied energy

Figure 18.24 The shift from low energy to zero carbon design

use, cost and environmental conditions, but also include the construction processes and the response of the occupants to their home. Projects such as Abertridwr and the EPAs, described earlier in this chapter, show how important monitoring performance has been in order to provide information that can inform the design process and the development of building regulations.

As the energy demand of housing is reduced, *new environmental systems* will be required to meet peoples' need for comfort, in a way that responds to this reduced demand. Achieving thermal comfort and good air quality needs to be assessed in the light of low carbon design. Research needs to be carried out on the most appropriate heating and ventilating systems, and their controls, to deliver comfortable and healthy environments, taking account of reduced energy demand and the increasing significance of internal and solar heat gains. The fluctuating supply from solar and wind and the need for energy storage, for both thermal and electrical power, is an area that needs development as well as introducing diversification in demand.

Embodied energy is becoming of increasing concern, as operating energy is reduced. There is a need to use materials and components that have a low embodied energy. Some materials such as timber are naturally low in embodied energy and can lock in carbon. Other materials such as steel and concrete will need to have production processes that reduce embodied energy and incorporate recycling. Materials should also be *disposable* without causing harm. We need to ensure that the materials that we use to achieve a low carbon design do not result in a legacy of poisonous substances that are difficult to dispose of in future.

The *cost of sustainable design* needs to be better understood in terms of a holistic whole building approach to costing and how costs can be reduced through increasing scale. For low carbon design, the cost implications of the split between building integrated solutions and allowable solutions (including grid-based green energy supply) needs to be assessed.

Our experiences so far indicate that most *projects don't deliver their design performance* in relation to reducing energy use and carbon dioxide emissions. This may be due to poor prediction, problems in design and construction, construction and equipment not performing as expected, or the building being used differently to design. In most cases it will be a combination of these factors. A greater understanding of this factor needs to be fed back into the design and construction process.

The concept of *design research* has developed to be able to understand the true performance of sustainable buildings in operation and to assess the effectiveness of the processes of planning, design, construction and operation. This involves integrating research into real design projects and using this experience to inform future research agendas. In this way the relevance of research to the needs of the industry is ensured and future research programmes can better inform industry through appropriate dissemination routes.

NOTES

1   *A Digest of United Kingdom Energy Statistics 2010*. National Statistics publication. London: TSO.
2   Our Energy Future: Creating a Low Carbon Economy. UK government White Paper, 2004.
3   Code for Sustainable Homes, Technical Guide Department for Communities and Local Government, May 2009.
4   Proposals to Amend Part L of the Building Regulations, Consultation Documents, ODPM, July 2004.
5   UK Building Regulations PART L1A, 2010.
6   Directive 2002/91/EC, Energy Performance of Buildings Directive, December 2002.
7   The Minergie Standard for Buildings, www.minergie.ch
8   Passivhaus Primer, http://www.passivhaus.org.uk/fileli-brary/BRE-PassivHaus-Primer.pdf.
9   Retrofit for the Future, Competition to Cut Carbon Emissions in Social Housing, Technology Strategy Board, 2009.
10   Revised Emission Factors for the National Calculation Methodologies, Technical Papers supporting SAP 2009, STP 09/CO201. SAP Crown copyright, 2005.

11 Solar Building Study St Michaels Close ETSU S 1163/SBS/9, 1992.
Solar Building Study Copper Beeches ETSU S 1163/SBS/2, 1990.
Solar Building Study Warmhome 200 ETSU S 1160/25, 1992.
Solar Building Study The Solaire House ETSU S 1163/SBS/6, 1991.
Solar Building Study Old Farm Road ETSU S 1160/10, 1990.
12 Solar Building Study Solar Cottage ETSU S 1160/5, 1991.
Solar Building Study Spinney Gardens ETSU S 1163/SBS/17, 1990.
13 Solar Building Study Albert Hall Memorial Housing ETSU S 1163/SBS/29, 1992.
14 WWF 1000000 million sustainable homes, WWF campaign document, 2004.
15 *Building a Future for Wales: A Strategy for Sustainable Housing*. Welsh School of Architecture for the WWF, 2005.
16 Carbon Compliance: What is the Appropriate Level for 2016. Interim Report, Zero carbon Hub, December 2010.
17 Operation Zero Carbon, Government Business, Vol 8.1, http://www.governmentbusiness.co.uk/content/view/1476/7/
18 Cost Analysis for the Code for Sustainable Homes. Department for Communities and Local Government, July 2008.

REFERENCES

Dunster B, et al. (2007) *The ZEDbook: Solutions for a Shrinking World*. London: Taylor & Francis.

Jones Phil, Paulo Pinho, Jo Patterson, Chris Tweed (eds), (2009) Low Carbon Urban Built Environment, European Carbon Atlas, COST 23. Welsh School of Architecture.

Jones, P. J., Patterson, J. L., Lannon, S. (2007) Modelling the built environment at an urban scale – Energy and health impacts in relation to housing, *Landscape and Urban Planning* 83, 39–49.

Jones, P. J., O'Sullivan. P. (1986) The role of trickle ventilators in domestic ventilation design, Occupant interactions with ventilation systems. 7th AIC Conference.

Jones, P. J., McGeevor, P. A. and O'Sullivan. P. (1985) The effect of low emissivity glass on energy usage in housing. Final SRC Report GR/C/21946.

Jones, P. J., McGeevor, P. A. and O'Sullivan. P. (1982) Better insulated houses, Abertridwr, monitoring of domes-tic central heating systems. Final SRC Report GR/A85360.

McAlister Isabel. (2009) Sustainability zero carbon homes, *Building Magazine*, 17 July.

McDonough, W. and Braungart, M. (2002) *Cradle to Cradle*, North Point Press.

Our Common Future (1987) Oxford: Oxford University Press.

O'Sullivan, P. and Jones, P. J. (1982) The ventilation perform-ance of houses – A case study energy efficient domestic ventilation systems for achieving accepta-ble indoor air quality. 3rd AIC Conference.

O'Sullivan, P. and Jones, P. J. (1981) Measurements of boiler efficiency in well-insulated houses. CIB-S-17 Heating and Climatisation, Delft.

Patterson, J. (2008) Evaluation of an energy efficiency scheme to upgrade the existing domestic building stock of a local authority region. Welsh School of Architecture.

Patterson, J., (2010) Cost of Refurbishing Existing Housing, report for the Welsh Assembly Government.

Pérez-Lombard L, Ortiz J and Pout C. (2008) A review on buildings energy consumption information, *Energy and Buildings*, 40(3): 394–398.

Ravetz, J. (2008) State of the stock – What do we know about existing buildings and their future prospects? *Energy Policy* 36: 4462–4470.

Schmidt, T. et al. (2003) Seasonal Thermal Energy Storage in Germany, ISES Solar World Congress P 7.

SECTION 4

Policy Issues

Kenneth Gibb

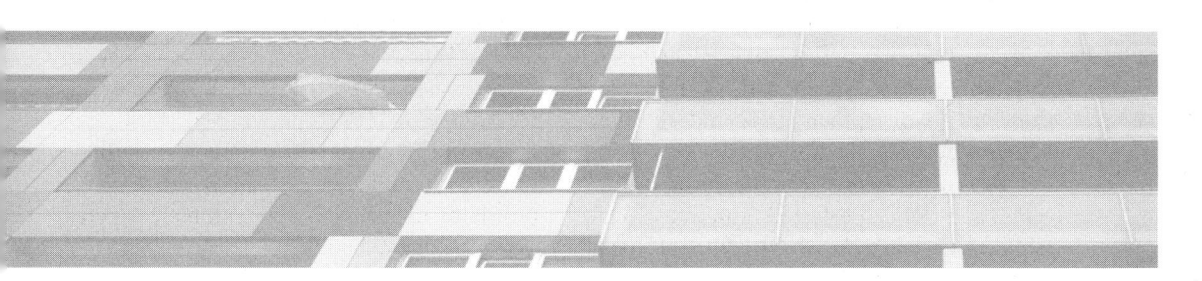

INTRODUCTION TO SECTION 4

Housing as a social concern, or indeed as an important economic activity – is unavoidably political and therefore closely associated with policy and policymaking. This section presents housing policy not as a grand overview of contrasting analytical perspectives on what housing policy is but rather from the point of view of a series of policy issues that have taken on particular significance in recent times: homelessness, affordability, ethnic segregation, etc. Several texts can help with the former approach (e.g. Lund, 2006; Mullins and Murie, 2006; Hudson and Lowe, 2009) and in this Introduction we make a few complementary points as background to the six substantive chapters that follow.

There are many different lenses through which to view policy process and outcomes associated with the housing sphere broadly conceived. Housing may be impacted by broader economic and social policies emanating from local, regional national and, even, international lawmaking. Of course, policies may be enacted at one scale (e.g. locally) to counteract intended or unintended consequences from higher levels above (as can happen when different tiers of government are in conflict or in response to unintended consequences). A theme of public policy literature in recent years has been that of fragmentation and the hollowing-out of the state – and given that governments typically adopt the subsidiarity principle when looking at housing governance, it is perhaps not surprising that in different countries a plethora of different elected and unelected bodies locally and regionally have power to enact policy, to regulate and in some cases directly provide housing.

Into this complex housing governance of different actors (also including trade bodies, professional institutes, the private sector and other constituencies) are a range of ideological perspectives and values framed by local–national contexts or path dependencies, which turn on questions to do with, among other things, the appropriate role of the state and the market. Housing policy tends to be organised through sponsoring government departments, which in different settings and eras enjoys more or less political priority (e.g. rebuilding after a war, following an affordability crisis and more negatively as a major loser when public spending crises require capital funding cuts). Of course, aspects of housing may not be organised as policy from within the sponsoring department, e.g. fiscal policy or social security – which can be an important source of unintended consequences and policy mismanagement. This can be further exacerbated by federal or devolved systems of government.

Academics and policy advisors may also influence policy design and its thrust by drawing on disciplinary and indeed more composite academic traditions when trying to explicate but also promote certain problems and their preferred solutions. One perspective might be the traditional social policy school (see Chapter 9) alongside the more political science public policy approach embracing concepts such as the above-mentioned notions of hollowing-out, fragmentation, actor networks and webs of regulation, to name but a few strands of the analysis that has been adapted to study housing policy. As elsewhere in social policy, economists have been influential through their application of the welfare economics of market and state failure, cost–benefit analysis, value for money and general principles of opportunity cost and inter-temporal investment analysis.

It is also useful to recognise that housing plays different roles in a policy setting, depending on the direct or indirect part in plays in the wider policy process. Housing might be at the centre of the policy: for example, a programme of new build specifically aimed at reducing unmet housing need or a policy of specific regulation to improve housing standards, perhaps among private landlords providing shared accommodation. Alternatively, housing may be the location but not the prime mover of a wider set of spatial, social or economic policies. Thus, a set of actions aimed at spatial regeneration may involve housing more or less centrally and as a necessary part of the programme but other areas such as education, labour market, policing or transport may be the policy coordinator. In this section, we look at several examples of this latter housing role. For instance, homelessness in some respects is a quintessential housing policy but its causes and solutions are in part nothing to do with housing though it is a necessary condition of any individual tailored response to the lack of a permanent home.

The first chapter in the Policy Issues section, Chapter 19, is by Suzanne Fitzpatrick and is 'Homelessness'. It is concerned with homelessness in the UK, but also elsewhere in Europe, North America and Australia. It sets out international variations in definitions of homelessness and describes the profile of homeless people and their experiences, also debating the causes of the complex phenomenon of homelessness. Fitzpatrick argues that the concept of 'homelessness pathways' is a helpful way to analyse homelessness. In addition to highlighting the substantive differences that exist across the countries in terms of policy approach, Fitzpatrick also identifies the importance as well as the potential pitfalls of comparative policy analysis in complex multidimensional policy arenas such as homelessness. The chapter concludes with a strong case for further comparative research that will inform policy and also additional calls to strengthen theoretically informed analysis of homelessness and to consolidate, extend and improve quantitative data that can underpin research.

Chapter 20 is 'Affordable Housing' and is by Chris Leishman and Steven Rowley. Affordability is an exemplar of policy and analytical non-clarity in terms of meaning and actual use of the term. Arguably, this is because it refers to housing costs but also to household resources (including savings) as well as housing quality. Some commentators, such as Duncan Maclennan, actually believe that the term is so misused and unhelpful that it should not be used at all. The authors here argue that the highly contested term 'affordability' is best thought of as a label for a number of closely related housing, social and economic issues. Like the previous chapter, the authors have taken an explicitly comparative approach, looking at affordable housing policies in different countries. They do this by examining the rationale, form and consequences of affordable housing policies and assessing their impacts. Fleishman and Rowley also present a UK affordability case study focusing on the use of planning agreements in the UK as a policy lever to deliver a greater supply of affordable housing units by different means of using quotas such that private sector housebuilders have to make a form of betterment or planning gain to the community, in this case through making an allowance for affordable, usually social housing.

In an authoritative chapter on housing subsidies, Judith Yates engages with a wide-ranging international literature. There are three main elements to Chapter 21: a helpful taxonomy of housing subsidy (distinguishing demand and supply subsidies and direct assistance vs indirect subsidies such as tax expenditures and housing finance subsidies, for instance, mortgage guarantees); an analysis of the rationale for housing subsidies (following Mayo by contrasting traditional with enabling arguments); and, critically, an assessment of the consequences of subsidies. Two key findings might be usefully stressed. First, it remains unwise to categorically favour demand relative to supply subsidies, since the outcome depends so much on local context, institutional design and the operation of markets. Second, causality is difficult to disentangle when one is trying to connect housing and its subsidy to non-shelter outcomes such as improved health, neighbourhood quality or education.

There then follow two complementary contributions: 'Ethnic Residential Segregation' by Sako Musterd and 'Social Consequences of Residential Segregation and Mixed Neighbourhoods' by Ronald van Kempen and Gideon Bolt. Musterd's Chapter 22 also complements Galster's neighbourhood's Chapter 5 in Section 1 of the Handbook. Musterd seeks to help us understand the meaning of the complex concept of segregation and then to apply it to residential neighbourhoods in terms of ethnic divisions. The chapter reviews and reflects on the empirical evidence from Europe and North America and how urban and housing policies aimed at alleviating ethnic segregation have fared. This leads Musterd to question whether the dominant policy discourse of mixing neighbourhoods to reduce ethnic segregation can, and indeed, should work. This is the key question also for van Kempen and Bolt.

Van Kempen and Bolt's specific contribution, Chapter 23, is to overview the international literature on the social consequences of spatial segregation and concentration. The chief policy consequence of late in Western Europe and elsewhere has been to create mixed-income, often mixed-tenure, neighbourhoods or districts. At times it seems like this is a universalist solution that hardly need to be justified, so obvious is its utility. The authors argue that the reasons behind such 'mixing' are complex and operate on several levels. However, they conclude that European models are rarely based on solid empirical evidence. Even so, the conceptual arguments used in defence of creating such mixed neighbourhoods can often be problematic. Moreover, the authors find that those areas of concentration by ethnic and/or socio-economic status are not necessarily negative and may even have advantages. This is a thought-provoking contribution that raises many serious questions about the efficacy of mixed neighbourhoods premised on what is often still elusive evidence on positive neighbourhood effects for the disadvantaged.

The final chapter is 'Managing Social Housing' by Hugo Priemus. Chapter 24 provides the reader with a wide-ranging overview of the history, evolution and structures associated with social housing management, including a case study of the policy framework in the Netherlands. The author correctly points out that research in this area has been primarily in the UK and the Netherlands, is often practice-based and technical in outlook. Academic work divides more between increasingly looking at the sector as a social business via economics and marketing concepts. Alternatively, social research has concentrated on the interface between social housing management and topical social problems such as anti-social behaviour and homelessness.

Taking these chapters together, a number of common themes emerge. First, comparative policy research and evidence is essential across the housing policy sphere. Equally, learning the lessons from the public policy literature on the careful use of policy transfer across nations, institutions and contexts is vital to progress. Second, alongside the great debates about whether housing should be studied via the core social sciences disciplines or rather that there should be a search for an interdisciplinary core to housing studies, similar controversies about the disciplinary, interdisciplinary or indeed multidisciplinary nature of the optimal way to conduct housing policy analysis are all too apparent from the material surveyed in the six chapters of this section. Finally, the policy areas examined here are often multidimensional and complex – housing is the site or location of the policy problem but not necessarily its entirety. This is why clear evidence-based policy research on neighbourhoods, mixing, homelessness, affordability, segregation and many other issues is so elusive but also so important to avoiding policy mistakes. This continues to be the key challenge for policy-oriented housing researchers.

REFERENCES

Hudson, J and Lowe, S (2009) *Understanding the Policy Process*. Bristol: Policy Press.
Lund, B (2006) *Understanding Housing Policy*. Bristol: Policy Press.
Mullins, D and Murie, A (2006) *Housing Policy in the UK*. Basingstoke: Palgrave Macmillan.

Homelessness

Suzanne Fitzpatrick

INTRODUCTION

This chapter focuses on homelessness in the developed world, and more particularly in the UK, elsewhere in Europe, North America and Australia. It commences with a discussion of international variations in definitions of homelessness, and moves on to reflect on the causes of homelessness, highlighting both the theoretical and empirical challenges in explaining this complex phenomenon. The next section summarises current evidence on the profile of the homeless population, before reviewing the experiences of homeless people, where it is suggested that the concept of 'homelessness pathways' is a particularly fruitful analytical framework. The chapter also provides an overview of key policy approaches to addressing homelessness, before concluding with a consideration of outstanding theoretical and empirical challenges in research in this area.

DEFINITIONS OF HOMELESSNESS

Definitions of homelessness differ very considerably across the developed world, and can be drawn variously from legal sources, national surveys or censuses, policy statements, or common usage. The most commonly understood definition of homelessness is that of 'literal homelessness', which has its origins in the USA and comprises (Shinn, 2007; Toro, 2007):

- people sleeping rough; and
- those using homeless shelters/accommodation.

In an international review of homelessness and social housing policies (Fitzpatrick & Stephens, 2007), most of the 12 OECD (Organisation for Economic Cooperation and Development) countries surveyed used something akin to this definition of literal homelessness for both policy and research purposes, albeit that all definitions varied in detailed respects (see also Minnery & Greenhalgh, 2007). However, a number of surveyed countries use wider definitions of homelessness for at least some purposes. In Sweden, for example, the definition used in national surveys includes the 'houseless' living in various institutional settings, as well as some of those living temporarily with friends or relatives. In Australia, homelessness is broadly defined, for service provision purposes, as having '*inadequate access to safe and secure housing*', and the national census counts people staying temporarily with friends/relatives, and those living in low-quality 'boarding houses' as 'homeless'.

By international standards, the 'statutory' definition of homelessness in the UK is exceptionally wide, as it encompasses all those who do not have 'reasonable' accommodation in which to live with their families:[1]

> Broadly speaking, somebody is statutorily homeless if they do not have accommodation that they have a legal right to occupy, which is accessible and physically available to them (and their household) and which it would be reasonable for them to continue to live in. It would not be reasonable for someone to continue to live in their home, for example, if that was likely to lead to violence against them (or a member of their family). (Department for Communities and Local Government (DCLG), Department for Education & Skills (DfES), Department of Health (DoH), 2006, p. 10)

The difficulties of comparing a very narrow concept like literal homelessness to the much wider definitions of homelessness used in the UK and Australia, for example, highlights the serious obstacles to cross-national research on this topic. However, in Europe there has been some significant definitional progress in recent years with the development of the ETHOS typology of homelessness, which comprises four main categories – rooflessness, houselessness, insecure accommodation and inadequate accommodation – and more detailed subcategories (see Table 19.1).

While ETHOS has now been formally adopted by the European Commission and the Council (2010), its key utility lies not so much in imposing a uniform definition of homelessness on all countries, but rather in providing a common framework within which definitions can be compared systematically. The existence of the ETHOS typology means that, though national definitions of homelessness vary considerably in their coverage, one can now, at least in principle, 'make sense' of this in cross-national research by identifying which categories of ETHOS are included (see, for example, Stephens et al., 2010).

THE CAUSES OF HOMELESSNESS

It is an extremely complex matter, in both theoretical and empirical terms, to analyse the causes of homelessness, particularly when one attempts to do so across countries. To start with, there is the obvious point that, as countries vary so much in the definitions of homelessness that they employ, they are focusing to some extent on explanations of different types of phenomena. Moreover, the interpretation of causes may well be influenced by the dominant research traditions and ideological assumptions in different national contexts, as much as by the varying 'realities' of homelessness (Fitzpatrick & Christian, 2006).

Bearing in mind these caveats, this section attempts to summarise existing knowledge on the causes of homelessness in the developed world. It begins by focusing on the relatively straightforward issue of the immediate causes ('triggers') for homelessness, which in fact display a degree of consistency across developed countries. It then moves onto the far trickier territory of the more fundamental ('underlying') causes of homelessness.

Triggers to homelessness

A range of research evidence indicates that the main 'triggers' to homelessness – i.e. the reasons why homeless people lost their last settled housing – are fairly consistent across developed countries. The key direct causes are (Fitzpatrick & Stephens, 2007):

- eviction from rented properties;
- relationship breakdown; and, to a lesser extent,
- loss of employment.

Table 19.1 ETHOS – European Typology on Homelessness and Housing Exclusion

ROOFLESS	1	People living rough
	2	People staying in a night shelter
HOUSELESS	3	People in accommodation for the homeless
	4	People in women's shelter
	5	People in accommodation for immigrants
	6	People due to be released from institutions
	7	People receiving support (due to homelessness)
INSECURE	8	People living in insecure accommodation
	9	People living under threat of eviction
	10	People living under threat of violence
INADEQUATE	11	People living in temporary/non-standard structures
	12	People living in unfit housing
	13	People living in extreme overcrowding

Source: Edgar et al., 2007b.

Eviction from rented properties is often cited as the largest direct cause of homelessness in developed countries, with most of these evictions prompted by rent arrears. The UK is, however, an exception here, as rent arrears are a relatively minor homelessness trigger, most probably because of the protective role of the housing benefit system (Busch-Geertsema & Fitzpatrick, 2008), although that protection is now likely to be undermined by restrictions on housing benefit planned by the current Conservative-led coalition government.

Relationship breakdown is very prominent as a cause of homelessness in virtually all countries, and most commonly involves relationship breakdown with spouses/partners (both violent and non-violent) or exclusion by parents. However, while the 'exhaustion' of family relationships (sudden or gradual) is a widespread trigger to homelessness, it should also be noted that evidence from a range of countries indicates that most homeless people have some ongoing contact with family members, even if it is not always positive (Firdion & Marpsat, 2007; Toro, 2007).

Homelessness – particularly amongst men (Philippot et al., 2007) – is sometimes attributed directly to the loss of a job or other sharp decreases in income, such as those attributable to severe health problems when they compromise earning potential in the context of weak social protection (Fitzpatrick & Stephens, 2007). Loss of paid work certainly seems to be the overwhelming immediate cause of homelessness in Japan, reflecting the close link between employment and housing, via 'tied' or 'company' housing, with mainly older men affected (Okamoto, 2007). But persistent poverty or long-term worklessness seems more often to be the key issue in developed countries, rather than the loss of a particular job (Stephens et al., 2010), placing these economic factors in the category of more 'fundamental causes' (see below).

In some countries, particularly those which focus on narrow definitions of 'literal homelessness', drug, alcohol and mental health problems, and leaving institutions such as prison or hospital, are often identified as key direct causes of homelessness (Stephens et al., 2010). For specific groups of homeless people, such as older homeless people, bereavement and other less common triggers may be especially important (Crane et al., 2005).

Interestingly, at least within Europe, even in those countries with very high rates of homeownership (e.g. the UK and much of southern and eastern Europe), mortgage arrears are seldom cited as a major trigger for homelessness, though large proportions of homeowners are of course outright owners (Stephens et al., 2010). There has been a particularly sharp upward trend in mortgage repossessions as a consequence of the credit crunch in the UK, but even here ex-homeowners still comprise a very small proportion of households accepted by local authorities as 'statutorily homeless' (under 5%) (Wilcox & Fitzpatrick, 2010). That said, in central and eastern Europe, in particular, there are many very poor homeowners who face high risks of homelessness and destitution because of unaffordable utility charges and housing maintenance costs (Edgar et al., 2007a).

Underlying causes of homelessness

Looking now at the longer-term, more 'fundamental' causes of homelessness, a much more complex and contestable picture emerges. These underlying causes of homelessness have been much discussed within the literature, but the debate has been hampered by a lack of conceptual and theoretical clarity (Neale, 1997), and by the adoption of polarised positions whereby some commentators assume that the causes are entirely 'structural' in origin, and others that they are entirely 'individual' (Fitzpatrick, 2005).

From an international perspective, it is clear that homelessness in some countries is interpreted as essentially a 'social' problem (i.e. related mainly to personal/individual factors), whereas in others it is viewed as mainly a 'housing' problem (with its roots in housing and welfare structures) (Stephens et al., 2010).

Within the UK, for example, there seems to be a broad-based consensus that structural factors, especially a shortage of affordable housing, are the fundamental drivers of the overall scale of homelessness, albeit that personal problems increase an individual's vulnerability to these structural factors and therefore to homelessness (Pleace, 2000; Fitzpatrick, 2005). A similar structurally focused analysis now seems to be coming to the fore in the USA (Metraux & Culhane, 1999; Quigley & Raphael, 2001), although this is a relatively recent development, as a more 'individualistic' account prevailed for many years (Fitzpatrick & Christian, 2006), and to some extent still does (Shinn, 2007; Toro, 2007). In the USA, and also in Canada, the concern with housing supply and affordability is accompanied by a recognition that the weak mainstream welfare provision for poorer groups, which has contracted in recent years, is also a key factor (Fitzpatrick & Stephens, 2007). (For a fuller discussion of affordable housing, see Chapter 20.)

The Netherlands is at the opposite end of this spectrum, whereby it is suggested that 'economic' or 'housing' problems alone are hardly ever a reason for homelessness, with almost all homeless people having additional personal support needs (Stephens et al., forthcoming). In Sweden, likewise, there is a strong emphasis on 'social' reasons for homelessness, such as drug addiction and mental health problems (albeit that some commentators argue that access to regular rental housing is also a key problem for some groups; Sahlin, 2005a).

Can these differing national perspectives on causation be reconciled and explained? Possibly, yes. I have hypothesised in series of publications that countries with benign social and economic conditions – well-functioning housing and labour markets, relatively low levels of poverty and inequality and generous social security policies – will have a low overall prevalence of homelessness, but that a high proportion of their (relatively) small homeless populations will have complex personal problems (Fitzpatrick, 1998; Fitzpatrick & Stephens, 2007; Stephens & Fitzpatrick, 2007). I posited that the reverse will hold true (high prevalence/low proportion with support needs) in countries with a more difficult structural context (a similar hypothesis has been forwarded by US authors; see Shinn, 2007).

While the international research evidence is not sufficient to test this hypothesis in a rigorous manner, existing knowledge does fit this broad hypothesis. Thus, Shinn's (2007) recent international review is consistent with the overall hypothesis, as is Milburn et al.'s (2007) cross-national comparison of risk-taking behaviours amongst homeless young people in the USA and Australia (which, highly unusually, comprised simultaneous primary data collection using consistent methods in both countries). Milburn et al. found that, as predicted by the second part of the hypothesis, young homeless people in Australia, where there is a relatively strong welfare safety net, were a more vulnerable group than their peers in the USA, with its much narrower welfare safety net that leaves a broader swathe of young people vulnerable to homelessness. While their study was not designed to compare overall prevalence rates of homelessness, they note that Toro et al.'s (2007) international comparative study, employing telephone surveys in five developed countries, found that 'lifetime homelessness' in the USA and UK was considerably higher than in Belgium, Germany and Italy, thus providing some support for the first part of the hypothesis. Shinn (2007) and Toro (2007) suggest that the telephone survey findings may be linked to the higher levels of poverty and income inequality found in English-speaking countries as compared with other developed economies.[2]

The 'critical realist' framework recommended below, as a means of providing a deeper, more theoretically grounded understanding of the causes of homelessness (Fitzpatrick, 2005) (and see Chapter 11), is also consistent with these international patterns as it allows for the possibility that both individual and structural factors can be causes of homelessness, without the need to assume that one is 'prior' in importance to the other. Thus, for some groups, and also in some countries, structural factors may be 'all important' in homelessness and in other circumstances it may be far more 'individual' in origin.

THE CHARACTERISTICS OF HOMELESS PEOPLE

The profile of homeless people appears to be remarkably consistent across Europe, Australia and the USA, at least when a narrow definition of 'literal homelessness' is employed (Fitzpatrick & Stephens, 2007; Philipott et al., 2007; Toro, 2007). The majority of homeless people fall into the following groups:

- Men: while women are often said to comprise a growing proportion of the homeless population, this is usually from a low base, so that a large majority are still men. Homeless women are usually younger than homeless men.
- Single: that is, never married, divorced or separated, and living in a childless household.
- Unemployed or long-term sick/disabled: this has changed in recent years in northern Europe, where more homeless people used to engage in at least casual or itinerant work. It is noticeable that in countries such as the USA, Canada and Portugal, with less welfare protection, there are still higher proportions of homeless people in work.
- Middle aged: while young people tend to be somewhat over-represented, and older people under-represented, the majority of these single homeless men are in their middle years (i.e. between 30 and 60 years old).
- Ethnic minorities – including immigrants and indigenous peoples – tend to be heavily over-represented.

These first and last points are worth dwelling on briefly.

Taking gender issues first, feminist academics (in the UK at least) have long argued that women are often powerless to define their own housing needs or to house themselves independently from a man because of their weak economic position and the patriarchal assumptions embedded in housing policy and practice (Watson with Austerberry, 1986; Webb, 1994; Tomas & Dittmar, 1995; Watson, 1999). These factors, together with women's vulnerability to domestic abuse and violence, have led numerous mainstream as well as feminist authors to identify being female as a particular risk factor predisposing a person to homelessness. However, these attempts to establish the special vulnerability of women to homelessness do not stand up to empirical scrutiny. As Philipott et al. (2007) comment:

> In most Western countries, women appear to be at a lower risk for [sic] homelessness [than men] (p. 490).

An important point, seldom acknowledged in the literature, is that some gendered factors associated with homelessness almost certainly disadvantage men. This includes the 'bias' in favour of women, particularly single mothers, in welfare and housing provision in many countries, and also the fact women also tend to have more access to family and other forms of social support than men (Neale, 1997; Fitzpatrick, 2000; Cramer & Carter, 2001; Firdion & Marpsat, 2007).

On the other hand, gender and household type are closely related with respect to homelessness, and it is notable that where definitions of homelessness are wider – such as in the UK and Germany – the proportion of the homeless population comprised of families with children tends to be larger than in countries where the focus is on literal homelessness, and many of these families are headed by lone women. In the UK, for example, families with dependent children or containing a pregnant woman comprise almost two-thirds of those accepted as statutorily homeless by local authorities. Most of these families with children are headed by female lone parents, with one or two young children. Unlike many single homeless people, particularly rough sleepers, these statutorily homeless families generally do not appear to have complex personal problems (Pleace et al., 2008). In Germany, while single men predominate amongst the clients of NGOs (non-governmental organisations) and in temporary accommodation provided by municipalities, female lone parents are also over-represented in the municipal statistics (though families with children constitute a declining proportion of homeless households, overall) (Busch-Geertsema & Fitzpatrick, 2008). But in the USA, even with its narrow 'literal' definition of homelessness, there appears to be a higher number of homeless families than in other developed countries (Toro, 2007). This is likely to reflect its very weak welfare state safety net, especially with respect to poor families, which leaves a great many vulnerable to homelessness (Shinn, 2007). There is also shocking evidence from the USA of families very often having to be broken up to be accommodated in shelters, a practice that was once common in the UK, for example, but was effectively ended by legislation back in 1977.

With respect to ethnicity, the relevant issues vary significantly between different developed countries, though in most instances there is at least one ethnic minority with a heightened risk of homelessness (Edgar et al., 2005; see also Shinn, 2007). Perhaps the most striking example is the USA, where around two-fifths of homeless people are African-Americans, as compared to only approximately 12 per cent of the total US population (Fitzpatrick & Stephens, 2007). This over-representation has strong historical roots in the enslavement and oppression of black people in the USA, and the consequent discrimination and economic disadvantage they have faced (Hopper & Milburn, 1996). Extraordinarily high levels of incarceration of African-Americans also seem to play a key role there (Shinn, 2007). In the UK (or, more precisely, in England), likewise, black and black British people have a much greater risk of homelessness than white people or other ethnic minorities (Pleace et al., 2008).

Elsewhere, it is other traditionally disadvantaged ethnic minorities who are at greatest risk. In Hungary, for example, a key homeless group are Roma people, whose housing circumstances are much poorer than that of the general population (Edgar et al., 2005). In Australia, Aborigines and other indigenous people are heavily over-represented in the homeless population (2 per cent of Australia's population identify as indigenous, but 16 per cent of people receiving homelessness services were indigenous in 2003/2004 (Fitzpatrick & Stephens, 2007)), and there is disturbing evidence on the extreme and tragic nature of their plight (Memmott et al., 2004). There is a similar pattern in Canada and in the USA, too, whereby native peoples are disproportionately found in the homeless population (Toro, 2007).

New immigrants are at a heightened risk of homelessness in many countries. For example, the proportion of homeless people reported to be of a 'foreign nationality' (often African) is very high in southern European countries such as Spain, Portugal and Italy, as well as in France (Fitzpatrick & Stephens, 2007). In the UK, there are currently great concerns about homelessness amongst vulnerable migrants, particularly refused asylum seekers, illegal immigrants and economic migrants from Eastern European countries (especially Poland) (McNaughton-Nicholls & Quilgars, 2009). Similar reports of homelessness amongst East European migrants, particularly Poles, are now emerging elsewhere in northern Europe, such as the Netherlands, as the UK economy falters and sterling weakens against the euro (Stephens et al., 2010).

In most developed countries, there appears to be a relatively consistent pattern with respect to the key individual or interpersonal factors associated with a heightened risk of homelessness (albeit that their perceived importance relative to structural factors in the causation of homelessness varies):

- addictions (drugs and alcohol);
- mental health problems;
- institutional living (especially prison and local authority care as a child); and
- traumatic experiences, especially childhood abuse.

It should be noted that, whereas the experience of homelessness very often exacerbates people's mental health or substance misuse problems (Pleace, 2008), evidence from a range of developed countries consistently indicates that these problems overwhelmingly pre-exist homelessness (supporting what is often characterised by psychologists as the 'social selection' hypothesis) (Philipott et al., 2007).

THE EXPERIENCES OF HOMELESS PEOPLE: CAREERS, TRAJECTORIES AND PATHWAYS

The information in the previous section on the 'causes' of homelessness and the 'characteristics' of homeless people gives only a very minimal flavour of the nature of the homeless experiences and the diversity of these experiences. 'Pathways' analysis has been proposed as a helpful means of framing and exploring these experiences – focusing on routes into, through and out of homelessness – offering a considerable improvement on the 'cross-sectional' emphasis in much homelessness research.

A pathways framework essentially charts the progress over time of an individual or household through both 'housed' and 'homeless' situations, and it has been argued that a principal strength of this perspective is that homeless 'episodes' can be 'related both to each other and to the housing circumstances both before and after' (Fitzpatrick & Clapham, 1999, p. 174). Such an approach can also bring to the fore more 'hidden' forms of homelessness, such as staying temporarily with friends or relatives (Robinson, forthcoming). An emphasis on homelessness pathways reflects the widespread recognition that homelessness is not a 'static' phenomenon, but is instead a dynamic and (for some) long-term experience. The pathways approach also reinforces the importance of taking a 'life-course' approach to understanding homelessness, and the need to view homeless experiences holistically, integrating them with other key aspects of people's lives (particularly work/employment and household/family formation). While notions of a homelessness/housing 'career' or 'trajectory' have sometimes been used to capture a similar point, particularly in relation to youth homelessness (Hutson & Liddiard, 1994), the more neutral term 'pathway' is now often preferred as it avoids the 'deterministic' or linear implications of the other terms, which can sometimes appear to imply an inevitable 'downward spiral' (Clapham, 2005; Maycock & O'Sullivan, 2007; Pillinger, 2007).

Anderson and Tulloch (2000) provided a useful summary of a range of potential homelessness pathways, arguing (convincingly) that the most fundamental factor affecting these pathways is the age at which the person first experiences homelessness. They thus categorise homelessness pathways into three broad groups – youth pathways, adult pathways and later life pathways – albeit that there is considerable diversity within each of these categories. They note that *pathways into* homelessness are often better understood than *pathways out* of homelessness (see also Rosengard et al., 2002), not least because of the relative lack of (prospective) longitudinal research on homelessness outside of the USA (see below).

Clapham (2005) has emphasised the merits of the 'housing pathways' approach from a 'social constructionist' perspective, focusing on the ways in which people interpret and understand their homeless and other housing experiences, foregrounding 'meaning, identity and lifestyle' (p. 237). However, as he also argues, the pathways approach to housing enables one to examine '…the interaction between households and the structures that influence the opportunities and constraints they face' (phrasing which highlights the influence of Giddens (1984) on this perspective) (p. 239). This capacity of housing pathways analysis to take account of forces operating at a wide range of societal levels – from macroeconomic structures, through to individuals' attributes, attitudes and behaviours (including their employment of 'strategies' and 'coping mechanisms') – renders it compatible with the realist analysis of causation advocated below[3] (see Chapter 9).

STATE POLICIES ON HOMELESSNESS

FEANTSA (the European Federation of National Organisations Working with the Homeless), in common with many national-level advocates and pressure groups, have for many years been advocating a 'rights-based' approach to addressing homelessness (Fitzpatrick & Stephens, 2007).[4] However, what is meant by a 'right to housing' by these advocates is not always clear, and there is often extreme vagueness in the arguments used to support this approach (Bengtsson et al., forthcoming; Fitzpatrick & Watts, forthcoming).

Bengtsson (2001) has drawn a useful clarifying distinction between what he has called 'legalistic' and 'social' rights to housing, which he argues are, respectively, associated with 'selective' and 'universal' housing policies. In the former, the state provides a legally 'protected' minimum entitlement to housing for poorer households as a complement to the general market, whereas in the latter it focuses on correctives to the general housing market, with the right to housing viewed not as an entitlement for individual households, but rather as an obligation of the state towards society as a whole.

Enforceable 'legalistic' rights – i.e. rights which courts of law will enforce on behalf of individual households – remain in fact relatively unusual in the housing and homelessness field.[5] While in many European countries there is a 'right' to housing contained in the national constitution, no legal mechanisms ('remedies') are provided to enable homeless individuals to enforce these constitutional rights. They are therefore akin to what Bengtsson (2001) has described as 'social' rights, and best understood as political 'marker[s] of concern' (p. 261).

The UK is probably the archetype with respect to the provision of a: '… legalistic safety net for households that find it hard to cope in the market' (Bengtsson, 2001, p. 262). Most unusually, it provides enforceable rights for homeless people, the ultimate discharge of which involves making available 'settled' housing to qualifying households. In order to qualify for this 'main homelessness duty', households must be 'eligible' for assistance (certain 'persons from abroad', including asylum seekers, are ineligible), 'unintentionally homeless' (i.e. have not brought about their homelessness through their own actions or inaction), and in 'priority need' (the principal priority need groups are households which contain dependent children, a pregnant woman or a 'vulnerable' adult). In Scotland, but not elsewhere in the UK, there are plans to gradually expand and then abolish the 'priority need' criterion so that virtually all homeless households will be entitled to settled housing by 2012 (Anderson, 2009).

The closest equivalent to these UK statutory rights is in France, where a highly charged protest campaign and media pressure resulted in emergency legislation being passed in 2007 which aimed to establish a legally enforceable right to housing. From January 2012, all social housing applicants who have experienced 'an abnormally long delay' in being allocated accommodation can apply to an administrative tribunal to demand that the state provide them with housing, and certain 'priority' categories, including homeless people, have benefited from these rights against the state from December 2008. This legislation was passed very quickly, and there are concerns that its vagueness in key areas will frustrate its implementation (Loison-Leruste & Quilgars, 2009).

However, while enforceable rights linked to the provision of settled housing seem limited to the UK and France, there are enforceable rights to *emergency accommodation* in a number of the other European countries. In Germany, for example, local authorities have a legally enforceable obligation (under police laws) to accommodate homeless persons who would otherwise be roofless. In Sweden, similarly, social services legislation impose a 'roof over head' obligation on local authorities. There are also some similar rights in Eastern Europe: in Poland, social welfare law obliges communes to offer shelter to homeless people in hostels, refuges and other institutional settings, and there is an enforceable duty in Hungary that resembles this approach. A single jurisdiction within the USA – New York City – provides a legally enforceable right to accommodation for the 'truly homeless' who have absolutely nowhere else to go.

Notwithstanding these fairly limited legal 'rights' to housing for homeless people, across Europe, North America and Australia there is extensive state-funded assistance available to tackle homelessness (Fitzpatrick & Stephens, 2007). The governance of such services tends to follow a consistent pattern across these developed countries:

- central/federal government establishes a national strategic and/or legal framework, and provides financial subsidies for homelessness services;
- local authorities are the key strategic players and 'enablers' of homelessness services; and
- direct provision is often undertaken by NGOs, particularly for single homeless people, with municipalities more often directly providing services to families with children.

While there is still evidence in some countries of services focusing on providing only emergency assistance to homeless people (i.e. food and basic shelter), in many developed countries there is now a strong emphasis on 'reintegration', and to a lesser extent 'prevention', within homelessness policy and practice frameworks. This is true, for example, in the UK where discharge of the statutory duty ultimately leads, in most cases, to the offer of settled housing, and the 'Supporting People' programme delivers housing-related assistance to help people sustain their accommodation. Also relevant here is a series of special initiatives established by central government to help rough sleepers to sustain lifestyles away from the streets (Jones & Johnsen, 2009), and the increasing focus on resettlement, employment and other purposeful activity within hostels policies (Fitzpatrick et al., 2009). At the same time, there has been a recent strong push towards preventative policies in the UK – employing techniques such as family mediation and improved access to the private rented sector – particularly in England (Pawson, 2009).

This focus on reintegration and prevention, as well as emergency provision, can also be found in other western European countries. In Germany, for example, the importance of reintegration into permanent housing is recognized, with 'floating support' for ex-homeless people living in self-contained accommodation available in many areas. In addition, local authorities now place a great emphasis on homelessness prevention services, usually focusing on dealing with rent arrears, which has demonstrably paid dividends, particularly with respect to family homelessness, which has declined considerably (Busch-Geertsema & Fitzpatrick, 2008). In Sweden there is, in principle, a strong emphasis on reintegration, encapsulated in its concept of a 'staircase' of provision, with emergency shelters at the bottom, intermediate forms of tenancy in the middle, and the top step comprising 'regular' rental flats and homeownership for those homeless people who are considered 'housing ready'. However, this linear, staircase model has come under heavy criticism, with evidence indicating that only a small minority of homeless people actually manage to 'climb all the stairs' to a dwelling of their own (Sahlin, 2005b).

In central European countries, provision is far more basic and crisis-focused than in western Europe, but things do seem to be changing (Fitzpatrick & Wygnanska, 2007). In Hungary and Poland, for example, there has been a rapid expansion of homelessness services over the past two decades, and social services legislation in the Czech Republic specifies a range of provision to be made available to homeless people, supported by funding from central government, including day centres, night shelters, 'asylum housing' (with a reintegrative function, helping clients find work and mainstream housing), and half-way houses (aimed mainly at people leaving institutions). The rate of move-on from temporary accommodation is reported to be extremely low in central European countries (this is a common problem across Europe; see also Sahlin, 2005b; Busch-Geertsema & Sahlin, 2007). In southern Europe, there tends to be very limited state support for homeless people, with an absence of national homelessness programmes. But local schemes are often developed, usually by the Catholic Church or NGOs, and some local authorities, particularly in the large cities, also fund provision for homeless people. Portugal has recently 'opened a window' in southern Europe by establishing a national homelessness strategy (Fitzpatrick, 2011).

Both Australia and the USA have relatively comprehensive and sophisticated programmes to help homeless people, with a clear emphasis on reintegration. The national Australian programme provides transitional accommodation and a range of forms of support (including mediation, counselling and advocacy) aimed at helping homeless people achieve maximum independence (Minnery & Greenhalgh, 2007). The Australian government has made addressing homelessness a key priority, with a target to reduce homelessness by half by 2020. The focus within policy has been to promote early intervention, significantly enhance the capacity and coordination of homelessness services and improve crisis intervention systems (Department of Families, Housing, Community Services and Indigenous Affairs, 2008).

In the USA, there has been a massive growth in homelessness services since the early 1990s, based largely on the idea of local 'continuums of care'. Since 1999, at least 30 per cent of federal funds in this area have been devoted to 'permanent supportive housing' – indicating the priority to be given to people with long-term ('chronic') homelessness histories and 'disabilities'. This is also linked to the increasing influence of the 'Housing First' approach in the USA which involves rapid access to permanent housing with *voluntary* access to a variety of (intensive) support services.

There seems to be encouraging evidence of significant success with this Housing First approach, as compared with more traditional 'transitional' models, particularly with respect to those homeless people with the most complex and challenging needs (Tsemberis et al., 2004; Atherton & McNaughton-Nicholls, 2008; although see Kertesz et al., 2009 for a more sceptical view). However, there are long-standing concerns in the USA that the development of these specialist homelessness services has run parallel with cuts in mainstream benefits that have impacted very negatively on homeless people. Another overall weakness of the current US framework is that it still overwhelmingly focuses on those who are already homeless, rather than on stemming the flow of people into homelessness (Shinn, 2007), though the Obama administration has begun to rectify this (Culhane et al., forthcoming).

Robust data are often very scarce on the outcomes of these homelessness policies (the USA being the exception, where robust longitudinal evaluations are quite common; see further below), but there are indications of success in some areas. For example, in both Germany and England homelessness prevention policies seem to have met with some considerable success (Busch-Geertsema & Fitzpatrick, 2008). Encouragingly, and perhaps surprisingly, it seems that these positive outcomes were achieved even in the face of unhelpful structural trends (worsening housing affordability in England; rising unemployment and poverty in Germany). There is also evidence of significant reductions in rough sleeping in both England and the Netherlands, following targeted programmes in both countries to help this group in major cities and other areas of concentration (Stephens et al., 2010). Thus, it seems that homelessness can be significantly reduced by targeted policy action, so long as such policies are backed by appropriate resources and have an effective governance framework for implementation (Busch-Geertsema & Fitzpatrick, 2008).

FUTURE RESEARCH: THEORETICAL AND EMPIRICAL PRIORITIES

Homelessness at a global level, or even just within the developed world, represents a massive potential research agenda which it would be foolish to attempt to summarise comprehensively. I will instead confine myself to identifying three broad priorities for future research in this field:

- theoretically informed explorations of causation;
- improved quantitative/statistical evidence; and
- international comparative research.

Theoretically informed investigations of causation

As social science, and indeed science as a whole, is often characterised as the 'search for causes' (Williams & May, 1996, p. 53), it is perhaps axiomatic to identify causation as a key research priority. Understanding the causes of homelessness is of course crucial to tackling and preventing it, and thus has a strong policy basis as a research priority. However, I would argue that practically useful research on the causes of homelessness also requires a strong theoretical basis because 'causation' is a matter of complex ontology and epistemology in any aspect of the social world, and homelessness is no exception. It is apparent that in most academic and policy discussions of the 'causes' of homelessness, very little attention is paid to what is actually meant by the notion of a 'cause', and this is a serious weakness in the international literature on this topic.

As has been argued in a previous paper (Fitzpatrick, 2005), 'critical realism' provides a useful theoretical framework for analysing the causation of homelessness because of its robust conceptualisation of 'causation' in both the material and social worlds (Bhaskar, 1989; Archer, 1995). Realists regard '*real*' causal powers as *necessary tendencies* of social objects and structures which may or may not be activated (and produce '*actual*' effects) depending on *contingent conditions* (Sayer, 2000).[6] Realists would therefore argue that the presence (or absence) of empirical regularities is not a reliable guide to the (non-) existence of causal powers as the presence of other causal mechanisms may often – or even always – prevent correspondence between cause and effect. Instead, they contend that potential causal mechanisms should be 'abducted' from the 'concrete' case in order to facilitate 'qualitative' examination – i.e. close scrutiny of *what is it about* this mechanism that may *tend to* cause the relevant phenomenon.

Realist explanations of actual social events and phenomena are not 'mono-causal' and deterministic, but rather contingent (given the 'open' nature of social systems), and also 'complex', with multiple (and multidirectional) causal mechanisms. They may also involve 'non-linear dynamics', meaning that small changes can potentially result in dramatically varying outcomes (Byrne, 1998). Realism also places great emphasis on 'emergence': from this complexity new phenomena emerge which have a reality over and above any individual component, carrying causal powers which cannot be deduced from taking these components separately (Williams, 2001, 2003; though see Van Wezemael's (2009) recent challenge to realists' preoccupation with systems-level emergence, which he terms 'romantic'). Central to this complexity is the likelihood of 'feedback loops' and causal interrelationships between various potential causal factors in homelessness. The challenge is to seek identifiable patterns in this complexity.

A particularly important characteristic of realist ontology is its positing of a layered (social as well as physical) reality (Pawson & Tilley, 2007). Thus, the central ontological assumption of realists is that the world is structured, differentiated and stratified, and no one strata is assumed to be logically prior to any other. This is a crucial point with respect to the causation of homelessness whereby the current orthodox position, at least in the UK and USA, tends to assume that structural causes are somehow more 'fundamental' than more personal or individual ones (see above). In contrast, a realist ontology allows for causal factors operating at a range of different levels to be explored in an open-minded way, without assuming that any one level necessarily 'trumps' another. To be clear: while it may be that, *in fact*, factors operating at a macro-structural level are more *important* (in scale) and/or *powerful* (in predictive strength) in the generation of homelessness than those operating at a lower (micro) level, these are empirical questions, to be settled by the evidence, rather than matters for a priori assumptions.

However, despite critical realism's theoretical elegance, it is not a philosophical programme that translates easily into empirical research (Williams & May, 1996). It is demanding because it requires not only a description of social relations and events but also a commitment to explaining them by means of uncovering 'hidden' dimensions of social reality. Theory-building is needed to postulate 'abstracted' aspects of reality in order to define necessary ('internal') tendencies which may constitute causal mechanisms. Attempts then must be made to demonstrate the existence and mode of operation of these hypothetical mechanisms through empirical testing and the elimination of alternative plausible explanations, using techniques such as contrastive and counterfactual questioning (Lawson, 2006).

It might reasonably be argued that critical realist research, focused as it is on hypothesis development and empirical testing, is little different from more traditional methodologies. However, it is at the level of theorisation and interpretation that realism differs profoundly from more traditionally 'empiricist' approaches (Pawson & Tilley, 1996). Perhaps the most important distinguishing feature of critical realist approaches to social science is the close attention paid to conceptual validity and clarity, particularly with regards to the 'qualitative nature' of the social object under scrutiny.

Following on from this, Williams (2001, 2003) has mounted an important challenge to the assumption that homelessness is a 'realistic category' amenable to causal analysis. The crux of his argument is that homelessness is a '*bad abstraction*', meaning that it '...arbitrarily divides the indivisible and/or lumps together the unrelated and the inessential' (Sayer, 1992, p.138). However, it is unclear from Williams' papers whether he views homelessness as a bad abstraction because it can arise from distinctive causal processes, or because, as an emergent condition, it lacks conceptual 'unity and autonomous force' (Sayer, 1992, p.138). With respect to the first point, one could argue that this is not central to the 'realistic' meaningfulness of a social object or property, because a realist analysis of causation can be 'complicated' (comprising a range of separate causal processes) as well as 'complex' (a result of interacting feedback loops between interrelated causal components). However, the conceptual coherence of the emergent condition of homelessness is, in contrast, crucial to its categorisation as a 'real' property appropriate for causal investigation (Fitzpatrick, 2005).

Is there such conceptual coherence in the 'universal' category we currently define as homelessness? Possibly not. It may well be that a focus on more internally homogeneous subgroups within the 'homeless' population would yield better explanations of the social problems associated with 'suboptimal' housing circumstances. So, if, for example, single people sleeping rough or living in shelters or hostels shared many similar experiences, and exhibited similar health and other impacts of their experience of homelessness, they may constitute a 'real' category which could, for instance, be entirely separate from that of families living in temporary accommodation. Systematic investigation of this point would require, as Williams has argued, empirically informed theorising about meaningful categorisations within the homeless experience, and a re-analysis of existing empirical material with this critical realist framework in mind; new data collection is also likely to be required to fulfil this demanding realist approach.

Improved quantitative evidence

A second research priority should, in my view, be increased and improved quantitative data on homelessness. The availability of robust statistical evidence on homelessness is extremely patchy, even if one confines oneself to the developed world. The USA has by far the most best quantitative research, based on large sample sizes and rigorous methodologies. This is rooted in a strong tradition of robust quantitative research on homelessness, including the use of experimental, quasi-experimental and control/comparison group methodologies to assess rigorously the effectiveness of specific homelessness programmes, and large-scale longitudinal evaluations to track the progress of homeless households over a number of years (e.g. Shinn et al., 1998; Tsemberis et al., 2004; see discussion in Philippot et al., 2007; Toro, 2007).

Elsewhere, there is a dearth of quantitative research on homelessness, aside from basic, descriptive work on the characteristics of homeless people which is available in a number of countries (see Philipott et al., 2007; Shinn, 2007). This is true even in the UK, which has the second largest extant literature on homelessness (Pleace & Quilgars, 2003; Fitzpatrick & Christian, 2006; Philipott et al., 2007), but little by way of large-scale quantitative research, notwithstanding a few notable exceptions (Anderson et al., 1993; O'Callaghan et al., 1996; Pleace et al., 2008). In most countries, such quantitative research as exists is limited to one-off, generalist surveys, rather than involving the routine use of robust quantitative methods (especially longitudinal quantitative methods) to investigate specific research questions and to evaluate responses to homelessness. Where survey methods are employed, they are often poorly designed, though the UK is a partial exception to this, as is France, where demographers have conducted some large and robust surveys of homelessness (Philipott et al., 2007).

Both the UK and Australia have relatively good administrative statistics on the homeless population (Minnery & Greenhalgh, 2007), and a range of European countries are seeking to improve their administrative data on homelessness, in part as a result of a European Commission (EC)-funded project to promote better information systems on homelessness at both member state and European Union (EU) level (Edgar et al., 2008). One aim of this MPHASIS project is to move all EU countries towards providing at least a minimum of some standardised 'core' data on the homeless population (Edgar et al., 2007). However, while this MPHASIS project appears to have enjoyed some considerable success with respect to its primary aim of improving the 'measurement of homelessness' within EU countries, its (implicit) secondary objective of providing a harmonised quantitative data set on homelessness across Europe that can be interrogated for comparative research purposes seems unlikely to be met for some considerable time (Stephens et al., 2010; see further below).

Thus, in the UK and across much of the rest of Europe, the majority of homelessness research is qualitative in nature, and is very often highly policy-driven (Philippot et al., 2007). This imbalance towards qualitative methods has some obvious consequences with respect to the international evidence base on homelessness. Thus, while qualitative research is well-suited to providing in-depth, nuanced information about the nature of individual experiences and perceptions, it is not designed to provide statistically robust information on the scale of a phenomenon such as homelessness. Likewise, assumptions about the general pattern of needs and experiences of homeless households, or particular sub-populations of homeless people, are quite likely to mislead if routinely based on samples which are not designed to be representative (Pleace et al., 2008).

While the routine use of experimental methods in UK and European homelessness research seems a long way off for both financial and ethical reasons (Fitzpatrick & Christian, 2006), it is crucial that robust quantitative components are incorporated insofar as possible (including longitudinal, chronological and comparison group elements where appropriate), without losing present strengths with respect to qualitative insights. Cost–benefit analysis, and associated economic techniques designed to demonstrate the efficient use of public resources, are a key concern in this regard. These types of economic analyses are relatively well developed within the homelessness sector in Australia (Flateau & Zaretzky, 2008) as well as in the USA (Culhane, 2009), but are only just emerging in the UK and in Europe, and (as things stand) researchers there rarely have access to the financial and longitudinal outcome data required to make robust assessments of the costs and benefits of particular interventions. While the increasing emphasis on cost–benefit/effectiveness within homelessness is controversial (Aldridge, 2008), it seems inevitable that its importance will grow in the coming years across Europe, and will present significant challenges for researchers, research funders and practitioners alike.

International comparative research

Finally, there is a clear need for comparative, empirical research on homelessness (both qualitative and quantitative). As Shinn (2007, p. 674) has commented, comparative work is '…invaluable in challenging local assumptions and broadening the focus of work on homelessness'. More specifically, there are some key research questions germane to both academic and policy debates which cannot be answered without it, including with respect to the hypothesis on the impact of structural contexts on the scale and nature of homelessness advanced above (Stephens & Fitzpatrick, 2007). There is also the important and vexed issue of policy transfer in the homelessness field. While there have been some obvious examples of this (such as the incorporation into the UK of the 'foyer' concept for young homeless people from France), these have occurred without the benefit of robust comparative research detailing the policy, institutional, economic and cultural contexts within which such targeted interventions may or may not 'work'. There is a huge amount of current interest across Europe in the 'Housing First' approach that has been developed in the USA, as noted above, but again robust comparative research would be extremely useful in analysing the effectiveness or otherwise of this approach in differing national and local contexts (see European Consensus Conference: Policy Recommendations of the Jury, http://www.housingeurope.eu/www.housingeurope.eu/uploads/file_/2011_02_08_FINAL_Consensus_Conference_Jury_Recommendations_EN.pdf).

Despite the best efforts of FEANTSA and the European Observatory on Homelessness (EOH) (EOH is the research arm of FEANTSA) over many years, within even the European context there is very little proper 'comparative' research on homelessness. To conduct empirical comparative research systematically over several countries, whether qualitative or quantitative, requires significant resources, which are rarely made available. A 'juxtapositional' approach tends to be pursued on homelessness, employing 'national experts' in each relevant country to provide relevant information that is then synthesised into an overview report. In the EOH this broad approach was used for its principal outputs for many years (with national reports and thematic overview reports), although it has now moved to a more academic style with an annual *European Journal of Homelessness* a key output, including refereed journal articles. However, the fundamental limitation remains the same – there are no substantial resources available for primary empirical research, so these papers rely mainly on country-specific (existing) literature and data, which of course vary hugely in coverage, methods and robustness, rather than original, comparative research conducted systematically across countries.

While there was an interesting special edition of the US-based *Journal of Social Issues* in September 2007, which contained some very useful cross-national reviews of literature, policy or national homelessness data (Minnery & Greenhalgh, 2007; Okamoto, 2007; Philipott et al., 2007; Shinn, 2007; Toro, 2007), only two papers contained cross-national primary data collection (Milburn et al., 2007; Toro et al., 2007). There are few other examples of cross-country empirical research on homelessness, though it is worth noting here Crane et al.'s (2005) analysis of the causes of homelessness amongst older people in England, the USA and Australia. However, there are also some other signs of progress, at least within Europe, with the EC funding a number of relevant pieces of work relevant to homelessness with an empirical, comparative element. For example, a recent EC-funded research project, which sought to investigate the interactions between welfare, labour market and housing policies in six EU member states, included some primary qualitative research on homelessness, employing the 'vignette' technique to compare systematically institutional responses to homeless households in similar circumstances across countries (Stephens et al., 2010). The EU has also funded a consortium to undertake research on combating social exclusion among young homeless populations in the UK, the Netherlands, Portugal and the Czech Republic.

But this is all still very limited with respect to primary comparative research on homelessness, and any substantial progress will require a major investment of resources. Of course, even if resources could be made available to conduct such primary comparative research on homelessness, there would still be considerable methodological challenges to overcome, with respect to conceptual equivalence, data harmonisation, language barriers (inhibiting precision in argument) and, perhaps most profoundly, institutional divergence (Busch-Geertsema & Fitzpatrick, 2008). As Firdion and Marpsat (2007, p. 571) have commented:

> International comparisons suffer from two kinds of problems, which make it difficult to establish and interpret comparable results: those arising from differences in methodology, definitions and sampling; and those arising from differences in policies designed to relieve poverty, help homeless people, and deal with immigration or mental illness.

However, there are many other areas of housing studies where such barriers are, if not overcome, at least worked around in order to deliver interesting comparative findings (Doling, 1997), such as on social housing (Stephens et al., 2002) and homeownership (Elsinga et al., 2007). There is, in principle, no reason why similar progress cannot be made in the homelessness field. One potential way forward, at least within Europe, would be to add a module on homelessness to the EU-SILC survey (there were some questions on housing exclusion but not homelessness in 2009). This would provide at least some statistical data on homelessness in a consistent manner across Europe, and the ETHOS typologies could be used as a means of identifying key categories of interest across the EU. Similar exercises, using modules in national household surveys, have previously revealed interesting findings on the prevalence of homelessness at national level (e.g. Burrows, 1996).

CONCLUSION

This chapter has taken a wide-ranging approach to the topic of homelessness, focusing on Europe, North America and Australia. It has outlined the challenges inherent in defining homelessness, but also the recent progress made in this respect, at least within Europe. It has highlighted areas where there is a reasonable degree of understanding about homelessness (the basic characteristics of homeless people, and the immediate 'triggers' to homelessness), and areas where far less is known (overall prevalence, underlying causation and robust evaluations of specific interventions). Finally, an agenda was set out for future research which prioritises empirically informed theorising about causation, quantitative methodologies and international comparative primary research.

NOTES

1 Though to be entitled to help under this UK legislation there are additional criteria that legally 'homeless' households have to fulfil.

2 Toro et al.'s survey had a range of limitations, not least that response rates were relatively low, the sample sizes in individual countries were quite small, it was restricted to those ex-homeless people who had access to a telephone, and those who were currently homeless or living in institutions were excluded (possibly depressing the homelessness rate in the USA, with its exceptionally high levels of incarceration; Shinn, 2007). Nonetheless, it remains the only credible attempt to provide estimates of overall levels of homelessness in different countries using a comparable methodology.

3 As I have argued elsewhere, 'weak constructionism' (Lupton, 1999) (such as that expounded by Clapham, 2005) and 'critical realism' disagree about little at the ontological and epistemological levels (both admit of an underlying 'reality' but also acknowledge that we cannot know it directly as it is mediated through social and cultural processes) (Fitzpatrick, 2005). They tend to focus on different issues as most worthwhile for social scientists to pursue: either 'meaning' (constructionists) or 'causation' (realists). This can mean that they can sometimes 'talk past each other', but both in fact have complementary insights.

4 Though there are counter voices: see O'Sullivan (2008).

5 It is also worth making the point that attempts to harness international law to establish an enforceable 'right to housing' for homeless people, routinely applicable in domestic courts, have thus far been largely unsuccessful (Kenna, 2005).

6 See Van Wezemaeal (2009, p. 95) for a recent application of such a realist ontology within housing studies. In the context of his discussion of rival conceptions of 'complexity' ('romantic' vs 'baroque'), Van Wezemaael posited that the 'real' comprised both

a 'field of actualities' and 'a field of virtuality', with the 'virtual' understood as 'unactualized tendencies' (termed 'singularities'). Lawson (2006) has also provided a sustained analysis of housing development in Australia and the UK based on a realist framework.

REFERENCES

Aldridge, R. (2008) 'The limitations of cost analysis in relation to homelessness', *European Journal of Homelessness*, 2: 275–287.

Anderson, I. (2009) 'Homelessness policy in Scotland: A complete state safety net by 2012', in S. Fitzpatrick, D. Quilgars & N. Pleace (eds), *Homelessness in the UK: Problems and Solutions*. Coventry: Chartered Institute for Housing.

Anderson, I. & Tulloch, D. (2000) *Pathways Through Homelessness: A Review of the Research Evidence*. Edinburgh: Scottish Homes.

Archer, M. (1995) *Realist Social Theory: The Morphogenetic Approach*. Cambridge: Cambridge University Press.

Atherton, I. & McNaughton-Nicholls, C. (2008) 'Housing First as a means of addressing multiple needs and homelessness', *European Journal of Homelessness*, 2: 289–303.

Bengtsson, B. (2001) 'Housing as a social right: Implications for welfare state theory', *Scandinavian Political Studies*, 24(4): 255–275.

Bengtsson, B., Fitzpatrick, S. & Watts, B. (forthcoming) 'Shelter, rights and citizenship', in S. Smith (editor-in-chief), *International Encyclopaedia of Housing and Home*. Oxford: Elsevier.

Bhaskar, R. (1989) *Reclaiming Reality*. London: Verso.

Burrows, R. (1997) 'The social distribution of the experience of homelessness', in R. Burrows, N. Pleace & D. Quilgars (eds), *Homelessness and Social Policy*. London: Routledge.

Busch-Geertsema, V. & Fitzpatrick, S. (2008) 'Effective homelessness prevention? Explaining reductions in homelessness in Germany and England', *European Journal of Homelessness*, 2: 69–95.

Busch-Geertsema, V. & Sahlin, I. (2007) 'The role of hostels and temporary accommodation', *European Journal of Homelessness*, 1: 67–93.

Byrne, D. (1999) *Social Exclusion*. Buckingham: Open University Press.

Byrne, D.S. (1998) *Complexity Theory and the Social Sciences*. London: Routledge.

Clapham, D. (2005) *The Meaning of Housing: A Pathways Approach*. Bristol: Policy Press.

Cramer, H. & Carter, M. (2001) *Homelessness: What's Gender Got to Do With It?* London: Shelter.

Crane, M., Byrne, K., Fu, R., et al. (2005) 'The causes of homelessness in later life: Findings from a three-nation study', *Journal of Gerontology*, 60B(3): 152–159.

Culhane, D. (2008) 'The costs of homelessness: A perspective from the United States', *European Journal of Homelessness*, 2: 97–114.

Culhane, D.P., Metraux, S. & Byrne, T. (forthcoming) 'A prevention-centered approach to homelessness assistance: A paradigm shift?', *Housing Policy Debate*

Department for Communities and Local Government, Department of Health, and Department for Education and Skills (2006) *Homelessness Code of Guidance for Local Authorities*. London: DCLG, DoH, DfES.

Department of Families, Housing, Community Services and Indigenous Affairs (2008) The Road Home: Homelessness White Paper. Canberra, Australia: FaHCSIA.

Doling, J. (1997) *Comparative Housing Policy: Government and Housing in Advanced Industrialized Countries*. Basingstoke & London: Macmillan.

Edgar, B. & Doherty, J. (2001) *Women & Homelessness in Europe*. Bristol: The Polity Press.

Edgar, W., Doherty, J. & Meert, H. (2005) *Immigration and Homelessness in Europe*. Bristol: The Policy Press.

Edgar, B. with Filopovic, M. & Dandolova, I. (2007a) 'Home ownership and marginalisation', *European Journal of Homelessness*, 1: 141–160.

Edgar, W., Harrison, M., Watson, P. & Busch-Geertsema, V. (2007b) *Measurement of Homelessness at European Union Level*. Brussels: European Commission, download under http://ec.europa.eu/employment_social/social_inclusion/docs/2007/study_homelessness_en.pdf

Edgar, W., Illsley, B., Busch-Geertsema, V., Harrison, M, & Watson, P. (2008) MPHASIS: Mutual Progress on Homelessness through Advancing and Strengthening Information Systems. How to Improve the Information Base on Homelessness on a Regional, National and European Level. Background Paper to Guide the National Seminars. download under http://www.trp.dundee.ac.uk/research/mphasis/papers/synthesis-engfinal150508.pdf

Elsinga, M., De Decker, P., Teller, N. & Toussaint, J. (2007) *Home Ownership beyond Asset and Security: Perceptions of Housing-Related Security and Insecurity in Eight European Countries*. Delft: Delft University Press.

European Commission and the Council (2010) *Joint Report on Social Protection and Social Inclusion 2010*. Brussels: EC.

Firdion, J.M. & Marpsat, M. (2007) 'A research programme on homelessness in France', *Journal of Social Issues*, 63(3): 567–588.

Fitzpatrick, S. (1998) 'Homelessness in the European Union', in M. Kleinman, W. Mattznetter & M. Stephens (eds), *European Integration and Housing Policy*. London and New York: Routledge, pp. 197–214.

Fitzpatrick, S. (2005) 'Explaining homelessness: a critical realist perspective', *Housing, Theory & Society*, 22(1):1–17.

Fitzpatrick, S. (2009) 'Homelessness policy in the UK in an international context', in S. Fitzpatrick, D. Quilgars & N. Pleace (eds), *Homelessness in the UK: Problems and Solutions*. Coventry: Chartered Institute for Housing.

Fitzpatrick. S. (2011) *Portugal 2010: Building a Comprehensive and Participative Strategy on Homelessness*. Synthesis Report. Brussels: European Commission.

Fitzpatrick, S. & Christian, J. (2006) 'Comparing homelessness research in the US and Britain', *European Journal of Housing Policy*, 6(3): 315–336.

Fitzpatrick, S. & Clapham, D. (1999) 'Young people and pathways through homelessness', in D. Clapham & S. Hutson (eds), *Homelessness: Public Policies and Private Troubles*. London: Cassals.

Fitzpatrick, S., Kemp, P. A. & Klinker, S. (2000) *Single Homelessness: An Overview of Research in Britain*. Bristol: The Policy Press.

Fitzpatrick, S. & Stephens, M. (2007) *An International Review of Homelessness and Social Housing Policy*. London: CLG.

Fitzpatrick, S. & Watts, B. (forthcoming) 'The 'Right to Housing' for homeless people', in E. O'Sullivan et al. (eds), *Homelessness Research in Europe*. Brussels: FEANTSA.

Fitzpatrick, S. & Wygnanska, J. (2007) 'Harmonising hostels standards: comparing the UK and Poland', *European Journal of Homelessness*, 1: 41–66.

Flateau, P. & Zaretzky, K. (2008) 'The economic evaluation of homelessness programmes', *European Journal of Homelessness*, 2: 305–320.

Giddens, A. (1984) *The Constitution of Society: Outline of the Theory of Structuration*. Cambridge: Polity Press.

Hopper, K. & Milburn, N.G. (1996) 'Homelessness among African-Americans: A historical and contemporary perspective', in J. Baumohl (ed.), *Homelessness in America*. Phoenix, AZ: Oryx Press.

Hutson, S. & Liddiard, M. (1994) *Youth Homelessness: The Construction of a Social Issue*. Basingstoke: Macmillan.

Jones, A. & Johnsen, S. (2009) 'Street homelessness', in Fitzpatrick, S., Quilgars, D. & Pleace, N. (Eds.) (2009) *Homelessness in the UK: Problems and Solutions*. Coventry: Chartered Institute for Housing.

Kenna, P. (2005) *Housing Rights and Human Rights*. Brussels: FEANTSA.

Kertesz, S.G., Crouch, K., Milby, J.B., Cusimano, R.E. & Schumacher, J.E. (2009) 'Housing First for homeless persons with active addiction: Are we overreaching?', *The Milbank Quarterly*, 87(2): 495–534.

Loison-Leruste, M. & Quilgars, D. (2009) 'Increasing access to housing – implementing the right to housing in England and France', *European Journal of Homelessness*, 3: 75–100.

Lupton, D. (1999) *Risk*. London: Routledge.

McNaughton-Nicholls, C. & Quilgars, D. (2009) 'Homelessness among minority ethnic groups', in S. Fitzpatrick et al. (eds), *Homelessness in the UK: Problems and Solutions*. London: Chartered Institute of Housing.

Maycock, P. & O'Sullivan, E. (2007) *Lives in Crisis: Homeless Young People in Dublin*. Dublin: The Liffey Press.

Memmott, P., Long, S., Chambers, C. & Spring, F. (2004) 'Re-thinking indigenous homelessness, *AHURI Research and Policy Bulletin*, 42, May. Melbourne: Australian Housing and Urban Research Institute.

Metraux, S. & Culhane, D.P. (1999). 'Family dynamics, housing, and recurring homelessness among women in New York City homeless shelters', *Journal of Family Issues*, 20: 371–396.

Milburn, N.G., Stein, J.A., Rice, E., et al. (2007) 'AIDS risk behaviours among American and Australian homeless youth', *Journal of Social Issues*, 63(3): 543–566.

Minnery, J. & Greenhalgh, E. (2007) 'Approaches to homelessness policy in Europe, the United States, and Australia', *Journal of Social Issues*, 63(3): 641–655.

Neale, J. (1997) 'Theorising homelessness: Contemporary sociological and feminist perspectives', in R. Burrows, N. Pleace & D. Quilgars (eds), *Homelessness and Social Policy*. London: Routledge.

Okamoto, Y. (2007) 'A comparative study of homelessness in the United Kingdom and Japan', *Journal of Social Issues*, 63(3): 525–542.

O'Sullivan, E. (2008) 'Sustainable solutions to homelessness: The Irish case', *European Journal of Homelessness*, 2: 205–234.

Pawson, H., Netto, G., Jones, C., et al. (2007) *Evaluating Homelessness Prevention.* London: Communities and Local Government.

Pawson, R. & Tilley, N. (2007) *Realistic Evaluation.* London: Sage.

Pawson, H. (2009) 'Homelessness policy in England: Promoting 'gatekeeping' or effective prevention', in Fitzpatrick, S., Quilgars, D. & Pleace, N. (Eds.) (2009) *Homelessness in the UK: Problems and Solutions.* Coventry: Chartered Institute for Housing.

Philippot, P., Lecocq, C., Sempoux, F., Nachtergael, H. & Galand, B. (2007) 'Psychological research on homelessness in western Europe: A review from 1970 to 2001', *Journal of Social Issues*, 63(3): 483–504.

Pillinger, J. (2007) *Homeless Pathways: Developing Effective Strategies to Address Pathways into, through and out of Homelessness.* Dublin: Focus Ireland.

Pleace, N. (2000) 'The new consensus, the old consensus and the provision of services for people sleeping rough', *Housing Studies*, 15: 581–594.

Pleace, N. (2008) *Effective Services for Substance Misuse and Homelessness in Scotland.* Edinburgh: Scottish Government.

Pleace, N., Fitzpatrick, S., Johnsen, S., Quilgars, D. & Sanderson, D. (2008) *Statutory Homelessness in England: The Experience of Families and 16–17 Year Olds.* London: Communities and Local Government.

Quigley, J.M. & Raphael, S. (2001) 'The economics of homelessness: The evidence from North America', *European Journal of Housing Policy*, 1: 323–336.

Robinson, D. (forthcoming) 'Staying temporarily with friends/relatives as a form of 'hidden' homelessness', in S. Smith (editor-in-chief), *International Encyclopaedia of Housing and Home.* Oxford: Elsevier.

Rosengard, A., Laing, I., Jackson, A.A. & Jones, N. (2002) *Routes out of Homelessness.* Edinburgh: Scottish Executive.

Sayer, A. (2000) *Realism and Social Science.* London: Sage.

Sahlin, I. (2005a) *Homelessness and the Changing Role of the State in Sweden.* European Observatory on Homelessness Thematic Paper. Brussels: FEANTSA.

Sahlin, I. (2005b) 'The staircase of transition: Survival through failure', *Innovation*, 18(2): 115–136.

Shinn, M. (2007) 'International homelessness: Policy, socio-cultural, and individual perspectives', *Journal of Social Issues*, 63(3): 657–677.

Shinn, M., Weitzman, B.C., Stojanovic, D., et al. (1998). Predictors of homelessness among families in New York City: From shelter request to housing stability. *American Journal of Public Health*, 88: 1651–1657.

Stephens, M. & Fitzpatrick, S. (2007) 'Welfare regimes, housing systems and homelessness: How are they linked?', *European Journal of Homelessness*, 1: 201–212.

Stephens, M., Burns, N. & MacKay, L. (2002) *Social Market or Safety Net? British Social Rented Housing in a European Context.* Bristol: Policy Press.

Stephens, M., Elsinga, M., Fitzpatrick, S., van Steen, G. & Chzhen, Y. (2010) Study on Housing and Exclusion: Welfare Policies, *Housing Provision and Labour Markets.* Brussels: European Commission.

Stephens, M., Fitzpatrick, S., Elsinga, M., Steen, G.V. and Chzhen, Y. (2010) Study on Housing Exclusion: Welfare policies, *Labour Market and Housing Provision.* Brussels: European Commission. [Available as free download from http://www.york.ac.uk/inst/chp/]

Tomas, A. & Dittmar, H. (1995) 'The experience of homeless women: An exploration of housing histories and the meaning of home', *Housing Studies*, 10(4): 471–491.

Toro, P.A. (2007) 'Toward an international understanding of homelessness', *Journal of Social Issues*, 63(3): 461–481.

Toro, P.A., Tompsett, C.J., Philippot, P., et al. (2007) 'Homelessness in Europe and the United States: A comparison of prevalence and public opinion', *Journal of Social Issues*, 63(3): 505–524.

Tsemberis, S., Gulcur, L. & Nakae, M. (2004) 'Housing first, consumer choice, and harm reduction for homeless individuals with a dual diagnosis', *American Journal of Public Health*, 94(4): 651–656.

Van Wezemaal, J. (2009) 'Housing studies between Romantic and Baroque complexity', *Housing, Theory and Society*, 26(2): 81–99.

Walby, S. (1990) *Theorizing Patriarchy.* Oxford: Blackwell.

Wardhaugh, J. (1999) 'The unaccommodated woman: Home, homelessness and identity', *The Sociological Review*, 47(1): 91–109.

Watson, S. (1999) 'A home is where the heart is: Engendering notions of homelessness', in P. Kennett & A. Marsh (eds), *Homelessness: Exploring the New Terrain.* Bristol: Policy Press.

Watson, S. with Austerberry, H. (1986) *Housing and Homelessness: A Feminist Perspective.* London: Routledge and Kegan Paul.

Webb, S. (1994) *My Address is Not My Home: Hidden Homelessness and Single Women in Scotland*. Edinburgh: SCSH and GCSH.

Wilcox, S. & Fitzpatrick, S. with Stephens, M., Pleace, N., Wallace, A. & Rhodes, D. (2010) *The Impact of Devolution: Housing and Homelessness*. York: Joseph Rowntree Foundation.

Williams, M. (2001).'Complexity, probability and causation: Implications for homelessness research', *Journal of Social Issues*, http://www.whb.co.uk/socialissues/mv.htm

Williams, M. (2003) 'The problem of representation: Realism and operationalism in survey research', *Sociological Research Online*, 8(1) http://www.socresonline.org.uk/8/1/williams.html

Williams, M. & May, T. (1996) *Introduction to the Philosophy of Social Research*. London: UCL Press.

Affordable Housing

Chris Leishman and Steven Rowley

DEFINING THE HOUSING AFFORDABILITY PROBLEM

The implementation of affordable housing policies has grown apace during the past two decades, with housing affordability as a policy issue rising ever more quickly on the agendas of numerous governments in very recent years. Before examining the rationale, form and consequences of affordable housing policies later in the chapter, we consider first the meaning of affordability. In particular, the chapter puts forward the idea that this commonly used term is really a label for a number of closely related housing, social and economic issues. The chapter goes on to examine affordable housing policies in a number of countries, and to assess the impacts of these. The chapter presents a case study of the use of planning agreements in the UK as a policy lever to deliver a greater supply of affordable housing units.

At a simple level, the housing affordability problem relates partly to the ongoing cost of housing, and partly to household income levels. Ongoing housing costs may take the form of rents or monthly mortgage payments. Of course, residential landlords may be private companies or individuals levying market rents, or social or other not-for-profit landlords charging below market rents with allocations policies reflecting housing needs. The monthly cost of housing to owners will largely reflect house price and mortgage interest rate levels; however, other factors come into play because we should expect a relationship between housing quality and ongoing maintenance costs, and between the income or credit worthiness of households and their marginal mortgage costs. Returning to the original point, a simple definition of housing affordability is based on the cost of housing, given household income. For this reason, ratios of housing costs (or prices) to household incomes are a popular, but problematic, measure of housing affordability problems in many countries. Some adjustment to such measures is possible in an effort to improve the responsiveness of indicators to the true incidence of housing affordability problems. For example, Meen et al. (2005) put forward the lower quartile owner-occupied house price to lower quartile household earnings as a preferred measure. Others have defined affordability as meaning rent levels that can be met by working households without support from state benefits.

A number of important factors combine to further complicate the issue, hence appropriate definition, of housing affordability. One of these factors is that the housing stock in most developed countries tends to be diverse in terms of the size, age and quality of housing units. Given that the stock is inherently durable, any process of change in terms of household composition or location represents potential for mismatch between demand and the supply possibilities that can be generated from the housing stock. Allied to this, housing units of similar size, age and design are generally not scattered randomly within an urban area, but tend to be found in spatial clusters (see Chapter 2). This gives rise to the possibility that mismatch between supply and demand will not necessarily be uniform within an urban housing market, but may vary at the neighbourhood level.

This 'spatial mismatch' argument for state intervention to promote a supply of affordable housing has become a cornerstone for policy intervention in recent years, particularly in the UK. It has been argued that an adequate supply of affordable housing is necessary to ensure the attraction and retention of 'key workers' (Barker, 2004). The issue here is that many such workers have nationally negotiated income levels that do not fully reflect regional differences in housing costs (Fingleton, 2008). In a particularly expensive region, or in a region based around an extensive metropolitan housing system, accessing affordable housing either locally or with the benefit of commuting can become literally impossible for key workers such as local government employees, school teachers, emergency services employees and so on. One implicit argument in the rationale for 'mixed communities' policies in the UK is that social welfare is enhanced when there is adequate provision of locally available services in all residential locations.

There is an inherently spatial dimension to the concept of housing affordability. Given that housing units are spatially fixed, occupancy of a given unit implies consumption of neighbourhood-level attributes and services at a level and quality available in the particular neighbourhood in which that housing unit is located. This potentially gives rise to difficult and normative policy questions: Is a low income household always to be considered adequately housed if their physical housing requirements are met? Accessibility to schooling, healthcare, public transportation, amenities and employment opportunities vary spatially within urban housing markets. This particular issue raises a related question over the appropriate unit of geography in which to calculate or measure affordability-related housing problems. When house prices and rents are high, a logical housing strategy for some low-income households may be to consume physically adequate housing in locations with a poor level of local services, amenities and employment opportunities. Indeed, reporting primarily on the US experience, Bogdon and Can (1997) point out that spatial clustering of low-income households in inner-city locations acts to deprive low-income households of decentralised employment opportunities as well as higher-quality services and living environments. They also argue that very-low-income renters are more likely to report neighbourhood problems and to assign a lower rating of their own neighbourhood than higher-income renters (see a discussion of the socio-spatial interpretations of housing spaces in Chapter 8).

It is important to note that households, like the housing stock, are also compositionally diverse. It does not follow that each member of a given household will alter the households' housing requirements or its equivalent income in a uniform way. For example, addition of children or elderly relatives to a household will increase housing requirements, but not necessarily household income or perhaps in only a modest fashion. Addition of a working adult to a single working adult household may have little or no impact on housing requirements, but will increase household income. This fact suggests a need for the consideration of household composition in an adequate definition of housing affordability, an argument examined in more detail later in the chapter.

Returning to the issue of defining housing affordability, it is clear that the term describes a complex and inter-related set of housing, social and economic issues. Bogdon and Can (1997) highlight three dimensions of housing problems often considered in assessment of housing need: physical adequacy, affordability and overcrowding. They note that, in 1990, 90% of households reporting one of these problems faced an affordability problem in particular, which seems to emphasise the housing costs and household income dimension of the problem. Yet, to some households a deliberate strategy of under-consuming housing (overcrowding) or consuming housing with poor amenities will be a logical response to high housing costs relative to income. For this reason, the concept of housing affordability potentially encompasses official definitions of the minimum tolerable quantity and quality of housing that a household should expect to access. Some commentators have emphasised the importance of housing need and housing quality in relation to the definition of housing affordability. For example, Stone (2006a: 151) defines housing affordability as: '... an expression of the social and material experiences of people, constituted as households, in relation to their individual housing situations.' This definition succinctly moves the focus from the simple level of house prices or rents given income and suggests the roles of housing size, quality, location, neighbourhood effects and household size in determining affordability.

CAUSES OF AFFORDABILITY PROBLEMS AND JUSTIFICATIONS FOR INTERVENTION

Policy interest in the concept of housing affordability can be justified on a number of grounds, as briefly outlined in the previous section. A leading argument put forward by the Barker Review of Housing Supply and Affordability in the UK (Barker, 2004) centres around the accessibility of housing to 'key workers', or public service employees with administratively rather than market-set income levels. As mentioned in the last section, this argument emphasises social welfare ideas that are also reflected in the UK's planning policies designed to promote mixed communities. An underlying argument is that housing can be viewed as a merit good, such that the welfare of society as a whole can be considered as higher if it can be demonstrated that all households can access a defined minimum standard of housing (Whitehead, 2007). Whitehead (2007) summarises two other leading arguments. The first is that housing costs represent a large proportion of most households' living costs with the result that a rise in house prices (or rents) has the potential to have a disproportionate impact on the standard of living, particularly of low-income households. The second is that household income levels are distributed unevenly. Households on low incomes may be left unable to afford necessities even after securing the minimum available quantity and quality of housing given that the house price and rent level will be set by demand from the majority of households in society.

In the UK in particular, there has been sustained debate about the underlying causes of declining levels of housing affordability. Focusing mainly on the ratio of owner-occupied house prices to household incomes, the Barker Review (2004) examined the supply side of the housing market in some detail. Among the key conclusions of the Barker Review were the arguments that the low level of new-build housing supply and low responsiveness to house price change in the UK have been leading factors in the high levels of growth in real house prices in the long run, together with associated declining housing affordability. The Barker Review, having been commissioned by HM Treasury, sets out a number of largely economic impacts, including escalating latent housing demand and restricted labour mobility. The key recommendations of the Barker Review focus particularly on the planning system, acknowledging that land supply is the main constraint to increasing the supply of housing. Among other things, the Barker Review proposed regional affordability targets (now abolished by the UK Coalition Government elected in 2010) and called for a stronger evidence base to monitor the levels of construction output required to deliver improved affordability.

The UK Government's decision to commission the Barker and Miles Reviews (Barker, 2004; Miles, 2004) might be interpreted as an underlying suspicion that there is 'something different' about the housing market in the UK. While Barker focused on the apparently low level of new-build supply and low price elasticity, Miles examined the speculative and short-term nature of the mortgage market in the UK, characterised at the time by the image of householders aggressively pursuing the most competitive remortgage deals every couple of years as introductory rates ended.

Returning to some of the Barker conclusions, other analysts have emphasised the role of the demand side of the housing market. For example, Matlack and Vigdor (2008) note that inelastic supply, in the context of stable demand, will not necessarily lead to a crisis of affordability. Their work focuses on the demand side, and they put forward the hypothesis that outcomes in one market sector may depend on demand in other market sectors. More specifically, they contend that high demand in the upper end of the market may cause a rise in prices at the lower end of the market. This argument finds sympathy in other branches of housing economics research (see Rothenberg et al., 1991, for example) and it seems no coincidence that the recent surge of interest in housing affordability has been paced with the publication of many studies examining the growth of second homes and holiday homes, suburbanisation and declining affordability in rural housing markets, and the growth of private residential investment. Indeed, adopting a behavioural analytical standpoint, it is easy to understand how society's wealthier households, having driven up prices (and therefore capital returns) in the upper end of the housing market, would seek new investment opportunities. Thus, the coincident growth of the 'buy to let' market in the UK and rising incidence of second and holiday homes plausibly be regarded as having some impact on affordability in housing markets and market segments not traditionally in demand by wealthier households.

Matlack and Vigdor (2008) limit their reasoning to direct occupation demand and the issues of substitutability and filtering. They argue that, as demand rises for upper end of the market properties, the extent to which prices will rise in other market segments depends on how far households in the upper end of the market can view alternative properties (or market segments) as substitutes. A second way in which demand in one market segment may overflow to other segments is through the conjectural process of 'filtering'. This concept argues that as society's wealthiest households periodically trade up into the highest available quality housing, so they leave behind what was previously the highest available quality as an opportunity for society's next wealthiest stratum to trade into. Through this process, new development or refurbishment aimed at the highest income groups of society may create new housing opportunities for households of all, or most, income groups. Extending this line of reasoning, sustained growth in the income of society's wealthiest households will cause these households to seek out higher-quality housing options. What is less clear is the process by which this could cause a rise in prices of lower housing market segments. Despite this, Matlack and Vigdor (2008) present empirical results, in a US context, suggestive that low-income households begin to reduce consumption on housing as income inequality rises. They also find that rents in the market as a whole respond to a rise in income in the right-hand tail of the income distribution.

Some further evidence of potential overstatement of the importance of the supply inelasticity argument is also presented in the case of the Republic of Ireland. Norris and Shiels (2007) point out that the supply response in that country was relatively elastic during the 1990s, owing partly to a more permissive planning system compared with the UK and partly to interest rate reductions during this period. Their conclusion is that a combination of macroeconomic conditions and inflationary fiscal policies is largely to blame for diminishing levels of housing affordability as these fuelled house prices, partly by encouraging growth in second homes.

Perhaps the most commonly cited argument about the underlying causes of declining housing affordability relates to the role of land-use planning. In the UK, theoretical and empirical studies have featured prominently in the literature since the early 1980s (see, for example, Cheshire and Sheppard, 1989; Evans, 1991). A key argument is that planning, by reducing the supply of land and the responsiveness of land supply for a particular use, acts to reduce the supply of new-build housing. In the long run, this reduced supply of new-build housing gradually builds latent demand such that pressure within the system, or mismatch between the needs of households and the profile of the housing stock, drives up prices or rents. Beyond the UK, Moore and Staburskis (2004) note that zoning ordinances in Canada set a minimum quality threshold for housing development. They point out that if this level is set too high, then low-income households may not be able to afford the defined minimum quality level of housing.

This line of reasoning introduces an interesting paradox because an important justification for land-use planning and development control is that state intervention to promote the separation of incompatible land uses, ordering of urban growth and design standards should increase social welfare. Yet, Gurran et al. (2008) make the point that when affordable housing is spatially separated from centres of employment opportunities, then traffic congestion and pollution can be expected to occur – a widely accepted set of consequences acting to lower social welfare. Quigley et al. (2001) and Moore and Staburskis (2004) note that growth in affordability problems increases the risk of homelessness, though not necessarily in a straightforward way. In addition, Stone (2006a) makes the point that housing deprivation is not restricted to poor affordability. Overcrowding, insecurity of tenure, poor housing quality and unsafe or inaccessible locations are also important aspects of deprivation. Households with the means to purchase adequate housing, but failing to do so, can be deemed as having pursued this path through choice. Otherwise, an aspect of housing deprivation is revealed. A further interesting dilemma is posed by Stone (2006a), by referring to: '... those households that *do* appear to have an affordability problem, yet are 'overhoused'...' (Stone, 2006a: 155).

Assuming that land-use planning really is partly responsible for the growth of affordability problems, it seems compellingly appropriate that planning should be used to mitigate them. Interestingly, this family of arguments also appears to lie at the root of the justification for what has become a prominent set of housing affordability interventions in the UK: the use of planning agreements to promote affordable housing supply. Crook and Whitehead (2002) summarise this set of arguments effectively by suggesting that the capture of betterment value for rechannelling into affordable housing provision may partially justify the inflationary effect of local planning policies on house prices.

There has been a long debate in the UK regarding appropriate policy interventions intended to capture betterment, for channelling into affordable housing, infrastructure and other forms of planning gain. This debate has resulted in a sustained rise in the use of planning agreements in the UK, a form of legal contract in which developers receive planning permission while committing to a range of obligations. These policies are examined in more detail later in the chapter. Yet, some commentators have sounded a cautionary note, particularly in response to the notion of national-level planning gain policies. For example, Crook and Whitehead (2002) have shown that a flat rate levy designed to pay for affordable housing would reduce economic rent of landowners with a minor impact on supply only in high-demand housing market areas. In lower-demand areas, the effect of a flat rate would be to reduce supply. This part of the debate helped to lead the then Office of the Deputy Prime Minister, now Communities and Local Government, to consider the introduction of 'market signals' into the planning system. Among the ideas considered were the possibility that the planning system could be compelled to identify and release more land for housing development if affordability became a particular problem in a local authority area.

Meanwhile, evidence reviewed by Newhaven Research (2008) suggests that the economic costs of procuring affordable housing through the planning system may not simply be transferred to landowners, but may have impacts on product quality, developers' profits and the purchasers of 'non-affordable' units on sites with an affordable housing component. They also point to evidence that a rise in affordable housing completions through the use of planning agreements in the UK has been at least partially offset by a reduction in 'traditional' affordable housing developments by housing associations, relying on social housing grant. They go further, making the point that affordable housing units delivered through planning agreements may be more expensive than those procured through the traditional route, potentially leading to a reduction in affordable supply overall.

DEFINING HOUSING AFFORDABILITY PROBLEMS

Earlier in the chapter, a simple approach to defining housing affordability was defined: this was based on construction of measures of the ratio of house prices to household incomes. Some of the difficulties inherent in this approach were also introduced. In this section, the arguments are developed further and a number of alternative measures of housing affordability are examined.

Perhaps the most striking difference between the UK-, European- and Australian-based studies, and those originating in North America, is the relative importance of housing costs as a proportion of income. Implicit in this difference in approaches are the issues of housing quality and standards. For example, Stone (2006a) criticises the UK approach to affordable housing policy for ignoring the question of housing quality and goes on to note that the issue of housing affordability is not practically separable from the issue of housing standards.

Over the past 10 years or so, a broad consensus has emerged in North America that housing costs with respect to income are a more important measure than simpler price-to-income ratios. Stone (2006a) notes that in the USA there is a widely accepted view that the ratio of housing cost to income is the appropriate indicator of affordability. He notes that a ratio of 25% of income until the early 1980s, and 30% since then, is an accepted indicator of affordability. Bogdon and Can (1997) describe households paying more than 30% of income for housing as facing an 'excess cost burden', and those paying more than 50% a 'severe cost burden'.

Policymakers and researchers in Australia have adopted a similar measure for quantifying housing affordability: housing stress. Housing stress can be broken down into mortgage and rental stress. The measure typically defines households to be in housing stress if they pay over 30% of their gross household income on housing costs (Yates and Gabriel, 2006). As many households in higher-income brackets may actually make a choice to spend over 30% of gross income on housing costs, the measure is usually refined to incorporate only those households in the lowest two income quintiles paying at least 30% of their income on housing costs. This is known as the 30/40 rule (Yates, 2007).

The housing costs to income indicator has a number of practical, as well as intuitively pleasing, aspects. For example, Bogdon and Can (1997) point out that ad hoc limits on income are often used by landlords and mortgage providers to ensure that renters or borrowers are likely to have the means to pay the rent or mortgage. Indeed, banks and other mortgage lenders often refer to these calculations as 'affordability checks'.

The use of an arbitrary benchmark of housing costs as a proportion of income effectively removes the focus from housing costs, to the ability of households to pay for other, non-housing, goods and services. This can be defined as the 'budget standards' approach to housing affordability (Stone, 2006a). This approach encapsulates the residual income concept. Given the cost of a standardised basket of household consumer items (such as food, clothing, utility bills and so on), the amount remaining from a household's income can be viewed as a residual that might be directed towards the consumption of housing. If this residual is inadequate to secure sufficient quality and quantity of housing, then a given household is taken as unable to access affordable housing, or might be described as being unable to access affordable housing of a minimum desirable quality and quantity. An alternative viewpoint is that if households, having met their essential housing costs, cannot then afford to purchase what is defined as an essential basket of goods and services, then this household can be defined as in 'housing-induced poverty'. This concept was introduced by Kutty (2005) as an indicator of households without the resources to consume a minimum or subsistence level of non-housing goods and services after paying for housing costs. This follows Stone's (1993) earlier definition of 'shelter poverty', but is calculated slightly differently using a more up-to-date basket of non-housing goods and prices.

Despite their intuitive appeal, the budget standards approach is not without either conceptual or empirical difficulties. Bogdon and Can (1997) describe percentage of income affordability measures as conceptually flawed given that these do not control for differences in preferences between households or for variation in housing quality. As examples, they suggest that households deliberately consuming more housing, or higher-quality housing, may misleadingly appear to have an affordability problem based on ratio of housing costs to income. A potentially more serious problem is that some households may have such a low income that they cannot realistically approach the expenditure of 30% of their income on housing and yet cover the cost of necessities.

Stone (2006a) makes the point that what many households pay for housing is not necessarily what they can afford, but a function of economic and social circumstances. Some households will over-consume, while others under-consume. An important argument is that a normative standard of housing affordability is therefore meaningless, assuming that households are rational utility maximisers – some households will deliberately choose to under-consume housing, or consume poor-quality housing, in order to promote consumption of other goods and services. However, Stone (2006a) also notes the greater flexibility with which households can address such choices as household income rises. It is also worth noting that Kutty (2005) argues for housing-induced poverty as a measure of household distress, but not necessarily a good indicator of well-being. This is because spatial variation in house prices, rents and housing quality imply potentially different levels of well-being, even holding affordability constant. Underlying this set of arguments is the idea that a perfectly rational, utility-maximising household may choose to under-consume housing in a bid to consume a desired level of neighbourhood-level services. This poses a considerable policy difficulty: such a household might appear to be in housing-induced poverty and/or in housing distress, but as a consequence of a non-housing-related consumption choice.

Empirical difficulties with the budget constraints approach emphasise measurement issues, particularly in relation to income. For example, Bogdon and Can (1997) note that percentage of income affordability measures are based on current, rather than permanent, income. Logically, long-term affordability problems are of greater concern to policymakers than short-term or transitory difficulties. They describe a combined supply- and demand-side indicator which they refer to as a 'housing affordability mismatch' indicator (see also Nelson, 1994). This form of indicator is constructed by dividing renting households into a number of income categories, and housing units into rent and size categories. It is assumed that housing units are allocated to households based on match between household size, and the size of the housing unit, but subject to the constraint that households will not pay more than 30% of their income. The affordability mismatch indicator is simply the ratio of the number of housing units affordable to the households of a given income category (with values below 1.0 taken as suggestive of an affordability problem).

In an effort to abstract the analysis of affordability from the issue of household choice, Thalmann (2003) uses a residual income standard and examines the problem from the point of view of affordability of a basic physical housing standard given household income. This clarifies the issue by moving the focus away from actual housing costs, given income, towards hypothetical housing costs, and effectively controls for the issues of deliberate housing under- or over-consumption, as well as the issue of housing quality. Earlier work (Thalmann, 1999) emphasised a proposed composite affordability indicator, including rent-to-income ratio, a measure of housing quality and housing consumption elements.

Bogdon and Can (1997) note the potential use of supply-side measures as indicators of affordability problems in the USA. In particular, they suggest that vacancy rates provide a measure of household difficulty in accessing housing in a market overall. They go on to suggest that vacancy rates at different levels will be useful for revealing if there are specific difficulties accessing affordable housing for lower-income households. This is suggestive of the idea that housing markets have a 'natural' or equilibrium vacancy rate – an idea widely applied in the analysis of housing (and commercial real estate) markets, particularly in the North American context. Bogdon and Can (1997) also describe more direct measures of housing affordability, including the estimated number of unsubsidised housing units renting for below a threshold monthly rent considered affordable for low-income households. However, they point out similar difficulties with the supply-side measures to those affecting demand-side indicators. For example, these indicators say little about the size, location or quality of housing units.

As briefly mentioned earlier in the chapter, one potentially fundamental problem with price-to-income measures of affordability is their ignorance of housing circumstances, including household composition and size. Stone (2006a) concludes that housing affordability, as a concept, is sensitive to both household composition and income level. Stone (2006b) further argues that larger and lower-income households can afford less than 25% of income for housing than smaller and higher-income households. He emphasises the non-linearity between disposable income and ability to pay for housing. This line of reasoning emphasises the potentially important role of income inequality in the housing affordability problem. It also argues for measurement of housing affordability on the basis of price to equivalent income – an adjusted measure of income accounting for household size and composition. The residual income approach to calculating housing affordability has growing support in Australia. This approach applies budget standards to different household types – e.g. two adults and two children – which, when removed from disposable income, determines the residual income remaining to pay for mortgage or rental costs (Hulse et al., 2010). This residual can then be compared to actual housing expenditure or potential expenditure to determine affordability.

Matlack and Vigdor (2008) describe the development of affordable housing policy in the USA as being prompted by post-1980 trends of declining housing quality and rising housing costs for lower-income households. They contend that the same period has seen a significant rise in inequality, defined both in income and housing terms. Moore and Staburskis (2004) also argue that, in Canada, rising income inequality is closely associated with rising incidence of households with affordability problems. They point out that house prices were stable during much of the 1990s, yet growing income inequality gave rise to marked growth in affordability problems. Using traditional North American measures of housing affordability, they focus particular attention on households paying more than 30% and more than 50%, respectively, of their gross income on shelter. They find that the number of households paying more than 50% tripled between 1982 and 1999.

APPROACHES TO STATE INTERVENTION

Whitehead (2007) outlines three broad category of policy interventions that might be used to tackle housing affordability problems: (i) actions to reduce the average price of housing; (ii) policies designed to promote higher household incomes or to lower house prices (or rents) specifically for households unable to access housing; and (iii) policies intended to reduce housing costs to allow the consumption of housing in line with defined minimum standards. In a detailed international review of housing affordability policies, Gurran et al. (2008) categorise policies as:

- housing supply levers
- barrier reduction strategies
- preserving and offsetting the loss of low-value housing
- incentives for new-build affordable housing
- incentives for dedicated affordable housing within new developments.

They describe housing supply levers as policies designed '... to enable a steady release of new land for housing to stabilise the land market. To be effective, the land must be located in areas where existing or potential demand is focused' (Gurran et al., 2008: 28). This form of intervention lies at the heart of proposals set out by Barker (2004) and followed up in a more formal research context by Meen et al. (2005) and Leishman et al. (2008). Thus, in the UK, affordability targets have been linked explicitly with rates of owner-occupied, new-build housing supply in the long run. More precisely, the long-run econometric models supporting these policy discussions postulate the ratio of house price to household earnings as a partial function of the ratio of households to dwellings. This, of course, is subject to change over time through demographic and migratory effects, and through the rate of net additions to the housing stock (new-build completions less demolitions).

Barrier reduction strategies (Gurran et al., 2008) might be viewed as a form of 'positive planning' and could include speedier planning consents for preferred forms of development. However, speedier consents linked with more heavily public sector initiated or controlled development processes might also fit under this description. Incentives for new affordable housing encompass direct or positive incentivisation policies such as the experimental Housing and Planning Delivery Grant[1] in the UK. In countries with more strictly defined land-use policies, or zoning, enhancements in permitted development densities in return for development designs that include elements of affordable housing could be described as a form of direct incentive.

Gurran et al. (2008) suggest that affordable housing policies in the USA emphasise two main areas: the reduction of barriers to affordable housing development (particularly through the offering of tax credits to developers of such housing) and the use of 'inclusionary zoning' (the exaction of voluntary or mandatory developer contributions through the planning process). However, rent control and rent subsidy policies are also in use, though with mixed results. For example, Kutty (2005) presents empirical evidence that seems to support the idea that direct rent subsidies reduce housing-induced poverty, but that rent control policies have no clear impact.

What is clear from the review of literature presented in this chapter is that affordable housing policies in many countries tend to emphasise the role of housing supply, and are often geared towards boosting the supply of specifically affordable new-build housing units. Yet, it is worth sounding two cautionary notes.

First, a set of policies predicated on booming housing market conditions may become ineffective following a fundamental change in such conditions (as evident at the time of writing). Crook et al. (2002) and Lerman (2006) point out that strong macroeconomic and local housing market conditions are necessary to sustain the effective use of planning approaches to facilitate private sector contribution to affordable housing supply.

Second, a well-designed policy intervention should target underlying problems, rather than merely the most clearly evident symptoms. To understand fully the importance of this, it is worth returning to the discussion about the causes of affordability problems earlier in the chapter. In particular, we should consider whether low and irresponsive supply of new-build housing is the main root cause, or whether housing affordability problems are driven more heavily by growing income and wealth inequality than currently acknowledged. The former, of course, suggests a form of policy intervention that emphasises the promotion of new-build housing supply generally. Policies designed to encourage provision of affordable units specifically are a special case of this justification. The latter (income and wealth inequality) can be broken down further. Rising inequality could be the result of a general societal rise in income and wealth that stops short of society's poorest households, thus leaving them further behind over time. Alternatively, inequality may result if society's wealthiest households see a rate of income and wealth rise that outstrips all other households.

This additional question of whether it is the left- or the right-hand side of the income distribution that is changing has important implications for appropriate policy interventions. In the first of these hypothetical examples, policy interventions might logically boost the income of society's poorest households to ensure consumption of an adequate quantity and quality of housing. In the second of the examples, a form of redistributive taxation might be a more appropriate intervention than the promotion of additional affordable housing units.

AFFORDABLE HOUSING DELIVERY IN THE UK

In the UK around 60% of all affordable housing is delivered through planning policy. In England and Wales, the main legal basis for delivery is set out in Section 106 (S106) of the Town and Country Planning Act 1990. The original intention of the policy was to mitigate the loss or damage to the local area caused by a development but the policy now ensures that planning agreements negotiated between the developer, landowner and local authority address a wide range of issues by placing obligations on the developer of a specific site. A planning agreement contains a wide range of these obligations and is negotiated between the local planning authority, the landowner, developer and any other body with a legal interest in the land. Obligations can include financial payments to the local authority for specific services – for example, contributions to local education services – or may be physical works completed by the developer themselves such as the provision of open space within a development or the construction of a local library. Affordable housing is just one of many obligations that may form a planning agreement but, unlike the majority of obligations, it is a material consideration and the local planning authority can refuse planning permission on the grounds that the development contributes insufficient affordable housing given local housing need.

The use of S106 agreements has grown rapidly since their introduction and especially in the last 10 years. The most recent study estimating the value of developer/landowner contributions through the policy placed the sum at £5 billion in England alone for 2007/08 (Crook et al., 2010). Affordable housing was the single biggest contributor at around £2.6 billion, followed by obligations linked to transport and open space. A new system designed to deliver local infrastructure, the Community Infrastructure Levy (CIL), was introduced in April 2010. The CIL allows a charging authority to levy a fee on development to fund local infrastructure. This replaces S106 agreements, although affordable housing contributions fall outside the CIL and will continue to be negotiated between the landowner, developer and local authority. Following the change of government in 2010, the future of the CIL looks uncertain.

The actual provision of affordable housing as part of a development is a complex, negotiated process. Almost all local authorities in England and Wales now have an affordable housing policy written into their development plan documents and almost two-thirds have a planning officer in-house to monitor agreements (Crook et al., 2010). Local planning authorities typically set out their affordable housing requirements as a percentage of the total residential development. For example, a requirement of 30% affordable housing would seek a contribution of 30 affordable units out of a total of 100 units developed on a site. The policy may also define a required tenure balance between social rented units and other forms of affordable housing such as key worker accommodation. The policy must be supported by evidence of local housing need, traditionally gathered through specific housing need studies but now more likely through housing market assessments. These studies lay the foundation for the affordable housing requirements of individual authorities, although the policy is also influenced by regional guidance. Table 20.1 describes some typical affordable housing requirements in England (see also Monk et al., 2008).

Affordable housing contributions are negotiated and can be delivered in a number of ways, including:

- on-site provision of completed units transferred to a registered social landlord (RSL)
- on-site provision of land transferred to the local authority or a RSL
- provision of completed affordable units off site
- off-site provision of land transferred to the local authority or a RSL
- payment of a financial sum.

The funding of units is complex but usually involves a combination of developer/landowner subsidy and government grant. The developer/landowner will often provide the land for free and sometimes a subsidy on the cost of constructing the units. A combination of central government funding and RSL resources are used to purchase the affordable units from the developer. One of the main benefits of the S106 policy is the development of affordable units in areas that would normally be outside the cost limits of RSL organisations, usually because of the land cost element. The developer subsidy brings

Table 20.1 Affordable housing policy examples

Local authority	Land value	Affordable housing requirement	Method of provision and tenure
South East, commuter belt	High	30%	Completed units sold to a RSL at an 'appropriate' price. Tenure to be negotiated
East Midlands, rural town	Medium	35%	Developer provides on-site land or completed units. 50/50 split between social rented and shared ownership
South West, small city	Medium to high	40%	Ideally 75/25 social rented/shared ownership. Units on site constructed by developer. Sold to RSL at reduced cost, to be agreed between RSL and developer
East, urban commuter belt	High	30%	On-site provision with social rented housing forming 75% of the contribution. Developer has to build units. Completed units purchased by RSL at an agreed price
Inner London	Very high	50%	Tenure split of 70/30 social rented/intermediate ownership. This is to be provided in the form of free land, given to a RSL, or in the form of completed units, sold to the RSL at a price agreed between the RSL and developer
North, large city	Medium	25%	Affordable housing must contribute towards creating a mix of housing. Exceptionally, off-site provision or a financial contribution in lieu of on-site provision may be accepted

RSL, registered social landlord.
Source: Data collected as part of research for Crook et al. (2006, 2008, 2010) and Monk et al. (2008).

costs within acceptable limits, widening the geography of affordable housing provision (Crook et al., 2006).

The size of the final developer subsidy will depend upon the negotiation process and the economics of the development. Contributions are maximised where the developer has been able to negotiate a land price with the landowner that reflects the contributions required by the local authority. In this case it is the landowner rather than the developer subsidising the affordable housing and other planning obligations. This is why the most effective policies are those which provide the developer with the greatest level of clarity and certainty. Where the developer has already purchased the land, any contributions not factored into the purchase price will come from the developer's profit margin, so resulting negotiations with the local authority are fierce. Financial appraisals are a common negotiating tool, with developers using them to demonstrate how a contribution will undermine the viability of a development, and local authorities (many of which employ consultants due to a lack of in-house skills) countering with their own financial assessments.

Although a local authority may have a clear policy within its development documents, the final outcome may be very different because of the specific economics of the site; there may be unusual development costs for example, and also the relative negotiating skills of the parties. In a strong housing market with rising house prices and land values, the developer will be reluctant to let a profitable development opportunity pass and may agree to all contributions required by the local authority. In a market where the developer has purchased land at a price which no longer reflects the current development value due to falling house prices, the developer will do everything he can to minimise contributions, as otherwise the development profit may be eroded entirely.

The success of the S106 policy is due, in part, to a period of rising land and house prices. In a declining market, affordable housing policies have the potential to delay or even postpone development unless a local authority adopts a flexible approach. It remains to be seen how the current market downturn affects affordable housing contributions.

Table 20.2 shows the outcome of a number of development applications gathered from recent research, including details of agreed planning obligation contributions (Crook et al., 2006, 2008, 2010; Monk et al., 2006, 2008). It should be noted that local authorities with strong housing markets that have built up an experienced negotiating team tend to secure more planning obligation contributions. This reflects first, what the development site can contribute in terms of value and second, the negotiating skills of the local authority (see Crook et al., 2006, 2008, 2010).

S106 affordable housing contributions have become increasingly important to the overall delivery of affordable accommodation in England. Table 20.3 shows how the number of affordable units completed through S106 contributions has grown threefold between the 2000/01 and the latter part of that decade. There is a regional pattern to contributions due to land values in the South being able to support higher contributions, but also the overall geography of housing completions in England.

Table 20.4 describes the proportion of all affordable housing delivered through the planning system. S106 contributions to all affordable housing peaked at 65% in 2006/07, followed closely by 2008/09. The table shows how the government has become increasingly reliant on private sector contributions to deliver affordable housing. Although the government still provides funding for the majority of S106 units, these units require not only the provision of land, often for free within market housing developments, but also construction cost subsidies in high value areas.

There are a number of arguments against relying on the planning system and the private sector to deliver affordable housing. Using the planning system to levy a tax, albeit a hypothecated one, sits uncomfortably with many, particularly those that end up paying. However, the policy has been used successfully to arrest a steep decline in the total supply of affordable housing. Supply fell to under 30,000 units in 2002/03 but rose to over 50,000 in 2008/09 and 2009/10 due to a combination of increased S106 contributions and government funding. The policy has also contributed to the balanced and mixed communities policy of the UK government by integrating affordable and market housing on many development sites and delivering affordable housing in areas that would otherwise have been too expensive for RSLs to develop units. Outcomes rely on a clearly defined policy with a strong evidence base and lengthy negotiations between the relevant parties and, as a result, is costly in terms of resources. Outcomes also rely on a rising housing market to maximise contributions and the housing conditions of 2008/10 may well have a significant effect on the future provision of affordable housing through S106.

CONCLUSIONS

This chapter has examined causes and definitions of housing affordability as a policy relevant to the social and housing market issue. In fact, the idea that housing affordability is not a single issue was set out very early in the chapter. It is now widely accepted that 'affordability' describes a collection of related housing, social and economic issues and that the issue of housing affordability is not readily separable from related problems such as housing quality minima and overcrowding. The chapter goes further by noting the role that some commentators ascribe to household income, wealth inequality and household composition. In particular, there is some evidence to suggest that single measures of affordability may be inadequate to

Table 20.2 S106 residential contribution examples

Authority	Development	Affordable housing contribution	Other planning obligations
Rural, South East	102 residential units	40% affordable housing	Provision of car parking, open space and landscaping
London	Residential development, 92 units	37% affordable housing	Public art, environmental improvements, footways
Urban, West Midlands	Residential development 61 units	25% affordable housing	Creation of a pedestrian/cycle route, education contribution
Urban, North East	Residential development of 149 units	20% affordable housing	Football pitch; recreational equipment; bus subsidy; community facilities
Urban, East Midlands	Residential development of 476 dwellings	28% affordable housing	Education contribution, public open space contribution, highways contribution, public transport contribution, replacement scout hut, management and retention of swimming pool, public art contribution
Rural, East	Residential development of 119 dwellings on a brownfield, green belt site	80% affordable housing	Highway works, education contribution, sustainability issues
Urban, South West	Residential development, 60 units	25% affordable housing	Highway works contribution, near-site leisure contribution, on-site play equipment, education contribution, green travel pack
Rural, East	Residential development 15 dwellings	35% affordable housing	Education and public open space contribution
London	371 residential units	35% affordable housing	Financial contributions to education, employment, healthcare, public transport, air quality monitoring, environmental sustainability practices, public realm, public art, construction charter, and equal opportunities statement
London	Residential development, 204 units	35% affordable housing	Parking restrictions, public art (in-kind), health contribution, education contribution, local employment and training clause
Rural, South East	Residential development of 269 houses/61 flats	25% affordable housing	Extension of burial ground, highway works, bus service, education, extension of doctor's surgery
Urban , South East	Residential development of 68 units	30% affordable housing	Carbon neutrality contribution, education contribution, leisure and sport contribution, public transport contribution, social infrastructure contribution
Urban, Yorkshire	Residential development of 38 units	15% affordable housing	Legal costs, public open space contribution
Rural, South West	Residential development of 152 dwellings	33.3% affordable housing	Provision of sports facilities including football pitches, cricket square, pavilion and car parking. Contributions towards education, dog and litter bins, libraries, green commuting, public art, waste recycling
Rural, West Midlands	Residential development of 20 units	30% affordable housing	Contributions for cycling, education, off-site POS and recycling
Rural, South East	Residential development of 64 dwellings	30% affordable housing	Contributions to transport strategy, community facilities, open space provision

Source: Crook et al. (2006, 2008, 2010) and Monk et al. (2006, 2008).

Table 20.3 Affordable units completed in England through S106 agreements

Government office region	2000/01	2001/02	2002/03	2003/04	2004/05	2005/06	2006/07	2007/08	2008/09	2009/10
North East	290	206	160	133	186	269	594	450	504	871
North West	777	785	733	812	631	1097	624	998	1,016	1,145
Yorkshire & the Humber	336	502	515	760	681	1039	797	1,009	878	437
East Midlands	778	761	1,155	898	1,294	1,914	2,089	2,605	2,601	2,471
West Midlands	660	985	1,117	1,199	1,672	2,046	1,610	1,950	2,314	2,046
East of England	1,103	1,511	1,780	2,426	2,710	3,229	4,018	4,236	4,216	4,607
London	1,958	1,904	3,153	3,895	3,725	4,981	7,468	6,774	9,851	8,212
South East	2,298	2,394	2,923	3,577	5,327	6,168	5,569	5,884	7,439	5,912
South West	1,097	1,255	1,056	2,680	1,949	3,126	3,069	3,204	3,467	3,366
England	9,297	10,303	12,592	16,380	18,175	23,869	25,838	27,110	32,286	29,067

Source: Housing Strategy Statistical Appendix, Communities and Local Government, 2001/02–2009/10. http://www.communities.gov.uk/housing/housingresearch/housingstatistics/housingstatisticsby/localauthorityhousing/dataforms/

capture the complexity of housing problems more widely defined.

To an extent, the complexity of housing-related problems may lie at the root of what is, for some, a search for an appropriate set of indicators of housing affordability. As noted above, ratios of house prices to incomes may not adequately capture the importance of diverse household composition in defining housing problems. The 'budget constraints' or 'residual income' approaches to defining affordability move the focus away from

Table 20.4 S106 completions as a proportion of all affordable units in England

Government office region	2000/01	2001/02	2002/03	2003/04	2004/05	2005/06	2006/07	2007/08	2008/09	2009/10
North East	13%	33%	49%	23%	29%	38%	65%	49%	37%	50%
North West	14%	33%	24%	32%	25%	37%	26%	26%	26%	27%
Yorkshire & the Humber	17%	34%	39%	44%	55%	65%	41%	39%	32%	16%
East Midlands	18%	41%	63%	47%	72%	74%	78%	73%	72%	63%
West Midlands	12%	34%	40%	42%	49%	60%	59%	48%	49%	42%
East of England	25%	51%	64%	70%	70%	70%	74%	66%	67%	72%
London	21%	27%	43%	44%	44%	57%	67%	58%	78%	64%
South East	29%	34%	48%	49%	70%	72%	66%	66%	70%	63%
South West	28%	35%	33%	79%	56%	72%	75%	52%	60%	58%
England	21%	35%	44%	50%	55%	64%	65%	56%	63%	56%

Source: Housing Strategy Statistical Appendix, Communities and Local Government, 2001/02–2009/10. http://www.communities.gov.uk/housing/housingresearch/housingstatistics/housingstatisticsby/localauthorityhousing/dataforms/

costs, to ability to pay for non-housing consumption. Housing stress is conceptually similar and applies notional maximum housing costs as a proportion of income, often only to households in the lower quartiles of income. This restriction effectively deals with higher-income group households deliberately spending a high proportion of their income on housing. However, the fact that some lower-income households may underconsume housing is more difficult to deal with, particularly where such choices lead to the consumption of very poor quality housing, or insufficient housing given household size and composition.

Social welfare arguments represent a key justification for state intervention designed to promote a defined minimum provision of housing at a defined affordable price. In addition, affordability problems may have wider impacts on access to employment opportunities, access to public services, levels of urban congestion and the incidence of homelessness. In the UK, in particular, the importance of attracting key workers with largely nationally agreed pay structures features prominently in the arguments for policy intervention.

Common examples of affordability policy interventions include those designed to promote supply generally and policies aimed at promoting supply of specifically affordable units. In the UK, low and irresponsive supply levels are a leading justification for policy intervention and the case study summarised in this chapter shows that these policies have been remarkably successful over recent years: in England and Wales, around 60% of all affordable housing is delivered through planning policy. However, there are significant regional differences and, in particular, Scotland and Northern Ireland have adopted a more cautious approach to the procurement of affordable housing units through the planning system. Despite these differences, using the planning system as a policy tool to promote affordable housing arguably fits well with the logic of having a planning system to raise social welfare by ordering and regulating land use and development. It also accords with the principles of betterment taxation.

While the case study shown in this chapter focuses on much of the UK, affordable housing policies in many countries emphasise the role of housing supply, and are often geared towards boosting the supply of specifically affordable new-build housing units. However, there must now be concerns that changing market conditions will undermine the effectiveness of such policies.

Despite the international dominance of supply-side policies, the review in this chapter suggests the need for periodic critical appraisal of policy interventions. The discussion has examined evidence that rising income inequality may pull up rents or house prices in the market as a whole. It may be appropriate to view this evidence alongside the fact that growth of policy interest in affordability has come alongside growing incidence of second homes and the continued development of private residential investment markets in many countries. There therefore exists some tentative evidence to suggest that the growth of affordability problems may relate not to the circumstances of lower-income households per se, but to the circumstances of those that are better off in society. In that context, the international plethora of housing affordability policies designed to promote supply to lower-income households seems to address a symptom, rather than a cause, of housing market inequalities.

NOTE

1   The Housing and Planning Delivery Grant was announced by the UK Government in 2006. Initially devised as an experimental three-year programme, its purpose was to 'provide an incentive to local authorities and other bodies to respond more effectively to local housing pressures to meet local demands and to incentivise improvements in the planning system' (improve delivery of housing and

other planning outcomes (Communities and Local Government, 2006: 5). The UK Government's allocation of £146 million for the third year of the grant (2010/11) was cut in June 2010, meaning that the programme ran for only two years of the intended initial three years.

REFERENCES

Barker, K. (2004) *Review of Housing Supply. Delivering Stability: Securing our Future Housing Needs. Final Report – Recommendations*. London: HM Treasury.

Bogdon, A.S. and Can, A. (1997) Indicators of local housing affordability: comparative and spatial approaches, *Real Estate Economics*, Vol. 25, No. 1, pp. 43–80.

Cheshire, P. and Sheppard, S. (1989) British planning policy and access to housing: Some empirical estimates, *Urban Studies*, Vol. 26, pp. 469–485.

Communities and Local Government (2006) *Housing and Planning Delivery Grant: Consultation Paper*. London: Communities and Local Government.

Crook, A. and Whitehead, C. (2002) Social housing and planning gain: Is this an appropriate way of providing affordable housing? *Environment and Planning A*, Vol. 34, pp. 1259–1279.

Crook, A., Currie, J., Jackson, A., et al. (2002) *Planning Gain and Affordable Housing: Making it Count*. York: Joseph Rowntree Foundation.

Crook, A.D.H., Monk, S., Rowley, S. and Whitehead, C.M.E. (2006) Planning gain and the supply of new affordable housing in England: Understanding the numbers. *Town Planning Review*, Vol. 77, No. 3, pp. 353–373.

Crook, A.D.H., Rowley, S., Henneberry, J.M.H. and Watkins, C.A. (2008) *Valuing Planning Obligations in England 2005/6 Update*. London: Communities and Local Government.

Crook, A.D.H., Rowley, S., Henneberry, J.M.H., Watkins, C.A. and Smith, R. (2010) *The Incidence, Value and Delivery of Planning Obligations in England in 2007–08: Final Report*. London: Communities and Local Government.

Evans, A.W. (1991) 'Rabbit hutches on postage stamps': planning, development and political economy, *Urban Studies*, Vol. 28, No. 8, pp. 853–870.

Fingleton, B. (2008) Housing supply, demand and affordability, *Urban Studies*, Vol. 45, No. 8, pp. 1545–1563.

Gurran, N., Milligan, V., Baker, D., Bugg, L.B. and Christensen, S. (2008) *New Directions in Planning for Affordable Housing: Australian and International Evidence and Implications. AURI Final Report No. 120*. Sydney: Australian Housing and Urban Research Institute.

Hulse, K., et al. (2010) *The Benefits and Risks of Home Ownership for Low-Moderate Income Households. AHURI Final Report No. 154*. Melbourne: Australian Housing and Urban Research Institute.

Kutty, N.K. (2005) A new measure of housing affordability: Estimates and analytical results, *Housing Policy Debate*, Vol. 16, Issue 1, pp. 113–142.

Leishman, C., Gibb, K., Meen, G., O'Sullivan, T., Young, G., Chen, Y., Orr, A., and Wright, R.E. (2008) Scottish model of housing supply and affordability: final report, Edinburgh: Scottish Government.

Lerman, B.R. (2006) Mandatory inclusionary zoning – the answer to the affordable housing problem, *Boston College Environmental Affairs Law Review*, Vol. 33, No. 2, pp. 383–416.

Matlack, J.L. and Vigdor, J.L. (2008) Do rising tides lift prices? Income inequality and housing affordability, *Journal of Housing Economics*, Vol. 17, No. 3, pp. 212–224.

Meen, G. et al (2005) *Affordability Targets: Implications for Housing Supply*. London: Office of the Deputy Prime Minister.

Miles, D. (2004) *The UK Mortgage Market: Taking a Longer-Term View. Final Report and Recommendations*. London: HM Treasury.

Monk, S., Crook, A.D.H., Lister, D., et al. (2006) *Delivering Affordable Housing through Planning Policy: Outputs and Outcomes*. York: Joseph Rowntree Foundation.

Monk, S., Burgess, G., Crook, A.D.H., Rowley, S. and Whitehead, C.M.E. (2008) *Common Starting Points for S106 Affordable Housing Negotiations*. London: Communities and Local Government.

Moore, E. and Staburskis, A. (2004) Canada's increasing housing affordability burdens, *Housing Studies*, Vol. 19, No. 3, pp. 395–413.

Nelson, K.P. (1994) Whose shortage of affordable housing, *Housing Policy Debate*, Vol. 5, No. 4, pp. 401–442.

Newhaven Research (2008) *Delivering Affordable Housing through the Planning System in Scotland*. Edinburgh: Chartered Institute of Housing.

Norris, M. and Shiels, P. (2007) Housing affordability in the Republic of Ireland: Is planning part of the problem or part of the solution, *Housing Studies*, Vol. 22, No. 1, pp. 45–62.

Quigley, J.M., Raphael, S. and Smolensky, E. (2001) Homeless in America, Homeless in California, *Review of Economics and Statistics*, Vol. 83, No. 1, pp. 37–51.

Rothenberg, J., Galster, G.C., Butler, R.V. and Pitkin, J.R. (1991) *The Maze of Urban Housing Markets: Theory, Evidence and Policy*. Chicago, IL: University of Chicago Press.

Stone, M.E. (1993) *Shelter Poverty: New Ideas on Housing Affordability*. Philadelphia, PA: Temple University Press.

Stone, M.E. (2006a) What is housing affordability? The case for the residual income approach, *Housing Policy Debate*, Vol. 17, No. 1, pp. 151–184.

Stone, M.E. (2006b) A housing affordability standard for the UK, *Housing Studies*, Vol. 21, No. 4, pp. 453–476.

Thalmann, P. (1999) Identifying households which need housing assistance, *Urban Studies*, Vol. 36, No. 11, pp. 1933–1947.

Thalmann, P. (2003) "House poor" or simply "poor"? *Journal of Housing Economics*, Vol. 12, No. 4, pp. 291–317.

Whitehead, C.M.E. (2007) Planning policies and affordable housing: England as a successful case study, *Housing Studies*, Vol. 22, No. 1, pp. 25–44.

Yates, J. (2007) *Housing Affordability and Financial Stress. Research Paper No. 6*. Sydney: Australian Housing and Urban Research Institute.

Yates, J. and Gabriel, M. (2006) *Housing Affordability in Australia. Research Paper No. 3 for National Research Venture 3: Housing Affordability for Lower Income Australians*. Sydney: Australian Housing and Urban Research Institute

21

Housing Subsidies

Judith Yates

INTRODUCTION

Governments at all levels and of all persuasions use a wide array of financial and other incentives to reduce the cost of housing. These range from explicit grants directed towards provision of housing for the most disadvantaged in society to implicit tax concessions that benefit the most advantaged. Over time, the rationale for such intervention in the housing market has shifted as economic, social and political circumstances have changed. This, in turn, has resulted in shifts of the relative importance of different types of assistance over time. In light of the instability and uncertainty surrounding housing and finance markets in the first decade of the 21st century, an assessment of what subsidies are currently provided, the question of what subsidies should be available and a re-examination of what their purpose should be is one that has become increasingly important.

Section 2 (Types of subsidies) begins by presenting a taxonomy of demand-side and supply-side subsidies provided directly or indirectly as upfront or recurrent grants, tax breaks and other more or less explicit financial support to different parts of the housing sector. This is followed by an indication of the rationales used to justify these interventions in housing markets in which traditional rationales (such as the classic public finance equity, efficiency and stabilisation roles) that influence market outcomes but leave stakeholders free to operate within the constraints defined by the market are distinguished from enabling rationales that improve the operation of the housing market. The scope of these rationales highlights the broad range of objectives that housing subsidies might be used to address. Section 3 (Rationales for housing subsidies) concludes with a brief overview of how the types of subsidies employed and the objectives they were intended to meet have changed in the past 50 or so years. These changes have resulted from changes in political, ideological and economic frameworks but have also been in response to an increased understanding of the impact that housing has on a broad range of non-shelter as well as shelter outcomes and to increasing evidence on the consequences of different subsidies in relation to objectives related to both sets of outcomes.

The substantive part of the chapter is Section 4 (Examining the consequences of housing subsidies), which provides a review of this evidence. It examines separately the evidence for subsidies targeted specifically to address the shelter needs of lower-income households and that for subsidies provided more generally. Targeted subsidies are dominated by explicit assistance provided through both demand and supply subsidies to renters. Untargeted subsidies are dominated by implicit assistance provided to homeowners through the tax system.

The results of the review point to the conditions under which explicit demand- or supply-side subsidies might be more effective in meeting shelter needs but also highlight the importance of examining the impact of each on the non-shelter outcomes identified as some of the rationales for intervening in housing markets. They suggest that much of the evidence on non-shelter outcomes is conflicting and fragmented and suffers from considerable methodological problems. Many of these problems arise because of the difficulties of identifying the ways in which the assistance provided has an impact. These difficulties arise because of the multi-dimensional nature of outcomes associated with, and characteristics of, housing. The results of the implicit assistance provided, however, are clear cut. There is relatively little evidence that it serves any of the stated objectives related to either shelter or non-shelter outcomes.

The chapter concludes by raising a number of questions that need to be asked in relation to the types of subsidies provided for housing, by pointing to a number of unresolved issues and to the research than might be undertaken to resolve these and by highlighting the methodological problems that such research will need to address.

TYPES OF SUBSIDIES

Classification of the vast array of subsidies that apply to housing is by no means simple because of the variety of instruments that are employed and the range of functions that they are intended to serve. Subsidies can be classified by the manner in which they are provided (explicitly or implicitly), by whether they are targeted at housing consumers or producers, according to whether they are directed to renters or owners, or whether they are provided on an upfront basis or on a recurrent basis as an ongoing means of support. They can also be classified according to the objectives they are intended to serve. This section focuses primarily on the first set of criteria. The range of functions they are intended to serve is covered in Section 3 (Rationales for housing subsidies). Evaluation of the different approaches follows in Section 4 (Examining the consequences of housing subsidies).

Explicit and implicit subsidies

Subsidies to housing drive a wedge between the market price and cost of production and both change the level of output from that which would have occurred in the absence of the intervention. In this subsection, subsidies are described as explicit or implicit (direct or indirect), according to whether or not the revenue obtained from the tax or the cost of providing a subsidy appears in government budget statements.

The term 'subsidy' is widely used as a means of describing the wide range of financial and other incentives that governments provide to reduce the cost of housing. At the simplest level, subsidies can be defined as payments or financial aid given by the government to individuals or groups, often with the proviso that the activity or enterprise being supported is in the public interest. At a broader level, however, subsidies might be regarded as any measure that affects consumption or production of housing.[1]

The simpler of these definitions confines analysis of housing subsidies to explicit grants such as housing allowances provided to consumers of housing services to improve affordability, deposit assistance provided to purchasers of housing to improve access to owner-occupied housing or direct grants to social housing producers and other such forms of intervention. The extent of such assistance is simple to measure: it is reflected in government budgets and hence is transparent.

The broader definition expands the analysis to implicit subsidies that may not involve explicit budgetary outlays. It adds such forms of assistance as cost- or income-geared rents (at below market rates) to tenants of publicly owned housing, subsidised loans to home purchasers and tax concessions to consumers and producers of housing, none of which appear as budget outlays but all of which reduce the cost of housing to the end user. These forms of intervention result in particular individuals or groups being treated more favourably than would have been the case without government intervention. The extent of such assistance, however, is more difficult to measure, not least because the benchmark against which such assistance should be measured can be (but is not always) more difficult to define. For example, estimating market rent for public housing in regions where there is no substantive and comparable private rental market can be difficult. In turn, this makes it difficult (but not impossible) to determine the extent of the implicit subsidy for a tenant paying what is presumed to be a below-market rent. By way of contrast, determination of the extent of the subsidies to recipients of below-market rate loans, at least in principle, is more straightforward because of the ubiquity of market-based financial institutions. In practice, however, the variety of mortgage instruments and the likelihood that different lending criteria (regarding loan-to-valuation ratios, etc.) are applied can make even this not a straightforward exercise.

The most significant implicit subsidies that benefit housing consumers, however, are those that arise from so-called tax expenditures. Tax expenditures occur when departures from the generally accepted or benchmark tax structure produce a favourable tax treatment of particular types of activities or groups of taxpayers. Examples of the ways in which tax expenditures arise are through tax exemptions, concessions and deductions, which reduce taxable income; preferential tax rates, allowances, rebates or offsets, which reduce the tax payable on income; tax credits, which are subtracted from taxes due; and tax deferrals arising from delayed recognition of income or from allowing in the current year deductions that are properly attributable to a future year. Tax expenditures subsidise both consumers and producers of housing. Examples of the former are those that exempt owner-occupiers from various taxes; examples of the latter are income tax credits for investors in affordable housing. The former, however, dominate.

Demand- and supply-side subsidies

Subsidies that are directed towards consumers of housing are often described as subject-oriented subsidies, or demand-side subsidies; those directed towards producers of housing are often described as object-oriented subsidies, or supply-side subsidies. Together, economic circumstances, economic ideology and changing objectives for housing policies have resulted in significant shifts in the relative emphasis placed on supply-side or demand-side subsidies over time, at least in relation to explicit subsidies. Supply-side subsidies in the form of direct government grants for provision of social housing were dominant during the 1950s and 1960s, but during the 1970s and 1980s there was a switch towards increased use of explicit demand-side subsidies, primarily in the form of housing allowances directed towards individuals (for example, Hills et al., 1990; Oxley, 2007; Stephens et al., 2005). Since then, however, an increasing awareness of the weaknesses of 'a one size fits all' approach to housing policy, partly as a result of an increasing awareness of the different strengths and weaknesses of each approach in different circumstances and partly because of a broadening of the objectives of housing policy, has resulted in a less ideological approach and moves towards using both demand and supply subsidies in conjunction with each other (for example, Lawson and Milligan, 2007).

Increasingly, supply-side subsidies are being provided less explicitly, often as an inducement to encourage private investment to achieve specific goals (such as provision of affordable housing or urban renewal). Examples are the use of tax concessions for investors in affordable housing (such as the low-income housing tax credits) and the provision of government-owned land for affordable housing. These are often supplemented with housing allowances, which remain a common form of direct demand-side assistance, albeit one that is often limited to renter households and not always available to owners.

Many purchasers, however, benefit directly from demand-side assistance in the form of upfront grants for deposit assistance to first home buyers and through subsidies that affect the cost and supply of finance for housing. Examples are the use of subsidised savings for home purchase and subsidised mortgages for lower-income buyers. Implicit subsidies that reduce the cost of finance for purchasers (such as mortgage guarantees) also should be regarded as implicit demand-side subsidies, as they generally result in an increased demand for housing. Many of these subsidies are targeted to specific groups such as low- or moderate-income households.

In many countries, however, the implicit tax expenditures indicated above (Explicit and implicit subsidies) outweigh all other demand-side subsidies. While estimates of these vary according to the institutional tax arrangements in each country, and according to whether they are measured depending on whether housing is regarded as a consumption good or an investment good, there is widespread agreement about the extent to which tax expenditures to owner-occupiers outweigh any other form of housing assistance provided.[2] Carasso et al. (2005) and Yates (2003) provide examples of the extent to which tax expenditures outweigh other forms of assistance for, respectively, the USA and Australia. Haffner (2002) and Ellis (2006) provide overviews of the tax treatment of housing in a range of countries.

Summary

The above description of housing subsidies has classified these according to whether they were provided explicitly or implicitly, whether they were directed primarily towards consumers or producers of housing and, within each of these classifications, whether they were focused specifically on owners or renters. Similar classifications have been employed in many of the substantive studies of housing subsidies. Recent examples can be found in Carasso et al. (2005), Gibb and Whitehead (2007), Hoek-Smit and Diamond (2003), Katz and Turner (2003), Le Blanc (2005) and Mayo (1999). A number of these studies omit the important implicit subsidies to owners and others add variations to the list. Gibb and Whitehead (2007) and Katz and Turner (2003), for example, add regulation as a separate category. Hoek-Smit and Diamond (2003) treat separately subsidies that are targeted to specific locations from those that are directed towards specific individual households and distinguish between entitlement and budget-constrained subsidies. They also treat separately those that operate through the housing finance system. For the purposes of this chapter, these differences are immaterial. The key purpose of this chapter is to provide a broad assessment of the general approach to providing housing subsidies against the reasons for why such subsidies might be thought to be needed.

RATIONALES FOR HOUSING SUBSIDIES

One of the reasons for such a wide array of approaches to providing housing assistance is that there are as many reasons why governments intervene in housing markets as there are ways of doing this.

In his report prepared for the World Bank, for example, Mayo (1999) distinguishes justifications and motivations for housing subsidies on the basis of both 'traditional' and 'enabling' rationales. The report provided background material for a 1988 United Nations policy document, in which it was recognised that 'good' housing policy was important not only for the performance of the housing sector but also for the economy as a whole. The economic events emerging from the sub-prime crisis of two decades later have served to highlight the importance of this broad view of why intervention in housing markets might be important.

Each of these rationales is consistent with what Berry (1983) describes, respectively, as 'market-supplementing' and 'market-supporting' policies. The focus on these two rationales reflects a trend towards increased reliance on the market and away from a third rationale that can be added to these two: that of 'market-replacement', which covers those forms of intervention designed to override the outcomes that arise from price and income interventions. Direct provision of public housing allocated by administratively determined criteria rather than market-based criteria is a classic example of a market replacement approach. One justification for such an approach could be a desire to provide renters with greater security of tenure than might be possible because of the inherent conflict over property use and exchange rights when housing is provided by a private landlord. Because there is often a fine line between market-supporting and market-replacement approaches, these two are combined below under the enabling rationales.

Traditional rationales

Traditionally, market-supplementing policies have been implemented to improve allocative and productive efficiency and to affect what would be the outcomes of the market in the absence of government intervention (see, for example, Gibb and Whitehead, 2007; Grigsby and Bourassa, 2003; Le Blanc, 2005; Mayo, 1999).

In relation to the efficiency rationales, they serve to address sources of market failure arising, for example, from negative and positive externalities such as:[3]

- health outcomes arising, for example, from dwelling standards;
- education outcomes arising, for example, from the contribution of security of tenure to a stable learning environment;
- the impact of housing on labour markets arising, for example, from the relation between location of housing and employment opportunities;
- the impact of housing on community cohesion arising, for example, from linkages between housing and crime, or social capital, or neighbourhood effects.

In the main, these rationales provide a justification for subsidies that are directed towards housing that, typically, is at the lower end of the market but, to a lesser extent, are also used to justify intervention that supports a particular tenure because of its specific characteristics (such as homeownership or social housing). Although interventions to improve health or education outcomes, access to employment and community cohesion can be justified on the grounds of the positive and negative externalities associated with these outcomes, they can also be justified on the grounds of improving fairness and increasing equality of opportunity.

The role of housing subsidies in improving equity or reducing societal injustice provides the second of the traditional rationales for intervention. Such intervention is justified to:

- promote improved housing as a so-called 'merit good', consumption of which is considered beneficial to society as a whole;
- promote opportunities for the generation of income and accumulation of wealth through homeownership; and to

- ensure that housing does not undermine wider equity objectives related to the distribution of income and wealth.

Associated with these criteria is a concern that households have access to adequate and affordable housing.

The type of interventions for these purposes vary because of the dual role of housing as an investment good (providing a source of wealth accumulation) and as a consumption good (providing shelter). In order to meet the first of these roles, homeownership must be accessible (and sustainable). In order to meet the second of these roles, housing must be affordable (hence, the focus on cost and price). Indirectly, intervention for these two purposes is consistent with the traditional public finance rationale for government intervention for distributional purposes.

A further traditional rationale is that of stabilisation (and growth enhancement). This provides a justification for using housing subsidies to:

- stimulate the economy and/or to protect vulnerable households when recession looms in order to mitigate the impact of any downturn and to
- encourage housing investment in order to address housing shortages and to stimulate growth.

Enabling rationales

This role of housing subsidies in promoting stabilisation and growth is consistent with, but considerably different from, the second of Mayo's overarching rationales for justifying government intervention through housing subsidies. In broad terms, traditional rationales justify market supplementing subsidies that alter the parameters within which the market operates but leave the various stakeholders free to operate within the constraints defined by the market (these stakeholders are the consumers, producers, financers and regulators of housing). Enabling rationales, on the other hand, justify market-supporting subsidies that affect the constraints within which these stakeholders operate.[4]

Many of the subsidies directed towards enabling policies arise because of a shift towards increased reliance on the market and a desire to directly address perceived sources of inefficiency in the market rather than concentrating on the consequences. They recognise that housing markets do not operate in a vacuum but are defined by a set of legal and institutional constraints that define their operation. In affecting these constraints, enabling rationales for housing subsidies tend to be broader than traditional rationales.

In broad terms, an efficient housing market is one which responds quickly to changes in demand by providing housing at the lowest cost possible where and when it is demanded. Because of specific characteristics of housing, housing markets, however, do not always exhibit this feature.[5]

A market-supporting approach to policy, for example, recognises that a well-functioning mortgage market is required in order for potential housing demand to be translated into effective demand. A well-developed planning system (with serviced land ready when and where required) is essential to ensure that increases in housing demand can be translated into increases in housing supply. A well-developed system of property rights is required to ensure that housing consumers and producers can be confident about their housing decisions. Enabling policies assist in meeting these requirements.

With existing mortgage markets, for example, marginal borrowers may be unable to borrow to their capacity because they are seen as being more likely to default when there are adverse economic circumstances beyond their control. Subsidies that provide guarantees to lending institutions or that provide mortgage insurance to low-income borrowers and, more generally, approaches to facilitate risk management in mortgage markets are examples of enabling policies that facilitate the operation of mortgage markets. Housing finance subsidies are particularly important in relation to facilitating access to housing as an investment asset. In a series of papers, Hoek-Smit and Diamond provide a comprehensive overview of some of the types of subsidies employed, the failures in the housing finance market that they address and why housing finance rather than housing might be subsidised (Hoek Smit, 2003, 2006; Hoek-Smit and Diamond, 2003).

Within the planning system, recognition of housing as providing access to a range of services and employment opportunities and its role in contributing to the efficient operation of the labour market by ensuring essential workers can be housed where they are needed have led to an increased focus on the role of planning as an enabling policy to override the outcomes of the uncontrolled operation of the housing market. Additional justifications for land-use intervention are provided in terms of broader objectives of reducing social exclusion, ensuring community involvement, supporting local democracy and protecting and enhancing the environment. Interventions via the planning system, and particularly those that improve supply responses, have also been justified as a response to the extent to which changes in house prices have contributed to inequalities in wealth (for example, Barker, 2004: 1).

Changing objectives

Emphasis on the various rationales for intervention in housing markets has changed over time within countries, with the result that there has been a change in the types of housing subsidies employed.[6] For example, the earliest forms of intervention were implemented in response to the emerging public health problems arising from poor sanitation and overcrowding associated with industrialisation and its associated urbanisation. Most of this was in the form of regulations associated with building codes and town planning. In the more immediate past, intervention in the post-war period of the 1950s and, to a lesser extent, the 1960s, was justified to redress extreme shortages of housing, to promote economic growth as part of the post-war reconstruction and to provide 'homes fit for heroes'. In many countries this was achieved primarily through direct provision of public housing, although early schemes to promote homeownership were also implemented.

Throughout the 1970s and 1980s, however, many of the immediate supply problems had been resolved and moves towards neo-liberal economic and political ideologies centred on free markets, self-sufficiency and choice led to attempts to reduce public spending and to a switch from production to consumer subsidies. Housing allowances (often a surrogate for income supplements) replaced the earlier 'bricks and mortar' subsidies (for example, Kemp, 2000). In Maclennan's view, these 'shifts in housing and related policies reduced not just the scale but the scope, vision and effectiveness of housing policies.' (Maclennan, 2008: 424). During this period, it could also be argued that the emergence of high inflation contributed to a change in the focus on housing from its role as a consumption good providing shelter to a role as an investment good providing a hedge against inflation. Alongside of this came a change in focus from policies directed towards (social) rental housing to those directed towards homeownership. As Santiago and Galster (2003) have argued, housing goals evolved from providing public housing for shelter to providing opportunities for escaping from welfare and buying one's own home (and associated moves to self-sufficiency). This switch was often connected to subsidy rationales associated with a desire to improve education and labour market outcomes. Because of the constraints that high inflation imposed on access to mortgage finance (through front-end loading) much of the emphasis on housing subsidies to support access to homeownership was directed through housing finance subsidies.

Many of the constraints within the mortgage market, however, were removed by the enabling policies associated with the financial deregulation and liberalisation of the 1990s and reductions in nominal interest rates as inflation decreased. This resulted in a significant increase in the availability of credit for housing which, along with a number of underlying structural factors, was a major contributor to the widespread *fin de siècle* house price boom (see, for example, Ellis, 2006; Chambers et al., 2007).[7]

By the 1990s, declining affordability and increasing housing cost burdens resulted in a shift in the focus of housing policies to access and affordability. Policies to improve affordability generally, but not exclusively, focused on renter households, initially in the form of demand-side subsidies (such as rent allowances or their equivalent), consistent with earlier moves away from supply-side subsidies (often associated with declining public support of social rental housing). Policies to improve access generally, but not exclusively, have been targeted at home buyers, again often in the form of demand-side subsidies such as deposit assistance grants (in the extreme case through the deep discounts provided in the UK Right-to-Buy policies introduced in the 1980s) or through policies that assisted with increasing access to housing finance.

At the risk of oversimplification it could be argued that, by the turn of the century, the effects of broad economic changes and the effects of past housing policies had contributed to a significant redirection in housing policies. These effects of different types of housing subsidies are considered in the following section. By the turn of the new century, Maclennan (2008: 424) has suggested that, although the focus on addressing rental burdens for low-income households remained, a number of countries were again rethinking their housing policies and were focusing, instead, on the role of housing reinvestment in neighbourhood renewal.[8] Likewise, Turner (2007) has suggested that, increasingly, intervention in housing is being justified on grounds that go well beyond narrow concerns such as affordability:

> Increasingly, however, researchers, policymakers, and advocates outside traditional housing policy circles are recognizing that housing is critical to advancing other national issues and agendas. In general, the lack of affordable housing stands in the way of economic productivity and undermines the fundamental premise that full-time workers should be able to achieve a decent standard of living for themselves and their families. More specifically, the concentration of affordable housing in distressed inner-city neighborhoods traps low-income children in places where public schools are failing and life-chances are limited. The lack of affordable housing in the right places also contributes to environmentally and fiscally wasteful patterns of sprawl and decentralization (Turner, 2007: 6).

Since the 1970s, however, when the wealth accumulation role of housing began to emerge, very little attention has been paid to the impact of the increasing implicit subsidies that have grown as homeownership has grown and as housing has become the major form of wealth accumulation for most households. High housing costs and low affordability have their corollary in substantial increases in the wealth levels of residential property owners. This results in a widening gap between them and the sizeable minority of households who do not own residential property. Increasing disparities in wealth add to the risks of a loss of social cohesion (for example, Forrest and Kearns, 2001: 2128) and to social polarisation (for example, Marsh and Mullins, 1998). In addition, intergenerational equity is compromised by the increasing disparities between those who gain access to homeownership and those who do not.

By the end of the noughties, the dominance of the impact of the sub-prime crisis in the USA on global financial and housing markets (and economies) had resulted in increased recognition of the impact of housing on the economy in general and on financial markets in particular. It has led to a questioning of lending practices that have encouraged vulnerable households into homeownership and to a reassessment of the importance of policies directed towards sustaining rather than promoting homeownership.

EXAMINING THE CONSEQUENCES OF HOUSING SUBSIDIES

As suggested above, changes in direction in the objectives of housing policies (and hence the rationale for intervention) have reflected greater attention being paid both to the effectiveness of different types of subsidies on housing specific objectives and to their impact on what are being recognised as important supplementary objectives. Direct provision of public housing in large estates in the 1950s, for example, served to meet immediate shortages of housing but created neighbourhoods of disadvantage that have had counterproductive effects on many public housing tenants. The switch to greater reliance on housing allowances in the 1970s had the potential to create greater housing choice for eligible recipients but often introduced high effective marginal tax rates with a capacity to create workforce disincentives and poverty traps.

Changes in direction in the objectives of housing policies also reflect greater attention being paid to the need for a clearer understanding of the factors that contribute to the source of the problems being addressed. Hoek-Smit and Diamond (2003: 4) illustrate this by pointing to the need to understand, for example, whether building codes and land-use regulation intended to ensure dwellings meet minimum standards or address environmental concerns contribute to a shortage of affordable rental housing or whether problems in accessing housing finance are due to incomplete housing finance markets, inadequate property rights or to macroeconomic conditions that have little to do with the housing finance system. This explanation of a change in direction can be interpreted as needing to keep in mind the enabling role as well as the traditional roles of subsidies.

Analysis of the consequences of different forms of intervention needs to take both of these explanations for changes in the direction of housing policies into account. Because many of the reasons for subsidy intervention focus on outcomes for lower-income households, they are examined first for subsidies targeted specifically at lower-income households and then by untargeted subsidies. Both can be provided directly or indirectly and delivered as demand- or supply-side subsidies and both can have significant impacts on housing markets.[9]

Targeted subsidies

One of the major concerns with assistance provided in the form of demand-side subsidies to lower income renters (as a means of addressing many of the efficiency issues associated with housing consumption or with a desire to improve affordability for those unable to provide themselves with adequate and affordable housing) is that such assistance increases the demand for housing and, in the absence of a supply-side response, is capitalised into rents and is therefore counterproductive. Similarly, subsidies designed to increase access to homeownership for first-time buyers may simply increase house prices not only rendering the assistance ineffective for those who receive such grants but also adding to the barriers faced by would-be home purchasers in the future.

One of the major concerns with supply-side subsidies is that they crowd out private investment that would otherwise have occurred or they displace those who are already disadvantaged in the housing market. Public housing construction programmes, for example, may result in no increase in the total housing stock if they result in an offsetting decline in private housing construction. Urban renewal programmes might be so effective in improving neighbourhoods that, as with a process of gentrification, they displace lower-income households who may be unable to find alternative affordable housing.

Well-established theories suggest that the market impact of housing assistance will depend on two main factors. On the demand side, it will depend on the extent to which the assistance generates an increase in housing consumption. On the supply side, it will depend on the underlying elasticity of supply in the relevant submarket.

Demand-side subsidies

Less than a decade ago, Olsen (2001) published a review of some 75 studies that examined the impact of housing subsidies provided to low-income households. All of those reviewed are now more than two decades old (and many date back to the early 1970s). He found that all housing programmes result in substantially improved housing for the recipients of the assistance provided and that there was relatively little resultant upward pressure on rents. In part this can be attributed to the fact that take-up rates were relatively low, many of those who participated were already in adequate standard housing and did not have to move and the programmes reviewed ran for only a limited length of time.

In a study which examines impacts at a low–middle–high submarket level of disaggregation for 90 metropolitan areas, Susin (2002) suggests, on the other hand, that rent assistance provided through vouchers increased rent levels by up to 16 per cent in the low-income housing market as a result of a low elasticity of supply of low-income housing. Laferrère and Le Blanc (2004) also find evidence that increases in housing allowances contribute to increases in rents. They attribute this to collusion between landlords and tenants. From their review of the evidence of the impact of housing assistance on non-shelter outcomes, Bridge et al. (2003: xiv) conclude that the market effects of demand-side assistance remain unresolved. This reinforces the conclusion that outcomes cannot be generalised but depend on the specific contexts or location of the programmes being evaluated.

Galster et al. (1999) raise methodological concerns in examining the impact of subsidies that arise from issues of endogeneity. Their study, motivated by a concern with the impact of mobility strategies in the USA, showed there was a tendency for assisted, or subsidised, tenants, to locate in less desirable, weaker submarkets. To determine whether or not this is the case requires determination of causality. It is not clear whether low-income neighbourhoods result from an increase in the number of assisted households or whether assisted households are attracted to low-income households because that is all that is affordable. In their analysis (which addressed this issue of causality), they were unable to distinguish between a number of alternative and opposing hypotheses regarding the direction of causality and the rationale for this. One of the key methodological issues that arise from their analysis is that results can be affected by the proportion of subsidised tenants in the neighbourhood. Thus, studies that ignore this are likely to yield misleading results. Methodological issues in addressing the impact of subsidies will be returned to below (Issues). These concerns notwithstanding, Galster (1997) concluded that demand-side subsidies are unambiguously best. For some of the reasons that will be covered below, Yates and Whitehead (1998) argue that his conclusion is explained by his US view of how housing systems work and is justified only when a limited range of objectives is considered.

Supply-side subsidies

Evidence on the impact of supply-side assistance is equally problematic. The issues that have been addressed in the US literature on supply-side assistance have dealt with the market impact of public housing construction and of private construction undertaken as a result of tax credit incentives, although there is also a sparse literature on the impact of urban renewal construction programmes.

Supply-side interventions, such as direct provision of public housing or tax incentives to encourage provision of private housing affordable for lower-income households, have the potential to have a different impact from demand-side interventions. A number of studies have attempted to identify these effects with one of the key concerns being whether such supply-side assistance increases the net stock of housing or whether it simply displaces private construction that would have taken place in any case.

Murray (1999) compares the market impacts of public housing targeted on low-income households with subsidised private housing for moderate-income households and concludes that the former adds to the overall stock of housing whereas the latter crowds out unsubsidised privately provided housing.[10] He suggests this outcome arises because the former primarily provides dwellings predominantly for single parents and elderly persons, and enables these low-income tenants who are a source of latent or unmet demand to form separate households. Their doing so means that there is no reduction of demand in the private rental market. Subsidised housing for moderate-income households, on the other hand, is targeted to already-existing households. This explanation raises the possibility that housing assistance and household formation are interdependent. It also highlights the importance of recognising there are distinct submarkets within 'the' housing market.

Critics of his approach, however, have suggested that his statistical method raises some difficulties. Sinai and Waldfogel (2005) suggest that, contrary to prior expectations, demand-side programmes are more effective than supply-side programmes in creating new additions to the stock. However, they acknowledge that their result depends on the extent of excess demand from low-income households in the locality in which the impact of the assistance is felt and suggest that their attempts to control for endogeneity were, in their words, 'less than successful'. Malpezzi and Vandell (2002) are unable to reject either the hypothesis that there is either full crowding out, or that there is no crowding out associated with use of the low-income tax credit to stimulate housing production. Neither of these two studies recognises Murray's distinction between low- and moderate-income housing submarkets.

DiPasquale (1999) addresses the question of why we don't know more about housing supply in her critical review of the literature on the impact of housing assistance on housing supply. She is particularly concerned with literature that compares the impact of assistance provided through direct expenditures, with that provided by tax credits to private producers. She suggests there is support for the claim that production subsidies targeted at housing for other than low-income households tend to displace private construction, and result in no increase in stock. Housing assistance for low-income households provided through public housing, on the other hand, tends to increase the overall stock of housing. Her results and explanation are consistent with those of Murray (1999).

Overview

Based on evidence from a more recent review of US literature, Khadduri et al. (2003) outline the conditions under which demand- or supply-side subsidies might be expected to be most and least effective. Khadduri and Wilkins (2007) provide an update. This evidence suggests demand-side subsidies are generally more effective in meeting affordability objectives than are supply-side subsidies because they can be well targeted (providing support only to those who need it) and are more cost-effective than supply-side subsidies in terms of their impact on government budgets. However, they are less effective in tight housing markets (where vacancy rates are low) and in housing markets where the elasticity of affordable housing supply is low. In such cases, they could increase the cost of housing in the affordable segment of the housing market and result in a net loss of stock affordable for low-income households.

Supply-side subsidies are more effective in avoiding rent escalation in markets where the private market supply response is not adequate to meet increasing demand. They are also more effective in supporting comprehensive neighbourhood revitalization efforts and in providing opportunities for low-income people to live in neighbourhoods in which they would have difficulty using a demand-side subsidy.

These overviews focus primarily on the impact of subsidies on affordability outcomes, on the quality and quantity of housing consumed by lower-income households (usually renters) and on the budgetary costs of subsidies. They do not consider the impact of different types of subsidies on some of the broader issues raised in Section 3 (Rationales for housing subsidies) or the impact of subsidies that are not as clearly focused on lower-income households (covered below – Untargeted subsidies).

On the former, one characteristic of the changing analysis of the impact of housing subsidies has been the attention paid to their effect on broader objectives. In a review essay that summarises (US-based) literature on the impacts of housing assistance, Shroder (2002) examined not only the effects on shelter needs but also effects on a broader range of objectives including, inter alia, labour supply and human capital accumulation. He concluded that housing assistance 'is not persuasively associated with any effect on employment: positive or negative. Evidence on human capital accumulation remains conflicting and fragmentary' (Shroder, 2002: 383).

Nordvik and Århén (2005) provide evidence from Norway to support these claims in terms of labour market incentives. Stephens (2005: 122) suggests that the evidence is weak for the UK. Haffner and Boelhouwer (2005) reach the conclusion that the evidence is mixed for the US, the UK and the Netherlands. For Australia, however, Hulse and Randolph (2005: 162) found that at least a subset of recipients (viz. unemployed renters) 'face significant disincentives to working through the interaction of the tax and income support systems, with housing allowances in the private sector extending the reach of the poverty trap for private renters, and public housing rent setting deepening the trap for public renters.' Whelan (2004: 58) reaches a similar conclusion about outcomes but is more cautious about drawing conclusions about the impact of housing assistance because of difficulty of separating such assistance from receipt of more general income support.

These potentially conflicting results highlight the importance of taking into account both how different types of targeted subsidies are provided and how institutional arrangements which affect their provision might affect results.

Bridge et al. (2003) provide a review of evidence on the impact of targeted housing assistance on additional non-shelter outcomes. They also provide some insights into the possible linkages between observed effects. Questions of how or whether housing subsidies affect work incentives, for example, might be related to their impact on housing mobility. Their evidence-based review suggests (inter alia) that:

- supply-side subsidies provided through public housing are more likely to reduce household mobility than are demand-side subsidies;
- education outcomes are more likely to be associated with (both measured and unmeasured) characteristics of housing assistance recipients than with the assistance itself;
- there is evidence on the relationship between housing and health (particularly in relation to location, overcrowding and dwelling quality and design) but little evidence on the effects of housing assistance on health;
- there is some evidence of a relation between a lack of sense of community and crime, with the implication that it is allocation policies that co-locate those recipients of housing assistance who do not have a sense of community responsibility rather than the assistance itself that may contribute to poor crime outcomes;
- there is reasonable evidence that neighbourhood has an important impact on outcomes for children and adults, but attempts to

identify which neighbourhood characteristics matter and the way in which these operate have been inconclusive.

Quigley (2007: 12), for example, supports the conclusion reached in relation to neighbourhood characteristics, arguing that the externalities associated with poor housing and poor neighbourhoods (particularly those associated with high concentrations of poverty) were generally presumed large but recent (US-based) studies have failed to find strong and systematic evidence of a causal nature.

With the exception of an examination of the role of homeownership, attempts to relate neighbourhood characteristics specifically to the impact of different types of housing assistance are unchartered waters. The role of homeownership is covered below.

Untargeted subsidies

Possibly the most obvious of subsidies that are not targeted at the most disadvantaged households are explicit demand-side subsidies that support access to homeownership (such as deposit assistance schemes or subsidised home saver accounts) and implicit subsidies that reduce the cost of housing for established homeowners (such as the tax concessions leading to tax expenditures). These will be the primary focus of this section. However, there are forms of assistance that can be regarded as untargeted supply-side subsidies, such as the public provision of the infrastructure that converts raw land into serviced land and any publicly provided local infrastructure. On the supply side, much has been written on the impact of specific taxes (and, especially, on the impact of property taxes generally, and of developer charges or impact fees particularly, in relation to affordable housing) on housing supply. However, relatively little has been written on the impact of untargeted supply-side subsidies and so these are not covered here.[11]

While there is an emerging consensus that both demand-side and supply-side subsidies, along with appropriate regulatory policies, are all likely to be needed to achieve sustainable affordability outcomes in the rental sector, the issue of subsidies for owner-occupation, which result in a shift from a focus on housing as providing shelter to housing as an asset, is more problematic.

Demand-side subsidies

Demand-side subsidies that facilitate access are often seen as inequitable (in that they provide support to households with fewer affordability problems and more choices than many of those in the rental market), inefficient (in that they simply add to price pressures in the housing market) and ineffective (in that they merely bring forward purchases that would have occurred in any case). There are also concerns that encouraging vulnerable households into homeownership and exposing them to the associated risks may not be in their best interests.[12] Post 2007 events after the sub-prime crisis suggest that it also might not be in the best interest of the economy as a whole.

Belsky et al. (2005) argue that there are few studies of the financial returns to homeownership and those that do exist are strongly influenced by the cyclical behaviour of rents, house prices and interest rates following purchase as well as on the terms of their mortgage and how long they hold the home. However, they do conclude there is enough evidence (in the US environment where the income tax system allows housing costs that exceed a standard deduction to be deducted from income) to suggest:

> low-income homeowners typically gain less from owning than high-income owners who buy and sell in the same years because they get no additional value from deducting mortgage interest and property taxes. Those who end up with sub-prime loans benefit far less than owners who do not. And those who miss opportunities to refinance to lower prime rates for whatever reason come out further behind still (Belsky et al., 2005: 17).

A recent paper by Turner and Luea (2009), which addresses many of the methodological concerns of earlier studies, suggests that homeownership had an independent effect on the ability of low- and moderate-income households (in the USA) to accumulate wealth during the mid-to-late 1990s, with this being higher for each additional year of ownership and higher for high-income households than for others.[13]

Demand-side subsidies that benefit established homeowners are potentially even more problematic than subsidies that assist with access to homeownership. A number of studies have been concerned with the impact of indirect housing assistance provided to homeownership through the tax system both at an aggregate and macroeconomic level and through their distributional impact at an individual household level.

In his seminal paper on this topic, Rosen (1979) estimated that both homeownership rates and dwelling prices were higher than they would otherwise have been in the absence of the assistance provided to homeownership through the tax system. These results have been confirmed by later studies and have been updated by Green and Vandell (1999) and Capozza et al. (1997) who suggest that tax expenditures have increased US house prices by up to 15 per cent in high house price areas.[14] Bourassa and Hendershott (1992, 1995) provide supporting evidence for Australia.

Additional adverse effects of such subsidies have been well rehearsed in the economics literature. They tend to be pro-cyclical, with the result that they contribute to the boom-bust cycle in housing in relation to the capital gains tax provisions (for example, HM Treasury, 2003). Listokin (2009) suggests that they have contributed to the reduced effectiveness of automatic stabilisers in government budgets. This is of particular concern in the current economic environment, with its return to fiscal stimulation to reduce the impact of impending recession.

Subsidies such as those covered in this chapter have the capacity to increase investment in housing, and particularly in owner-occupied housing, at the expense of investment in more productive areas. In principle, this leads to a lower rate of economic growth than would otherwise be possible. McCarthy et al. (2001) provide a review of some of the literature on this issue. They also add to the economic incentive for a renter to become a homeowner sooner than they otherwise might. Dietz and Haurin (2003) suggest this might generate impacts on labour supply, wealth, fertility, investment risk and mobility.

In a formal theoretical framework, Voith (1999a) suggests they may have contributed to greater lot sizes, and hence to suburban sprawl. Voith (1999b) and Voith and Gyourko (2002) suggest they create incentives for communities to enact exclusionary zoning, which contributes to geographic sorting of households by income. These effects depend on the extent to which subsidies are capitalised into land and house prices and this, in turn, depends on the relevant supply elasticities. This conceptual work, however, has yet to be empirically tested (as claimed by Dietz and Haurin, 2003, in their systematic review of the literature on the impacts of homeownership assistance on non-shelter outcomes).

The perverse distributional outcomes associated with these subsidies have been well documented (see, for example, Carasso et al., 2005; Gale et al., 2007; Reynolds, 2007; and Yates, 2003 for recent analyses). Conclusions regarding the age of beneficiaries vary according to whether tax expenditures are assessed on the basis of housing as a consumption or investment good but unequivocally they benefit mostly those with high incomes. As Carasso et al. have argued in relation to US subsidies:

> Federal housing benefits are not distributed very rationally, efficiently, or equitably. Instead, the government bestows some rental subsidies in the form of direct outlays on only some households with modest means, while providing generous ownership subsidies in the form of tax incentives to most of those with ample means. The rental subsidies in and of themselves provide an additional barrier for low-income families to

own, while the ownership subsidies encourage excessive borrowing and inefficient wealth allocation among households that by and large already possess the means to own a home. While home-ownership is not realistic for all people – given the costs of ownership and risks involved and particular needs of some households – there is little excuse for creating a subsidy system that strongly discourages many moderate-income people from owning (Carasso et al., 2005: 15).

The key arguments for assistance that supports homeowners generally rely on the perceived economic and social benefits associated with homeownership. Comprehensive reviews of the economic and social benefits of home ownership can be found in Dietz and Haurin (2003), McCarthy et al. (2001) and Rohe et al. (2002). Increasingly, however, the methodologies that have led to these conclusions are being questioned. Aaronson (2000) and Apgar (2004) point to omitted variable biases, as does Shlay (2006: 511), who suggests that [the] 'alleged effects of homeownership may be artefacts of self-selection and the conflation of homeownership with unobserved characteristics coincident with buying homes.' Issues of the direction of causality are also of concern.

Even the informed media has begun to raise questions about the rationale for providing subsidies to support homeownership. A recent article in *The Economist* points to studies that purport to show the social benefits of homeownership and suggests that, 'on the face of it, the evidence for these claims is strong'. However, it also questions these conclusions:

> These studies, though, are not the last word. They find a link between children's education and home-owning. But is this because, as some suggest, home ownership requires parents to possess managerial or financial skills that they pass on to their children? Or is it because the people with those skills help their children at school and also buy houses? No one knows.
>
> Nor is it certain that owners always take better care of their neighbourhoods than renters do. Some studies claim that the effect in fact depends on a few public-spirited people willing to set an example. Renters can be public-spirited too.

In America areas with lots of renters tend to be transient because the typical rental period is short. In Germany, though, people rent for years. Stable neighbourhoods and widespread home ownership can go together but do not need to. As Bill Rohe of the University of North Carolina, Chapel Hill puts it, 'evidence regarding the societal benefits of home ownership is highly conjectural' (*The Economist*, 2009).

Overview

To the extent that any of the arguments in favour of homeownership can be supported, they provide an argument in favour of using subsidies to assist those who would not otherwise become homeowners into homeownership. However, the structure of assistance provided by indirect tax expenditures to owner-occupiers does not do this. The greatest support goes to households who are already homeowners. The least support goes to young lower-income home purchasers or to renters. The implicit subsidies provided through the tax system benefit homeowners, not homeownership.

As demand-side subsidies that create an economic incentive to increasing consumption of housing through homeownership, they add to price pressures in the housing market and thereby contribute to the affordability constraints faced by aspiring homeowners. This is particularly likely in areas where the supply of land is restricted, as is the case in the more central of the built-up areas of major metropolitan regions. They therefore have the potential to contribute to the forces that push lower-income households to residential location and dwelling quality decisions that are likely to be riskier in terms of the potential they provide for economic gain (Shlay, 2006: 522–524).

Recent events following the sub-prime crisis in the US have highlighted the economic and social costs (at both and individual and economy-wide level) of encouraging homeownership by lower- and moderate-income households and of failing to recognise the risks associated with such a policy.[15]

RESEARCH GAPS AND ISSUES

A few key observations can be drawn from the above overview of the evidence on the consequences of the broad range of housing subsidies that are widely employed.

Gaps

There is increasingly good evidence on the impact of housing subsidies on objectives related to a range of shelter outcomes (particularly, for example, in relation to housing consumption, housing quality, crowding and affordability). Newman (2008) provides an excellent assessment of the literature on the last three of these attributes of housing (she also covers self-sufficiency and homeownership). There is, however, less work on questioning these objectives by relating them back to the conventional rationales for intervention in housing markets. Attempting to answer this question is more likely to lead research into the more problematic area of non-shelter outcomes.

There is, for example, a considerable amount of research on the relation between housing quality and health, but there has been less focus on the causal relationships between these factors (Newman, 2008: 901) and on the relationship between the types of housing assistance provided and health outcomes (Bridge et al., 2003: 140). Similar problems arise in relation to crowding (Newman, 2008: 903).

While there is some research on issues associated with measuring or defining outcomes such as affordability, less attention is paid to asking why affordability should be an objective and for whom it should be a concern. Unaffordable housing for lower-income households might be a problem, for example, because it means such households have insufficient resources to pay for other necessities (such as health and education), to participate in community activities or to access available employment opportunities. The importance of these outcomes will vary by household type (for example, whether there are children in the household) and by the age of those in the household. Many of the concerns that might be associated with housing affordability problems are likely to arise over time. What is needed, therefore, is more use of longitudinal studies that are able to separate out (often unobservable) household characteristics that might affect outcomes from those more conventionally included in analyses.

In summary, there is a general lack of conceptual understanding about how different dimensions of housing assistance are linked to different attributes of housing and how both are linked to different non-shelter outcomes. This suggests analysis of the impact of subsidies could also benefit from greater attention being paid to the need for a clearer understanding of the factors that contribute to the problems being addressed. This can be interpreted as needing to keep in mind the enabling role as well as the traditional roles of subsidies. Hoek-Smit and Diamond (2003: 4) make a similar claim. They point to the need to understand, for example, whether building codes and land-use regulation intended to ensure dwellings meet minimum standards or address environmental concerns contribute to, say, a shortage of affordable rental housing or whether problems in accessing housing finance due to incomplete housing finance markets, inadequate property rights or to macroeconomic conditions that have little to do with the housing finance system.

Table 21.1 provides an indication of the different attributes of housing that might have an impact on a range of non-shelter outcomes. Figure 21.1 highlights some of the possible interactions between housing subsidies and shelter and non-shelter outcomes.

More needs to be known about how different forms of assistance affect these different attributes and how they, in turn, affect a range of non-shelter outcomes.

Table 21.1 Illustrative dimensions of shelter and non-shelter outcomes

Shelter attributes	Non-shelter outcomes
Tenure	Health
Tenure mix	Education
Security of tenure	Employment
Physical design	Crime
Dwelling quality	Social cohesion
Adequacy	Income/wealth distribution
Affordability	Locational advantage
Appropriateness	
Location	
Level of control	

Source: based on Bridge et al. (2003: 8).

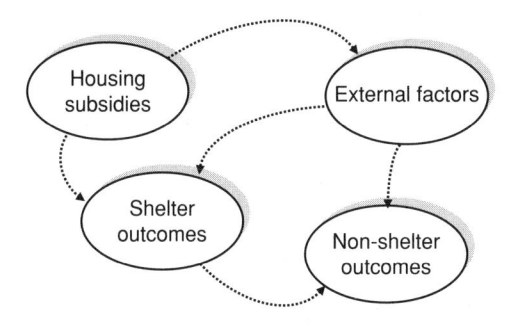

Figure 21.1 Potential causal links between housing subsidies, shelter and non-shelter outcomes.

Source: Bridge et al., 2003: 5.

Issues

Even when there is a good theoretical understanding of linkages between housing and non-shelter outcomes, however, establishing the magnitude and direction of impacts has proved problematic. A number of excellent overviews highlight the methodological difficulties that arise (for example, Bridge et al., 2003; Dietz and Haurin, 2003; Newman, 2008)

These include the following factors:

- Omitted variables: factors other than subsidies can affect both shelter and non-shelter outcomes, which is a particular problem if assistance is correlated with the omitted factor.
- Endogeneity: housing subsidies and their consequences can have an impact on relevant explanatory variables, which raises issues of causality.
- Measurement errors: there is little agreement on how quantifiable factors (such as housing quality, crowding or affordability) should be measured; factors such as cultural values that affect social norms about some of these measures are even more difficult to measure.
- Dynamic effects and cumulative causation.

A key factor that underpins all of these issues is the need to recognise the differences in local housing markets and to avoid generalising results when this is not applicable. In housing, space matters.

CONCLUSIONS

Much of the early research on the impacts of housing subsidies was undertaken at a highly aggregative level. Increasingly, it is being realised that an assessment of the impact of housing subsidies requires much more attention being paid to the ways in which these interventions are undertaken; of the institutional environment within which they operate; of the characteristics of the local, national (and even global) economy which affects the impact they have and, importantly, of identifying the pathways through which they have their effects. Only by understanding the complex system within which housing subsidies operate and the complex and competing objectives they are intended to serve and on which they have an effects, intended or otherwise, will true progress be made.

Complex policy problems are often described as 'wicked' problems, after the terminology introduced by Rittel and Webber as far back as 1973. In contrast with 'tame' problems, which are tightly defined and have readily identifiable solutions, wicked problems are difficult to define, are socially complex, are often multi-causal with many interdependencies, are often not stable or involve changing behaviour, and hardly ever sit within the responsibility of any one organisation or level of government. Finally, attempts to address wicked problems often lead to unforeseen consequences.[16] Many of the rationales used to justify a specific form of subsidy can be equated to attempting to apply a tame solution to what is a wicked problem. Not only do a number of types of subsidies employed not solve the problem but also they often exacerbate it.

Considerable progress has been made in understanding these issues over the past 50 years. Hopefully, this will continue.

NOTES

1 Although subsidies need not only cover assistance provided by governments, only such assistance will be covered in this chapter. Thus, subsidies provided by gifts or charitable donations (such as might arise if an organisation charges zero or below market value for land for affordable housing) are excluded as are examples of cross-subsidisation where one group is subsidised at the expense of another but where there is no government support provided. Haffner and Oxley (1999) discuss different ways in which the term 'subsidy' is used.

2 In most (but not all) countries, owner-occupied housing is exempted from capital gains taxes (or benefits from significant deferral of any liability); in more countries (but not all), imputed rent from owner-occupied housing is not subject to taxation but sometimes owners are permitted to deduct their housing costs. While some authors regard the tax deductibility of mortgage interest as the key tax expenditure (consistent with treating housing as a consumption good), most authors regard the non-taxation of capital gains and the non-taxation of net imputed rent (i.e. after costs are taken into account) as the more appropriate way to estimate tax expenditures. This is consistent with treating housing as an asset or investment good.

3 Bridge et al. (2003) provide a systematic review of the literature on housing assistance and non-shelter outcomes. More details on these externalities with a particular reference to homeownership can be found, for example, in Dietz and Haurin (2003) or Rohe et al. (2002).

4 Enabling policies need not only be provided through subsidies; they also are, or can be, implemented through regulation. However, in the same way that subsidies involve a transfer of resources to one party (the beneficiary of the subsidy) from another (via taxation used to fund the subsidies), regulation also essentially results in a transfer or redistribution of benefits and costs. Barr (1992) provides an argument for matching the type of intervention (e.g. regulation, direct provision, or subsidy) to specific types of market failure.

5 The standard characteristics that are seen to contribute to market inefficiencies are its heterogeneity, spatial fixity, durability, its indivisibility and its illiquidity. These contribute to 'thin' housing markets where there are only a few buyers and sellers for particular types of dwellings in any location. In such markets, prices are often volatile and assets are less liquid, with the result that prices are not known with any certainty.

6 It has also varied between countries, but this variation will be ignored here in the interests of highlighting broad common trends in OECD (Organisation for Economic Cooperation and Development) countries.

7 Ellis (2006: 4–6) provides an explanation of the relation between asymmetric information in finance markets and credit rationing. An (unintended) outcome of house price inflation is a reduction in the user cost of owner-occupied housing brought about by the interaction of house price inflation and tax expenditures which exempted owner-occupiers from capital gains taxes. This, then, added to the factors that increased demand for housing. Intended and unintended consequences of both implicit and explicit subsidies are covered in more detail in Section 4 (Examining the consequences of housing subsidies).

8 Homelessness has also emerged as a growing issue but is covered here only in so far as it is an extreme outcome of housing affordability problems.

9 Much of the material in the following sections relies heavily on the systematic review of housing and non-shelter outcomes reported in Bridge et al. (2003).

10 This study represents a return to a less sophisticated study undertaken some 15 years earlier (Murray, 1983) which concluded that all publicly assisted production crowded out private construction but which also failed to recognise the relevance of distinct submarkets in the housing system.

11 On the basis of a recent exploratory study, Goodman (2005: 19), for example, concludes that the residential property tax, as implemented, promotes low-density development, disproportionately burdens lower-valued properties and may impose higher taxes on apartment residents than on homeowners of identical incomes. For the UK, much of this is covered by the Barker Review (2004). Muellbauer (2005) provides a critique of the Barker proposals for property tax reform from the point of view of the objectives of macroeconomic stability, resource allocation, economic inequality and the environment. A recent UK official report on fiscal

stabilisation and the Economic and Monetary Union (EMU) (HM Treasury, 2003) raised the possibility of using taxes on housing to stabilise the housing sector (and therefore the economy). This report focused on the role of tax expenditures rather than on taxes, and the same approach is taken here.

12   A series of edited books in the Delft University Press Housing and Urban Policy Studies series, beginning with Doling and Ford (2003), cover many of these concerns.

13   Care needs to be taken in extrapolating results from US studies to other countries because of key differences in the system of housing finance. In the USA, for example, mortgage finance often is provided as a non-recourse loan, which means the downside risk for borrowers is limited. The predominant form of lending is also on a fixed rate mortgage, which means that households do not face interest rate risk.

14   Green and Vandell (1999) show that a revenue neutral redistribution of tax expenditures associated with mortgage interest deduction in the USA would increase house values by 10.4 per cent for low-income households. Capozza et al. (1997) impose variations in taxes across regions in the USA on a formal asset price model that takes into account variations in supply elasticities. They estimate that a 0.03 decrease in the average marginal federal tax rate would result in an overall decrease in real house prices by 5.5 per cent, with declines of up to 12.5 per cent in high-price regions. Removal of the property tax exemption would reduce overall house prices by 4.7 per cent, with declines of up to 15 per cent in high-cost regions.

15   While there is some debate over the economic benefits or otherwise of low-income households being assisted into homeownership (often because of the risks associated with such ownership), there is increasing evidence that households who become homeowners have greater household net wealth than do renters with similar socio-economic and demographic characteristics (for example, Di, 2006).

16   Rittel and Webber identify 10 characteristics of wicked problems. Those identified here are taken from Australian Government (2007).

REFERENCES

Aaronson, D. (2000) 'A note on the benefit of homeownership', *Journal of Urban Economics*, 47(3): 356–369.

Apgar, W. (2004) 'Rethinking rental housing: Expanding the ability of rental housing to serve as a pathway to economic and social opportunity', Working Paper w04-11, Joint Center for Housing Studies, Harvard University. At: http://www.jchs.harvard.edu/publications/markets/w04-11.pdf. Downloaded 28 April 2009.

Australian Government (2007) *Tackling Wicked Problems: A Public Policy Perspective*. Australian Public Service Commission, At: http://www.apsc.gov.au/publications07/wickedproblems.pdf. Downloaded 27 July 2009.

Barker, K. (2004) *Review of Housing Supply, Final Report*. HM Treasury. At: http://www.hm-treasury.gov.uk/d/barker_review_report_494.pdf. Downloaded 20 February 2009.

Barr, N. (1992) 'Economic theory and the welfare state: A survey and interpretation', *Journal of Economic Literature*, 30(2): 741–803.

Belsky, E., Retsinas, N. and Duda, M. (2005) "The Financial Returns to Low-Income Homeownership", Joint Center for Housing Studies, Working Paper W05-9, Harvard University. At http://www.jchs.harvard.edu/publications/finance/w05-9.pdf. Downloaded 29 July 2009.

Berry, M. (1983) 'Posing the housing question in Australia', in L. Sandercock and M. Berry (eds), *Urban Political Economy*. Sydney: Allen and Unwin.

Bourassa, S. and Hendershott, P. (1992) 'Overinvestment in Australian housing?', National Housing Strategy Background Paper. Canberra: Australian Government Publishing Service.

Bourassa, S. and Hendershott, P. (1995) 'Australian capital city real house prices, 1979–1993', *Australian Economic Review*, 95(3):16–26.

Bridge, C., Flatau, P., Whelan, S., Wood, G. and Yates, J. (2003) *Housing Assistance and Non-Shelter Outcomes*. Australian Housing and Urban Research Institute Final Report, June 2003. At: http://www.ahuri.edu.au. Downloaded 2 November 2005.

Capozza, D., Green, R. and Hendershott, P. (1997) 'Income taxes and house prices', mimeo. At: http://www.bus.wisc.edu/realestate/pdf/pdf/income.pdf. Downloaded 2 November 2005.

Carasso, A. Steuerle, E. and Bell, E. (2005) 'Making tax incentives for homeownership more equitable and efficient', Tax Policy Center Discussion Paper No. 21. At: http://www.taxpolicycenter.org/UploadedPDF/411180_TPC_DiscussionPaper_21.pdf.

Chambers, M., Garriga, C. and Schlagenhauf, D. (2007) 'Accounting for changes in the homeownership rate'. Available at SSRN: http://ssrn.com/abstract=1010966. Downloaded 9 June 2009.

Di, Z. (2006) 'The role of housing as a component of household wealth', Working Paper 01–6, Joint Center for Housing Studies, Harvard University. At: http://www.jchs.harvard.edu/publications/markets/di_w01-6.pdf. Accessed 5 January 2009.

Dietz, R. and Haurin, D. (2003) 'The social and private micro-level consequences of homeownership', *Journal of Urban Economics*, 54(3): 401–450.

DiPasquale, D. (1999) 'Why don't we know more about housing supply? *Journal of Real Estate Economics*, 18(1): 9–23.

Doling, J. and Ford, J. (eds) (2003) *Globalisation and Home Ownership*. Delft: DUP Science.

The Economist (2009) 'Home ownership: Shelter, or burden?', 16 April 2009. At: http://www.economist.com/businessfinance/PrinterFriendly.cfm?story_id=13491933.

Ellis, L. (2006) 'Housing and housing finance: The view from Australia and beyond', Reserve Bank Discussion Paper, RDP 2006-12. At: http://www.rba.gov.au/PublicationsAndResearch/RDP/RDP2006-12.html.

Forrest, R. and Kearns, A. (2001) "Social Cohesion, Social Capital and the Neighbourhood", *Urban Studies*, 38(12): 2125–2144.

Gale, W., Gruber, J. and Stephens-Davidowitz, S. (2007) 'Encouraging homeownership through the tax code', *Tax Notes*, 18 June 2007. At: http://www.urban.org/UploadedPDF/1001084_Encouraging_Homeownership.pdf. Downloaded 9 June 2009.

Galster, G. (1997) "Comparing demand-side and supply-side housing policies: Sub-market and spatial perspectives" *Housing Studies*, 12(4): 561–577.

Galster, G., Tatian, P. and Smith, R. (1999) 'The impact of neighbours who use section 8 certificates on property values', *Housing Policy Debate*, 10(4): 879–918.

Gibb, K. and Whitehead, C. (2007) 'Towards the more effective use of housing finance and subsidy', *Housing Studies*, 22(2): 183–200.

Goodman, J. (2005) 'Houses, apartments, and property tax incidence', Working Paper W05-2, Joint Center for Housing Studies, Harvard University. At: http://www.jchs.harvard.edu/publications/finance/w05-2.pdf. Downloaded 29 July 2009.

Green, R. and Vandell, K. (1999) 'Giving households credit: How changes in the US tax code could promote homeownership', *Regional Science and Urban Economics*, 29(4), 419–444.

Grigsby, W. and Bourassa, S. (2003) 'Trying to understand low-income housing subsidies: Lessons from the United States', *Urban Studies*, 40(5–6): 973–992.

Haffner, M. (2002) 'Dutch personal income tax reform 2001: An exceptional position for owner-occupied housing', *Housing Studies*, 17(3): 521–534.

Haffner, M. and Boelhouwer, P. (2006) 'Housing allowances and economic efficiency', *International Journal of Urban and Regional Research*, 30(4): 944–959.

Haffner M, and Oxley M, (1999) "Housing Subsidies: Definitions and Comparisons", *Housing Studies*, 14(2): 145–162.

Hendershott, P. and White, W. (2000) 'Taxing and subsidizing housing investment: The rise and fall of housing's favored status', NBER Working Paper 7928. At: http://www.nber.org/papers/w7928. Downloaded 29 July 2009.

Hills, J., Hubert, F., Tomann, H. and Whitehead, C. (1990) 'Shifting subsidies from bricks and mortar to people', *Housing Studies*, 5(1): 147–167.

Hoek-Smit, M. (2003) 'Subsidizing housing: Why, when and how', Presentation to World Bank Seminar on Housing Finance, 10–13 March, 2003. At: http://info.worldbank.org/etools/docs/library/156603/housing/pdf/HoekSmit.ppt#544,9, Demand or Supply-Oriented Subsidies? Accessed 1 March 2009.

Hoek-Smit, M. (2006) 'Setting the framework: Connecting public and private sector', Paper prepared for the 2006 KfW Financial Sector Development Symposium Financing Housing for the Poor: Connecting Low-Income-Groups to Markets, 9–10 November 2006, KfW, Berlin. At: http://www.kfw-entwicklungsbank.de/EN_Home/Topics/Financial_Sector/Events/Pdf_documents_Symposium_2007/Session2_Hoek_Smit_Paper.pdf. Accessed 31 March 2009.

Hoek-Smit, M. and Diamond, D. (2003) 'The design and implementation of subsidies for housing finance', Paper prepared for the World Bank Seminar on Housing Finance, 10–13 March 2003. At: http://housingfinance.wharton.upenn.edu/Documents/design%20and%20implementation%20of%20subsidies%20for%20housing%20finance.pdf. Accessed 31 March 2009.

Hulse, K. and Randolph, B. (2005) 'Workforce disincentive effects of housing allowances and public housing for low income households in Australia', *European Journal of Housing Policy*, 5(2): 147–165.

Katz, B. and Turner, M. (2003) 'Rethinking local affordable housing strategies: lessons from 70 years of policy and practice', Discussion paper prepared for the Brookings Institute Center on Urban and Metropolitan Policy and the Urban Institute. At: http://www.brookings.edu/dybdocroot/es/urban/knight/housingreview.pdf Accessed 26 January 2004.

Kemp, P. (2000) 'The role and design of income-related housing allowances', *International Social Security Review*, 50(3): 43–57.

Khadduri, J. and Wilkins, C. (2007) 'Designing subsidized rental housing programs: What have we learned?', Paper prepared for Revisiting Rental Housing: A National Policy Summit, November 2006, Joint Center for Housing Studies. At: http://www.jchs.harvard.edu/publications/rental/revisiting_rental_symposium/papers/rr07-5_khadduri.pdf. Accessed 20 November 2008.

Khadduri, J., Burnett, K. and Rodda, D. (2003) 'Targeting housing production subsidies: Literature review', Paper prepared for US Department of Housing and Urban Development Office of Policy Development and Research, Abt Associates, Inc. At: http://www.huduser.org/Publications/pdf/TargetingLitReview.pdf. Accessed 20 November 2008.

Laferrère, A. and Le Blanc, D. (2004) 'How do housing allowances affect rents? An empirical analysis of the French case', *Journal of Housing Economics,* 13(1): 36–67.

Lawson, J. and Milligan, V. (2007) *International Trends in Housing and Policy Responses.* Australian Housing and Urban Research Institute Final Report No. 110. At: http://www.ahuri.edu.au. Accessed 12 November 2007.

Le Blanc, D. (2005) *Economic Evaluation of Housing Subsidy Systems: A Methodology with Application to Morocco.* World Bank Policy Research Working Paper No. 3529, World Bank , February 2005.

Listokin, Y. (2009) 'Tax expenditures and business cycle fluctuations', Available at SSRN: http://ssrn.com/abstract=1372782. Downloaded 29 May 2009.

McCarthy, G., van Zandt, S. and Rohe, W. (2001) *The Economic Benefits and Costs of Homeownership*, Working Paper No. 01–02. Arlington: Research Institute for Housing America. At: http://www.housingamerica.org/docs/RIHAwp00-01.pdf. Downloaded 15 March 2003.

Maclennan, D. (2008) "Trunks, Tails, and Elephants: Modernising Housing Policies", *European Journal of Housing Policy*, Volume 8(4): 423–440.

Malpezzi, S. and Vandell, K. (2002) 'Does the low-income housing tax credit increase the supply of housing?' *Journal of Housing Economics,* 11(4): 360–380.

Marsh, A and Mullins, D. (1998) 'The social exclusion perspective and housing studies: Origins, applications and limitations', *Housing Studies*, 13(6): 749–759.

Mayo, S. (1999) *Subsidies in Housing.* Inter-American Development Bank, Washington, DC. Sustainable Development Department Technical Papers Series, Publication No. SOC-112. At http://www.iadb.org/sds/doc/soc112e.pdf. Downloaded 23 June 2009.

Muellbauer, J. (2005) 'Property taxation and the economy after the Barker Review', *Economic Journal*, 115(502): C99–C117.

Murray, M. (1999) 'Subsidized and unsubsidized housing stocks 1935 to 1987: Crowding out and cointegration', *Journal of Real Estate Finance and Economics*, 18(1): 107–124.

Murray, M. (1983) 'Subsidized and unsubsidized housing starts: 1961–1977', *Review of Economics and Statistics*, 65(4): 590–597.

Newman, S. (2008) 'Does housing matter for poor families? A critical summary of research and issues still to be resolved', *Journal of Policy Analysis and Management*, 27(4): 895–925.

Nordvik, V. and Åhrén, P. (2005) 'The duration of housing allowance claims and labour market disincentives: The Norwegian case', *European Journal of Housing Policy*, 5(2): 131–146.

Olsen, E. (2001) 'Housing programs for low-income households', NBER Working Paper No. w8208. At: http://www.nber.org/papers/w8208. Accessed 26 January 2003.

Oxley, M. (2007) 'Social housing versus housing allowances: What determines the result?', Paper prepared for the ENHR conference on Sustainable Urban Areas held in Rotterdam, 25–28 June 2007. At: http://www.enhr2007rotterdam.nl/documents/W12_paper_Oxley.pdf. Downloaded 29 July 2009.

Quigley, J. (2007) 'Just suppose: Housing subsidies for low income renters.' Paper prepared for Revisiting Rental Housing: A National Policy Summit, November 2006, At: http://www.jchs.harvard.edu/publications/rental/revisiting_rental_symposium/papers/rr07-9_quigley.pdf. Downloaded 23 June 2009.

Reynolds, G. (2007) *Federal Housing Subsidies: To Rent or To Own?* Urban Institute. At: http://www.urban.org/publications/411592.html. Downloaded 9 June 2009.

Rittel, H. and Webber, M. (1973) 'Dilemmas in a general theory of planning', *Policy Sciences*, 4(2): 155–169, cited in Australian Government (2007).

Rohe, W., van Zandt, S. and McCarthy, G. (2002) 'Social benefits and costs of homeownership' in N. Retsinas, and E. Belsky (eds), *Low-Income Homeownership: Examining the Unexamined Goal.* Washington, DC: The Brookings Institution.

Rosen, H. (1979) 'Housing decisions and the U.S. income tax: An econometric analysis', *Journal of Public Economics*, 11(1): 1–23.

Santiago, A. and Galster, G. (2003) 'Moving from public housing to homeownership: Perceived barriers to program participation and success', National Poverty Center Working Paper Series #03-6. At: http://www.npc.umich.edu/publications/working_papers/paper6/03-06.pdf. Downloaded 23 June 2009.

Sinai, T. and Waldfogel, J. (2005) 'Do low-income housing subsidies increase the occupied housing stock?', *Journal of Public Economics*, 89(11–12): 2137–2164.

Shlay, A. (2006) 'Low-income homeownership: American dream or delusion?' *Urban Studies*, 43(3): 511–531.

Shroder, M. (2002) 'Does housing assistance perversely affect self-sufficiency? A review essay', *Journal of Housing Economics*, 11(4): 381–417.

Stephens, M. (2005) 'An assessment of the British housing benefit system', *European Journal of Housing Policy*, 5(2): 111–129.

Stephens, M., Whitehead, C. and Munro, M, (2005) *Lessons from the Past, Challenges for the Future for Housing Policy*. London: Office of the Deputy Prime Minister. At: http://www.communities.gov.uk/documents/housing/pdf/138130.pdf. Downloaded 24 March 2009.

Susin, S (2002) 'Rent vouchers and the price of low-income housing', *Journal of Public Economics*, 83(2): 109–152.

HM Treasury (2003) *Housing Consumption and EMU: EMU Study*. London: HM Treasury. At: http://www.hm-treasury.gov.uk/media/3/1/ACF1951.pdf. Downloaded 20 November 2007.

Turner, M. (2007) *Current Rental Housing Market Challenges and the Need for a New Federal Policy Response*. Testimony before the US House Committee on Appropriations, Urban Institute. At: http://www.urban.org/url.cfm?ID=901048. Downloaded 9 June 2009.

Turner, T. and Luea, H. (2009) "Homeownership, wealth accumulation and income status", *Journal of Housing Economics*, 18(2): 104–114.

United Nations Center for Human Settlements (1988) *A Global Shelter Strategy towards the Year 2000*. Nairobi, UN. Cited in Mayo (1999).

Voith, R. (1999a) 'Does the federal tax treatment of housing affect the pattern of metropolitan development?', *Business Review (Federal Reserve Bank of Philadelphia)*, March–April, p3(1). At: http://www.phil.frb.org/files/br/brma99rv.pdf.

Voith, R. (1999b) *Does the Tax Treatment of Housing Create an Incentive for Exclusionary Zoning and Increased Decentralization?* Federal Reserve Bank of Philadelphia Research Working Paper No. 99–22. At: http://www.phil.frb.org/files/wps/1999/wp99-22.pdf.

Voith, R. and Gyourko, J. (2002) 'Capitalization of federal taxes, the relative price of housing, and urban form: Density and sorting effects', *Regional Science and Urban Economics*, 32: 673–690.

Whelan, S. (2004) *An Analysis of the Determinants of the Labour Market Activities of Housing Assistance Recipients*. Australian Housing and Urban Research Institute Final Report No. 70. At: http://www.ahuri.edu.au. Accessed 12 November 2007.

Yates, J. (2003) 'The more things change? An overview of Australia's recent home ownership policies.' *European Journal of Housing Policy*, 3(1): 1–33.

Yates, J. and Whitehead, C. (1998) 'In defence of greater agnosticism', *Housing Studies*, 13(3): 415–423.

22

Ethnic Residential Segregation – Reflections on Concepts, Levels and Effects

Sako Musterd

INTRODUCTION

Segregation has become a key concept in social, geographical and political research and in numerous societal debates. Because of its predominant, though not its sole, use as a means to refer to uneven residential distributions of individuals or households, it has become a major issue in housing studies as well. Segregation is a difficult concept, both because of the variety of ways segregation can be measured, and due to the variety of contexts in which the concept is applied. This complicates each study of residential segregation and the interpretation of the measures of segregation (see Chapter 23).

Because of its use in a wide range of debates, it is crucial to try to get a better understanding of the various forms of segregation, and its meanings in various contexts and to help create awareness of the different ways segregation can be approached, both in theoretical terms and in a paradigmatic sense. It is my objective to contribute to such awareness while focusing on the following two questions:

- How is the concept of segregation used and measured in societal and scientific debates and how do these uses relate to each other?
- What are the dimensions brought forward for the understanding of the various concepts of segregation?

However, this is not the only focus of this contribution. The second part of the chapter will address segregation issues in an empirical way. The most commonly applied and some more innovative – more spatial – concepts of segregation will be taken as a start for the presentation of figures on segregation and segregation dynamics in the North American and European contexts in particular. The focus will be on ethnic segregation. The leading question is:

- What are the levels of ethnic segregation in various urban contexts in North America and Europe and how are these developing?

Finally, I will deal briefly with the way the concepts are applied in governmental policies, mainly housing and urban policies aimed at reducing problems in the city. Here the question is:

- What are typical policy responses to segregation dynamics and how are these related to conceptual, methodological and empirical debates we refer to in this chapter?

CONCEPTS AND MEASURES OF SEGREGATION

The use of the concept of 'segregation' for the description of unequal spatial distributions of population categories has, over the decades, developed from a fairly technically defined exercise to express inequality of entire spatial distributions of two population categories, into a metaphor, which is frequently meant to express 'problematic' population compositions in certain urban areas. The metaphoric use of the concept, favoured in political arenas, often creates confusion and therefore a need for more rigid definitions of the concepts and for more awareness that different concepts should be used for different purposes. This brings us back to the 'technical' exercises. A wide variety of ways of measuring spatial inequalities has been developed over time (for older and for more recent overviews see, for example, Duncan and Duncan 1955; Taeuber and Taeuber 1965; Massey and Denton 1988; Wong 1993; Iceland et al. 2002; Reardon and O'Sullivan 2004; Johnston et al. 2004, 2005, 2007a; Deurloo and de Vos 2008).

Duncan and Duncan (1955) can be regarded the 'godfathers' of the dissimilarity index, which is by far the most widely used index to express levels of segregation or separation between two population categories. In their widely quoted article in the *American Sociological Review* they presented the dissimilarity index D as one way of using the information provided by the segregation curve and the theoretical situation of non-segregation. The segregation curve is defined as $Y_i = f(X_i)$, where X_i is the cumulative proportion of population category X in spatial unit i when the spatial units are ordered to the share of the population category relative to the total population of that spatial unit; and Y_i is the cumulative proportion of the second population category in spatial unit i. The theoretical situation of non-segregation is a special case of the function $Y_i = f(X_i)$, i.e. in which $Y_i = X_i$ for each value of i (see Figure 22.1). The D is the value of the maximum vertical distance between the curve and the diagonal and can also be calculated with not cumulated proportions of both population categories per spatial unit and this is the familiar formula for calculating the dissimilarity index:

$$D = 0.5 * \Sigma_{i=1...n} |x_i/X - y_i/Y|$$

where:

X = number of people in the first category
x_i = number of people in the first category in spatial unit i
Y = number of people in the second category
y_i = number of people in the second category in spatial unit i
i = a spatial unit
n = number of units.

The graphic presentation is attractive to illustrate other, related measures of (spatial) inequality, such as the Gini coefficient, which measures the area between the segregation curve and the diagonal.

Apart from the dissimilarity index D, there is another measure of segregation which has been frequently applied, and which may even be the measure for segregation which is most often used implicitly in wider public debates on segregation. That is the index of isolation $_xP_x^*$, defined as:

$$_xP_x^* = \Sigma_{i=1...n} (x_i/X * x_i/t_i)$$

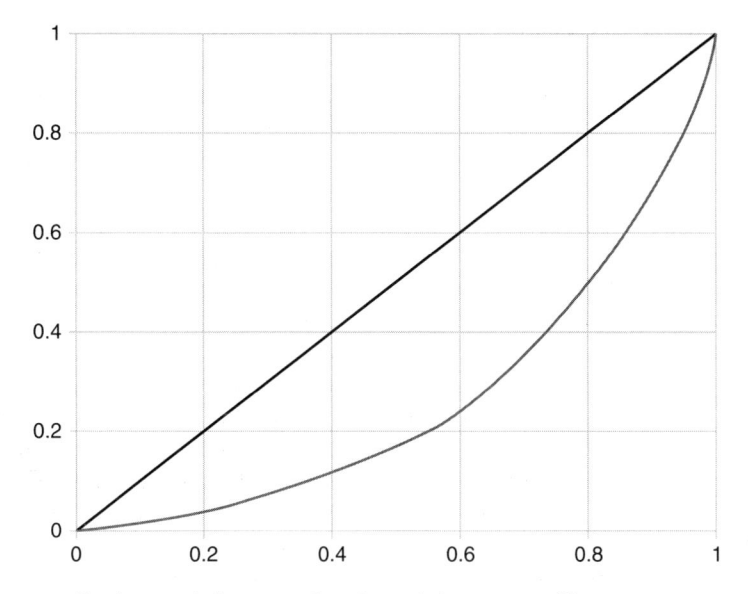

X-axis: cumulative proportion of population category X
Y-axis: cumulative proportion of population category Y
Diagonal: equality line (no segregation)
Curve: $Y_i = f(X_i)$

Figure 22.1 Segregation curve (Lorentz curve)

where:

X = number of people in the category considered
x_i = number of people in the category considered in spatial unit i
t_i = total population in spatial unit i
i = a spatial unit
n = number of units

This measure expresses the probability that a person of category X meets someone else of category X in spatial unit i, summed up across all units i. Unlike the D, this index $_xP_x^*$ is dependent on the relative size of the population categories under consideration.

If exposure of a person of category X is not calculated relative to other persons who belong to X, but instead to persons belonging to another category Y, the index transforms to the index of exposure.

$$_xP_y^* = \Sigma_{i = 1...n} (x_i/X * y_i/t_i)$$

where:

X = number of people in the first category
x_i = number of people in the first category in spatial unit i
y_i = number of people in the second category in spatial unit i
t_i = total population in spatial unit i
i = a spatial unit
n = number of units

Where the D is a symmetric measure, the index of exposure is an asymmetric measure, which expresses the probability that a person of category X meets someone of category Y in area i. Obviously this probability will be different if we start with a person of category Y and calculate the chance of meeting someone from category X.

These measures focus on only two categories of the population and are to be regarded as 'crude' measures of inequality in the entire spatial system. Some debates on segregation and integration appear to require more, and aim to include measures of diversity in a more encompassing way, including all categories that are regarded important to distinguish. One of the indexes developed for that purpose is the information measure H, also known as the entropy index (Theil 1972). This is also an index of evenness (like the D and the Gini coefficient) but measures homogeneity or heterogeneity in spatial units. The index is defined as:

$$H(X) = - \Sigma p_j \ln p_j$$

where p_j = the probability of an observation belonging to category j of variable X (here population category j of the set of population categories distinguished).

Standardisation can be obtained by dividing H(X) by the maximum attainable value, which is dependent on the number of categories (ln J). The resulting scale reflects scores between maximum homogeneity (value 0) and maximum heterogeneity (value 1). This measure can also be applied to calculate (weighted) average entropy scores for spatial units in a spatial system as a whole.

The measures referred to here are part of a system of measurement methods that in its basic form was presented by Massey and Denton (1988), when they distinguished measures for levels of unevenness (the dissimilarity and Gini and entropy indexes are representing this), exposure (including the index of isolation), and various measures of concentration, centralization and clustering. These dimensions express different aspects of segregation and therefore have different meanings, although they frequently overlap.

In their book on *American Apartheid* (1993), Massey and Denton argued that cities with high scores on all of these five dimensions (for which they used selected indicators), should be labelled as 'hyper-segregated' cities. With reference to the black population, cities like Chicago and Detroit were mentioned as typical examples of 'hyper-segregated' cities. In a more recent study, Wilkes and Iceland (2004) found that blacks in the USA were hyper-segregated in 29 metropolitan areas, whereas Hispanics were hyper-segregated in two. They argued that socio-economic difference could not explain the difference. Recently, Johnston et al. (2007b) reanalysed the interrelations between the five dimensions and the five indicators chosen to represent them and asked the question whether these really were independent, although related? When focusing on the indicators, they found that, in fact, two composite concepts should be distinguished: 'separateness' and 'location'. The first concept includes Massey and Denton's notions of unevenness, isolation and clustering and refers to the degree to which members of an ethnic group live apart from the remainder of the population in a specific urban area. The second concept includes notions of concentration and centralisation, and refers to 'the degree to which members of the group are congregated (irrespective of their degree of isolation) into high-density, inner-city areas' (p. 498). This finding thus challenges the value of the concept hyper-segregation.

The discussions just referred to indicate that measures of segregation are not without criticism. Much attention has, for example, been given to the fact that almost all of the measures are dependent on the size of the spatial units that are applied. The D value, for example, will get higher when the area size gets smaller (see Woods 1976). In a study in Amsterdam, Van Daalen et al. (1995) found that raising the number of units from 111 to 369 and then to 1216, resulted in a rise of the D (relative to the rest of the population) for Surinamese from 35 to 36 to 38, respectively; for Turks from 40 to 42 to 45;

and for Moroccans from 38 to 42 to 45. In addition, most of the measures do not take into account the location of areas relative to other areas and are in fact aspatial. Concentrations of a specific population category may be located next to each other or not, while the same value for D or $_xP_x^*$ will result. This is known as the checkerboard problem. The dependence of the indexes on the size and also on form and location of the unit, the Modifiable Areal Unit Problem (MAUP) (Openshaw 1984), is regarded a major drawback. As a result, several alternative measures have been suggested to overcome the aspatial character and to capture variation across neighbourhoods (see, for example, O'Sullivan and Wong 2007; Wong 2008). The objectives of the alternative measures are to overcome the negative impacts of boundaries between units, arbitrariness as regard the size and form of units, and the lack of information about the (spatial) relations between the units. More recently, new comments relate to the fact that existing summary measures are not suitable for the analyses of inequality in small areas and also that they are unfit for comprehensive use of all the information that is available in newer and also spatially more detailed data sets.

Johnston et al. (2008) are among those who are critical of the use of 'classic' indexes for larger urban systems, first of all because the calculations discard the richness of information in the data that is used to calculate the indexes; however, they also state that the indexes are often difficult to interpret, and that the indexes are not directly related to the definition of segregation they prefer ('isolation of one group from another'; p. 2037). For them it would be more helpful to develop instruments that can be used to identify the extent to which members of a population category live apart from others and how that is changing over time using as much of the information as possible and approaching segregation as a process.

Similar comments formed the basis for alternative ways of measuring segregation, assimilation and integration in the recent work of Philpott (1978), Peach (1996), Deurloo and Musterd (1998), Poulsen et al. (2001) and Deurloo and de Vos (2008). The last-mentioned authors deserve some specific attention. They adapted the so-called M index (initially developed by Marcon and Puech 2003), which can be used to express the level of statistical 'attraction' or 'repulsion' between different categories in a delineated area. They started with producing these delineated areas and then constructed 'ethnic clusters'. For each of 18,000 six-digit postcode areas in the city of Amsterdam they calculated whether there was an overrepresentation of non-Western immigrants or not; overrepresented areas were joined into larger areas when adjacent, with help of GIS tools. The resulting uniquely shaped clusters (see Figure 22.2) formed the delineated areas for calculating the M scores.

For each of the delineated areas, they then drew circles with radius r around each individual member of population category X and counted the number of other people of category X and the number of people of category Y within the circle boundary. These numbers were used to calculate the quotient for each member of category X; this was followed by measuring the average of the quotients over all circles. That average was divided by the expected proportion of the two categories in the case of a random distribution. In formal terms the M-measure is defined as follows:

$$M_{xy} = ((1/n \ \Sigma_{i=1...n} \ (y_i/x_i)) / (Y/(X-1)))$$

where:

X = number of people in category X in the whole research area
Y = number of people in category Y in the whole research area
x_i = number of other people in category X in a circle r around the i-th person of category X
y_i = number of people in category Y in a circle r around the i-th person of category X
n = number of people in category X

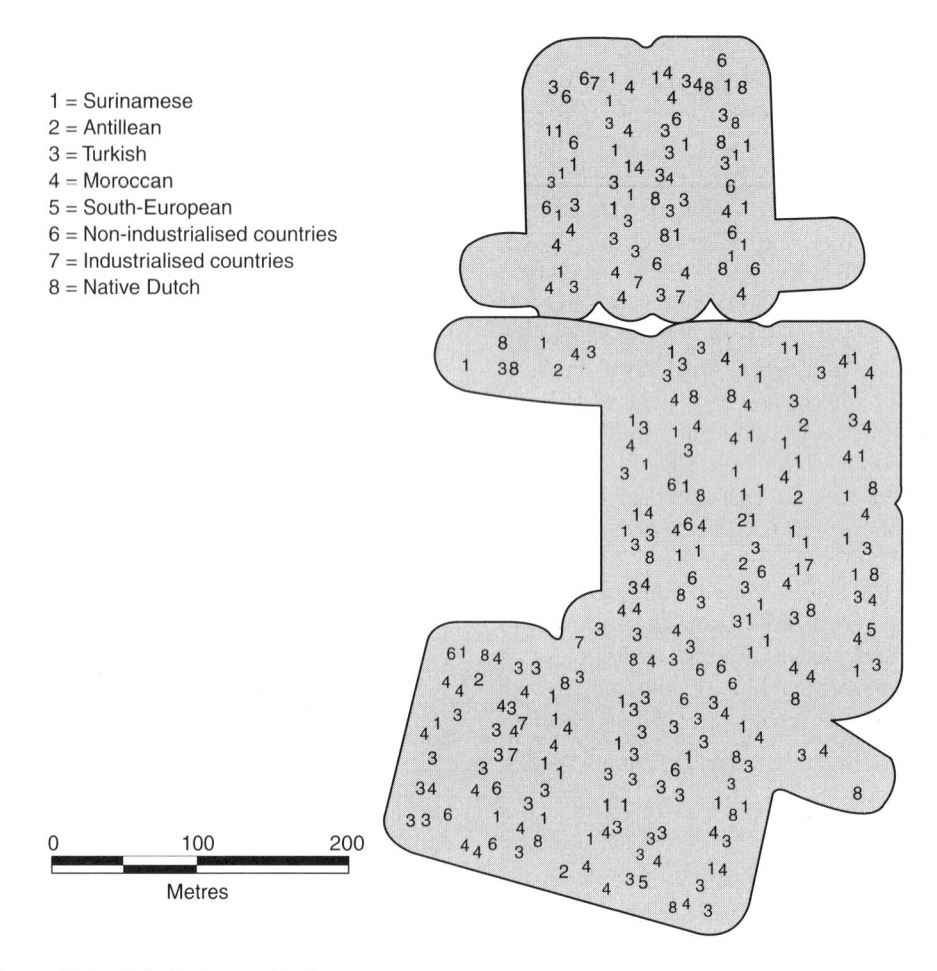

1 = Surinamese
2 = Antillean
3 = Turkish
4 = Moroccan
5 = South-European
6 = Non-industrialised countries
7 = Industrialised countries
8 = Native Dutch

Figure 22.2 Ethnic cluster '415'

Source: Deurloo and de Vos, 2008, Figure 2.

The M-measure can be calculated for various radius values and expresses levels of attraction or repulsion between two population categories. For more empirical detail I refer to Deurloo and de Vos (2008). They could show, for example, that in one of the delineated areas Dutch inhabitants were clearly separated from Turkish and Moroccan inhabitants, but only up to a distance of 200 metres (p. 341). In another area, separation turned out to be much more moderate.

These and related comments and new approaches will bring the debate on segregation a step further, and this is an argument for providing some additional empirical examples of these new approaches in Section 4 (Levels of segregation) as well. However, as Johnston et al. (2008, p. 2037) state: 'in certain circumstances' the use of the 'classic' indexes may still be helpful. Some of the comments, notably those related to size and form of the areas under consideration, are less disturbing when comparisons over time can be made and where the boundaries do not change. Moreover, it is true that data reduction (modelling) implies loss of information, but also often results in a gain of insight, at least in a crude way. It is – relatively – easy to obtain information that can be used for the calculation of D and $_xP_x^*$; this certainly is another factor explaining why these indexes are still being used rather frequently. For those reasons I will also pay some attention to these indexes in Section 4. Before turning to the empirical section, I will first refer to some literature that focuses on understanding residential segregation and the various meanings attached to it. This may help to get to grips with the wider public and political debates on segregation, which will be dealt with in Section 5 (Public debates on segregation) and where it is clarified what the explicit and implicit connotations are that politicians give to the concept of segregation.

UNDERSTANDING URBAN SEGREGATION: CAUSES AND EFFECTS

'Causes'

Because of the wide variety of concepts used to refer to segregation, it is logically difficult to explain segregation, its levels and segregation as a process. This is not just related to the variety of concepts, though. There are also many different perspectives on explaining segregation (Burgers and Musterd 2002) and there is an ongoing debate about the impact of various dimensions. At least four different perspectives may be discerned. The first perspective refers to behavioural theories in which individual behaviour, preferences, tolerance, choices and some constraints are key concepts (see, for example, Clark 2009). In this view, the separation should at least partly be ascribed to different orientations based on lifestyles, socio-economic position (income) and other characteristics that match and result in ethnic enclaves and specific residential domains. The supply side cannot be disregarded in this perspective, since the supply of dwelling types and residential milieus and the behaviour of various actors and gatekeepers will be crucial conditions for the settlement of the various household types referred to as well. Clark (2007) argues that 'separation in the residential fabric is not the outcome, alone, of income, affordability, social status, or preferences; it is the outcome of the mixture of these factors tempered by the myriad daily decisions in the rental and owner markets of American cities' (see discussions of neighbourhood change in Chapters 4 and 5).

The second perspective is embedded in structural processes and stresses the impact of major economic transformation processes, globalisation and related positions of households in urban societies (Wilson 1987, Sassen 1991, Hamnett 1994). The polarising impacts of these structural processes will create different positions in society and subsequently different spatial patterns and spatial mismatches (Kain 1968), which will – because 'race and class' are interrelated to some extent – also be reflected in ethnic residential segregation.

A third perspective refers to institutional structures that 'produce' segregation outcomes. The role of the state, welfare regimes and the functioning of various institutions that have a say in what will happen in spatial terms may all have serious impacts on patterns and processes of segregation (Musterd and Ostendorf 1998). Especially, the distinction between types of welfare states (ranging from residual to universal) may have strong impact on inequalities, which will also be expressed spatially. Universal welfare states are known for their redistributing character through the application of generous social and unemployment benefit systems, high-level minimum wages, elaborate pension systems and a range of housing subsidies and individual rent subsidies; residual models are characterised by the opposite and tend to generate much more inequality (see Esping-Andersen 1990). Institutional factors may also be central in discrimination practices, or even racism. 'White flight' and 'white avoidance' co-produce segregation and these behaviours might be partly explained by discriminatory practices (see Andersson 2006). The overall political and policy discourses on (spatial) diversity should perhaps be regarded to be part of this perspective as well.

Finally, we could refer to explanations in which the place-specific or context-specific historically grown and path-dependent realities are referred to in an effort to understand life chances and the variety of segregation levels and dynamics. This type of explanation also seems to fit some findings by Johnston et al. (2007a) when they found that the level of segregation must be partly ascribed to the relative size of the category under consideration, the urban size and the urban ethnic diversity in the area under consideration. In addition, country-specific variations would play a role. All of these factors will have developed over time and thus require a kind of historical perspective as well.

One can imagine that in reality dimensions of all of these perspectives are pushed forward to feed the discussion on what factors are (or are not) relevant to the understanding of segregation. In the scholarly literature, interesting debates can be found between key players in this research field. A core issue in these debates is whether, and to what extent, own choice, based on demographic, socio-economic and housing characteristics, or discrimination on the basis of race, explain the variation in ethnic spatial segregation. These debates (for examples, see Galster 1988, 1989; Clark 1989, 2007; Dawkins 2004) are helpful in shaping new research agendas.

'Effects'

One of the reasons why segregation is receiving so much attention is that there are distinct opinions about the relationship between 'residential environments' and 'effects'. There is some consensus that impacts of the segregated local environment of individuals may be shaped via at least three mechanisms: first, socialisation processes through which commonality of norms may be reached; secondly, stigmatisation and the internal and external perception of neighbourhoods as deviant places connected with crime, disorder and physical and social decay; and thirdly, the impact through social networks – in that sphere, social ties and interrelationships would help residents by bringing them in contact with the wider society (Ellen and Turner 1997; Friedrichs et al. 2005). Whether these mechanisms result in positive or negative outcomes is less clear.

One extreme position is that major negative effects are associated with the segregated environment (Massey and Denton 1993). Segregation, particularly ethnic segregation, would contribute to the development of 'counter cultures', in which norms and values that deviate from those that can be found in the mainstream would be celebrated. Growing up in an ethnic (and poor) ghetto would result in a higher probability to leave school prematurely; to stay unemployed; to earn a low income at adult age; to get into early pregnancy; to become a single mother; or to end up in prison. Many others, especially politicians, but including scholars such as Julius Wilson (1987), share this opinion and suggest that segregation causes the reproduction of inequality by its negative effects on social norms, attitudes towards society and social mobility in general.

A less extreme position is taken when urban marginality, also in ethnic (ghetto) neighbourhoods, is considered to have a range of backgrounds, which are not necessarily all related to concentrations in terms of ethnicity, but instead may be due to structural conditions related to factors such as access to jobs, media coverage of life in ethnic neighbourhoods, level of state intervention and discrimination (see Wacquant 2008). In that view, the effects of segregation on individuals' perspectives are not necessarily negative, especially for those who are living in ethnic neighbourhoods that are embedded in strong welfare states. This position is supported by other logics, again especially in state contexts in which inequalities are relatively small. In several European contexts segregation levels appear to be moderate and not very persistent. Ethnic concentrations are, in other words, limited and not always spatially fixed (Musterd and de Vos 2007). Consequently, one would expect limited effects from these conditions. Yet there are, occasionally, serious problems in cities, which seem to be associated with ethnic segregation, even where levels are moderate. The latest riots in cities such as Bradford, Antwerp and the Paris 'banlieues' are cases in point. Some of the riots occurred in moderately segregated areas and similarly segregated areas elsewhere did not show these tensions, which implies that the associations should be interpreted with caution.

At the other extreme position of the scale we find authors who state that ethnic segregation may actually have positive effects on those who reside in ethnic concentrations: for example, because the concentration of 'ethnic capital' may contribute to the formation of other capital, such as ethnic entrepreneurships, as well (Portes and Zhou 1992; Portes and Sensenbrenner 1993; Borjas 1998; Kloosterman and Rath 2003).

Thus, there is no consensus over the positive or negative effects of (ethnic) segregation. An important factor for the lack of consensus is research itself. It is very difficult to test the effects of segregation because the analyses are highly demanding in terms of data; moreover, self-selection processes may hide that unmeasured individual characteristics are in fact responsible for both the neighbourhood selection and the social outcomes. Ideal neighbourhood effect research should apply large and rich individual and longitudinal data sets, which can be connected with various data available or constructed for different geographical units. Detailed geo-information should also be available. Individuals with a variety of individual characteristics, with a variety of household characteristics, experiencing their lives in various residential environments ought to be followed during a range of years, and specific techniques such as 'differencing' in regression models should be used to eliminate the potential impact of unobserved, time-invariant characteristics. Differencing implies measuring differences between two periods for dependent and independent variables in regression models (see, for example, Galster et al. 2008).

These requirements are seldom met. However, there are exceptions, notably in Scandinavian countries and more recently also in the Netherlands. Longitudinal data are available for the entire population, at the individual level, and the required multi-level analyses can be carried out, while controlling for a wide range of individual characteristics. Among the most far-reaching research experiences are analyses with Swedish data. Although inequalities in Sweden are moderate and the welfare state strong, there is a big debate about the potential impacts of ethnic (and social) segregation (Andersson 2006). The question is whether there is a sound basis for that debate. In an effort to provide an answer to this question, Andersson et al. (2007), Galster et al. (2008) and Musterd et al. (2008) carried out a series of large-scale longitudinal studies. The last-mentioned study focused on the question, 'Are Ethnic Enclaves Good or Bad?' Multiple measures of the spatial context in which immigrants reside were developed and their contribution to average earnings of immigrant individuals in the three large Swedish metropolitan areas were assessed, controlling for individual and regional labour market characteristics. Longitudinal information during the 1995–2002 period was used. It was found that immigrants who enter the country and settle in an ethnic enclave would typically benefit from that position, but only if they were not staying in the enclave for too long. A longer stay of more than approximately two years would result in negative effects on their economic career. This study supports work done by Clark and Drinkwater (2002) and Galster et al. (1999), but surprisingly has opposite outcomes compared to what Borjas (1995, 1998) found, while he also based his conclusions on extensive longitudinal studies. The time element in the study may be of crucial importance. The findings from the Swedish study fit into ideas that immigrants may indeed benefit from other immigrants in an early phase of their settlement, because they can profit from experiences with the new situation acquired by former immigrants; however, after initial gains, a lasting position in an encapsulated enclave may prevent full participation in the wider society, which may eventually result in negative effects from staying in such enclaves.

LEVELS OF SEGREGATION: SOME EMPIRICAL EXAMPLES

Segregation varies across social and political contexts and also varies over time. A presentation of 'classic' measures (D and $_xP_x\,*$) and time-series data on segregation in cities in the USA and the European Union (EU) may illustrate the importance of such variations. A focus on dynamics is important to the wider political debate about segregation, which is often characterised by an 'automatic' assumption that 'segregation is increasing', although this seems to be dependent on context and measurement instrument.

Empirical data tell us three important things: first, that outcomes are not similar when measures of dissimilarity and measures of isolation are used – these tell us different stories; secondly, that it is important to consider the differences between population categories; and thirdly, that segregation levels are not uniformly going up or down within one state context, which illustrates the importance of local-level impacts.

Table 22.1 reveals that that there is a clear reduction of the level of segregation in US metropolitan areas: i.e. if we measure this for blacks and if we base the definition on the D index (Iceland et al. 2002). Almost all metropolitan areas (New York is one of the few exceptions) show a reduction of D values over the period 1980–2000. Such a reduction, however, cannot be shown for Hispanics and for Asians and Pacific Islanders. There we see more or less stable values of D. When reading the $_xP_x\,*$ values (index of isolation), we may notice – again except New York – that black isolation from the rest of the population is still high, but also slowly decreasing. For the other population categories we see strong increases of the level of isolation. This must at least partly be ascribed to a general increase of the number of migrants in these categories.

What about the levels of segregation in European metropolitan areas? This is a question which is far less easy to answer. There still is no single European standard for registering levels of segregation. The European Statistical Office (Eurostat) does not provide data on D or $_xP_x\,*$ values. This must partly be ascribed to the recent existence of the EU. Until now (cities in) individual EU member states, which are characterised by their own and very different migration histories, have calculated their own measures of inequality. In many cities, information on D values is available, but the way these values are calculated differs. Some distinguish between categories on the basis of nationality, whereas others apply country of origin and yet others use self-identification information. In short, definitions differ and categories are difficult to compare. Moreover, there is no unique way of defining metropolitan areas or the tracks within these areas and timing of measuring levels of segregation is also highly varied. Some cities use registers; others base their reports on census data. All of these factors have implications for comparing segregation levels of European cities with American cities (see also Musterd 2005). Although efforts were made to apply criteria which allow for the best possible comparison (size of units, definitions, year of measurement), it was inevitable to use a range of independent sources. For these reasons, the information in Table 22.2 should just be read as a set of indications of levels of segregation.

Table 22.1 Levels of dissimilarity and isolation for three population categories in selected US metropolitan areas, 1980–2000

Area	Dissimilarity index D			Isolation index $_xP_x$ *		
	1980	1990	2000	1980	1990	2000
Blacks						
All 220 metropolitan areas1	0.73	0.68	0.65	0.66	0.66	0.60
Largest metro areas > 1 mln.[2]	0.78	0.73	0.69	0.72	0.68	0.66
Five large metro areas with highest D scores (2000)						
Chicago	0.88	0.84	0.80	0.86	0.81	0.78
Detroit	0.87	0.87	0.85	0.81	0.82	0.81
Milwaukee	0.84	0.83	0.82	0.72	0.73	0.72
New York	0.81	0.81	0.81	0.79	0.82	0.83
Newark	0.83	0.83	0.80	0.77	0.78	0.78
Hispanics						
All 123 metropolitan areas	0.51	0.51	0.52	0.48	0.53	0.59
All metro areas > 1 mln.[3]	0.54	0.54	0.55	0.48	0.55	0.60
Five large metro areas with highest D scores (2000)						
Chicago	0.64	0.62	0.61	0.44	0.49	0.55
Hartford	0.66	0.66	0.64	0.38	0.44	0.45
Los Angeles-Long Beach	0.57	0.61	0.63	0.60	0.72	0.78
New York	0.65	0.66	0.67	0.60	0.67	0.71
Newark	0.67	0.67	0.65	0.41	0.48	0.53
Asians and Pacific Islanders						
All 30 metropolitan areas	0.42	0.42	0.43	0.29	0.33	0.40
All metro areas > 1 mln.[4]	0.43	0.43	0.44	0.19	0.28	0.36
Five large metro areas highest D scores (2000)						
Houston	0.42	0.46	0.48	0.09	0.16	0.28
Los Angeles-Long Beach	0.47	0.46	0.48	0.28	0.41	0.50
New York	0.49	0.48	0.51	0.23	0.33	0.44
San Diego	0.46	0.48	0.46	0.18	0.29	0.36
San Francisco	0.51	0.50	0.48	0.37	0.46	0.52

[1] Selected when there are at least 10 tracts and 3% or 20,000 or more of the category (blacks and African Americans, respectively, Hispanics and Latinos, respectively, Asians and Pacific Islanders) in 1980; reference group is white non-Hispanic; group averages are weighted averages.
[2] 43 metropolitan areas.
[3] 36 metropolitan areas.
[4] 20 metropolitan areas.

Source: Iceland, J., Weinberg, D.H. & Steinmetz, E. (2002) *Racial and Ethnic Residential Segregation in the United States: 1980–2000*. Washington, DC: US Census Bureau, Series CENSR-3, US Government Printing Office.

Only D values are presented, since $_xP_x$ * is not available for most of the cities. In a separate comparison of segregation levels in the cities of Amsterdam and Rotterdam (both in the Netherlands), for which comparable data are available, I will also investigate the $_xP_x$ * development.

Overall, segregation levels are relatively low in EU cities when compared to US cities. Exceptions may be found for UK cities, where we find relatively high scores for Bangladeshi; and in new immigration environments, such as in Barcelona, where Moroccans and Pakistani show high levels

Table 22.2 Dissimilarity index for selected cities and selected migrant categories, 1986–2004

Area	Dissimilarity index D			
	1986/92	1993/94	1995/98	2000/04
Amsterdam				
Turks	0.39	0.41	0.45	0.48
Moroccans	0.37	0.40	0.41	0.45
Rotterdam				
Turks		0.59	0.59	0.55
Moroccans		0.57	0.56	0.51
Brussels				
Moroccans	0.59		0.43	
London				
Bangladeshi	0.75			0.70
Indians	0.54			0.56
Black Caribbean	0.49			0.53
Birmingham				
Bangladeshi	0.79			0.61
Indians	0.56			0.42
Leeds				
Bangladeshi	0.67			0.61
Pakistani	0.61			0.42
Cologne				
Turks	0.37	0.33	0.35	0.35
Yugoslavs	0.27	0.26	0.29	0.26
Italians	0.31	0.27	0.28	0.26
Frankfurt				
Turks		0.19		
Yugoslavs		0.23		
Lisbon Metro				
Brazilians	0.33			0.28
Guineans	0.51			0.46
Indians	0.54			0.54
Madrid				
Peruvians			0.22	
Moroccans			0.27	
Barcelona				
Peruvians			0.23	0.38
Colombia				0.35
Moroccans			0.57	0.60
Pakistani				0.80
Rome				
Moroccans			0.40	
Uppsala				
foreign born			0.35	

Sources: Peach (1996); Gullberg (2002); Malheiros (2002a, 2002b); Martori et al. (2005); Burgess et al. (2005); Musterd (2005); Stillwell & Phillips (2006); Arbaci (2007); Peach (2007); Bolt et al. (2008).

of segregation. Housing conditions in rather unregulated housing market environments seem to play a key role in the explanation. As far as dynamics are concerned, the general tendency is one of stabilising or decreasing levels of segregation, pointing at ongoing integration or, at least, local cohabitation in the urban societies. Amsterdam and Barcelona seem to be exceptions, but most recent trends for Amsterdam show a decrease as well.

For Amsterdam, and for Rotterdam, we were able to calculate longer time series for both the D and the $_xP_x$ * for the four largest immigrant categories in both cities. Results are shown in Figure 22.3.

The interesting findings include, first, a clear difference between the levels of segregation when measured with different instruments. D values in Amsterdam started at a lower level compared to those in Rotterdam, but directions of development of the level of segregation of Turkish and Moroccan residents are almost opposite. Secondly, the index of isolation values in the two largest Dutch cities are very low when compared to those of various population categories in US cities. Thirdly, the D and $_xP_x$ * do not show similar patterns in all contexts. In Amsterdam, where, until recently, D values tended to increase for Turkish and Moroccan residents,

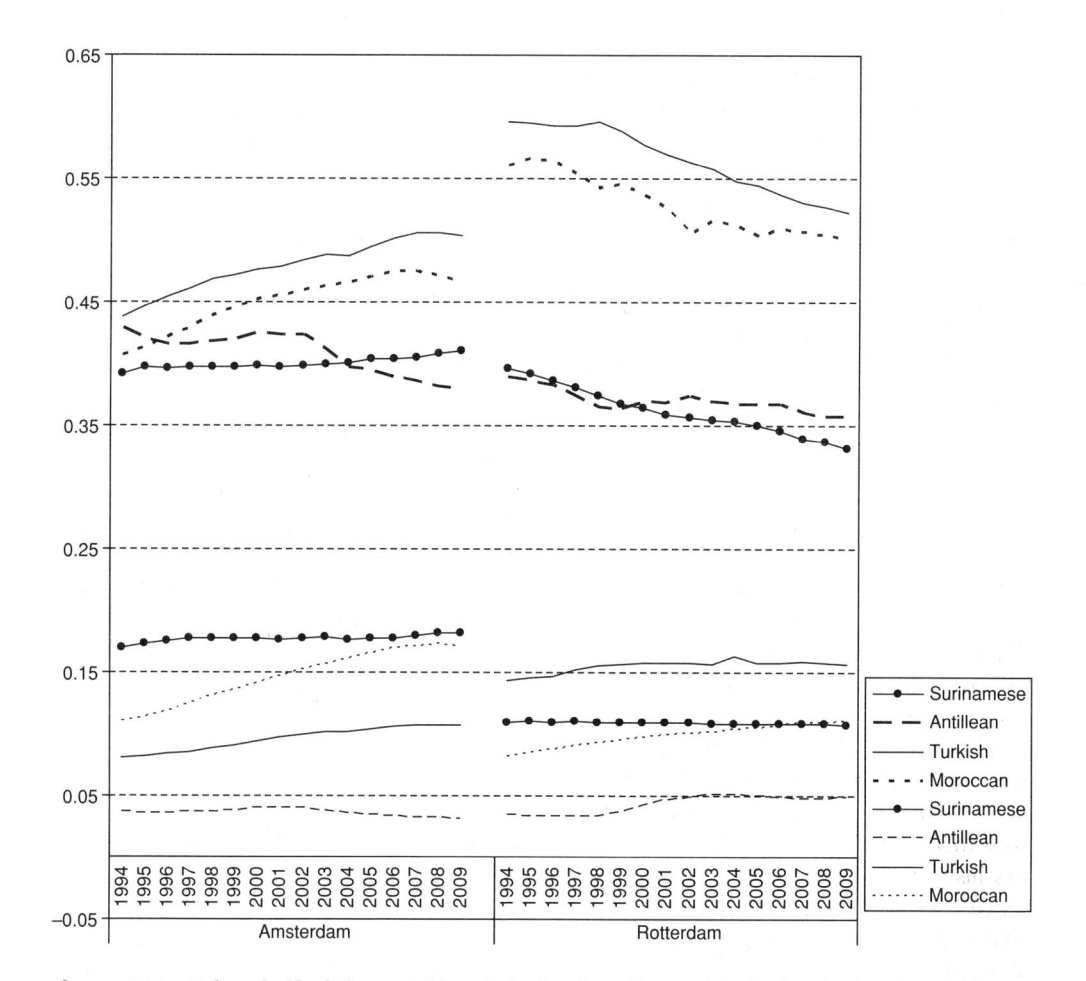

Figure 22.3 D (top half of the graph) and $_xP_x$ * values (bottom half) for Amsterdam and Rotterdam, 1994–2009

Source: author's calculations; Amsterdam: Onderzoek + Statistiek; Rotterdam: gemeentelijke basisadministratie.

but not for Antilleans, the $_xP_x$* shows relatively similar patterns; in Rotterdam, however, D values clearly dropped, whereas $_xP_x$* values were stable or rising. This finding contrasts to what Johnston et al. (2008) found in the USA; they stated that 'those two indices are strongly correlated across all US metropolitan areas for various ethnic groups: places high on dissimilarity are also high on isolation'(p. 2039).

Although these time-series overviews provide relevant data to be used in judging changing levels of segregation, separation or integration, we agree with commentators who argue that often more information can be pulled out of the existing data sets. In this section, I provide some recent examples of studies carried out by researchers of my own institute, where this objective was made central. The methods used by Deurloo and de Vos (2008), which were referred to above, seem to be particularly helpful, but also other analyses that build on similar data, and similar initial steps in the analyses, can contribute to the insights. The initial steps refer to the GIS-based calculation of so-called concentration areas on the basis of detailed spatial data. When these concentration areas have been formed, they can be used for various subsequent analyses. I already referred to the calculation of the M-measure. Other examples of analyses are focusing on the dynamics with regard to the concentrations. In several Dutch context studies, more detail could be shown about the instability of these concentrations. Demographic change due to birth, death and migration of a range of population categories could be measured for individual concentrations and this has led to insights that in Amsterdam, for example, Turkish concentrations that existed in 1994 tended to become less instead of more Turkish over the period between 1994 and 2004 (Musterd and de Vos 2007). Musterd and Deurloo (2002) and Musterd and Ostendorf (2009) started their analyses with similar concentrations and followed ideas of Philpott (1978) and Peach (1996) to say more about isolation, separation and encapsulation. Figure 22.4 shows an example of the analysis of the dynamics of 'encapsulation', here measured as the category's percentage living in concentration areas of the category.

In 2008, for example, 67,153 people of Moroccan origin were living in the city of Amsterdam. This was 9 per cent of the total population. It could be calculated that 30,920 of them (46 per cent) lived in an area that could be labelled 'a Moroccan concentration area'; these concentrations were contiguous areas, built up from the six-digit postcode level on the basis of the criterion that the share of Moroccans should be at least four standard deviations above the mean. Figure 22.4 shows the degree to which a population category is separated from others: or in other words, the degree to which they are settled among residents of the same origin. The time frame (2000–2008) is interesting, since after the Al Qaeda attacks of 9/11 and subsequent bombings and social unrest in many places in the world, including Amsterdam, xenophobia and a generally more negative attitude towards immigrants, especially those with an Islamic background, increased significantly. This may have led to stronger encapsulation, especially among Islamic residents, in the Netherlands, who typically originate from Turkey and Morocco. Such a tendency can be shown for Moroccans, but not immediately for Turkish citizens. From 2007 onwards, the share of Moroccan origin living in clear Moroccan concentration areas is declining again. Integration processes seem particularly strong for the Antillean population.

PUBLIC DEBATES ON SEGREGATION

In North America and Europe the public and political debates about ethnic segregation are characterised by expressions of both worries about the level of segregation and about the development of segregation. Although, as we have seen in the former

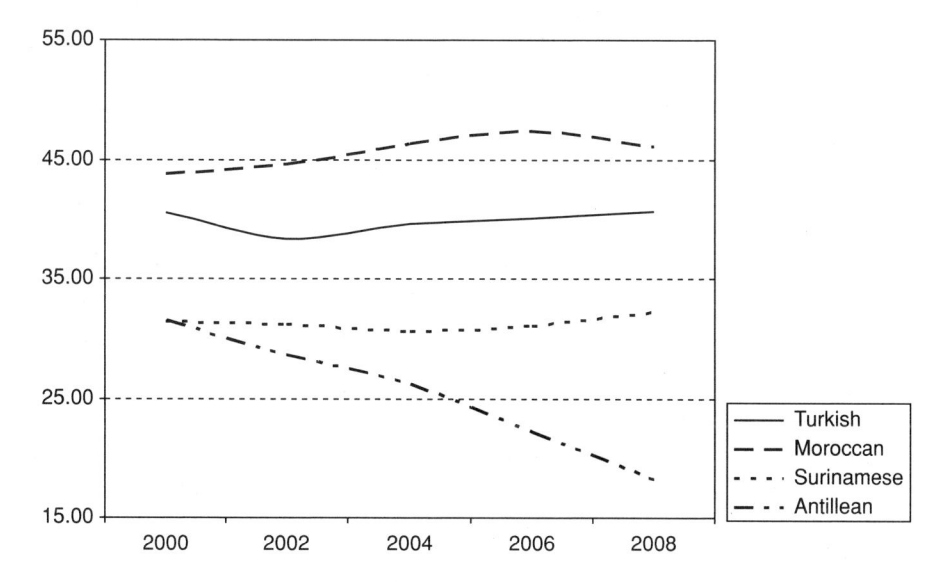

Figure 22.4 ▢ Percentage of a population category living in a concentration of that category, Amsterdam, 2000–2008

Source: author's calculations; City Monitor Amsterdam. Geography, University of Amsterdam and O+S Amsterdam.

sections, not everyone agrees that segregation is a negative thing per se, most of the wider public debates are characterised by a view that segregation is a bad thing. Especially in countries with an interventionist tradition in many spheres of life, policymakers tend to develop strategies to 'do something about it', to restore the 'balanced community'. The reasons for addressing ethnic segregation are different though. Some respond because of a fear for the development of so-called parallel societies; they use concepts such as 'apartheid', dual cities and divided societies to underline how serious and dangerous the segregation levels are. Many fear that the integration in the wider, or mainstream, society will be hampered by high levels of segregation, often – however – without measuring the level and dynamics of segregation (see Peach 2009). Others touch upon similar fears, but develop anti-immigrant sentiments as well. In that construction of reality, immigrants tend to be stereotyped, stigmatised and blamed for the problems that occur in urban neighbourhoods, or for the problems they experience themselves. Again, others try to clarify that social processes in society have different backgrounds and that residential segregation may have little connection to the problems such as unemployment and criminality that can be shown in some neighbourhoods. Some believe that different ethnic categories have chosen their own destiny, also in spatial terms, while others believe that structural and institutional forces have produced their (spatial) destiny (Préteceille 2003).

It is striking that debates about the relation between levels of segregation and levels of integration are not confined to societies or cities that experience high and increasing levels of segregation; similar debates can be shown in contexts where segregation levels are moderate and not generally increasing. This illustrates that the concept 'segregation' is increasingly used as a metaphor to point to a wide variety of 'rising neighbourhood problems'. In this way it is blurring the discussion of segregation and its effects. Nevertheless, the metaphoric use of the concept of segregation has become more favoured over the past decade, especially in Europe, where several political movements wanted to move away from so-called multicultural models of integration (Alexander 2003). It was felt that multiculturalism was preventing real integration and would lead to the development of parallel societies with various 'fundamentalist' fractions being part of that. This also resulted in a more open discussion about potentially harmful levels of ethnic segregation, and led to a call for more assimilation. In former times these open debates were regarded 'not done'.

As a result of the discussions, many plead for the reduction of levels of segregation. In Europe, these efforts were typically connected to policies aimed at changing the population structure of certain neighbourhoods and increasing the ethnic (and social) mix, often through housing restructuring or even demolition and newly built housing; in the US, programmes such as Moving to Opportunity and HOPE VI were aimed at similar results, but with a greater focus on opportunities for individuals. However, these debates seem to be disconnected from real levels of residential segregation and real processes of increase or decrease of the levels of segregation. However, the metaphoric use of the concept of segregation is likely to hide what are the serious causes of social neighbourhood problems.

As far as measures of segregation are used in political debates, it is still highly important to make clear what exactly is the kind of concept used and what precisely is the debate about. Is it about unequal spatial distributions of categories of residents, which may say something about the level of spatial integration, and about the deliberate development of separate societies within the wider society? Or is it about the level of isolation from others, which may say something about the relative share of different population categories in specific cities and neighbourhoods? These are different things, although they are both presented as 'segregation'.

In practice, the concepts of segregation in the meaning of D and P* are mixed up with each other as well as with other concepts such as concentration and integration. In the wider public debates, a rising share of a certain population category in the city as a whole may already be presented as increasing segregation. This is not necessarily true, though. If the newcomers follow the existing spatial distribution of those who were already settled in certain neighbourhoods in the city, the D will not change; the newcomers might even settle in such a way that the D values will decline. However, if the newcomers would follow the spatial distribution of the same category already residing in the city, the $_xP_x$* index of isolation will – *ceteris paribus* – rise, because the probability that someone belonging to X will meet another person of category X will increase, simply because of the rise of the share of X in general; this may happen without any deliberate effort from the side of the immigrants to create separate residential milieus. More detailed analyses in which, for example, the share of a population category that resides in so-called concentration areas of that population category is measured, may help to say more about levels of isolation than summarizing indexes might do. However, even when we focus more deeply at specific rising concentrations of a population category in particular neighbourhoods in the city we must refrain from interpreting this as increasing segregation per se. In terms of the D values, this will not be true if the relative spatial distribution remains unchanged. In many debates about segregation effects, the actual argument is that effects are expected that relate to shares and absolute levels of a population category in neighbourhoods in the city that exceed certain thresholds. In public debates, reference is being made more frequently to concentrations rather than to a particular form of segregation.

A concrete example of the disconnection between the public debate and actual development of segregation can be shown for the city of Rotterdam in the Netherlands. Local politicians in that city continue to argue that segregation levels are high and increasing and that separate societies are developing. This is, however, not true when measured through the D value; there are some signs of increasing segregation when measured in terms of $_xP_x$ *; however, this seems mainly due to a general increase of specific categories of immigrants in the city as a whole; the spatial patterns of the largest immigrant categories – as expressed by the D value – are actually becoming more similar to the mainstream society than before. The sentiment is, therefore, directed towards the immigrant category as a whole.

CONCLUSION

This chapter had four objectives:

- to clarify the nature of several concepts and measures of segregation, all with their own characteristics, meanings and potential uses;
- to discuss selected literature on causes and effects of segregation;
- to provide some empirical information about levels of segregation and isolation in American and European cities;
- and to discuss the typical constructions of 'segregation' in policy and political circles.

The variety of concepts and the metaphoric use of segregation sometimes creates confusion. This is a reason on its own to be as explicit as possible when dealing with segregation as a concept. It is also an argument to dig deeper into the questions that are related to segregation and to search for a better use of the information that is available in current data.

High levels of segregation are often presented as detrimental to a variety of integration processes. However, when concepts are used vaguely there is little basis for testing these visions. Where concepts of segregation have been made more explicit, as was done in a recent study we were involved in, hardly any relation between segregation and levels of participation in economic or cultural spheres could be shown (Musterd and Ostendorf 2009).

While multiple concepts of segregation can be distinguished, and multiple theoretical perspectives on explaining segregation exist, the theoretical debate regarding segregation is not expected to come to an end soon. The resulting wide array of explanations that can be provided in fact requires new large-scale integrated research, aimed at improving our understanding of segregation in all its forms.

In the meantime, the main reason for arguing that segregation is problematic is related to the negative effects assumed to go with it. Indeed, in many academic and societal debates it is hypothesised that certain levels of segregation (or homogeneity or concentration) would – after reaching specific saturation or tipping points – reduce the opportunities to participate in society at the required level. This persistently is the reason why national and local politicians are developing policies aimed at changing the segregation levels or population composition in certain neighbourhoods or why they want people to move to 'opportunity'. In this chapter, however, we argue that we should be aware of the fact that the assertion that there are 'dangerously high levels of segregation' that are continuously increasing and causing a lot of trouble is a typical policy construction of segregation in the first place.

Based on the complexities we refer to in this contribution, it makes sense to ask the question whether current policy interventions aimed at reducing levels of segregation can be effective in reducing the problems found in certain neighbourhoods? The dominant policy response in both the USA and Europe, which is in the affirmative, seems to be based on the philosophy that mixing the population is preferable in order to reduce the problems that occur in certain neighbourhoods. Housing and social mix, usually through tenure diversification, sometimes combined with demolition programmes, are regarded as the best answer. Offering positive role models, using networks of the 'good examples' and reducing negative stigmatisation through mixing would all explain the preference for mixed and unsegregated or balanced neighbourhoods. However, it remains to be seen whether this is a good strategy to solve local problems. First, it remains to be seen whether the population mix helps to bring people better lives; secondly, if mixing would be better for some purposes, it remains to be seen whether it is good for all purposes. After all, social theory tells us that interactions between people are easier and more effective if social distances between individuals are not too big. Finally, a key question remains of how far social and ethnic spatial engineering can go, whether strong interventions reduce or increase the negative stigma of a neighbourhood, or more generally, if interventions aimed at reducing levels of segregation produce more negative externalities than they take away. If that were be true, alternative strategies would have to be considered.

ACKNOWLEDGEMENT

I would like to thank Bill Clark for his most valuable comments on an earlier version of this contribution.

REFERENCES

Alexander, M. (2003) Local policies towards migrants as an expression of host–stranger relations: A proposed typology. *Journal of Ethnic and Migration Studies*, 29 (3), pp. 411–430.

Andersson, R. (2006) 'Breaking segregation' — rhetorical construct or effective policy? The case of the metropolitan development initiative in Sweden. *Urban Studies*, 43 (4), pp. 787–799.

Andersson, R., Musterd, S., Galster, G. & Kauppinen, T. (2007) What mix matters? Exploring the relationships between individual's incomes and different measures of their neighbourhood context. *Housing Studies*, 22 (5), pp. 637–660.

Arbaci, S. (2007) The residential insertion of immigrants in Europe: Patterns and mechanisms in southern European cities. PhD thesis, The Bartlett School of Planning, University College London.

Bolt, G., van Kempen, R. & van Ham, M. (2008) Minority ethnic groups in the Dutch housing market: Spatial segregation, relocation dynamics and housing policy. *Urban Studies*, 45 (7), pp. 1359–1384.

Borjas, G. (1995) Ethnicity, neighborhoods, and human capital externalities. *American Economic Review*, 85, pp. 365–390.

Borjas, G. (1998) To ghetto or not to ghetto: Ethnicity and residential segregation. *Journal of Urban Economics*, 44, pp. 228–253.

Burgers, J. & Musterd, S. (2002) Understanding urban inequality: A model based on existing theories and an empirical illustration. *International Journal of Urban and Regional Research*, 26 (2), pp. 403–413.

Burgess, S., Wilson, D. & Lupton, R. (2005) Parallel lives? Ethnic segregation in schools and neighbourhoods. *Urban Studies*, 42 (7), pp. 1027–1056.

Clark, K. & Drinkwater, S. (2002) Enclaves, neighborhood effects and employment outcomes: Ethnic minorities in England and Wales. *Journal of Population Economics,* 15, pp. 5 – 29.

Clark, W.A.V. (1989) Residential segregation in American cities: Common ground and differences in interpretation. *Population Research and Policy Review*, 8, pp. 193–197.

Clark, W.A.V. (2007) Race, class, and pace: Evaluating mobility outcomes for African Americans. *Urban Affairs Review*, 42 (3), pp. 295–314.

Clark, W.A.V. (2009) Changing residential preferences across income, education, and age: Findings from the multi-city study of urban inequality. *Urban Affairs Review*, 44 (3), pp. 334–355.

Dawkins, C.J. (2004) Recent evidence on the continuing causes of black–white residential segregation. *Journal of Urban Affairs*, 26 (3), pp. 379–400.

Daalen, G. van, Deurloo, M.C. & Musterd, S. (1995) Segregatie op microniveau. Amsterdam: AME-Universiteit van Amsterdam.

Deurloo, M.C. & de Vos, S. (2008) Measuring segregation at the micro level: An application of the M measure to multi-ethnic residential neighbourhoods in Amsterdam. *Tijdschrift voor Economische en Sociale Geografie*, 99 (3) pp. 329–347.

Deurloo, M.C. & Musterd, S. (1998) Ethnic clusters in Amsterdam, 1994–96: A micro-area analysis. *Urban Studies*, 35, pp. 385–396.

Duncan, O.D. & Duncan, B. (1955) A methodological analysis of segregation indexes. *American Sociological Review*, 20, pp. 210–217.

Ellen, I.G. & Turner, M.A. (1997) Does neighborhood matter? Assessing recent evidence. *Housing Policy Debate*, 8, pp. 833–866.

Esping-Andersen, G. (1990) *The Three Worlds of Welfare Capitalism*. Cambridge: Polity Press.

Friedrichs J., Galster, G. & Musterd, S. (eds) (2005) *Life in Poverty Neighbourhoods: European and American Perspectives*. London and New York: Routledge.

Galster, G. (1988) Residential segregation in American cities: A contrary review. *Population Research and Policy Review*, 7, pp. 93–112.

Galster, G. (1989) Residential segregation in American cities: A further response to Clark. *Population Research and Policy Review*, 8, pp. 181–192.

Galster G., Metzger, K. & Waite, R. (1999) Neighborhood opportunity structures and immigrants' socioeconomic advancement. *Journal of Housing Research*, 10, pp. 95–127.

Galster, G., Kauppinen, T., Musterd, S. & Andersson, R. (2008) Does neighborhood income mix affect earnings of adults? A new approach using evidence from Sweden. *Journal of Urban Economics*, 63, pp. 858–870.

Gullberg, A. (2002) Chapter 8. Housing segregation. *International Journal of Social Welfare*, Vol. 11, pp. 90–100.

Hamnett, C. 1994) Social polarization in global cities: Theory and evidence. *Urban Studies*, 31, pp. 401–425.

Iceland, J., Weinberg, D.II. & Steinmetz, E. (2002) *Racial and Ethnic Residential Segregation in the United States: 1980–2000*. Washington, DC: US Census Bureau, Series CENSR-3, US Government Printing Office.

Johnston, R.J., Poulsen, M.F. & Forrest, J. (2004) The comparative study of ethnic residential segregation in the United States 1980–2000. *Tijdschrift voor Economische en Sociale Geografie*, 95, pp. 550–569.

Johnston, R.J., Poulsen, M.F. & Forrest, J. (2005) On the measurement and meaning of segregation: A response to Simpson. *Urban Studies*, 42, pp. 1221–1227.

Johnston, R.J., Poulsen, M.F. & Forrest, J. (2007a) The geography of ethnic residential segregation: A comparative study of five countries. *Annals of the Association of American Geographers*, 97, pp. 713–738.

Johnston, R.J., Poulsen, M.F. & Forrest, J. (2007b) Ethnic and racial segregation in U.S. metropolitan areas, 1980–2000: The dimensions of segregation revisited. *Urban Affairs Review*, 42 (4), pp. 479–504.

Johnston, R.J., Poulsen, M.F. & Forrest, J. (2008) Back to basics: A response to Watts. *Environment and Planning A*, 40, pp. 2037–2041.

Kain, J.F. (1968) Housing segregation, negro employment, and metropolitan decentralization. *Quarterly Journal of Economics*, 82 (2), pp. 175–197.

Kloosterman, R. & Rath, J. (eds) (2003) *Immigrant Entrepreneurs: Venturing Abroad in the Age of Globalization*. Oxford: Berg.

Malheiros, J. (2002a) Ethni-cities: Residential patterns in the Northern European and Mediterranean metropolises – Implications for policy design. *International Journal of Population Geography*, 8, pp. 107–134.

Malheiros, J.M. (2002b) Immigration and city change: The Lisbon metropolis at the turn of the twentieth century. *Journal of Ethnic and Migration Studies*, 30 (6), pp. 1065–1086.

Marcon, E. & Puech, F. (2003) Evaluating the geographic concentration of industries using distance-based methods. *Journal of Economic Geography*, 3, pp. 409–428.

Martori, J.C., Hoberg, K. & Suriñach, J. (2005) Segregation measures and spatial autocorrelation. Location patterns of immigrant minorities in the Barcelona region. Paper presented at the 45th Congress of the European Regional Science Association, 23–27 August, 2005, Amsterdam, the Netherlands.

Massey, D.S. & Denton, N.A. (1988) The dimensions of residential segregation. *Social Forces*, 67, pp. 281–315.

Massey, D.S. & Denton, N.A. (1993) *American Apartheid: Segregation and the Making of the Underclass*. Cambridge, MA: Harvard University Press.

Musterd, S. (2005) Social and ethnic segregation in Europe: Levels, causes, and effects. *Journal of Urban Affairs*, 27 (3), pp. 331–348.

Musterd, S. & de Vos, S. (2007) Residential dynamics in ethnic concentrations. *Housing Studies*, 22 (3), pp. 333–353.

Musterd, S. & Deurloo, M.C. (2002) Instable immigrant concentrations in Amsterdam: Spatial segregation and integration of newcomers. *Housing Studies*, 17 (3), pp. 487–503.

Musterd, S. & Ostendorf, W. (eds) (1998) *Urban Segregation and the Welfare State: Inequality and Exclusion in Western Cities*. London: Routledge.

Musterd, S. & Ostendorf, W. (2009) Spatial segregation and integration in the Netherlands. *Journal of Ethnic and Migration Studies*, 35 (9), pp. 1515–1532.

Musterd, S., Andersson, R., Galster, G. & Kauppinen, T. (2008) Are immigrants' earnings influenced by the characteristics of their neighbours? *Environment and Planning A*, 40, pp. 785–805.

Openshaw, S. (1984) *The Modifiable Areal Unit Problem. Concepts and Techniques in Modern Geography 38*. Norwich: GeoBooks.

O'Sullivan, D. & Wong, D.W.S. (2007) A surface-based approach to measuring spatial Segregation. *Geographical Analysis*, 39, pp. 147–168.

Peach, C. (1996) Does Britain have ghettos? *Transactions, Institute of British Geographers*, 21, pp. 216–235.

Peach, C. (2009) Slippery segregation: Discovering or manufacturing ghettos? *Journal of Ethnic and Migration Studies*, 35 (9), pp. 1381–1395.

Philpott, T.L. (1978) *The Slum and the Ghetto: Neighborhood Deterioration and Middle Class Reform, Chicago, 1880–1930*. New York: Oxford University Press.

Portes A. & Sensenbrenner, J. (1993) Embeddedness and immigration: Notes on the social determinants of economic action. *American Journal of Sociology*, 98, pp. 1320–1350.

Portes A. & Zhou, M. (1992) Gaining the upper hand: Economic mobility among immigrant and domestic minorities. *Ethnic and Racial Studies*, 15, pp. 491–522.

Poulsen, M., Johnston, R. & Forrest, J. (2001) Intraurban ethnic enclaves: Introducing a knowledge-based classification method. *Environment and Planning A*, 33, pp. 2071–2082.

Préteceille, E. (2003) *La Division Sociale de l'Espace Francilien: Typologie Socioprofessionnelle 1999 et Transformations de l'Espace Residential 1990–99*. Paris: Fondation Nationale des Sciences Politiques, Centre National de la Recherche Scientifique, Observatoire Sociologique du Changement.

Reardon, S.F. & O'Sullivan, D. (2004) Measures of spatial segregation. *Sociological Methodology* 34, pp. 121–162.

Sassen, S. (1991) *The Global City: New York, London, Tokyo*. Princeton, NJ: Princeton University Press.

Stillwell, J. & Phillips, D. (2006) Diversity and change: Understanding the ethnic geographies of Leeds. *Journal of Ethnic and Migration Studies*, 32 (7), pp. 1131–1152.

Taeuber, K.E. & Taeuber, A.F. (1965) *Negroes in Cities*. Chicago: Aldine.

Theil, H. (1972) *Statistical Decomposition Analysis*. Amsterdam: North-Holland Publishing Company.

Wacquant, L. (2008) *Urban Outcasts: A Comparative Sociology of Advanced Marginality*. Cambridge: Polity Press.

Wilkes, R. & Iceland, J. (2004) Hypersegregation in the twenty-first century. *Demography*, 41 (1) pp. 23–36.

Wilson, W.J. (1987) *The Truly Disadvantaged*. Chicago, IL: University of Chicago Press.

Wong, D.W.S. (1993) Spatial indices of segregation. *Urban Studies*, 30 (3), pp. 559–572.

Wong, D.W.S. (2008) A local multidimensional approach to evaluate changes in segregation. *Urban Geography*, 29(5), pp. 455–472.

Woods, R.I. (1976) Aspects of the scale problem in the calculation of segregation indices: London and Birmingham, 1961 and 1971. *Tijdschrift voor Economische en Sociale Geografie*, 67, pp. 169–174.

Social Consequences of Residential Segregation and Mixed Neighborhoods

Ronald van Kempen and Gideon Bolt

INTRODUCTION

While patterns of segregation can tell us a great deal about the housing market and its differentiation, there are additional issues raised by the *social consequences* of these patterns. Does segregation impede social cohesion between different groups? Will it increase social contacts within groups? Are these differential patterns of contact detrimental or helpful for other aspects in the life of individuals? How, for example, does living in neighborhoods of poverty or ethnically homogeneous neighborhoods have implications for education and the educational life trajectory of children? How does the residential structure help or impede labor market careers? These are the kinds of questions that are central in this chapter. We will focus also on the relevance of residential mix strategies for cohesion, contact patterns and educational and labor careers. By comparing results from mainly Western European and American research we will give a clear picture of the relevance of the neighborhood, and especially of patterns of segregation and concentration of income and ethnic groups, for social and socio-economic issues. The conclusion of the chapter is that, especially in the Western European context, there is not so much evidence of the relevance of the neighborhood for the social conditions of its inhabitants.

Nobody wants an underclass. And if segregation and concentration are responsible for the creation of such an underclass, it is clear that those manifestations should be attacked and corrected to the extent that we can intervene in the urban fabric. William Julius Wilson (1987, 1996) provided evidence that spatial concentrations of the poor do lead to negative effects: without the buffer of the middle class, the poor suffer a damaging social isolation (see also Friedrichs, 1998; Atkinson and Kintrea, 2000). In his famous book The Truly Disadvantaged, Wilson (1987) wrote about what is maybe the most extreme spatial outcome of processes of segregation: the ghetto. He defined the ghetto as a spatial concentration of poor blacks. Also, in other writings, the ghetto is defined as a 'racial' or ethnic concentration of poor households (e.g., Clark, 1989; Wacquant, 1997; Marcuse, 2002). Because of their low incomes and because of racial discrimination, these poor households are forced to live in such areas; there are no alternatives on the urban housing market. In the footsteps of Kenneth Clark (1989), Wilson writes a clear account on the negative sides of the ghetto. He stresses the fact that living in a ghetto very seriously impedes the social and economic opportunities of its residents.

How does this work? Why is it so that people are negatively influenced by those living in proximity? In much of the literature the lack of good role models in the vicinity is mentioned as the principal factor (e.g., Wilson, 1987). Neighbors and other residents in the neighborhoods often do not have a job. They support themselves by crime and other anti-social behaviors. Thus, some inhabitants of the ghetto see crime as an alternative to a regular job and they do not see, through the lack of good examples, that there are other, legal ways to earn their livelihood. People are thus influenced in a negative way by those around them. Other authors do not stress the good and bad role models, but focus more on issues from outside: the inhabitants of a ghetto are stigmatized by people from outside their neighborhood and therefore have to fight a continuing battle against prejudices, stereotyping, and 'racial' and ethnic discrimination (e.g., Andersson, 2001).

The fear of the effects of segregation and spatial concentrations of poor and minority ethnic households and the concomitant wish of many policymakers to create mixed urban neighborhoods in European cities is for a large part based on the American literature (e.g., Van der Laan Bouma-Doff, 2007). Ideas about the formation of ghettos and the negative ideas of living in ghettos are easily transported to Europe and taken over by politicians and policymakers in Europe and by some scientists. European cities are definitely characterized by areas that can be called poor, distressed or disadvantaged and do contain concentrations of poor and minority ethnic groups. The reasoning is easy then: if so many problems emerge from those concentration areas, as exemplified in the American literature, then something must be done to break these patterns of socio-economic and ethnic segregation and concentration. The logical alternative then is to create a social and ethnic mix. Indeed, the creation of areas with mixed tenure, sometimes called 'balanced communities', seems to be popular. The policy philosophy of the former British government is formulated as follows:

> Part of what makes a community sustainable is a well-integrated mix of decent housing of different types and tenures to support a wide range of households of different sizes, ages and incomes (Office of the Deputy Prime Minister, 2005, p. 9).

This philosophy can also be found in European countries like Belgium, Denmark, Luxembourg, Finland, France, Ireland, the Netherlands and Sweden (Veldboer et al., 2002; Graham et al., 2009) and in Australia (Wood, 2003; Arthurson, 2007).

Perhaps some areas in British cities and some in France do share many characteristics with the American ghetto,[1] but the majority of concentration areas in European cities are better places to live than the American ghetto. Some areas with about 80–90 percent of the population belonging to minority ethnic groups exist in, for example, Dutch cities, but these are exceptions. Moreover, anyone walking in the most problematic Dutch, Swedish, German, Spanish, and Hungarian neighborhoods (or in neighborhoods of any other European country) will have to admit that these areas are not comparable to the ghettos in the USA, with respect to, for example, size and character of the built environment. A 'black' (i.e. Turkish/Moroccan) area like Kanaleneiland in the Dutch city of Utrecht only has about

7,000 inhabitants. Also, the housing in the area looks neat and tidy and is well cared for. And despite some rubbish in the streets, the area is quite clean. We should also not forget that the American society is quite differently organized from most European welfare states. To be poor in the market-driven USA is probably much harsher than in most European countries, where the poor can profit much more from many kinds of welfare state arrangements.

In this chapter, we give an overview of the literature on the effects of spatial segregation and concentration. We make clear which motivations are used for creating mixed districts. Our discussion is organized around three perspectives. First, we make clear that the motivations used by policymakers are, at least in European countries, rarely based on empirical evidence. Secondly, we show that the arguments themselves for creating mixed neighborhoods are problematic. Thirdly, we demonstrate that areas of concentration of ethnic and socio-economic status are not necessarily negative and may even have advantages. We end the chapter by reviewing the possible intersection of policy and mixed areas. We begin with a general overview of the literature on the importance of the neighborhood in the lives of individuals.

THE RELEVANCE OF THE NEIGHBORHOOD

How important is the neighborhood for the people who live there? For answering this question, we can use three sets of literature. A first set indicates that the neighborhood is not important, or is becoming less important. A second set has the main message that the neighborhood has some importance at the margin after the effects of individual and family variables have been accounted for. A third set of literature states that the neighborhood is of prime importance in organizing urban social life (see discussion of neighbourhood change in Chapters 4 and 5).

Research that asserts that the neighborhood is not important or is becoming less important

It seemed in the 1960s and early 1970s that the neighborhood was gradually becoming less important; abilities to move over greater distances were enhanced, mainly because of joint developments in the fields of transport – including the mass purchase of automobiles – and infrastructure (Webber, 1963; Stein, 1972). This has led, in the words of Janelle (1973, p. 8.) to 'human extensibility', which refers to the increased opportunities for interaction among people and places. The number of social relations at the level of the neighborhood is expected to decline, as social life has no clear spatial boundaries anymore (Keller, 1968) (see Chapter 17).

In the last few years there has been an additional perspective; thanks to information technology, people do not need to use the street, the shopping center or the neighborhood so much. Graham and Marvin (1996, p. 207) argue that this will shift the focus of individuals more and more from the community to the home:

> As families get smaller, new technologies allow the home to emerge as center for communications, receiving information and entertainment, obtaining goods and services, and even linking in with workplaces and employment. Advances in telecommunications, and, more particularly, the way they are being socially shaped and marketed to be individualized services to households, can be seen directly to support this shift toward home-centredness.

The warning that the internet damages community seems to be supported by a few empirical studies, which have shown that use of the internet is negatively associated with the size of social circles (Kraut et al., 1998) and the frequency of attending community events (Nie and Erbring, 2000). In short, the neighborhood is steadily becoming less important.

Research in which it is shown that the neighborhood is of some importance

In this second set of studies, the neighborhood is considered to be of *some* importance. An important question addressed in this sort of research is: Can impoverished neighborhoods make their residents worse off (Friedrichs, 1998)? In such research, neighborhood effects being sought are: To what extent does a neighborhood exert an extra influence over and above the personal and household characteristics of the residents on their labor market position or income? From different studies come different results. Some older studies in Germany, for example, indicate that individual traits of Yugoslav and Turkish guest workers (such as education) had a much greater effect in explaining the degree of a minority member's assimilation in the host society than the population composition of the neighborhood. In this case the influence of the neighborhood only reaches 10 percent of the total variance (Alpheis, 1990). Jencks and Mayer (1990) have indicated that that we should not forget schools when looking at neighborhood effects: if the influence of schools is controlled for, neighborhood effects may be close to zero.

Another example of a neighborhood effect study is the article by Hogan and Kitagawa (1985) who investigated teenage pregnancy of unmarried female blacks aged 13–19 in Chicago. Neighborhood effects seemed to be present when using bivariate analyses, but when controlling for other variables, neighborhood effects disappeared (see also Friedrichs, 1997). More recently, a study in Sweden on the effects of income mix on the earnings of adults has indicated that neighborhood effects are present, but quite low (Galster et al., 2008). Urban (2009) also found only a small effect of the childhood neighborhood on the level of income and unemployment risks in Stockholm. Next to that, the ethnic make-up of the neighborhood had even a smaller impact than the socio-economic composition. Oberwittler (2007) found evidence of both neighborhood and school contextual effects on adolescent delinquency in Germany. However, the effect of neighborhood was only found for native adolescents and not for immigrant adolescents.

Also in the literature in which neighborhood effects for children are central, the conclusion is in most cases that these effects are small. Leventhal and Brooks-Gunn (2000) have given an extensive overview of research on the effects of neighborhoods on children's and adolescent's outcomes. After controlling for individual and family-level characteristics, in general not more than a few percent of the outcome – such as children's IQ, school achievement, verbal ability and reading recognition scores – is explained by neighborhood effects. Socio-economic neighborhood variables seem to be more influential than ethnic variables or residential instability of the neighborhood.

The dominant conclusion seems to be: there are neighborhood effects, but these are small in comparison with individual characteristics such as education and age and household characteristics such as income (Brooks-Gunn et al., 1997; Ellen and Turner, 1997; Jargowsky, 1997; Friedrichs, 1998; Andersson, 2001; Friedrichs et al., 2003; Musterd et al., 2008).

Research in which the neighborhood is of primary importance

In some studies it transpires that neighborhoods can have very important effects on the lives of individuals and families. These studies thus question the assumed limited or decreasing importance of the neighborhood. Cities can be world cities, play an important part in the world economy, and be recognized as such by everyone; nevertheless, there remain neighborhoods within these cities that are recognizable, unique, and of importance for their residents, whether they be poor or prosperous (see Castells, 2002). The increase in working at home can lead to greater interest in the neighborhood, because the home-based worker looks for leisure and relaxation outside the house (Forrest and Kearns, 2001). Next to that, the idea that the internet destructs communities is refuted by scholars who found that the internet has the effect of enhancing existing relationships (Wellman and Haythornthwaite, 2002). Hampton and Wellman's (2003, p. 305) research in a Toronto suburb ('Netville') even shows that the internet can have a very positive effect on neighborhood-based interactions:

> Netville's local computer network reduced the cost and increased the speed of grassroots collective action. Spatial, temporal, and social barriers to community organizing were overcome through the use of Internet. Internet use did not inhibit or substitute for other forms of social contact, in person or over the telephone. Contact led to contact through the interplay of online and offline encounters.

In more general terms Forrest and Kearns (2001) point out that, in times of (assumed) increasing influence from all kinds of macro developments, people are beginning to find the neighborhood to be of greater importance as a place where they feel safe and at their ease. The degree to which a neighborhood can function as a safe haven depends very much on its degree of social organization, as shown by Robert Sampson and his colleagues (Sampson et al., 1997). The work of Sampson differs from the mainstream literature on neighborhood effects (as described above) in the sense that it does not focus on the individual level, but on neighborhood crime. Whereas the effect of the neighborhood on individual outcomes is usually found to be small, crime rates can to a large extent be attributed to community characteristics, like the level of social organization and collective efficacy (Sampson, 2008; Sampson and Raudenbusch, 2004).

It does appear from many studies that the neighborhood is certainly of importance, in particular for poorer households (see, for example, Henning and Lieberg, 1996; Ellen and Turner, 1997; Guest and Wierzbicki, 1999). This literature focuses on the fact that the neighborhood provides important social contacts for the inhabitants. Neighbors have the opportunity for social interaction, for doing things together, and for helping each other – for example, with a small loan, Less well educated people and lower-income groups often have more contacts within the neighborhood than do those with a higher educational level and a higher income. Households with a lower income in general need survival strategies, and the neighborhood can be of essential importance in that respect. People on a low income often turn to the neighborhood, because they do not have the financial opportunities to travel elsewhere, even if the inner city is just a 10 km distance away, such as in the Dutch case of Rotterdam (Botman and Van Kempen, 2001) (see Chapter 17).

Ethnic groups feature prominently in much of the literature on the importance of the neighborhood. The spatial segregation of immigrants finds its basis in a multitude of factors, but for recent immigrants in particular the finding of mutual support is an important factor. It can be a matter of receiving help in finding a (temporary) place to live or a first job. Immigrants who cannot speak the language of the host country adequately and those with a low level of education have a particular tendency to make (in the first instance) for a neighborhood where many compatriots already live, in the expectation that they will be more likely to receive social, economic, and emotional support there (Dahya, 1974; Enchautegui, 1997; Fong and Gulia, 1999).

When people not only reside in a neighborhood (sleep there), but also live there (make use of it), it may be assumed to exert some influence on their lives. Wilson (1987) has shown that American deprived neighborhoods can be characterized by the more frequent occurrence of deviant behavior, more school dropouts, more teenage pregnancies, more crime, and more neglect of dwellings and buildings than in other neighborhoods. He asserts, furthermore, that deviant norms in such neighborhoods can readily become dominant so that the neighborhood becomes isolated from the rest of the city. Living in an impoverished environment with a high percentage of unemployed neighbors would not, for example, encourage people to go out and look for a job (Friedrichs, 1998). Precisely because contact networks are limited to the neighborhood, there is no further influence from outside. Neighborhood residents who resemble each other closely attract each other and find role models in each other. In short: the neighborhood is of importance, but not necessarily in a positive manner.

From the three strands of literature that have been briefly outlined above, no clear conclusion can be drawn. It seems that we have three different kinds of research lines. It is interesting to see, however, that most authors who claim that the neighborhood is not important at all do not base their statement on empirical research. Those who make advanced statistical analyses usually arrive at the conclusion that the effect of the neighborhood is marginal. Such studies usually investigate in a quantitative manner how the neighborhood influence (on, for example, the socio-economic position) is related to the influence of personal and household variables. From other, more qualitative, studies it becomes clear that for specific groups (low income, immigrants) the neighborhood makes a difference for various reasons. In a positive sense, the neighborhood can lead to support, reception, and social contacts, and in a negative sense, the development of deviant norms and values, as a consequence of contacts between people in situations of deprivation.

INITIATIVES TO COUNTER SEGREGATION AND CONCENTRATION AND TO CREATE MIXED DISTRICTS

Policymakers have outlined several arguments to support their focus on countering spatial segregation and concentration. Underlying these arguments is an overarching view that creating mixed districts will enhance the living condition of its inhabitants. These arguments range from creating a mixed housing stock to increasing social capital and social mobility. In this section we focus briefly on the most important of these arguments. The question becomes simply: Why should we create mixed districts? Later in the chapter we consider whether the expectations and arguments are realistic. First we discuss the most important advantages of mixed districts (for a fuller discussion of socio-spatial dimensions of housing spaces, see Chapter 8).

Providing opportunities for a housing career in the district

Some urban districts are highly homogeneous with respect to their housing stock. In countries like the Netherlands and Sweden, for example, many urban districts consist to a large extent of social housing in monotonous apartment blocks. There are obvious concentrations of low-income households and minority ethnic groups in these dwellings. But in the same housing stock live a number of people who want to make a housing career and are, because they have a better income, able to do so: they want to move to better, more expensive, even owner-occupied dwellings (Musterd and Van Kempen, 2007). In many cases, at the same time, they want to stay in their present district or neighborhood: for example, because they like the area for one or more reasons, or because they are just used to living there. But if there are no opportunities to move to a better house, they have to look for a dwelling in another district or neighborhood (Bolt et al., 2009).

Demolition of part of the existing (social-rented) stock and new dwellings in the more expensive sector do provide opportunities for making a housing career for these groups.

The demolition of relatively inexpensive rental dwellings and the building of more upmarket housing in the owner-occupied sector is a main policy in post World War II areas in Western European cities (see, e.g., Van Beckhoven and Van Kempen, 2003; Bolt et al., 2009; Van Gent, 2009). Especially in the Netherlands, plans for demolition and restructuring the housing stock are manifold and in many cases in full swing (like in the Bijlmermeer in Amsterdam, Hoograven in Utrecht, Bouwlust in The Hague, and Pendrecht in Rotterdam). In general, these restructured areas are able to keep (or to attract) a significant number of middle-income households (see, e.g., Van Kempen et al., 2009).

New population: better services

A population change in a neighborhood almost automatically leads to a change in the level of services in the area. When an area is characterized by an outflow of poor households and an inflow of middle- and high-income households, there will be a situation of more income to be spent in the area. This enhances the possibilities for amenities like cafés, restaurants, and luxurious shops. A new, richer, population can thus lead to a higher quantity as well as higher quantity of amenities (Arthurson, 2002). The process of gentrification in the Alberta neighborhood of Portland has, for instance, led to an expansion of galleries, coffeehouses, and restaurants (Sullivan, 2006). Likewise, Battersea in London has become known as an area with high-quality local amenities and shops (Butler and Robson, 2001).

The inflow of higher-income households may not only attract commercial facilities but also potentially increases the political power of a community to improve municipal services. Although there is hardly any research on this issue, there are some indications that social mix produces more effective collective action (Jupp, 1999; Smith, 2002).

More social contacts and social cohesion

Social cohesion is a difficult concept. In its most general meaning it refers to a kind of glue, holding society together (Maloutas and Malouta, 2004; see also Dekker, 2006). According to the influential work of Kearns and Forrest (2000), social cohesion comprises shared norms and values, social solidarity, social control, social networks, and a feeling of belonging to each other through a common identity and a strong bonding with the place where one lives (see also Forrest and Kearns, 2001). These aspects reinforce each other: whenever people have, for example, the same ideas about life (shared norms and values), the chance of making social contacts is greater and so the feeling of being part of a certain group or a particular neighborhood or district is reinforced (see also Atkinson and Kintrea, 2002).[2] In urban policies, social cohesion is almost always used as a concept that is of relevance at the level of the urban neighborhood or urban district (for another discussion of social cohesion and neighborhoods, see Chapter 17).

Mixed districts are said to improve contacts between different groups of people; the formation of social networks becomes possible. Spatial proximity stimulates contacts, social interaction, and social networks. This is a positive thing, because social networks lead to the possibility of profiting from each other; people can, for example, borrow things from each other and learn from each other. Social networks can be seen as one of the dimensions of social cohesion and it is even possible to see these networks as the basis for other aspects of social cohesion (Kearns and Forrest, 2000).

One of these aspects is social control. Wilson (in Tunstall, 2003) notes that people in mixed neighborhoods more often point to deviant behavior than people in homogeneous poor neighborhoods. Another aspect of social cohesion is the bonding with the place where one lives. This aspect is related closely to the numbers and kinds of social contacts in the area. The reasoning is as follows: people with many contacts in the neighborhood have a bigger chance for a strong bonding with the neighborhood than people without such contacts (Van Kempen and Bolt, 2009).

Social capital and social mobility

Related to the concept of social cohesion is the concept of social capital. This term refers to the means persons or households have as a consequence of social networks and to reciprocity, norms, and trust (Kleinhans et al., 2007; see also Bourdieu, 1986; Coleman, 1988; Putnam, 2000). It is thus more than just a set of social contacts. Most authors refer to two different kinds of capital: bonding and bridging capital. Bonding capital refers to the strong bonding between people that produces very little new information. This bonding is strong within a particular group, but easily leads to social fragmentation in the broader society. Bridging capital, in contrast, refers to weak bonding, but in relationships that do provide information on the wider world, such as the availability of jobs (Granovetter, 1973).

For people on a low income in particular, a neighborhood functions more as a source of bonding capital than as a platform for bridging capital (Burns et al., 2001). Mixed districts should lead to more social capital, because there are simply more opportunities for contacts between different kinds of people – such as workers and the unemployed – and in particular to bridging capital (Campbell et al., 1986; Van Eijk and Blokland, 2007). Unemployed people can be helped to find a job, for example, by those who already have one. This can work in a direct way (e.g., by giving information about a job vacancy in the firm where one works), or indirectly (e.g., because someone assists in the process of applying for a job). The idea is that these help functions do not work in a segregated neighborhood but have much more chance of happening in more mixed neighborhoods. This is of course especially advantageous for those in a disadvantaged position.

Thus, the idea is that by having the right contacts in the neighborhood, residents can climb the social ladder. Even without having real contact with each other, mixed districts can be advantageous because they can provide positive role models. A situation where people see their neighbor go out of the door every day to go to work is different from one in which everyone around you is poor and criminal acts are considered normal. Despite the fact that in these times many role models are probably found on television and the internet, it is still possible that they can be found in the neighborhood or district.

Spatial concentrations of minority ethnic groups can have their advantages, but can also be disadvantageous for contacts between members of these groups and natives (De Souza Briggs, 2003, 2005). Indeed, research from the Netherlands indicates that minority ethnic groups living in concentration neighborhoods have only few contacts with natives (Dagevos, 2005; Van der Laan Bouma-Doff, 2007). Whether this lack of contact has negative effects on their labor market career, school career or housing career has hardly been investigated in the European context. Van Tubergen and Kalmijn (2002) did find that the number of members of minority ethnic groups in a neighborhood affects the language ability of Turks and Moroccans of the first generation. Also, a high presence of non-Western minority ethnic groups in the vicinity affects the number of people belonging to minority ethnic groups that visits a church, mosque, or temple positively (Van Tubergen, 2007).[3]

The text in this section has made clear that in principle enough motivations exist to try and change patterns of segregation and concentration and to strive for more mixed neighborhoods. A more diverse neighborhood in terms of housing type and population may create positive effects for its inhabitants.

WHAT DOES THE CURRENT LITERATURE REPORT ABOUT MIXED NEIGHBORHOODS?

The expectations and ideas about the advantages of mixed neighborhoods seem to be reasonable interpretations of what the neighborhood can do for families. But what does the empirical literature tell us? Are the advantages suggested by proponents of mixed neighborhoods found in empirical research? In the following section we review the research results on housing careers, neighborhood services, social contacts, and social cohesion and social mobility.

Mixed neighborhoods and housing careers

When the housing stock of an area with an overwhelming majority of inexpensive rental dwellings becomes more differentiated – through demolition and building more expensive alternatives – households waiting for a better home can make a housing career within the neighborhood. They move to better dwellings, often also from rented to owner-occupied dwellings (Bolt et al., 2009). Demolition often leads to a selection process: those who can afford the new dwellings and who prefer to stay in the neighborhood find a new home there. At the same time, other households may be attracted to the new parts of the neighborhood. Such a process also implies that those with lower incomes have to leave the area, because there are no affordable dwellings in that area anymore. In European cities, this is often done on purpose: concentrations of low-income households have to be broken, because negative effects seem to result from such concentrations.[4] The result is a more mixed neighborhood in terms of income (see earlier in this chapter for some examples).

Transforming a monotonous neighborhood in terms of housing type and tenure thus makes a housing career possible: especially those with higher incomes seem to profit. The income mix in a restructured neighborhood does not always go along with a stronger ethnic mix. It has been indicated in some studies that new dwellings in a restructured area seem to attract many minority ethnic households (Gijsberts and Dagevos, 2007). They have often lived in the area for a relatively long time and now make the step to owner-occupation. Because they are used to living in the area, and often like to live there, they are happy to move to a better dwelling a few streets further. These minority ethnic movers clearly belong to the groups that have a relatively good economic position, otherwise they could not afford to live in the more expensive new dwellings. They could be regarded as successful members of an ethnic group that might have the ability to serve as a role model for the rest of the group.

When the creation of mixed neighborhoods goes hand in hand with demolition of inexpensive dwellings and building more expensive dwellings, those who cannot afford to live in the renewed neighborhood have to leave the area and find a place to live somewhere else. In general, these forced movers are assisted in their search very well, at least in most civilized countries (Kleinhans, 2005). This means that most of the displaced people often find an alternative home pretty soon, because they have absolute priority in the system of housing allocation. However, those who do not have this absolute priority status, i.e. the regular renters who are looking for a home (e.g., because their family has grown), may face increasing lengths of waiting lists. They have to wait until the urgent families have been re-housed (Arthurson, 2002). This indirect housing market effect of demolition has hardly been researched.

Thus, although the evidence is not that impressive, creating a mixed housing stock in areas that were dominated by low-rent housing does seem to be successful in attracting (or at least keeping) households that have higher incomes. This is a quite logical result: if more expensive dwellings are built, low-income households cannot afford to live there. But success is not guaranteed: building new expensive dwellings could result in vacancies, because nobody wants to live there. From the research literature we have no evidence for such a situation, however. Generally, builders carry out some market research before they start building. In that way risks are minimized.

Mixed neighborhoods, better services?

Services need people. Without customers, commercial services will disappear quickly from the neighborhood. A new population may generate more demand, but more differentiation in the neighborhood will also lead to a differentiated demand. Doucet (2009) indicates this for the gentrified area of Leith in Edinburgh, where the old and new inhabitants clearly do not mix and make use of different leisure facilities within the same area: the wine bars for the gentrifiers, the pubs for the traditional local poor population. Within mixed-tenure regeneration areas, it also appears that new inhabitants of the area are less prone to shop in the area and prefer to do that elsewhere (Atkinson and Kintrea, 2000; Van Beckhoven and Van Kempen, 2003; Camina and Wood, 2009), especially also in their former neighborhood, the city center or, increasingly in specific places like mega-markets and filling stations. The disappearance of shops because of a lack in demand can lead to unattractive vacant shopping centers and to unsafe places in the neighborhood (Atkinson, 2000). Van Kempen et al. (2009) found that the satisfaction with shopping facilities in five out of their six research areas has not improved, and in some cases even deteriorated, since the start of the regeneration process. The claim that social mix leads to better facilities is, at least for the case of the UK, further undermined by the finding that the access of facilities is not associated with the level of neighborhood deprivation (Macintyre et al., 2008).

Social contacts in mixed neighborhoods

Many perceived disadvantages of spatial concentrations are in terms of lack of contacts with the outside world. Many advantages of mixed neighborhoods are related to the idea of the existence of social contacts between all kinds of different people, such as old and new inhabitants, old and young ones, owners and renters, native and minority ethnic groups. However, the gap between ideas and ideals, on the one hand, and empirical research, on the other hand, is quite striking. In a large number of papers, researchers have stated that contacts between different kinds of groups often hardly exist and are difficult to generate. Probably this lack of contact has to do with differences in lifestyles, orientations, values, and norms between members of different groups. Living together in one block, street, or neighborhood is definitely not automatically leading to intensive social contacts. On the contrary, people seem to avoid each other; they live parallel lives. Some examples follow below.

In the UK researchers found out that owners and renters have totally different activity patterns, which means that they hardly ever meet (Atkinson and Kintrea, 1998, 2000; Jupp, 1999; Hiscock, 2001). In the words of Atkinson and Kintrea (2000, p. 104):

> Owners do occupy largely different social worlds and play only a small part in the social interaction that goes on in the estates. They are away from the estates, at work and leisure, more often than renters, and use the local facilities far less.

Also in Australia, there is empirical evidence that owners and renters in mixed neighborhoods have not much in common (Arthurson, 2007). In the Netherlands, researchers discovered that in post World War II neighborhoods new inhabitants more often have their social contacts in their former neighborhood or elsewhere in the city than in the present neighborhood (Van Beckhoven and Van Kempen, 2003). New inhabitants are just not interested in the old inhabitants of the area (Kleinhans et al., 2007).

In the USA, a large number of researchers have indicated that there is not much interaction between different income groups in a mixed neighborhood (e.g., Brophy and Smith, 1997; De Souza Briggs, 1997; Schwartz and Tajbakhsh, 1997; Rosenbaum et al., 1998; Popkin et al., 2002). It is not only the new people that are not enthusiastic about new contacts but also the older residents of the area are often not interested: they often have an extensive and long-standing social network within the neighborhood and there seems to be no room for new contacts (Bolt and Van Kempen, 2008). The conclusions of all these researchers add up to a pessimistic picture: it is quite unlikely that mixed neighborhoods will quickly lead to new communities of new and old inhabitants (see also Jupp, 1999; Arthurson, 2002; Van Eijk and Blokland, 2007). A divided neighborhood is a more logical result than a more cohesive community (Wood and Vamplew, 1999).

Monotonous neighborhoods often have a strong social cohesion. This is at least partly due to the fact that residents have the same lifestyle. Cohesion can be so strong that contacts with people outside the area – with people belonging to other ethnic groups or different social classes – hardly exist and have to exist. This kind of neighborhood is characterized by a large amount of bonding capital and not so much bridging capital. In some cases the wish to create mixed neighborhoods is generated especially to break these concentrations in order to facilitate the generation of more bridging capital. It is then (deliberately) forgotten that this goes together with the breaking up of intensive (for the people involved) social ties. Although the creation of mixed neighborhoods can often be seen as a deliberate attempt to break up existing communities, it should also be recognized that social structures that are important for the residents will also disappear. Social contacts that have been built up in years and decades may be frustrated when suddenly a part of the population of the neighborhood has to move out and find a new place in another part of the city. Those who are dependent on family support in the neighborhood (such as taking care of the children when the parents are not at home) suddenly find themselves in a difficult situation (Dawkins, 2006; see also Gans, 1962).

Also the research by Putnam (2007) does not lead to optimistic views on the relation between mixed neighborhoods and social cohesion. He found out that a higher ethnic diversity in the neighborhood goes hand in hand with less trust in local politicians. Ethnic heterogeneity, furthermore, affects negatively the number of friends and acquaintances and the willingness to do something for the neighborhood or to work with voluntary organizations. Diversity does not only lead to less trust in the so-called out-group (e.g., people with a different ethnicity) but also to distrust in the in-group. Putnam (2007, p. 140) concludes:

> Diversity seems to trigger not in-group/out-group division, but anomie or social isolation. In colloquial language, people living in ethnically diverse settings appear to 'hunker down' – that is, to pull in like a turtle.

Also in the Netherlands research has indicated that ethnic heterogeneity within a neighborhood has a negative effect on social cohesion. More ethnic heterogeneity leads to less trust in the direct neighbors and to a less strong attachment to the neighborhood (Lancee and Dronkers, 2008).

The end result of creating a mixed community might be a division of a neighborhood: the old, poor, dilapidated neighborhood with many poor households and the new area in which the new inhabitants are totally different and have nothing to do with the inhabitants of the old part of the area. Within one neighborhood dividing lines may appear, at least in the eyes of the inhabitants (Goodchild and Cole, 2001).

It has already been indicated that the mixing of population groups within neighborhoods can lead to avoidance and parallel lives instead of social contact, because most people only want contacts with people who are like themselves. The effects of living in each other's vicinity can also be somewhat heftier. People can be disturbed by each other lifestyles: not everybody likes garden parties with loud music at night and not everybody thinks that public squares are for children playing football and the bus stops are for hanging out. The use of alcohol in public may annoy Muslims, while Muslims wearing a burka may annoy natives. Confrontations between different groups are more common in areas with a mixed population than in monoethnic areas. Living closer together may mean that people are more aware of differences between themselves and others (Arthurson, 2002, 2007). Interethnic tensions and discriminatory and cultural isolation behavior may be the result (Rosenbaum et al., 1998; Amin, 2002). There thus seems to be clear limits to how far social or community cohesion can become the basis of living with differences in mixed neighborhoods (Amin, 2002).

Mixed neighborhoods and social mobility

When social contacts hardly occur between different groups in a neighborhood it becomes quite difficult to arrive at a process of social mobility. Social mobility in mixed neighborhoods is still possible, because of the existence of local role models, with whom contact is not necessary. Whether this works in practice is still unclear: there is hardly empirical evidence for this.

Despite the lack of knowledge of the working of mechanisms, it has become clear from the literature that 'the neighborhood' can influence social mobility. However, this effect is small. Musterd et al. (2003) have for example indicated that neighborhood variables do affect social mobility, but that individual characteristics (such as years of schooling) and structural characteristics of the labor market are much more influential. For the USA, Galster (2005, 2007a) has indicated that many studies have found that a concentration of non-whites negatively affects the labor market position and chances of the inhabitants of such concentrations. Musterd et al. (2008) discovered that living in a concentration area positively affects the chances on the labor market in the first years, but that a longer stay in such an area creates negative effects. In general, American research seems to arrive at larger neighborhood affects than European research, although some American researchers also make clear that a mix of different groups is definitely no guarantee for higher social mobility (Goetz, 2003; Orr et al., 2003).

A side effect: waterbed effects

Creating mixed neighborhoods can have unwanted side effects in other neighborhoods (Bolt and Van Kempen, 2010). Spatial concentrations of low-income households or minority ethnic groups may disappear in areas where an increasing differentiation of the housing stock (and the population) is an important aim. But these concentrations may then appear in other neighborhoods, where affordable dwellings are still available. The same holds for schools: black schools may be closed in a neighborhood with many minorities, but concentration of minorities may then go to a limited number of other schools, creating again black schools. And increasing police surveillance in a neighborhood may displace criminal acts to adjacent neighborhoods. Politicians and policymakers hardly pay attention to these 'waterbed effects'. In a way this is logical, because it is quite an uneasy issue. Usually an area-based policy is aimed at making an area a better place to live, and then there is no interest in what is happening in other areas.

Summary

Mixed neighborhoods seem to give the possibility of pursuing a housing career within the neighborhood. But other positive effects of mixed neighborhoods seem to be difficult to find. This means that we should be extremely careful with creating mixed neighborhoods and attaching great expectations for the inhabitants of these neighborhoods. Ideas and ideals that are often formulated for mixed neighborhoods are in general not based on empirical results and are therefore only wobbly pillars. In the words of Rebecca Tunstall:

> The limits to the evidence for the neighborhood effects of mixed tenure means that policy to promote mixed tenure has been largely based on conviction (Tunstall, 2003, p. 157; see also Galster, 2007b, p. 35; Graham et al., 2009, pp. 142, 161).

POSSIBLE GAINS FROM ENCLAVES AND ETHNIC CONCENTRATIONS

Until now we have reviewed the advantages and disadvantages of mixed neighborhoods. But what can be said about areas which are not mixed across ethnicity and socio-economic status? While some of the advantages are simply the mirror image of the disadvantages of mixed areas, there are especially some advantages of concentrations of ethnic groups (Boal, 1976; Bolt et al., 1998). It is acknowledged in the literature that the positive aspects of ethnic clustering are largely ignored in research (Peach, 1996; Dunn, 1998).

First, spatial concentrations may serve as a starting point for immigrants who do not speak the language of the guest country. These immigrants often start their life in the new country in cities and neighborhoods with concentrations of their fellow-countrymen. Those neighborhoods serve as ports of entry to the new country (Dunn, 1998). Here they expect to receive a (temporary) place to sleep and social, economic, and emotional support from family members, friends or even vague acquaintances (Dahya, 1974; Enchautegui, 1997; Fong and Gulia, 1999; Zorlu and Mulder, 2008). Spatial concentrations of minority ethnic groups can thus have an important function for the first step of integration of immigrants belonging to the same group in a new society.

Secondly, spatial concentrations of people who are more or less alike facilitate social contacts between these people. As said earlier in this chapter, people generally like people who are like themselves and therefore it is nice when these people are close by. The possibility to have contacts with people you like can be an important contributor to people's feelings of happiness and control (Gans, 1962; Guest and Wierzbicki, 1999). Kinship networks can also be important: they may induce people to stay in the same neighborhood as their parents live, as has been put forward for Pakistanis in Birmingham, in the UK (Cole and Ferrari, 2008).

Thirdly, spatial concentrations of minority ethnic groups give the possibility to save the culture and identity of specific groups. Inhabitants of such concentrations can preserve habits, values, and norms of their own culture or even of their mother country (Boal, 1976). This may lead to neighborhoods with a very specific ethnic signature, such as Chinatowns and Little Italies. Neighborhoods not only may contain a population that overwhelmingly belongs to the same ethnic category but also may contain all kinds of group-specific elements, like churches that are an exact copy of the church in the homeland and shops with names in the group's language. People might even wear clothing that is typical for the place they originate from (Suttles, 1974). All these elements may create a feeling of security or even a place of home for the residents of that area. In a study in Toronto, Murdie (2002) indicates that living in an area with a 'Polish' character is emphasized by many Poles as an important contributor to housing satisfaction.

Fourthly, spatial concentrations of a specific minority group can create a critical mass for commercial services, such as shops, which offer an alternative for people unable to access formal provisions (Wilson and Portes, 1980; Robinson, 2008). Starting a new enterprise is not only a route for individual social mobility but also has a positive impact on the wider ethnic community:

> Once in a place, the immigrant sector has grown as a self-feeding process. Newcomers take up work in immigrant firms, and workers who have gained skills and experience working for co-ethnic owners set up a new business of their own (Bailey and Waldinger, 1991, p. 443).

The literature on minority ethnic businesses confirms the association between segregation and ethnic entrepreneurship. Wilson and Portes (1980), for instance, showed that ethnic businesses in Miami were mainly in highly concentrated Cuban neighborhoods. In Toronto, most Portuguese real estate companies are located in Portuguese concentrated neighborhoods (Teixeira, 1998). Fong et al. (2005) have found in their research in Scarborough (Canada) that the number of Chinese businesses in the neighborhood is positively associated with the number of Chinese residents. In contrast to the enclave hypothesis of Wilson and Portes (1980), they found that the proportion of recent immigrants is negatively associated with Chinese businesses. They attribute that to the high level of human capital of immigrants, which implies that they cannot function as a cheap labor force as is witnessed in earlier immigration waves. In many concentration areas, numerous small shops are present, providing goods and services for the ethnic community. At the same time it is indicated that competition is often fierce, because so many immigrants see having a business as a way to earn their money (Dunn, 1998). Such spatial concentrations can also be important for preserving non-commercial institutions, such as churches, mosques, clubs, and specific schools. Moreover, clusters of services may attract people from elsewhere, to shop, to spend leisure time, or to attend a religious service, creating such neighborhoods in activity-space concentrations rather than residential concentrations (Zhou, 1992). Dunn (1998) describes this vividly for the Indo-Chinese neighborhood of Cabramatta in Sidney, Australia.

Fifthly, concentration areas can fulfill an important defensive function against acts of discrimination. In some parts of the city, minority ethnic groups feel unsafe, because they fear racial harassment and discrimination from natives (Phillips, 1998; Logan et al., 2002). In terms of Boal (1976, p. 46), a concentration area can then act as a 'safe haven'. It is not always clear if minorities choose to settle in such 'safe' areas, or if they feel more or less forced to settle there, as Kundnani (2001) and Amin (2002) state for English cities (Oldham, Burnley, Bradford) in which, in the summer of 2001, race disturbances broke out.

Finally, concentrations of minority ethnic groups can protect against psychotic disorders.[5] Members of minority ethnic groups living in areas that are almost entirely native have a larger chance for developing schizophrenia than minority ethnic groups living in concentration areas of minorities (Veling et al., 2008; Bécares et al., 2009). More research is necessary to find out if there is a causal connection here, because it is as yet unclear why this is the case. One hypothesis is that minorities living in ethnic concentration areas can more easily fall back on their own ethnic group, which creates positive identities. An alternative explanation is that minority ethnic groups in native neighborhoods experience more discrimination, which increases the possibility for psychotic disorders.

DISCUSSION AND CONCLUSIONS

American researchers have repeatedly indicated that living in neighborhoods with concentrations of low-income and/or minority ethnic groups can have detrimental effects on a number of aspects of the lives of inhabitants of these areas. For researchers in Europe it is not yet quite clear how important these effects are. The conclusion is often that the neighborhood makes a non-trivial difference for a variety of outcomes, but that other characteristics, on the individual as well as on the level of the world (economic crisis), are more important (Friedrichs et al., 2003).

Especially from European research, there is not much evidence that mixed neighborhoods are much better places to live in than unmixed neighborhoods, in terms of socio-economic and ethnic variables. Despite this, many policies on national and local levels are aimed at creating socio-economically and/or ethnically mixed areas, sometimes called 'balanced' communities. Physical measures, such as large-scale renovation or demolition, have a prominent place on many urban policy agendas in European countries. There seems to be a big gap between what policymakers think and want, on the one hand, and the empirical research evidence, on the other hand. The increasing number of articles and reports that warn against the big expectations of mixed neighborhoods do not seem to prevent the ongoing efforts of policymakers to create mixed neighborhoods.

Would there be some good arguments to demolish affordable housing in order to create mixed communities? Yes, there are. First, there is the argument of giving the opportunity for a housing career: demolition and creating a more diversified housing stock in a neighborhood provides alternatives to people who otherwise would have moved to another part of the city or region. Here, creating a mixed community helps to keep middle-class households, who are attached to the area, in the neighborhood. Secondly, demolition and large-scale renovations are necessary when the dwellings are in such a bad condition that it is impossible, or even dangerous, to live in them. Of course, it would be possible to build new affordable dwellings instead. But usually this does not happen. Thirdly, demolition is necessary in the case of large-scale vacancies. This is for example the case in Berlin, where especially the large, unattractive post World War II blocks in the former eastern part of the city are increasingly left by those who can afford to do so. Finally, there is some evidence that after demolition and creating more housing diversification in the area, the inhabitants of the area show more satisfaction and a lower propensity to move out of the area, creating more stable communities (Kleinhans, 2005).

It becomes more problematic when there are big expectations of mixed communities with respect to social and socio-economic effects. Governments and other bodies, such as housing associations, often find the positive effects of heterogeneous neighborhoods so clear and so important that they do not seem to be interested in empirical evidence that points to contrary results. In the Netherlands, for example, we have found out in a research in six urban restructuring areas in different cities that social cohesion and satisfaction with the neighborhood had not increased after the restructuring process (Van Kempen et al., 2009).

Other research has pointed out that minority ethnic groups living in ethnic concentration areas do have fewer social contacts with natives and do speak the language of the majority less well. This might be worrying. But the first question we have to ask here is the question of causality. Are fewer social contacts and less command of the language a consequence of ethnic concentration or has it been the case that those with fewer contacts and less language command have deliberately selected the neighborhood with many people in the same situation? The second question to be asked is: What effects do these, on first sight worrying, social consequences have?

A possible problem with research in European cities on the effects of living in mixed neighborhoods might be that the research took place too early. It would be possible that significant effects can only be found at a later stage: for example, after 10 years. A few older studies have, indeed, indicated that the number and character of social relations in a neighborhood depends heavily on the number of years a person has lived in the area (Shaw and McKay, 1969; Kasarda and Janowitz, 1974; Sampson, 1988). More recently, researchers have found a positive relation between the number of years living in an area and social capital (DiPasquale and Glaeser, 1999; Saegert and Winkel, 2004). A more long-term and a more longitudinal approach of the effects of urban restructuring and the advantages of mixed neighborhoods thus seems to be important.

At the moment we think that the mix doctrine is as yet insufficiently informed by scientific research and evidence. But even if future research will point out that mixing is better than concentration, it remains to be seen if large-scale urban restructuring is the most efficient means to reach big issues like less social polarisation, more cohesion, and higher social mobility. Big demolition and refurbishing efforts are needed to reach a substantial change of the population in a neighborhood (small-scale projects do not affect the population composition and segregation very much; see Galster and Zobel, 1998). Those enormous projects can lead to all kinds of negative side effects, like large numbers of forced moves to areas where households actually do not want to live, increasing waiting lists for affordable dwellings, a declining social cohesion and more social polarisation and inequality within a neighborhood. Demolition is a heavy means, while other kinds of measures – like a more socially oriented policy – are maybe equally effective and more cost-efficient. The British researcher Rob Rowlands (2008) talked about the relation between demolition and the possible positive social consequences as a situation of 'cracking a nut with a sledgehammer'. We tend to agree with this view. It would be nice if policymakers would be more precise about what they have in mind when demolishing a neighborhood. When they refrain from too big expectations, they might find more support for their increasing efforts to change the built environment of urban neighborhoods in which still many people are very satisfied with their dwelling and their environment.

NOTES

1 As Massey and Denton (1993, pp. 18–19) indicate, the term 'ghetto' means different things to different people. They define the ghetto as a set of neighborhoods that are exclusively inhabited by members of one group, within which virtually all members of that group live. They also indicate that many observers add that a ghetto is not only a 'black' area but also a very poor area, plagued by a host of social and economic problems. Still others do not use the criterion that all members of a certain group should live in the area. In our opinion, it is important to talk about a ghetto as an area that is inhabited by members of one group and as an area with enormous social and economic problems (see Clark, 1989 for an extensive overview of these problems).

2 Of course, there are many other definitions of 'social cohesion': the attractiveness of the use of this term by Kearns and Forrest lies in its multi-dimensionality, while still keeping clear what is meant. Several other European authors have used their definition, although in most cases they do not use all the elements (Bolt and Torrance, 2005; Dekker, 2006).

3 A major problem with these kinds of research results is that it is difficult to demonstrate that spatial concentrations have an independent effect. The causality could even be reversed: people who *do not* speak the language of the guest country very well might be prone to cluster together. It can thus be hypothesized that members of minority ethnic groups choose much more quickly for a concentration neighborhood when they are not so well integrated in terms of language, social contacts, and economic terms (Bolt et al., 2008). Relations between concentration and integration are then not the consequence of a concentration effect, but of a so-called selection effect.

4 In European countries, like the Netherlands and the UK, a shift from a program of rehabilitation

to a program of demolition has taken place, which is comparable to what Goetz (2003) has described for the American HOPE VI program.

5   Whereas ethnic concentration has been found to be positively associated with mental health, there is an abundance of evidence that living in deprived neighborhoods (in which minority ethnic groups are strongly represented) negatively affects all kind of health indicators (Diez-Roux, 1998; Sloggett and Joshi, 1998).

REFERENCES

Alpheis, H. (1990), Erschwert die ethnische Konzentration die Eingliedrung? [Does ethnic concentration make assimilation more difficult?]. In: H. Esser and J. Friedrichs (eds), *Generation und Identität* [Generation and Identity], pp. 147–184. Opladen: Deutscher Verlag.

Amin, A. (2002), Ethnicity and the multicultural city: living with diversity. In: *Environment and Planning A*, 34, pp. 959–980.

Andersson, R. (2001), Spaces of socialization and social network competition: A study of neighborhood effects in Stockholm, Sweden. In: H.T. Andersen and R. van Kempen (eds), *Governing European Cities: Social Fragmentation, Social Exclusion and Urban Governance*, pp. 149–188. Aldershot: Ashgate.

Arthurson, K. (2002), Creating inclusive communities through balancing social mix: A critical relationship or tenuous link? In: *Urban Policy and Research*, 20 (3), pp. 1–29.

Arthurson, K. (2007), Social mix and social interaction: Do residents living in different housing tenures mix? Paper for the conference of the European Network for Housing Research, Rotterdam, 25–28 June 2007.

Atkinson, R. (2000), The hidden costs of gentrification: Displacement in central London. In: *Journal of Housing and the Built Environment*, 15 (4), pp. 307–326.

Atkinson, R. and Kintrea, K. (1998), *Reconnecting Excluded Communities: The Neighborhood Impacts of Owner Occupation*. Edinburgh: Scottish Homes.

Atkinson, R. and Kintrea, K. (2000), Owner occupation, social mix and neighbourhood impacts. In: *Policy and Politics*, 28 (1), pp. 93–108.

Atkinson, R. and Kintrea, K. (2002), *'Opportunities and Despair, It's All in There', or, 'Every Area Has Its Problems': Everyday Experiences of Area Effects.* Glasgow: Department of Urban Studies, University of Glasgow.

Bailey, T. and Waldinger, R. (1991), Primary, secondary, and enclave labour markets: A training systems approach. In: *American Sociological Review*, 56 (4), pp. 432–445.

Bécares, L., Nazroo, J. and Stafford, M. (2009), The buffering effects of ethnic density on experienced racism and health. In: *Health & Place*, 15 (3), pp. 700–708.

Boal, F.W. (1976), Ethnic residential segregation. In: D.T. Herbert and R.J. Johnston (eds), *Social Areas in Cities*, pp. 41–79. London: John Wiley and Sons.

Bolt, G., Burgers, J. and Van Kempen, R. (1998), On the social significance of spatial location, spatial segregation and social inclusion. In: *Netherlands Journal of Housing and the Built Environment*, 13 (1), pp. 83–95.

Bolt, G. and Torrance, M. (2005), *Sociale cohesie en stedelijke herstructurering* [Social Cohesion and Urban Restructuring]. Utrecht/Den Haag: DGW/Nethur Partnership.

Bolt, G. and Van Kempen, R. (2008), *De mantra van de mix: ideeën, idealen en de praktijk* [The Mantra of the Mix: Ideas, Ideals and Practices]. Utrecht: Forum: Institute for Multicultural Development.

Bolt, G. and Van Kempen, R. (2010), Dispersal patterns of households who are forced to move: Desegregation by demolition: A case study of Dutch cities. In: *Housing Studies*, 25 (2), pp. 159-180.

Bolt, G., Van Kempen, R. and Van Ham, M. (2008), Minority ethnic groups in the Dutch housing market: Spatial segregation, relocation dynamics and housing policy. In: *Urban Studies*, 45 (7), pp.1359–1384.

Bolt, G., Van Kempen, R. and Van Weesep, J. (2009), After urban restructuring: Relocations and segregation in Dutch cities. In: *Tijdschrift voor Economische en Sociale Geografie*, 100 (4), pp. 502–518.

Botman, S. and van Kempen, R. (2001), *Spatial Dimensions of Urban Social Exclusion and Integration: The Case of Rotterdam.* Amsterdam: Amsterdam Study Centre for the Metropolitan Environment.

Bourdieu, P. (1986), The forms of capital. In: J.G. Richardson (ed.), *Handbook of Theory and Research for Sociology and Education*, pp. 241–258. New York: Greenwood Press.

Brooks-Gunn, J., Duncan, G. and Aber, J. (eds) (1997), *Neighborhood Poverty: Volume 1, Context and Consequences for Children*. New York: Russell Sage.

Brophy, P. and Smith, R. (1997), Mixed income housing factors for success. In: *CityScape*, 3 (2), pp. 3–32.

Burns, D., Forrest, R., Flint, J. and Kearns, A. (2001), *Empowering Communities: The Impact of Registered Social Landlords on Social Capital*. Edinburgh: Scottish Homes.

Butler, T. and Robson, G. (2001), Social capital, gentrification and neighbourhood change in London. In: *Urban Studies*, 38 (12), pp. 2145–2162.

Camina, M.M. and Wood, M.J. (2009), Parallel lives: Towards a greater understanding of what mixed communities can offer. In: *Urban Studies*, 46 (2), pp. 459–480.

Campbell, K., Marsden, P. and Hurlbert, J. (1986), Social resources and socioeconomic status. In: *Social Networks*, 8, pp. 97–117.

Castells, M. (2002), Local and global: Cities in the network society. In: *Tijdschrift voor Economische en Sociale Geografie*, 93 (5), pp. 546–556.

Clark, K.B. (1989), *Dark Ghetto: Dilemmas of Social Power* (second edition). Middletown: Wesleyan University Press.

Cole, I. & Ferrari, E. (2008), Connectivity of place and housing market change: The case of Birmingham. In: J. Flint & D. Robinson (eds), *Community Cohesion in Crisis? New Dimensions of Diversity and Difference*, pp. 57–79. Bristol: The Policy Press.

Coleman, J.S. (1988), Social capital and the creation of human capital. In: *American Journal of Sociology*, 94, pp. S95–S120.

Dagevos, J. (2005), Gescheiden werelden. De etnische signatuur van vrijetijdscontacten van minderheden [Separate Worlds: The Ethnic Signature of Leisure Contacts of Minority Ethnic Groups]. In: *Sociologie*, 1 (1), pp. 52–69.

Dahya B. (1974), The nature of Pakistani ethnicity in industrial cities in Britain. In: A. Cohen (ed.), *Urban Ethnicity*, pp. 77-118. London: Tavistock.

Dawkins, C.J. (2006), Are social networks the ties that bind families to neighborhoods? In: *Housing Studies*, 21 (6), pp. 867–881.

De Souza Briggs, X. (1997), *Yonkers Revisited: The Early Impacts of Scattered-site Public Housing on Families and Neighborhoods*. Ford Foundation (unpublished report).

De Souza Briggs, X. (2003), *Bridging Networks, Social Capital, and Racial Segregation in America*. Cambridge, MA: John F. Kennedy School of Government.

De Souza Briggs, X. (2005), *Who Bridges and How? Race, Friendships, and Segregation in American Communities*. Cambridge, MA: MIT.

Dekker (2006), *Governance as Glue: Urban Governance and Social Cohesion in Post-WWII Neighbourhoods in the Netherlands*. Utrecht: Faculty of Geosciences.

Diez-Roux, A. (1998), Bringing context back into epidemiology: Variables and fallacies in multi-level analysis. In: *American Journal of Public Health*, 88 (2), pp. 216–222.

DiPasquale, D. and Glaeser, E. (1999), Incentives and social capital: Are homeowners better citizens? In: *Journal of Urban Economics*, 45 (2), pp. 354–384.

Doucet, B. (2009), Living through gentrification: Subjective experiences of local, non-gentrifying residents in Leith, Edinburgh. In: *Journal of Housing and the Built Environment*, 24 (3), pp. 299–315.

Dunn, K.M. (1998), Rethinking ethnic concentration: The case of Cabramatta, Sydney. In: *Urban Studies*, 35 (3), pp. 503–527.

Ellen, I.G. and Turner, M.A. (1997), Does neighborhood matter? Assessing recent evidence. In: *Housing Policy Debate*, 8 (4), pp. 833–866.

Enchautegui, M.E. (1997), Latino neighborhoods and Latino neighborhood poverty. In: *Journal of Urban Affairs*, 19 (4), pp. 445–467.

Fong, E. and Gulia, M. (1999), Differences in neighborhood qualities among racial and ethnic groups in Canada. In: *Sociological Inquiry*, 69 (4), pp. 575–598.

Fong, E., Luk, C. and Oka, E. (2005), Spatial distribution of suburban ethnic businesses. In: *Social Science Research*, 34 (1), pp. 215–235.

Forrest, R. and Kearns, A. (2001), Social cohesion, social capital and the neighbourhood. In: *Urban Studies*, 38 (12), pp. 2125–2143.

Friedrichs, J. (1997), Context effects of poverty neighbourhoods on residents. In: H. Vestergaard (ed.), *Housing in Europe*, pp. 141–160. Horsholm: Danish Building Research Institute.

Friedrichs, J. (1998), Do poor neighbourhoods make their residents poorer? Context effects of poverty neighbourhoods on residents. In: H.-J. Andress (ed.), *Empirical Poverty Research in a Comparative Perspective*, pp. 77–99. Aldershot: Ashgate.

Friedrichs, J., Galster, G. and Musterd, S. (2003), Neighbourhood effects and social opportunities: The European and American research and policy context. In: *Housing Studies*, 18 (6), pp. 797–806.

Galster, G. (2005), *Neighborhood Mix, Social Opportunities, and the Policy Challenges of an Increasingly Diverse Amsterdam. Wibaut Lecture*. Amsterdam: AMIDSt.

Galster, G. (2007a), Should policy makers strive for neighborhood social mix? An analysis of the Western European evidence base. In: *Housing Studies*, 22 (4), pp. 523–545.

Galster, G. (2007b), Neighborhood social mix as a goal for housing policy: A theoretical analysis.

In: *European Journal of Housing Policy*, 7 (1), pp. 19–43.

Galster, G. and Zobel, A. (1998), Will dispersed housing programmes reduce social problems in the US? In: *Housing Studies*, 13 (5), pp. 605–622.

Galster, G., Andersson, R., Musterd, S. and Kauppinen, T.M. (2008), Does neighborhood income mix affect earnings of adults? New evidence from Sweden. In: *Journal of Urban Economics*, 63, pp. 858–870.

Gans, H. (1962), *The Urban Villagers*. New York: The Free Press.

Gijsberts, M. and Dagevos, J. (eds) (2007), *Interventies voor integratie – het tegengaan van etnische concentratie en het bevorderen van interetnisch contact* [Interventions for Integration]. Den Haag: Sociaal en Cultureel Planbureau.

Goetz, E.G. (2003), *Clearing the Way: Deconcentrating the Poor in Urban America*. Washington, DC: The Urban Institute.

Goodchild, B. and Cole, I. (2001), Social balance and mixed neighbourhoods in Britain since 1979: A review of discourse and practice in social housing. In: *Environment and Planning D: Society and Space*, 19 (1), pp. 103–121.

Graham, S. and Marvin, S. (1996), *Telecommunications and The City: Electronic Spaces, Urban Places*. London: Routledge.

Graham, E., Manley, D., Hiscock, R., Boyle, P. and Doherty, J. (2009), Mixing housing tenures: Is it good for social well-being? In: *Urban Studies*, 46 (1), pp. 139–165.

Granovetter, M.S. (1973), The strength of weak ties. In: *American Journal of Sociology*, 78 (6), pp. 1360–1380.

Guest, A.M. and Wierzbicki, S.K. (1999), Social ties at the neighborhood level: Two decades of GSS evidence. In: *Urban Affairs Review*, 35 (1), pp. 92–111.

Hampton, K. and Wellman, B. (2003), Neighboring in Netville: How the internet supports community and social capital in a wired suburb. In: *City & Community*, 2 (4), pp. 277–311.

Henning, C. and Lieberg, M. (1996), Strong ties or weak ties? Neighbourhood networks in a new perspective. In: *Scandinavian Housing and Planning Research*, 13, pp. 3–26.

Hiscock, R. (2001), Are mixed tenure estates likely to enhance the social capital of the residents? Paper for the HAS Conference, Cardiff, 3–4 September.

Hogan, D.P. and Kitagawa, E.M. (1985), The impact of social status, family structure, and the neighborhood on the fertility of Black adolescents. In: *American Journal of Sociology*, 90, pp. 825–855.

Janelle, D.G. (1973), Measuring human extensibility in a shrinking world. In: *The Journal of Geography*, 72 (5), pp. 8–15.

Jargowsky, P.A. (1997), *Poverty and Place: Ghettos, Barrios and the American City*. New York: Russell Sage.

Jencks, C. and Mayer, S.E. (1990), The social consequences of growing up in a poor neighborhood. In: L.E. Lynn and M.G.H. McGeary (eds), *Inner-City Poverty in the United States*, pp. 111–186. Washington, DC: National Academy Press.

Jupp, B. (1999), *Living Together: Community Life on Mixed Housing Estates*. London: Demos.

Kasarda, J. and Janowitz, M. (1974), Community attachment in mass society. In: *American Sociological Review*, 39 (3), pp. 328–339.

Kearns, A. and Forrest, R. (2000), Social cohesion and multilevel urban governance. In: *Urban Studies*, 37 (5/6), pp. 995–1017.

Keller, S. (1968), *The Urban Neighborhood: A Sociological Perspective*. New York: Random House.

Kleinhans, R. (2005), *Sociale implicaties van herstructurering en herhuisvesting* [Social Implications of Restructuring and Rehousing]. Delft: Delftse Universitaire Pers Science.

Kleinhans, R., Priemus, H. and Engbersen, G. (2007), Understanding social capital in recently restructured urban neighbourhoods: Two case studies in Rotterdam. In: *Urban Studies*, 44 (5/6), pp. 1069–1091.

Kraut, R., Patterson, M., Landmark, V., et al. (1998), Internet paradox: A social technology that reduces social involvement and psychological well-being? In: *American Psychologist*, 53 (9), pp. 1017–1031.

Kundnani, A. (2001), From Oldham to Bradford: The violence of the violated. In: *Race and Class*, 43 (2), pp. 105–131.

Lancee, B. and Dronkers, J. (2008), Ethnic diversity in neighborhoods and individual trust of immigrants and natives: A replication of Putnam (2007) in a West-European country. Paper presented at the International Conference on Theoretical Perspectives on Social Cohesion and Social Capital, Brussels, 15 May 2008.

Leventhal, T. and Brooks-Gunn, J. (2000), The neighborhoods they live in: The effects of neighborhood residence on child and adolescent outcomes. In: *Psychological Bulletin*, 126 (2), pp. 309–337.

Logan, J.R., Alba, R.D. and Zwan, W. (2002), Immigrant enclaves and ethnic communities in New York and Los Angeles. In: *American Sociological Review*, 67, pp. 299–322.

Macintyre, S., MacDonald, L. and Ellaway, A. (2008), Do poorer people have poorer access to local resources and facilities? The distribution of local resources by area deprivation in Glasgow, Scotland. *Social Science & Medicine*, 67 (6), pp. 900–914.

Maloutas, T. and Malouta, M.P. (2004), The glass menagerie of urban governance and social cohesion: Concepts and stakes/concepts as stakes. In: *International Journal of Urban and Regional Research*, 28 (2), pp. 449–465.

Marcuse P. (2002), The shifting meaning of the black ghetto in the United States. In: P. Marcuse and R. van Kempen (eds), *Of States and Cities: The Partitioning of Urban Space*, pp. 109-142. Oxford: Oxford University Press.

Massey, D.S. and Denton, N.A. (1993), *American Apartheid: Segregation and the Making of the Underclass*. Cambridge, MA: Harvard University Press.

Murdie, R.A. (2002), The housing careers of Polish and Somali newcomers in Toronto's rental market. In: *Housing Studies*, 17 (3), pp. 423–443.

Musterd, S. and Van Kempen, R. (2007), Trapped or on the springboard? Housing careers in large housing estates in European cities. In: *Journal of Urban Affairs*, 29 (3), pp. 311–329.

Musterd, S., Ostendorf, W. and de Vos, S. (2003), Environmental effects and social mobility. In: *Housing Studies*, 18 (6), pp. 877–892.

Musterd, S., Andersson, R., Galster, G. and Kauppinen, T. (2008), Are immigrants' earnings influenced by the characteristics of their neighbors? In: *Environment and Planning A*, 40, pp. 785–805.

Nie, N. and Erbring, L. (2000), *Internet and Society: A Preliminary Report*. Stanford, CA: Stanford University.

Oberwittler, D. (2007), The effects of neighbourhood poverty on adolescent problem behaviours: A multi-level analysis differentiated by gender and ethnicity. In: *Housing Studies*, 22 (5), pp. 781–803.

Office of the Deputy Prime Minister (2005), *Planning for Mixed Communities*. London: ODPM.

Orr, L., Feins, J.D., Jacob, R., et al. (2003), *Moving to Opportunity for Fair Housing Demonstration Program. Interim Impacts Evaluation*. Washington, DC: US Department.

Peach, C. (1996), Does Britain have ghettos? In: *Transactions of the Institute of British Geographers*, 21, pp. 216–235.

Phillips, D. (1998), Black minority ethnic concentration and dispersal in Britain. In: *Urban Studies*, 35 (10), pp. 1681–1702.

Popkin, S., Harris, J. and Cunningham, M. (2002), *Families in Transition: A Qualitative Analysis of the MTO Experience, Final Report*. Washington, DC: US Department of Housing and Urban Development.

Putnam, R.D. (2000), *Bowling Alone: The Collapse and Revival of American Community*. New York: Simon and Schuster.

Putnam, R.D. (2007), E pluribus unum: Diversity and community in the twenty-first century. The 2006 Johan Skytte Prize lecture. In: *Scandinavian Political Studies*, 30 (2), pp. 137–174.

Robinson, D. (2008), Community cohesion and the politics of communitarianism. In: J. Flint & D. Robinson (eds), *Community Cohesion in Crisis? New Dimensions of Diversity and Difference*, pp. 15–33. Bristol: The Policy Press.

Rosenbaum, J., Stroh, L. and Flynn, C. (1998), Lake Parc Place: A study of mixed-income housing. In: *Housing Policy Debate*, 9 (4), pp. 703–772.

Rowlands, R. (2008), The sledgehammer and the nut: A story of the contribution of mix in planning the sustainable community. Paper for the Housing Studies Association Conference, York, 2–4 April 2008.

Saegert, S. and Winkel, G. (2004), Crime, social capital and community participation. In: *American Journal of Community Psychology*, 34 (3/4), pp. 219–233.

Sampson, R.J. (1988), Local friendship ties and community attachment in mass society: A multilevel systemic model. In: *American Sociological Review*, 53 (5), pp. 766–779.

Sampson, R.J. (2008), Moving to inequality: Neighborhood effects and experiments meet social structure. In: *American Journal of Sociology*, 114 (1), pp. 189–231.

Sampson, R.J. and Raudenbusch, S.W. (2004), Seeing disorder: Neighborhood stigma and the social construction of 'broken windows'. In: *Social Psychology Quarterly*, 67 (4), pp. 319–342.

Sampson, R.J., Raudenbush, S.W. and Earls, F. (1997), Neighborhoods and violent crime: A multilevel study of collective efficacy. In: *Science*, 277 (5328), pp. 918–924.

Schwartz, A. and Tajbakhsh, K. (1997), Mixed income housing: Unanswered questions. In: *CityScape*, 3 (2), pp. 71–92.

Shaw, C.R. and McKay, H. (1969), *Juvenile Deliquency and Urban Areas*. Chicago, IL: University of Chicago Press.

Sloggett, A. and Joshi, H. (1998), Deprivation indicators as predictors of life events 1981–1992 based on the UK ONS longitudinal study. In: *Journal of Epidemiology and Community Health*, 52 (4), pp. 228–233.

Smith, A. (2002), *Mixed-Income Housing Developments: Promise and Reality*. Cambridge, MA: Harvard University.

Stein, M. (1972), *The Eclipse of Community*. Princeton, NJ: Princeton University Press.

Sullivan, D.M. (2006), Assessing residents' opinions on changes in a gentrifying neighborhood: A case study of the Alberta neighborhood in Portland, Oregan. In: *Housing Policy Debate*, 17 (3), pp. 595–624.

Suttles, G.D. (1974), *The Social Order of the Slum: Ethnicity and Territory in the Inner City*. Chicago, IL: University of Chicago Press.

Teixeira, C. (1998), Cultural resources and ethnic entrepreneurship: A case study of the Portuguese real estate industry in Toronto. In: *The Canadian Geographer*, 41 (3), pp. 267–281.

Tunstall, R. (2003), 'Mixed tenure' policy in the UK: Privatisation, pluralism or euphemism? In: *Housing, Theory and Society*, 20, pp. 153–159.

Urban, S. (2009), Is the neighbourhood effect an economic or an immigrant issue? A study of the importance of the childhood neighbourhood for future integration into the labour market. In: *Urban Studies*, 46 (3), pp. 583–603.

Van Beckhoven, E. and Van Kempen, R. (2003), Social effects of urban restructuring: A case study in Amsterdam and Utrecht, the Netherlands. In: *Housing Studies*, 18 (6), pp. 853–875.

Van der Laan Bouma-Doff, W. (2007), Confined contact: Residential segregation and ethnic bridges in the Netherlands. In: *Urban Studies*, 44 (5/6), pp. 997–1017.

Van Eijk, G. and Blokland, T. (2007), Poor people's bridging ties: An exploration of poor people's networks in a poverty neighborhood and a mixed neighborhood in Rotterdam, the Netherlands. Paper for the conference of the European Network for Housing Research, Rotterdam, 25–28 June 2007.

Van Gent, W.P.C. (2009), *Realistic Restructuring: The Social Outcomes and Housing Context of Neighbourhood Interventions in Western European Cities*. Amsterdam: Amsterdam Institute for Metropolitan and International Development Studies, Universiteit van Amsterdam.

Van Kempen, R. and Bolt, G. (2009), Social cohesion, social mix, and urban policies in the Netherlands. In: *Journal of Housing and the Built Environment*, 24 (4), pp. 457-475.

Van Kempen, R., Bolt, G., Van Bergeijk, E. and Kokx, A. (2009), Does Urban Restructuring Work? Effects of Urban Policies in Deprived Neighborhoods in Dutch Cities. Paper for the Urban Affairs Association Conference in Chicago, 4–8 March 2009.

Van Tubergen, F. (2007), Religious affiliation and participation among immigrants in a secular society. In: *Journal of Ethnic and Migration Studies*, 33 (5), pp. 747–765.

Van Tubergen, F. and Kalmijn, M. (2002), Tweede taalverwerving en taalgebruik onder Turkse en Marokkaanse immigranten in Nederland: Investering of gelegenheid? In: *Migrantenstudies*, 18(3), pp. 156–177.

Veldboer, L., Kleinhans, R. and Duyvendak, J.W. (2002), The diversified neighborhood in Western Europe and the United States: How countries deal with the spatial distribution of economic and cultural differences. In: *Journal of International Migration and Integration*, 3 (1), pp. 41–64.

Veling, W., Susser, E., van Os, J., et al. (2008), Ethnic density of neighborhoods and incidence of psychotic disorders among immigrants. In: *American Psychiatric Association*, 165 (1), pp. 66–73.

Wacquant, L.J.D. (1997), Three pernicious premises in the study of the American ghetto. In: *International Journal of Urban and Regional Research*, 21 (2), pp. 341–353.

Webber, M.M. (1963), Order in diversity: Community without propinquity. In: L. Wingo (ed.), *Cities and Space: The Future Use of Urban Land*, pp. 23–54. Baltimore, MD: Johns Hopkins University Press.

Wellman, B. and Haythornthwaite, C. (2002), *The Internet in Everyday Life*. Oxford: Blackwell.

Wilson, K.L. and Portes, A. (1980), Immigrant enclaves: An analysis of the labor markets experiences of Cubans in Miami. In: *American Journal of Sociology*, 86 (2), pp. 295–319.

Wilson, W.J. (1987), *The Truly Disadvantaged: The Inner City, the Underclass, and Public Policy*. Chicago, IL: University of Chicago Press.

Wilson, W.J. (1996), *When Work Disappears: The World of the New Urban Poor*. New York: Knopf.

Wood, M. (2003), A balancing act? Tenure diversification in Australia and the UK. In: *Urban Policy and Research*, 21 (1), pp. 45–56.

Wood, M. and Vamplew, C. (1999), *Neighbourhood Images in Teesside: Regeneration and Decline?* York: Joseph Rowntree Foundation.

Zhou, M. (1992), *Chinatown: The Socioeconomic Potential of an Urban Enclave*. Philadelphia, PA: Temple University Press.

Zorlu, A. and Mulder, C.H. (2008), Initial and subsequent location choices of immigrants to the Netherlands. In: *Regional Studies*, 42 (2), pp. 245–264.

24

Managing Social Housing

Hugo Priemus

INTRODUCTION

Harriott et al. (1998: 151–153) give an overview of definitions of 'housing management':

> the central tasks of housing management.... Letting houses, repairing them and collecting rent – are the core of a rather wider range of functions normally constituting 'housing management' (Department of the Environment, 1990:16);
>
> For the purpose of this study, 'housing management' has been defined to encompass the core landlord activities of letting houses, collecting rents and carrying out repairs. These functions are clearly integral to the management of housing (Centre for Housing Policy, University of York; 1993: 13)

Harriott et al. (1998: 152–153) present the following specification:

Letting of properties

- waiting lists and selection
- transfers and exchanges
- void property management.

Rent collection and arrears control

- rent collection and arrears recovery
- benefit advice
- tenants welfare.

Repairs and maintenance

- estate management
- repairs inspection and ordering.

Tenancy management

- neighbourhood disputes and harassment
- tenancy enforcement
- tenant consultation and participation.

Housing management, then, is essentially about four key tasks:

- letting houses
- collecting the rent
- maintaining the properties in good condition
- managing tenancies.

Housing management can also be subdivided into four other categories:

- *technical management* – maintenance, renovation, demolition, enlargement, restoration, splitting and combining housing units
- *social management* – dealing with future and sitting tenants through marketing, information, communication, the encouragement of tenant participation, housing allocation, target group selection, reducing anti-social behaviour, the administration of tenancy agreements, and finally the clearance of dwellings

- *financial management* – everything relating to housing finance, lending and borrowing, treasury management and rent policy
- *tenure management* – the purchase and sale of properties, the adoption of mixed and experimental tenures such as sheltered ownership and tenant ownership of the interior of dwellings.

Housing management can also be split into day-to-day management and strategic management: there are short-term decisions and medium- and long-term management policies. Strategic management sets the priorities and charts the course for the future (5–10 years). Though short-term decisions are responses to everyday problems, they still have to fit in with the long-term policies.

Priemus et al. (1999: 211) define the management of social housing as: *the full array of activities designed to produce and allocate housing services from the social housing stock*. The management of social housing excludes all activities connected with the development of new social housing. It is also distinct from the pure consumption of housing services, although it should be borne in mind that tenants are responsible for some elements of social housing management, such as certain maintenance activities.

Housing management in the social rented sector is usually the responsibility of private or public managers who work in housing associations, housing corporations, municipal companies or local housing authorities (CHR, 1989; Bines et al., 1993; Clapham et al., 1995).

Housing management is not the sole territory of social housing organizations. It involves relationships and interdependencies with various stakeholders, such as tenants, home-seekers, municipalities, the Ministry of Housing (including housing inspectors and regulators), financiers, guarantee providers and housing organization employees. Housing management, especially strategic management, reflects the way a housing organization deals with its stakeholders.

There are many studies on social housing, social housing policy and social housing management, including historical overviews, such as Burnett (1978), Merrett (1979), Balchin (1990), Power (1993) and Pooley (1992). These studies will not be recapitulated in this chapter.

This chapter opens with an overview of tenures (Section 2). This is followed by an introduction to technical management and strategic housing stock policy (Section 3). Section 4 reviews developments in social housing and social housing management. Section 5 discusses the changing socio-economic and ethnic composition of tenants in the (European) social housing stock. In the UK these changes have been associated since about 1980 with residualization in the social housing sector. Section 6 presents three models of landlord–tenant relationships. In Section 7 social housing management is accorded a position between citizenship and managerialism. Section 8 describes the service-oriented approach. Section 9 elaborates on the conceptual model of service quality and Section 10 addresses the service–profit chain in social housing management. Section 11 presents an analysis of the bureaucratic discourse and shows how social housing management is socially constructed.

Some social housing estates have degenerated into problem areas, thereby accelerating the implementation of strategic housing management (Section 12). In Section 13 the public framework for social housing is described on the basis of the situation in the Netherlands. The chapter ends with conclusions in Section 14.

SOCIAL RENTED SECTOR – COMMERCIAL RENTED SECTOR – OWNER-OCCUPIER SECTOR

In theory, people can choose to either rent or buy a dwelling. Many of those who can afford to live in the owner-occupier sector will choose to buy. Many housing consumers see a home in the owner-occupier sector as having certain important advantages compared with a rented home. Boumeester et al. (1998) cite various motives for choosing to buy instead of rent. First of all, a homeowner has maximum control over his home and can make his own decisions on the quality of the fittings and finishing. Secondly, in many countries there are special tax arrangements which make the long-term cost of homeownership more attractive than the cost of renting. Fluctuations in the interest rate mean that, over time, housing costs for owner-occupiers are usually more irregular than for tenants. Potential owner-occupiers also have a wider range of choice than potential tenants. Finally, the purchase of a home is often seen as an excellent long-term investment, a way of accumulating capital.

However, a rented home also has certain advantages. Boumeester et al. (1998) point out that consumers who cannot afford to buy a home are often able to rent one thanks to rent allowances. In addition, tenants have more freedom than owner-occupiers as it is generally much easier to cancel a tenancy agreement than to sell a house.

Moreover, tenants can call upon the services of a landlord and need not worry about maintenance and maintenance costs. Some tenants even receive services which go beyond what the landlord is obliged to provide. Often these services are customized to their own needs.

In the rented sector social housing is separate from commercial housing. The commercial sector consists of dwellings let by institutional investors and by (usually small-scale) private landlords. The social rented sector is run by public and private organizations. The private organizations are subject to legislation that promotes affordable housing for households with a modest income and/or handicaps (see Section 13).

The main difference between profit-making and non-profit-making landlords is – as the adjective suggests – that the primary aim of the former is to make money.

In the Netherlands any financial surplus recorded by non-profit-making landlords must be spent in accordance with the stipulations of the Housing Act, which states that housing associations are required to spend any financial surplus 'exclusively in the interest of housing'.

TECHNICAL MANAGEMENT AND STRATEGIC HOUSING STOCK POLICY

Straub (2002) argues that technical management is directly linked to the strategic housing stock policy, which is developed from the 'top-down' (Figure 24.1), in contrast with the situation in the past, when the management of existing stock was more of a routine activity carried out at operational level in the organization. The housing association builds a picture of the desired housing portfolio and works out market strategies for product lines, e.g. investment in growth or divestment. The desired quality of housing complexes and dwellings may depend on the product line to which the complex belongs. Housing complex and maintenance strategies are the result of market strategies formulated from the 'top-down' and product and exploitation analyses carried out at operational level. The current policy might not be appropriate for the predicted future developments. Besides maintenance strategies, design proposals for major improvements are derived from the housing complex strategies.

The technical exploitation of complexes by housing associations falls into two main categories – ongoing exploitation and limited exploitation – ending with, for instance, demolition or sale. The strategy for a housing complex due to be exploited over a long-time horizon is dictated by whether the technical performance is to be maintained or altered and whether the dwellings in the complex are to be allocated to the existing client group or to a new one (Figure 24.2). A housing association strives for a level of quality that is commensurate with the current position of

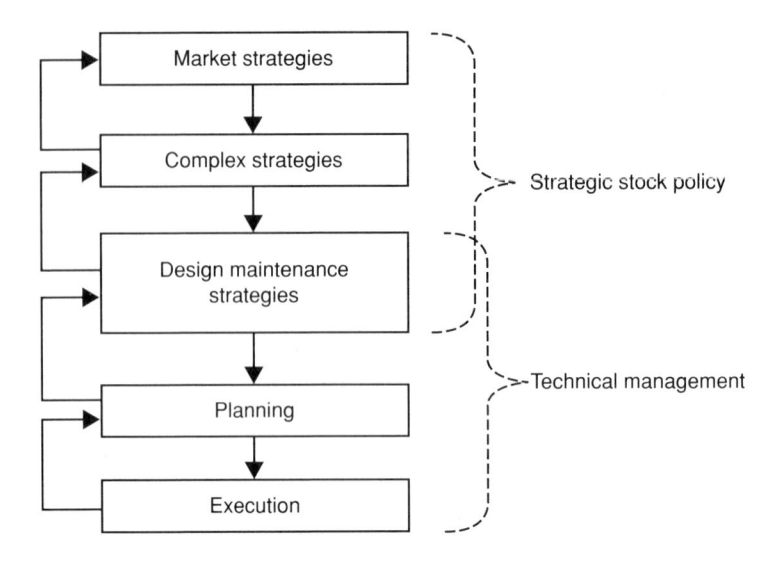

Figure 24.1 Strategic stock policy and technical management
Source: Straub, 2002.

the complex on the housing market or the position that is aspired to in the future. At the same time, this market position determines the deviation margins for dwellings. A property manager can cater to the wishes of individual clients by upgrading individual parts of a dwelling. This client-centred approach has implications for relet maintenance and for the housing association's policy on home alterations undertaken by tenants who are vacating the property.

The housing association ought to align maintenance with one of the housing complex strategies. The maintenance strategy depends on anticipated interventions or the product line or the specific client group or individual client. This is sometimes referred to as intervention-oriented, market-oriented and client (group)-oriented maintenance. Figure 24.3 presents a diagram of successive complex strategies, maintenance strategies and activities. Even after selling dwellings to individual buyers, the housing associations may still be involved in the maintenance of communal parts of the building and the exterior. In the near future, housing associations may play a dominant role in the technical maintenance of entire housing estates with several owners.

Maintenance strategies can be devised to achieve a desired basic quality for communal areas, entries, common space, building services and the surroundings, and a desired basic and top quality for parts of individual dwellings. The housing association can also match the maintenance levels with the different client (user/occupant) groups in the strategic stock policy. The strategies must be applied in line with the different maintenance types: responsive maintenance, relet maintenance (including altered performance) and planned maintenance.

Performance measurement

Strategic and maintenance policy should be based on objective, reliable information on the performance of housing complexes and building components. Data collected during an on-site assessment survey are needed for strategic policymaking and maintenance planning. Additional information is needed for the actual maintenance work. A condition-dependent approach to maintenance planning leads to a separation between quality assessment and the determination of maintenance activities. A condition assessment survey is a

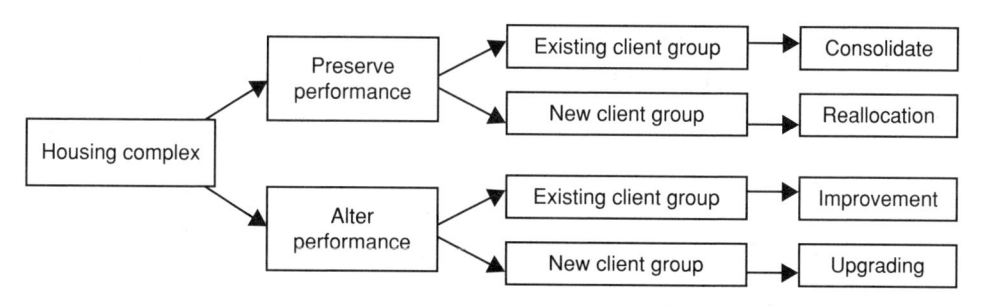

Figure 24.2 Strategies for the ongoing exploitation of housing complexes
Source: Straub, 2002.

tool that gauges the technical performance of properties in order to underpin the long-term maintenance expectations. Hence, its main purpose is not to draw up the annual maintenance budget and plan the work. It is, first and foremost, a strategic management tool (Chandler, 1995; Shen & Spedding, 1998). Additional information is needed for the preparation of remedial work.

All building components have to contend with loss of performance through ageing, usage, weather and other external factors. The relationship between defects and loss of performance has been explored by many researchers (e.g. Addleon, 1989; Hermans, 1995; Damen Consultants, 1996), but these studies often do little more than observe that loss of performance is not the same as defects. However, we distinguish different kinds of maintenance performance and link them to different kinds of maintenance. In general, acceptable loss of performance and the implementation of appropriate maintenance activities depend on legal requirements, technical and functional considerations, and environmental objectives. The international ISO 6241 (ISO, 1984) standard lists the following performance categories for building components: technical performance, fire safety, utilization safety, social safety, health, indoor environment, functionality, availability, maintainability, aesthetic performance, energy performance, water performance and sustainable use of materials.

These performance categories also apply to maintenance activities.

Process model

Complex and maintenance strategies can be developed in an entirely 'top-down' process, so that one model can be established for 'strategic technical management'. This model leads to the choice of housing complex strategy, maintenance strategy, maintenance performance level, basic quality for the building and basic and top quality for the dwellings. Maintenance and improvement budgets are worked out at the same time (Figure 24.4).

Processes at tactical and operational level involve the planning, scheduling, calculation and execution of technical interventions and technical maintenance. There are five independent processes:

- alterations per housing complex
- relet maintenance and alterations per dwelling
- responsive and emergency maintenance
- planned maintenance
- scheduling and execution of planned maintenance.

To implement these processes, data are required on the technical condition of the building components, the quality of the housing, the quality of the environment and the complex and maintenance strategy.

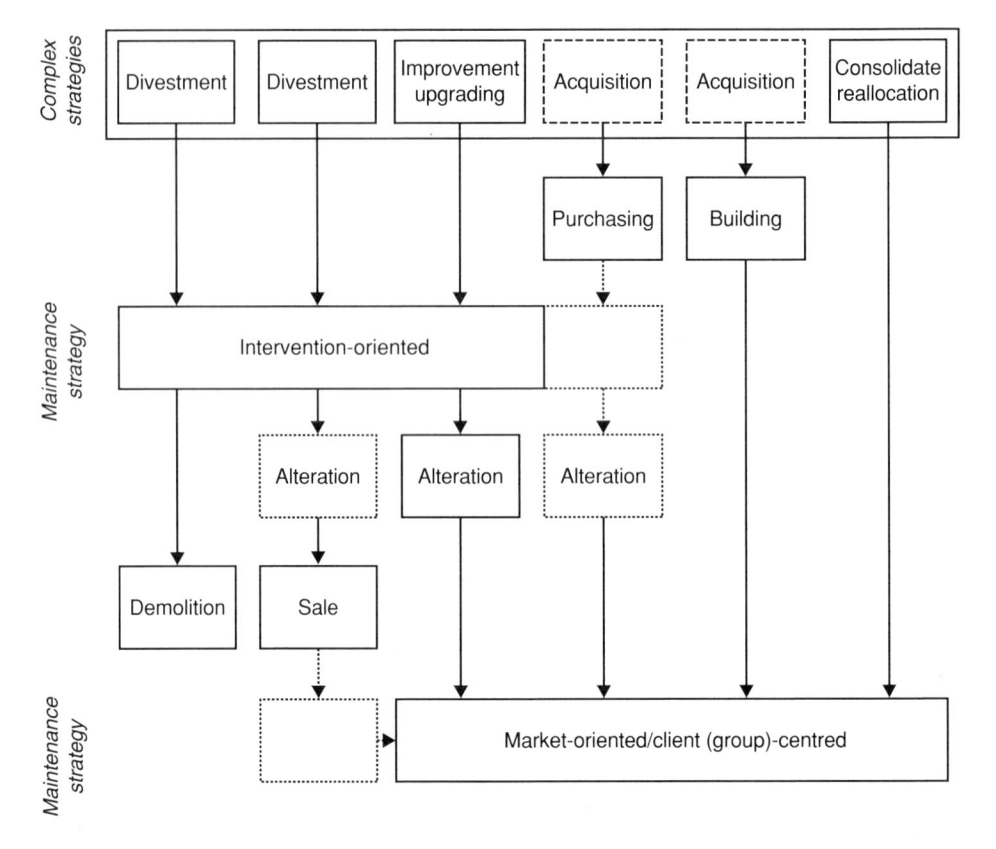

Figure 24.3 Process complex strategies and maintenance strategies

Source: Straub, 2002.

CURRENT DEVELOPMENTS IN SOCIAL HOUSING AND SOCIAL MANAGEMENT

The changes in social housing management are closely related to the changes in social housing. These changes have been analysed in various studies (see Lundqvist, 1992; Pearl, 1997; Priemus & Dieleman, 1997, 1999; Harriott et al., 1998; Priemus & Boelhouwer, 1999) and can be summarized as follows:

- *Property management is becoming increasingly market-oriented.* Social housing organizations and social housing managers are acting more as entrepreneurs, trying to meet the market demands of tenants and future tenants.
- *A shift from public responsibility to privatization and increasing independence from public authorities.* Public finance is being replaced by private finance. Traditional brick-and-mortar subsidies are making way for housing allowances, housing benefit and housing vouchers, which are less disruptive of market relationships. Financial risks are moving from central government to housing organizations; public values have to be safeguarded by governments.
- *Changing housing markets, from suction to pressure*: from a general shortage to equilibrium and even an oversupply in some submarkets. Housing service providers are focusing more on owner-occupiers. Every effort is being made to prevent or minimize vacancies.
- *A generally declining market share for social housing.* This shift is bringing about a reorientation from real-estate development towards strategic housing management, including the

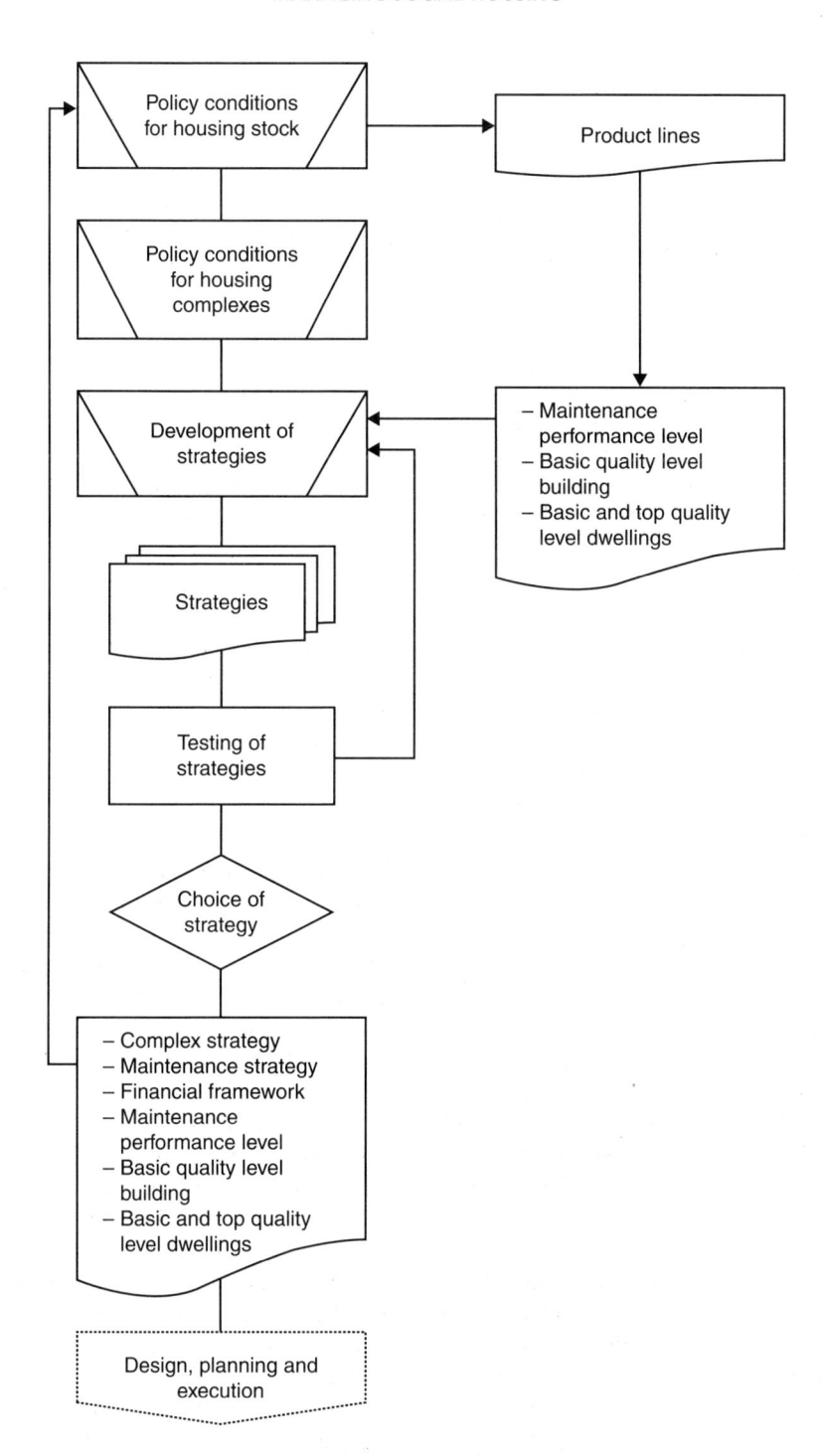

Figure 24.4 Process model for strategic technical management

Source: Straub, 2002.

restructuring and redifferentiation of the housing stock. Sometimes strategic cooperation is stimulated and mergers may even take place between housing organizations. This shift may pave the way for new subsidiary activities, such as the development of (expensive) housing for sale. The development of new social housing is on the decline in most European Union (EU) countries.

- The diminishing share of the social rented sector in the housing market as a consequence of meagre new building projects and the sale and demolition of social rented dwellings goes hand in hand with the *increasing concentration of lower-income groups in social housing* (residualization). This trend is adding to the problems of the housing managers. In the UK residualization in the social housing stock began during the Thatcher era. It then drifted over to the continent, where the share of the social rented sector in the Swedish and Dutch markets also started to decline, prompting (some) politicians and housing managers to express growing fears of social polarization (Van Kempen & Priemus, 2002). The continuing success of homeownership is prompting middle- and higher-income groups to vacate social housing and is thus widening the gap in income, employment and ethnicity between the occupants of social housing and those of other tenures.
- Often, the increasing emphasis on occupants and target groups leads to *more differentiation in housing services*, including activities in the housing environment (cleaning, greening and surveillance to promote social safety) and various care and cure arrangements. Some countries are forging stronger connections between housing provision and housing policies in order to promote the economic and social vitality of cities.

These are general observations which have not been pinpointed in time or place. First one needs to establish that there are still substantial differences between the countries of Northwest and Southern Europe. The above changes seem to be taking place primarily in Northwest Europe, but it is not inconceivable that they will appear in the social rented sector in Southern Europe as well. In Northwest Europe, the UK is clearly the front runner. With the introduction of the Right-to-Buy in 1980 and countless other policy regulations, the UK government set a policy course which put the council housing sector strongly on the defensive. It is therefore not surprising that British writers were the first to stress the increasing residualization in the social housing stock (Murie, 1975; Holmans, 1987; Forrest & Murie, 1988) – even though the market share of social rented dwellings in Belgium has always been much lower than in the UK.

Another precursor, often overlooked, is (West) Germany, which has a long tradition of social housing (*Gemeinnütziges Wohnungswesen*), but where the dividing line between the social and the (commercial) private rented sector soon started to fade. The effects of market forces quickly spread to the social rented sector (Dorn, 1997). The above changes have all manifested themselves in the social rented sector in France, where a shift to the customer and the market took place in the 1990s and looks set to continue.

The latecomers are Sweden and the Netherlands, traditional bastions of social rented housing, where the changes have only recently become apparent, although they have taken place in an intense, almost revolutionary form. In Sweden the position of municipal housing companies came under attack in the late 1990s (Turner, 1997). In the Netherlands the position of the housing associations has only recently become a topic of debate (Boelhouwer, 1992; Conijn, 1994; Dieleman, 1994; Priemus, 1995).

Though the exact form of these changes and the rate at which they occur differ from country to country, it may still be concluded that they represent a general trend of development in Northwest Europe.

In general, we are witnessing a growing sensitivity to competition in social housing organizations: they are competing with one another, with commercial landlords, and in particular, with the owner-occupier sector, which is growing apace as a result of government policy and favourable market conditions. The social housing sector is losing ground in the competition with the owner-occupier sector. Social housing managers are fighting back to try to maintain or regain a strong position in the market.

THE CHANGING SOCIO-ECONOMIC AND ETHNIC COMPOSITION OF TENANTS IN THE SOCIAL HOUSING STOCK

The mounting competition between the owner-occupier sector and the social rented sector, observable in many countries in Northwest Europe, is changing the socio-economic and ethnic mix of tenants in the social rented sector. There is extensive evidence in the literature of an increase in low-income households, the unemployed, the elderly, single parents and ethnic minorities among social housing tenants. At the same time, middle- and higher-income households are increasingly more likely to opt for the owner-occupied or the private rental sector (see Van Kempen et al., 2000 for a review of the literature). Needless to say, a sector that houses a substantial portion of the less well-off – in other words, a sector with a primarily 'safety net role' (Malpass, 1983: 44) – is more difficult to manage than a sector with tenants who represent a broad mix of income groups and occupations (see discussions of ethnic residential segregation in Chapters 22 and 23).

In fact, many of the first occupants of the new social housing estates built in Northwest Europe in the 1950s and 1960s were from high- and middle-income rather than low-income groups. Consider, for example, the HLM sector in France. In 1973, 60 per cent of the tenants came from the two highest income quartiles of the population. Only 15 years later, 63 per cent came from the two lowest quartiles (Dieleman, 1997). A similar major trend is occurring in other countries, although the differences in the role of social housing in each country should not be ignored. For example, in the Netherlands, with its mass supply of social housing, the social rented sector has always housed and continues to house more middle- and higher-income households than in the UK, where the social rented sector serves a predominantly lower-income population (Meusen & Van Kempen, 1995). It looks, however, as if the Netherlands is now moving in the same direction as the UK (Van Kempen & Priemus, 2002).

There are three main factors that seem to be causing the social rented sector to drift towards providing housing services mainly for lower-income groups: (i) changes in the housing hierarchy; (ii) unemployment and income polarization; and (iii) demographic change. These three factors are discussed below.

When social housing first assumed a prominent role in the provision of housing in Northwest Europe in the 1950s and 1960s – the heyday of the social rented sector (Priemus & Dieleman, 1997) – the owner-occupier sector was still relatively small and (older) private rented housing was still fairly plentiful. The new social rented sector came to occupy a relatively high position in the housing hierarchy; many households improved their housing situation by moving from the private rented sector to better-quality accommodation in the social rented sector, which offered excellent value for money, especially in countries, where rents were kept at a low level. The growth of the owner-occupier sector, the declining position of (older) private rented housing and ageing in part of the social rented stock in later decades have caused the stock in the social rented sector to move down the housing hierarchy. Nowadays, middle- and higher-income households often find better value for money in owner-occupation than in social rented housing, especially if mortgage interest rates are low and tax-deductible and if equity is increased by house price inflation. In such a situation social housing ends up serving low-income groups, which cannot afford to buy, and households with a lower preference for owner-occupier housing (younger and older persons in particular).

Some authors argue that increasing segmentation in housing tenure, with higher-income households living predominantly in owner-occupier housing and lower-income households in social housing, is mirroring the emergence of a more polarized and dual society (O'Loughlin & Friedrichs, 1996; Van Kempen et al., 2000). The retrenchment of the welfare state and the change from an industrial to a service economy are pushing up unemployment rates and causing more income polarization, which is reflected in the housing market. As cities seem to show more income polarization than elsewhere, one would expect to see more and more low-income households in (older parts of) social housing in cities in particular. It is uncertain if this argument holds for all cities in Northwest Europe; Van Kempen et al. (2000) show that, as the social rented sector is so large in the cities in the Netherlands, it still accommodates a relatively high proportion of high-income households.

The third factor relates to demographic changes. Inevitably, rapid changes in the composition of the house-seeking population will lead to changes in the tenant mix in the social housing stock. The first major change in household structure in Europe began in the 1960s, when birth rates dropped and many young and old single persons started to live independently. One- and two-person households increased dramatically in number and there was a proportional drop in the number of families with children. Social housing was strongly affected by this change. Families with children have a particular preference for single-family housing and owner-occupation. Thus, many such families left the social rented sector, which was increasingly serving one- and two-person households. Young households are often very mobile and tend to move house frequently. Hence, some social housing estates are populated by highly mobile groups of occupants, which put a strain on the management of parts of the stock.

The second major demographic change was the arrival of large immigrant populations in the countries of Northwest Europe from the 1960s. Immigrant groups tend to concentrate in cities, where they now frequently constitute more than 20–30 per cent of the population (Özüekren & Van Kempen, 1997; Musterd et al., 1998). When social housing is a large and well-maintained sector, as in the cities in the Netherlands, immigrants can profit from the availability of stock and can move into this sector in large numbers (Zetter & Pearl, 2002). In the four largest cities in the Netherlands, 40 per cent of Mediterranean households lived in social housing in 1981 compared with 82 per cent in 1994 (Van Kempen et al., 2000). So, there was a massive influx of immigrants into the social sector, a phenomenon not unusual in other countries in Europe either. Obviously, such dramatic changes in tenant population call for a commensurate change in the attitudes and practices of the managers who let the social rented stock.

TENANT–LANDLORD RELATIONSHIPS

Cairncross et al. (1997) reach a number of conclusions on landlord–tenant relationships and the future of council housing. They describe three ideal types of local authority roles and landlord–tenant relationships.

Table 24.1 presents three models for local authority roles: traditionalism, consumerism and citizenship.

Each of these models is elaborated for landlord–tenant relationships (Tables 24.2–24.4).

Cairncross et al. (1997: 46) wrote:

> One factor which all the approaches to tenant participation have in common is the belief that some form of tenant involvement in the management of council housing leads to better housing management.

Of the three forms of tenant participation outlined here, the 'traditionalist' approach is

Table 24.1 Models of local authority roles

	Traditionalism	Consumerism	Citizenship
Primary focus	Producers, i.e. housing managers and councillors	Role of consumer	Consumer and citizen
View of tenants	Focus on needs of tenants as a whole	Focus on individual tenant	Focus on tenants individually and collectively
	Paternalist and authoritarian	Emphasis on tenant choice	Tenants' rights and obligations
Information flows	Reliance on political and professional judgements	Market research	Dialogue
	Information transmitted through professional and formal political channels, i.e. ballot box	Advertising	Two-way information flow through many channels
Issue focus	General issues relating to tenants as a whole	Issues directly relevant to individual tenants	Individual and collective issues

Source: Cairncross et al. (1997: 27).

essentially an attempt to retain existing power relationships as much as possible. In consumerism, local authorities are intent on treating rented housing as a tradable commodity, which is not a subject of political debate or collective action. The citizenship approach involves the engagement of landlords in a dialogue with tenants' representatives. The emphasis here is on tenants acting collectively as well as individually (Cairncross et al., 1997: 46–47; see also Goodlad & Rosengard, 1994).

Around the turn of the 21st century David Clapham, Philippa O'Neill and Nic Bliss conducted a study on the ways in which tenant control impacts on social exclusion. The study was commissioned by the Confederation of Co-operative Housing in an attempt to bring tenant control into the debate on social exclusion (see also Lee & Murie, 1997; Bolt et al., 1998). The aims were:

- to ascertain what tenants and residents involved in tenant-controlled organizations considered to be the most pressing issues in their neighbourhoods
- to assess levels of understanding within tenant-controlled organizations about the concept of social exclusion
- to investigate the impact of tenant-controlled organizations on social exclusion.

A fourth objective materialized in the course of the research:

- to examine the relationship between tenant-controlled organizations and wider neighbourhood partnership frameworks.

Table 24.2 Traditionalist tenant participation

Structures	Processes	Objectives (councillors, officers)
Letters	Information provision	Better housing management
Leaflets	Listening	Tenant satisfaction
Handbooks	Seeking information	Community development (tied up to previous two)
Most participation around:		
Modernization		(Tenants)
Difficult-to-let estates		Better housing

Source: Cairncross et al. (1997: 37).

Table 24.3 Consumerist tenant participation

Structures	Processes	Objectives (councillors, officers)
Letters	Providing information	Better housing management
Leaflets	Seeking information	
Handbooks/information packs	Listening (to individuals)	Expand choice
Advertisements/newsletter	Choice	Tenant satisfaction
Surveys		(Tenants)
Meetings with individual tenants		Better housing
Issues which impact on individual tenants rather than general policy		

Source: Cairncross et al. (1997: 40).

The main conclusions were as follows:

1. Members of tenant-controlled organizations see housing, crime and the lack of facilities for young people as the key issues facing their community.
2. They place a very high value on the sense of community, personal responsibility and well-being that their organizations have created.
3. Most of the interviewed tenants did not understand the concept of social exclusion. When it was explained to them, they all said that they did not feel socially excluded. They feel that they are either solving the key issues in their community, or that their organization has given them a sense of control over their neighbourhoods and their future which makes other issues irrelevant.
4. All the tenant-controlled organizations in the study had a significant impact on crime and fear of crime.
5. Only larger tenant-controlled organizations had a significant impact on unemployment or health issues.
6. Local Strategic Partnerships are strengthened by the involvement of tenant-controlled organizations, especially where they are a key driving force.
7. Tenants who are actively involved in tenant-controlled or other community organizations may already be overstretched and find it hard to spare the time to get voluntarily involved with Local Strategic Partnerships.

CITIZENSHIP, MANAGERIALISM AND HOUSING MANAGEMENT

Goodlad (1999) places housing management in the context of citizenship and

Table 24.4 Citizenship tenant participation

Structures	Processes	Objectives (councillors, officers)
Letters	Providing information	Community development
Leaflets	Seeking information	Better housing management
Handbooks	Listening	Empowering tenants
Newsletter	Consultation	Tenant satisfaction
Tenant representation	Dialogue	
Regular meeting	Joint management	(Tenants)
	(Control)	Better housing
Covers whole range of issues from practical to policy		

Source: Cairncross et al. (1997: 43).

managerialism. She addresses three neglected issues in the restructuring of the housing policy and the housing provision in the UK in the 1980s and 1990s:

1. The relationship between welfare restructuring and management regimes.
2. The nature of local variations in the impact of welfare restructuring.
3. The significance of human agency interpretations of change.

She examines changing notions of welfare using three competing conceptions of citizenship rights: market efficiency, institutionalized rights and the radical challenge set by social movements.

A four-part typology of the main concepts and themes in the 'new public management'—namely, efficiency, downsizing and decentralization, excellence and public service – is used to present the main components of change in management regimes (Osborne & Graebler, 1993; Ferlie et al., 1996; Walker, 1998).

Citizenship concerns the duties and obligations of citizens and the state and how they are to be fulfilled.

Managerialism concerns the search for the conditions that allow managers to manage effectively (Pahl, 1975; Pollitt, 1990).

Goodlad (1999) concludes by identifying three emergent developments:

1. Management regimes were deeply implicated in attempts to create new forms of housing welfare in the 1980s and 1990s. New management regimes have been created through the reform of existing institutions and the establishment of new ones. But the reforms have not always worked out as intended, since alternative concepts of citizenship and management effectiveness have been promoted at local level by various players competing for legitimacy. Management regimes may then be created through a combination of welfare state restructuring *and the reaction to it.*
2. Management regimes differ from locality to locality in ways that cannot be explained only in terms of national and global forces, be they economic, social or political. Local variations in the impact of welfare restructuring require local explanations.
3. These local explanations can be found in the interactions of local players, traditions and social relations. We have seen the potential impact of human agency factors, such as the nature of landlord–tenant and employer–employee relationships, public resistance to certain changes and the impact of local movements seeking to extend social rights.

Local social movements and housing managers have played a role in shaping the new housing welfare market. The 'complex mixed economy' and 'the capitalist world' (Saunders, 1981: 135) continue to be crucial, but a role in shaping them is opening up for citizens and human agency within the creation of welfare states.

SOCIAL HOUSING MANAGEMENT AND HOUSING SERVICES

For a long time real estate lay at the heart of the traditional approach to social housing management. As rents became more aligned with the market and as the demands of (aspiring) tenants became more differentiated, attention shifted more and more to services. In a supply market the letting and management of dwellings is regarded as a product- and process-based business (Anderson et al., 1992). Landlord services have always been geared to the actions and procedures considered necessary to initiate and maintain the rental process for each tenant and to terminate it when the tenancy agreement expires (Dogge, 2003).

The more competition social landlords encounter from their commercial counterparts and from segments in the owner-occupier sector, the more they seem to adopt a market-oriented approach. More and more social landlords are using strategic stock policy to bring their stock in the short and long term into line with the dynamic demand and corporate goals (Van den Broeke, 1998). Higher housing satisfaction leads to more loyalty from the tenants, which, in turn, eases the burden of costs for the landlord (Hooley et al., 1998). Social landlords are also trying to develop and improve the service–profit chain (Heskett et al., 1994, 1997) and to procure housing services (Van Mossel, 2008) with treasury policy, right up to the sale of real estate to tenants and – in exceptional cases – evictions.

As Dogge (2003: 3) wrote:

> Landlords are no longer organizations in which the tangible product 'the dwelling' is central. They are evolving into more customer-oriented organizations in which the importance of services is clearly rising.

Service is defined as follows in the service marketing literature: (Grönroos, 1990):

> A service is an activity or series of activities of more or less intangible nature that normally, but not necessarily, take place in interactions between the customer and service employees and/or physical resources or goods and/or systems of the service provider, which are provided as solutions to customer problems.

Van den Broeke (1992) describes housing association services as:

> Social, technical and financial activities carried out by the housing association for the benefit of the tenant from the date he registers as a home-seeker up to the expiry date of the tenancy agreement. These activities consist of emergency services, information, and dealing with complaints of a social, technical and financial nature

Pott and Smeets (1995) define the services of landlords as:

> The full complement of core, support and emergency services geared to the accessibility, interaction and participation needs of the different target groups in the different phases of the rental process.

Besides the more general term of 'service provision', the term 'housing services' is applied regularly in relation to the letting of property (Van der Schaar, 1987; Conijn, 1995). Van der Schaar splits the housing market into two parts: one part involving the transaction of ownership rights and the other involving the transaction of user rights. He claims that the housing service provided by the landlord to the customer is 'the right to use a dwelling for a fixed or indeterminate period'. Conijn (1995) expands this definition into: 'user rights with an accompanying package of services for a fixed or indeterminate period'.

Dogge (2003) defines the service provision of housing associations as:

> All acts, activities and procedures carried out by landlords during all phases of the rental process, from the preliminary phase to the termination of the tenancy agreement, to benefit and promote the interests of (potential) customers.

The marketing literature in general mentions four characteristics that distinguish services from goods (Zeithaml et al., 1985):

1 *Intangibility.* Services are intangible. Unlike physical goods, they are experienced; they are not objects that can be owned.
2 *Inseparability.* Production and consumption are inseparable in the case of services. Goods are produced first and then consumed.
3 *Heterogeneity.* The quality of a service can vary from day to day, from provider to provider, and from consumer to consumer.
4 *Perishability.* As services are experienced, they cannot be kept or stored. As a result, providers may find it difficult to match demand (especially quantitative demand) with supply.

Intangibility is considered the most crucial difference between services and goods (Bateson, 1977; Zeithaml et al., 1985). The other three are regarded as consequences of intangibility.

There are very few organizations that provide only services or only tangible goods. Social housing managers provide a mix of goods (mainly real estate) and services. Strictly speaking, landlords do not offer real estate (unless they intend to sell it), but housing services. They might therefore be described as providers of real-estate-intensive services (Dogge, 2003).

These can be split into three categories (Dogge, 2003: 8):

1 Core services: pleasurable housing/housing facilities.
2 Support services/support goods/support environment: dwellings/semi-public space; location/living environment/tenancy-related services.
3 Additional services/goods: additional housing-related services/other additional services.

SERVICE QUALITY

The *Conceptual Model of Service Quality* (Parasuraman et al., 1985), which is regarded as the standard service quality model par excellence, combines the tangible product-based, the production-based and the user-based approach.

This model consists of perceived *service quality* (*Gap* 5), on the one hand, and four internal gaps (*Gaps* 1–4) on the other. It indicates that the service perceived by the consumer is the result of the size and trend of internal *Gaps* 1–4:

1 *Marketing Information Gap* (*Gap* 1): the difference between the actual expectations of the customer and the management's perception of the customer's expectations.
2 *Standards Gap* (*Gap* 2): the difference between the management's perception of the customer's expectations and the description of the quality of the services.
3 *Service Performance Gap* (*Gap* 3): the difference between the description of the quality of the services and the actual services.
4 *Communication Gap* (*Gap* 4): the difference between the services that are actually provided and the way these are communicated to the customer.

When we refer to quality or *service quality* we mean the *perceived service quality*. It is generally assumed that service quality is the outcome of a comparison that customers draw between their expectations of the service and their perception of the actual service they receive (Parasuraman et al., 1985).

Information and Communication Technology can play an increasing role in providing a better service quality (Scanlon & Pearl, 2002).

SERVICE–PROFIT CHAIN

The *service–profit chain* has been introduced (Heskett et al., 1994, 1997, Hallowell & Schlesinger, 2000) as a conceptual framework. The service–profit chain sheds light on the factors that influence the value that a customer attaches to the product provided by the service organization. It also shows that customer value leads to customer satisfaction, which then leads to an increase in customer loyalty and hence to a better market position for the service provider. Dogge (2003) uses these assumed relationships in the service–profit chain as a starting point for his work on social housing management in the Netherlands.

Theoretically, landlords can offer the customer superior value in various ways. Thus, it is possible to differentiate in the physical supply of real estate, the price, the promotion or the services surrounding the physical product.

Marketability goes hand in hand with the ambition to achieve sustainable, added value for the customer. Eventually, this added value should theoretically generate a profit for profit-making organizations and should enable the survival of non-profit-making organizations. Amongst other things, Dogge (2003) uses the service–profit chain (Heskett et al., 1994, 1997, Hallowell & Schlesinger, 2000) as a conceptual framework to gain insight into profitability and survival.

The theory behind the service–profit chain is based on the assumption that the quality of internal services (*internal service quality*), the performance of the service personnel, the quality of the external services (*external service quality*), customer value, customer satisfaction, customer loyalty and a better market position (measured in income growth and/or profitability) are linked successively in a chain.

The service–profit chain assumes that a direct and robust connection exists between profit, growth, loyalty, customer satisfaction, the value of the services delivered to the customer, the quality of these services, and the expertise, satisfaction, loyalty and productivity of the service personnel. Various authors have separately identified and described the relationships between the different elements. Heskett et al. (1994, 1997) eventually combined them in one model called the service–profit chain.

The service–profit chain suggests that the quality of the services, as experienced by the customer, i.e. the external service quality, is influenced by the expertise, satisfaction, loyalty and productivity of the employees in the organization. These elements also influence one another. For example, a skilled or competent employee will be happier in his job than an employee who is working above his capacity. A satisfied employee is more likely to be loyal to the employer and will be more productive than a dissatisfied employee. The internal service quality is also important for the performance of the personnel as it creates the working conditions within which the employee operates.

SOCIAL CONSTRUCTION OF HOUSING MANAGEMENT: ANALYSIS OF BUREAUCRATIC DISCOURSE

Social housing has been analysed not only in economic, legal and political terms. Some researchers have examined the way in which housing management is socially constructed by looking closely at the use of language in policy documents. Saugeres and Clapham (1999: 174) analysed the semantics in the *British Housing Management Standards Manual*, produced by the Chartered Institute of Housing and found four main themes which consistently recur in the manual. The first is that housing management is bureaucratically framed in terms of written procedures, policies, rules and predefined categories. Secondly, housing officers are presented as experts and hence are deemed able to identify and define people's needs and to make rational and objective decisions. Thirdly, the attitude to tenants is paternalistic, so housing officers are assigned a role in the maintenance of social control. Fourthly, there is a strong orientation towards consumerism (Saugeres & Clapham, 1999: 261).

The analysis of the *Manual* exposes the influence of background factors which are confronting housing management in the UK and elsewhere, such as economic change, government policy and the restructuring of public sector management.

One striking contradiction in the *Manual* is that whereas landlords are expected to take account of individual circumstances when deciding on allocation, rehousing, customer care, homelessness or special needs, any decisions on tenants' views and the tenants themselves must be taken in accordance with predefined policies and formal procedures (Saugeres & Clapham, 1999: 262).

A second contradiction is that the *Manual* tells landlords to involve tenants in decision-making and the management of their homes, to encourage the formation of tenants' associations, to listen to the tenants' views, to respect their choices and to treat them as equals. However, at the same time, it adopts a paternalistic approach towards social tenants, who come across as irresponsible, potentially uncontrollable, and thus, dangerous because they do not conform to acceptable codes of behaviour.

A third contradiction is that there is a tension between the welfare role and the bricks-and-mortar role of housing managers. The primary concern of housing management seems to be property. People are seen merely as tenants who occupy it (Power, 1987). The concern with tenants is that they might damage the property, they might not pay the rent and they might indulge in anti-social behaviour which will make people leave the estate, resulting in a high proportion of vacant properties and lost revenue for the organization. At the same time, the *Manual* does not speak about tenants only as secondary to property; it also recognizes that social tenants may have different needs and vulnerabilities which should be considered.

Saugeres and Clapham (1999) conclude:

> Public rented housing provides accommodation for the poorest members of society and is thus implicated in social control. At the same time, as with other public services, it reinforces the market ideology and is therefore expected to adopt at least the rhetoric and the image of competition and consumer choice, although (...) contradictions with other elements of the role indicate that there are limits to how far this can be taken in practice. Overlaying this is the professional ethos of housing management, which emphasizes the expertise of the rational and objective professional in undertaking these roles.

FROM PROBLEM ESTATES TO STRATEGIC HOUSING MANAGEMENT

Residualization in the social housing sector is taking place at a varying pace across Europe. Large differences are discernible in the property holdings of social housing organizations. Some housing estates are still operating well, serving satisfied tenants from high-income groups, who would not even think about moving house. In other estates the problems seem to be piling up. Here we see a deterioration in the residential climate with noise nuisance, vandalism, drug dealing and drug abuse, petty and sometimes serious crime and general feelings of insecurity (Newman, 1972; Prak & Priemus, 1985; Elsinga & Wassenberg, 1991; Danermark & Elander, 1994).

The management problems in the Pruitt–Igoe public housing project in St. Louis (Missouri, USA) – problems that led to the demolition of no fewer than 2,870 dwellings in 1974 – are world renowned (Rainwater, 1970; Meehan, 1974; Priemus, 1986). Since then, a stigma has clung to American public housing. It was also around this time that the decline of the public housing sector began in earnest. Problem estates also sprung up in Western Europe, mostly in the 1980s, first in the UK (Coleman, 1985), and soon after in the Netherlands, France (*the grands ensembles*) and Sweden as well as in East Germany, particularly after reunification. For the first time since World War II there was massive under-occupation in some complexes. In contrast with the United States, however, that did not spell the end of social housing building projects.

In Western European countries social housing organizations tried, often in close cooperation with local government, to solve the problems and improve the conditions in the social housing sector. The housing estate caretaker was reinstated and many housing estates and environments were redesigned; there was a broader commitment to involving tenants in housing management issues, the promotion of employment and educational improvement (Krantz et al., 1999).

Ever-encroaching residualization in the social housing sector increased the proportion of lower-income groups, unemployed and ethnic minorities in social housing estates. Many tenants were seen as part of the solution, but others were seen, not without reason, as part of the problem. Some households maintained a lifestyle that was not only a nuisance to the landlord but also a source of torment to fellow residents. Housing managers tried to identify the problem tenants, to communicate with them, educate them, and, when all else failed, did not hesitate to evict them. When social housing managers allocated housing, they checked more scrupulously than in the past whether the candidate-tenants had paid their rent to their former landlord and had behaved in a socially acceptable manner. Housing rules and norms for tenants were reinvented at the same time as tenant participation was encouraged by many housing managers.

Saugeres and Clapham (1999) show how contradictions emerged between an emancipatory approach (stimulating tenant participation) and a paternalistic approach (imposing behavioural norms and rules on the tenants) in social housing management.

The problems with some categories of tenants were exacerbated by an unhappy combination of an irresponsible lifestyle and technical shortcomings in some of the social housing stock. In many countries privately owned dwellings are, almost by definition, single-family dwellings. In the social housing sector a substantial part of the stock consists of multifamily housing. During the post-war housing shortage, quantity took precedence over quality in housing production. Many cheap, monotonous, multi-family blocks were built in mono-functional housing areas, sometimes at unpopular locations. A number of labour-saving production techniques and materials were introduced, such as prefab concrete, system building and on-site casting – but some of them were still suffering from teething troubles. Thermal bridges became damp from condensation and draughts whistled through cracks in the wall, making the physical indoor climate far from ideal. Noise was a common problem in these apartment blocks, so tenants became extremely sensitive to the boisterous behaviour of some of their neighbours. The combination of problem tenants and deficient apartment blocks (the very environment which demands a quiet way of life) created huge problems for managers of social housing. Sometimes eviction was the only answer; at other times solutions were sought in drastic renovation programmes. Specially adapted systems of housing allocation were introduced to deal with the problems, together with direct confrontation with the anti-social tenants. The housing managers discovered, especially in the 1970s and 1980s, that there is a lot more to housing management than rent collecting and maintenance and repairs. They have now taken on a much broader remit in collaboration with municipal services.

The problems seem to be concentrated primarily in and around the cities. This is because low-income households and immigrant populations are usually overrepresented in cities, and most of the high-rise estates in the social rented sector are situated in metropolitan regions. Housing problems have become more closely intertwined with urban problems. Since the 1980s, in particular, housing organizations and municipalities in many EU countries have sought to integrate housing and urban policy.

Housing organizations now look farther ahead and develop a longer-term strategic housing policy. Which target groups are to be served? Which niches in the market need to be addressed? What implications do the answers to these questions have for the composition of the housing stock? Which dwellings can be disposed of (clearance and sale), which need to be acquired (purchase, construction) and which need to be renovated? And how will these actions affect rent policy, services and the urban design of the neighbourhood?

The presence of a limited number of problem estates with many vacant dwellings has forced social housing managers to take more notice of the market. Social housing managers in EU countries are fast discovering that they are operating in a variety of markets and that the best way to survive is to meet the demand in all of them.

PUBLIC FRAMEWORK FOR SOCIAL HOUSING: THE CASE OF THE NETHERLANDS

In every country social housing is anchored in public legislation (Merrett, 1979; Clapham and English, 1987; Balchin, 1990; Malpass and Murie, 1994). In the Netherlands, the old legislation (BTIV) was replaced in 1993 by the Social Housing Management Decree (*Besluit Beheer Sociale Huurwoningen/ BBSH*), an Order in Council, which is based on the Housing Act and which has regulated the supervision of approved housing organizations since January 1993. The BBSH states that the working domain of these organizations extends solely to public housing and includes:

1. The construction, acquisition, encumbrance and demolition of housing and real-estate appurtenances.
2. The provision and maintenance of facilities in the organization's own housing and real-estate appurtenances and in those of third parties.
3. The maintenance and improvement of the direct environment of the housing and the real-estate appurtenances.
4. The management, allocation and letting of housing and real-estate appurtenances.
5. The alienation of housing and real-estate appurtenances.
6. The provision of dwelling-related services to the inhabitants of the housing administered by the approved organizations and the provision of dwelling-related services to persons who state that they wish to occupy such housing.
7. The activities arising from the execution of the activities in Points 1–6.

The BBSH imposes certain obligations on housing organizations. The list has been extended twice since the BBSH came into force. The current obligations (in random order) are as follows:

1. To assure good quality in all dwellings.
2. To guarantee the financial continuity of the organization.
3. To accord priority to housing the primary target group defined in public housing policy.
4. To involve residents in the policy and management of the organization.
5. To enhance quality of life in the neighbourhoods and districts where the housing is situated (since 1997).
6. To contribute within reason to housing the elderly, the disabled and people who require care or supervision (since 2001).

The housing association can, either alone or with other housing associations, enter performance agreements with the municipality. These performance agreements are based on a Housing Vision which the municipality is required to draw up periodically.

The national government supervises the implementation of the BBSH, which states that, every year, the approved organizations must send their financial statements to the Minister of Housing, who assesses the performance of the individual organizations and of the sector as a whole.

Two organizations need information on the financial position of the housing associations: the Social Housing Guarantee Fund (*Stichting Waarborgfonds Sociale Woningbouw*, hereinafter WSW) and the Central Fund for Housing (*Centraal Fonds voor de Volkshuisvesting*, hereinafter CFV). The WSW was set up in 1983 by the predecessors of Aedes, the umbrella organization for housing associations. The task of the WSW is to help housing associations to gain entry to the capital market at the lowest possible costs. The WSW provides guarantees for financiers of new building projects, housing upgrades and the purchase of housing, care homes and nursing homes with a social function (non-dwellings). The CFV annually assesses the financial position of the housing associations, both individually and collectively, and screens intended mergers for financial feasibility. The BBSH requires housing associations to submit an overview of core data and a prognosis besides the annual report and the financial statements.

At the request of the Housing Minister, the CFV may give project-linked support to housing associations with insufficient financial resources to meet their public housing remit. This may be combined with an (additional) levy on wealthier associations.

In April 2000, Johan Remkes, at that time State Secretary for Housing, signed a covenant with Aedes and the Association of Netherlands Municipalities to guarantee that individual differences between the investment capacity of 'rich' and 'poor' housing associations would not lead to underachievement in the regions and that the performance would, somehow or other, be delivered regardless of the possibilities of the individual housing associations. The covenant also guaranteed that differences in the financial position of the housing associations would not lead to differences in the treatment of the households in the target group. The covenant led to the appointment of a board (*College Sluitend Stelsel*) to assess and advise on obstacles that housing associations, municipalities or central government reported as standing in the way of the local housing remit.

The *College Sluitend Stelsel* has certainly not been overworked. In the Netherlands the surplus capital of housing associations has become a much greater problem than lack of resources in getting important social housing projects off the ground.

CONCLUSION

It may be concluded generally that research into social housing management is taking place mainly in the sphere of consultancy and is strongly oriented to practice. Social housing management has only recently become an independent research theme. Leaving aside the question of rent control, rent regulation and rent policy, it has not been intensively explored in economic research since the turn of the 21st century.

Academic research is focusing on the business–economics aspects, where marketing and service quality play a key role. The service–profit chain is proving a workable concept in this domain.

The second approach is geared more to the technical aspects, stretching across the entire spectrum, from maintenance to renovation and refurbishment, and often including the rehabilitation of the housing environment.

The third approach, which is geared primarily to social research, includes the social construction of housing management, the positioning of housing management between citizenship and managerialism, and issues of tenant control, anti-social behaviour and social exclusion.

So far, most of the academic research on social housing management has taken place in the UK and the Netherlands.

REFERENCES

Addleon, L., 1989, *Building Failures: A Guide to Diagnosis, Remedy, and Prevention*, London (Butterworth Architecture).

Anderson, E.W., Fornell, C. and Lehman, D.R., 1992, Customer satisfaction, market share, and profitability: Findings from Sweden, *Journal of Marketing*, 58, (3): 53–66.

Balchin, P., 1990, *Housing Policy: an Introduction*, London (Routledge).

Bateson, J.E.G., 1977, Do we need service marketing? in: *Marketing Consumer Services: New Insights*, Report No. 77–115, Marketing Science Institute, Cambridge.

Bines, W., Kemp, P., Pleace, N. and Radley, C., 1993, *Managing Social Housing*, London (HMSO).

Boelhouwer, P.J., 1992, *Vervroegde aflossing van rijksleningen in de sociale huursector, omvang-aard-aanwending* [Accelerated repayment of government loans in the social rental sector, extent-nature-application], Zoetermeer (Ministerie van VROM).

Bolt, G.S., van Kempen, R. and Burgers, J., 1998, On the social significance of spatial location: Spatial segregation and social exclusion, *Netherlands Journal of Housing and the Built Environment*, 13: 83–95.

Boumeester, H., Elsinga, M. and Priemus, H., 1998, *Woonproducten voor de toekomst: marktperspectieven voor woningcorporaties* [Housing products for the future: market perspectives for housing associations], Woningraad Extra nr. 83, NWR, Almere.

Burnett, J., 1978, *A Social History of Housing, 1815–1970*, Newton Abbot, Devon (David and Charles).

Cairncross, L., Clapham, D. and Goodlad, R., 1997, *Housing Management, Consumers and Citizens*, London (Routledge).

Centre for Housing Policy, University of York. 1993, *Managing Social Housing*, London (HMSO).

Centre for Housing Research (CHR), 1989, *The Nature and Effectiveness of Housing Management in England*, London (HMSO).

Chandler, I., 1995, The generation and use of stock condition surveys, *Journal of the Institute of Maintenance and Building Management*, 1 (1).

Clapham, D. and English, J. (eds), 1987, *Public Housing – Current Trends and Future Developments*, London (Croom Helm).

Clapham, D., Kintrea, K., Malcolm, J., Parkey, H. and Scott, S., 1995, *A Baseline Study of Housing Management in Scotland*, Edinburgh (Scottish Office).

Clapham, D., O'Neill, P. and Bliss, N. (no year), *Tenant Control & Social Exclusion*, London (Confederation of Co-operative Housing).

Coleman, A., 1985, *Utopia on Trial*, London (Hilary Shipman).

Conijn, J.B.S., 1994, *De verzwegen problemen van de brutering* [The concealed problems of grossing], Delft (Delft University Press).

Conijn, J.B.S., 1995, *Enkele financieel-economische grondslagen van de volkshuisvesting* [Basic financial-economic principles of housing], Delft (Delft University Press).

Damen Consultants, 1996, *Brite Euram Project 4213 Condition Assessment and Maintenance Strategies for Building and Building Components*, Rotterdam (Damen Consultants).

Danermark, B. and Elander, I. (eds), 1994, *Social Rented Housing in Europe: Policy, Tenure and Design*, Housing and Urban Policy Studies, 9, Delft (Delft University Press).

Department of the Environment, 1990, *Efficiency Report and Action Plan: Training, Education and Performance in Housing Management*, London (Department of the Environment).

Dieleman, F.M., 1994, Social rented housing: Valuable asset or unsustainable burden? *Urban Studies*, 31: 447–463.

Dieleman, F.M., 1997, European housing market developments, in: H. Vestergaard (ed.), *Housing in Europe*, Report of the ENHR Housing Research Conference in Denmark, 26–31 August 1996, pp. 43–56.

Dogge, P.J.C., 2003, *Van Woningverhuurder naar Aanbieder van Woongenot. De strategische mogelijkheden en beperkingen van de inzet van diensten ter verbetering van de marktpositie* [From landlord to provider of pleasurable housing. Strategic possibilities and limitations of the deployment of services in order to improve the market position], Eindhoven (PhD dissertation TU Eindhoven).

Dorn, V., 1997, Changes in the social rented sector in Germany, *Housing Studies*, 12, (4): 463–475.

Elsinga, M.G. and Wassenberg, F.A.G., 1991, Tackling crime and vandalism in post-war housing estates: The Dutch approach, *Netherlands Journal of Housing and the Built Environment*, 6: 159–175.

Ferlie, E., Ashburner, L., Fitzgerald, L. and Pettigrew, A., 1996, *The New Public Management in Action*, Oxford (Oxford University Press).

Forrest, R. and Murie, A., 1988, *Selling the Welfare State*, London (Routledge).

Goodlad, R., 1999, Housing management matters: Citizenship and managerialism in the new welfare market, *Netherlands Journal of Housing and the Built Environment*, 14, (3): 241–256.

Goodlad, R. and Rosengard, A., 1994, Tenant involvement in compulsory competitive tendering, in: *Housing Management Compulsory Competitive Tendering*, module 8, London (Association of District Councils and Chartered Institute of Housing).

Grönroos, C., 1990, *Service Management and Marketing: Managing Moments of Truth in Service Competition*, Lexington (Lexington Books).

Hallowell, R. and Schlesinger, L.A., 2000, The service profit chain: Intellectual roots, current realities, and future prospects, in: T.A. Swartz and D. Lacobucci (eds), *Handbook of Services Marketing & Management*, London (Sage Publications Inc.), pp. 203–221.

Harriott, S., Matthews, L. and Grainger, P., 1998, *Social Housing: An Introduction*, Harlow, Essex (Longman).

Hermans, M.H., 1995, *Deterioration Characteristics of Building Components: A Data Collection Model to Support Performance Management*, Eindhoven (PhD dissertation TU Eindhoven).

Heskett, J.L., Jones, T.O., Loveman, G.W., Sasser, W.E. and Schlesinger, L.A., 1994, Putting the service profit chain to work, *Harvard Business Review*, 72, (2): 164–174.

Heskett, J.L., Sasser, W.E. and Schlesinger, L.A., 1997, *The Service Profit Chain*, New York (Free Press).

Holmans, A.E., 1987, *Housing Policy in Britain: A History*, London (Croom Helm).

Hooley, G.J., Saunders, J.A. and Piercy, N.F., 1998, *Marketing Strategy & Competitive Positioning*, London (Prentice Hall Europe).

International Organization of Standardization (ISO), 1984, *International Standard ISO 6241, Performance Standards in Building – Principles for Their Preparation and Factors to be Considered*.

Krantz, B., Öresjö, E. and Priemus, H. (eds.), 1999, *Large Scale Housing Estates in Northwest Europe: Problems, Interventions and Experiences*, Housing

and Urban Policy Studies 17, Delft (Delft University Press).
Lee, P. and Murie, A., 1997, *Poverty, Housing Tenure and Social Exclusion*, Bristol (The Policy Press).
Lundqvist, L.J., 1992, *Dislodging the Welfare State? Housing and Privatization in Four European Nations*, Housing and Urban Policy Studies 3, Delft (Delft University Press).
Malpass, P., 1983, Residualisation and the restructuring of housing tenure, *Housing Review*, March–April: 44–45.
Malpass, P. and Murie, A., 1994, *Housing Policy and Practice*, 4th edn, Basingstoke (Macmillan).
Meehan, E.J., 1974, *Public Housing Policy; Convention versus Reality*, New Brunswick, NJ (Center for Urban Policy Research, Rutgers University).
Merrett, S., 1979, *State Housing in Britain*, London (Routledge & Kegan Paul).
Meusen, H. and van Kempen, R., 1995, Towards residual housing? A comparison of Britain and the Netherlands, *Netherlands Journal of Housing and the Built Environment*, 10, (3): 239–258.
Murie, A., 1975, *The State of Council Houses. A Study in Social Policy*, Birmingham (CURS/University of Birmingham).
Musterd, S., Ostendorf, W. and Breebaart, M., 1998, *Multi-ethnic Metropolis: Patterns and Policies*, Dordrecht (Kluwer).
Newman, O., 1972, *Defensible Space*, New York (Macmillan).
O'Loughlin, J. and Friedrichs, J. (eds), 1996, *Social Polarization in Post-Industrial Metropolises*, Berlin and New York (De Gruyter).
Osborne, D. and Graebler, T., 1993, *Reinventing Government: How the Entrepreneurial Spirit is Transforming the Public Sector*, London (Plume).
Özüekren, A.Ş. and van Kempen, R., 1997, *Turks in European Cities: Housing and Urban Segregation*, Utrecht (European Research Centre on Migration and Ethnic Relation).
Pahl, R., 1975, *Whose City?* 2nd edn, London (Penguin).
Parasuraman, A., Berry, L.L. and Zeithami, V.A., 1985, A conceptual model of service quality and its implications for future research, *Journal of Marketing*, 49, (4): 41–50.
Pearl, M., 1997, *Social Housing Management: A Critical Appraisal of Housing Practice*, Basingstoke (Macmillan).
Pollitt, C., 1990, *Managerialism and the Public Services*, Oxford (Basil Blackwell).

Pooley, C.G. (ed.), 1992, *Housing Strategies in Europe 1880–1930*, Leicester, London & New York (Leicester University Press).
Pott, M. and Smeets, J., 1995, Dienstverlening als strategisch concurrentievoordeel van corporaties [Service as a strategic competitive advantage for housing associations], *Service Magazine*, No. 3, March: 32–36.
Power, A., 1987, *Property before People*, London (Allen and Unwin).
Power, A., 1993, *Hovels to High Rise: State Housing in Europe since 1850*, London (Routledge)
Prak, N. and Priemus, H. (eds), 1985, *Post-war Public Housing in Trouble*, Delft (Delft University Press).
Priemus, H., 1986, *The Spirit of St. Louis: De neergang van Pruitt-Igoe* [The Spirit of St. Louis: The Downfall of Pruitt-Igoe], Onderzoeksgroep Exploitatieproblemen Naoorlogse Woningen, Delft (Delft University Press).
Priemus, H., 1995, How to abolish social housing? The Dutch case, *International Journal of Urban and Regional Research*, 19, (1): 145–155.
Priemus, H. and Boelhouwer, P., 1999, Social housing finance in Europe: Trends and opportunities, *Urban Studies*, 36, (4): 633–645.
Priemus, H. and Dieleman, F.M., 1997, Social rented housing: Recent changes in Western Europe, Special Issue *Housing Studies*, 12, (4), 421–560.
Priemus, H. and Dieleman, F.M., 1999, Social housing finance in the European Union: Developments and prospects, *Urban Studies*, 36, (4): 623–631.
Priemus, H., Dieleman, F. and Clapham, D., 1999, Current developments in social housing management, *Netherlands Journal of Housing and the Built Environment*, 14, (3): 211–223.
Rainwater, L., 1970, *Behind Ghetto Walls; Black Families in a Federal Slum*, Chicago (Aldine).
Saugeres, L. and Clapham, D., 1999, Themes and contradictions in housing management: An analysis of bureaucratic discourse, *Netherlands Journal of Housing and the Built Environment*, 14, (3): 257–276.
Saunders, P., 1981, *Social Theory and the Urban Question*, London (Hutchinson).
Scanlon, M. and Pearl, M., 2002, *Remote Control: Housing Associations and E-governance*, Bristol (The Policy Press).
Shen, Q. and Spedding, A., 1998, Priority setting in maintenance – practical issues in using the multi-attribute approach, *Building Research & Information*, 26: 169–180.

Straub, A., 2002, Strategic technical management of housing stock: Lessons from Dutch housing associations, *Building Research & Information*, 30, (5): 372–381.

Turner, B., 1997, Municipal housing companies in Sweden: On or off the market?, *Housing Studies*, 12, (4): 477–488.

Van den Broeke, R.A., 1992, *Dienstverlening woningcorporaties en huurderswaardering* [Services, Housing Associations and Tenant Ratings], Delft (Delft University Press).

Van den Broeke, R.A., 1998, *Strategisch voorraadbeleid van woningcorporaties: informatievoorziening en instrumenten*, translated title: [Strategic housing stock management of housing associations: information provision and instruments]. Delft (Delft University Press).

Van der Schaar, J., 1987, *Groei en bloei van het Nederlandse volkshuisvestingsbeleid* [Growth and Development of the Dutch Housing Policy], Delft (Delft University Press).

Van Kempen, R. and Priemus, H., 2002, Revolution in social housing in the Netherlands: Possible effects of new housing policies, *Urban Studies*, 39, (2): 237–253.

Van Kempen, R., Schutjens, V.A.J.M. and van Weesep, J., 2000, The changing tenant mix in Dutch social rented housing, *Housing Studies*, 15: 505–531.

Van Mossel, J.H., 2008, *The purchasing of maintenance service delivery in the Dutch social housing sector. Optimising commodity strategies for delivering maintenance services to tenants*, PhD dissertation TU Delft, Amsterdam (IOS Press BV).

Walker, R., 1998, New public management and housing associations: From comfort to competition, *Policy and Politics*, 26, (1): 71–87.

Zeithaml, V.A., Parasuraman, A. and Berry, L.L., 1985, Problems and strategies in services marketing, *Journal of Marketing*, 49: 33–46.

Zetter, R. and Pearl, M., 2002, *Managing to Survive: Asylum Seekers, Refugees and Access to Social Housing*, Bristol (The Policy Press).

Conclusion

David Clapham

The primary aim of this collection has been to provide a 'state-of-the-art' review of research on housing as well as to highlight some of the key issues and approaches for the future. So, what kind of state is housing studies in?

The collection was intended to be as comprehensive as possible, given the constraints of space, but it is clear that there are gaps in our coverage. Nevertheless, the wide scope of the contributions shows the complexity of housing analysis. Some of this complexity relates to the nature of housing itself. Many chapters have reflected on the wide array of benefits or attributes that a house and home have for individuals and households.

It is this complexity that is one reason why the house purchase decision is a difficult and protracted process that is difficult to model accurately. But housing is also complex because it impacts on many areas of private and public life. The complexity of housing has problems and opportunities for housing analysis. It precludes partial or simplistic analysis, but it provides an incentive and opportunity to undertake comprehensive and trans-disciplinary research.

Section 1 showed that the basic concepts underlying our understanding of housing are contested. For example, there is no consensus on the nature of the micro foundations of the housing market. The traditional neo-liberal approaches have been increasingly criticised by adherents of behavioural economics and other approaches such as material sociology. There is agreement that housing as a commodity has many features that differentiate it from other commodities. For example, Whitehead in Chapter 6 gives a list which includes its longevity, its complexity and the difficulties of information collection by buyers. People do not move home often and each time will have to update their knowledge of the market and the movement of house prices. These issues lead to complex patterns of consumer behaviour which most analysts accept are not reflected accurately in neo-liberal models, which assume perfect information and rational choices. However, the disagreement seems to be over whether this matters. Whitehead argues that the test of such models is not whether they seem to conform to reality, but rather whether they provide accurate predictions. It is difficult to see how they could do the one without the other, although I suppose that it could be argued that neo-liberal models just simplify by ignoring factors that cancel each other out. It is clear that this is an important argument that will run for some time. Progress in reaching a satisfactory conclusion will depend on two things that are highlighted in this volume.

The first is more empirical work on actual local housing markets. Surprisingly, there is little empirical work in this area and, without it, the quest for a deeper understanding of market functioning seems to be futile. Neoliberal analysts have tended just to assume the nature of markets, but the new approaches in economics outlined in Chapter 13, with their psychological and sociological borrowings, offer the beginnings of a way of approaching the study of real markets. Therefore, the second important factor necessary for an understanding of housing markets is trans-disciplinary analysis. The effective fusing together of insights from different disciplines is necessary to understand the complexities of consumer behaviour and the actions and interactions of different agents in the housing market. Behavioural and new institutional economics provide a starting point for this, but have so far been very limited in their scope. The need is for a wider framework that incorporates insights from material sociology and other approaches. However, trans-disciplinary work is not easy and there are many barriers to be overcome.

Section 2 showed the wide array of theoretical perspectives that have been used to illuminate housing and, again, although we have attempted to be as comprehensive as possible, there are inevitably gaps in our coverage. The large number of approaches reflects the complexity of housing and the many different analytical or policy questions that it poses. Even single issues such as consumer market behaviour can be viewed in many different ways and each can offer its own particular insights. So the approach taken is often dictated by the precise research question being addressed. Nevertheless, the lack of a coherent and comprehensive theoretical framework for the analysis of housing is a substantial weakness, because it becomes impossible to transcend the individual partial analyses. How do you put together different insights to understand how they relate together? How do you devise a policy when all you have to go on are partial insights?

Of course the lack of a comprehensive framework reflects the situation in the social sciences more broadly and there is a strong argument that transcendence needs to start at that level. However, it has been argued in this Handbook that housing is a good place to start because of the need for a comprehensive analysis and the existing inter-disciplinary networks that have formed around it. Housing has already been the focus of transdisciplinary work in behavioural and institutional economics because of its unique features. Also, King (2009) has argued that housing provides a good base from which to devise theory because of its particular nature. Moreover, King argues for the need to devise a specific theory of housing, because it requires more than the application of general theory. Therefore, there is a strong argument for housing studies to be at the forefront of trans-disciplinary theory generation and research.

However, the difficulties of undertaking trans-disciplinary research must not be underestimated. The reason that some psychological theories have been incorporated into behavioural economics is that they share common epistemologies and ontologies. The reason that sociological and geographical theories have not been incorporated is because of the lack of this common underpinning. In Chapter 10 in this Handbook and in a previous article (Clapham, 2009), I have attempted to outline the conditions necessary to combine a positivist economics and psychology with a social constructionist sociology, and have used the terms 'limited positivism' and 'fixed constructionism' to indicate the possibility of transcendence. Social constructionism accepts that certain elements of social life become 'reified' or accepted as fact in certain places at certain times. Is it then possible for social constructionists to accept positivism in these fixed or situated circumstances? Clearly there is much work to be done before progress can be made in this direction, but housing has proved to be a good testing ground for such endeavours.

Section 3 examined the context of housing. An issue which has come to the fore in recent years and is reflected in many contributions here is the embededness of housing in the global and national economies. This has created a situation of volatility in housing markets and a need for households to manage risk. There is an ongoing debate, reflected in this Handbook, about the cause of the boom and bust cycles in many national housing markets. Some analysts situate their analysis in a neo-liberal assessment of changes in the 'fundamentals' of housing demand and supply. Behavioural economists focus on consumer behaviour and 'irrational exuberance' in creating booms. Yet others focus on the globalisation of finance markets brought about by their deregulation and internationalisation. The result has been massive flows of capital across space and in some instances risky investment that, when it has gone 'bad' as in the sub-prime mortgage market in the USA, has had deleterious impacts on housing markets and national economies. Clearly what is needed here is the trans-disciplinary analysis posited earlier that can incorporate all of these factors.

Section 3 has also shown some of the public policy areas that relate to the field of housing. The most obvious are the economy and welfare policies, but others are coming more to the fore, such as the increasing concern with the environmental agenda.

One element of the context facing housing markets has only been touched on in this collection, but could become a major research focus in the near future. This is the environmental impact of housing. Here we have focused on current interest in carbon reduction in housing design, but the need to tackle climate change and the increasing price of oil and other materials and energy sources could result in change in many aspects of housing production and consumer behaviour.

A number of chapters have focused on the neighbourhood as a key component of the attributes of housing. But the location of households in space is a key element in the social impact of housing and so has been the focus of much government policy attention. Three chapters have focused on the social and ethnic segregation of households as 'a problem' sometimes for the households involved, but often for the wider society. It is likely that a concern with the neighbourhood as an important mechanism for social cohesion at a time of increasing individualism and mobility will be a key feature of government policy on housing. The neighbourhood may also be a key element in the search for a more environmentally sustainable form of living in cities. Therefore, it is a concern that government policies towards neighbourhoods seem to have had limited success. Policies designed to promote a mixed population have not succeeded in promoting personal interaction, although they do seem to have overcome some problems of stigma. There is little evidence that ethnic segregation is declining at a time when ethnic conflict is perceived as being a major problem. Therefore, further research on the causes and consequences of segregation, as well as on the mechanisms of location selection by consumers, is required in order to be able to identify effective intervention mechanisms for governments to pursue.

Two chapters in Section 4 focused on government policies towards low-income households. In many countries social rented housing is the preserve of the poorest sections of the population and has been stigmatised. How to provide quality housing and services to this population within the constraints of declining public expenditures is a crucial issue, as of course is dealing with those people who become homeless. Despite the increased quantity and quality of housing in many countries, homelessness persists. Increasingly, the focus is on inequalities in housing opportunities that exclude some people from adequate housing and on the personal attributes and problems such as drug abuse and poor mental health that hinder some people in their pursuit of somewhere to live. Here is another example of the need for trans-disciplinary research to provide the holistic analysis to allow for all the complex factors involved in homelessness to be understood and related together.

So this review finds housing studies in a robust state of health, as shown by the wealth of research covered here. But there is the potential for a greater contribution. There have been examples where housing studies have been at the forefront of trans-disciplinary thinking and research and there is a wide scope for this approach in the future.

REFERENCES

Clapham D (2009) "A Theory of Housing: Problems and Potential", *Housing, Theory and Society* vol. 26, no.1 pp. 1–9.

King P. (2009) "Using theory or making theory: can there be theories of housing", *Housing, Theory and Society* vol. 26, no. 1 pp. 41–52.

Index

Aalbers, M. B. 197, 287
Aaronson, D. 411
abandonment 90, 92
Abbot-Chapman, J. 321
Abertridwr housing project 332–6, 353
Abrahmson, P. 281
accessibility 74, 90
access-space model 15
Acorn 160
actor–network relationships 132, 143, 181, 183–4, 190
Adams, D. 132–3, 135
addictions *see* alcohol; drugs
adolescents 321, 442–3
aesthetic value 155, 231, 237, 239, 338, 465
 and sustainable housing 327
affluence 34, 147, 246, 315, 322–3
affordability 76–7, 192, 240, 246, 248, 355–7, 391–4
 affordable housing in the UK 357, 379–81, 383–4, 387–94
 approaches to state intervention 387–8
 causes of problems 381–4
 definition of 379–81
 and homelessness 362, 369
 and migration 296, 298, 304–5, 309–10
 and people–environment studies 232–3
 problems with 384–7
 and segregation 447, 450, 453–4
 and subsidies 400, 402, 404–5, 407–9, 412–13
age (of houses) 73, 155, 380, 469
age (of people) 85, 109, 260, 279, 306, 320, 324, 366
 and housing demand 296–9
 and migration 300, 307–8
 and mobility 66, 68, 70–2, 75
 see also life-course approach; old age
agent-based models 74–5
agents 11, 101, 136
agriculture 44
air quality 231, 353
Aitken, A. 13
Akerlof, G. A. 261
Al Qaeda 432
Alberstlund 337
alcohol 361, 365
Allen, C. 196, 199
Allen, J. 279–80, 286

allowances 211, 239, 278, 289, 403, 405
Alonso, W. 15, 148, 154
Althusser, L. P. 189
Ambrose, P. 194
amenities 298–9, 307, 380, 445
America *see* USA
American Apartheid 422
American Dream 51
American Economics Association 132
American Sociological Review 420
Amin, A. 452
Anderson, I. 366
Andersson, R. 427
Andrew, M. 264
antisocial behaviour 237, 357, 440, 443, 446, 476–7, 480
 see also crime
Antonides, G. 8
Aoki, K. 260
apartheid 216, 433
apartment blocks 67–8, 71, 150–1, 246, 248, 444, 478
 and building 27, 33–4, 37, 39
 and social life 321, 323
Apgar, W. 411
appliances 331, 341, 343, 345, 351
Arbaci, S. 283–4
architects 28, 34, 184, 230, 232, 237–40, 323
Århén, P. 408
Arthur, W. B. 269
Artle, R. 256
Asia 153, 281
 see also individual countries
aspirations 199, 232, 240, 322
 see also status
asylum seekers 154, 365
Atkinson, R. 323, 448
attachment costs 209–10
Attanasio, O. 260
auctions 8, 20
Australia 68–9, 215, 247
 and affordable housing 384–5, 387
 and building 33, 37
 and homelessness 356, 359–60, 363–5, 367–8, 372–4
 and housing markets 11, 13–14
 and segregation 440, 449, 452

and structurally inspired approaches 193, 199
and subsidies 400, 408, 410
and welfare states 280, 283
Austria 3, 7, 199, 337
and welfare states 282–3, 285, 289
automata models 74–5

baby boom generation 246, 248, 295, 297, 309–10
Baker, R. 137
Balchin, P. 462
Ball, M. 2–3, 13, 135–7, 193, 211
Bank of England 55
banks 6, 14, 197, 267–70
Barker Review 13, 263, 268, 381–2, 387
Barlow, J. 283
Bartlett, W. 138
Basset, K. 191–2
Bauman, Z. 177
Baumgarter, M. 322
Beddington Zero Energy Development (BedZED) 338–9, 351
bedrooms 47, 50, 335, 338
behaviour 2, 47–50, 93
　future research 58–60
　and the housing market 47, 50, 53–5, 57–8
　housing needs and preferences 50–2
　resources and restrictions 52–3
　tenure choice in a life-course perspective 55–8
behavioural economics 2–3, 107, 132–3, 140, 142
Behring, K. 290
Belgium 363, 440, 468
Bell, W. 51
Belsky, E. 409–11
benefit system 54, 276, 361, 379
Bengtsson, B. 110–11, 181, 198, 201, 209, 211, 215–16, 366
Benito, A. 256, 259, 261
Benjamin, D. 234
bereavement 361
Berger, M. C. 299
Berger, P. 175–6, 182
Berry, M. 193, 401
Beveridge, W. 277–8
bid rent 148
Bismarck–Beveridge divide 277–8, 280
Bitter, C. 246, 248
Black, J. 266
Blandy, S. 323
Bliss, N. 471
Blokland, T. 314
Bloomquist, G. C. 299
Blumer, H. 175–6
Boal, F. W. 151, 452
Boehm, T. P. 53
Boelhouwer, P. 195, 408
Bogdon, A. S. 380–1, 384–6
Böheim, R. 264–5
boilers 328, 334, 349
Bolt, G. 357

Bonoli, G. 277
boom-and-bust cycles 7, 22, 41, 152, 252–3, 264, 268, 295, 297, 299, 305, 404, 410
Borchert, J. 278
Borjas, G. 427–8
borrowing rates 7, 149
Boumeester, H. 463
bounded rationality 132–3, 142
Bourassa, S. 17, 410
Bourdieu, P. 151, 157–8, 196–7
Bover, O. 265
Boyer, R. 192
Boyle, P. 77
Bramley, G. 23
Brenner, N. 288
Bridge, C. 406, 408, 413
Bridge, G. 157
Britain *see* UK
British Attitude Survey 318
British Household Panel Study (BHPS) 318
British Housing Management Standards Manual 476–7
Brito, P. M. B. 266
Brooks-Gunn, J. 442
Brown, T. 54
brownfield schemes 34, 37, 39
Brundtland Report 328
Bryman, A. 166–7
bubbles 121, 124, 141, 261, 263, 268–9, 299
building 2, 27–30, 44–5, 109, 137, 191, 199, 249, 448
　firms 3, 6, 28–30, 32–8
　functional continuity 31–2
　importance of viability and risk in 38–41
　process of 30–1
　subcontracting *see* subcontractors
　see also construction sector
Building Research Establishment (BRE) 348–9
building societies 267
　see also financial institutions
Buiter, W. H. 22
Burgess, E. W. 148
Burj Khalifa 32
Burnett, J. 462
Burns, A. F. 6
Butler, D. 157
Butler, R. 91
Butler, T. 108–9, 156, 315
buy-to-let 11, 159, 382

Cairncross, L. 216, 470
Callcutt Review 41
Callon, M. 139
Cameron, G. 264–5, 268
Campbell, J. Y. 260
Can, A. 380–1, 384–6
Canada 33, 68, 283, 320, 383, 452
　and homelessness 362–3, 365
　and housing politics 8, 11, 14
　and segregation 69, 443
capital gains tax 78, 86, 265, 410

capitalism 149, 193–4, 197
Capozza, D. 410
car ownership 246, 286, 322, 441
car sharing 351
Carasso, A. 400, 410–11
carbon charging 16
carbon emissions 245, 249, 327–8, 330–31, 340, 343, 345, 347–8, 351–2
    see also zero carbon housing
Case, K. E. 23, 259, 268
Castells, M. 189, 192–3, 217, 317
Castles, F. G. 279–80, 286, 290
Catholic Church 275, 279, 368
Cathy Come Home 171
census data 43, 77, 166, 248, 297, 300, 306–7, 359–60, 428
central heating *see* heating
Chadwick, E. 165
Chan, S. 265
charities 109, 166, 171, 288
Chartered Institute of Housing 476
Cheshire, P. 18
Chicago School 109, 148
childbirth 48, 67–8, 73–4, 78–9, 470
    see also pregnancy
childless couples 52, 68, 75, 310
children 51, 57, 60, 276, 320–21, 380, 408, 411
    and homelessness 364, 367
    and migration 296, 307
    and mobility 68–9, 71–2
    and neighbourhoods 84, 99, 101
    and segregation 439, 442, 449–50
China 316, 320
cities 5, 94, 233, 248, 283, 287, 296, 470
    and building 33, 37
    and household behaviour 48, 51, 53
    and housing politics 206, 217, 219
    and mobility 66, 69, 71, 79–81
    and segregation 420, 425, 427–9, 434–5, 440, 443, 445, 447, 449, 451–4
    and social geographic interpretations 148–9, 153, 155, 159
    and social life 314–16, 319, 324
    and structurally inspired approaches 191–2, 195
citizenship 110, 137, 171–2, 216–17, 219–20, 472–3, 480
    and housing politics 207
Clampet-Lundquist, S. 99
Clapham, D. 109–10, 164, 180, 185–6, 216, 366, 471, 476–8
Claritas 158, 322
Clark, K. 427, 440
Clark, W. A. V. 2–3, 51, 60, 78, 300, 425
class 155, 158–9, 188–9, 191–2, 196, 199, 275, 278, 317, 449
    see also status
class monopoly rents 197
Clegg, S. 184, 216
climate change 245, 327–8, 338–9, 351

Cloke, P. 196
clustering 422–4, 451–2
Coase, R. 133
Cocco, J. F. 260
Code for Sustainable Homes 328, 330–31, 337, 343
Coed Cymru 351
cognitive dissonance reduction 49
cohabitation 56–8, 67–9
Cole, I. 288
Collin, F. 181
comfort 50, 333, 335, 338
    and sustainable housing 353
commodification 110, 189
commuting time 10, 12, 47–8, 53, 70, 77, 148, 156–7, 237, 313, 322–3, 325, 339, 380, 383, 392, 426
comparative historical analysis 189–90, 197
competition 27, 191, 282, 452, 468, 473
composition of households 85, 101, 238
    and affordable housing 381, 387, 391, 394
    and mobility 67–8, 71
Conceptual Model of Service Quality 475
Condition of the Working Class in England 165
Confederation of Co-operative Housing 471
Confucian cultural heritage 281
Conijn, J. B. S. 474
conservative–corporatist welfare states 274–5, 279, 285, 290
construction sector 7, 13, 28, 30, 32, 36, 41–3, 66, 89–90, 199, 230, 234, 236, 238–9, 246, 263–4, 274, 406, 479
    and sustainable housing 327, 342, 351, 353
    see also building
consumption 50, 72, 141, 286
    and affordability 380, 382
    and the economy 251–4, 256–61, 263, 267
    and housing politics 214–15
    and structurally inspired approaches 189–91, 193–4, 196–7, 199
    and subsidies 406, 408, 412
contagion models 93
contractors 38, 40, 42, 210, 239
    see also subcontractors
cooling 331, 337, 342–3, 345
Cooper, C. 217
cooperative housing 211, 217, 288
Core-Based Statistical Areas (CBSAs) 301–2, 304
corporatism 213–14, 218, 283, 285
cost-benefit analysis 169, 237, 372
cost-effectiveness analysis 169–70, 372
costs of housing 56, 133, 136, 239
    and building 27, 31–2, 35–6, 40, 43
    and migration 76–7
cottages 154
council housing 139, 149, 153–4, 158, 214, 216, 468
    see also social housing
council tax 268
Courgeau, D. 52
cradle to cradle approach 351
Crane, J. 93

Crane, M. 373
credit crunch 246, 251–2, 255, 263, 266–7, 270, 362
   see also financial crisis
crime 12, 79, 93, 98–9, 165, 237, 320, 322, 401, 408, 413, 426, 433, 440, 443, 446, 450, 472, 477
   see also antisocial behaviour
critical realism 110–11, 168, 170–1, 178, 199–201, 369–70
Crook, A. 383–4, 388, 390, 392
crowding 151, 381, 383, 403, 408, 412–13
crowding out 264, 266, 407
cultural issues 37, 51, 67, 152, 156–7, 180, 199, 230–4, 236, 315, 327, 435, 451
cybernetic approach 169
cyberspace *see* internet
Czasny, K. 289
Czech Republic 368, 373

DataBuild 335
Davies, R. B. 49
Davies Withers, S. 78
Davis, M. 200
De Jong, G. F. 50
de Meza, D. 266
de Vos, S. 423–4, 432
death 78, 297, 361
debt 7, 40, 260, 267, 269
decentralization 16, 288, 404
decommodification 193–4, 201, 221, 274–6, 279, 282, 289–90
defaults 197, 267, 402
Della Vigna, S. 142
demand 18, 53, 231, 248, 357
   and affordability 380, 382, 384
   and the economy 251–62, 267
   and life-course approach 295–9
   and migration 298, 309–10
demand-side subsidies 399–400, 404, 406–11
democracy 51, 110, 169, 194, 200, 207–8, 217–20, 403
demolition 153, 387, 435, 445, 447, 453–4, 477, 479
Denmark 56, 214, 216, 285, 288, 337, 440
Denton, N. A. 422
deposits 55, 252, 255, 257, 259–61, 266, 398
deprived neighbourhoods 47, 218, 266, 409, 443–4, 446, 448, 455
deregulation 108, 252, 404
desegregation *see* mixed districts; segregation
design 136, 184, 380, 408, 413
   and building 28, 32–4, 43
   and people–environment studies 230–1, 233, 237–8
   and sustainable housing 327, 352–3
detached houses 54, 56, 150, 286, 304–5, 322, 345
Deurloo, M. C. 423–4, 432
developers 29, 32–6, 38–9, 41–2, 44, 94, 136, 143, 149, 191, 383, 389
deviant behaviour *see* antisocial behaviour
Dewilde, C. 58
Diamond, D. 400, 403, 405, 412

Dickens, P. 213, 217
Dieleman, F. M. 51
Dietz, R. 410–11
dilapidation 92, 94–5
DiPasquale, D. 19, 264, 407
disability 164, 181, 183, 281, 338, 363
discourse 110, 178–9
discrete choice models 73
discrimination 2, 55, 150, 157, 279, 286, 425–6, 440, 452, 479
disequilibrium models 72–3
disinvestment 155
displacement 69–70, 96, 155–6, 405, 447
dissatisfaction *see* satisfaction
divorce 48, 52, 57–60, 67, 73–4, 78
Dogge, P. J. C. 474–5
Doling, J. 194, 289
domestic hot water 331, 337, 347
Donald Review 13
Donnison, D. V. 313
Dorling, D. 53
Doucet, B. 448
Dougherty, A. 253
down payments 255–7, 280, 308
Downs, A. 85
downsizing 53, 55, 57, 92, 260, 473
Drinkwater, S. 427
drugs 79, 98, 361–2, 365, 477
dual-earner households 53, 71, 75, 77
Dubai 32
Duncan, B. 420
Duncan, O. D. 420
Duncan, S. 283
Dunham, J. 94
Dunleavy, P. 217
Dunn, K. M. 452
Dunster, B. 338
durability 1, 10–13, 15, 88, 100
Dynarski, M. 210

Eccles, R G. 43
econometric models 97
Economic and Monetary Union (EMU) 251
economic crisis *see* financial crisis
Economist, The 411
economy
   housing and aggregate demand 251–62
   housing and aggregate supply 262–6
   and housing policy 267–9
   see also credit crunch; financial crisis
eco-villages 323
education 52, 85, 164, 237, 247, 281, 308, 392, 477
   and mobility 66, 68, 70–1, 79
   and neighbourhoods 86, 98
   and segregation 439, 442
   and social geographic interpretations 155, 157
   and social life 314, 319, 322
   and subsidies 357, 401, 408, 411–13
   see also schools

elasticity
  of demand 18
  of prices 262–3
  of supply 297, 406–7, 410
elderly people *see* old age
elective belonging 151, 156–8, 160
electricity 331, 345
Ellis, L. 400
Elsinga, M. 286, 289
embodied energy 331, 340–41, 343, 345–7, 351–2, 353
emergency accommodation 367–8
emotional attachments 71, 85, 100, 157, 181, 265–6, 315
empiricism 166–9
employment 52–3, 57, 74, 76, 78–9, 85, 164, 198–200, 238, 264–5, 279, 320, 361, 365, 401, 403, 412–13, 443
  access to *see* commuting time
  changes in 68, 70, 75–6, 78, 265, 298
  rates of 97
  and social housing 468, 477
  workforce attachment 77–8
  working from home 313, 323, 443
  see also labour markets; unemployment
empty-nester stage 296, 301–2, 309
endowment effects 141
energy efficiency 249, 329–30, 343, 345
  energy efficient housing 330–37
  see also energy use; sustainable housing
Energy Performance Assessments (EPAs) 335–7, 353
Energy Performance of Buildings Directive (EPBD) 330
Energy Technology Support Unit (ETSU) 335
energy use 30, 238, 245, 310, 323, 327–8, 332–3, 347–8, 350, 353, 465
  see also energy efficiency
Engelhardt, G. 142, 310
Engels, F. 165
England 78, 139, 231, 260, 265, 288, 315
  and affordable housing 388–9, 391, 393–4
  and building 31, 37–8
  and homelessness 364, 368–9, 373
  and social geographic interpretations 147, 157–8
  and social policy approaches 165, 170
  and sustainable housing 328, 343
  see also UK
entertainment *see* recreation
entrepreneurship 41–2
Environmental Design Research Association (EDRA) 231
environmental issues 74, 85, 88, 90, 201, 231, 239, 249, 310, 383, 403, 405, 468
  see also carbon emissions; climate change
ergonomics 230, 237, 239
Esping-Andersen, G. 179, 198, 211, 274–83, 285, 290
estates 206, 218, 232, 234, 319–20, 405, 448, 462, 464, 477
Etherington, D. 288

ethical issues 24, 50, 163, 171–2, 200, 372
ethnic minorities 85, 88, 171, 197, 232, 249
  and homelessness 363–4
  and household behaviour 48, 55
  and housing politics 216
  and mobility 75, 81
  and social geographic interpretations 147–8, 154–6, 158–9
  and social housing 468–70, 477
  and social life 316, 319–20, 324
  see also ethnic segregation; racial issues
ethnic segregation 79, 97, 151, 216, 283, 355, 357, 435–6, 439–41
  causes and effects of 425–8
  concepts and measures of 420–5
  initiatives to counter segregation 444–7
  levels of 428–32
  possible gains from 451–2
  public debates of 432–5
ETHOS typology 360
E-topia 323
Europe 34–5, 58, 100, 139, 233, 245–7, 297, 300, 319, 384
  and the economy 251, 259, 268
  and homelessness 356, 359, 361–3, 367–8, 372–4
  and housing politics 212, 214, 216
  and mobility 69–70, 75, 78
  and segregation 357, 419, 427–8, 432–5, 439–41, 445–7, 453–4
  and social geographic interpretations 149, 152–3
  and social housing 462, 468–70, 477
  and structurally inspired approaches 191, 195–8
  and sustainable housing 330, 337, 342, 351
  and welfare states 274–6, 278–82, 285–6, 288–90
  see also individual countries
European Commission 360, 372
European Community Household Panel 285, 289
European Journal of Homelessness 373
European Journal of Housing Policy 207
European Observatory on Homelessness (EOH) 373
European Parliament 330
European Union (EU) 214, 218, 280–2, 288, 372–4, 428–9, 468, 478
Europeanization 278
Evans, A. 15
Evers, A. 275
evictions 78, 360–1, 474
exclusion 119, 153, 164, 284, 361, 373–4, 403, 471–2, 480
Experien 322
explicit subsidies 398–9

Fabian socialist tradition 165, 167
Facebook 316
families 3, 111, 246–8, 325, 451, 470
  and homelessness 154, 364, 367
  and household behaviour 51, 54, 58
  and life-course approach 296, 300–1
  and migration 300, 308

and mobility 68–9, 71–6
and welfare states 275–6, 279–83, 285
Fawcett, J. T. 50
FEANTSA 366, 373
Federal Reserve 7
feed-in tariffs 351
Feijten, P. 57, 60
Feins, J. 99
feminism 201, 363
Ferrera, M. 279
fertility events *see* childbirth; pregnancy
filtering 91–2, 192, 382
financial crisis 3, 5, 7, 22, 27, 38, 197, 246, 261, 286
    see also credit crunch
financial institutions 6, 14, 197, 267–70, 269
Financial Services Authority 261
Fincher, R. 199
Fine, G. 176
Finland 440
Firdion, J. M. 374
fire risk 30, 237
first-time buyers 48, 55–7, 255, 257, 259–60, 280, 296, 405
fittings 30–1
Fitzpatrick, S. 356
fixed rate mortgages 269, 415
fixity *see* spatial fixity
flats *see* apartment blocks
Fleishman, C. 357
Flint, J. 323
floor plans 237, 239
Fopp, R. 181, 201
Ford, H. 150
foreclosures 4, 246
Forrest, R. 246, 248, 443, 445
fossil fuels 327, 331, 340
Foucault, M. 177–8, 182, 184
fragmentation 13, 36–7, 199–200, 282, 355–6, 398, 408, 446
framing analysis 219, 223
France 34, 44, 193, 214, 331, 440
    and homelessness 365, 367, 372–3
    and social geographic interpretations 147, 153
    and social housing 468–9
    and welfare states 283, 289
free market economies 152
Frey, W. H. 151
Fried, M. 322
Fukayama, F. 316, 324
furnishings 231–3, 241–2

Gabriel, M. 181, 184
Gabriel, S. 299–300
Galster, G. 2–3, 10, 91, 314, 403, 406, 427, 450
game theory 110–11
gaming models 93–5, 100–1
gardens 38, 56, 154, 315, 321
Garfinkel, H. 177, 212
gated communities 315, 323

GEAR urban renewal projects 170
gender 171, 188, 190, 194, 196, 199, 232, 275–6, 279, 286, 315, 320, 324, 363–4
General Household Survey (GHS) 318–19
General Social Survey 318
Gennetian, L. 97–9
Genovese, D. 142
gentrification 108, 149, 152, 154–60, 189, 405–6, 448
geographic information systems (GIS) 17, 86, 88, 347, 423, 432
geography 27, 44, 80, 156–7, 159, 168, 192, 207, 231, 323
Germany 34, 56, 153, 214, 411
    and building 44
    and homelessness 363–4, 367–9
    and segregation 430, 440, 442, 453
    and social housing 468, 477
    and sustainable housing 330, 337, 340
    and welfare states 285, 289
ghettos 426, 440, 454
Gibb, K. 8, 108, 137–8, 142, 264
Gibson, J. 183
Giddens, A. 177, 180, 184, 366
Glaeser, E. L. 13, 22, 297
Glass, R. 154
glazing *see* windows
global financial crisis *see* financial crisis
globalization 150, 157, 180, 197, 247, 269, 278, 281, 425
glocalization 193, 197
Goering, J. 99
Golab, C. 85
Golden Age of Welfare 194, 278, 288, 302
Goodlad, R. 216, 472–3
Goodman, A. C. 17, 263
Goodman, J. 75
Goodwin, M. 196
Gordon, A. 328
Gough, I. 281
governance 134–5, 137–8, 179, 196, 355, 367, 369
    and housing politics 206–8, 216–20
governments 35, 40, 79, 81, 109, 136, 154, 246, 249, 263, 288, 355–6
    and affordable housing 379, 382, 384, 389, 391
    and homelessness 367–8
    and household behaviour 51, 54–5
    and housing markets 6–7, 9, 23
    and housing politics 207, 210–12, 214
    intervention *see* state intervention
    and neighbourhoods 86, 90, 100–1
    and people–environment studies 237, 239
    and segregation 420, 440, 453
    and social housing 466, 468, 477, 479
    and social policy approaches 163–6, 168–71
    and subsidies 397–9, 410
    and sustainable housing 327–30, 332, 339, 343, 345–6, 348
    and welfare states 288
    see also housing politics; policies
Graham, E. 441

Granovetter, M. 317
grants 397, 399
Grayson, J. 217
Great Britain *see* UK
Great Depression 269
Great Financial Crash (GFC) *see* financial crisis
Greece 56, 279, 337
Green, R. K. 51, 410
green issues *see* environmental issues
greenfield building 29, 152
Grimes, A. 13
Grönroos, C. 474
gross domestic product (GDP) 246, 251, 263–4, 274
Guest, A. M. 318–19
Gurran, N. 387–8
Gustavsson, S. 212
Gwalia Housing Association 342
Gyourko, J. 410

Haffner, M. 400, 408
Halfacre, K. 78
Hall, R. E. 254, 256
Hallman, H. 85
Hamilton, W. 132
Hamnett, C. 108–9, 155–6
Hamnett, S. 199
Hampton, K. 443
Handbook of European Welfare Systems 281, 288
Handbook of Social Theory 175
Hanuschek, E. 72
Hardy, D. 231–2, 240
Harloe, M. 194–5, 213
Harriott, S. 461
Hartig, T. 238
Harvey, D. 149–50, 152, 155, 189, 192–3, 197
Haurin, D. 410–11
Haworth, A. 179
Hawtin, M. 217
Hayden, D. 199
Headey, B. 212
Healey, P. 136
health 58, 78, 99, 109, 168, 237–8, 247, 286–7, 314, 361, 380, 392, 465
    mental health 99, 361–2, 365, 374, 452
    and people–environment studies 231–2, 239
    and social policy approaches 164–5
    and subsidies 357, 401, 403, 408, 412–13
    and sustainable housing 327, 338, 348, 351
    and welfare states 276, 281
heating 11, 328–9, 331–7, 341, 343, 345, 347, 353
hedonic studies 10–11, 15, 17–19, 48, 108, 299
Hegedüs, J. 285
Heidenheimer, A. J. 274
Heins, F. 301
Helbrecht, I. 290
Helderman, A. 53, 57–8
Hendershott, P. 410
Henley, A. 265
Henning, C. 317

herd behaviour 95, 141
Hertting, N. 218
Heskett, J. L. 476
Hess, K. 85
heterogeneity 1, 36, 136, 320, 449, 453
heuristics 140–1
Hicks, A. 278
high-income households 148, 156, 257, 322, 409–10, 469–70, 477
    and affordable housing 380, 382, 385, 388, 394
    and neighbourhoods 91–2, 95
    and segregation 443, 445
    and social housing 468
Hills, J. 137
Himmelberg, C. 268
historical institutionalism 214–15, 218–19
HM Treasury 381, 410
Hodgson, G. 132–3, 135, 139
Hoek-Smit, M. 400, 403, 405, 412
Hoekstra, J. 279, 283, 285, 289
Hogan, D. P. 442
holiday homes 382
holistic approach 109, 174, 180, 233, 327, 336–9, 342, 345, 351–3, 365
homelessness 48, 109, 154, 166–8, 171–2, 178, 186, 200, 313, 355–6, 383, 394
    causes of 360–3
    characteristics of homeless people 363–5
    definitions of 359–60
    experiences of homeless people 365–6
    future research agenda 369–74
    and housing politics 216
    and social housing 357, 359, 367, 374, 476
    state policies on 366–9
homeownership 98, 137, 168, 246–7, 296, 324, 463
    and the economy 257, 260, 265
    and housing politics 211, 215
    and migration 305, 308
    and mobility 66–8
    rates of 56, 98, 257, 260, 265, 285, 289, 296, 305, 361, 410
    and social geographic interpretations 153–4
    and structurally inspired approaches 193, 197–8
    and subsidies 401–5, 409–12
    and welfare states 285–7, 289
    see also first-time buyers; owner-occupiers
Hong Kong 153, 316, 323
Hooimeijer, P. 52
Hoover, H. 51
HOPE VI 100, 434
housebuilding *see* building
household behaviour *see* behaviour
Housing Act (1980) 55, 154
Housing and Planning Delivery Grant 387
Housing and Social Theory 282
housing associations 55, 137–9, 214, 216, 284, 384, 453, 463–4, 479
housing career 51–2, 55–6, 58–60, 66–7, 69, 444–7, 451, 453

Housing First approach 368–9, 373
Housing Market Renewal Programme 170
housing markets 1, 5–15, 95, 108–9, 135, 209, 231, 245–6
   and affordability 380, 382, 391
   and building 37, 39–41
   crisis 53, 57, 59, 71, 101
   and the economy 257, 261–2, 264
   and household behaviour 47, 50, 53–5, 57–8
   and life-course approach 295–7
   metropolitan markets and local market analysis 15–22
   and migration 19, 297–309
   and mobility *see* mobility
   and neighbourhoods 88, 91
   and segregation 431, 440
   and social geographic interpretations 149–50, 158
   and social housing 464, 466, 470
   and structurally inspired approaches 189
   and subsidies 397, 404, 407, 411
   vacancy chains 2, 54, 81
   and welfare states 282, 287
housing politics 110–11, 206
   policy orientation of housing studies 207–8
   political perspective on housing provision 208–10
   studies on the macro level 210–15
   studies on the micro and meso levels 215–20
   see also policies
Housing Theory and Society 201
Hoyt, H. 148
Huang, Y. 78
Hughes, G. A. 265
Hulse, K. 283, 408
Hungary 56, 364, 367–8, 440
hybrid organizations 216, 219–20
hyper-segregation 422

Iceland, J. 422
identification with place *see* emotional attachments
immigration 90, 309–10
   and homelessness 363, 365, 374
   and segregation 427–8, 432–3, 442–3, 451–2
   and social housing 470, 478
impact fees 31, 40
implicit subsidies 398–9
incentives 29, 41, 327, 330, 397, 406
income tax 409
incomes 164, 191, 246, 276, 287, 296, 347, 361, 363
   and affordable housing 379–81, 383–8, 391, 393–4
   and the economy 257, 259, 267–8
   and household behaviour 47, 52, 56–7, 59
   and housing markets 7, 16–19, 22, 24
   and migration 299, 305, 308
   and mobility 66–7, 71–3, 78–9, 81
   and neighbourhoods 85–6, 88–90, 100
   and people–environment studies 238–9
   and segregation 425, 439, 442, 449
   and social geographic interpretations 147–8, 150–1, 154

   and social housing 468–9, 475
   and subsidies 403, 408, 410, 413
indigenous peoples 363–5
individualism 132, 236, 248
industrialization 324, 352, 403
inflation 267, 403–4
inheritance 53
inner-city living 52, 54, 75, 148–50, 153–8, 314–15, 380, 404, 422, 448
institutional economics 107–8, 131–3, 142–3
   applications to housing 135–9
   extensions, possible developments and agendas 139–42
   new institutional economics (NIE) 108, 133–5, 142–3, 269
   old institutional economics (OIE) 131–2, 135
institutional layering 197–8
insulation 239, 333–5, 337, 348–9
   thermal insulation 328–9, 332, 334, 347
insurance 84, 90, 101, 274, 277, 287, 402
integration *see* ethnic segregation; mixed districts; segregation
interest rates 40, 149, 256–7, 262–4, 266–7, 404
   and affordable housing 379
   and household behaviour 55, 57, 59
   and housing markets 22
   real interest rates 124, 254, 256, 261–2, 266–7
   and social housing 463, 469
Internal Review Service 78
International Association for People–Environment Studies (IAPS) 231
International Monetary Fund (IMF) 7
internet 8, 316, 441, 443
Interstate system 152
investors 85, 87, 95, 100
isolation 422, 428, 432, 434–5, 439
Italy 34, 56, 279, 363, 365, 430

Jacobs, K. 178, 181–2, 184
Janelle, D. G. 441
Japan 70, 281, 361
Jencks, C. 442
Jensen, L. 216
Jessop, B. 196, 200
jobs *see* employment
Johnston, R. J. 422–4, 426, 432
joint ventures 35–6
Jones, C. 17
Jones, P. 245–6, 249
Journal of Housing and the Built Environment 207
Journal of Social Issues 373
journals 207, 373, 411, 420
journey to work *see* commuting time
Jurjevich, J. R. 301

Kahneman, D. 140–1
Kallus, R. 314
Kalmijn, M. 446
Katz, B. 400

Kearns, A. 443, 445
Keller, S. 85
Kemeny, J. 49, 163, 166–7, 171, 174, 178–9, 181–2, 195, 198, 211–13, 216, 219–20, 282, 284–6, 288
Kemp, J. 51
Kemp, P. 164
key worker accommodation 380–1, 389
Keynesian Welfare National State (KWNS) 288
Khadduri, J. 407
King, M. 259
King, P. 54, 180, 182–3
kinship 188, 234, 280–2, 451
Kintrea, K. 448
Kitagawa, E. M. 442
Kitsuse, J. 178
Kleinman, M. 214
Kramer, J. 153
Ku, Y. 281
Kumar, K. 324
Kundnani, A. 452
Kutty, N. K. 385, 388

labour markets 30, 68, 75–8, 98, 299–300, 403, 408, 410, 439
 see also employment
labour unions 214
Lachmann, L. M. 7
Laferrère, A. 406
Lancaster, K. 85
land 2, 27, 41–2, 44, 90
 acquisition of 29, 32, 36
 cost of 7, 148, 246, 389–90
land developers *see* developers
Land Registry 17
landlords 54, 110, 136, 149, 172, 195, 199, 240, 290, 356
 and affordable housing 379, 385
 and housing politics 209–10, 216
 registered social landlords (RSLs) 389, 391
 and social housing 463, 473–7
 tenant–landlord relationships 470–2
landowners 35, 136, 149, 199, 213, 384, 389
land-use 74–5, 91, 100, 191, 198, 232, 240, 264, 388, 403
land-use planning 29, 40, 43, 74, 143, 165, 383
language 110, 176–7, 183, 234
language barriers 320, 373–4, 443, 446, 451, 453
Lasch, C. 324
Latin America 281
Lawrence, R. 111, 189, 237–40
Lawson, J. 110, 190, 196, 198, 215
Law-Yone, H. 314
layout of houses 10, 232, 237, 337
Le Blanc, D. 400, 406
Le Grand, J. 138
leaving parental home 48, 51, 56, 68, 257, 301–2
Lee, B. H. 74
Lee, Y. 281
Lees, L. 156–7

Leibfried, S. 279
Leishman, C. 356, 387
leisure facilities *see* recreation
lenders 101, 197, 199, 214, 255, 298, 385
 see also banks; mortgages
Lerman, B. R. 388
Leventhal, T. 442
Ley, D. 155, 157
liberal welfare states 274–5, 278, 280, 283, 285
Lieberg, M. 317
life-course approach
 and household behaviour 47, 49–52, 55–60
 and migration 295–8, 300–8
 and mobility 66–71, 76–7
 and social life 319, 324
 see also age (of people)
life-cycle approach 86, 155, 236, 247, 252, 257, 259–61, 286
 and household behaviour 51–2, 55
lifestyles 51, 286, 350, 425
 and homelessness 366–7
 and housing markets 12, 16, 18
 and people–environment studies 230, 232–3
 and social housing 477–8
 and social life 314–15, 321–5
lighting 331, 338, 343, 347
Lindblom, C. 170, 186
Lindbom, A. 215
Linz Solar City 337
Lipsky, M. 217, 219
Listokin, Y. 410
Lithuania 56
loans 40, 44, 237, 239, 257, 259–60, 267, 399, 443
 see also mortgages
Local Strategic Partnerships 472
locality studies 195
location 2, 298–9, 322, 408, 423, 478
 and affordability 381, 383
 and household behaviour 47–8, 50, 52–3
 and housing markets 8, 10, 12
 and mobility 67, 75
 and people–environment studies 233–4
 see also neighbourhoods
Lockwood, D. 155
long-distance migration 57, 75–6, 248, 264
longevity 247, 265, 313
Low, L. 281
Low, S. 155
Low Carbon Urban Built Environments (LCUBE) 330
low energy housing 328, 330, 332–6, 339, 350, 352
 see also sustainable housing; zero carbon housing
Lowe, S. 211, 214
Lowi, T. J. 208
low-income households 21, 79, 95–7, 232, 246, 257, 284
 and affordable housing 380–2, 386–8, 394
 and segregation 426, 440, 443–4, 446–8, 450, 453
 and social geographic interpretations 149–51, 153–4
 and social housing 468–70, 477–8

and social policy approaches 165–6, 171
and subsidies 400, 402, 404–12
Luckmann, T. 175–6, 182
Ludwig, J. 97–9
Luea, H. 409–10
Lundqvist, L. J. 212

Maclennan, D. 1–3, 10, 16, 137–8, 356, 404
MacRae, C. 94
macroeconomics 22–3, 152, 251, 263–4, 267, 383, 388, 410, 412
Mahoney, J. 201
maintenance 95, 194, 254, 362, 379
of social housing 461–5
Malpass, P. 284
Malpezzi, S. 18, 407
managerialism 29, 472–3, 480
Mankiw, N. G. 295
Manley, D. 60
Manor, O. 320
Manski, S. 73
Manzi, A. 178–9, 181–2
Marcon, E. 423
Marcuse, P. 212
market failure 13, 15, 24, 101, 114, 125, 133–4, 142, 401, 414
marketability 31, 38–9, 475
Marpsat, M. 374
marriage 56–7, 59–60, 67–8, 72–3, 75, 234
Marsh, A. 137, 142
Marshall, T. H. 216
Martin, D. 176
Martinez, M. 320
Marvin, S. 441
Marxism 149, 189, 191–3, 196, 213
Maslow, A. H. 50
Massey, D. 99, 422
materiality 139–40, 189, 191, 193
Matlack, J. L. 382–3, 387
Matznetter, W. 245, 282
Mayer, C. 142
Mayer, S. E. 442
Mayo, S. 400–1
McCarthy, G. 410–11
McCormick, B. 265
McFedden, D. 73
Mead, G. 175
means-testing 280, 284, 367
media 5, 51, 68
Meen, G. 23, 245–7, 264, 267–8, 379, 387
mental health 99, 361–2, 365, 374, 452
Merrett, S. 462
Mesch, G. 320
metropolitan statistical areas (MSAs) 297
mews houses 154
Michelson, W. 238–9
microclimates 233
microcomputing 88
microeconomics 9, 24, 92, 211

micro-simulation software 92
middle classes 108–9, 148, 153–8, 165, 317, 322, 325, 453
Middle East 28
migration 148, 246, 248, 308–10, 316
and the economy 264–6, 270
and housing costs 76–7
and housing markets 19, 297–308
and life-course approach 295–8, 300–8, 306
long-distance migration 57, 75–6, 248, 264
and mobility 69, 72, 75–8
and segregation 428, 432
Milburn, N. G. 363
Miles, D. 256
Miles Review 382
Mills, C. W. 208
Minergie Standard for Buildings 330
Mishkin, F. 259, 263, 268
Mishra, R. 167
Mitchell, D. 280
Mitchell, W. C. 6
Mitchell, W. J. 323–4
mixed districts 151, 357, 381, 436, 441, 444–51, 453–4
mixed-use schemes 32, 35, 38, 143, 319, 325
MMC 351
mobile homes 305
mobility 2, 66–7, 157, 231, 246–8, 265, 300–1, 321, 382, 406, 410, 470
classic and contemporary models 72–5
correlates of 69–72
lessons from recent research 75–9
and life-course approach 295
and migration 69, 72, 75–8
and neighbourhoods 67, 69, 71, 75, 77, 79–81, 88, 98–9
and policy 79–81
and segregation 426, 444, 446–7, 450
theory and the life course 67–9
modelling 42, 108, 190, 219, 255, 261, 424
and household behaviour 58–9
and housing markets 9, 22–4
and mobility 72–5
moderate-income households 407, 410–11, 445, 468–9
modernism 192
modernization 200, 282
modes of social regulation (MSR) 195–6
Modifiable Areal Unit Problem (MAUP) 423
Monk, S. 390, 392
monopolies 13–15, 24, 191–3, 198
Moore, E. 383, 387
Moore, R. 149
morality *see* ethical issues
More, A. 138
Morris, D. 85
mortgages 44, 66, 84, 141, 246, 298, 362
100% mortgages 57
and affordable housing 379, 385, 387
and the economy 252, 255, 259, 266–7, 270
fixed rate mortgages 269

mortgages (Cont'd)
    and household behaviour 47, 53, 55–7, 59
    and housing politics 211, 214
    mortgage market 189, 197, 247, 254, 269, 402–4
    and neighbourhoods 90
    and social geographic interpretations 149, 159
    and subsidies 400, 402–3, 409
    and welfare states 280, 286
Mosaic 158, 160
moving house *see* migration; mobility
Moving to Opportunity 79–80, 98–9, 434
MPHASIS project 372
Muellbauer, J. 7, 23, 264–5, 268
Mulder, C. 52–3
multi-family dwellings 58, 356, 478
multiple births 78–9
multiple classification approach 73–4
Mundt, A. 245
Murdie, R. A. 452
Murie, A. 137
Murray, M. 407
Musterd, S. 357, 427, 432, 450
Muth, R. 15
Myers, D. 296–7

National Federation of Non-Profit Housing Associations 214
National Health Service 277
National House Building Council 37
national insurance 277
National Union of Tenants 214
natural disasters 237
Neale, M. 142
negative equity 59, 265, 287, 298
neighbourhood watch committees 316
neighbourhoods 2, 74, 84–5, 136, 143, 157, 164, 247–9, 266, 323, 338, 381
    boundaries of 86–8
    change in 3, 72, 81, 86, 90–6, 100, 314, 425
    creation of 89–90
    definition of 85–6, 314
    and household behaviour 47–8, 51–2, 55
    and housing markets 11–13, 15, 17, 21, 91
    idiosyncrasies of 88–9
    and mobility 67, 69, 71, 75, 77, 79–81, 88, 98–9
    and people–environment studies 230, 232, 237, 239
    renewal programmes 22, 218, 288, 318, 404–6, 408
        see also urban renewal
    segregation in *see* ethnic segregation; segregation
    and social life 313–19, 322, 324
    and subsidies 357, 405, 409, 411
neighbours 10, 51, 249, 477
    and housing markets 12, 19
    and people–environment studies 232–3, 236
    and segregation 440, 443
    and social life 313, 315–19, 324
neo-classicalism 7–8, 11, 13, 16, 73, 132, 135–6, 148, 150, 192, 197, 252, 261

neo-liberalism 107–8, 197
nest leavers *see* leaving parental home
nested logistic models 67, 72, 74
Netherlands 35, 74, 139, 195, 199, 215, 408
    and homelessness 362, 365, 369, 373
    and household behaviour 53, 56–8
    and segregation 422, 427, 429–32, 434–5, 440–1, 443–6, 449, 453
    and social geographic interpretations 152–3
    and social housing 357, 463, 468–70, 475, 477–80
    and welfare states 283, 285, 287
new institutional economics (NIE) 108, 133–5, 142–3, 269
new public management (NPM) 218
New Zealand 68–9, 247, 280, 283
new-build housing 67, 81, 215, 248–9, 263, 283, 319–20
    and affordability 382–3, 387–8
    and household behaviour 54–5
    and neighbourhoods 89, 91
    and social policy approaches 165, 170
    and sustainable housing 327–9, 331, 348
Newhaven Research 384
Newman, S. 412
Nieboer, N. 196
Nieuwenhuysen, J. 199
NIMBY syndrome 218
noise 85, 231, 233, 237, 477–8
non-governmental organizations (NGOs) 210, 214, 364, 367–8
Nordvik, V. 408
Norris, M. 383
North, D. 133
North America 16, 69, 274
    and affordable housing 384, 386–7
    and homelessness 356, 359, 367, 374
    and segregation 357, 419, 432
    and social geographic interpretations 152, 155
    see also individual countries
Northcraft, G. 142
Northern Ireland 394
    see also UK
Norway 219, 331, 408
Novy-Marx, R. 16
Nozick, R. 180
nuclear energy 331
Nygaard, C. 138–9

Obama, B. 369
Oberwittler, D. 442
occupation *see* employment
OECD countries 69, 274, 281, 286, 359
oil crisis 328, 335
Okuyama, T. 266
old age 50, 57–8, 60, 69, 170, 181, 215, 260, 276, 287, 297, 301, 380, 407, 470, 479
    baby boom generation 246, 248, 295, 297, 309–10
    care of elderly 68, 76, 286
    empty-nester stage 296, 301–2, 309

and social life 313, 316, 318
  and social policy approaches 164
  see also population aging; retirement
old institutional economics (OIE) 131–2, 135
Olsen, E. 406
O'Neill, P. 471
orientation 19–20
Orr, L. 80
Ostendorf, W. 432
Oswald, A. 265
OTB Institute 286
Our Common Future see Brundtland Report
outdoor areas 237, 321, 338, 389, 450
  see also gardens; parks
overcrowding *see* crowding
owner-occupiers 33, 76, 180, 246, 379, 387
  and the economy 257, 259, 265
  and household behaviour 47–8, 54–5, 57–8, 60
  and housing politics 210, 213–14, 218
  and mobility 71, 73
  and neighbourhoods 84–6, 90, 93, 100–1
  and segregation 447, 449
  and social geographic interpretations 153, 159
  and social housing 462–3, 466, 468–70
  and subsidies 398–400, 410–11
  and welfare states 279–80, 282, 285, 287
  see also homeownership
Oxley, M. 211

Pahl, R. 149, 317, 319
Panel Study of Income Dynamics (PSID) 78–9
panic selling 95
parameterization 18
parental assistance 57, 260
Park, R. 148
parking 32
parks 85, 238
partnerships 35–6, 42
part-time employment 320
Passivhaus standard 330–31, 335–7, 340, 342, 351–2
paternalism 476, 478
path dependence 110, 197–8, 208, 214–15, 218–19
  and welfare states 276–8
pathways approach 180, 193
  and homelessness 356, 365–6
patriarchy 200
Patterson, K. 256
Peach, C. 423, 432
Pefki Solar Village 337
Peng, I. 281
pensions 50, 215, 274, 276, 281, 286–7
people–environment studies 107, 111, 183, 230–1, 241–2
  built environment of housing 236–8
  critique of recent architectural and psycho-sociological contributions 238–9
  and housing quality 231, 239–40
  interdisciplinarity and transdisciplinarity 240–1
  rethinking housing–people relations 231–6

Pereira, A. M. 266
performativity 139
period housing 155
phenomenology 177
Philipott, P. 364
Phillipson, C. 315
philosophy 108, 132, 199–200
Philpott, T. L. 423, 432
photovoltaics 330, 342–3, 345, 347–8
Pickles, A. R. 49
Pickvance, C. 219
Pitkin, J. 91
Plane, D. 246, 248, 301
planning 247, 262–3, 265, 345
  and affordable housing 382–4, 390–1, 394
  and building 27, 29, 32–3
  and housing politics 208, 210–11, 217
  and people–environment studies 231–2, 240
  and social life 323, 325
  and subsidies 402–3
planning permission 30–2, 34, 384
Poland 365, 367–8
policies 54, 154, 169, 212, 215, 239, 399–400, 402, 404, 411, 420, 468, 473
  and the economy 267–9
  on homelessness 366–9
  and mobility 79–81
  policy orientation of housing studies 207–8
  Right to Buy 55, 153–4, 172, 404, 468
  and social constructivism 179, 185–6
  social policies *see* social policy approaches
  and welfare states 279, 281–2, 290
pollution *see* environmental issues
Pooley, C. G. 462
poor neighbourhoods *see* deprived neighbourhoods
population aging 71, 248, 278, 295–6, 300, 325
  see also old age
Portes, A. 452
Portugal 279, 363, 365, 368, 373
positivism 166–9, 171, 175, 181, 184–5
post-modernism 177, 189
post-socialism 152, 280
post-structuralism 189, 200
Potepan, M. 300
Poterba, J. M. 262
Pott, M. 474
poverty 2–3, 109, 147, 165–6, 200, 439
  and affordable housing 385–6, 388
  and homelessness 361, 363, 369, 374
  and mobility 79–81
  and neighbourhoods 98–9
  and social policy approaches 163–5, 171–2
  and subsidies 405, 408–9
power 132, 182, 184, 188, 199, 201, 207–8, 210–11, 213–14, 216–18, 220
Power, A. 216, 462
preference models 94
pregnancy 78, 364, 367, 426, 442–4
pressure groups 109, 169–70, 179

prices 18, 53–4, 91, 137, 287, 297
    and affordability 381, 385, 390–1, 393
    and the economy 251–3, 257, 259–61, 263–5, 267–8
    and migration 298–300, 307–9
    and mobility 68, 74
    and social geographic interpretations 156, 159
    and subsidies 402–3, 405, 409–10
Priemus, H. 357, 462
prisons 302, 361, 365, 426
privacy 232, 236, 321
private rental market 153, 198, 211, 257, 264–5, 283–4, 287, 315, 368, 399, 407–8, 463, 469
privatization 108, 165, 247, 274, 282, 284, 286, 466
profitability 31–2, 38–9, 50, 476
property rights 32, 133, 136, 142–3, 198, 215, 247, 265, 412
proximity of job *see* commuting time
Pryce, G. 17, 264, 266
psychology 21, 88, 107, 111, 151, 168, 175–6, 183, 230–1, 238–9, 261, 365
psychotic disorders *see* mental health
public housing 97–8, 100, 152, 159, 166, 263–4, 276
    and subsidies 399, 401, 403, 405–8
    see also social housing
public sector 42, 149, 171
public services 84–5, 88, 90, 166, 381, 394
public spaces 86, 232, 450
public–private partnerships 36
Puech, F. 423
Putnam, R. 316, 449

quality of housing 27, 192, 307, 478–9
    and affordability 379–85, 387
    and household behaviour 48, 55
    and neighbourhoods 88, 92, 95
    and people–environment studies 231, 239–40
    and subsidies 408, 412–13
quality of life 77, 84, 86, 96, 147, 231, 237, 240–1, 338
    see also standard of living; well-being
quantity of housing 88, 381, 385, 408, 478
quasi-random assignment natural experiments 97–8
questionnaires *see* surveys
Quigley, J. 10, 23, 72, 99, 383, 409

racial issues 79, 85–6, 94–6, 98, 109, 147–8, 150, 154, 157, 159, 197, 425–6, 440, 452
    see also discrimination; ethnic segregation
Randolph, B. 199, 408
random assignment experiments 98–9
random utility theory 48, 73
Raphael, S. 99
rates of return 38–9, 91
Rawls, J. 171
real estate investment trusts (REITs) 33
real interest rates 124, 254, 256, 261–2, 266–7
recession 156, 253, 402, 410
    see also credit crunch; financial crisis
recreation 10, 85, 155–6, 217, 237, 308, 313, 315, 320–23, 392, 443, 448, 452

recycling 323, 353, 392
redlining 55
reductionism 22–4
refugees 154, 316
refurbishment 249, 327, 382, 454, 480
regeneration 35–6, 448
regimes of capital accumulation (RCA) 195–6
registered social landlords (RSLs) 389, 391
regulation theory 110, 195–6
regulations 138, 247, 261, 297, 403
    and building 29–32, 36, 39–40, 43, 191, 249
    and people–environment studies 232, 240
    and sustainable housing 327–32, 340
rehabilitation 89–90, 480
relationship breakdown *see* divorce; separation
relativism 184–5
religion 85, 147, 150, 157, 171, 249, 316, 319, 450, 452
    Catholic Church 275, 279, 368
relocating *see* migration; mobility
remarriage 52, 59–60
Remkes, J. 479
renewable energy 330–31, 334, 338–40, 343, 345–7, 353
renewal programmes 22, 218, 288, 318, 404–6, 408
    see also urban renewal
renovation 95, 453, 461, 478, 480
rental markets 11, 52–8, 109, 136–7, 165, 247, 282–5, 297
    and affordable housing 379, 381–2, 384–8
    and building 33–4, 36
    and the economy 257, 259–60, 262
    and homelessness 360–2, 368
    and housing politics 210, 213, 216
    and migration 299, 305, 308
    and mobility 66, 71, 74, 79
    and neighbourhoods 86, 91, 95, 98
    and people–environment studies 231
    and segregation 447–9
    and structurally inspired approaches 191–2, 195
    and subsidies 398–9, 404–6, 408–11
    see also landlords; private rental market; social housing
repairs *see* maintenance
repossession 14, 197, 287, 362
representativeness 140–1
Republic of Ireland 33, 383
Rescaled Competition State Regimes (RCSR) 288
resident participation 206, 216–17, 219
residential mobility *see* mobility
residential mortgage-backed securities (RMBS) 197
Resmussen, K. 321
retail facilities 10, 38, 73, 85–6, 152, 164, 323, 448
retirement 51, 70, 248–9, 286, 295–6, 301, 303, 306, 309–10, 313, 319
    see also pensions
Retrofit for the Future 330, 350, 353
retrofitting 330, 345, 347–50, 352–3
revealed preference approach 148
Review of Housing Supply see Barker Review
Rex, J. 149, 152

Ricketts, M. 137
Right to Buy 55, 153–4, 172, 404, 468
riots 427, 452
risk 2–3, 12, 15, 41, 140–1, 200, 255, 287, 323, 364, 402
   and building 31, 35, 37–43, 45
   and household behaviour 56
   and neighbourhoods 84, 90
   and subsidies 409–11
Rittel, H. 413
Ritzer, G. 175
roads 31–2, 85, 87, 152
Robertson, M. 321
Robson, B. 148–9
Robson, G. 315
Rohe, B. 411
role models 102, 440, 444, 446–7, 450
rooms, number of *see* size of houses
Roosevelt, F. D. 51
Rosen, H. 410
Rosen, S. 264
Rosenbaum, J. 80
Rothenberg, J. 16, 91
rough sleeping 169, 359, 364, 369, 371
   see also homelessness
row housing 154
Rowlands, R. 454
Rowley, S. 356–7
Rowntree, S. 165
Rowntree Foundation 166, 172
Ruanovarra, H. 198
Rueschemeyer, D. 201
rural areas 37, 56, 230, 306, 315, 320–1, 350, 382, 390, 392
Ryu, S. 296–7

safety 30, 89, 99, 156, 200, 237, 338, 383, 443, 452, 465, 468
Sampson, R. 319, 443
Samuels, W. 132
Sanbonmatsu, L. 97–9
Sandefur, G. D. 52
Sandstrom, K. 176
Santiago, A. 100, 403
satisfaction 38, 78, 99, 247, 289, 448, 453, 473, 475
Saugeres, L. 476–8
Saunders, P. 51, 153, 168, 324
Saussure, F. 189
Savage, M. 151, 157–8, 160, 314, 317
savings 190–1, 215, 246, 253, 260, 286, 296, 308, 400
Sayer, A. 181, 200
Schelling, T. 94, 151
Schlottmann, A. M. 53
Schmidt, M. 276
Schmitter, P. 213
Schnare, A. 17, 94
Schoenberg, S. 85
schools 38, 164, 215, 237–8, 249, 286, 301, 380, 404
   and mobility 69, 73
   and neighbourhoods 85–6, 89, 98
   and segregation 426, 442, 450, 452
   and social life 313, 315, 321–2
   see also education
Schulte, B. 279
Schutz, A. 177, 182
Scotland 147, 170, 264, 367, 394, 448
   and housing markets 8, 17, 20
   see also UK
Scott, P. 136
Scott, W. J. 52
Searle, B. A. 5, 10
second homes 50, 280, 296, 310, 382, 394
Second World War 75, 152, 155, 215, 246, 277–8, 280, 445, 449, 453, 477
Section 8 vouchers *see* voucher programmes
Section 106 (Town and Country Planning Act) 30–1, 39, 345, 388–9, 391–3
securitization 269–70
security 56, 156, 231, 237, 247, 315, 317, 324, 401, 477
   see also safety
segregation 94, 100, 109, 148, 152, 157, 164, 284, 357, 419–20, 435–6, 439–41, 453–4
   causes and effects of 425–8
   concepts and measures of 420–5
   initiatives to counter segregation 444–7
   levels of 428–32
   possible gains from 451–2
   public debates of 432–5
   relevance of the neighbourhood 441–4
   see also ethnic segregation; mixed districts
selection bias 97, 99
self-building 27, 34–5, 37, 44
self-sufficiency 199, 403, 412
semi-detached housing 32, 150, 154
sentimental attachments *see* emotional attachments
separation 57–8, 60, 78, 360–1
service–profit chain 475–6
sewerage 232, 237
shared accommodation 58, 356, 478
Sheils, P. 383
Shelter 166, 171
Sheppard, S. 18
Shiller, R. J. 23, 140, 142, 261, 268
Shinn, M. 363, 372
Shlay, A. 411
Shleifer, A. 140
shops 10, 85–6, 152, 164, 323, 448
Short, J. 191–2
Shroder, M. 408
Simon, H. 133
simulation models 74
Sinai, T. 407
Singapore 153, 316
single people 48, 52, 56–7, 60, 68, 72, 322, 470
   and homelessness 363–4, 367, 371
single-family housing 58, 196, 246, 296, 304–5, 310, 478
   and building 33, 39–40, 44

single-parent families 57, 68, 75, 154, 364, 407, 426
size of households 17
    and affordability 381, 394
    and mobility 67
size of houses 2, 10, 148, 234, 289
    and affordability 380–1
    and household behaviour 47–8, 50, 53
    and migration 304–5
    and mobility 67, 71–2
Skjaeveland, O. 316
Skype 316
Slater, T. 156
sleeping rough *see* rough sleeping
Slovenia 56
slum areas 151, 165, 171
Smart, B. 175
Smeets, J. 474
Smith, A. 7
Smith, D. 78
Smith, N. 149, 155
Smith, R. J. 5
Smith, S. 139–40, 164
Smith, S. J. 10
social cohesion 314, 325, 404, 413, 439, 447, 453–4
social constructivism 109–10, 168, 170–1, 174–80, 183–4, 366
    and housing policy 185–6
    problems with 180–2
social geographic interpretations 89, 108–9, 147–50, 158–60
    choice and preference 150–1
    gentrification and suburbanization 154–8
    structure of housing supply 151–4
social groups 93, 147, 150, 170, 234, 314
social housing 1, 247, 357–8, 461–3
    and affordability 379, 384, 389
    bureaucratic discourse 476–7
    and building 33–5, 42
    changing composition of tenants 469–70
    citizenship, managerialism and housing management 472–3
    current developments in 466–9
    and the economy 257, 265
    and homelessness 357, 359, 367, 374, 476
    and household behaviour 47–8, 55–6, 58
    and housing politics 211, 213–16
    and institutional economics 137–9, 142–3
    maintenance of 461–5
    management and housing services 473–5
    and neighbourhoods 90, 100
    public framework for 478–80
    Right to Buy 55, 153–4, 172, 404, 468
    and segregation 444–5
    service–profit chain 475–6
    and social geographic interpretations 150, 152–4
    strategic housing management 477–8
    and structurally inspired approaches 194–6, 199
    and subsidies 399, 401, 403–4
    and sustainable housing 347
    technical management of 463–6
    tenant–landlord relationships 470–2
    and welfare states 278, 280, 282–4, 286–8, 470, 473
    see also council housing; public housing
social justice 110, 113, 149, 207, 219, 222
Social Justice and the City 149–50, 192
social life 198, 246, 248, 313–14, 324–5, 441
    decline of neighbouring 318–19
    differences in 319–21
    housing and the neighbourhood 314–15
    and lifestyle choices 314–15, 321–5
    neighbourly activity 315–18
social networks 85, 90, 137, 200, 316–20, 324, 426, 445–6, 449
social policy approaches 163–4, 356
    future of 171–2
    housing as social policy 164–5
    nature of social policy research 166–71
    and social constructivism 185–6
    social policy tradition 165–6
social relationships 10
social sciences 51, 85, 132–3, 135, 171, 184, 189, 193, 211, 238, 314, 333, 369
social services 164, 276, 278
social standing *see* status
social-democratic welfare states 274–5, 278, 283, 285, 290
socioeconomic groups 53, 70–1, 89, 91, 230, 249, 274, 276, 339, 357, 425, 439, 441–3, 451, 453, 469–70
sociology 49, 107–8, 133, 148, 157, 159, 168, 176, 189, 193, 199
    and housing politics 207–8
    and people–environment studies 231, 238–9
solar energy 334, 338, 340, 353
    see also photovoltaics
Sommerville, P. 181, 201
South Korea 281
sovereignty 196, 209, 241–2
space 11, 75, 77, 239, 296, 321
Spain 56, 279–80, 287, 365, 430–1
spatial fixity 1, 10–13, 15, 28, 247, 265–6, 269, 380
specifications 237
Spector, M. 178
speculators 41
Spencer, L. 317, 319
splitting up *see* divorce; separation
sprawl *see* urban sprawl
stability 60, 402
Staburskis, A. 383, 387
stamp duty 254, 268
standard of living 289
    see also quality of life
standards 356, 384, 405, 476–7
    Passivhaus standard 330–31, 335–7, 340, 342, 351–2
    and people–environment studies 237, 239–40
Stapleton, C. M. 52
state intervention 136, 152, 194–6, 247, 261, 283, 380, 387–8, 401, 426

status 12, 85, 89, 147, 151, 191, 231–2, 275
  and household behaviour 50–1, 56
  and social geographic interpretations 148, 154
  and social life 322, 324–5
Stegman, M. A. 51
Stephens, M. 408
stereotyping 433, 440
Stigler, G. 24
stock 66–7, 380, 407, 450, 478
Stone, M. E. 381, 384–6
Straszheim, M. 16
strategic housing management 477–8
Straub, A. 463, 465
Strauss, A. 177, 184
structurally inspired approaches 110, 182
  critical realism *see* critical realism
  criticisms of 200–1
  history of 189–91
  how structure informs housing analysis 188–9
  key texts 191–9
Struyk, R. 17
student housing 33–4
style of houses 10, 48
subcontractors 28–30, 32–4, 41–4
subjectivity 179
subprime lending 149
subsidies 36, 98, 237, 239, 283, 357, 388, 397–8, 413–14
  consequences of 405–11
  definition of 398–9
  rationales for 400–5
  research gaps and issues 412–13
  types of 398–400
substitutability 42, 91, 382
suburbanization 75, 152, 154–8, 382
suburbs 17, 37, 71, 248
  and household behaviour 48, 51, 54, 56, 60
  and social geographic interpretations 150, 155, 158–9
  and social life 315, 322–3
Sunbelt 309
super gentrification 156
supermarkets 38
superstructures 31, 33
supply chains 29, 31–2, 41–3
supply of housing 1, 7, 54, 109, 208, 239, 283, 295, 309, 362
  and affordability 380, 384, 386–8, 394
  and the economy 262–6
  elasticity of 297, 406–7, 410
  and social geographic interpretations 149–54
  and subsidies 357, 402–3, 406
  see also building
supply-side subsidies 399–400, 404–9
Supporting People programme 367
supranationalism 288
surveys 87, 92–4, 97, 137, 163, 232–4, 237, 257, 304, 318, 359, 363, 371–2, 374, 464–5
Susin, S. 406

sustainable housing 327–8
  definition of 337–8
  energy efficient housing 330–37
  Energy Performance Assessments (EPAs) 335–7, 353
  future research agenda 352–3
  house of the future 350–52
  regulations and other government drivers 328–30
  retrofitting existing housing stock 347–50
  see also low energy housing; zero carbon housing
Suttles, G. 87
Sweden 27, 56–7, 153, 195, 317, 440
  and homelessness 359, 362, 367–8
  and housing politics 212, 214–16, 219
  and segregation 427, 442, 444
  and social housing 468, 477
  and welfare states 283, 285, 289
Switzerland 195, 199, 285, 330

Taiwan 281
takeovers 37
Talen, E. 322
targeted subsidies 405–9
Tasmania 321
Tatch, J. 259
Taub, R. 94
tax concessions 397, 399–400, 406, 409
tax credits 399–400, 406–7
taxation 137, 209, 247, 268, 330, 391, 463
  and building 34, 39, 43
  and the economy 254, 266, 268
  and neighbourhoods 85–6, 88, 90
  and subsidies 398–9, 405, 408–11
  and welfare states 275–7, 280, 286, 289
Taylor, G. 94
Taylor, M. 264–5
Taylor, P. J. 154
Taylor Wimpey 30
technologies 28, 44, 248, 323, 351, 441, 475
teenagers *see* adolescents
Teich Adams, C. 274
Teller, N. 285
tenants 110, 168, 199, 240, 289
  and housing politics 214, 216–17
  and subsidies 399, 406
  tenant participation *see* resident participation
  tenant–landlord relationships 470–2
tenure 2, 20, 100, 137, 153, 168, 238, 296, 305, 320, 447
  and affordable housing 383, 389
  and the economy 260–1, 265, 268
  and household behaviour 47–8, 50–9
  and housing politics 209–11, 214–16, 218
  and mobility 70–3, 75, 77
  and social constructivism 178–9
  and social housing 462, 468
  and structurally inspired approaches 188–9, 191, 197
  and subsidies 401, 413
  and welfare states 279, 282, 285–6, 289

terraced housing 32, 154, 348–9
terrorism 432
Thaler, R. 140–1
Thalmann, P. 386
Thatcher, M. 55, 211
thermal insulation 328–9, 332, 334, 347
Thibodeau, T. G. 17, 263
Thomas, B. 53
Three Worlds of Welfare Capitalism, The 274
Tiebout, C. 81
Titmuss, R. 274
Titon trickle ventilators 332, 334–5
tolerance 94, 200, 425
Topel, R. 264
Torgersen, U. 209, 211, 215
Toro, P. A. 363
Torrens, P. 74–5
tourist developments 280
Toussaint, J. 286
Town and Country Planning Act 30–1, 39, 345, 388–9, 391–3
trade-offs 16, 35–6, 48, 52, 54, 148, 156
transport 85, 152, 286–7, 323, 325, 380, 383, 389, 392, 441
  and mobility 74–5
  and sustainable housing 338–9, 350
Travers, M. 182
Trifiletti, R. 279
triggers 73–5, 298, 360–2
Truly Disadvantaged, The 439
Tu, Y. 17
Tulloch, D. 366
Tunstall, R. 451
Turner, J. 231, 261
Turner, M. 400, 404
Turner, T. 409–10
turnkey projects 33
Turnovsky, S. J. 266
Tversky, A. 140–1
two-earner households *see* dual-earner households
Ty Unnos project 351

UK 68, 75, 137–9, 178, 193–4, 211–17, 249, 318–19, 322
  and affordable housing 357, 379–81, 383–4, 387–94
  and building 30, 33, 37, 42–3, 45
  and the economy 251, 254–5, 257, 259, 263–5, 267–70
  and homelessness 356, 359–68, 370–3
  and household behaviour 51, 53, 55–6
  and housing markets 11, 14, 16, 22
  and segregation 429–30, 440, 445, 448, 451
  and social geographic interpretations 147, 149, 151–9
  and social housing 357, 462, 468–9, 473, 477, 480
    see also council housing
  and social policy approaches 166, 170
  and subsidies 404, 408

  and sustainable housing 327, 330–32, 335, 337, 339–40, 342–3, 345–8, 350–51
  and welfare states 277, 280, 283, 286–9
  see also individual countries
underclass 79, 439
unemployment 77, 265, 270, 276, 319, 477
  and homelessness 360–1, 363, 369
  and segregation 426, 433, 440, 442–3, 446
United Nations 401
Universal Declaration of Human Rights 50
universities 166
untargeted subsidies 409–11
Upmystreet 322
Urban Process and Power 194
Urban Question, The 192
urban renewal 170, 178, 400, 405–6
urban sprawl 74, 404
urbanization 320, 325, 403
UrbanSim 74
USA 13, 142, 245–9, 283, 287, 477
  and affordable housing 380, 382, 384, 386–8
  and building 33, 37, 42–3
  and the economy 251, 255, 259, 263, 265, 268–9
  and homelessness 359, 362–8, 370–3
  and household behaviour 51, 53, 56–7
  and housing markets 11, 16
  and housing politics 211–12, 217, 219
  and life-course approach 295–8
  and migration 299–301, 305, 310
  and mobility 68–71, 75, 77, 79–80
  and neighbourhoods 94, 100
  and segregation 425, 428–9, 432, 434–5, 439–41, 443, 445, 449–50, 452–3
  and social geographic interpretations 147–8, 151–5, 157–8
  and social life 318, 322–3
  and structurally inspired approaches 197, 200
  and subsidies 400, 404, 406, 408–11
utilitarianism 217
utilities 31–2, 85, 362, 385

vacancies 12, 19–20, 54, 66, 81, 94, 98, 154, 265, 304–5, 345, 386, 407, 453, 466, 477
vacancy chains 2, 54, 81
van Daalen, G. 422
Van den Broeke, R. A. 474
Van den Schaar, J. 474
van der Heijden, H. 195
Van Ham, M. 2–3
Van Kempen, R. 357, 448, 470
Van Order, R. 253
Van Tubergen, F. 446
vandalism 477
Vandell, K. 407, 410
Varaiya, P. 256
Veblen, T. 133
ventilation 237, 331–2, 334–5, 337, 339, 342–3, 347, 353
viability 30–1, 38–41, 390
Vigdor, J. L. 382–3, 387

violence 79, 99
virtual reality techniques 19
Voith, R. 410
voucher programmes 79–81, 98, 406

Waddell, P. 74
Wagner, M. 52
Wainwright, T. 197
Waldfogel, J. 407
Wales 328, 343, 347–9, 351, 388–9, 394
   see also UK
Walker, B. 137
Walrasian theory 7–9
Ward, C. 231–2, 240
Warren, D. 85
water supply 165, 232, 237, 327, 331, 337, 339, 347
Watkins, C. A. 17
Watson, S. 199
Watt, P. 156
wealth 137, 141, 239, 246, 275, 391
   and the economy 251–2, 257, 259–61, 266
   and household behaviour 50, 52–3, 59
   and subsidies 401, 404, 410–11, 413
Wealth of Nations 7
Webb, B. 165
Webb, D. 266
Webb, S. 165
Webber, M. 413
Weber, G. 260
Webster, C. 139
Weil, D. 295
welfare states 58, 97, 110, 138, 152, 164–5, 179, 245, 247, 403
   and affordable housing 380, 383
   concept of welfare regimes 274–7
   evaluation of housing systems 288–9
   and homelessness 362–4, 367
   and homeownership 285–6
   and housing politics 208–9, 211–12, 216, 290
   and housing systems 282–5
   outlook for 290
   path dependency and path changes of 277–8
   range of 279–82
   rescaling welfare and housing 287–8
   and segregation 425, 427, 441
   and social housing 278, 280, 282–4, 286–8, 470, 473
   and structurally inspired approaches 191, 194, 197–9

well-being 22, 24, 90, 99, 249, 317, 385, 472
   and people–environment studies 237–8
   and sustainable housing 327, 338, 351
   see also quality of life; standard of living
Wellman, B. 443
Welsh School of Architecture 335, 342, 347, 351
Wheaton, W. C. 19, 264
Whelan, S. 408
White, M. J. 51
white flight 425
Whitehead, C. 108, 137, 383–4, 387, 400, 406
wicked problems 413–14
Wierzbicki, S. K. 318–19
Wilkes, R. 422
Wilkins, C. 407
Wilkinson, N. 141
Willekens, F. J. 52
Williams, M. 371
Williams, P. 149
Williamson, O. 134, 138
Williamson, P. 213
Wilson, J. Q. 208, 439–40
Wilson, K. L. 452
Wilson, W. J. 443, 445–6
windows 328, 332–6, 347, 349
Withers, S. 300
women 58, 76–8, 275, 279, 320, 363–4, 367
   see also gender
working classes 155–6, 159, 165–6, 278, 316
working from home 313, 323, 443
World Bank 401
World Economy Report 7, 9
World War II *see* Second World War
WWF 337

xenophobia 432

Yates, J. 357, 400, 406
Young, K. 153
young households 246, 257, 259–60, 265, 280, 287, 296–7, 300, 306, 411, 470

Zeithaml, V. A. 474
zero carbon housing 249, 328–31, 337–43, 350, 352, 343–7
   see also sustainable housing
Z-Factory 338
Zhang, J. 151
zoning 148–9, 152, 323–4, 383, 388, 410